Christia

EDITED BY SAMUEL WELLS

CHRISTIAN ETHICS

AN INTRODUCTORY READER

WILEY-BLACKWELL

A John Wiley & Sons, Ltd., Publication

Library of Congress Cataloging-in-Publication Data

Wells, Samuel, 1965–
    Christian ethics: an introductory reader / Samuel Wells.
        p. cm.
    Includes bibliographical references and index.
    ISBN 978-1-4051-6886-1 (hardcover: alk. paper) – ISBN 978-1-4051-6887-8 (pbk. : alk. paper)
1. Christian ethics–Textbooks.   I. Title.

    BJ1251.W443 2010
    241–dc22   2010001893

A catalogue record for this book is available from the British Library.

Set in 9.5/11.5 Minion by Toppan Best-set Premedia Limited

7   2017

For Laurence and Stephanie

Brief Contents

Contents

    Philosophical Ethics   52
        Plato, *The Republic*   52
        Aristotle, *The Nature of Virtue*   56

    Religious Ethics   59
        Sumner B. Twiss, *Comparison in Religious Ethics*   59
        Mohandas K. Gandhi, *Experiments With Truth*   62
        The Dalai Lama, *The Supreme Emotion*   65

    Professional Ethics   68
        Tom L. Beauchamp and James F. Childress, *Principles of Biomedical Ethics*   68
        Thomas F. McMahon, *A Brief History of American Business Ethics*   70

4   The Story of Christian Ethics   74
    Foundations   74
        Augustine, *The City of God*   75
        Thomas Aquinas, *Of War*   78

    Revisions   81
        Martin Luther, *Temporal Authority*   81
        Menno Simons, *A Kind Admonition on Church Discipline*   84

    Legacies of Division   86
        John Wesley, *The Use of Money*   87
        Reinhold Niebuhr, *The Conflict Between Individual and Social Morality*   89
        William Temple, *Christian Social Principles*   92

Part Two   The Questions Christian Ethics Asks   97

5   Universal Ethics   99
    Right Actions   99
        Karl Barth, *The Command of God*   99
        Thomas Aquinas, *The Natural Law*   103
        Thomas Hobbes, *Natural Law and Natural Right*   105
        Immanuel Kant, *The Categorical Imperative*   107

    Right Outcomes   110
        John Stuart Mill, *Utilitarianism*   111
        Richard A. McCormick, *Ambiguity in Moral Choice*   113
        Joseph Fletcher, *Situation Ethics*   116

    Right Relationships   119
        Pope Leo XIII, *Rerum Novarum (On Capital and Labor)*   119
        Bartolomé de las Casas, *History of the Indies*   122
        General Assembly of the United Nations, Universal Declaration of Human Rights   125
        John Rawls, *A Theory of Justice*   128

6   Subversive Ethics   131
    Class   131
        Gustavo Gutiérrez, *The Church in the Process of Liberation*   132

    Race   135
        James Cone, *Black Theology of Liberation*   135

    Rosemary Radford Ruether, *Sexism and God-Talk*   139
    Delores S. Williams, *Womanist Theology*   142
    Ada María Isasi-Díaz, *Mujerista Theology*   146

Age and Disability   149
    Jean Vanier, *In the Presence of the Poor*   149
    Rowan Williams, *The Gifts Reserved for Age*   151

7   Ecclesial Ethics   155
    Persuasive Narratives   155
        Alasdair MacIntyre, *After Virtue*   156
        John Milbank, *Theology as a Social Science*   159

    A New Aristotelianism   162
        Thomas Aquinas, *Of the Virtues*   163
        Samuel Wells, *Forming Habits*   166
        Stanley Hauerwas, *The Narrative Character of Christian Ethics*   169

    The Christological Turn   172
        John Howard Yoder, *The Possibility of a Messianic Ethic*   173

Part Three   The Questions Asked of Christian Ethics   177

8   Good Order   179
    The State   179
        Pope Pius XI, *Quadragesimo Anno (On Reconstruction of the Social Order)*; Pope John XXIII,
            Pacem in Terris (On Establishing Universal Peace in Truth, Justice, Charity, and Liberty)   180
        The Kairos Document   183
        The Barmen Declaration   186

    Justice and Punishment   189
        Oliver O'Donovan, *The Death Penalty in Evangelium Vitae*   189
        Daniel and Philip Berrigan, *Civil Disobedience*   193
        Timothy Gorringe, *Atonement, Retribution, and Forgiveness*   196

    War and Violence   199
        Paul Ramsey, *Justice in War*   200
        Camilo Torres, *Love and Revolution*   202
        Dorothy Day, *Our Country Passes from Undeclared War to Declared War; We Continue Our
            Christian Pacifist Stand*   205

9   Good Life   208
    Economics, Wealth, and Poverty   208
        Adam Smith, *The Invisible Hand*   209
        Medellín Conference   211
        Martin Luther King, Jr., *I See The Promised Land*   215

    Work, Business, and Management   217
        Max L. Stackhouse, *Spirituality and the Corporation*   218
        Miguel A. de la Torre, *Corporate Accountability*   221
        Alasdair MacIntyre, *"Fact," Explanation, and Expertise*   224

    Media   228
        Pope John Paul II, *Aetatis Novae (On Social Communications on the Twentieth Anniversary
            of Communio et Progressio)*   228

Preface

This is a reader for entry-level students in Christian ethics. It is designed for undergraduates and seminarians, in some cases pre-college students, and the elusive but much-coveted general reader. It is intended to be used in lay ministry courses, and a variety of lay educational and training courses, at diploma and informal levels.

It is designed to accompany a textbook, *Introducing Christian Ethics*, which attempts to offer an overview of the whole field of Christian ethics. Most textbooks provide a typology or a list of the sometimes bewilderingly diverse and complex assortment of theories quoted and employed in the discourse. Some work their way through a grab-bag of controversial issues and endeavor to present both balance and wisdom. Others again offer a sequence of great authors in the history of the discipline. *Introducing Christian Ethics* seeks to do all three of these things, and, in addition, to present a constructive proposal for perceiving three strands in Christian ethics – universal (ethics for anyone), subversive (ethics for the excluded), and ecclesial (ethics for the church).

Christian Ethics: An Introductory Reader is intended to provide a lively companion to the textbook, making life straightforward for teacher and student by supplying texts that are sufficiently linked to the subsections of the textbook to dovetail easily, but are of sufficient length to be worth sustained study on their own. At entry level this reader should be all the supplementary material the teacher needs: at more advanced levels the teacher will obviously be looking to provide extra resources from elsewhere, but there are also suggestions for further reading to help both teacher and student in these areas.

This reader also sets out to introduce accessible primary material from major figures in theological and ecclesial tradition. It is anticipated that this may be a student's first encounter with Augustine, Thomas Aquinas, Martin Luther, John Calvin, and Karl Barth, and the intention is to present the material in an attractive way that encourages the student to read primary texts themselves, rather than always rely on secondary treatments. Meanwhile, it introduces material from major contemporary figures in the field, such as Paul Ramsey, Jürgen Moltmann, Stanley Hauerwas, Rosemary Radford Ruether, John Howard Yoder, Oliver O'Donovan, John Milbank, and Wendell Berry. The aspiration is to show how these figures are participating in debates that have in many cases been going on a long time, but how they nonetheless have new things to say. This reader blends in a few surprises from figures who are famous but are not always thought of as specific authors in ethics, such as Gandhi, Philip and Daniel Berrigan, and Martin Luther King, Jr. This helps the students realize that there is a continuum rather than a distinction between practitioners (perhaps like themselves) and theorists. No attempt has been made to make the language ring with the inclusive tenor of contemporary theological convention: these are works of perennial significance, but nonetheless of their time.

This reader offers introductory material at the head of each section, designed to demonstrate explicitly the significance of the passages and how they relate to one another and to the subject in question; to make direct connections between the structure of the reader and the argument of the textbook; and to make it possible to use the reader alone, should for any reason the teacher choose not to use the textbook. The reader follows the same structure as the textbook, so that teacher and student can at every stage make close connections between the two. The whole two-volume project is conceived as a unit, but in such a way that either volume could be used alone if so desired. The structure of the textbook is as follows.

There is a story to be told about how Christian ethics came to be where it is today, and a good grasp of that story greatly empowers the student to set about the theoretical and practical aspects of the discipline with considerable confidence. Thus in Part One the book starts with four foundational stories. One is the story of the Bible, which some would see as the only story that matters. Another would be the story of ethics told from a philosophical or pluralist perspective, which others might see as a more comprehensive story. In between we give an account of the story of the church, the place where the two previous stories come together; and finally, acknowledging the role of significant texts and authors, the story of Christian ethics.

Part Two describes and locates the diverse range of approaches to the discipline. Here the aim is to give the student not only a framework through which to grasp the bewildering array of competing theories, but also a perspective that offers to upset the conventional approach to the discipline. First there is universal ethics: three headings summarize the conventional theories. But then under the headings of subversive and ecclesial ethics, voices from the margins or a renewed emphasis on the church provide thoroughgoing critiques of the whole enterprise. It is important to say that the universal-subversive-ecclesial typology cannot be read back into pre-Enlightenment texts without much caution. In significant ways the typology reflects a series of different strands that emerge from the philosophical legacy of the Enlightenment.

Part Three focuses on fifteen controversial issues widely regarded as significant in Christian ethics, arranged under five headings. Each one follows the categories established earlier in the book, so the student can begin to get a feeling for how the theoretical and practical aspects of the discipline interact and in fact blend into one another. While none of these treatments could hope to be comprehensive, the aim is to provide not only a balanced summary of the arguments on various sides, but also a provocative dimension that might facilitate discussion.

The selection of the specific texts is needless to say a matter of judgment, and a word on how some of those judgments came to be made may be helpful in case any of those judgments seem difficult to understand. The universal-subversive-ecclesial typology is by no means a watertight one. Many figures cross over between the categories, and that is not due to any inherent inconsistency in their arguments. The typology is designed to help beginners get a sense of the whole field, not to impoverish the field by suggesting there are only three ways to inhabit it. Reading an excerpt from Martin Luther King, Jr., under an ecclesial heading, for example, is not "claiming" him as an ecclesial figure, but is designed to expand the imagination of what these categories represent. Likewise placing a reading from John Howard Yoder in the "church" chapter is not necessarily endorsing his reading of church history, but instead recognizing that the passage in question is a fascinating and invigorating one that should be included in an introductory reader and this is the best section in which to put it. Selecting Camilo Torres in the subversive part of the treatment of war is not a suggestion that all liberation theologians are part of guerrilla movements, but simply an attempt to bring a diversity of perspective. Not all passages selected are representative: some are selected because they are constructively provocative. If this book inspires the teacher or student, out of joy or exasperation, to go out and create their own much better selection of readings under more fruitful headings and categories, it will have had a healthy outcome.

This book stands on the shoulders of four key friendships and collaborations. The idea for the book came from Rebecca Harkin. This is now the fourth book she and I have imagined, crafted, and completed together, and I am as grateful for her vision and encouragement as I am in awe of her skill and wisdom. The shaping of the book owed much to John Kiess, who chased up many blind alleys and consulted many helpful faculty colleagues in compiling an original list of texts and sources, and who has been a stimulating and challenging conversation partner throughout. The book was prepared alongside the textbook which I co-authored with Ben Quash, and his perception and companionship have enriched this volume too. But the greatest debt and the deepest thanks go to Rebekah Eklund, who has with insight, grace, humor, and immense patience and thoroughness translated a provisional list of possibilities into an edited book of texts of even length, difficulty, and format. It has been a larger project than I anticipated and one I could not have comprehended without her attention to detail, her willingness to prepare, alter, and sometimes jettison carefully edited material, and her facility with the technology of the process. Friends like Rebecca, John, Ben, and Rebekah make scholarship a daily privilege and joy.

If there is one context in which my wife Jo and I daily encounter the habits, practices, perspectives, and dilemmas of Christian ethics in all their universal, subversive, and particular realms, it is in the blessing and discovery of raising children. Every principle or insight discovered in the library or sanctuary comes to be tested in the kitchen or the back yard. To our children, in humble thanks and abiding wonder, this book is dedicated.

Part One

The Story of Christian Ethics

Chapter One

The Story of God

The Bible is the document that Christians believe shows them the character of God, and the nature of life under God. This is a tradition Christians inherit from Jews, although of course the text Jews recognize as authoritative is significantly different from the text Christians cherish. It is also worth noting that not all Christians recognize exactly the same text – for example, the status of the so-called Apocryphal writings is controversial.

Nonetheless the Bible is integral to Christian ethics. But what does *integral* mean? Does it mean comprehensive, indispensable, highly significant, or influential? This chapter considers the role of the Bible in Christian ethics.

There are many for whom Christian ethics simply means following Jesus. But beneath this apparently straightforward commitment lie a number of questions that are difficult to resolve. Three kinds of questions shape this chapter, and yield the three respective sections below:

1 What is the status of the Old Testament in the ethic of Jesus? In other words, is following Jesus identical to seeing the Bible as authoritative in ethics, or are some parts of the Bible more important than others?
2 If it is acknowledged that the New Testament has different emphases and even perhaps in occasional places contrary emphases to the Old, is the New Testament itself to be regarded as a seamless robe, or are different nuances to be highlighted, understood in context, or minimized?
3 Is Jesus primarily a figure who *made possible* a new life (through his death and resurrection, as Paul's

epistles generally emphasize) or did he also *model* a new life (as the narrative accounts of his ministry in the gospels might suggest)?

The readings in this chapter explore these kinds of questions. They are drawn from different periods and traditions of the church. They do not give a consistent answer to the questions raised above, but they do address the most significant questions. No excerpts from the Bible itself have been included in this volume; however, the volume assumes regular specific and general encounters with the scriptural text.

The People of God

This section concerns the Old Testament, sometimes known as the Hebrew Bible. There have been three broad approaches to the Old Testament from the point of view of Christian ethics. The first is separation. This view assumes the Old Testament should be considered independently of the New Testament. The subtle and affirming aspect of this view points out that God's revelation to Israel, at least as Jews understand it, has continued beyond the Old Testament into the Talmud and the Halakhah, and that the Old Testament cannot be read independently of this later Jewish tradition. The less subtle but older view is that the God of the Old Testament is wrathful and obsessed with ritual and is thus more or less a different God from the God of the New.

The second view sees a seamless transition between Old Testament and New. The first offers promise; the second brings fulfillment. The laws, the priests, the sacrifices, the Temple, the kings, and the prophets of the Old Testament were all fulfilled in Jesus. When it comes to the lengthy legal passages, the moral laws were simply part of natural law, and thus remained binding. The ceremonial laws applied specifically to ancient Israel and had no abiding authority.

The third view affirms the continuity of God's character from Old Testament to New, but sees a creative tension between the two testaments. The cautious aspect of this sees the primary value of the Old Testament in Christian ethics as a collection of salutary stories, challenging prophecies, and distilled wisdom, particularly concerning freedom for the oppressed, justice for the poor, compassion for the outcast, and regard for the whole earth. The less cautious view sees the Old Testament as the indispensable scene-setting for the New, with the overall continuous theme of God calling a people through whom the whole earth will be restored to well-being and healthy relationship.

The readings in this section address some of the most pertinent issues concerning the role of the Old Testament in Christian ethics. Tertullian is struggling with the question of whether the God of the Old Testament is a harsher God than that of the New. Karl Barth is concerned with the relationship of Israel and the church. John Howard Yoder focuses specifically on whether a pacifist can find resources in the Old Testament for an ethic based squarely around Jesus. And Oliver O'Donovan seeks to root political theology in the life of Israel under God.

Tertullian, *Against Marcion*

Tertullian (160–225) grew up in Carthage (in modern Tunisia) as the son of a Roman centurion. He became a Christian as a young adult and was the first great theologian to write in Latin. He was very influential in early formulations of the doctrine of the Trinity (he was the first to use the term) and he was the first to coin the terms Old and New Testaments. He ended his life as a Montanist, a member of an ecstatic sect that believed its prophecies had superseded the New Testament and was thus declared heretical.

In this text Tertullian is offering counter-arguments to Marcion. Marcion of Sinope (110–160) argued in the early second century that the creator God of the Old Testament was chiefly concerned with the law. Jesus came to displace the God of the Old Testament and inaugurate an era of love. Marcion's Bible had none of the eventual Old Testament and only parts of Luke and Paul in it.

The heart of Tertullian's argument lies in Book IV number 6, where he shows that Christ has no authority if it is not derived from the Creator, in other words the God of the Old Testament. His compelling conclusion is that "Christ must belong to Marcion or to the Creator, but not to both." While some of Tertullian's arguments may seem remote, it is vital to realize that Marcion's claim is very widely aired today; the notion that the God of the Old Testament is a wrathful (and thus a somehow lesser) God is by no means limited to the second century CE.

Tertullian. *Adversus Marcionem*. Ed. Ernest Evans. Oxford: Oxford University Press, 1972. From Book I Paragraph 10 (pp. 25–7); I.19 (pp. 49–51); IV.6–7 (pp. 257–85); IV.20 (pp. 365–71); IV.43 (p. 507). Available online at www.tertullian.org/articles/evans_marc/evans_marc_00index.htm. By permission of Oxford University Press.

Book I

10. For the fact is that ever since things have existed their Creator has become known along with them: for they were brought into being with the intent that God might be made known. Admittedly it is somewhat later that Moses before others is seen to have established the

God of the world in the temple of his writings: but we need not on that account reckon that the knowledge of him was born along with the Pentateuch, for Moses' writings as a whole do not initiate knowledge of the Creator, but rather describe it from the beginning, so that its age must be counted from Paradise and from Adam, not from Egypt and Moses. And again, the great majority of the human race, though ignorant even of Moses' name, not to mention his written works, do for all that know Moses' God. In spite of the darkness of idolatry, and its wide dominion, men do distinguish him by the name of God, as though this were a proper noun – "God of gods," and "If God grant it," and "What God will," and "I commit to God." Evidently they know him, for they testify that he can do all things: and this they owe not to any books of Moses, for man's soul was there before prophecy. The knowledge inherent in the soul since the beginning is God's endowment, the same and no other whether in Egyptians or Syrians or men of Pontus. It is the God of the Jews whom men's souls call God.

19. "Yes, but our god," the Marcionites rejoin, "though not revealed from the beginning, or by virtue of any creation, yet has by his own self been revealed in Christ Jesus." One of my books will have reference to Christ and all that he stands for: for the divisions of our subject have to be kept distinct, so as to receive more complete and orderly treatment. For the time it must suffice to follow up our present argument so far as to prove, and that in few words, that Christ Jesus is the representative of no other god than the Creator. ... The separation of Law and Gospel is the primary and principal exploit of Marcion. His disciples cannot deny this, which stands at the head of their document, that document by which they are inducted, into and confirmed in this heresy. For such are Marcion's Antitheses or Contrary Oppositions, which are designed to show the conflict and disagreement of the Gospel and the Law, so that from the diversity of principles between those two documents they may argue further for a diversity of gods. Therefore, as it is precisely this separation of Law and Gospel which has suggested a god of the Gospel, other than and in opposition to the God of the Law, it is evident that before that separation was made, that god was still unknown who has just come into notice in consequence of the argument for separation: and so he was not revealed by Christ, who came before the separation, but was invented by Marcion, who set up the separation in opposition to that peace between Gospel and Law which previously, from the appearance of Christ until the impudence of Marcion, had been

kept unimpaired and unshaken by virtue of that <sound> reasoning which refused to contemplate any other god of the Law and the Gospel than that Creator against whom after so long a time, by a man of Pontus, separation has been let loose.

Book IV

6. I now advance a step further, while I call to account, as I have promised, Marcion's gospel in his own version of it, with the design, even so, of proving it adulterated. Certainly the whole of the work he has done, including the prefixing of his Antitheses, he directs to the one purpose of setting up opposition between the Old Testament and the New, and thereby putting his Christ in separation from the Creator, as belonging to another god, and having no connection with the law and the prophets. Certainly that is why he has expunged all the things that oppose his view, that are in accord with the Creator, on the plea that they have been woven in by his partisans; but has retained those that accord with his opinion. These it is we shall call to account, with these we shall grapple, to see if they will favour my case, not his, to see if they will put a check on Marcion's pretensions. Then it will become clear that these things have been expunged by the same disease of heretical blindness by which the others have been retained. Such will be the purpose and plan of my treatise, on those precise terms which have been agreed by both parties. Marcion lays it down that there is one Christ who in the time of Tiberius was revealed by a god formerly unknown, for the salvation of all the nations; and another Christ who is destined by God the Creator to come at some time still future for the re-establishment of the Jewish kingdom. Between these he sets up a great and absolute opposition, such as that between justice and kindness, between law and gospel, between Judaism and Christianity. From this will also derive my statement of claim, by which I lay it down that the Christ of a different god has no right to have anything in common with the Creator; and again, that Christ must be adjudged to be the Creator's if he is found to have administered the Creator's ordinances, fulfilled his prophecies, supported his laws, given actuality to his promises, revived his miracles, given new expression to his judgements, and reproduced the lineaments of his character and attributes. I request you, my reader, always to bear in mind this undertaking, this statement of my case, and begin to be aware that Christ belongs either to Marcion or the Creator, but not to both.

7. [Luke 4:31–37] ... Also what had he to do with Galilee, if he was not the Creator's Christ, for whom

that province was predestined as the place for him to enter on his preaching? For Isaiah says: *Drink this first, do it quickly, province of Zebulon and land of Naphtali, and ye others who <dwell between> the sea-coast and Jordan, Galilee of the gentiles, ye people who sit in darkness, behold a great light: ye who inhabit the land, sitting in the shadow of death, a light has arisen upon you.* It is indeed to the good that Marcion's god too should be cited as one who gives light to the gentiles, for so there was the greater need for him to come down from heaven – though, if so, he ought to have come down into Pontus rather than Galilee. Yet since both that locality and that function of enlightenment do according to the prophecy have their bearing upon Christ, we at once begin to discern that it was he of whom the prophecy was made, when he makes it clear on his first appearance that he is come not to destroy the law and the prophets, but rather to fulfil them. For Marcion has blotted this out as an interpolation. But in vain will he deny that Christ said in words a thing which he at once partly accomplished in act. For in the meanwhile he fulfilled the prophecy in respect of place. From heaven straightway into the synagogue. As the saying goes, let us get down to it: to your task, Marcion: remove even this from the gospel, *I am not sent but to the lost sheep of the house of Israel,* and, *It is not <meet> to take away the children's bread and give it to dogs:* for this gives the impression that Christ belongs to Israel. I have plenty of acts, if you take away his words. Take away Christ's sayings, and the facts will speak; See how he enters into the synagogue: surely to the lost sheep of the house of Israel. See how he offers the bread of his doctrine to the Israelites first: surely he is giving them preference as sons. See how as yet he gives others no share of it: surely he is passing them by, like dogs. Yet on whom would he have been more ready to bestow it than on strangers to the Creator, if he himself had not above all else belonged to the Creator? Yet again how can he have obtained admittance into the synagogue, appearing so suddenly, so unknown, no one as yet having certain knowledge of his tribe, of his nation, of his house, or even of Caesar's census, which the Roman registry still has in keeping, a most faithful witness to our Lord's nativity? They remembered, surely, that unless they knew he was circumcised he must not be admitted into the most holy places. Or again, even if there were unlimited access to the synagogue, there was no permission to teach, except for one excellently well known, and tried, and approved, and already either for this occasion or by commendation from elsewhere invested with that function. "But they were all astonished at his doctrine."

Quite so. *Because,* it says, *his word was with power,* not because his teaching was directed against the law and the prophets. For in fact his divine manner of speaking did afford both power and grace, building up, much more than pulling down, the substance of the law and the prophets. Otherwise they would not have been astonished but horrified; would not have marvelled at, but immediately shrunk from, a destroyer of the law and the prophets – and above all else the preacher of a different god, because he could not have given teaching contrary to the law and the prophets, and, by that token, contrary to the Creator, without some previous profession of belief in an alien and hostile deity. As then the scripture gives no indication of this kind, but only that the power and authority of his speech were a matter of wonder, it more readily indicates that his teaching was in accordance with the Creator, since it does not deny that, than that it was opposed to the Creator, since it has not said so. It follows that he must either be acknowledged to belong to him in accordance with whom his teaching was given, or else judged a turn-coat if his teaching was in accordance with him whom he had come to oppose. …

20. [Luke 8:25–48] Now who is this, that commands even the winds and the sea? Some new ruler, perhaps, and impropriator of the elements which have belonged to that Creator who is now subdued and dispossessed? By no means. Those elements had recognized their author, even as they had of old been accustomed to obey his servants. Look at Exodus, Marcion: see how Moses' rod gave orders to the Red Sea, a much greater matter than all the ponds in Judaea, so that it was split to the bottom, was made firm with equal amazement on either side, and by a route through its midst let the people pass through on dry feet: and again at the command of the same rod its nature returned, and the flowing together of the waters overwhelmed the Egyptian host. To that Work also the south winds gave service. Read how for the dividing off of one tribe by lot there was a sword at their crossing of Jordan, after Joshua had clearly enjoined its current from above and below to stand still as the prophets passed over. What say you to this? If Christ belongs to you, you will not find him more powerful than these servants of the Creator. Now I might have been content with these instances, but that a prophecy of this actual walking upon the sea had anticipated Christ's action. When he crosses the sea, there is a psalm being fulfilled, *The Lord is upon many waters.* When he scatters its waves, Habakkuk is being fulfilled, *Scattering the waters by his passage.* When at his rebuke the sea is stricken down,

Nahum too is made complete, *He rebuketh the sea and maketh it dry*, along with those winds, of course, by which it was disquieted. By what evidence will you have me prove that Christ is mine? By the Creator's acts or by his prophets? ...

43. ... I have, I think, fulfilled my promise. I have set before you Jesus as the Christ of the prophets in his doctrines, his judgements, his affections, his feelings, his miracles, his sufferings, as also in his resurrection, none other than the Christ of the Creator. And so again, when sending forth his apostles to preach to all the nations, he fulfilled the psalm by his instruction that their sound must go out into all the world and their words unto the ends of the earth. I am sorry for you, Marcion: your labour has been in vain. Even in your gospel [the Gospel of Luke] Christ Jesus is mine.

Karl Barth, *Israel and the Church*

Karl Barth (1886–1968), a Swiss Presbyterian who spent much of his life in Germany and was closely involved in the German church struggle, is widely regarded as the most significant theologian of the twentieth century. The heart of his theology is the notion of election. For Barth, the decisive choice is God's choice never to be except to be for us in Christ. Our choice in return to follow Christ is secondary. Theology derives from the way God's life is shaped in order to be in relationship with us.

In this passage Barth elucidates the delicate relationship between Israel and the church, and thus between the Old and New Testaments. He sets out what we described above as the third approach to the Old Testament – the notion of the people of God as uniting the history of Israel and the history of the church. In a series of carefully worded formulations, Barth states both the continuities and the discontinuities of Israel and the church. He reiterates that God's election is definitively expressed in Christ; it "does not immediately envisage the election of the individual believer," but principally considers the community – "a fellowship elected by God in Jesus Christ and determined from all eternity for a particular service."

While Barth affirms that the community "is as Israel and the Church indissolubly one," he does not shy away from underlining the significant differences. Israel represents the divine judgment, the church the divine mercy; Israel is shaped by hearing, the church by believing; one form of the community of God is characterized by a passing form, another by a coming form.

Karl Barth. "Israel and the Church." *Church Dogmatics*. Volume 2, Part 2. Edinburgh: T & T Clark, 1949. From Section 34, "The Election of the Community," pages 195–205. By kind permission of Continuum International Publishing Group.

§ 34 The Election of the Community

The election of grace, as the election of Jesus Christ, is simultaneously the eternal election of the one community of God by the existence of which Jesus Christ is to be attested to the whole world and the whole world summoned to faith in Jesus Christ. This one community of God in its form as Israel has to serve the representation of the divine judgment, in its form as the Church the representation of the divine mercy. In its form as Israel it is determined for hearing, and in its form as the Church for believing the promise sent forth to man. To the one elected community of God is given in the one case its passing, and in the other its coming form.

I. Israel and the Church

The election of man is his election in Jesus Christ, for Jesus Christ is the eternally living beginning of man and of the whole creation. Electing means to elect "in Him." And election means to be elected "in Him." Yet there is "another" electing and election, not alongside or outside, but included in the election of Jesus Christ. Already we have found it impossible to speak of the latter in itself and as such without continually thinking of this "other" election. Materially, the self-giving of God determined in it concerns the man Jesus, but teleologically it concerns man in himself and as such created by and fallen away from God. It is to this man, to the plurality of these men, to each and all, that the eternal love of God is turned in Jesus Christ. And it is turned to them in such a way that in this name it is to be attested to everyone, and in this name it is to be believed by everyone. The way taken by the electing God is the way of witness to Jesus, the way of faith in Him. Included in His election there is, therefore, this "other" election, the election of the many (from whom none is excluded) whom the electing God meets on this way.

But if we keep to Holy Scripture, we find that unlike the classical doctrine of predestination it is in no hurry to busy itself with the "many" men elected in Jesus Christ, either in the singular or plural. It does do this, of course, and we shall have to do so. But starting from the election of Jesus Christ it does not immediately envisage the election of the individual believer (and in this too we shall have to follow it), but in the first place a mediate and mediating election. The Subject of this is indeed God in Jesus Christ, and its particular object is indeed men. But it is not men as private persons in the singular or plural. It is these men as a fellowship elected by God in Jesus Christ and determined from all eternity for a peculiar service, to be made capable of this service and to discharge it. According to Holy Scripture its life and function is the primary object of this "other" election which is included in the election of Jesus Christ. Only from the standpoint of this fellowship and with it in view is it possible to speak properly of the election of the individual believer (which tradition has been far too eager to treat as *the* problem of doctrine of predestination). To designate the object of this "other" election we choose the concept of the community because it covers the reality both of Israel and of the Church. The meaning of concept – given here only in outline – is as follows. The community is the human fellowship which in a particular way provisionally forms the natural and historical environment of the man Jesus Christ. Its particularity consists in the fact that by its existence it has to witness to Him in face of the whole world, to summon the whole world to faith in Him. Its provisional character consists in the fact that in virtue of this office and commission it points beyond itself to the fellowship of all men in face of which it is a witness and herald. The community which has to be described in this way forms

so to speak the inner circle of the "other" election which has taken place (and takes place) in and with the election of Jesus Christ. In so far as on the one hand it forms this special environment of the man Jesus, this inner circle, but on the other hand it is itself of the world or chosen from the world and composed of individual men, its election is to be described as mediate and mediating in respect of its mission and function. It is *mediate*, that is, in so far as it is the middle point between the election of Jesus Christ and (included in this) the election of those who have believed, and do and will believe, in Him. It is *mediating* in so far as the relation between the election of Jesus Christ and that of all believers (and vice versa) is mediated and conditioned by it.

… Again, the existence of the community cannot be regarded as an end in itself with respect to the world. It has been chosen out of the world for the very purpose of performing for the world the service which it most needs and which consists simply in giving it the testimony of Jesus Christ and summoning it to faith in Him. It has forgotten and forfeited its election if it is found existing for itself only and omitting this service, if it is no longer really mediating. The inner circle is nothing apart from the relation to the outer circle of the election which has taken place (and takes place) in Jesus Christ.

But this outer circle, too, is in its turn nothing without the inner one; all the election that has taken place and takes place in Jesus Christ is mediated, conditioned and bounded by the election of the community. It mirrors in its mediate and mediating character the existence of the one Mediator, Jesus Christ, Himself. In its particularity over against the world it reflects the freedom of the electing God, just as in its service to the world (that is, in the provisional nature of its particularity) it reflects His love. It is only in virtue of this reflection that witness to Jesus Christ, the summons to faith in Him and therefore the faith of the individual elect are achieved. …

Now just as the electing God is one and elected man is one, i.e., Jesus, so also the community as the primary object of the election which has taken place and takes place in Jesus Christ is one. Everything that is to be said of it in the light of the divine predestination will necessarily result in an emphasising of this unity. But we had to regard the divine predestination that is to be equated with the election of Jesus Christ as a double predestination, as the primal act of the free love of God in which He chooses for Himself fellowship with man and therefore the endurance of judgment, but for man fellowship with Himself and therefore the glory of His mercy. According to the first aspect of this act He determines man for the hearing of His promise, and according to the second aspect of the same act for faith in it. In the one He determines him for an old and passing form of existence, in the other for a new and coming (and abiding) form. If the election of the community is included in the election of Jesus Christ, if in and with Jesus Christ it is the object of this primal act of the free love of God, then we must inevitably expect that in its election too we will encounter this twofold (and in its twofoldness single) direction of the eternal will of God. This is indeed the state of affairs with which, according to Holy Scripture, we have to do.

Who and what is Jesus Christ Himself in His relation to the community of God? Here already we find unity and differentiation. He is the promised son of Abraham and David, the Messiah of Israel. And He is simultaneously the Head and Lord of the Church, called and gathered from Jews and Gentiles. In both these characters He is indissolubly one. And as the One He is ineffaceably both. As the Lord of the Church He is the Messiah of Israel, and as the Messiah of Israel He is the Lord of the Church. ...

To this unity and twofold form of Jesus Christ Himself there corresponds that of the community of God and its election. It exists according to God's eternal decree as the people of Israel (in the whole range of its history in past and future, *ante* and *post Christum natum*), and at the same time as the Church of Jews and Gentiles (from its revelation at Pentecost to its fulfilment by the second coming of Christ). In this its twofold (Old Testament and New Testament) form of existence there is reflected and repeated the twofold determination of Jesus Christ Himself. The community, too, is as Israel and as the Church indissolubly one. It, too, as the one is ineffaceably these two, Israel and the Church. It is as the Church indeed that it is Israel and as Israel indeed that it is the Church. This is the ecclesiological form of what we have previously described in christological terms. ...

The Church is the gathering of Jews and Gentiles called on the ground of its election. It is the community of God in so far as this community has to set forth to sinful man the good-will, readiness and honour of God. As Jesus Christ the crucified Messiah of Israel shows Himself in His resurrection to be the Lord of the Church, the latter can recognise and confess the divine mercy shown to man. And as it recognises and confesses that the divine Word is in its fulfilment stronger than the contradiction of its hearers, it can believe and keep and do it. It can reveal in its existence the coming of the new man accepted and received of God. The Church,

however, as the gathering of Jews and Gentiles, called on the ground of its election, is at the same time the revealed determination of Israel, which is established by it, as elected to bring forth Him in whose person God makes all human sin and need His own concern, as marked out by the hearing of His Word, which must in any case precede faith in it, as the form of the old man who in his passing makes room for the new and coming man.

... The object of election is neither Israel for itself nor the Church for itself, but both together in their unity. (In speaking of elected Israel or of the elected Church we must be clear that we are speaking "synecdochically.") What is elected in Jesus Christ (His "body") is the community which has the twofold form of Israel and the Church. The glory of the election, the love of God to man as the basis of the election, the bow of the covenant that God in His love to man has from eternity purposed and established – all these are the same in the one case as in the other, for in both cases it is Jesus Christ who originally and properly is both Elector and Elected, and in both cases we find ourselves in His environment. Admittedly everything has a different form in the two cases. This difference is in the relation of election to the rejection which inevitably accompanies it. And it is in the twofold determination of Christ Himself that this difference has its basis. It consists in the fact that the Israelite form of the elected community reveals its essence in its Old Testament determination, as determined from the side of elected man as such, whilst its Church form, on the other hand, reveals the same essence of the elected community in its New Testament determination, as determined by the electing God as such. This ineffaceable differentiation of its essence is made plain by the fact that the people of the Jews (delivering up Jesus Christ to the Gentiles to be put to death) resists its divine election, whereas the gathering of Jews and Gentiles (believing in the same Jesus Christ) is called on the ground of its election. The decisive factor in the former case is human turning away from the electing God, and in the latter case the turning of the electing God towards man. These are the two forms of the elected community, the two poles between which its history moves (in a unilateral direction, from here to there), but in such a way that the bow of the one covenant arches over the whole. ...

It is, moreover, implicit in the nature of the case that only in the knowledge of Jesus Christ and of His election, i.e., in the faith of the Church, is the differentiation as well as the unity of the elect community knowable and actually known. The bow of the covenant over the two is not a neutral area and observation point between them but the history which takes place between Israel and the Church. The way of this history is, however, the way of the knowledge of Jesus Christ. It leads from

Israel *to* the Church. Only in this movement, i.e., in practice only from the standpoint of the Church, can it be perceived, described and understood as the living way of the one elect community of God.

John Howard Yoder, *If Abraham is our Father*

John Howard Yoder (1927–1997) was a Mennonite biblical scholar and theologian shaped by his pacifist Anabaptist tradition, his ecumenical experiences in Europe, and his exposure to Roman Catholic faculty colleagues. He is most famous for his book *The Politics of Jesus* which reasserts the primacy of the example of Jesus for social ethics.

In this reading Yoder carefully examines in characteristic "list" style five approaches to the problem of the way the Hebrew Bible seems to foster and glorify violence. His concern is not so much with the wrathful God generally but with the violent, warmongering God more specifically. His central argument is that what God wanted of Israel, and wants of the church, is the conviction that "their survival could be entrusted to the care of Yahweh as their King." In the Old Testament narrative this is frequently expressed in the willingness to wage war against extraordinary odds; in the New Testament, when all people are seen as potential partakers of the covenant, "then the outsider can no longer be perceived as less than human or the object for sacrificing."

For Yoder, as for many other theologians, the most creative theology comes out of refusing to reject the legacy of the Old Testament and striving to articulate the theological continuities and historical developments that link the Old to the New.

John Howard Yoder. *The Original Revolution: Essays on Christian Pacifism*. Scottdale: Herald Press, 1972. From "If Abraham is our Father," pages 91–111. Copyright © 1971, 1977, 2003 by Herald Press, Scottdale, PA 15683. Used by permission.

One basic problem of interpretation, which cannot be avoided by Christians whose commitment to nonresistance or pacifism is oriented around loyalty to Jesus Christ, is the issue of the Old Testament. The entire impression left with the modern reader by the narrative of the Hebrew Bible is one of violence being not merely tolerated but fostered and glorified. This impression seems to be present throughout the Old Testament, and to constitute a logical unity. ...

In the face of this problem there seem to be only a certain number of possible explanations. They recur all through the centuries.

A. The New Dispensation

The Sermon on the Mount, in which we find the most concentrated statement of the ethical demand of

Jesus, repeats six times the formula, "You have learned that our forefathers were told. ... But what I tell you is this. ..." It has seemed self-evident to many that Jesus here is announcing the beginning of a new era or dispensation which purely and simply sets aside what went before. There need therefore be no embarrassment about the contradiction with the sacred writings of old; Jesus takes it upon Himself to declare them no longer binding. Thus in Peter of Cheltchitz, in some early Anabaptists and Quakers, in Tolstoy and numerous modern Protestants, the sweeping novelty of the new covenant is a total answer to this problem. ...

Thus both the claim of Jesus to represent the claim of fulfillment of Israelite faith and Jewish hope, and the claim of the God of the Bible to be a faithful and reliable witness are seriously jeopardized by a sweeping shift of dispensations, unless we are to be provided with some far more clear way of measuring the why and the wherefore of the shift, its extent and its character. On the face of the text, the words of Jesus in Matthew 5 do not suffice to sweep away our problem, for to do so would demand that they sweep away the entire Old Testament, which is clearly not their intent.

B. A Shift of Degree; Concession to Disobedience

It is possible to interpret Jesus' words, "But I say," not as a fundamental shift of the divine purpose but as pointing to a new stage in its definition and realization. We could say that the purpose of God has always been the same, but that He made a permissive concession to the unwillingness or unreadiness of men to accept or to obey His full intent. There is a shift from old to new, but that shift is the termination or the withdrawal of the concession.

C. The Pedagogical Concession

Perhaps God was making an adjustment not to a culpable hardness of heart but to an innocent primitive moral immaturity. Perhaps insight into the destructiveness of violence and the redemptiveness of love is a very refined kind of cultural understanding accessible only to cultures with a certain degree of advancement. It would have been too much to ask for the rough and illiterate tribesmen of the age of Moses and Joshua. For the age of Jesus, however, standing on the shoulders of the civilizing preparation of later prophets and the experience of exile and Roman rule, the nature of such an imperative became much more readily conceivable. ...

One difficulty with this kind of position is its traditional correlation with an evolutionist liberal theological perspective. To hold a view like this one must look down on the ancient Israelites with a sense of moral superiority which is difficult to justify on objective grounds. One must also take a rather cavalier attitude toward the authority of the scriptural narratives, which affirm explicit and affirmative divine instructions hardly able to be subsumed under the heading of "adjustment to immaturity." It could be pointed out also that the analogy of the child's use of fire is significantly reversed. In the case of Israelite warfare it is the command which comes early and the prohibition late. The same conception of the growing capacity to act with insight would not seem to fit as well in this case.

D. The Division of Levels or Realms

In view of the shortcomings of each of these views which seeks to interpret Old Testament warfare as somehow less binding or exemplary than New Testament nonresistance, it is no surprise that the main stream of Christian interpretation has resolved the question by dividing the materials into different levels. One has no difficulty in reconciling the Old Testament and the New if one notices they are simply talking on different subjects. ...

In the Old Testament we have narrative and imperative dealing with the civil life of the Hebrew people. The commands and permissions which enabled that civil order to defend itself, including the use of violence both against social offenders and against enemies, were not only legitimate for them but continue to give legitimacy to the use of the death penalty and military violence by the state in our age. The New Testament does not deny or retract any of this; it cannot since it is not on that subject. Nothing in the New Testament prescribes any standards for the civil order. The only New Testament texts which speak to that issue are those which recognize the civil order as being master in its own house. ("Render to Caesar that which is Caesar's," "Be subject to the powers that be"). The nonviolence, the renunciation of rights, and the willingness to suffer which are typical of the ethic of the New Testament are only imperatives for the Christian individual and apply only in his primary relationships or in the church. Thus there is no contradiction.

This approach has the great advantage of not really needing to solve the problem we have been working at. It merely sets it aside. It does have, however, some significant theological and logical shortcomings. One finds them when one attempts to neatly draw the line (which it takes for granted) between the individual and the social, or when one recognizes that the New Testament says far more about social and political orders than simply to command submission to Caesar. ...

E. The Concrete Historical Anthropological Meaning

... If we look at the Old Testament from the perspective of the New we are struck by the difference, and the difference seems to lie at the point of whether killing is forbidden or not. But if we were instead to look at the events of the old story as they happened, moving toward the new, we should have been struck by quite another kind of consideration. It is therefore more proper, in reading the Old Testament story, to ask not how it is different from what came later, but rather how it differs from what went *before* or what prevailed at the time, and how it moves toward what was to come later. If we put the question in this way, we then find that the diversity of imperatives regarding killing is not the basic issue. What is most fundamentally at stake is rather an understanding of the covenant community and its relationship to God who has called it and promised it His care.

… What kind of social phenomenon was holy war in ancient Israel? We should ask, we have said, not how it differed from New Testament discipleship but how it was original in its own cultural context. … We first observe that the issue of the rightness or wrongness of taking of life does not arise in these accounts. There is no discussion within them of any effort to relate these words to the teaching of the Decalogue which forbids killing. It is not argued that killing is wrong except in these circumstances (the lines of the later doctrine of the just war which was taken over from pagan philosophical tradition). The possibility had not yet come into view that the prohibition of killing in the Decalogue (as it was understood) would need somehow to be related to these wars.

The holy war of ancient Israel is a religious or a ritual event. Prominence is given in many of the accounts to the term *herem,* meaning "set apart" or *tabu;* before being attacked, a Canaanite city would be "devoted to Jahweh," a ceremony which made of that entire city, including its living inhabitants, a sacrificial object. The bloodshed which followed the victory was not conceived as the taking of the individual lives of persons, each of whom could be thought of as a father or a mother or a child; it was rather a vast, bloody sacrifice to the God who had "given the enemy into our hands." The enemy has been put to death not because he has been conceived of personally as an object of hate but because in a much more ritual way he becomes a human sacrifice.

This ritual context has in turn an economic side effect. If all the slaves and the flocks of the enemy are to be slaughtered in one vast sacrifice, there will then be no booty. The war does not become a source of immediate enrichment through plunder nor a source of squabbling among the soldiers about how to divide the spoils; for there are no spoils.

The holy war is not a result of strategic planning but an *ad hoc* charismatic event. Israel is under the pressure of a neighboring tribe; a leader arises who is not a part of any royal dynasty or professional military class, and in response to his call the men of Israel arrive bringing their own weapons, whatever tools (axes, hoes) they had just been using. There is no professional army and no military strategist. If Israel's forces win it is not because they were more expert or more numerous but because of a miracle: "Yahweh gave the enemy into their hands."

Sometimes, especially as in the parade around Jericho and the wars of Gideon, special symbolic measures are taken to dramatize the non-rational, nonprofessional, miraculous character of the entire sacramental battle. When the Israelites want to have a king like other kings and a standing army like other nations have, *the holy wars come to an end.*

What the original experience of the holy wars meant in the life of Israel was that even at the very crucial point of the bare existence of Israel as a people, their survival could be entrusted to the care of Yahweh as their King, even if He told them to have no other kings. They did not need to trust to their own institutional readiness or the solidarity of their royal house; Jahweh would provide.

This interpretation of the central permanent meaning of the holy war story is supported by the appeal which is made to the holy war tradition by the later prophets and by the writer of the Book of Chronicles. These later interpreters do not derive from the tradition the conclusion, "Israel slaughtered the Amalekites and therefore we should put to death all the enemies of God." The point made by the prophets is rather, "Jahweh has always taken care of us in the past; should we not be able to trust His providence for the immediate future?" Its impact in those later prophetic proclamations was to work *against* the development of a military caste, military alliances, and political designs based on the availability of military power. …

The Case for the Historical View

From this perspective we can avoid both the condescending and arbitrary approach of saying that the ancient Hebrews only thought that God told them to fight, and the concept of a "concession" in response to conscious disobedience. We can affirm that in these events there was, as the story says, a real word from the true Jahweh of hosts, speaking to His people in historically relevant terms.

The issue to which He spoke was not one of ethical generalizations and the limits of their validity. To place the question here is the source of our trouble. The issue to which this experience speaks is the readiness of God's people to be dependent upon miracles for survival. The holy war of Israel is the concrete experience of not needing any other crutches for one's identity and community as a people than trust in Jahweh as king, who makes it unnecessary to have earthly kings like the neighboring nations.

From the ancient Hebrews through the later prophets up to Jesus there was real historical movement, real "progress"; but the focus of this progress was not a changing of ethical codes but rather in an increasingly precise definition of the nature of peoplehood. The identification of the people of Israel with the state of Israel was progressively loosened by all of the events and prophecies of the Old Testament. It was loosened in a positive way by the development of an increasing vision for the concern of Yahweh for *all* peoples and by the promise of a time when *all* peoples would come to Jerusalem to learn the law; it was loosened as well in a negative direction by the development of a concept of the faithful remnant, no longer assuming that Israel as a geographical and ethnic body would be usable for Jahweh's purposes. These two changes in turn altered the relevance of the prohibition of killing. Once all men are seen as potential partakers of the covenant, then the outsider can no longer be perceived as less than human or as an object for sacrificing. Once one's own national existence is no longer seen as a guarantee of Jahweh's favor, then to save this national existence by a holy war is no longer a purpose for which miracles would be expected. Thus the dismantling of the applicability of the concept of the holy war takes place not by promulgation of a new ethical demand but by a restructuring of the Israelite perception of community under God. ...

Thus, instead of being struck by a categorical difference between an Old Testament which permits killing and a New Testament which does not, we will observe positive movement along coherent lines, beginning with what is novel in holy war itself and moving in continuous steps to what is novel about the man Jesus. Already in the very earliest legislation of early Israel there will be novelties, such as for instance the rejection of indirect retaliation which was a part of the contemporary laws of other peoples, and the greater dignity given to woman and the slave in Israelite legislation. Then progressively the prophetic line underlines these same dimensions as the story continues. Through the incorporation of persons of non-Israelite blood into the tribe, through the expansion of the world vision to include other nations, through the prophets' criticism of and history's destruction of kingship and territorial sovereignty as definitions of peoplehood, the movement continued through the centuries which was ultimately to culminate at the point where John the Baptist opened the door for Jesus.

"Do not claim that you are sons of Abraham; God can raise up sons of Abraham out of stones." To be the son of Abraham means to share the faith of Abraham. Thus the relativizing of the given ethnic-political peoplehood is completed in both directions. There is no one in any nation who is not a potential son of Abraham since that sonship is a miraculous gift which God can open up to Gentiles. On the other hand there is no given peoplehood which can defend itself against others as bearer of the Abrahamic covenant, since those who were born into that unity can and in fact already did jeopardize their claim to it by their unbelief. Thus the very willingness to trust God for the security and identity of one's peoplehood, which was the original concrete moral meaning of the sacrament of holy warfare, is now translated to become the willingness or readiness to renounce those definitions of one's own people and of the enemy which gave to the original sacrament its meaning.

Oliver O'Donovan, *Yhwh Reigns*

Oliver O'Donovan (b. 1945) is the leading theological ethicist currently at work in the United Kingdom, and his trilogy *Resurrection and Moral Order*, *The Desire of the Nations*, and *The Ways of Judgment* is the most accomplished contribution to Anglican ethics since World War II. He sees ethics in largely teleological terms, aspiring to the eschatological fulfillment of the created order, and seeks to recover the scriptural roots of Christian ethics. His project is to identify and articulate the distinctively political character of Christianity and the uniquely Christian character of politics.

In this passage O'Donovan resolves the political legacy of Israel into four terms – salvation, judgment, possession, and praise. The first three refer to God's exercise of kingship, the fourth to humanity's appropriate response. It is important to note that O'Donovan resolves the question of God's bellicose activity in a very different way from Yoder: for O'Donovan, the military face of God is just one aspect of a larger category called salvation. Likewise "possession" gives O'Donovan a subtle tool to handle the delicate question of the relationship of God's reign to the land of Israel. Meanwhile, "praise" offers potential for discussing civil religion and its equivalents. This is among the most ambitious attempts to harness the social and historical context of the Old Testament for contemporary political ethics.

Oliver O'Donovan. *The Desire of the Nations: Rediscovering the Roots of Political Theology.* Cambridge: Cambridge University Press, 1996, 2002. From pages 30–49. © Cambridge University Press, reproduced with permission.

"Yhwh reigns"

The cry *Yhwh mālak* ["Yhwh is king"] carried with it three kinds of association. In the first place it offered a geophysical reassurance about the stability of the natural order; in the second place, it offered a reassurance about the international political order, that the God of Israel was in control of the restless turbulence of the nations and their tutelary deities and could safeguard his people; in the third place, it was associated with the ordering of Israel's own social existence by justice and law, ensuring the protection of the oppressed and vulnerable. In the third of these lines of association lay the calling and the demand. …

We can explore the idea of Yhwh's kingship further … by identifying some leading political terms that are habitually grouped with it. We shall take three common Hebrew words as primary points of reference: *yᵉshū'āh* (salvation), *mishpāt* (judgment) and *naha̔lāh* (possession). Yhwh's authority as king is established by the accomplishment of victorious deliverance, by the presence of judicial discrimination and by the continuity of a community-possession. To these three primary terms I add a fourth, which identifies the human response and acknowledgment of Yhwh's reign: *tᵉhillāh* (praise). …

1. Let us begin with "salvation," the usual translation of a Hebrew word which often bears a military sense, "victory." Yhwh's kingship is established by the fact that he delivers his people from peril in conflict with their enemies. To be sure, this starting-point should not be construed in too narrowly military a sense, as though Yhwh's power was confined to the battlefield (though "warrior" is a title given him at Exod. 15:3; Jer. 20:11; Zeph. 3:17). Rather, as Buber expressed it (*The Kingship of God*, p. 101): "His natural potency is contained in his historical potency." To Yhwh belongs the power to initiate. He initiates and

leads his people in the face of opposition and obstacle. They come to be, and they go forward, in the wake of his call to follow, in defiance of all that would destroy and disintegrate them. The miracle of the Exodus, which is a military event only in an unconventional sense, is the paradigm of Yhwh's *yᵉshū'āh*. Miraculous and providential deliverance are a part of what that "right hand" and "strong arm" have accomplished, as much for the individual worshipper, beset by his "pursuers," as for the people as a whole. Yet, equally, it is clear that the primary political implication of *yᵉshū'āh* is Israel's power to win military engagements, especially engagements against the odds. …

Taking "salvation" as a point of reference, we can follow subsidiary parallels which help us explore the meaning of Yhwh's military victories. They were, in the first place, a sign of his *hesed* or "favour" (Pss. 13:5; 85:7). As has been constantly stressed, Yhwh's *hesed* is more than a momentary or occasional disposition of goodwill. It is his enduring commitment to those who lived within his covenant. (*Hesed*, "turn" often stands in parallel to *'ᵉmūnāh*, "faithfulness" (Ps. 98:3 e.g.), and the two words occur together in parallel with *yᵉshū'āh*.) In the second place it was an exercise of Yhwh's *tsedeq*. The group of words formed on the root *tsdq* are traditionally translated "righteousness" or "justice"; but their sense is often better caught by "vindication" or "justification," as Luther famously discovered. If with *hesed* we are in a relation known only from within, inscrutable to the outside world and private to Yhwh and his people, with *tsedeq* we are in the fully public realm of a world court. When Yhwh's right hand and holy arm have effected a victory for his people, it is a matter of international notice (Ps. 98:2). …

2. This brings us to our second primary point of reference: judgment. The *tsdq* words appear in connexion with the *ysh'* words from time to time; but they are continually associated with words formed on the root *shpt*, which have to do with judging. "To judge with *tsedeq*" is the usual phrase for "judging justly," as it might apply to anybody responsible for making decisions of any kind. But the successful dis-

charge of judicial duties, especially those of the monarch, is described in the Deuteronomic period by a favourite combination of two nouns and a verb, as "doing judgment and justice" (2 Sam. 8:15; I Kgs. 10:9; Jer. 22:3, 15; 23:5; 33:15; Ezek. 45:9). ... He is "a righteous judge ... who is angry every day" (Ps. 7:11), which is to say that, like his earthly counterpart, he is scrupulous to hold daily assizes (Zeph. 3:5, cf. Ps. 101:8). But his judicial role is also taken to include international and military exertions on behalf of his people as a whole. ...

A very similar assertion, however, can yield a very different inference. "He stands up to judge his people; he enters into judgment against the elders and leaders of his people," says Isaiah of Jerusalem (Isa. 3:13). The preexilic prophets often return to the theme of Yhwh's "controversy" with his people (Mic. 6:2; Jer. 2:9), which is taken up memorably in Psalm 50, where Elohim testifies against the consecrated people that makes sacrifices to him. Here the notion of an *objective right* comes to the fore. If it is true that Yhwh's *tsedeq* is his vindication of the righteous against their adversaries, it is also true that it is his vindication of the *righteous*, and that a faithless nation, though chosen of God, cannot escape God's judgment of its ways. Out of this delicately balanced tension springs the whole dynamic of Israel's election-consciousness – one could say, without exaggeration, the dynamic of the Gospel itself, which, through God's act in the death and resurrection of Jesus, addresses not only our need for comfort but our need for objective justice, that paradoxically twofold need which refuses, existentially or ontologically, to be reduced to simplicity one way or the other.

To judge is to make a distinction between the just and the unjust, or, more precisely, to bring the distinction which already exists between them into the daylight of public observation. ... *Mishpāt* is primarily a judicial *performance*. When "judgment" is present, it is not a state of affairs that obtains but an activity that is duly carried out. When it is absent, it is not imbalance or maldistribution that is complained of but the lapsing of a juridical function that always needs to be exercised. ...

The permanence of the law, then, was not a reflection of Yhwh's eternal unchangingness as such, but of his divine decisiveness. There is ... a theme of legal and cosmic stability in Israel's faith; yet it is not self-standing, but rests on the self-consistency of Israel's God, his *'emeth* and *'ᵉmūnāh*, truth and faithfulness, in confirming and upholding his own judgments. ...

3. This brings us to our third point of reference: without the consciousness of something *possessed* and handed on from generation to generation there could be a theology of divine judgments but not a political theology, since it would never be clear how the judgments of God could give order and structure to a community and sustain it in being. It was not always the case that this traditional possession was identified primarily as the law. Originally and fundamentally the existence of Israel as a people was mediated through the land. But between these two ideas there was more connexion than at first meets the eye. Possessing the land was a matter of observing that order of life which was established by Yhwh's judgments; possessing the law was a matter of enjoying that purchase on the conditions of life which was Yhwh's gift. ... The material and spiritual aspects of the Israelites' possession are held together, a thought which will deeply affect John Wyclif two millennia later.

We may say that the land was the material cause of Yhwh's kingly rule, as judgment was the formal cause and his victories the efficient cause. There never was a pure nomad-ideal in Israel's history. ... The land was Yhwh's sovereign gift to his people (Josh. 24:13 etc.), even though, exceptionally, it could be thought of as given solely on leasehold (Lev. 25:23), emphasising Yhwh's sovereign right of disposal. ...

Corresponding to the notion that the land as a whole is Israel's possession as a whole is an assertion that Israel itself is Yhwh's possession. Possessing the gift, she is possessed by the giver; and this is something that is either to be true of the whole nation or not to be true at all. Hence the stress on the common act of conquest the military self-commitment of the nation to the claiming of the land which preceded, according to the Deuteronomic historian, the act of division. And hence the emphasis, which became very important for the Deuteronomic reformers, on a united nation based on a single cult-centre. ...

4. ... So Yhwh's rule receives its answering recognition in the praises of his people. In a telling phrase a psalmist describes Yhwh as "enthroned upon the praises of Israel" (Ps. 22:3), an adaptation of the conventional designation, drawn from the sacred furniture of the First Temple, which has him "enthroned upon the cherubim" (i.e. of the Ark). The link which ties the exercise of Yhwh's kingly rule to the praise of his people is that as the people congregate to perform their act of praise, the political reality of Israel is displayed. "To you belongs praise, Elohim, in Zion ... to you shall all flesh come" (Ps. 65:1f.). The gathering of the

congregation is the moment at which the people's identity is disclosed (as in the late Psalm 149 the distinct identity of the warrior-saints ($h^a s \bar{\imath} d \bar{\imath} m$) is seen in the fact that they have their separate assembly of praise). Hence the importance of "gathering," both on annual pilgrimage and in a final and complete return from exile, to the hopes of the post-exilic community: "Gather us from the nations, that we may give thanks to your holy name and glory in your praise" (Ps. 106:47). The community is a political community by virtue of being a worshipping community; while the worship of the single believer, restored from some affliction and desiring to thank God, must, as it were, be politicised by being brought into the public arena of "the great congregation" (Pss. 35:18; 40:9f.) in "the gates of the daughter of Zion" (Ps. 9:14). Otherwise, the poet says, Yhwh's righteousness faithfulness, salvation, love and truth would be "hidden" and "concealed" (Ps. 40:10).

The congregation, however, forms the centre of a much wider community of praise which runs out as far as Yhwh's kingly rule is manifest. It is as though the assembly can extend itself to include communities of worship everywhere that have seen evidence of the divine rule. So the thought of the poet of Psalm 48 moves from the Temple, where worshippers "have thought on" Elohim's favour – "Like your name, Elohim, so your praise reaches to the ends of the earth. Your right hand is occupied with vindication" – and then back to the focal place of worship again: "Mount Zion shall rejoice" (9–11). ...

Praise is a kind of proving or demonstration of the fact of God's kingly rule. At no point is the suggestion allowed that the people, by their praises, have *made* Yhwh king, nor should that suggestion be inferred from the speculative hypothesis of an "enthronement ceremony." This fourth section of our discussion, then, has to be set apart from the three which preceded it, for it does not relate to them as they relate to each other. Victory, judgment and possession are what God has done "by his own right hand." In one sense everything is complete when he has done them. If Israel's praises did not follow, or were radically defective, then, as the prophet of Psalm 50 very well understands, God's position would not be weakened in the slightest. "The heavens" are sufficient to "declare his vindication" in an assembly where the supposedly "consecrated ones" can expect nothing but judgment for their meaningless

attempts at worship (Ps. 50:6). Yet the people's praise is more than "confirmation," if by that word we mean no more than a kind of public notification of something that has happened quite independently. The kingly rule of Yhwh *takes effect in* the praises of his people, so that ... praise is the final cause of God's kingdom. Deutero-Isaiah can say that Yhwh "formed" the people for himself "that they might declare my praise" (43:21). This is what God's reign is directed towards, an acclamation that unites the whole community. In giving himself as king, God sought acknowledgment from mankind. We can say that much without derogation from divine sovereignty, since it is the implication of the covenant by which sovereign and subject are bound together. So that even Psalm 50, which knows that Elohim will get his tribute of praise regardless of what Israel does, must renew the summons of the covenant: "He who brings thanksgiving as his sacrifice, honours me; to him who orders his way aright I will show Elohim's victory" (Ps. 50:23).

Shall we conclude, then, that within every political society there occurs, implicitly, an act of worship of divine rule? I think we may even venture as far as that. "State-authority," remarks Stephen Clark, "is what emerges when households, clans and crafts first recognise a sacred centre in their lives together and then forget where the centre gets its authority. ... The voice of the High God reminds us that the land is his" (*Civil Peace and Sacred Order*, p. 90). Certainly it explains, as very few attempts at theorising the foundations of politics ever do explain, the persistent cultural connexion between politics and religion. And it allows us to understand why it is precisely at this point that political loyalties can go so badly wrong; for a worship of divine rule which has failed to recollect or understand the divine purpose can only be an idolatrous worship which sanctions an idolatrous politics. It sheds light, too, on the nature of the impasse into which a politics constructed on an avowedly anti-sacred basis has now come. For without the act of worship political authority is unbelievable, so that binding political loyalties and obligations seem to be deprived of any point. The doctrine that *we* set up political authority, as a device to secure our own essentially private, local and unpolitical purposes, has left the Western democracies in a state of pervasive moral debilitation, which, from time to time, inevitably throws up idolatrous and authoritarian reactions.

God in Person

The key question regarding the gospels is whether and to what extent Jesus may be regarded as normative for Christian ethics. Looking at his life in four dimensions – his incarnation, his ministry, his death, and his resurrection – different theologians have stressed different dimensions as key, and among them some have seen the respective dimension as normative, while others have seen it as only illustrative of ethical foundations that were also available elsewhere. This distinction between normative and illustrative views of Jesus is very important for understanding the role of Jesus in ethics.

Thus, theologians such as Friedrich Schleiermacher and Karl Barth ground their understanding of the uniqueness and ethic of Jesus not so much on the outstanding features of his life but on his *incarnation* and birth – his very existence. Jesus for them was significant not for what he did but for who and what he was.

Meanwhile, theologians such as Walter Rauschenbusch and Elizabeth Schüssler Fiorenza place Jesus' ministry and *teaching* as central. For them, what was unique was the quality and ethos of the community he inaugurated and gathered around him.

For Reinhold Niebuhr, the *cross* is the key element of Christ's coming, since it illustrates the reality and consequences of sin and the paradox of finitude and freedom. The cross is also central for John Howard Yoder, but in a very different sense from Niebuhr: for Yoder, the definitive dimension of Jesus' ministry was his willingness to go to the cross as a form of revolutionary subordination rather than pursue a zealot's crusade or settle for establishment quietism.

Finally, there are those for whom the *resurrection* and ascension are the most important features. For Rudolf Bultmann, the resurrection wrests the imagination away from commitment to inauthentic existence; for Oliver O'Donovan, it is the key moment that restores creation (and thus keeps salvation this-worldly) and inaugurates the kingdom of God (and thus appeals to a world beyond).

In the selections below John Calvin outlines a comprehensive view of Jesus across these stages of his "career"; and Stanley Hauerwas similarly restores the role of Jesus' life prior to the cross as vital for ethics, incorporating his embodiment of Israel.

John Calvin, *The Purpose for which Christ was Sent by the Father*

Perhaps the most influential understanding of the significance of Jesus for Christian ethics has been that of John Calvin (1509–1564). In his *Institutes* Calvin sets out the ministry of Christ as prophet, priest, and king. In this he draws out the salient roles of Old Testament leadership – for the people who kept Israel faithful to God through the story of the Old Testament were, at different times, prophets, priests, and kings. All of these were anointed roles, and thus are linked to the most common title of Jesus – the Messiah, or Christ, which means the anointed one.

Calvin intended all three titles to apply to all aspects of Jesus' life – his birth, ministry, death, and resurrection. However, in the *Institutes* as they stand the prophetic ministry is linked most clearly to Jesus' life, the priestly ministry is connected most evidently to Jesus' death, and the kingly ministry is oriented most explicitly to Jesus' resurrection. The threefold office (or *munus triplex*) is not fully developed in the *Institutes*, and elsewhere in Calvin's work he largely settles for describing Christ as priest and king. The potential of the prophetic office may have appealed to Calvin as a basis for understanding the authority and role of Protestant ordained ministry (for which he was reluctant to use the term *priest*). Karl Barth was later to take up Calvin's unfinished project and develop a much more thorough account of Christ's threefold office.

John Calvin. *Institutes of the Christian Religion*. 2 vols. Ed. John T. McNeill. Trans. Ford Lewis Battles. The Library of Christian Classics 20. Philadelphia: Westminster Press, 1960. From Vol. 1, Book II, Chapter 15, pages 494–502. Available online at www.reformed.org/master/index.html?mainframe=/books/institutes/.

Book Two, Chapter XV: To Know The Purpose for Which Christ Was Sent by the Father, and What He Conferred Upon Us, We Must Look Above All at Three Things in Him: the Prophetic Office, Kingship, and Priesthood

(i. Christ's saving activity threefold: first the prophetic office, 1–2)

1. The need of understanding this doctrine: Scriptural passages applicable to Christ's prophetic office

… Therefore, in order that faith may find a firm basis for salvation in Christ, and thus rest in him, this principle must be laid down: the office enjoined upon Christ by the Father consists of three parts. For he was given to be prophet, king, and priest. …

We have already said that although God, by providing his people with an unbroken line of prophets, never left them without useful doctrine sufficient for salvation, yet the minds of the pious had always been imbued with the conviction that they were to hope for the full light of understanding only at the coming of the Messiah. This expectation penetrated even to the Samaritans, though they never had known the true religion, as appears from the words of the woman: "When the Messiah comes, he will teach us all things" [John 4:25 p.]. And the Jews did not rashly presume this in their minds; but, being taught by clear oracles, they so believed. Isaiah's saying is particularly well known: "Behold, I have made him a witness to the peoples, I have given him as a leader and commander for the peoples" [Isa. 55:4]. Elsewhere, Isaiah called him "messenger or interpreter of great counsel" [Isa. 9:6, conflated with Isa. 28:29 and Jer. 32:19]. For this reason, the apostle commends the perfection of the gospel doctrine, first saying: "In many and various ways God spoke of old to our fathers by the prophets" [Heb. 1:1]. Then he adds, "In these last days he has spoken to us through a beloved Son." [Heb. 1:2 p.] But, because the task common to the prophets was to hold the church in expectation and at the same time to support it until the Mediator's coming, we read that in their dispersion believers complained that they were deprived of that ordinary benefit: "We do not see our signs; there is no

… prophet among us, … there is no one … who knows how long" [Ps. 74:9]. But when Christ was no longer far off, a time was appointed for Daniel "to seal both vision and prophet" [Dan. 9:24], not only that the prophetic utterance there mentioned might be authoritatively established, but also that believers might patiently go without the prophets for a time because the fullness and culmination of all revelations was at hand.

2. The meaning of the prophetic office for us

Now it is to be noted that the title "Christ" pertains to these three offices: for we know that under the law prophets as well as priests and kings were anointed with holy oil. Hence the illustrious name of "Messiah" was also bestowed upon the promised Mediator. As I have elsewhere shown, I recognize that Christ was called Messiah especially with respect to, and by virtue of, his kingship. Yet his anointings as prophet and as priest have their place and must not be overlooked by us. Isaiah specifically mentions the former in these words: "The Spirit of the Lord Jehovah is upon me, because Jehovah has anointed me to preach to the humble, … to bring healing to the brokenhearted, to proclaim liberation to the captives … , to proclaim the year of the Lord's good pleasure," etc. [Isa. 61:1–2; cf. Luke 4:18]. We see that he was anointed by the Spirit to be herald and witness of the Father's grace. And that not in the common way – for he is distinguished from other teachers with a similar office. On the other hand, we must note this: he received anointing, not only for himself that he might carry out the office of teaching, but for his whole body that the power of the Spirit might be present in the continuing preaching of the gospel. …

(ii. The kingly office – its spiritual character, 3–5)

3. The eternity of Christ's dominion

I come now to kingship. It would be pointless to speak of this without first warning my readers that it is spiritual in nature. For from this we infer its efficacy and benefit for us, as well as its whole force and eternity. Now this eternity, which the angel in The Book of Daniel attributes to the person of Christ [Dan. 2:44], in the Gospel of Luke the angel justly applies to the salvation of the people [Luke 1:33]. But this eternity is also of two sorts or must be considered in two ways: the first pertains to the whole body of the church; the second belongs to each individual member. We must refer to the first kind the statement in The Psalms: "Once for all I have sworn by my holiness; I will not lie to David. His line shall endure forever, his throne as long as the sun before me. Like the moon, it shall be established forever; the witness of heaven is sure" [Ps. 89:35–37 p.]. God surely promises here that through the hand of his Son he will be the eternal protector and defender of his church. ...

Now with regard to the special application of this to each one of us – the same "eternity" ought to inspire us to hope for blessed immortality. For we see that whatever is earthly is of the world and of time, and is indeed fleeting. Therefore Christ, to lift our hope to heaven, declares that his "kingship is not of this world" [John 18:36]. In short, when any one of us hears that Christ's kingship is spiritual, aroused by this word let him attain to the hope of a better life; and since it is now protected by Christ's hand, let him await the full fruit of this grace in the age to come.

4. The blessing of Christ's kingly office for us

We have said that we can perceive the force and usefulness of Christ's kingship only when we recognize it to be spiritual. This is clear enough from the fact that, while we must fight throughout life under the cross, our condition is harsh and wretched. What, then, would it profit us to be gathered under the reign of the Heavenly King, unless beyond this earthly life we were certain of enjoying its benefits? For this reason we ought to know that the happiness promised us in Christ does not consist in outward advantages – such as leading a joyous and peaceful life, having rich possessions, being safe from all harm, and abounding with delights such as the flesh commonly longs after. No, our happiness belongs to the heavenly life! In the world the prosperity and well-being of a people depend partly on an abundance of all good things and domestic peace, partly on strong defenses that protect them from outside attacks. In like manner, Christ enriches his people with all things necessary for the eternal salvation of souls and fortifies them with courage to stand unconquerable against all the assaults of spiritual enemies. ...

5. The spiritual nature of his kingly office: the sovereignty of Christ and of the Father

Therefore the anointing of the king is not with oil or aromatic unguents. Rather, he is called "Anointed" [Christus] of God because "the spirit of wisdom and understanding, the spirit of counsel and might ... and of the fear of the Lord have rested upon him" [Isa. 11:2 p.]. This is "the oil of gladness" with which the psalm proclaims he "was anointed above his fellows" [Ps. 45:7], for if such excellence were not in him, all of us would be needy and hungry. As has already been said, he did not enrich himself for his own sake, but that he

might pour out his abundance upon the hungry and thirsty. The Father is said "not by measure to have given the Spirit to his Son" [John 3:34 p.]. The reason is expressed as follows: "That from his fullness we might all receive grace upon grace" [John 1:16 p.]. From this fountain flows that abundance of which Paul speaks: "Grace was given to each believer according to the measure of Christ's gift" [Eph. 4:7]. These statements quite sufficiently confirm what I have said: that Christ's Kingdom lies in the Spirit, not in earthly pleasures or pomp. Hence we must forsake the world if we are to share in the Kingdom. ...

And surely, to say that he sits at the right hand of the Father is equivalent to calling him the Father's deputy, who has in his possession the whole power of God's dominion. For God mediately, so to speak, wills to rule and protect the church in Christ's person. Paul explains in the first chapter of the letter to the Ephesians that Christ was placed "at the right hand of the Father" to be the "Head of the church, ... which is Christ's body" [vs. 20–23 p.]. He means the same thing when he teaches in another place: "God ... has bestowed upon him the name which is above every name, that at the name of Jesus every knee should bow ... and every tongue confess what is to the glory of God the Father" [Phil. 2:9–11 p.]. In these words Paul also commends the order in the Kingdom of Christ as necessary for our present weakness. Thus Paul rightly infers: God will then of himself become the sole Head of the church, since the duties of Christ in defending the church will have been accomplished. For the same reason, Scripture usually calls Christ "Lord" because the Father set Christ over us to exercise his dominion through his Son. Although there are many lordships celebrated in the world [cf. I Cor. 8:5], "for us there is one God, the Father, from whom are all things and we in him, and one Lord, Jesus Christ, through whom are all things and we through him" [I Cor. 8:6, cf. Vg.], says Paul. From this we duly infer that he is the same God who through the mouth of Isaiah declared himself to be king and lawgiver of the church [Isa. 33:22]. For even though [the Son] consistently calls all the power he holds "the benefit and gift of the Father," he merely means that he reigns by divine power. Why did he take the person of the Mediator? He descended from the bosom of the Father and from incomprehensible glory that he might draw near to us. All the more reason, then, is there that we should one and all resolve to obey, and to direct our obedience with the greatest eagerness to the divine will! Now Christ fulfills the combined duties of king and pastor for the godly who submit willingly and obediently; on the other hand, we hear that he carries a "rod of iron to break them and dash them all in pieces like a potter's vessel" [Ps. 2:9 p.]. We also hear that "he will execute judgment among the Gentiles, so that he fills the earth with corpses, and strikes down every height that opposes him" [Ps. 110:6 p.]. We see today several examples of this fact, but the full proof will appear at the Last Judgment, which may also be properly considered the last act of his reign.

(iii. The priestly office: reconciliation and intercession, 6)

6. Now we must speak briefly concerning the purpose and use of Christ's priestly office: as a pure and stainless Mediator he is by his holiness to reconcile us to God. But God's righteous curse bars our access to him, and God in his capacity as judge is angry toward us. Hence, an expiation must intervene in order that Christ as priest may obtain God's favor for us and appease his wrath. Thus Christ to perform this office had to come forward with a sacrifice. For under the law, also, the priest was forbidden to enter the sanctuary without blood [Heb. 9:7], that believers might know, even though the priest as their advocate stood between them and God, that they could not propitiate God unless their sins were expiated [Lev. 16: 2–3]. The apostle discusses this point at length in The Letter to the Hebrews, from the seventh almost to the end of the tenth chapter. To sum up his argument: The priestly office belongs to Christ alone because by the sacrifice of his death he blotted out our own guilt and made satisfaction for our sins [Heb. 9:22]. God's solemn oath, of which he "will not repent," warns us what a weighty matter this is: "You are a priest forever after the order of Melchizedek" [Ps. 110:4; cf. Heb. 5:6; 7:15]. God undoubtedly willed in these words to ordain the principal point on which, he knew, our whole salvation turns. For, as has been said, we or our prayers have no access to God unless Christ, as our High Priest, having washed away our sins, sanctifies us and obtains for us that grace from which the uncleanness of our transgressions and vices debars us. Thus we see that we must begin from the death of Christ in order that the efficacy and benefit of his priesthood may reach us.

Stanley Hauerwas, *Jesus: The Presence of the Peaceable Kingdom*

Stanley Hauerwas (b. 1940) began his career seeking to recover the tradition of the virtues and point out the weaknesses of approaches to Christian ethics that focused disproportionately on the moment of decision. This led him to explore how character is formed, focusing on narrative, tradition, and community, and more recently on worship. His work is largely expressed in essay form, but towards the end of the first period of his career he published a single volume, *The Peaceable Kingdom*, which remains the best introduction to his work.

In chapter 5 of *The Peaceable Kingdom* Hauerwas provides perhaps the single most eloquent summary of the convictions of ecclesial ethics. He begins by pointing out that "we only learn who Jesus is as he is reflected through the eyes of his followers" and argues that, far from being a problem, this is in fact "a theological necessity." In *The Peaceable Kingdom* he makes a transition from referring to narrative in general as significant in Christian ethics, to identifying the ways the narrative of Jesus, as disclosed through the gospels, is uniquely significant for ethics. While he argues that we should see in Jesus' cross "the summary of his whole life" (one can perceive the influence of Yoder here), Hauerwas goes on to highlight the importance of Jesus' resurrection, which he sees as God's Sabbath, offering the possibility of forgiveness and restoration for all creation.

It is important also to note another recurring theme in Hauerwas' writing: the role of Israel, historically and in the present, in locating and understanding both Jesus and the church.

Stanley Hauerwas. *The Peaceable Kingdom: A Primer in Christian Ethics*. Notre Dame: University of Notre Dame Press, 1983. From Chapter 5, "Jesus: The Presence of the Peaceable Kingdom," pages 72–90. Copyright © Stanley Hauerwas, 1983. Used by permission of Hymns Ancient & Modern Ltd.

1. The Ethical Significance of Jesus

It is not my intention to settle to what extent we can know the "real Jesus." I am quite content to assume that the Jesus we have in Scripture is the Jesus of the early church. Even more important, I want to maintain that it cannot or should not be otherwise, since the very demands Jesus placed on his followers means he cannot be known abstracted from the disciples' response. The historical fact that we only learn who Jesus is as he is reflected through the eyes of his followers, a fact that has driven many to despair because it seems they cannot know the real Jesus, in fact is a theological necessity. For the "real Jesus" did not come to leave us unchanged, but rather to transform us to be worthy members of the community of the new age.

It is a startling fact, so obvious that its significance is missed time and time again, that when the early Christians began to witness to the significance of Jesus for their lives they necessarily resorted to a telling of his life. Their "Christology" did not consist first in claims about Jesus' ontological status, though such claims were made; their Christology was not limited to assessing the significance of Jesus' death and resurrection, though certainly these were attributed great significance; rather their "Christology," if it can be called that, showed the story of Jesus as absolutely essential for depicting the kind of kingdom they now thought possible through his life, death, and resurrection. Therefore, though Jesus did not call attention to himself, the early Christians rightly saw that what Jesus came to proclaim, the kingdom of God as a present and future reality, could be grasped only by recognizing how Jesus exemplified in his life the standards of that kingdom.

But the situation is even more complex. The form of the Gospels as stories of a life are meant not only to display that life, but to train us to situate our lives in relation to that life. For it was assumed by the churches that gave us the Gospels that we cannot know who Jesus is and what he stands for without learning to be his followers. Hence the ironic form of Mark, which begins by announcing to the reader this is the "good news about Jesus, the anointed one, the son of God," but in depicting the disciples shows how difficult it is to

understand the significance of that news. You cannot know who Jesus is after the resurrection unless you have learned to follow Jesus during his life. His life and crucifixion are necessary to purge us, like his disciples and adversaries had to be purged, of false notions about what kind of kingdom Jesus has brought. Only by learning to follow him to Jerusalem, where he becomes subject to the powers of this world, do we learn what the kingdom entails, as well as what kind of messiah this Jesus is.

... To locate our lives in relation to his is already to be involved with the basic issues of Christian ethics. Jesus is he who comes to initiate and make present the kingdom of God through his healing of those possessed by demons, by calling disciples, telling parables, teaching the law, challenging the authorities of his day, and by being crucified at the hands of Roman and Jewish elites and raised from the grave. Insisting that Jesus is the initiator and presence of the kingdom, of course, does not mean he was not the Christ, or that he is not God incarnate, or that his death and resurrection has nothing to do with the forgiveness of sins, but it does mean that each of these claims are subsequent to the whole life of this man whom God has claimed as decisive to his own for the presence of his kingdom in this world.

... By learning to be followers of Jesus we learn to locate our lives within God's life, within the journey that comprises his kingdom. I will try to show how the very heart of following the way of God's kingdom involves nothing less than learning to be like God. We learn to be like God by following the teachings of Jesus and thus learning to be his disciples. ...

We are called to be like God: perfect as God is perfect [Matt 5:38–48]. It is a perfection that comes by learning to follow and be like this man whom God has sent to be our forerunner in the kingdom. That is why Christian ethics is not first of all an ethics of principles, laws, or values, but an ethic that demands we attend to the life of a particular individual – Jesus of Nazareth. It is only from him that we can learn perfection – which is at the very least nothing less than forgiving our enemies.

2. Jesus, Israel, and the Imitation of God

... To be like Jesus requires that I become part of a community that practices virtues, not that I copy his life point by point.

There is a deeper reason that I cannot and should not mimic Jesus. We are not called upon to be the initiators of the kingdom, we are not called upon to be God's anointed. We are called upon to be *like* Jesus, not to *be*

Jesus. As I will try to show, that likeness is of a very specific nature. It involves seeing in his cross the summary of his whole life. Thus to be like Jesus is to join him in the journey through which we are trained to be a people capable of claiming citizenship in God's kingdom of nonviolent love – a love that would overcome the powers of this world, not through coercion and force, but through the power of this one man's death.

A proper appreciation of the centrality of the theme of imitation must begin, however, not with Jesus but with Israel. For Jesus brought no new insights into the law or God's nature that Israel had not already known and revealed. The command to be perfect as God is perfect is not some new command, nor is the content of that command to love our enemies new. Both the structure and the content of the command draw from the long habits of thought developed in Israel through her experience with the Lord. Jesus' activity as presented in the Gospels makes no sense without assuming what Israel had long known, that any story worth telling about the way things are requires an account of God's activity as the necessary framework for that story.

… [T]he task for Israel, indeed the very thing that makes Israel Israel, is to walk in the way of the Lord, that is, to imitate God through the means of the prophet (Torah), the king (Sonship), and the priest (Knowledge). To walk in the way of God meant that Israel must be obedient to the commands (Deut. 8:6); to fear the Lord (Deut. 10:12); to love the Lord (Deut. 11:22); and thus to be perfect in the way (Gen. 17:1). But the way of obedience is also the way of intimacy, for Israel is nothing less than God's "first-born son" (Ex. 4:22). Moreover Israel has the knowledge of the Lord as a just and compassionate God and so Israel too must act justly and with compassion (Jer. 22:16).

Israel is Israel, therefore, just to the extent that she "remembers" the "way of the Lord," for by that remembering she in fact imitates God. Such a remembering was no simple mental recollection, rather the image remembered formed the soul and determined future direction. … Thus the call of the prophets to Israel was always a summons to return to the vocation of an *imitator Dei* … For Israel, therefore, to love God meant to learn to love as God loved and loves. …

It is against this background that the early Christians came to understand and believe in Jesus' life, death, and resurrection. They had found a continuation of Israel's vocation to imitate God and thus in a decisive way to depict God's kingdom for the world. Jesus' life was seen as the recapitulation of the life of Israel and thus presented the very life of God in the world. By learning to

imitate Jesus, to follow in his way, the early Christians believed they were learning to imitate God, who would have them be heirs of the kingdom. …

4. The Resurrection: The Establishment of a Kingdom of Forgiveness and Peace

Jesus' death was not a mistake but what was to be expected of a violent world which does not believe that this is God's world. In effect Jesus is nothing less than the embodiment of God's sabbath as a reality for all people. Jesus proclaims peace as a real alternative, because he has made it possible to rest – to have the confidence that our lives are in God's hands. No longer is the sabbath one day, but the form of life of a people on the move. God's kingdom, God's peace, is a movement of those who have found the confidence through the life of Jesus to make their lives a constant worship of God. We can rest in God because we are no longer driven by the assumption that we must be in control of history, that it is up to us to make things come out right.

Such a peace is not just that between people, but between people and our world. For it is a genuine eschatological peace that renews the peace of the beginning, where humans and animals do not depend on one another's destruction for their own survival (Gen. 29). …

Therefore the Christian commitment to the protection of life is an eschatological commitment. Our concern to protect and enhance life is a sign of our confidence that in fact we live in a new age in which it is possible to see the other as God's creation. We do not value life as an end in itself – there is much worth dying for – rather all life *is* valued, even the lives of our enemies, because God has valued them.

The risk of so valuing life can only be taken on the basis of the resurrection of Jesus as God's decisive eschatological act. For through Jesus' resurrection we see God's peace as a present reality. Though we continue to live in a time when the world does not dwell in peace, when the wolf cannot dwell with the lamb and a child cannot play over the hole of the asp, we believe nonetheless that peace has been made possible by the resurrection. Through this crucified but resurrected savior we see that God offers to all the possibility of living in peace by the power of forgiveness. …

Only if our Lord is a risen Lord, therefore, can we have the confidence and the power to be a community of forgiveness. For on the basis of the resurrection we have the presumption to believe that God has made us agents in the history of the kingdom. The resurrection is not a symbol or myth through which we can interpret our individual and collective dyings and risings. Rather the resurrection of Jesus is the ultimate sign that our salvation comes only when we cease trying to interpret Jesus' story in the light of our history, and instead we interpret ourselves in the light of his. For this is no dead Lord we follow but the living God, who having dwelt among us as an individual, is now eternally present to us making possible our living as forgiven agents of God's new creation.

Following Jesus

This section considers the significance of those aspects of the New Testament that are not precisely about the narrative of Jesus. One can trace New Testament ethics in broadly three strands: the Gospels (and the Acts of the Apostles), Paul's epistles, and the rest of the New Testament. The Gospels are characterized by their narrative form and the way they, unlike other parts of the New Testament, dwell extensively on Jesus' life and ministry and not just on his death and resurrection. Some of the passages most frequently cited in Christian ethics are in fact to be found in only one Gospel – for example the parable of the Good Samaritan is only to be found in Luke, while the parable of the last judgment, including the words "just as you did it to one of the least of these who are members of my family, you did it to me," is found only in Matthew. It is not clear whether such passages are any less authoritative than material found in all four Gospels.

Paul's epistles weave together crises in the early churches, discussing local problems in such a way as to bring together saving revelation with practical wisdom. In particular in 1 Corinthians, Paul proceeds through a sequence of pressing questions, including incest, lawsuits among believers, divorce, eating food previously sacrificed to idols, covering the head in worship, equal distribution of food at the Lord's Supper, and speaking in tongues. Paul's theological emphases can be outlined by describing where he perceives his readers to stand in relation to world history. In the (relatively recent) past lies the overwhelming event of Christ's cross; behind it lies the still very significant relationship of God to Israel.

In the (perhaps near) future lies the completion of God's work begun in creation and fully expressed in Christ. In the present lies the church, a reality most fully emphasized and explored in Ephesians (which may have been written by a follower of Paul), but assumed throughout the Pauline letters.

The rest of the New Testament is made up of diverse material taking a range of ethical approaches. Hebrews enjoins hospitality to strangers, solidarity with those suffering, the sharing of resources and obedience to leaders: but its emphasis is primarily on the inadequacy of the sacrifices made in the Jerusalem Temple, and on the sufficiency of the sacrifice made by Christ the great high priest. James lies in continuity with the wisdom tradition of the Old Testament, and especially emphasizes charity towards the poor. First Peter grounds a wide-ranging vision of faithful Christian discipleship explicitly in the life, death, resurrection, and ascension of Jesus. Revelation is deeply concerned with the nature of current suffering and the promise that God will intervene to vindicate the saints. There is a stark and uncompromising contrast between good and evil, light and darkness, God and Satan, church and world.

In the following readings, John Calvin attempts a summary of a New Testament ethic, striving to weave together the epistles' assumptions with those of the gospels. Dietrich Bonhoeffer is reacting against the Lutheran tendency to reduce the New Testament ethic to one element – grace – and thereby lose the need for costly human response.

John Calvin, *The Sum of the Christian Life: The Denial of Ourselves*

Calvin's *Institutes* begin with our knowledge of God the creator, before moving on to our knowledge of God the redeemer in Christ. Then comes the way in which we receive the grace of Christ, and finally the means (largely the church and its powers and sacraments) by which God invites us into Christ's society. This passage comes from the third of the four books, covering the ways in which we receive Christ's grace. After six introductory chapters about the nature of the Christian life, covering issues such as faith and repentance, Calvin begins in earnest with this chapter on the "Sum of the Christian Life." He goes on to explore in detail cross-bearing, the life to come, justification, freedom, eternal election, and resurrection.

Calvin begins this exposition with the principle that "we are not our own," citing 1 Corinthians 6:19 ("your body is a temple of the Holy Spirit within you, which you have from God, and that you are not your own"). He then moves on to the affirmation that "we are God's," and thus that we should live and die for God. The virtue Calvin commends is humility. He summarizes his words thus: "You will never attain true gentleness except by one path: a heart imbued with lowliness and with reverence for others."

John Calvin. *Institutes of the Christian Religion.* 2 vols. Ed. John T. McNeill. Trans. Ford Lewis Battles. The Library of Christian Classics 20. Philadelphia: Westminster Press, 1960. From Vol. 1, Book III, Chapter 7, pages 689–701. Available online at www.reformed.org/master/index.html?mainframe=/books/institutes/.

(The Christian philosophy of unworldliness and self-denial; we are not our own, we are God's, 1–3)

1. We are not our own masters, but belong to God

Even though the law of the Lord provides the finest and best-disposed method of ordering a man's life, it seemed good to the Heavenly Teacher to shape his people by an even more explicit plan to that rule which he had set forth in the law. Here, then, is the beginning of this plan: the duty of believers is "to present their bodies to God as a living sacrifice, holy and acceptable to him," and in this consists the lawful worship of him [Rom. 12:1]. From this is derived the basis of the exhortation that "they be not conformed to the fashion of this world, but be transformed by the renewal of their minds, so that they may prove what is the will of God" [Rom. 12:2]. Now the great thing is this: we are consecrated and dedicated to God in order that we may thereafter think, speak, meditate, and do, nothing except to his glory. For a sacred thing may not be applied to profane uses without marked injury to him.

If we, then, are not our own [cf. I Cor. 6:19] but the Lord's, it is clear what error we must flee, and whither we must direct all the acts of our life.

We are not our own: let not our reason nor our will, therefore, sway our plans and deeds. We are not our own: let us therefore not set it as our goal to seek what is expedient for us according to the flesh. We are not our own: in so far as we can, let us therefore forget ourselves and all that is ours.

Conversely, we are God's: let us therefore live for him and die for him. We are God's: let his wisdom and will therefore rule all our actions. We are God's: let all the parts of our life accordingly strive toward him as our only lawful goal [Rom. 14:8; cf. I Cor. 6:19]. Oh, how much has that man profited who, having been taught that he is not his own, has taken away dominion and rule from his own reason that he may yield it to God! For, as consulting our self-interest is the pestilence that most effectively leads to our destruction, so the sole haven of salvation is to be wise in nothing and to will nothing through ourselves but to follow the leading of the Lord alone. ...

2. Self-denial through devotion to God

From this also follows this second point: that we seek not the things that are ours but those which are of the Lord's will and will serve to advance his glory. This is also evidence of great progress: that, almost forgetful of ourselves, surely subordinating our self-concern, we try faithfully to devote our zeal to God and his commandments. For when Scripture bids us leave off self-concern, it not only erases from our minds the yearning to possess, the desire for power, and the favor of men, but it also uproots ambition and all craving for human glory and other more secret plagues. Accordingly, the Christian must surely be so disposed and minded that he feels within himself it is with God he has to deal throughout his life. ...

(The principle of self-denial in our relations with our fellow men, 4–7)

4. Self-denial gives us the right attitude toward our fellow men

Now in these words we perceive that denial of self has regard partly to men, partly, and chiefly, to God.

For when Scripture bids us act toward men so as to esteem them above ourselves [Phil. 2:3], and in good faith to apply ourselves wholly to doing them good [cf. Rom. 12:10], it gives us commandments of which our mind is quite incapable unless our mind be previously emptied of its natural feeling. For, such is the blindness with which we all rush into self-love that each one of us seems to himself to have just cause to be proud of himself and to despise all others in comparison. ... There is no other remedy than to tear out from our inward parts this most deadly pestilence of love of strife and love of self, even as it is plucked out by Scriptural teaching. For thus we are instructed to remember that those talents which God has bestowed upon us are not our own goods but the free gifts of God; and any persons who become proud of them show their ungratefulness. "Who causes you to excel?" Paul asks. "If you have received all things, why do you boast as if they were not given to you?" [I Cor. 4:7].

Let us, then, unremittingly examining our faults, call ourselves back to humility. Thus nothing will remain in us to puff us up; but there will be much occasion to be cast down. On the other hand, we are bidden so to esteem and regard whatever gifts of God we see in other men that we may honor those men in whom they reside. For it would be great depravity on our part to deprive them of that honor which the Lord has bestowed upon them. But we are taught to overlook their faults, certainly not flatteringly to cherish them; but not on account of such faults to revile men whom we ought to cherish with good will and honor. Thus it will come about that, whatever man we deal with, we shall treat him not only moderately and modestly but also cordially and as a friend. You will never attain true gentleness except by one path: a heart imbued with lowliness and with reverence for others.

5. Self-renunciation leads to proper helpfulness toward our neighbors

Now, in seeking to benefit one's neighbor, how difficult it is to do one's duty! Unless you give up all thought of self and, so to speak, get out of yourself, you will accomplish nothing here. For how can you perform those works which Paul teaches to be the works of love, unless you renounce yourself, and give yourself wholly to others? "Love," he says, "is patient and kind, not jealous or boastful, is not envious or puffed up, does not seek its own, is not irritable," etc. [I Cor. 13:4–5 p.]. If this is the one thing required – that we seek not what is our own – still we shall do no little violence to nature, which so inclines us to love of ourselves alone that it does not easily allow us to neglect ourselves and our possessions

in order to look after another's good, nay, to yield willingly what is ours by right and resign it to another. But Scripture, to lead us by the hand to this, warns that whatever benefits we obtain from the Lord have been entrusted to us on this condition: that they be applied to the common good of the church. And therefore the lawful use of all benefits consists in a liberal and kindly sharing of them with others. No surer rule and no more valid exhortation to keep it could be devised than when we are taught that all the gifts we possess have been bestowed by God and entrusted to us on condition that they be distributed for our neighbors' benefit [cf. I Peter 4:10].

But Scripture goes even farther by comparing them to the powers with which the members of the human body are endowed [I Cor. 12:12 ff.]. No member has this power for itself nor applies it to its own private use; but each pours it out to the fellow members. Nor does it take any profit from its power except what proceeds from the common advantage of the whole body. So, too, whatever a godly man can do he ought to be able to do for his brothers, providing for himself in no way other than to have his mind intent upon the common upbuilding of the church. Let this, therefore, be our rule for generosity and beneficence: We are the stewards of everything God has conferred on us by which we are able to help our neighbor, and are required to render account of our stewardship. Moreover, the only right stewardship is that which is tested by the rule of love. ...

(The principle of self-denial in our relation to God, 8–10)

8. Self-denial toward God: devotion to his will!

... To begin with, then, in seeking either the convenience or the tranquillity of the present life, Scripture calls us to resign ourselves and all our possessions to the Lord's will, and to yield to him the desires of our hearts to be tamed and subjugated. To covet wealth and honors, to strive for authority, to heap up riches, to gather together all those follies which seem to make for magnificence and pomp, our lust is mad, our desire boundless. On the other hand, wonderful is our fear, wonderful our hatred, of poverty, lowly birth, and humble condition! And we are spurred to rid ourselves of them by every means. Hence we can see how uneasy in mind all those persons are who order their lives according to their own plan. We can see how artfully they strive – to the point of weariness – to obtain the goal of their ambition or avarice, while, on the other hand, avoiding poverty and a lowly condition.

In order not to be caught in such snares, godly men must hold to this path. First of all, let them neither desire nor hope for, nor contemplate, any other way of prospering than by the Lord's blessing. Upon this, then, let them safely and confidently throw themselves and rest. For however beautifully the flesh may seem to suffice unto itself, while it either strives by its own effort for honors and riches or relies upon its diligence, or is aided by the favor of men, yet it is certain that all these things are nothing; nor will we benefit at all, either by skill or by labor, except in so far as the Lord prospers them both. ...

10. Self-denial helps us bear adversity

And for godly minds the peace and forbearance we have spoken of ought not to rest solely in this point; but it must also be extended to every occurrence to which the present life is subject. Therefore, he alone has duly denied himself who has so totally resigned himself to the Lord that he permits every part of his life to be governed by God's will. He who will be thus composed in mind, whatever happens, will not consider himself miserable nor complain of his lot with ill will toward God. How necessary this disposition is will appear if you weigh the many chance happenings to which we are subject. ... "Nevertheless we are in the Lord's protection, sheep brought up in his pastures" [Ps. 79:13]. The Lord will therefore supply food to us even in extreme barrenness. If he shall be afflicted by disease, he will not even then be so unmanned by the harshness of pain as to break forth into impatience and expostulate with God; but, by considering the righteousness and gentleness of God's chastening, he will recall himself to forbearance. In short, whatever happens, because he will know it ordained of God, he will undergo it with a peaceful and grateful mind so as not obstinately to resist the command of him into whose power he once for all surrendered himself and his every possession.

Dietrich Bonhoeffer, *Costly Grace*

Dietrich Bonhoeffer (1906–1945) was a German theologian and founder of the Confessing Church that opposed the Nazis. He established a Confessing Church seminary in Finkenwalde and on the von Blumenthal family estate in modern Poland. He was drawn into the plot to kill Adolf Hitler, and this led to his imprisonment in 1943 and his brutal execution in 1945, in the last weeks of the war.

He is best known today for his reflections on seminary existence, *Life Together*; for his extensive, wide-ranging, and allusive *Letters and Papers from Prison*; and for the text quoted here, the challenging and uncompromising *Cost of Discipleship* (1937), in which he coins the influential term "cheap grace." This last work is most famous for Bonhoeffer's unequivocal statement, "When Christ calls a man, he bids him come and die."

Bonhoeffer's Lutheran formation is evident in the passage below. Here we see him steering a course between a bland Protestant affirmation of humanity in the notion of grace and the much-feared (but no doubt caricatured) Roman Catholic notion of merit. Bonhoeffer is in no doubt that there is nothing the Christian can do to earn grace – and he credits Luther for demonstrating this conviction; but he is equally sure that while grace is free, it must never be regarded as cheap, and again he cites Luther as an example of how the burden of grace costs everything to the stability of life. Bonhoeffer cites the directness of Jesus with the urgency of Paul.

Dietrich Bonhoeffer. *The Cost of Discipleship*. London: SCM Press, 2001. From Chapter 1, "Costly Grace," pages 3–9. Available online at www.cross-road.to/Persecution/Bonhoffer.html. Reprinted by permission of the publisher SCM Press. Reprinted with the permission of Scribner, a Division of Simon & Schuster, Inc., from *The Cost of Discipleship* by Dietrich Bonhoeffer. Copyright © 1959 by SCM Press Ltd. All rights reserved.

Cheap grace is the deadly enemy of our Church. We are fighting to-day for costly grace.

Cheap grace means grace said on the market like cheapjack's wares. The sacraments, the forgiveness of sin, and the consolations of religion are thrown away at cut prices. Grace is represented as the Church's inexhaustible treasury, from which she showers blessings with generous hands, without asking questions or fixing limits. Grace without price; grace without cost! The essence of grace, we suppose, is that the account has been paid in advance; and, because it has been paid, everything can be had for nothing. Since the cost was infinite, the possibilities of using and spending it are infinite. What would grace be if it were not cheap?

Cheap grace means grace as a doctrine, a principle, a system. It means forgiveness of sins proclaimed as a general truth, the love of God taught as the Christian "conception" of God. An intellectual assent to that idea is held to be of itself sufficient to secure remission of sins. The Church which holds the correct doctrine of grace has, it is supposed, *ipso facto* a part in that grace. In such a Church the world finds a cheap covering for its sins; no contrition is required, still less any real desire to be delivered from sin. Cheap grace therefore amounts to a denial of the living Word of God, in fact, a denial of the Incarnation of the Word of God.

Cheap grace means the justification of sin without the justification of the sinner. Grace alone does everything, they say, and so everything can remain as it was before. "All for sin could not atone." The world goes on in the same old way, and we are still sinners "even in the best life" as Luther said. Well, then, let the Christian live like the rest of the world, let him model himself on the world's standards in every sphere of life, and not presumptuously aspire to live a different life under grace from his old life under sin. … Let the Christian rest content with his worldliness and with this renunciation of any higher standard than the world. He is doing it for the sake of the world rather than for the sake of grace. Let him be comforted and rest assured in his possession of this grace – for grace alone does every-

thing. Instead of following Christ, let the Christian enjoy the consolations of his grace! That is what we mean by cheap grace, the grace which amounts to the justification of sin without the justification of the repentant sinner who departs from sin and from whom sin departs. Cheap grace is not the kind of forgiveness of sin which frees us from the toils of sin. Cheap grace is the grace we bestow on ourselves.

Cheap grace is the preaching of forgiveness without requiring repentance, baptism without church discipline, Communion without confession, absolution without personal confession. Cheap grace is grace without discipleship, grace without the cross, grace without Jesus Christ, living and incarnate.

Costly grace is the treasure hidden in the field; for the sake of it a man will gladly go and sell all that he has. It is the pearl of great price to buy which the merchant will sell all his goods. It is the kingly rule of Christ, for whose sake a man will pluck out the eye which causes him to stumble, it is the call of Jesus Christ at which the disciple leaves his nets and follows him.

Costly grace is the gospel which must be *sought* again and again, the gift which must be asked for, the door at which a man must *knock*.

Such grace is *costly* because it calls us to follow, and it is *grace* because it calls us to follow *Jesus Christ*. It is costly because it costs a man his life, and it is grace because it gives a man the only true life. It is costly because it condemns sin, and grace because it justifies the sinner. Above all, it is *costly* because it cost God the life of his Son: "ye were bought at a price," and what has cost God much cannot be cheap for us. Above all, it is grace because God did not reckon his Son too dear a price to pay for our life, but delivered him up for us. Costly grace is the Incarnation of God.

Costly grace is the sanctuary of God; it has to be protected from the world, and not thrown to the dogs. It is therefore the living word, the Word of God, which he speaks as it pleases him. Costly grace confronts us as a gracious call to follow Jesus, it comes as a word of forgiveness to the broken spirit and the contrite heart. Grace is costly because it compels a man to submit to the yoke of Christ and follow him; it is grace because Jesus says: "My yoke is easy and my burden is light."

On two separate occasions Peter received the call, "Follow me." It was the first and last word Jesus spoke to his disciple (Mark 1:17; John 21:22). A whole life lies between these two calls. The first occasion was by the lake of Gennesareth, when Peter left his nets and his craft and followed Jesus at his word. The second occasion is when the Risen Lord finds him back again at his old trade. Once again it is by the lake of Gennesareth, and once again the call is "Follow me." Between the two calls lay a whole life of discipleship in the following of Christ. Half-way between them comes Peter's confession, when he acknowledged Jesus as the Christ of God. Three times Peter hears the same proclamation that Christ is his Lord and God – at the beginning, at the end, and at Caesarea Philippi. Each time it is the same grace of Christ which calls to him "Follow me" and which reveals itself to him in his confession of the Son of God. Three times on Peter's way did grace arrest him, the one grace proclaimed in three different ways.

This grace was certainly not self-bestowed. It was the grace of Christ himself, now prevailing upon the disciple to leave all and follow him, now working in him that confession which to the world must sound like the ultimate blasphemy, now inviting Peter to the supreme fellowship of martyrdom for the Lord he had denied, and thereby forgiving him all his sins. In the life of Peter grace and discipleship are inseparable. He had received the grace which costs. ...

When the Reformation came, the providence of God raised Martin Luther to restore the gospel of pure, costly grace. Luther passed through the cloister; he was a monk, and all this was part of the divine plan. Luther had left all to follow Christ on the path of absolute obedience. He had renounced the world in order to live the Christian life. He had learnt obedience to Christ and to his Church, because only he who is obedient can believe. The call to the cloister demanded of Luther the complete surrender of his life. But God shattered all his hopes. He showed him through the Scriptures that the following of Christ is not the achievement or merit of a select few, but the divine command to all Christians without distinction. ... The bottom having thus been knocked out of the religious life, Luther laid hold upon grace. Just as the whole world of monasticism was crashing about him in ruins, he saw God in Christ stretching forth his hand to save. He grasped that hand in faith, believing that "after all, nothing we can do is of any avail, however good a life we live." The grace which gave itself to him was a costly grace, and it shattered his whole existence. Once more he must leave his nets and follow. The first time was when he entered the monastery, when he had left everything behind except his pious self. This time even that was taken from him. He obeyed the call, not through any merit of his own, but simply through the grace of God. Luther did not

hear the word: "Of course you have sinned, but now everything is forgiven, so you can stay as you are and enjoy the consolations of forgiveness." No, Luther had to leave the cloister and go back to the world, not because the world in itself was good and holy, but because even the cloister was only a part of the world. ...

It is a fatal misunderstanding of Luther's action to suppose that his rediscovery of the gospel of pure grace offered a general dispensation from obedience to the command of Jesus, or that it was the great discovery of the Reformation that God's forgiving grace automatically conferred upon the world both righteousness and holiness. On the contrary, for Luther the Christian's worldly calling is sanctified only in so far as that calling registers the final, radical protest against the world. Only in so far as the Christian's secular calling is exercised in the following of Jesus does it receive from the gospel new sanction and justification. It was not the justification of sin, but the justification of the sinner that drove Luther from the cloister back into the world. The grace he had received was costly grace. It was grace, for it was like water on parched ground, comfort in tribulation, freedom from the bondage of a self-chosen way, and forgiveness of all his sins. And it was costly, for, so far from dispensing him from good works, it meant that he must take the call to discipleship more seriously than ever before. It was grace because it cost so much, and it cost so much because it was grace. That was the secret of the gospel of the Reformation – the justification of the sinner.

... When he spoke of grace, Luther always implied as a corollary that it cost him his own life, the life which was now for the first time subjected to the absolute obedience of Christ. Only so could he speak of grace. Luther had said that grace alone can save; his followers took up his doctrine and repeated it word for word. But they left out its invariable corollary, the obligation of discipleship. There was no need for Luther always to mention that corollary explicitly for he always spoke as one who had been led by grace to the strictest following of Christ. Judged by the standard of Luther's doctrine, that of his follower was unassailable, and yet their orthodoxy spelt the end and destruction of the Reformation as the revelation on earth of the costly grace of God. The justification of the sinner in the world degenerated into the justification of sin and the world. Costly grace was turned into cheap grace without discipleship.

Chapter Two

The Story of the Church

In the previous chapter we looked at the story of God – the Bible. In this chapter we look at the community which tells that story – the church. Christian ethics has been called "theology teaching by examples" – and in this sense, church history is crucial to understanding Christian ethics.

The church is the community in which Christian people are formed and transformed. It is a community that makes sense of who its members are and how they act. The content of its ethics involves claims about a kingdom, which fulfils the purposes of God by creating a sanctified people. But the way the church goes about this shaping of ethical lives has varied from place to place and from era to era. Three broad periods of time are identified in the present chapter:

1   The period before Christianity became the official religion of the Roman Empire under Constantine, during which Christianity was a minority religion and was often persecuted.
2   The period between Constantine and the time of the European wars of religion and the Enlightenment, during which Christianity was the dominant religion of the Mediterranean and then the European world.
3   The period of Western modernity, during which Christianity has faced a series of challenges to its intellectual and social hegemony, and has had to find a way of relating to multiple worldviews – some religious and some anti-religious – in a less Eurocentric world.

Minority Status

The life of the early church was marked by close-knit groups rejecting pagan cults and reluctant to participate in public entertainment and spectacles. There is no record of Christians serving regularly in the imperial armies until about 170 CE. There was highly effective pastoral care for the poor in their midst, and support for widows, orphans, and prisoners. Care for those outside the Christian community was significant. Persecution was sporadic but sometimes severe. Even in calmer times, there was a concern on the part of the first Christians not to be unnecessarily misunderstood.

Among many controversies were the questions of how close Christians should remain to Jews in their life and worship, and to what extent they could borrow pagan ideas and values. Meanwhile, in relation to the state, the church faced a tension between the extremes of provocation and compromise. In relation to issues such as money, slave-holding, and marriage, it faced the "already–not yet" tension of a community half-expecting the world to end soon, and half-preparing for a whole new order of society.

The texts in this section express the sociology of Christian belonging in this period. The Epistle to Diognetus carefully places the church in relation to the world, while the account of the martyrdom of Perpetua and her companions demonstrates vividly that the costs of upholding the faith could be very great. The words of Clement of Alexandria display another dimension of Christian existence in this period – the need to come to terms with the temptations of wealth.

The Epistle to Diognetus

This text, thought to have been written to the procurator of Alexandria in the late second century CE by an anonymous disciple, is one of the earliest apologetic writings defending the claims and activities of Christians against their critics and persecutors. It begins by locating Christian belief between what it calls the "superstitions of the Jews" and the "vanity of idols." Before setting out the fundamentals of Christian theology it pauses for the passage excerpted below, which sets out Christian habits and practices.

Echoing the style of Paul's epistles, the account describes the Christians as ones who "are poor, yet make many rich … are in lack of all things, and yet abound in all." As the soul is to the body, Christians are to the world. (Here the influence of Neoplatonism, with its firm soul–body distinction, is harmonized with a Christian social ethic.) The epistle shows the kind of dualist ethic and theology that emerged from a time of persecution. The writer has no triumphalist aspirations: he insists, "it is not by ruling over his neighbors, or by seeking to hold the supremacy over those that are weaker, or by being rich, and showing violence towards those that are inferior, that happiness is found."

The Epistle of Mathetes to Diognetus. Source: www. earlychristianwritings.com/text/diognetus-roberts. html.

Chapter 5. The Manners of the Christians

For the Christians are distinguished from other men neither by country, nor language, nor the customs which they observe. For they neither inhabit cities of their own, nor employ a peculiar form of speech, nor lead a life which is marked out by any singularity. The course of conduct which they follow has not been devised by any speculation or deliberation of inquisitive men; nor do they, like some, proclaim themselves the advocates of any merely human doctrines. But, inhabiting Greek as well as barbarian cities, according as the lot of each of them has determined, and following the customs of the natives in respect to clothing, food, and the rest of their ordinary conduct, they display to us their wonderful and confessedly striking method of life. They dwell in their own countries, but simply as sojourners. As citizens, they share in all things with others, and yet endure all things as if foreigners. Every foreign land is to them as their native country, and every land of their birth as a land of strangers. They marry, as do all [others]; they beget children; but they do not destroy their offspring. They have a common table, but not a common bed. They are in the flesh, but they do not live after the flesh. They pass their days on earth, but they are citizens of heaven. They obey the prescribed laws, and at the same time surpass the laws by their lives. They love all men, and are persecuted by all. They are unknown and condemned; they are put to death, and restored to life. They are poor, yet make many rich; they are in lack of all things, and yet abound in all; they are dishonoured, and yet in their very dishonour are glorified. They are evil spoken of, and yet are justified; they are reviled, and bless; they are insulted, and repay the insult with honour; they do good, yet are punished as evil-doers. When punished, they rejoice as if quickened into life; they are assailed by the Jews as foreigners, and are persecuted by the Greeks; yet those who hate them are unable to assign any reason for their hatred.

Chapter 6. The Relation of Christians to the World

To sum up all in one word – what the soul is in the body, that are Christians in the world. The soul is dispersed through all the members of the body, and Christians are scattered through all the cities of the world. The soul dwells in the body, yet is not of the body; and Christians dwell in the world, yet are not of the world. The invisible soul is guarded by the visible body, and Christians are known indeed to be in the world, but their godliness remains invisible. The flesh hates the soul, and wars against it, though itself suffering no injury, because it is prevented from enjoying pleasures; the world also hates the Christians, though in nowise injured, because they abjure pleasures. The soul loves the flesh that hates it, and [loves also] the members; Christians likewise love those that hate them. The soul is imprisoned in the body, yet preserves that very body; and Christians are confined in the world as in a prison, and yet they are the preservers of the world. The immortal soul dwells in a mortal tabernacle; and Christians dwell as sojourners in corruptible [bodies], looking for an incorruptible dwelling in the heavens. The soul, when but ill-provided with food and drink, becomes better; in like manner, the Christians, though subjected day by day to punishment, increase the more in number. God has assigned them this illustrious position, which it were unlawful for them to forsake.

Chapter 7. The Manifestation of Christ

For, as I said, this was no mere earthly invention which was delivered to them, nor is it a mere human system of opinion, which they judge it right to preserve so carefully, nor has a dispensation of mere human mysteries been committed to them, but truly God Himself, who is almighty, the Creator of all things, and invisible, has sent from heaven, and placed among men, [Him who is] the truth, and the holy and incomprehensible Word, and has firmly established Him in their hearts. He did not, as one might have imagined, send to men any servant, or angel, or ruler, or any one of those who bear sway over earthly things, or one of those to whom the government of things in the heavens has been entrusted, but the very Creator and Fashioner of all things – by whom He made the heavens – by whom he enclosed the sea within its proper bounds – whose ordinances all the stars faithfully observe – from whom the sun has received the measure of his daily course to be observed – whom the moon obeys, being commanded to shine in the night, and whom the stars also obey, following the moon in her course; by whom all things have been arranged, and placed within their proper limits, and to whom all are subject – the heavens and the things that are therein, the earth and the things that are therein, the sea and the things that are therein – fire, air, and the abyss – the things which are in the heights, the things which are in the depths, and the things which lie between. This [messenger] He sent to them. Was it then, as one might conceive, for the purpose of exercising tyranny, or of inspiring fear and terror? By no means, but under the influence of clemency and meekness. As a king sends his son, who is also a king, so sent He Him; as God He sent Him; as to men He sent Him; as a Saviour He sent Him, and as seeking to persuade, not to compel us; for violence has no place in the character of God. As calling us He sent Him, not as venge-fully pursuing us; as loving us He sent Him, not as judging us. For He will yet send Him to judge us, and who shall endure His appearing? ... Do you not see them exposed to wild beasts, that they may be persuaded to deny the Lord, and yet not overcome? Do you not see that the more of them are punished, the greater becomes the number of the rest? This does not seem to be the work of man: this is the power of God; these are the evidences of His manifestation.

Chapter 8. The Miserable State of Men before the Coming of the Word

For, who of men at all understood before His coming what God is? Do you accept of the vain and silly doctrines of those who are deemed trustworthy philosophers? Of whom some said that fire was God, calling that God to which they themselves were by and by to come; and some water; and others some other of the elements formed by God. But if any one of these theories be worthy of approbation, every one of the rest of created things might also be declared to be God. But such declarations are simply the startling and erroneous utterances of deceivers; and no man has either seen Him, or made Him known, but He has revealed Himself. And He has manifested Himself through faith, to which alone it is given to behold God. For God, the Lord and Fashioner of all things, who made all things, and assigned them their several positions, proved Himself not merely a friend of mankind, but also long-suffering [in His dealings with them]. Yea, He was always of such a character, and still is, and will ever be, kind and good, and free from wrath, and true, and the only one who is [absolutely] good; and He formed in His mind a great and unspeakable conception, which He communicated to His Son alone. As long, then, as He held and preserved His own wise counsel in concealment, He appeared to neglect us, and to have no care over us. But after He revealed and laid open, through His beloved Son, the things which had been prepared from the beginning, He conferred every blessing all at once upon us, so that we should both share in His benefits, and see and be active [in His service]. Who of us would ever have expected these things? He was aware, then, of all things in His own mind, along with His Son, according to the relation subsisting between them.

Chapter 10. The Blessings that will Flow from Faith

If you also desire [to possess] this faith, you likewise shall receive first of all the knowledge of the Father. For

God has loved mankind, on whose account He made the world, to whom He rendered subject all the things that are in it, to whom He gave reason and understanding, to whom alone He imparted the privilege of looking upwards to Himself, whom He formed after His own image, to whom He sent His only-begotten Son, to whom He has promised a kingdom in heaven, and will give it to those who have loved Him. And when you have attained this knowledge, with what joy do you think you will be filled? Or, how will you love Him who has first so loved you? And if you love Him, you will be an imitator of His kindness. And do not wonder that a man may become an imitator of God. He can, if he is willing. For it is not by ruling over his neighbours, or by seeking to hold the supremacy over those that are weaker, or by being rich, and showing violence towards those that are inferior, that happiness is found; nor can any one by these things become an imitator of God. But these things do not at all constitute His majesty. On the contrary he who takes upon himself the burden of his neighbour; he who, in whatsoever respect he may be superior, is ready to benefit another who is deficient; he who, whatsoever things he has received from God, by distributing these to the needy, becomes a god to those who receive [his benefits]: he is an imitator of God. Then thou shalt see, while still on earth, that God in the heavens rules over [the universe]; then thou shall begin to speak the mysteries of God; then shalt thou both love and admire those that suffer punishment because they will not deny God; then shall thou condemn the deceit and error of the world when thou shall know what it is to live truly in heaven, when thou shalt despise that which is here esteemed to be death, when thou shalt fear what is truly death, which is reserved for those who shall be condemned to the eternal fire, which shall afflict those even to the end that are committed to it. Then shalt thou admire those who for righteousness' sake endure the fire that is but for a moment, and shalt count them happy when thou shalt know [the nature of] that fire.

Perpetua, *The Martyrdom of Perpetua*

This is thought to be one of the earliest preserved pieces of writing by a Christian woman. Emperor Septimus Severus had forbidden any conversion to Christianity or Judaism. Perpetua (died ca. 203) was the wife of a wealthy man in Carthage (in modern Tunisia); she had a baby at the breast and she was accompanied by a slave named Felicity, who was heavily pregnant. It seems Perpetua wrote at least sections 3–10 of her own passion account herself. It is an archetypal piece of martyrology.

The significance of the passage lies not in suggesting that martyrdom was a daily threat for all Christians in the early centuries of the church – it clearly was not – but in perceiving the hold that these stories had over the imagination of the early Christians. When considering what it meant to live a good life they went immediately to the question of what it meant to die a good death. Proximity to death opened their lives to visions in which they communed with those already dead: it was the way the barrier of death and the threat of persecution were transcended.

Perpetua. "Martyrdom of Perpetua." From *In Her Words: Women's Writings in the History of Christian Thought*. Ed. Amy Oden. Nashville: Abingdon Press, 1994. From pages 26–37. Available online at www. newadvent.org/fathers/0324.htm.

2. Arrested were some young catechumens; Revocatus and Felicitas (both servants), Satuminus, Secundulus, and Vibia Perpetua, a young married woman about twenty years old, of good family and upbringing. She had a father, mother, two brothers (one was a catechumen like herself), and an infant son at the breast. The following account of her martyrdom is her own, a record in her own words of her perceptions of the event.

3. While I was still with the police authorities (she said) my father out of love for me tried to dissuade me from my resolution. "Father," I said, "do you see here, for example, this vase, or pitcher, or whatever it is?" "I see it," he said. "Can it be named anything else than

what it really is?," I asked, and he said, "No." "So I also cannot be called anything else than what I am, a Christian." Enraged by my words my father came at me as though to tear out my eyes. He only annoyed me, but he left, overpowered by his diabolical arguments. ...

A few days later we were imprisoned. I was terrified because never before had I experienced such darkness. What a terrible day! Because of crowded conditions and rough treatment by the soldiers the heat was unbearable. My condition was aggravated by my anxiety for my baby. Then Tertius and Pomponius, those kind deacons who were taking care of our needs, paid for us to be moved for a few hours to a better part of the prison where we might refresh ourselves. Leaving the dungeon we all went about our own business. I nursed my child, who was already weak from hunger. In my anxiety for the infant I spoke to my mother about him, tried to console my brother, and asked that they care for my son. I suffered intensely because I sensed their agony on my account. These were the trials I had to endure for many days. Then I was granted the privilege of having my son remain with me in prison. Being relieved of my anxiety and concern for the infant, I immediately regained my strength. Suddenly the prison became my palace, and I loved being there rather than any other place. ...

6. One day as we were eating we were suddenly rushed off for a hearing. We arrived at the forum and the news spread quickly throughout the area near the forum, and a huge crowd gathered. We went up to the prisoners' platform. All the others confessed when they were questioned. When my turn came my father appeared with my son. Dragging me from the step, he begged: "Have pity on your son!"

Hilarion, the governor, who assumed power after the death of the proconsul Minucius Timinianus, said, "Have pity on your father's grey head; have pity on your infant son; offer sacrifice for the emperors' welfare." But I answered, "I will not." Hilarion asked, "Are you a Christian?" And I answered, "I am a Christian." And when my father persisted in his attempts to dissuade me, Hilarion ordered him thrown out, and he was beaten with a rod. My father's injury hurt me as much as if I myself had been beaten, and I grieved because of his pathetic old age. Then the sentence was passed; all of us were condemned to the beasts. We were overjoyed as we went back to the prison cell. Since I was still nursing my child who was ordinarily in the cell with me, I quickly sent the deacon Pomponius to my father's house to ask for the baby, but my father refused to give him up. Then God saw to it that my child no longer

needed my nursing, nor were my breasts inflamed. After that I was no longer tortured by anxiety about my child or by pain in my breasts. ...

11. The saintly Saturus also related a vision which he had and it is recorded here in his own hand. Our suffering had ended (he said), and we were being carried towards the east by four angels whose hands never touched us. And we floated upward, not in a supine position, but as though we were climbing a gentle slope. As we left the earth's atmosphere we saw a brilliant light, and I said to Perpetua who was at my side, "This is what the Lord promised us. We have received his promise."

And while we were being carried along by those four angels we saw a large open space like a splendid garden landscaped with rose trees and every variety of flower. The trees were as tall as cypresses whose leaves rustled gently and incessantly. And there in that garden-sanctuary were four other angels, more dazzling than the rest. And when they saw us they showed us honor, saying to the other angels in admiration, "Here they are! They have arrived."

And those four angels who were carrying us began trembling in awe and set us down. And we walked through a violet-strewn field where we met Jocundus, Saturninus, and Artaxius who were burned alive in that same persecution, and Quintus, also a martyr, who had died in prison. We were asking them where they had been, when the other angels said to us, "First, come this way. Go in and greet the Lord."

12. We went up to a place where the walls seemed constructed of light. At the entrance of the place stood four angels who put white robes on those who entered. We went in and heard a unified voice chanting endlessly, "Holy, holy, holy." We saw a white haired man sitting there who, in spite of his snowy white hair, had the features of a young man. His feet were not visible. On his right and left were four elderly gentlemen and behind them stood many more. As we entered we stood in amazement before the throne. Four angels supported us as we went up to kiss the aged man, and he gently stroked our faces with his hands. The other elderly men said to us, "Stand up." We rose and gave the kiss of peace. Then they told us to enjoy ourselves. I said to Perpetua, "You have your wish." She answered, "I thank God, for although I was happy on earth, I am much happier here right now." ...

17. On the day before the public games, as they were eating the last meal commonly called the free meal, they tried as much as possible to make it instead an *agape*. In the same spirit they were exhorting the people,

warning them to remember the judgment of God, asking them to be witnesses to the prisoners' joy in suffering, and ridiculing the curiosity of the crowd. Saturus told them, "Won't tomorrow's view be enough for you? Why are you so eager to see something you hate? Friends today, enemies tomorrow! Take a good look so you'll recognize us on that day." Then they all left the prison amazed, and many of them began to believe.

18. The day of their victory dawned, and with joyful countenances they marched from the prison to the arena as though on their way to heaven. If there was any trembling it was from joy, not fear. Perpetua followed with quick step as a true spouse of Christ, the darling of God, her brightly flashing eyes quelling the gaze of the crowd. Felicitas too, joyful because she had safely survived child-birth and was now able to participate in the contest with the wild animals, passed from one shedding of blood to another; from midwife to gladiator, about to be purified after child-birth by a second baptism. As they were led through the gate they were ordered to put on different clothes; the men, those priests of Saturn, the women, those of the priestesses of Ceres. But that noble woman stubbornly resisted even to the end. She said, "We've come this far voluntarily in order to protect our rights, and we've pledged our lives not to recapitulate on any such matter as this. We made this agreement with you." Injustice bowed to justice and the guard conceded that they could enter the arena in their ordinary dress. Perpetua was singing victory psalms as if already crushing the head of the Egyptian. Revocatus, Saturninus and Saturus were warning the spectators, and as they came within sight of Hilarion they informed him by nods and gestures: "You condemn us; God condemns you." This so infuriated the crowds that they demanded the scourging of these men in front of the line of gladiators. But the ones so punished rejoiced in that they had obtained yet another share in the Lord's suffering. ...

20. For the young women the devil had readied a mad cow, an animal not usually used at these games, but selected so that the women's sex would be matched with that of the animal. After being stripped and enmeshed in nets, the women were led into the arena. How horrified the people were as they saw that one was a young girl and the other, her breasts dripping with milk, had just recently given birth to a child. Consequently both were recalled and dressed in loosely fitting gowns.

Perpetua was tossed first and fell on her back. She sat up, and being more concerned with her sense of modesty than with her pain, covered her thighs with her gown which had been torn down one side. Then finding her hair-clip which had fallen out, she pinned back her loose hair thinking it not proper for a martyr to suffer with dishevelled hair; it might seem that she was mourning in her hour of triumph. Then she stood up. Noticing that Felicitas was badly bruised, she went to her, reached out her hands and helped her to her feet. As they stood there the cruelty of the crowds seemed to be appeased and they were sent to the Sanavivarian Gate. There Perpetua was taken care of by a certain catechumen, Rusticus, who stayed near her. She seemed to be waking from a deep sleep (so completely had she been entranced and imbued with the Spirit). She began to look around her and to everyone's astonishment asked, "When are we going to be led out to that cow, or whatever it is." She would not believe that it had already happened until she saw the various markings of the tossing on her body and clothing. Then calling for her brother she said to him and to the catechumen, "Remain strong in your faith and love one another. Do not let our excruciating sufferings become a stumbling block for you."

21. ... And when the crowd demanded that the prisoners be brought out into the open so that they might feast their eyes on death by the sword, they voluntarily arose and moved where the crowd wanted them. Before doing so they kissed each other so that their martyrdom would be completely perfected by the rite of the kiss of peace.

The others, without making any movement or sound, were killed by the sword. Saturus in particular, since he had been the first to climb the ladder and was to be Perpetua's encouragement, was the first to die. But Perpetua, in order to feel some of the pain, groaning as she was struck between the ribs, took the gladiator's trembling hand [and] guided it to her throat. Perhaps it was that so great a woman, feared as she was by the unclean spirit, could not have been slain had she not herself willed it.

O brave and fortunate martyrs, truly called and chosen to give honor to our Lord Jesus Christ! And anyone who is elaborating upon, or who reverences or worships that honor, should read these more recent examples, along with the ancient, as sources of encouragement for the Christian community. In this way, there will be new examples of courage witnessing to the fact that even in our day the same Holy Spirit is still efficaciously present, along with the all powerful God the Father and Jesus Christ our Lord, to whom there will always be glory and endless power. Amen.

Clement of Alexandria, *Who is the Rich Man That Shall Be Saved?*

This piece was written around the same time as the foregoing pieces. Clement of Alexandria (ca. 150–215) – not to be confused with Clement of Rome, who lived a hundred years earlier – is one of the theologians sometimes known as the "Early Fathers" and is most often cited as the teacher of the great theologian Origen (185–254).

In this discussion of wealth and resources, Clement shows the way Platonic and Stoic influences were drawn together in shaping the ethic of the early church. Clement sees Christianity as focused ultimately on becoming like God and even becoming part of God – this is the Platonic influence. Likewise, early in this excerpt Clement distinguishes between the "outer act" and the greater "stripping off of the passions." The Stoic influence is visible in the way Clement distinguishes between the possession of wealth and its use. Like the Stoics, Clement believed it was possible to be appropriately detached from one's wealth so that the simple possession of wealth was not an inherent problem: the issue was about the development of wisdom. In many ways his discussion anticipates many later treatments of this issue in Christian ethics (see, for example, the passage from John Wesley in Chapter 4), in that it makes clear money is not an evil in itself, but is also very aware of the temptations open to the one who is wealthy.

St. Clement of Alexandria, "Who is the Rich Man That Shall Be Saved?" Source: www.earlychristianwritings. com/text/clement-richman.html. Originally published by Eerdmans Pub. Co. Scotland, 1867.

[Clement recounts the story of the rich man in Mark 10:17–22, to whom Jesus says, "Go, sell what you own, and give the money to the poor, and you will have treasure in heaven; then come, follow me," and who "was shocked and went away grieving, for he had many possessions."]

XI. What then was it which persuaded him [the rich man] to flight, and made him depart from the Master, from the entreaty, the hope, the life, previously pursued with ardour? – "Sell thy possessions." And what is this? He does not, as some conceive off-hand, bid him throw away the substance he possessed, and abandon his property; but bids him banish from his soul his notions about wealth, his excitement and morbid feeling about it, the anxieties, which are the thorns of existence, which choke the seed of life. For it is no great thing or desirable to be destitute of wealth, if without a special object, – not except on account of life. For thus those who have nothing at all, but are destitute, and beggars for their daily bread, the poor dispersed on the streets, who know not God and God's righteousness, simply on account of their extreme want and destitution of subsistence, and lack even of the smallest things, were most

blessed and most dear to God, and sole possessors of everlasting life.

Nor was the renunciation of wealth and the bestowment of it on the poor or needy a new thing; for many did so before the Saviour's advent, – some because of the leisure (thereby obtained) for learning, and on account of a dead wisdom; and others for empty fame and vainglory, as the Anaxagorases, the Democriti, and the Crateses.

XII. Why then command as new, as divine, as alone life-giving, what did not save those of former days? And what peculiar thing is it that the new creature, the Son of God, intimates and teaches? It is not the outward act which others have done, but something else indicated by it, greater, more godlike, more perfect, the stripping off of the passions from the soul itself and from the disposition, and the cutting up by the roots and casting out of what is alien to the mind. For this is the lesson peculiar to the believer, and the instruction worthy of the Saviour. For those who formerly despised external things relinquished and squandered their property, but the passions of the soul, I believe, they intensified. For they indulged in arrogance, pretension, and vainglory, and in contempt of the rest of mankind, as if they had done something superhuman. How then would the Saviour have enjoined on those destined to tire for ever what was injurious and hurtful with reference to the life which He promised? For although such is the case, one, after ridding himself of the burden of wealth, may nonetheless have still the lust and desire for money innate and living; and may have abandoned the use of it, but being at once destitute of and desiring what he spent, may doubly grieve both on account of the absence of attendance, and the presence of regret. For it is impossible and inconceivable that those in want of the necessaries of life should not be harassed in mind, and hindered from better things in the endeavour to provide them somehow, and from some source.

XIII. And how much more beneficial the opposite case, for a man, through possessing a competency, both not himself to be in straits about money, and also to give assistance to those to whom it is requisite so to do! For if no one had anything, what room would be left among men for giving? And how can this dogma fail to be found plainly opposed to and conflicting with many other excellent teachings of the Lord? "Make to yourselves friends of the mammon of unrighteousness, that when ye fail, they may receive you into the everlasting habitations." "Acquire treasures in heaven, where neither moth nor rust destroys, nor thieves break through." How could one give food to the hungry, and drink to the thirsty, clothe the naked, and shelter the houseless, for not doing which He threatens with fire and the outer darkness, if each man first divested himself of all these things? Nay, He bids Zacchaeus and Matthew, the rich tax-gatherers, entertain Him hospitably. And He does not bid them part with their property, but, applying the just and removing the unjust judgment, He subjoins, "To-day salvation has come to this house, forasmuch as he also is a son of Abraham." He so praises the use of property as to enjoin, along with this addition, the giving a share of it, to give drink to the thirsty, bread to the hungry, to take the houseless in, and clothe the naked. But if it is not possible to supply those needs without substance, and He bids people abandon their substance, what else would the Lord be doing than exhorting to give and not to give the same things, to feed and not to feed, to take in and to shut out, to share and not to share? which were the most irrational of all things.

XIV. Riches, then, which benefit also our neighbours, are not to be thrown away. For they are possessions, inasmuch as they are possessed, and goods, inasmuch as they are useful and provided by God for the use of men; and they lie to our hand, and are put under our power, as material and instruments which are for good use to those who know the instrument. If you use it skillfully, it is skillful; if you are deficient in skill, it is affected by your want of skill, being itself destitute of blame. Such an instrument is wealth. Are you able to make a right use of it? It is subservient to righteousness. Does one make a wrong use of it? It is, on the other hand, a minister of wrong. For its nature is to be subservient, not to rule. That then which of itself has neither good nor evil, being blameless, ought not to be blamed; but that which has the power of using it well and ill, by reason of its possessing voluntary choice. And this is the mind and judgment of man, which has freedom in itself and self-determination in the treatment of what is assigned to it. So let no man destroy wealth, rather than the passions of the soul, which are incompatible with the better use of wealth. So that, becoming virtuous and good, he may be able to make a good use of these riches. The renunciation, then, and selling of all possessions, is to be understood as spoken of the passions of the soul. ...

XVI. The presence of wealth in these is deadly to all, the loss of it salutary. Of which, making the soul pure, – that is, poor and bare, – we must hear the Saviour speaking thus, "Come, follow Me." For to the pure in heart He now becomes the way. But into the impure soul the grace of God finds no entrance. And that (soul) is unclean which is rich in lusts, and is in the throes of many worldly affections. For he who holds possessions, and gold, and silver, and houses, as the gifts of God; and ministers from them to the God who gives them for the salvation of men; and knows that he possesses them more for the sake of the brethren than his own; and is superior to the possession of them, not the slave of the things he possesses; and does not carry them about in his soul, nor bind and circumscribe his life within them, but is ever labouring at some good and divine work, even should he be necessarily some time or other deprived of them, is able with cheerful mind to bear their removal equally with their abundance. This is he who is blessed by the Lord, and cared poor in spirit, a meet heir of the kingdom of heaven, not one who could not live rich.

XVII. But he who carries his riches in his soul, and instead of God's Spirit bears in his heart gold or land, and is always acquiring possessions without end, and is perpetually on the outlook for more, bending downwards and fettered in the toils of the world, being earth and destined to depart to earth, – whence can he be able to desire and to mind the kingdom of heaven, – a man who carries not a heart, but land or metal, who must perforce be found in the midst of the objects he has chosen? For where the mind of man is, there is also his treasure. The Lord acknowledges a twofold treasure, – the good: "For the good man, out of the good treasure of his heart, bringeth forth good;" and the evil: for "the evil man, out of the evil treasure, bringeth forth evil: for out of the abundance of the heart the mouth speaketh." As then treasure is not one with Him, as also it is with us, that which gives the unexpected great gain in the finding, but also a second, which is profitless and undesirable, an evil acquisition, hurtful; so also there is a richness in good things, and a richness in bad things, since we know that riches and treasure are not by nature separated from each other. And the one sort of riches is to be possessed and acquired, and the other not to be possessed, but to be cast away. ...

XXIV. You may even go against wealth. Say, "Certainly Christ does not debar me from property. The Lord does not envy." But do you see yourself overcome and overthrown by it? Leave it, throw it away, hate, renounce, flee. "Even if thy right eye offend thee," quickly "cut it out." Better is the kingdom of God to a man with one eye, than the fire to one who is unmutilated. Whether hand, or foot, or soul, hate it. For if it is destroyed here for Christ's sake, it will be restored to life yonder. ...

XXVI. ... I think that our proposition has been demonstrated in no way inferior to what we promised, that the Saviour by no means has excluded the rich on account of wealth itself, and the possession of property, nor fenced off salvation against them; if they are able and willing to submit their life to God's commandments, and prefer them to transitory objects, and if they would look to the Lord with steady eye, as those who look for the nod of a good helmsman, what he wishes, what he orders, what he indicates, what signal he gives his mariners, where and whence he directs the ship's course. For what harm does one do, who, previous to faith, by applying his mind and by saving has collected a competency? Or what is much less reprehensible than this, if at once by God, who gave him his life, he has had his home given him in the house of such men, among wealthy people, powerful in substance, and pre-eminent in opulence? For if, in consequence of his involuntary birth in wealth, a man is banished from life, rather is he wronged by God, who created him, in having vouchsafed to him temporary enjoyment, and in being deprived of eternal life. And why should wealth have ever sprung from the earth at all, if it is the author and patron of death?

But if one is able in the midst of wealth to turn from its power, and to entertain moderate sentiments, and to exercise self-command, and to seek God alone, and to breathe God and walk with God, such a poor man submits to the commandments, being free, unsubdued, free of disease, unwounded by wealth. But if not, "sooner shall a camel enter through a needle's eye, than such a rich man reach the kingdom of God."

Christendom

The early centuries after Christianity became closely linked with the Roman Empire and were marked initially by a major transformation (as noted in the Yoder text, below), but thereafter were profoundly affected by the decline and fall of the Roman Empire. Monasticism was a vital force in sustaining the Christian faith through this period and in restoring Western civilization as it entered the medieval period. The evolving practices of confession and penance emerged out of the monasteries and became a vital part of the practice of moral theology. The Crusades, aimed at reclaiming Jerusalem from Turkish rule, sent a long shadow over the early centuries of the new millennium, as did chronic persecution of the Jews.

The Reformation brought a major change in the notion of authority, as the Bible became for Protestants the source of most of what Catholics had always derived from the officers of the church. In triggering the rise of the nation-state and in turning attention from the practice of the church to the faith of the believer, the Reformation ushered in the period now known as modernity.

The texts below illustrate these themes. Eusebius is the great advocate for how a ruler can advance the kingdom of God. Benedict's *Rule* is a key text for understanding how the church survived the disintegration of the Roman Empire, and for perceiving how Christian community could be founded on humane guidelines. Yoder's more polemical text is a bold attempt to narrate the significance of the Constantinian transformation for today. While "Constantinianism" is a multivalent term, it broadly identifies the state of mind that sees majoritarian thinking by Christians and an inclination to see matters from the ruler's point of view as natural, healthy, and good.

Eusebius of Caesarea, *A Speech on the Dedication of the Holy Sepulchre Church*

No one epitomizes the Constantinian shift in Christian history and ethics more than Eusebius of Caesarea (ca. 263–ca. 339). He became bishop of Caesarea in northern Palestine around 313 and was closely involved in drafting the Nicene Creed in 325. In his rejection of tritheism he steered close to the unitarian heresy of Arianism. He wrote a very influential history of the church from its beginnings to 325. To this he added an unfinished biography of Constantine, which praised the emperor in glowing terms, seeing his conversion to Christianity as the climax of church history. This work, along with his apparently selective reading of history, incurred the wrath of famous critics such as Edward Gibbon and Jakob Burckhardt.

This passage gives a sense of Eusebius' view of history as a march of progress through the unspeakable shortcomings of the variously governed peoples, to the revelation of Christ and finally the coming together of Christian peace under the unity of the one Roman ruler. It is easy to see how Eusebius came to be regarded as the high watermark of state theology.

Eusebius of Caesarea. "A Speech on the Dedication of the Holy Sepulchre Church." In *From Irenaeus to Grotius: A Sourcebook in Christian Political Thought 100–1625*. Ed. Oliver O'Donovan and Joan Lockwood O'Donovan. Translation adapted from E. C. Richardson, *Nicene and Post-Nicene Fathers*. Grand Rapids: Eerdmans, 1999. From pages 58–65.

16. Of old the nations of the earth, the entire human race, were variously distributed into provincial, national, and local governments, subject to kingdoms and principalities of many kinds. The consequences of this variety were war and strife, depopulation and captivity, which raged in country and city with unceasing fury. Hence, too, the countless subjects of history, adulteries and rapes of women; hence the woes of Troy and the ancient tragedies so known among all peoples. The origin of these may justly be ascribed to the delusion of polytheistic error. But when that instrument of our redemption, the thrice-holy body of Christ, which proved itself superior to all Satanic fraud and free from evil both in word and deed, was raised, at once for the abolition of ancient evils and in token of his victory over the powers of darkness; the energy of these evil spirits was at once destroyed. The manifold forms of government, the tyrannies and republics, the siege of cities and devastation of countries caused thereby, were now no more, and one God was proclaimed to all mankind. At the same time one universal power, the Roman empire, arose and flourished, while the enduring and implac-able hatred of nation against nation was now removed; and as the knowledge of one God and one way of religion and salvation, even the doctrine of Christ, was made known to all mankind; so at the self-same period the entire dominion of the Roman empire being vested in a single sovereign, profound peace reigned throughout the world. And thus by the express appointment of the same God, two roots of blessing, the Roman empire and the doctrine of Christian piety, sprang up together for the benefit of men. For before this time the various countries of the world, as Syria, Asia, Macedonia, Egypt and Arabia, had been severally subject to different rulers. The Jewish people, again, had established their dominion in the land of Palestine. And these nations, in every village, city and district, actuated by some insane spirit, were engaged in incessant and murderous war and conflict. But two mighty powers starting from the same point, the Roman empire which henceforth was swayed by a single sovereign and the Christian religion, subdued and reconciled these contending elements. Our Saviour's mighty power destroyed at once the many governments and the many gods of the powers of darkness, and proclaimed to all men, both rude and civilized, to the extremities of the earth, the sole sovereignty of God himself. Meantime the Roman empire, the causes of multiplied governments being thus removed, effected an easy conquest of those which yet remained its object being to unite all nations in one harmonious whole, an object in great measure already secured and destined to be still more perfectly attained, even to the final conquest of the ends of the habitable

world, by means of the salutary doctrine and through the aid of that divine power which facilitates and smoothes its way.

And surely this must appear a wondrous fact to those who will examine the question in the love of truth and desire not to cavil at these blessings. The falsehood of demon superstition was convicted; the inveterate strife and mutual hatred of the nations was removed; at the same time one God and the knowledge of that God were proclaimed to all; one universal empire prevailed; and the whole human race, subdued by the controlling power of peace and concord, received one another as brethren and responded to the feelings of their common nature. Hence as children of one God and Father, and owning true religion as their common mother, they saluted and welcomed each other with words of peace. Thus the whole world appeared like one well-ordered and united family; each one might journey unhindered as far as and whithersoever he pleased; men might securely travel from West to East and from East to West, as to their own native country; in short, the ancient oracles and predictions of the prophets were fulfilled, more numerous than we can at present cite, and those especially which speak as follows concerning the saving Word: "He shall have dominion from sea to sea and from the river to the ends of the earth" (Ps. 72:8). And again: "In his days shall righteousness flourish, and abundance of peace" (Ps. 72:7). "And they shall beat their swords into ploughshares, and their spears into pruning-hooks; nation shall not lift up sword against nation, neither shall they learn war any more" (Isa. 2:4). [...]

Who else but our Saviour has taught his followers to offer those bloodless and reasonable sacrifices which are performed by prayer and the secret worship of God? Hence is it that throughout the habitable world altars are erected and churches dedicated wherein these spiritual and rational sacrifices are offered as a sacred service by every nation to the one supreme God. Once more, who but he, with invisible and secret power, has suppressed and utterly abolished those bloody sacrifices which were offered with fire and smoke as well as the cruel and senseless immolation of human victims; a fact which is attested by the heathen historians themselves? For it was not till after the publication of the Saviour's divine doctrine, about the time of Hadrian's reign, that the practice of human sacrifice was universally abandoned. Such and so manifest are the proofs of our Saviour's power and energy after death. Who, then, can be found of spirit so obdurate as to withhold his assent to the truth, and refuse to acknowledge his life to be divine? Such deeds as I have described are done by the living, not the dead, and visible acts are to us as evidence of those which we cannot see. It is as it were an event of yesterday that an impious and godless race disturbed and confounded the peace of human society, and possessed mighty power. But these, as soon as life departed, lay prostrate on the earth, worthless as dung, breathless, motionless, bereft of speech, and have left neither fame nor memorial behind.

The Rule of St. Benedict

Benedict of Nursia (ca. 480–ca. 547) came from the region of Umbria in central Italy. In around 500 he abandoned the studies that had him headed for the life of a Roman noble and spent three years as a hermit in Subiaco, near Rome. He accepted an invitation to become abbot of a monastery and thereafter established twelve monasteries, notably his first at Monte Cassino.

Benedict's *Rule* is made up of 73 brief chapters, concerning holiness, obedience, worship, the role of the abbot, and the regular life of a monastic community. It has been the most influential of all monastic handbooks, even though it is unlikely Benedict believed he was founding an order. The model is the family, with the abbot as father. Several features of the *Rule* have been widely influential beyond the cloister: it contributed to the tradition of a written constitution, offered a modest but significant dimension of democracy, modeled a notion of authority exercised within the constraints of law, and pointed towards the right of subjects to redress against unjust rulers.

The excerpt below sets out twelve steps by which the monk may practice and embody humility. The style is notable for its short sentences and practical injunctions. Obedience is stressed throughout, together with dependence on others as agents of grace. The final paragraph anticipates the commitments of ecclesial ethics to be found in Chapter Seven, below. Benedict's words, "all the things he did out of fear he will begin to perform without effort, out of habit and naturally," are a model of virtue ethics.

The Rule of St. Benedict. **Trans. Caroline White. New York: Penguin Books, 2008. From Chapter 4, "The Tools for Good Works" (pages 17–18) and Chapter 7, "Humility" (pages 22–6). Available online in multiple versions at www.osb.org/rb/.**

4. The tools for good works

First of all, "love the Lord God with all your heart, with all your soul and with all your strength," then "love your neighbour as yourself" (Matt. 22:37, 39; Mark 12:30–31; Luke 10:27).

"Do not kill, do not commit adultery, do not steal or covet, do not give false evidence about each other" (Rom. 13:9). "Honour all men" (1 Pet. 2:17) and "do not do to someone else what you do not want done to you" (Tob. 4:15). "Deny yourself so as to follow Christ" (Matt. 16:24; Luke 9:2–3), "discipline the body" (1 Cor. 9:27) and do not be self-indulgent; put a high value on fasting. Relieve the poor, clothe those who are in need of clothing, visit the sick and bury the dead; help those in trouble and console those who grieve. Do not be guided in your actions by the values of this world, and do not value anything more highly than the love of Christ.

Do not act in anger or harbour a grudge. Do not allow deceit to lurk in your heart, and do not make peace if it is not genuine. Do not abandon love. Do not swear, in case you perjure yourself. Speak the truth from heart and mouth. "Do not repay one wrong with another" (1 Thess. 5:15; 1 Pet. 3:9). Do not do wrong to anyone but bear patiently any wrongs done to you. "Love your enemies" (Matt. 5:44; Luke 6:27). Do not repay insults with insults but rather with kind words. Endure persecution for the sake of justice (Matt. 5:10). "Do not be arrogant or drunken" (Titus 1:7) or greedy. Do not be lazy or a grumbler. Do not cast aspersions on others. Put your hope in God. If you notice anything good in yourself, give the credit to God, not to yourself. Be aware that the wrongs you commit are always your own and admit to them.

Fear the Day of Judgement and be terrified of hell. Long for eternal life with all your spiritual desire. Each day remind yourself of your mortality. Keep a watch on the actions of your life at all times. Be aware that God can certainly see you wherever you are. As soon as wicked thoughts spring into your heart, dash them against Christ. Guard your mouth from all wicked or warped words. Do not take pleasure in talking a lot. Do not say foolish things or things that are intended to cause laughter. Do not take pleasure in excessive or unrestrained laughter. Enjoy listening to holy readings. Pray frequently. Confess your past sins to God each day in prayer with tears and sighs. Correct your faults for the future. "Do not indulge the desires of the flesh" (Gal. 5:16). Hate your own will. Obey the abbot's commands in all circumstances, even if he (which God forbid) does not act in accordance with them. Remember the Lord's words, "Do what they say and not what they do" (Matt. 23:3). Do not strive to be referred to as holy before you are so: be holy first, so that you may more accurately be referred to as holy.

Carry out God's commandments in what you do every day. Embrace chastity. Hate no one. Do not be jealous or give in to feelings of envy. Do not take pleasure in disputes. Avoid pride, respect your elders and care for those younger than yourself. Pray for your enemies in the love of Christ. Before the day's end be reconciled with anyone with whom you have a disagreement. Never despair of God's mercy. …

7. Humility

… The first step towards humility is to keep the fear of God in mind at all times. There must be absolutely no room for forgetfulness, and one must always remember everything that God has commanded. Do not forget that those who are scornful of God will burn in hell for their sins. Keep in mind the eternal life that God has prepared for those who fear him. Guard yourself at all times from sins and vices, whether of thought or speech or hands or feet or of self-will, as well as of desire of the body. Remember that God is watching you from heaven at every moment, and that wherever you are your actions can be seen by the Divine Being and are being reported by the angels at all times. The prophet teaches us this when he shows that God is always present in our thoughts, "God searches the mind and tests the heart" (Ps. 7:9), he says, and similarly, "The Lord knows the thoughts of men" (Ps. 94:11). He also says, "You have understood my thoughts from afar" (Ps. 139:2), and "A man's thought will confess to you." To guard against bad thoughts, the good brother should constantly repeat in his heart, "If I keep myself from wickedness, then I will be perfect in his sight" (Ps. 18:23).

We are forbidden to do our own will, for Scripture says to us, "Turn away from your own will" (Sir. 18:30). Similarly in the Lord's Prayer we ask God that his will be done in us (Matt. 6:10). It is right that we are taught not to do our own will since we are afraid of that saying of Scripture, "There are ways that seem straight to men but which lead down to the depths of hell" (Prov. 16:25), and we also tremble at what is said of those who fail to take notice, "They are corrupt and have become abominable in their pleasures" (Ps. 14:1). …

The second step towards humility is not to love your own will and not to take pleasure in satisfying your own desires. Instead, imitate in your actions the voice of the Lord when he says, "I have not come to do my will but that of the one who sent me" (John 6:38). And again Scripture says, "Self-indulgence has its own punishment and necessity wins the prize."

The third step towards humility is to submit to your superior with complete obedience out of love for God, imitating the Lord of whom the Apostle says, "He was made obedient even to the point of death" (Phil. 2:8).

The fourth step towards humility is to cling to patience with equanimity, practising obedience when you encounter painful and difficult experiences and even unjust treatment. You should endure all this without growing angry or running away, for Scripture says, "He who stands firm right until the end will be saved" (Matt. 10:22), and similarly, "Let your heart be comforted and wait for the Lord" (Ps. 27:14). To indicate that the person who is faithful ought to endure all things, however difficult, for the Lord's sake, Scripture says in the person of those who suffer, "For your sake we face death all day. We are regarded as lambs for the slaughter" (Rom. 8:36). Confident in their hope of divine reward, they go forward with joy, saying, "But in all these things we are victorious because of him who loved us" (Rom. 8:37). Similarly in another passage of Scripture, "You have tested us, Lord; you have tried us in the fire; you have led us into a snare; you have laid troubles on our back" (Ps. 66:10–11). And to show that we ought to live under the guidance of a prior, it goes on to say, "You have set men over our heads" (Ps.

66:12). Carrying out the Lord's commands in adversity and persecution, when struck on one cheek they offer the other, when someone takes their tunic they offer their cloak as well, when forced to walk a mile, they walk two, and they join the Apostle Paul in "putting up with false brothers" (2 Cor. 11:26) and "blessing those who curse them" (1 Cor. 4:12).

The fifth step towards humility is to confess humbly to the abbot all the wicked thoughts that spring to mind and anything you have secretly done wrong, as Scripture encourages us to do when it says, "Reveal to the Lord your path and put your hope in him" (Ps. 37:5). Similarly it says, "Confess to the Lord for he is good and his mercy lasts forever" (Ps. 106:1). As the prophet says, "I have revealed to you my faults and I have not concealed the unjust things I have done. I said, I will accuse myself of my wrongs to the Lord and you forgave the wickedness of my heart" (Ps. 32:5).

The sixth step towards humility is for the monk to be content with the lowest position and most menial treatment, and to consider himself incompetent and worthless with regard to everything he is told to do, saying to himself in the words of the prophet, "I have been reduced to nothing and I know nothing. I am regarded as a beast of burden in your eyes; yet I am always with you" (Ps. 73:22–23).

The seventh step towards humility is for him not only to claim that he is beneath everyone else and worse than them, but also to be convinced of this deep in his heart, humbling himself and saying with the prophet, "I am a worm and not a man, hated by others and a laughing-stock to the people" (Ps. 22:6). "I have been raised up and then humiliated and thrown into confusion" (Ps. 88:15), and also "It is good for me that you have humiliated me so that I might learn your commandments" (Ps. 119:71).

The eighth step towards humility is for the monk to do only what is commended by the common rule of the monastery and the example of his superiors.

The ninth step towards humility is for the monk to keep his tongue in check and to refrain from speaking. He should only speak when questioned, as Scripture demonstrates for "you will not escape sin if you talk too much" (Prov. 10:19) and "a talkative man loses his way on earth" (Ps. 140:11).

The tenth step towards humility is to avoid being easily provoked to laughter, for it says in Scripture that "the person who raises his voice in laughter is a fool" (Sir. 21:20).

The eleventh step towards humility is for the monk to speak gently and without laughter, but with humility and seriousness, saying only a few, reasonable words, and not speaking in a loud voice, for as it is written, "The wise man is recognized by his few words."

The twelfth step towards humility is for the monk always to display humility, both in his attitude and his behaviour, to those who see him. In other words, in the work of God, in the oratory, in the monastery, in the garden, on the road, in the fields, or anywhere else, whether sitting, walking or standing, he should always have his head bent, his eyes fixed on the ground, regarding himself at all times as guilty of his sins, and imagining that he is already appearing before the dread judgement. He should constantly repeat to himself in his heart the words of the publican in the

Gospels who said, with his eyes fixed on the ground, "Lord, I am a sinner and not worthy to raise my eyes to heaven" (Luke 18:13), and also the words of the prophet, "I am bowed down and utterly humiliated" (Ps. 38:6).

When the monk has climbed up all these steps of humility, he will reach "the perfect love of God which casts out all fear" (1 John 4:18). As a result, all the things he did out of fear he will begin to perform without effort, out of habit and naturally, no longer out of the fear of hell but as a good habit out of the love of Christ and delight in virtue. The Lord in his kindness will by the Holy Spirit give evidence of this in his workman, now cleansed from vices and sins.

John Howard Yoder, *The Constantinian Sources of Western Social Ethics*

Yoder's Mennonite commitments predispose him to a suspicion of the Constantinian settlement and the era of Christendom that followed. Whether such a single phenomenon as "Constantinianism" can be identified has proved a controversial claim, and a number of theologians sympathetic to Yoder have begun to doubt its usefulness. But there is no doubt Yoder's attack on Constantinianism is at least as compelling as Eusebius' euphoria at its inception.

Yoder's summary description of the Constantinian shift is one of the most striking insights in all his writing. "Before Constantine, one knew as a fact of everyday experience that there was a believing Christian community but one had to 'take it on faith' that God was governing history. After Constantine, one had to believe without seeing that there was a community of believers, within the larger nominally Christian mass, but one knew for a fact that God was in control of history." It introduces Yoder's characteristic question, "What if nobody else acted like a Christian, but we did?"

John Howard Yoder. *The Priestly Kingdom.* 2nd edn. Notre Dame: University of Notre Dame Press, 1984, 2001. From Chapter 7, "The Constantinian Sources of Western Social Ethics," pages 135–47.

Christians in the first century were a minority in a hostile world. Their ethical views were attuned to that context. In the twentieth century, Christians – especially if by that noun we refer to people voluntarily committing themselves, at some cost, to living in the light of their confession of Christ – are also in a minority in a world committed to other loyalties, yet we do not reason as the early Christians did. This study shall

seek to show summarily how some of the axioms of Western social thought are the product of the deep shift in the relation of church and world for which Constantine soon became the symbol. ...

This new era was to include far-reaching changes in Christian social ethics. For example, the pre-Constantinian Christians had been pacifists, rejecting the violence of army and empire not only because they had no share of power, but because they considered it morally wrong; the post-Constantinian Christians considered imperial violence to be not only morally tolerable but a positive good and a Christian duty. But our attention must move deeper, to the levels of ecclesiology and eschatology.

The New Ecclesiology

Obviously the composition of the church changed. Before, Christians had been a minority – some scholars estimate no more than ten percent of the empire's population – and intermittent persecution worked against making anyone's adherence cheap. It took at least a degree of conviction to belong. After Constantine the church was everybody. Being counted as "Christian" was the rule, not an exception. Paganism was soon declared illegal, and within another century the government was actively repressing heresies, i.e., ruling on what constitutes orthodox belief and punishing dissent. Henceforth, it would take exceptional conviction not to be counted as Christian. ...

The New Eschatology

The apostolic church confessed Jesus Christ as Lord; risen, ascended, sitting at the right hand of the Father, i.e., ruling (1 Cor. 15:25ff.) over the not yet subdued *kosmos*. The principalities and powers, though not manifestly confessing His Lordship, could not escape from His hidden control or from the promise of His ultimate victory. In ways that took account of their rebelliousness He denied them free rein, using even their self-glorifying designs within His purpose. A later term for this same idea was "Providence." But with the age of Constantine, Providence no longer needed to be an object of faith, for God's governance of history had become empirically evident in the person of the Christian ruler of the world. The concept of millennium was soon pulled back from the future (whether distant or imminent) into the present. All that God can possibly have in store for a future victory is more of what has already been won.

We are in a position now to capsule in a phrase the reversal of ecclesiology and eschatology underlying the changes in ethics and in dogma. Before Constantine, one knew as a fact of everyday experience that there was a believing Christian community but one had to "take it on faith" that God was governing history. After Constantine, one had to believe without seeing that there was a community of believers, within the larger nominally Christian mass, but one knew for a fact that God was in control of history. Ethics had to change because one must aim one's behavior at strengthening the regime, and because the ruler himself must have very soon some approbation and perhaps some guidance as he does things the earlier church would have disapproved of. The conception of a distinctive life-style befitting Christian confession had to be sweepingly redefined. It could no longer be identified with baptism and church membership, since many who are "Christian" in that sense have not themselves chosen to follow Christ. Its definition will tend to be transmuted in the definition of inwardness. Its outward expression will tend to be assigned to a minority of special "religious" people. "Mission" in the sense of calling one's hearers to faith in Jesus Christ as Lord must also be redefined. Beyond the limits of empire it had become identical with the expansion of Rome's sway. Within Christendom, since outward allegiance to Christ is universal, compulsory, the concern of the preacher will be with "renewal," i.e., with adding inner authenticity to an outward profession which is already there, because obligatory.

Two further symbolic shifts spell out the implications of the Constantinian age at the borders of Christendom. Once "Christendom" means Empire, non-empire is a new challenge. The era of Charlemagne demonstrates the option of annexation and fusion. Germanic values, legal traditions, social structures, and ruling families are "baptized" globally. This does not mean, at least not for most of them, conversion in any deep sense. It rather means that the *name* of Jesus is now intoned over a Germanic culture without changing its inner content, as it had been intoned over Graeco-Roman culture for half a millennium before. "Syncretism" is probably not the best label for the resulting mixture, since there is not so much genuine fusion and reconception as there is an overlaying of two cultures.

The other symbolically powerful event is the Crusade. When the other "world" at the border is not open to interpenetration, the collision becomes a holy war. Mohammed will have to be met on his own terms. The outsider is not only no longer privileged, as he had been for Jesus and Paul, as the test of one's love (Matt. 5:43ff., Luke 6:32ff.) or as the proof of the new age's having come (Eph. 2). The outsider is not simply ignored, or disregarded as "barbarian" or heretical, as Christian Rome had largely done. Now the outsider has become the "infidel," the incarnation of anti-faith. To destroy him, or to give one's life in the attempt, has become a positively virtuous undertaking, quite without regard for the ordinary criteria of justifiable violence (the so-called just war theory). Our world has a divinely imparted duty to destroy or to rule over their world. ...

A New Universality

After Constantine not only is the ruler the bearer of history; the nonsovereign ethical agent has changed as well. The "Christian" used to be a minority figure, with numerous resources not generally available to all people: personal commitment, regeneration, the guidance of the Holy Spirit, the consolation and encouragement of the brotherhood, training in a discipleship life-style. But now that Christianity is dominant, the bearer of history is Everyman – baptized but not necessarily thereby possessed of the resources of faith. Ethical discourse must now meet two more tests:

1. Can you ask such behavior of everyone? Are not servanthood and the love of enemy, or even contentment and monogamy, more than we have the right to expect of everyone? Is not the love ethic of the New Testament unrealistic, too heroic? The pressure builds rapidly for a duality in ethics. The "evangelical counsels" will be commended to the religious and the highly motivated. The "precepts," less demanding, will suffice for catechesis and the confessional. Two levels, two kinds of motivations and sanctions will be discerned, entailing different specific duties (contradictory ones, in fact, at points such as power, property, marriage, bloodshed, which were morally proper for the laity but not for the religious). Then the Reformation polemic against works of righteousness and monasticism removed the upper, more demanding, level.

2. What would happen if everyone did it? If everyone gave their wealth away what would we do for capital? If everyone loved their enemies who would ward off the Communists? This argument could be met on other levels, but here our only point is to observe that such reasoning would have been preposterous in the early church and remains ludicrous wherever committed Christians accept realistically their minority status. For more fitting than "What if everybody did it" would be its inverse, "What if nobody else acted like a Christian, but we did?"

A New Value for Effectiveness

A third dimension of the great reversal is the transformation of moral deliberation into utilitarianism. Minorities and the weak have numerous languages for moral discourse:

* conscience, intention, inspiration, and other similar "subjective" measures of right action;
* revelation, "nature," "wisdom," and other "received" standards;
* covenant, tradition, "style," reputation, training, and other "community-maintenance" criteria.

Each of these ways of moral reasoning has its logical and psychological strengths and limits. We cannot evaluate them here. Yet it is important that each can, in given circumstances, lead persons to act sacrificially, for the sake of others, or for the sake of a "cause" more important than the individual. Each can lift decision and action above immediate cost/benefit calculation. But once the evident course of history is held to be empirically discernible, and the prosperity of our regime is the measure of good, all morality boils down to efficacy. Right action is what works; what does not promise results can hardly be right.

Perhaps the most evident example of the dominion of this axiom is today's debate about revolution, liberation, and violence. Any ethic, any tactic, is, in the minds of many, self-evidently to be tested by its promised results. To them, the rejection of violence is morally sustainable only if nonviolent techniques are available which are able to promise an equally rapid "revolution." Again it would be petitionary to argue that the utilitarian world view is "wrong" or that an ethic of "principles" would be "right." For the present our concern is only to report that the dominance of the engineering approach to ethics, reducing all values to the calculation of pressures promising to bring about imperative results, is itself a long-range echo of the Constantinian wedding of piety with power; it is an approach foreign to the biblical thought world and makes no sense in a missionary situation where believers are few and powerless.

A New Metaphysic

A fourth, more doctrinal implication of the Constantinian reversal must be named: it is the victory of metaphysical dualism. Historically the source of this view is predominantly Neoplatonism. But naming its source does not explain its success. Certainly one reason it took over was the usefulness of dualism to justify the new social arrangement and resolve the problems it raised. The church we see is not the believing community; the visible/invisible duality names, and thereby justifies, the tension. The dominant ethic is different from the New Testament in content (Lordship is glorified rather than servanthood) as in source (reason and the "orders of creation" are normative, rather than the particularity of Jesus' and the apostles' guidance). What could be easier than to reserve the ethics of love for the inward or for the personal, while the ethics of power are for the outward world of structures? Interiorization and individualization, like the developments of the special worlds of cult and meditation, were not purely philosophical invasions which took over because they were intellectually convincing. They did so also because they were functional. They explained and justified the growing distance from Jesus and his replacement by other authorities and another political vision than that of the Kingdom of God. ...

A New Start

The intention of this text is descriptive only. What a coherent non- or anti-Constantinian option would be, would demand a quite different study. For present purposes it must suffice to have sustained two theses:

1   that the fourth-century shift continues to explain much if not most of the distance between biblical Christianity and ourselves, which is a distance not simply of time and organic development, but of disavowal and apostasy;
2   that many efforts to renew Christian thought regarding power and society remain the captives of the fallen system they mean to reject.

Still another study would be needed to unfold the specific missiological perspectives of the disavowal of Constantine. On the one hand "mission" by definition should mean a forsaking of the Constantinian setting for a pilgrim status in someone else's world. The "forsaking" in mission has been as complex and as bur-

dened with unpurged vestiges as the "overcoming" in Western experience. Suffice it to suggest that "to deconstantinize" or "to disestablish" might be a more concretely usable verb for the critical changes still needed than are the more current verbs "to contextualize" or "to indigenize," because the changes include:

- an element of repentance and judgment on the Western past;
- an awareness of the centrality of the power problem (whereas some discussion of "contextualizing" is often more narrowly semantic);
- a warning against a too easy conformity (to the indigenous scheme) to correct for the old ("foreign") one.

To conclude with a biblical vocabulary: if *kenosis* is the shape of God's own self-sending, then any strategy of Lordship, like that of the kings of this world, is not only a strategic mistake likely to backfire but a denial of gospel substance, a denial which has failed even where it succeeded. What the churches accepted in the Constantinian shift is what Jesus had rejected, seizing godlikeness, moving *in hoc signo* from Golgotha to the battlefield. If this diagnosis is correct, then the cure is not to update the fourth-century mistake by adding another "neo-" but to repent of the whole "where it's at" style and to begin again with *kenosis*.

The Church in Western Modernity

Modernity names the time since when public ideas about meaning, truth, and purpose began to be expressed most commonly in terms that did not require God. This was sometimes because God was associated with traditions and superstitions that constrained knowledge and growth; sometimes because religion seemed to be the source of conflict; and sometimes because of the desire to establish universal truths that required no supernatural starting point. Whether God seemed problematic morally, historically, scientifically, or philosophically, an era of public life arose where God became largely confined to the personal, psychological, and "spiritual."

The church's encounter with a fast-changing world was affected by industrialization and the breakdown in

traditional rural society, by global expansion, by encounter with other faiths, and by the broadening political base on which societies were coming to rest.

The readings below strive to take stock and make a virtue of these new sociological realities. They represent what might be called the conventional (or "universal") understanding of the place of the church in modernity – very different from what we shall later in this book call the "subversive" or "ecclesial" approaches. Ernst Troeltsch assumes churches are organized societies for the sanctification of individual souls. H. R. Niebuhr identifies the appropriate role of the church in society by distinguishing it from four less satisfactory models. These two accounts have been immensely influential.

Ernst Troeltsch, *The Gospel Ethic*

Ernst Troeltsch (1865–1923) wove together the theology of Albrecht Ritschl with the sociology of Max Weber. His magisterial two-volume *The Social Teaching of the Christian Churches* (1912), a landmark text in the sociology of religion, is significant for Christian ethics for two reasons. Today, it gives an insight into a classic late nineteenth-century perception of the ethic of Jesus and the kingdom. The passage quoted below expresses a view very widely held then (and now) that Jesus had no specific political agenda and was largely concerned with saving souls. It shows how the assumption that Jesus had no particular political agenda quickly leads to political agendas of other kinds becoming nonetheless associated with Jesus.

In its time, however, especially for those theologians such as Reinhold Niebuhr who were able to read it in German before it came to be published in an English translation, it offered a highly influential threefold typology of Christian social engagement. In addition to the "mystical" type of Christianity, which is concerned only with inward and personal experiences, there were two rivals: the "sect" type, which is set apart from the world and emphasizes law rather than grace, and the "church" type, which resembles early twentieth-century established Christianity. The first two types are, in truth, devices to set the church type in positive relief. The common anxiety about sectarian ethics, as some forms of ecclesial ethics are sometimes portrayed today, is rooted in this Troeltschian typology.

Ernst Troeltsch. *The Social Teaching of the Christian Churches.* Vol. 1. Trans. Olive Wyon. New York: Macmillan, 1931. From Chapter 1, "The Foundations in the Early Church"; Part 1: The Gospel. Page 61.

Amidst all the uncertainties of tradition the fundamental idea underlying the preaching of Jesus is easy to discern. It deals with the proclamation of the great final Judgment of the coming of the "Kingdom of God," by which is meant that state of life in which God will have supreme control, when His Will will be done on earth, as it is now being done only in heaven; in this "Kingdom" sin, suffering, and pain will have been overcome, and the true spiritual values, combined with single-eyed devotion to the Will of God, will shine out in the glory that is their due. That is why sinful men who acknowledge their sinfulness, and those who have learned the lessons of submission and humility through their experience of sorrow and poverty, will enter the Kingdom of God before the self-satisfied and the righteous as well as before the rich and the great ones of the earth.

Further, the message of Jesus also deals with the formation of the community based on the Hope of the Kingdom, which, in the meantime, possesses both the pledge of the Kingdom and the preparation for its coming in Jesus Himself. This community is to be founded by the missionary efforts of the narrower circle of the immediate disciples and followers of Jesus; they therefore are entrusted with the special duties which devolve upon the heralds of the Kingdom. With their help the Kingdom is preached everywhere. Jesus does not speculate about the nature of the Kingdom of God; it simply includes all ethical and religious ideals, among which freedom from suffering is certainly one aspect of the message. ... All the emphasis is laid on preparing for the Kingdom of God, and this preparation is so thorough that the community which is "looking out for the Kingdom of God" can already in anticipation be described as the "Kingdom of God." There is no desire to organize a special group of chosen souls; the way that leads to salvation, and the rock upon which men ought to build, is to be made plain to as many as possible. ...

[Jesus'] fundamental moral demand, briefly expressed, is the sanctification of the individual in all his moral activity for the sake of God, or that "purity of heart" which, when the Kingdom has actually come, will enable a man to "see God." The moral commandments themselves are conceived from the point of view of ordinary practice and general human interest, but they are illuminated by the fact that as they are obeyed with devotion and inner simplicity, all that is done takes place under the Eye of God, which penetrates every disguise and tests human motives to the utmost; thus the will is given to God in absolute obedience, in order that it may attain the real and true life, its real spiritual eternal value in the sight of God. Hence the ethic of the Gospel is marked by emphasis on purity of intention and a greatly intensified reverence for all moral commands, without any allowance for conflicting motives or for expediency. Above all, it connects this moral conduct with its supreme object – a personal relation with God and the supreme value of the soul, "for what is a man profited if he shall gain the whole world and lose his own soul?" …

Sociological Characteristics of the Gospel Ethic

These ideas determine the form of the sociological structure. Its first outstanding characteristic is an unlimited, unqualified individualism. The standard of this individualism is wholly self-contained, determined simply by its own sense of that which will further its consecration to God. It is bound to go all lengths in obedience to the demands of the Gospel. Its basis and its justification lie in the fact that man is called to fellowship with God, or, as it is here expressed, to be the child of God, and in the eternal value of the soul which this filial relation confers. The individual as a child of God may regard himself as infinitely precious, but he reaches this goal only through self-abnegation in unconditional obedience to the Holy Will of God.

It is clear that an individualism of this kind is entirely radical, and that it transcends all natural barriers and differences, through the ideal of the religious value of the soul. It is also clear that such an individualism is only possible at all upon this religious basis. It is only fellowship with God which gives value to the individual, and it is only in common relationship with God, in a realm of supernatural values, that natural differences disappear. Where this kind of individualism prevails all earthly differences are swallowed up in the Divine power and love which reduce all other distinctions to nothing. … From the very outset this was not an ideal for the masses. Faced by the extreme tension of these demands, we must also remember that they were formulated in the expectation of the final Judgment of the imminent End of the World. However little these demands may have been due to this expectation, we must realize that their radicalism and their indifference towards questions of practicability can only be understood from this point of view. The feeling is that the sphere in which they are to be realized will not last long and has no intrinsic value of its own. This absolute

religious individualism, however, which removes all distinctions by concentrating entirely upon differences in character in individuals, each of whom has his own value, also contains within itself a strong idea of fellowship; this idea is based just as clearly upon the specifically religious fundamental idea. This cannot be explained simply by pointing out that the altruistic commandments are bound up with the commands to consecrate the self to God – commands which have to be obeyed to the uttermost limits in self-purification and self-denial. In the last resort the idea of fellowship springs from the fact that those who are being purified for the sake of God meet in Him; and since the dominating thought of God is not that of a peaceful happiness into which souls are gathered but that of a creative will, so those who are united in God must be inspired by the Will and the Spirit of God, and must actively fulfil the loving Will of God. Therefore for the children of God there is no law and no pressure, no war and no conflict, but only an urgent love and a conquest of evil by good, demands which the Sermon on the Mount illustrates by giving extreme instances. Since, as we have seen, absolute individualism springs from the religious idea of pure-hearted self-surrender to Him who seeks men's souls and to the Fatherly Will which calls them to the vocation of being His children, so from this same fundamental idea this absolute individualism leads to just as absolute a fellowship of love among those who are united in God; from this springs an active realization of the love of God even towards strangers and enemies, because only through the revelation of absolute love can a true understanding of God be awakened and the way opened to Him. …

Thus out of an absolute individualism there arises a universalism which is equally absolute. Both these aspects of the Gospel are based entirely upon religion; their support is the thought of the Holy Divine Will of Love, and they mutually aid each other quite logically; we cannot here pursue any farther the particular question of the extent to which Jesus really abrogated the Jewish position of privilege. The interesting point for us is simply the fact that absolute individualism and universalism spring directly out of the religious idea, and that this fact has, sociologically, a double aspect. Both require each other. For individualism only becomes absolute through the ethical surrender of the individual to God, and being filled with God; and on the other hand, in possession of the Absolute, individual differences merge into an unlimited love whose prototype is the Father-God Himself, to whom souls are drawn and in whom they are united. This lesson must be learnt by all who desire to save their souls at the Judgment and have their part in the Kingdom of God; and those who do this are His brothers and sisters, and therefore the firstborn of the coming Kingdom of God. ...

The Gospel Ethic and General Social Values

From this point of view it is easy to forecast what form the Christian attitude will take towards social problems which belong to an entirely different group of interests. These problems belong to the world and will perish with the world. As the world itself is a mixture of good and evil, so the whole social order, with its pleasure and its labour, has its good points. On the other hand, it is also full of danger; its bad side is manifest in its tendency to distract the hearts of men from the one thing needful. Jesus does not preach asceticism; in His teaching there is no trace of contempt for the life of the senses or for pleasure as such, nor does He glorify poverty for its own sake. But He teaches quite plainly that food and work are only of value in so far as they are necessary to life; otherwise they have no ethical value. This point of view is characteristic of popular Oriental feeling with its depreciation of the claims of a higher civilization; it is also the expression of that religious radicalism which cannot see any ethical value at all in anything which is not directly connected with religion.

The ethic of Jesus is heroic rather than ascetic. The heroic aspect is softened only by the gentler elements of trust in the Fatherly Love of God and faith in the forgiveness of sins, but not by any compromise with the claims of the life of the world and the "nature of things."

From this point of view we can see plainly the attitude of Jesus towards the State, Society, labour, and the possession of property. There is no thought of the State at all. Jewish nationalism and all its expectations are ignored entirely, even though Israel appears as the germ of the new world that is to be. In the thought of Jesus the Kingdom of God is the rule of God and not the rule of the Jewish people. Jesus makes it perfectly plain that the Roman Empire exists, and has a right to exist, because God permits it; but while He admits this He also adds the injunction: "Render to God the things that are God's." ...

It is therefore clear that the message of Jesus is not a programme of social reform. It is rather the summons to prepare for the coming of the Kingdom of God; this preparation, however, is to take place quietly within the framework of the present world-order, in a purely religious fellowship of love, with an earnest endeavour to conquer self and cultivate the Christian virtues. Even the Kingdom of God itself is not (for its part at least) the new social order founded by God. It creates a new order upon earth, but it is an order which is not concerned with the State, with Society, or with the family at all. How this will work out in detail is God's affair; man's duty is simply to prepare for it. It is, of course, true that Jesus promises that the poor and the suffering shall have their tears wiped away and all their desires satisfied; but after all this is only natural in a message addressed to the poor; it is not the chief point. The centre of His Message was the glory of God's final victory, and the conquest of demons.

H. Richard Niebuhr, *Christ the Transformer of Culture*

The typologies created by H. Richard Niebuhr (1894–1962) were as significant in the second half of the twentieth century as those of Ernst Troeltsch were in the first half. Niebuhr outlined five types – although it has been strongly argued by J. H. Yoder and others that the first four types are merely foils to highlight the fifth.

Christ against Culture is the exclusive stance. History narrates the rise of the church and the fall of pagan civilization. *Christ of Culture* is a much more accommodating stance, which sees history as G. W. F. Hegel saw it, as the unfolding story of the Spirit's encounter with nature. The synthesist advocates *Christ above Culture*, which regards history as a long preparation under law, reason, gospel, and church for an ultimate communion of the soul with God. The dualist places *Christ and Culture in Paradox*, and perceives history as the time of struggle between faith and unbelief.

Niebuhr himself favors the conversionist stance of *Christ Transforming Culture*. History is humanity's more or less adequate response to God's mighty deeds. Conversionists are less concerned with prehistory or the end times than with the present moment.

I. Theological Convictions

The conversionists' understanding of the relations of Christ and culture is most closely akin to dualism, but it also has affinities with the other great Christian attitudes. That it represents a distinct *motif*, however, becomes apparent when one moves from the Gospel of Matthew and the Letter of James through Paul's epistles to the Fourth Gospel, or proceeds from Tertullian, the Gnostics, and Clement to Augustine, or from Tolstoy, Ritschl, and Kierkegaard to F. D. Maurice. The men who offer what we are calling the conversionist answer to the problem of Christ and culture evidently belong to the great central tradition of the church. Though they hold fast to the radical distinction between God's work in Christ and man's work in culture, they do not take the road of exclusive Christianity into isolation from civilization, or reject its institutions with Tolstoyan bitterness. Though they accept their station in society with its duties in obedience to their Lord, they do not seek to modify Jesus Christ's sharp judgment of the world and all its ways. In their Christology they are like synthesists and dualists; they refer to the Redeemer more than to the giver of a new law, and to the God whom men encounter more than to the representative of the best spiritual resources in humanity. They understand that his work is concerned not with the specious, external aspects of human behavior in the first place, but that he tries the hearts and judges the subconscious life; that he deals with what is deepest and most fundamental in man. He heals the most stubborn and virulent human disease, the phthisis of the spirit, the sickness unto death; he forgives the most hidden and proliferous sin, the distrust, lovelessness, and hopelessness of man in his relation to God. And this he does not simply by offering ideas, counsel, and laws; but by living with men in great humility, enduring death for their sakes, and rising again from the grave in a demonstration of God's grace rather than an argument about it. In their understanding of sin the conversionists are more like dualists than synthesists. They note that it is deeply rooted in the human soul, that it pervades all man's work, and that there are no gradations of corruption, however

various its symptoms. Hence they also discern how all cultural work in which men promote their own glory, whether individualistically or socially, whether as members of the nation or of humanity, lies under the judgment of God – who does not seek His own profit. They see the self-destructiveness in its self-contradictoriness. Yet they believe also that such culture is under God's sovereign rule, and that the Christian must carry on cultural work in obedience to the Lord.

What distinguishes conversionists from dualists is their more positive and hopeful attitude toward culture. Their more affirmative stand seems to be closely connected with three theological convictions. The first of these relates to creation. The dualist tends so to concentrate on redemption through Christ's cross and resurrection that creation becomes for him a kind of prologue to the one mighty deed of atonement. Though with Paul he affirms that in Christ "all things were created, in heaven and on earth, visible and invisible, whether thrones or dominions or principalities or authorities – all things were created through him and for him," yet this is a relatively unemphasized idea, used mostly to introduce the great theme of reconciliation. For the conversionist, however, the creative activity of God and of Christ-in-God is a major theme, neither overpowered by nor overpowering the idea of atonement. Hence man the creature, working in a created world, lives, as the conversionist sees it, under the rule of Christ and by the creative power and ordering of the divine Word, even though in his unredeemed mind he may believe that he lives among vain things under divine wrath. To be sure, the dualist often also says something like this; but he tends to qualify it so much by references to God's anger as peculiarly manifest in the physical world that the beneficence of the Ruler of nature becomes somewhat doubtful. The effect of the conversionist's theory of culture on his positive thought about creation is considerable. He finds room for affirmative and ordered response on the part of created man to the creative, ordering work of God; even though the creature may go about his work unwillingly as he tills the ground, cultivates his mind, and organizes his society, and though he may administer perversely the order given him with his existence. In connection with this interest in creation, the conversionist tends to develop a phase of Christology neglected by the dualist. On the one hand he emphasizes the participation of the Word, the Son of God, in creation, not as this took place once upon a time but as it occurs in the immediate origin, the logical and momentary beginning of everything, in the mind and power of God. On the other hand he is concerned with the redemptive work of God in the incarnation of the Son, and not merely with redemption in his death, resurrection, and return in power. Not that the conversionist turns from the historical Jesus to the Logos that was in the beginning, or that he denies the wonder of the cross in marveling at the birth in a barn; he seeks to hold together in one movement the various themes of creation and redemption, of incarnation and atonement. The effect of this understanding of the work of Christ in incarnation as well as creation on conversionist thought about culture is unmistakable. The Word that became flesh and dwelt among us, the Son who does the work of the Father in the world of creation, has entered into a human culture that has never been without his ordering action.

The second theological conviction that modifies the conversionist view of human work and custom is its understanding of the nature of man's fall from his created goodness. As we have noted, dualism often brings creation and fall into such close proximity that it is tempted to speak in almost Gnostic terms, as if creation of finite selfhood or matter involved fall. To be in the body is to be away from Christ; nothing good dwells in the flesh; to be carnal is to be sold under sin. All this is true for a Paul and a Luther not only because the spirit of man that dwells in his body is sinful but because the body offers unconquerable temptation to sin. Hence such Christians tend to think of the institutions of culture as having largely a negative function in a temporal and corrupt world. They are orders for corruption, preventatives of anarchy, directives for the physical life, concerned wholly with temporal matters. The conversionist agrees with the dualist in asserting a doctrine of a radical fall of man. But he distinguishes the fall very sharply from creation, and from the conditions of life in the body. It is a kind of reversal of creation for him, and in no sense its continuation. It is entirely the action of man, and in no way an action of God's. It is moral and personal, not physical and metaphysical, though it does have physical consequences. The results of man's defection from God, moreover, all occur on man's side and not on God's. The word that must be used here to designate the consequences of the fall is "corruption." Man's good nature has become corrupted; it is not bad, as something that ought not to exist, but warped, twisted, and misdirected. He loves with the love that is given him in his creation, but loves beings wrongly, in the wrong order; he desires good with the desire given him by his Maker, but aims at goods that are not good for him and misses his true good; he produces fruit, but it is misshapen and bitter; he organizes society with the aid of his practical reason,

but works against the grain of things in self-willed forcing of his reason into irrational paths, and thus disorganizes things in his very acts of organization. Hence his culture is all corrupted order rather than order for corruption, as it is for dualists. It is perverted good, not evil; or it is evil as perversion and not as badness of being. The problem of culture is therefore the problem of its conversion, not of its replacement by a new creation; though the conversion is so radical that it amounts to a kind of rebirth.

With these convictions about creation and fall the conversionists combine a third: a view of history that holds that to God all things are possible in a history that is fundamentally not a course of merely human events but always a dramatic interaction between God and men. For the exclusive Christian, history is the story of a rising church or Christian culture and a dying pagan civilization; for the cultural Christian, it is the story of the spirit's encounter with nature; for the synthesist, it is a period of preparation under law, reason, gospel, and church for an ultimate communion of the soul with God; for the dualist, history is the time of struggle between faith and unbelief, a period between the giving of the promise of life and its fulfillment. For the conversionist, history is the story of God's mighty deeds and of man's responses to them. He lives somewhat less "between the times" and somewhat more in the divine "Now" than do his brother Christians. The eschatological future has become for him an eschatological present. Eternity means for him less the action of God before time and less the life with God after time, and more the presence of God in time. Eternal life is a quality of existence in the here and now. Hence the conversionist is less concerned with conservation of what has been given in creation, less with preparation for what will be given in a final redemption, than with the divine possibility of a present renewal. Such differences of orientation in time are not to be defined with nice precision. There is a strain toward the future in every Christian life, as well as a reliance upon the God of Abraham, Isaac, and Jacob and the recognition that this is the day of salvation. But there is a difference between Paul's expectation of the time when the last enemy, death, will have been destroyed by Christ, and John's understanding of Christ's last words upon the cross, "It is finished." The conversionist, with his view of history as the present encounter with God in Christ, does not live so much in expectation of a final ending of the world of creation and culture as in awareness of the power of the Lord to transform all things by lifting them up to himself. His imagery is spatial and not temporal; and the movement of life he finds to be issuing from Jesus Christ is an upward movement, the rising of men's souls and deeds and thoughts in a mighty surge of adoration and glorification of the One who draws them to himself. This is what human culture can be – a transformed human life in and to the glory of God. For man it is impossible, but all things are possible to God, who has created man, body and soul, for Himself, and sent his Son into the world that the world through him might be saved.

Chapter Three

The Story of Ethics

The role of this chapter is not to argue that there is only one way to tell the story of ethics. It is to survey those dimensions of ethics of which Christians must be aware but which could easily be overlooked in an outline of Christian ethics, narrowly understood. The readings in this chapter cover three aspects which, while not being integral to the discipline of Christian ethics, are highly significant for comprehending its emergence, development, and current context. The first area is the largely pre-Christian classical philosophical tradition. The second is the concurrent development of ethical ideas and practices in faith traditions other than Christianity. And the third is the emergence of disciplinary or professional ethics, perhaps the most prominent area in which ethics is taught and discussed today.

Philosophical Ethics

The Western tradition of philosophical ethics, within which Christian ethics was to take its place, is generally acknowledged to begin in Athens in the fifth century BCE. The key movements are those of Plato and Aristotle, of the Epicureans and Stoics, and finally of Plotinus. Christianity is sometimes seen as a fusion of Judaism and classical thinking; while this is too simple a description, a sense of the key themes in classical ethics is nonetheless vital to an understanding of how a Jewish body gained classical philosophical legs.

The readings in this section are taken from Plato and Aristotle. In very broad and perhaps simplistic terms, these two philosophers could be regarded as setting the contours of Christian ethics. For example, when the Christian life is thought of as spiritual, other-worldly, and seeking an ideal, such a portrayal is usually traceable to Platonic assumptions. When Christianity is assumed to be about practical matters, being a good neighbor, and making healthy communities, such a perception is often rooted in an Aristotelian view of the world.

Plato, *The Republic*

Plato (ca. 428–ca. 348 BCE), who described himself as a devoted pupil of Socrates (ca. 470–399 BCE), wrote many dialogues in which Socrates discusses and disputes with a range of partners. They are set out not as continuous prose but more in the form of a dramatic script. In the *Republic* Socrates' disputants include Plato's brothers Glaucon (with whom he shares the discussion below) and Adeimantus.

The *Republic* addresses the question, fascinating to many later Christian readers, of why one should be good, given that the wicked seem to prosper. Plato sees this as fundamentally a question of the ordering of the city-state, and only secondarily a question of personal well-being. Socrates goes to considerable lengths to argue that a just city and a just person are both good and possible. The work is concerned with the nature and value of justice.

The passages quoted below introduce themes that came to be significant for later Christian ethics. Plato sees the body as distinct from the soul, and the soul as the higher of the two. (This view came to be expanded by Neoplatonism, and is the source of much neglect or denigration of the body in Christian ethics.) Here we see Plato's understanding of the soul, and, in his famous parable of the cave, we see the significance of the soul for leading human beings into contact with the eternal forms (goodness, truth, and beauty), on which abiding life rests.

Plato. *The Republic*. Provided by the Internet Classics Archive. www.classics.mit.edu//Plato/republic.html. From Book IX and Book VII.

From Book IX

[Socrates – *Glaucon*]

Need we hire a herald, or shall I announce, that the son of Ariston (the best) has decided that the best and justest is also the happiest, and that this is he who is the most royal man and king over himself; and that the worst and most unjust man is also the most miserable, and that this is he who being the greatest tyrant of himself is also the greatest tyrant of his State? ... Then this, I said, will be our first proof; and there is another, which may also have some weight.

What is that?

The second proof is derived from the nature of the soul: seeing that the individual soul, like the State, has been divided by us into three principles, the division may, I think, furnish a new demonstration.

Of what nature?

It seems to me that to these three principles three pleasures correspond; also three desires and governing powers.

How do you mean? he said.

There is one principle with which, as we were saying, a man learns, another with which he is angry; the third, having many forms, has no special name, but is denoted by the general term appetitive, from the extraordinary strength and vehemence of the desires of eating and drinking and the other sensual appetites which are the main elements of it; also money-loving, because such desires are generally satisfied by the help of money.

That is true, he said.

If we were to say that the loves and pleasures of this third part were concerned with gain, we should then be able to fall back on a single notion; and might truly and intelligibly describe this part of the soul as loving gain or money.

I agree with you.

Again, is not the passionate element wholly set on ruling and conquering and getting fame?

True.

Suppose we call it the contentious or ambitious – would the term be suitable?

Extremely suitable.

On the other hand, every one sees that the principle of knowledge is wholly directed to the truth, and cares less than either of the others for gain or fame.

Far less.

"Lover of wisdom," "lover of knowledge," are titles which we may fitly apply to that part of the soul?

Certainly.

One principle prevails in the souls of one class of men, another in others, as may happen?

Yes.

Then we may begin by assuming that there are three classes of men – lovers of wisdom, lovers of honour, lovers of gain?

Exactly. ...

You would allow, I said, that there is in nature an upper and lower and middle region?

I should.

And if a person were to go from the lower to the middle region, would he not imagine that he is going up; and he who is standing in the middle and sees whence he has come, would imagine that he is already in the upper region, if he has never seen the true upper world?

To be sure, he said; how can he think otherwise?

But if he were taken back again he would imagine, and truly imagine, that he was descending?

No doubt.

All that would arise out of his ignorance of the true upper and middle and lower regions?

Yes. …

Look at the matter thus: – Hunger, thirst, and the like, are inanitions of the bodily state?

Yes.

And ignorance and folly are inanitions of the soul?

True.

And food and wisdom are the corresponding satisfactions of either?

Certainly.

And is the satisfaction derived from that which has less or from that which has more existence the truer?

Clearly, from that which has more.

What classes of things have a greater share of pure existence in your judgment – those of which food and drink and condiments and all kinds of sustenance are examples, or the class which contains true opinion and knowledge and mind and all the different kinds of virtue? Put the question in this way: – Which has a more pure being – that which is concerned with the invariable, the immortal, and the true, and is of such a nature, and is found in such natures; or that which is concerned with and found in the variable and mortal, and is itself variable and mortal?

Far purer, he replied, is the being of that which is concerned with the invariable.

And does the essence of the invariable partake of knowledge in the same degree as of essence?

Yes, of knowledge in the same degree.

And of truth in the same degree?

Yes.

And, conversely, that which has less of truth will also have less of essence?

Necessarily.

Then, in general, those kinds of things which are in the service of the body have less of truth and essence than those which are in the service of the soul?

Far less.

And has not the body itself less of truth and essence than the soul?

Yes.

What is filled with more real existence, and actually has a more real existence, is more really filled than that which is filled with less real existence and is less real?

Of course.

And if there be a pleasure in being filled with that which is according to nature, that which is more really filled with more real being will more really and truly enjoy true pleasure; whereas that which participates in less real being will be less truly and surely satisfied, and will participate in an illusory and less real pleasure?

Unquestionably.

Those then who know not wisdom and virtue, and are always busy with gluttony and sensuality, go down and up again as far as the mean; and in this region they move at random throughout life, but they never pass into the true upper world; thither they neither look, nor do they ever find their way, neither are they truly filled with true being, nor do they taste of pure and abiding pleasure. … For they fill themselves with that which is not substantial, and the part of themselves which they fill is also unsubstantial and incontinent. … And must not the like happen with the spirited or passionate element of the soul? Will not the passionate man who carries his passion into action, be in the like case, whether he is envious and ambitious, or violent and contentious, or angry and discontented, if he be seeking to attain honour and victory and the satisfaction of his anger without reason or sense?

Yes, he said, the same will happen with the spirited element also.

Then may we not confidently assert that the lovers of money and honour, when they seek their pleasures under the guidance and in the company of reason and knowledge, and pursue after and win the pleasures which wisdom shows them, will also have the truest pleasures in the highest degree which is attainable to them, inasmuch as they follow truth; and they will have the pleasures which are natural to them, if that which is best for each one is also most natural to him?

Yes, certainly; the best is the most natural.

And when the whole soul follows the philosophical principle, and there is no division, the several parts are just, and do each of them their own business, and enjoy severally the best and truest pleasures of which they are capable?

Exactly.

From Book VII

[Socrates – *Glaucon*]

And now, I said, let me show in a figure how far our nature is enlightened or unenlightened: – Behold! human beings living in an underground den, which has a mouth open towards the light and reaching all along the den; here they have been from their child-hood, and have their legs and necks chained so that they cannot move, and can only see before them, being prevented by the chains from turning round their heads. Above and behind them a fire is blazing at a distance, and between the fire and the prisoners there is a raised way; and you will see, if you look, a low wall built along the way, like the screen which marionette players have in front of them, over which they show the puppets.

I see.

And do you see, I said, men passing along the wall carrying all sorts of vessels, and statues and figures of animals made of wood and stone and various materials, which appear over the wall? Some of them are talking, others silent.

You have shown me a strange image, and they are strange prisoners.

Like ourselves, I replied; and they see only their own shadows, or the shadows of one another, which the fire throws on the opposite wall of the cave?

True, he said; how could they see anything but the shadows if they were never allowed to move their heads?

And of the objects which are being carried in like manner they would only see the shadows?

Yes, he said.

And if they were able to converse with one another, would they not suppose that they were naming what was actually before them?

Very true.

And suppose further that the prison had an echo which came from the other side, would they not be sure to fancy when one of the passers-by spoke that the voice which they heard came from the passing shadow?

No question, he replied.

To them, I said, the truth would be literally nothing but the shadows of the images.

That is certain.

And now look again, and see what will naturally follow it; the prisoners are released and disabused of their error. At first, when any of them is liberated and compelled suddenly to stand up and turn his neck round and walk and look towards the light, he will suffer sharp pains; the glare will distress him, and he will be unable to see the realities of which in his former state he had seen the shadows; and then con-ceive some one saying to him, that what he saw before was an illusion, but that now, when he is approaching nearer to being and his eye is turned towards more

real existence, he has a clearer vision, – what will be his reply? And you may further imagine that his instructor is pointing to the objects as they pass and requiring him to name them, – will he not be per-plexed? Will he not fancy that the shadows which he formerly saw are truer than the objects which are now shown to him?

Far truer.

And if he is compelled to look straight at the light, will he not have a pain in his eyes which will make him turn away to take and take in the objects of vision which he can see, and which he will conceive to be in reality clearer than the things which are now being shown to him? … And suppose once more, that he is reluctantly dragged up a steep and rugged ascent, and held fast until he's forced into the presence of the sun himself, is he not likely to be pained and irritated? When he approaches the light his eyes will be dazzled, and he will not be able to see anything at all of what are now called realities.

Not all in a moment, he said.

He will require to grow accustomed to the sight of the upper world. And first he will see the shadows best, next the reflections of men and other objects in the water, and then the objects themselves; then he will gaze upon the light of the moon and the stars and the span-gled heaven; and he will see the sky and the stars by night better than the sun or the light of the sun by day?

Certainly.

Last of all he will be able to see the sun, and not mere reflections of him in the water, but he will see him in his own proper place, and not in another; and he will contemplate him as he is. … This entire alle-gory, I said, you may now append, dear Glaucon, to the previous argument; the prison-house is the world of sight, the light of the fire is the sun, and you will not misapprehend me if you interpret the journey upwards to be the ascent of the soul into the intellec-tual world according to my poor belief, which, at your desire, I have expressed whether rightly or wrongly God knows. But, whether true or false, my opinion is that in the world of knowledge the idea of good appears last of all, and is seen only with an effort; and, when seen, is also inferred to be the universal author of all things beautiful and right, parent of light and of the lord of light in this visible world, and the immedi-ate source of reason and truth in the intellectual; and that this is the power upon which he who would act rationally, either in public or private life must have his eye fixed.

Aristotle, *The Nature of Virtue*

Plato's pupil Aristotle (384–322 BCE) laid the foundations of a comprehensive system of knowledge, covering arts, sciences, logic, metaphysics, and ethics. His significance for Christian ethics lies both in the fact that his work was not available to those who shaped the faith in the early centuries – notably Augustine – who were influenced instead by Plato; and in the profound degree to which his work framed the consciousness of medieval theologians – notably Thomas Aquinas.

Aristotle's discussion of virtue is by no means his only contribution to contemporary debates in ethics, but it is the most frequently cited. Here he outlines his theory of habituation. Virtue of character arises not naturally, but through practice: "we become just by doing just actions, temperate by temperate actions, and courageous by courageous actions." He also describes his notion of the mean. Virtue lies at an appropriate point between excess and deficiency. To attain the mean means to experience feelings "at the right time, about the right things, towards the right people, for the right end, and in the right way."

Aristotle acknowledges "it is hard to be good, because in each case it is hard to find the middle point." His notion of virtue has experienced a revival in recent ethical discussion, notably in the field of ecclesial ethics. The following is excerpted from his *Nicomachean Ethics*.

Aristotle. *Nicomachean Ethics*. Cambridge Texts in the History of Philosophy. Ed. Roger Crisp. Cambridge: Cambridge University Press, 2000. From Book II, pages 23–35. Available online at www.classics.mit.edu/Aristotle/nicomachean.html through the Internet Classics Archive. © Cambridge University Press, reproduced with permission.

Chapter 1

Virtue, then, is of two kinds: that of the intellect and that of character. Intellectual virtue owes its origin and development mainly to teaching, for which reason its attainment requires experience and time; virtue of character (*ethos*) is a result of habituation (*ethos*), for which reason it has acquired its name through a small variation on "*ethos*." From this it is clear that none of the virtues of character arises in us by nature. For nothing natural can be made to behave differently by habituation. For example, a stone that naturally falls downwards could not be made by habituation to rise upwards, not even if one tried to habituate it by throwing it up ten thousand times; nor can fire be habituated to burn downwards, nor anything else that naturally behaves in one way be habituated to behave differently. So virtues arise in us neither by nature nor contrary to nature, but nature gives us the capacity to acquire them, and completion comes through habituation.

Again, in all the cases where something arises in us by nature, we first acquire the capacities and later exhibit the activities. This is clear in the case of the senses, since we did not acquire them by seeing often or hearing often; we had them before we used them, and did not acquire them by using them. Virtues, however, we acquire by first exercising them. The same is true with skills, since what we need to learn before doing, we learn by doing; for example, we become builders by building, and lyre-players by playing the lyre. So too we become just by doing just actions, temperate by temperate actions, and courageous by courageous actions. ...

Chapter 2

... First, then, let us consider this – the fact that states like this are naturally corrupted by deficiency and excess, as we see in the cases of strength and health (we must use clear examples to illustrate the unclear); for both too much exercise and too little ruin one's strength, and likewise too much food and drink and too little ruin one's health, while the right amount produces, increases and preserves it. The same goes, then, for temperance, courage and the other virtues: the person who avoids and fears everything, never standing his ground, becomes cowardly, while he who fears nothing, but confronts every danger becomes rash. In the same way, the person who enjoys every pleasure and never restrains himself becomes intemperate, while he who avoids all pleasure – as boors do – becomes, as it were, insensible. Temperance and courage, then, are ruined by excess and deficiency, and preserved by the mean.

Not only are virtues produced and developed from the same origins and by the same means as those from which and by which they are corrupted, but the activities that flow from them will consist in the same things. For this is also true in other more obvious cases, like that of strength. It is produced by eating a great deal and going through a great deal of strenuous exercise, and it is the strong person who will be most able to do these very things. The same applies to virtues. By abstaining from pleasures we become temperate, and having become so we are most able to abstain from them. Similarly with courage: by becoming habituated to make light of what is fearful and to face up to it, we become courageous; and when we are, we shall be most able to face up to it. …

Chapter 5

Next we must consider what virtue is. There are three things to be found in the soul – feelings, capacities, and states – so virtue should be one of these. By feelings, I mean appetite, anger, fear, confidence, envy, joy, love, hate, longing, emulation, pity, and in general things accompanied by pleasure or pain. By capacities, I mean the things on the basis of which we are described as being capable of experiencing these feelings – on the basis of which, for example, we are described as capable of feeling anger, fear or pity. And by states I mean those things in respect of which we are well or badly disposed in relation to feelings. If, for example, in relation to anger, we feel it too much or too little, we are badly disposed; but if we are between the two, then well disposed. And the same goes for the other cases.

Neither the virtues nor the vices are feelings, because we are called good or bad on the basis not of our feelings, but of our virtues and vices; and also because we are neither praised nor blamed on the basis of our feelings (the person who is afraid or angry is not praised, and the person who is angry without qualification is not blamed but rather the person who is angry in a certain way), but we are praised and blamed on the basis of our virtues and vices. Again, we become angry or afraid without rational choice, while the virtues are rational choices or at any rate involve rational choice. Again, in respect of our feelings, we are said to be moved, while in respect of our virtues and vices we are said not to be moved but to be in a certain state.

For these reasons they are not capacities either. For we are not called either good or bad, nor are we praised or blamed, through being capable of experiencing things, without qualification. Again, while we have this capacity by nature, we do not become good or bad by nature; we spoke about this earlier.

So if the virtues are neither feelings nor capacities, it remains that they are states. We have thus described what virtue is generically.

Chapter 6

But we must say not just that virtue is a state, but what kind of state. We should mention, then, that every virtue causes that of which it is a virtue to be in a good state, and to perform its characteristic activity well. The virtue of the eye, for example, makes it and its characteristic activity good, because it is through the virtue of the eye that we see well. Likewise, the virtue of the horse makes a horse good – good at running, at carrying its rider and at facing the enemy. If this is so in all cases, then the virtue of a human being too will be the state that makes a human being good and makes him perform his characteristic activity well.

We have already said how this will happen, and it will be clear also from what follows, if we consider what the nature of virtue is like.

In everything continuous and divisible, one can take more, less, or an equal amount, and each either in respect of the thing itself or relative to us; and the equal is a sort of mean between excess and deficiency. By the mean in respect of the thing itself I mean that which is equidistant from each of the extremes, this being one single thing and the same for everyone, and by the mean relative to us I mean that which is neither excessive nor deficient – and this is not one single thing, nor is it the same for all. If, for example, ten are many and two are few, six is the mean if one takes it in respect of the thing, because it is by the same amount that it exceeds the one number and is exceeded by the other. This is the mean according to arithmetic progression. The mean relative to us, however, is not to be obtained in this way. For if ten pounds of food is a lot for someone to eat, and two pounds a little, the trainer will not necessarily prescribe six; for this may be a lot or a little for the person about to eat it – for Milo [a famous athlete of Croton in the late 6th century], a little, for a beginner at gymnastics, a lot. The same goes for running and wrestling. In this way every expert in a science avoids excess and deficiency, and aims for the mean and chooses it – the mean, that is, not in the thing itself but relative to us.

If, then, every science does its job well in this way, with its eye on the mean and judging its products by this criterion (which explains both why people are inclined to say of successful products that nothing can be added or taken away from them, implying that excess and deficiency ruin what is good in them, while the mean preserves it, and why those who are good at the skills have their eye on this, as we say, in turning out their product), and if virtue, like nature, is more precise and superior to any skill, it will also be the sort of thing that is able to hit the mean.

I am talking here about virtue of character, since it is this that is concerned with feelings and actions, and it is in these that we find excess, deficiency and the mean. For example, fear, confidence, appetite, anger, pity, and in general pleasure and pain can be experienced too much or too little, and in both ways not well. But to have them at the right time, about the right things, towards the right people, for the right end, and in the right way, is the mean and best; and this is the business of virtue. Similarly, there is an excess, a deficiency and a mean in actions. Virtue is concerned with feelings and actions, in which excess and deficiency constitute misses of the mark, while the mean is praised and on target, both of which are characteristics of virtue. Virtue, then, is a kind of mean, at least in the sense that it is the sort of thing that is able to hit a mean.

Again, one can miss the mark in many ways (since the bad belongs to the unlimited, as the Pythagoreans portrayed it, and the good to the limited), but one can get things right in only one (for which reason one is easy and the other difficult missing the target easy, hitting it difficult). For these reasons as well, then, excess and deficiency are characteristics of vice, the mean characteristic of virtue: for good people are just good, while bad people are bad in all sorts of ways.

Virtue, then, is a state involving rational choice, consisting in a mean relative to us and determined by reason – the reason, that is, by reference to which the practically wise person would determine it. It is a mean between two vices, one of excess, the other of deficiency. It is a mean also in that some vices fall short of what is right in feelings and actions, and others exceed it, while virtue both attains and chooses the mean. So, in respect of its essence and the definition of its substance, virtue is a mean, while with regard to what is best and good it is an extreme.

But not every action or feeling admits of a mean. For some have names immediately connected with depravity, such as spite, shamelessness, envy, and, among actions, adultery, theft, homicide. All these, and others like them, are so called because they themselves, and not their excesses or deficiencies, are bad. In their case, then, one can never hit the mark, but always misses.

Nor is there a good or bad way to go about such things – committing adultery, say, with the right woman, at the right time, or in the right way. Rather, doing one of them, without qualification, is to miss the mark.

It would be equally wrong, therefore, to expect there to be a mean, an excess and a deficiency in committing injustice, being a coward, and being intemperate, since then there would be a mean of excess and a mean of deficiency, an excess of excess and a deficiency of deficiency. Rather, just as there is no excess and deficiency of temperance and courage, because the mean is, in a sense, an extreme, so too there is no mean, excess or deficiency in the cases above. However they are done, one misses the mark, because, generally speaking, there is neither a mean of excess or deficiency, nor an excess or deficiency of a mean.

Chapter 7

… In fear and confidence, courage is the mean. Of those who exceed it, the person who exceeds in fearlessness has no name (many cases lack names), while the one who exceeds in confidence is rash. He who exceeds in being afraid and is deficient in confidence is a coward.

With respect to pleasures and pains – not all of them, and less so with pains – the mean is temperance, the excess intemperance. People deficient with regard to pleasures are not very common, and so do not even have a name; let us call them insensible.

In giving and taking money, the mean is generosity, while the excess and deficiency are wastefulness and stinginess. People with these qualities are excessive and deficient in contrary ways to one another. The wasteful person exceeds in giving away and falls short in taking, while the stingy person exceeds in taking and falls short in giving away. …

Chapter 9

Enough has been said, then, to show that virtue of character is a mean, and in what sense it is so; that it is a mean between two vices, one of excess and one of deficiency; and that it is such because it is the sort of thing able to hit the mean in feelings and actions. This is why it is hard to be good, because in each case it is hard to find the middle point; for instance, not everyone can find the centre of a circle, but only the person with knowledge. So too anyone can get angry, or give and spend money – these are easy; but doing them in relation to the right person, in the right amount, at the right time, with the right aim in view, and in the right way – that is not something anyone can do, nor is it easy. This is why excellence in these things is rare, praiseworthy and noble.

Religious Ethics

Religion is a disputed notion. It refers to broad similarities of form in relation to observable behavior and central texts, in terms of ritual, divinity, worship, doctrine, faith, devotion, and so on. Some seek a stricter definition of religion, which seeks to articulate and identify common denominators of religious expression and then use such a normative model as a way of assessing and quantifying religions new and old. Such a notion of religion comes largely from secular observation and is not internal to any of the specific traditions.

There are a variety of ways in which religion has been regarded as being more or less identical with ethics. This recognizes the practical aspect of the major traditions of

faith, and the reality that the founders of many of the great world traditions were themselves historical figures with pressing personal and political issues to address. Some would say that without religion, there can be no ethics. Others would take the opposite view and seek an ethic that was not based on a specific religious tradition.

These readings give an introduction to the kinds of directions religious ethics tends to take and a taste of some of its more illustrious exponents. Sumner Twiss provides an overview of what it means to set religious traditions in ethics side-by-side. Mahatma Gandhi and the Dalai Lama offer constructive accounts of ethics from beyond the Abrahamic perspective.

Sumner B. Twiss, *Comparison in Religious Ethics*

Sumner B. Twiss (b. 1944) taught for many years at Brown University in Providence, Rhode Island, and now teaches at Florida State University in Tallahassee. This passage offers a brief history, a contemporary overview, and a prospectus for the field of comparative religious ethics.

In some ways comparative religious ethics mirrors the threefold typology employed in this volume. One approach mirrors what we are calling "universal ethics," in that it seeks to articulate a template for what might be regarded as "religion," and then to offer a definition of ethics, and subsequently to draw similarities and differences across different traditions, sometimes accompanied by an overarching theory of religion or ethics, sometimes not. Another approach, more like what we are calling "subversive ethics," is much more suspicious of (often Western, academic, and apparently privileged, typically white male) attempts to define and prescribe forms of religion and ethics, and is more concerned with difference and context. A third, more like what we are calling "ecclesial ethics," distrusts the desire to step outside any one particular tradition to make so-called objective judgments.

Sumner B. Twiss. "Comparison in Religious Ethics." Chapter 16 in *The Blackwell Companion to Religious Ethics*, ed. William Schweiker. Oxford: Blackwell, 2005. Pages 148–54.

History

From the period of classical social theory and philosophy, the illustrative landmark figures are Emile Durkheim, Max Weber and Ernst Troeltsch, and Edward Westermarck and L. T. Hobhouse. Durkheim pioneered the idea of developing a positive science of social life. A science of morality should treat moral and religious beliefs and practices as natural phenomena for which were sought the causes, functions, and laws on a

sui generis social plane. From Durkheim's perspective, the science of morality provided an intellectual basis for guiding enlightened social and political policy. In fact, he played a significant role as a transformative public intellectual during the period of the Third French Republic.

Unlike Durkheim, Weber distinguished between politics and scholarship. He developed a program of value-neutral scientific inquiry into social phenomena. Weber's distinctive methodology of *Verstehen* uncovered the subjective motives of agents – complemented by causal and historical explanation and involving the use of ideal types of rational behavior. Using this methodology, Weber pioneered sociological inquiry into distinctive types of religious ethical systems within correlated political economies. This was informed by an overarching evolutionary view of rational social development.

Although in significant agreement with Weber's method, Troeltsch crystallized the meaning and challenge of historicism for dealing with the moral and religious diversity and the internal development of supposedly absolute ethical and religious values. Unlike Weber, Troeltsch was not shy about playing a public intellectual role in German political society, particularly after World War I.

While not trained social scientists, philosophers Westermarck and Hobhouse undertook comparative surveys of moral phenomena all over the world. Their contrasting normative and theoretical conclusions – ethical relativism and moral universalism, respectively – illustrated the challenge of Troeltsch's "crisis of historicism" for the field of ethics. Both Westermarck and Hobhouse played significant public intellectual roles in, respectively, Finnish and English politics. ...

The second phase is marked by anthropological interventions, whether pursued by professional anthropologists or by philosophers guided by such professionals. Two philosophers, Richard Brandt and John Ladd, did limited fieldwork among the Hopi and Navajo, respectively, utilizing Western moral theory (theory types) to expose the logical structure of the reasoning and worldviews of their subjects. Both were widely read in the ethnographic literature and used informants and professional translators for limited periods of field research. Both used "ideal types" to guide their inquiry and to analyze their results. They regarded their studies as forays into what was called "descriptive ethics," that is, analyzing the moral reasoning of subjective agents from their internal perspective. Yet their work also compared Western patterns of reasoning and justification with those of indigenous peoples. Neither Brandt nor Ladd envisioned himself as a transformative intellectual.

By contrast, the anthropologist Bronislaw Malinowski undertook intensive field studies of the people of Melanesia. Curtailing the use of theoretical ideas and professional informants, he relied on long-term participant observation in order to ascertain how they reasoned and made sense of their world. Malinowski's ethnographic method was influenced by American pragmatism (specifically, William James). He attempted to determine how his subjects' behavior made sense or was reasonable inasmuch as it pragmatically satisfied their basic needs. The total field of data was scrutinized from the perspective of how the data fit holistically and pragmatically in order to form an intelligible world. Malinowski was not interested in comparison per se, or in using ideal types as bridges of comprehension, which might distort the data and do an injustice to the way his subjects actually reasoned. ...

The third phase of development begins with [the publication in 1978 of *Religious Reason: The Rational and Moral Basis of Religious Belief* by R. M. Green, *Comparative Ethics in Hindu and Buddhist Traditions* by R. Hindery, and *Comparative Religious Ethics: A New Method* by D. Little and S. B. Twiss], followed by intensive scrutiny of their presuppositions, methods, and results. Ronald Green's book was predicated on a theory of moral and religious rationality derived from Kant's moral philosophy (and to a lesser extent John Rawls' theory of justice). This theory was used to probe the structure of reasoning in Judaism, Christianity, and the religions of India.

Roderick Hindery was guided in part by Weber's work on religious ethics, as well as other methodological studies. He used primary sources and history of religions literature to challenge simplistic views of the ethics of Hindu and Buddhist traditions.

David Little and Sumner Twiss explicitly adapted Ladd's descriptive ethics – by adding definitions of certain key concepts (morality, law, religion) – to probe the reasoning and justificatory patterns of selected data from three moral traditions: the Navajo, early Christianity, and Theravāda Buddhism. This study was also informed by contemporary ethnological and historical scholarship.

The response to some of these works was immediate and sustained. Green was criticized for imposing an *a priori* and ethnocentric account of rationality on religious-moral traditions that distorted their views. Little and Twiss' study was criticized for being overly positivistic and deploying categories and ideal-typical structures of reasoning that were too static and unnuanced to capture the dynamics of reasoning within the complex worldviews in which they are embedded.

In reaction to these criticisms, Robin Lovin and Frank Reynolds published an anthology of essays in 1985 on cosmogonies and ethics that explicitly propounded a Malinowski-like pragmatic holism as the proper way to study texts and phenomena within diverse moral traditions. This continued the suspicion of systematic comparative work in ethics, while opening the possibility that pragmatic holism could be used for non-systematic comparison in the future. The majority of essays in their anthology were particularistic studies of limited texts and traditions (considered within themselves), not explicit comparisons across traditions or cultures. The majority of the authors were historians of religions and anthropologists. For this phase as a whole, none of the scholars advocated the role of the comparative ethicist as a transformative intellectual.

A number of trends are remarkable in light of the preceding phases: a continuing interest in a grand theoretical (although not explicitly evolutionary) account of morality across traditions; the continuing use of ideal types (even if challenged) in comparative ethics; and a continuing interest in deploying less systematic and more pragmatic approaches to the subject. In addition, the theme of universality versus relativism carried through many of these works. Green's theory presupposed moral universalism. Little and Twiss' patterns of moral reasoning were portrayed as descriptive universals. Lovin and Reynolds worried about the possible relativistic implications of their pragmatic holism.

Contemporary Situation

… As scholarship has progressed, and as appropriate in a world characterized by global intercultural communication, transport, and education, non-Western scholars have entered the conversation of comparative religious ethics. They are guided by similar or analogous aims, methods, and categories, although now enriched by indigenous social and intellectual locations. This trend is likely to continue and strengthen, eroding perceptions (or misperceptions) of the hegemony of Western scholarship. This trend, in turn, has surfaced – or at least emphasized – the fact that non-Western traditions embody diverse sub-traditions (an internal moral pluralism) that accounts for the fact that previous scholars have offered seemingly competing readings of non-Western traditions, thinkers, and texts. Monolithic interpretation of these traditions is forever eroded.

Some of the most important work in comparative ethics is now being done by indigenous scholars interested in philosophical and practical issues and the way that their societies and traditions deviate from Western moral reasoning and praxis. This scholarship is complemented by Western scholars equally interested in the reasons for such deviation, as well as being alert to ways that Western reasoning and praxis might have something to learn from non-Western traditions or at least be enriched by them. Illustrative examples of this development range from comparative studies of the self (relevant to moral psychology), to cross-cultural studies of human rights and just war theory (relevant to political ethics), to comparative studies of health, medicine, and

healthcare delivery (relevant to biomedical ethics), to cross-cultural studies of ecological thought and practice (relevant to environmental ethics). …

Future

In order to concretize further the maturity attained by comparative religious ethics and to illustrate directions for future scholarship, it is necessary to note in more detail work now being pursued. As mentioned previously, comparative ethics is now being undertaken in substantive focal areas of concern.

(1) Comparative inquiry into selfhood and moral agency subsumes study of particular topics, such as self-cultivation, the sources of human moral evil, particular virtues, notions of conscience and their analogues, among others. Much of this work constitutes rather thin comparisons between non-Western conceptions of self and related phenomena, on the one hand, and somewhat broadly cast notions of Western metaphysics and virtue theory, on the other. By contrast, other studies are much thicker and more robust comparisons between particular thinkers or key normative concepts from two different traditions – for example, Mencius and Aquinas, Augustine and Xunzi, *jen* (Confucian humaneness) and *agape* (Christian neighbor-love). These studies push comparisons in the direction of trying to solve a genuine human problem, such as how to relate reason and emotion, how to overcome moral evil, or how to sustain the project of becoming a good person. …

(2) The emergence of social, applied, or practical ethics from the perspective of non-Western moral traditions, while not explicitly comparative, is a phenomenon worthy of note. It portends the general potential for scholars of non-Western and Western traditions to collaborate on seeking answers to shared moral dilemmas cutting across traditional and cultural boundaries. It is simply a fact, for example, that scholars of Buddhism, Confucianism, and Hinduism – whatever their social and intellectual location – are probing moral issues concerning medicine and healthcare, ecology, statecraft, business, and human rights. Given the processes of globalization one can easily anticipate an explosion of such work that can only benefit the scope and quality of comparative inquiry in applied ethics. …

(3) One encounters similar developments in the area of ecological and environmental ethics, although with a twist. Disenchanted environmentally minded Western scholars are taking the lead in looking toward non-Western traditions for conceptual and practical resources to mitigate environmental pollution, ecologi-

cal destruction, species extinction, and depletion of non-renewable energy sources that are exacerbated by modern industrialized economies. The hope is that comparative study of non-Western moral traditions will yield new ways of conceptualizing a positive regard for nature, as well as correlated practical strategies for reining in energy and resource-hungry Western societies. There is a spate of studies on non-Western traditions focusing on conceptions of nature, ecological balance, appropriate land use, and harmony between humans and other species, among other related topics. As the environmental crisis constitutes a worldwide problem, one can, again, anticipate increasingly robust comparative work in this area.

(4) Comparative ethics and political theory has been high on the agenda of comparativists for the last two decades. It has been intensified by recent political, military, and terrorist events. Amid claims of an inevitable clash of civilizations, scholars of comparative ethics have been patiently addressing issues of war and statecraft – just war theory and its analogues – and human rights that are increasingly translated into discourse for public consumption and education. With respect to just war thinking, the comparative work thus far is focused on Islam, Christianity (or Western tradition more broadly), and Buddhism. In regard to human rights,

comparative work has focused on the enlightened retrospective interpretation of myriad non-Western and Western moral and religious traditions in light of their congruence with or deviation from traditions of international law and human rights. ...

(5) The final substantive area – search for a common morality – brings us full circle to a perdurable concern of comparative religious ethics since its earliest inception: universality versus relativism. While theoretical in tone, this issue has a very practical moral dimension, since if there is (or can be) a universal, common, or global ethic or morality, a strong groundwork is provided for intercultural moral dialogue and praxis. Comparativists have been working on the prospects for a common morality from a number of angles: deploying diverse philosophical theories (Kantian, Aristotelian) informed by comparative data; forging a practical overlapping normative consensus among diverse moral and political traditions; showing pragmatically that a common set of moral norms is the best way to solve shared problems and advance human well-being. In addition, this search – which is likely to continue into the foreseeable future – continues to press the theoretical issue about whether comparative ethics can produce generalizable moral knowledge indicating some deep truths about our human moral nature.

Mohandas K. Gandhi, *Experiments With Truth*

Mohandas Karamchand Gandhi (1869–1948) was raised in Gujarat, India, in Jain traditions. He came to London at the age of 19 to study law and was introduced to social organizing through the Vegetarian Society. He read widely in religious thought. After returning to India he traveled to South Africa at the age of 24. After experiencing significant racial prejudice and brutality he quickly began to organize the Indian community in South Africa into a political force. In 1906 he adopted his non-violent approach to social protest, known as *satyagraha* (devotion to the truth), and began a seven-year struggle for Indian civil rights in the Transvaal region of northern South Africa. He returned to India in 1915, and spent the rest of his life at the center of the independence movement.

Hinduism was key to Gandhi's ethics. "Hinduism as I know it entirely satisfies my soul, fills my whole being. ... When doubts haunt me, when disappointments stare me in the face, and when I see not one ray of light on the horizon, I turn to the *Bhagavad Gita*, and find a verse to comfort me; and I immediately begin to smile in the midst of overwhelming sorrow." Among ethical commitments related to his Hinduism was simplicity: he dressed to be accepted by the poorest person in India, at the same time challenging Indians to strengthen their economy by wearing simple Indian-made clothes. Non-violence (*ahimsa*) is especially associated with Gandhi, as is, controversially, spiritual and practical purity, particularly chastity (*brahmacharya*).

Mohandas K. Gandhi. *An Autobiography: The Story of My Experiments With Truth*. Trans. Mahadev Desai. Boston: Beacon Press, 1957. From pages xii–xiv, 135–8, 159–60, 503–5. Reprinted by permission of the Navajivan Trust.

Introduction

What I want to achieve, – what I have been striving and pining to achieve these thirty years, – is self-realization, to see God face to face, to attain *Moksha* [i.e., freedom from birth and death]. I live and move and have my being in pursuit of this goal. All that I do by way of speaking and writing, and all my ventures in the political field, are directed to this same end. But as I have all along believed that what is possible for one is possible for all, my experiments have not been conducted in the closet, but in the open; and I do not think that this fact detracts from their spiritual value. There are some things which are known only to oneself and one's Maker. These are clearly incommunicable. The experiments I am about to relate are not such. But they are spiritual, or rather moral; for the essence of religion is morality. ...

If I had only to discuss academic principles, I should clearly not attempt an autobiography. But my purpose being to give an account of various practical applications of these principles, I have given the chapters I propose to write the title of *The Story of My Experiments with Truth*. These will of course include experiments with nonviolence, celibacy and other principles of conduct believed to be distinct from truth. But for me, truth is the sovereign principle, which includes numerous other principles. This truth is not only truthfulness in word, but truthfulness in thought also, and not only the relative truth of our conception, but the Absolute Truth, the Eternal Principle, that is God. There are innumerable definitions of God, because His manifestations are innumerable. They overwhelm me with wonder and awe and for a moment stun me. But I worship God as Truth only. I have not yet found Him, but I am seeking after Him. I am prepared to sacrifice the things dearest to me in pursuit of this quest. Even if the sacrifice demanded be my very life, I hope I may be prepared to give it. But as long as I have not realized this Absolute Truth, so long must I hold by the relative truth as I have conceived it. That relative truth must, meanwhile, be my beacon, my shield and buckler. Though this path is strait and narrow and sharp as the razor's edge, for me it has been the quickest and easiest. Even my Himalayan blunders have seemed trifling to me because I have kept strictly to this path. For the path has saved me from coming to grief, and I have gone forward according to my light. Often in my progress I have had faint glimpses of the Absolute Truth, God, and daily the conviction is growing upon me that He alone is real and all else is unreal. ...

Religious Ferment

It is now time to turn again to my experiences with Christian friends.

Mr. Baker was getting anxious about my future. He took me to the Wellington Convention. The Protestant Christians organize such gatherings every few years for religious enlightenment or, in other words, self-purification. ...

This Convention was an assemblage of devout Christians. I was delighted at their faith. I met the Rev. Murray. I saw that many were praying for me. I liked some of their hymns, they were very sweet.

The Convention lasted for three days. I could understand and appreciate the devoutness of those who attended it. But I saw no reason for changing my belief – my religion. It was impossible for me to believe that I could go to heaven or attain salvation only by becoming a Christian. When I frankly said so to some of the good Christian friends, they were shocked. But there was no help for it.

My difficulties lay deeper. It was more than I could believe that Jesus was the only incarnate son of God, and that only he who believed in him would have everlasting life. If God could have sons, all of us were His sons. If Jesus was like God, or God Himself, then all men were like God and could be God Himself. My reason was not ready to believe literally that Jesus by his death and by his blood redeemed the sins of the world. Metaphorically there might be some truth in it. ... The pious lives of Christians did not give me anything that the lives of men of other faiths had failed to give. I had seen in other lives just the same reformation that I had heard of among Christians. Philosophically there was nothing extraordinary in Christian principles. From the point of view of sacrifice, it seemed to me that the Hindus greatly surpassed the Christians. It was impossible for me to regard Christianity as a perfect religion or the greatest of all religions. ...

Thus if I could not accept Christianity either as a perfect, or the greatest religion, neither was I then convinced of Hinduism being such. Hindu defects were pressingly visible to me. If untouchability could be a part of Hinduism, it could but be a rotten part or an excrescence. I could not understand the *raison d'être* of a multitude of sects and castes. What was the meaning of saying that the Vedas were the inspired Word of God? If they were inspired, why not also the Bible and the Koran?

As Christian friends were endeavouring to convert me, even so were Musalman friends. Abdulla Sheth had kept on inducing me to study Islam, and of course he had always something to say regarding its beauty.

I expressed my difficulties in a letter to Raychandbhai. I also corresponded with other religious authorities in India and received answers from them. Raychandbhai's letter somewhat pacified me. He asked me to be patient and to study Hinduism more deeply. One of his sentences was to this effect: "On a dispassionate view of the question I am convinced that no other religion has the subtle and profound thought of Hinduism, its vision of the soul, or its charity."

I purchased Sale's translation of the Koran and began reading it. I also obtained other books on Islam. I communicated with Christian friends in England. One of them introduced me to Edward Maitland, with whom I opened correspondence. He sent me *The Perfect Way*, a book he had written in collaboration with Anna Kingsford. The book was a repudiation of the current Christian belief. He also sent me another book, *The New Interpretation of the Bible*. I liked both. They seemed to support Hinduism. Tolstoy's *The Kingdom of God is Within You* overwhelmed me. It left an abiding impression on me. ...

Though I took a path my Christian friends had not intended for me, I have remained for ever indebted to them for the religious quest that they awakened in me. I shall always cherish the memory of their contact. The years that followed had more, not less, of such sweet and sacred contacts in store for me. ...

Comparative Study of Religions

If I found myself entirely absorbed in the service of the community, the reason behind it was my desire for self-realization. I had made the religion of service my own, as I felt that God could be realized only through service. And service for me was the service of India, because it came to me without my seeking, because I had an aptitude for it. I had gone to South Africa for travel, for finding escape from Kathiawad intrigues and for gaining my own livelihood. But as I have said, I found myself in search of God and striving for self-realization. ...

Thus I gained more knowledge of the different religions. The study stimulated my self-introspection and fostered in me the habit of putting into practice whatever appealed to me in my studies. Thus I began some

of the Yogic practices, as well as I could understand them from a reading of the Hindu books. But I could not get on very far, and decided to follow them with the help of some expert when I returned to India. The desire has never been fulfilled.

I made too an intensive study of Tolstoy's books. *The Gospels in Brief, What to Do?* and other books made a deep impression on me. I began to realize more and more the infinite possibilities of universal love. ...

Farewell

... It is not without a wrench that I have to take leave of the reader. I set a high value on my experiments. I do not know whether I have been able to do justice to them. I can only say that I have spared no pains to give a faithful narrative. To describe truth, as it has appeared to me, and in the exact manner in which I have arrived at it, has been my ceaseless effort. The exercise has given me ineffable mental peace, because, it has been my fond hope that it might bring faith in Truth and Ahimsa [nonviolence] to waverers.

My uniform experience has convinced me that there is no other God than Truth. And if every page of these chapters does not proclaim to the reader that the only means for the realization of Truth is Ahimsa, I shall deem all my labour in writing these chapters to have been in vain. And, even though my efforts in this behalf may prove fruitless, let the readers know that the vehicle, not the great principle, is at fault. After all, however sincere my strivings after Ahimsa may have been, they have still been imperfect and inadequate. The little fleeting glimpses, therefore, that I have been able to have of Truth can hardly convey an idea of the indescribable lustre of Truth, a million times more intense than that of the sun we daily see with our eyes. In fact what I have caught is only the faintest glimmer of that mighty effulgence. But this much I can say with assurance, as a result of all my experiments, that a perfect vision of Truth can only follow a complete realization of Ahimsa.

To see the universal and all-pervading Spirit of Truth face to face one must be able to love the meanest of creation as oneself. And a man who aspires after that cannot afford to keep out of any field of life. That is why my devotion to Truth has drawn me into the field of politics; and I can say without the slightest hesitation, and yet in all humility, that those who say that religion has nothing to do with politics do not know what religion means.

Identification with everything that lives is impossible without self-purification; without self-purification the observance of the law of Ahimsa must remain an empty dream; God can never be realized by one who is not pure of heart. Self-purification therefore must mean purification in all the walks of life. And purification being highly infectious, purification of oneself necessarily leads to the purification of one's surroundings.

But the path of self-purification is hard and steep. To attain to perfect purity one has to become absolutely passion-free in thought, speech and action; to rise above the opposing currents of love and hatred, attachment and repulsion. I know that I have not in me as yet that triple purity, in spite of constant ceaseless striving for it. That is why the world's praise fails to move me,

indeed it very often stings me. To conquer the subtle passions seems to me to be harder far than the physical conquest of the world by the force of arms. Ever since my return to India I have had experiences of the dormant passions lying hidden within me. The knowledge of them has made me feel humiliated though not defeated. The experiences and experiments have sustained me and given me great joy. But I know that I have still before me a difficult path to traverse. I must reduce myself to zero. So long as a man does not of his own free will put himself last among his fellow creatures, there is no salvation for him. Ahimsa is the farthest limit of humility.

The Dalai Lama, *The Supreme Emotion*

Tenzin Gyatso (b. 1935) was the fifth of 16 children born to a farming family in Qinghai province, Tibet. He was proclaimed the reincarnation of the thirteenth Dalai Lama two years after he was born. On November 17, 1950, at the age of 15, only one month after the Chinese invasion of Tibet, he was enthroned as the Dalai Lama, Tibet's most prominent spiritual leader and political ruler. He has become a significant international spokesperson on Tibetan affairs, global ethics, and interfaith dialogue.

He has shown sympathy towards Marxism, noting that, unlike capitalism, it is founded on moral principles. The flawed regimes in China, the USSR, and Vietnam were "more concerned with their narrow national interests than with the Workers' International," and "placed too much emphasis on the need to destroy the ruling class, on class struggle, and this causes them to encourage hatred and to neglect compassion," with the result that they simply impoverished their people.

While the Dalai Lama is the leading voice in Tibetan Buddhism, he is not an officially recognized spokesperson for Buddhism more generally. Buddhism is now a truly global faith, with a wide diversity of expressions and traditions.

His Holiness The Dalai Lama. *Ethics for the New Millennium.* New York: Riverhead Books, 1999. From Chapter Five, "The Supreme Emotion," pages 64–8, 70–4.

Events such as those which occurred at Auschwitz are violent reminders of what can happen when individuals – and by extension, whole societies – lose touch with basic human feeling. But although it is necessary to have legislation and international conventions in place as safeguards against future disasters of this kind, we have all seen that atrocities continue in spite of them. Much

more effective and important than such legislation is our regard for one another's feelings at a simple human level.

When I speak of basic human feeling, I am not only thinking of something fleeting and vague, however. I refer to the capacity we all have to empathize with one another, which, in Tibetan we call *shen dug ngal wa la mi sö pa*. Translated literally, this means "the inability to bear the sight of another's suffering." Given that this is what enables us to enter into, and to some extent participate, in others' pain, it is one of our most significant characteristics. It is what causes us to start at the sound of a cry for help, to recoil at the sight of harm done to another, to suffer when confronted with others' suffering. And it is what compels us to shut our eyes even when we want to ignore others' distress.

... It is certainly possible to imagine people who, after enduring years of warfare, are no longer moved at the sight of others' suffering. The same could be true of those who live in places where there is an atmosphere of violence and indifference to others. It is even possible to imagine a few who would exult at the sight of another's suffering. This does not prove that the capacity for empathy is not present in such people. That we all, excepting perhaps only the most disturbed, appreciate being shown kindness, suggests that however hardened we may become, the capacity for empathy remains.

This characteristic of appreciating others' concern is, I believe, a reflection of our "inability to bear the sight of another's suffering." I say this because alongside our natural ability to empathize with others, we also have a need for others' kindness, which runs like a thread throughout our whole life. It is most apparent when we are young and when we are old. But we have only to fall ill to be reminded of how important it is to be loved and cared about even during our prime years. Though it may seem a virtue to be able to do without affection, in reality a life lacking this precious ingredient must be a miserable one. It is surely not a coincidence that the lives of most criminals turn out to have been lonely and lacking in love. ...

Despite the body of opinion suggesting that human nature is basically aggressive and competitive, my own view is that our appreciation for affection and love is so profound that it begins even before our birth. Indeed, according to some scientist friends of mine, there is strong evidence to suggest that a mother's mental and emotional state greatly affects the wellbeing of her unborn child, that it benefits her baby if she maintains a warm and gentle state of mind. A happy mother bears a happy child. On the other hand, frustration and anger are harmful to the healthy development of the baby. Similarly, during the first weeks after birth, warmth and affection continue to play a supreme role in the infant's physical development. At this stage, the brain is growing very rapidly, a function which doctors believe is somehow assisted by the constant touch of the mother or surrogate. This shows that though the baby may not know or care who is who, it has a clear physical need of affection. Perhaps, too, it explains why even the most fractious, agitated, and paranoid individuals respond positively to the affection and care of others. As infants

they must have been nurtured by someone. Should a baby be neglected during this critical period, clearly it could not survive.

Fortunately, this is very rarely the case. Almost without exception, the mother's first act is to offer her baby her nourishing milk – an act which to me symbolizes unconditional love. Her affection here is totally genuine and uncalculating: she expects nothing in return. As for the baby, it is drawn naturally to its mother's breast. Why? Of course we can speak of the survival instinct. But in addition I think it reasonable to conjecture a degree of affection on the part of the infant toward its mother. If it felt aversion, surely it would not suckle? And if the mother felt aversion, it is doubtful her milk would flow freely. What we see instead is a relationship based on love and mutual tenderness, which is totally spontaneous. It is not learned from others, no religion requires it, no laws impose it, no schools have taught it. It arises quite naturally.

This instinctual care of mother for child – shared it seems with many animals – is crucial because it suggests that alongside the baby's fundamental need of love in order to survive, there exists an innate capacity on the part of the mother to give love. So powerful is it that we might almost suppose a biological component is at work. Of course it could be argued that this reciprocal love is nothing more than a survival mechanism. That could well be so. But that is not to deny its existence. Nor indeed does it undermine my conviction that this need and capacity for love suggest that we are, in fact, loving by nature. ...

In all of what I have said about our basic nature, I do not mean to suggest that I believe it has no negative aspects. Where there is consciousness, hatred, ignorance, and violence do indeed arise naturally. This is why, although our nature is basically disposed toward kindness and compassion, we are all capable of cruelty and hatred. It is why we have to struggle to better our conduct. It also explains how individuals raised in a strictly non-violent environment have turned into the most horrible butchers. ...

To say that basic human nature is not only non-violent but actually disposed toward love and compassion, kindness, gentleness, affection, creation, and so on does, of course, imply a general principle which must, by definition, be applicable to each individual human being. What, then, are we to say about those individuals whose lives seem to be given over wholly to violence and aggression? During the past century alone there are several obvious examples to consider. What of Hitler and his plan to exterminate the entire Jewish race? What of Stalin and his pogroms? What of Chairman Mao, the man I once knew and admired, and the barbarous insanity of the Cultural Revolution? What of Pol Pot, architect of the Killing Fields? And what about those who torture and kill for pleasure?

Here I must admit that I can think of no single explanation to account for the monstrous acts of these people. However, we must recognize two things. Firstly, such people do not come from nowhere but from within a particular society at a particular time and in a particular place. Their actions need to be considered in relation to these circumstances. Secondly, we need to recognize the role of the imaginative faculty in their actions. Their schemes were and are carried out in accordance with a vision, albeit a perverted one. Notwithstanding the fact that nothing could justify the suffering they instigated, whatever their explanation might be and whatever positive intentions they could point to, Hitler, Stalin, Mao, and Pol Pot each had goals toward which they were working. If we examine those actions which are uniquely human, which animals cannot perform, we find that this imaginative faculty plays a vital role. The faculty itself is a unique asset. But the use to which it is put determines whether the actions it conceives are positive or negative, ethical or unethical. The individual's motivation (kun long) is thus the governing factor. And whereas a vision properly motivated – which recognizes others' desire for and equal right to happiness and to be free of suffering – can lead to wonders, when divorced from basic human feeling the potential for destruction cannot be overestimated.

As for those who kill for pleasure or, worse, for no reason at all, we can only conjecture a deep submergence of the basic impulse toward care and affection for others. Still this need not mean that it is entirely extinguished. As I pointed out earlier, except perhaps in the most extreme cases, it is possible to imagine even these people appreciating being shown affection. The disposition remains.

Actually, the reader does not need to accept my proposition that human nature is basically disposed toward love and compassion to see that the capacity for empathy which underlies it is of crucial importance when it comes to ethics. We saw earlier how an ethical act is a non-harming act. But how are we to determine whether an act is genuinely non-harming? We find that in practice, if we are not able to connect with others to some extent, if we cannot at least imagine the potential impact of our actions on others, then we have no means to discriminate between right and wrong, between what

is appropriate and what is not, between harming and non-harming. It follows, therefore, that if we could enhance the capacity – that is to say, our sensitivity toward others' suffering – the more we did so, the less we could tolerate seeing others' pain and the more we would be concerned to ensure that no action of ours caused harm to others.

The fact that we can indeed enhance our capacity for empathy becomes obvious when we consider its nature. We experience it mainly as a feeling. And, as we all know, to a greater or lesser extent we can not only restrain our feelings through reasoning, but we can enhance them in the same way. Our desire for objects – perhaps a new car – is enhanced by our turning it over and over in our imagination. Similarly, when, as it were, we direct our mental faculties onto our feelings of empathy, we find that not only can we enhance them, but we can transform them into love and compassion itself.

As such, our innate capacity for empathy is the source of that most precious of all human qualities, which in Tibetan we call *nying je*. Now while generally translated simply as "compassion," the term *nying je* has a wealth of meaning that is difficult to convey succinctly, though the ideas it contains are universally understood. It connotes love, affection, kindness, gentleness, generosity of spirit, and warm-heartedness. It is also used as a term of both sympathy and of endearment. On the other hand, it does not imply "pity" as the word compassion may. There is no sense of condescension. On the contrary, *nying je* denotes a feeling of connection with others, reflecting its origins in empathy. Thus while we might say, "I love my house" or "I have strong feelings of affection for this place," we cannot say, "I have compassion" for these things. Having no feelings themselves, we cannot empathize with objects. We cannot, therefore, speak of having compassion for them.

Although it is clear from this description that *nying je*, or love and compassion, is understood as an emotion, it belongs to that category of emotions which have a more developed cognitive component. Some emotions, such as the revulsion we tend to feel at the sight of blood, are basically instinctual. Others, such as fear of poverty, have this more developed cognitive component. We can thus understand *nying je* in terms of a combination of empathy and reason. We can think of empathy as the characteristic of a very honest person; reason as that of someone who is very practical. When the two are put together, the combination is highly effective. As such, *nying je* is quite different from those random feelings, like anger and lust, which, far from bringing us happiness, only trouble us and destroy our peace of mind.

To me, this suggests that by means of sustained reflection on, and familiarization with, compassion,

through rehearsal and practice we can develop our innate ability to connect with others, a fact which is of supreme importance given the approach to ethics I have described. The more we develop compassion, the more genuinely ethical our conduct will be.

Professional Ethics

While contemporary life is marked by fragmentation – the loss of a single purpose or community around which ethical practice and theory can coalesce – there are nonetheless significant areas of common agreement. Notable among these are the professions – law, medicine, and so on – and other areas that might be called quasi-professions, such as executive roles in business.

The rapid range of social change, the increased level of technology, and the higher expectation of public scrutiny and accountability (not to mention litigation) has made professional ethics a prominent concern particularly in professional schools. The following readings give a flavor of the concerns that arise in such discourses.

Tom L. Beauchamp and James F. Childress, *Principles of Biomedical Ethics*

Tom Beauchamp (b. 1939) is based at Georgetown University's Kennedy Institute of Ethics. James Childress (b.1940) is a long-serving faculty member at the University of Virginia. Their influential study in medical ethics shows a notable confidence in what they call "the common morality" – that is, universal norms that are "accepted by all morally serious persons" as binding on all persons in all places and are "not grounded in a particular philosophical or theological theory or doctrine." There is no doubt that autonomy has become the single most significant value in medical ethics, as this passage demonstrates.

Tom L. Beauchamp and James F. Childress. *Principles of Biomedical Ethics*. 5th edn. Oxford: Oxford University Press, 2001. From pages 342–50. By permission of Oxford University Press, Inc.

A Framework of Moral Principles

The common morality contains a set of moral norms that includes principles that are basic for biomedical ethics. Most classical ethical theories include these principles in some form, and traditional medical codes presuppose at least some of them.

Basic Principles

A set of principles in a moral account should function as an analytical framework that expresses the general values underlying rules in the common morality. These principles can then function as guidelines for professional ethics. ... [W]e defend four clusters of moral

principles that serve this function. The four clusters are (1) *respect for autonomy* (a norm of respecting the decision-making capacities of autonomous persons), (2) *nonmaleficence* (a norm of avoiding the causation of harm), (3) *beneficence* (a group of norms for providing benefits and balancing benefits against risks and costs), and (4) *justice* (a group of norms for distributing benefits, risks, and costs fairly).

Nonmaleficence and beneficence have played a central historical role in medical ethics, whereas respect for autonomy and justice were neglected in traditional medical ethics but came into prominence because of recent developments. To illustrate this traditional neglect, consider the work of British physician Thomas Percival. In 1803, he published *Medical Ethics,* which was the first well-formed account of medical ethics in the long history of the subject. This book served as the prototype for the American Medical Association's

(AMA) first code of ethics in 1847. Easily the dominant influence in both British and American medical ethics of the period, Percival argued (using somewhat different language) that nonmaleficence and beneficence fix the physician's primary obligations and triumph over the patient's preferences and decision-making rights in circumstances of serious conflict. Percival failed to appreciate the power of principles of respect for autonomy and distributive justice, but, in fairness to him, we must acknowledge that these considerations are now ubiquitous in discussions of biomedical ethics in a way they were not when he wrote at the turn of the nineteenth century.

That four clusters of moral "principles" are central to biomedical ethics is a conclusion the authors of this work have reached by examining *considered moral judgments* and the way *moral beliefs cohere*. ...

Rules

Our framework encompasses several types of moral norms, including principles, rules, rights, virtues, and moral ideals. Rules, rights, and virtues are very important in the framework, though we believe that principles provide the most general and comprehensive norms. We also operate with only a loose distinction between rules and principles. Both are general norms that guide actions. The difference is that rules are more specific in content and more restricted in scope than principles. Principles are general norms that leave considerable room for judgment in many cases. They thus do not function as precise action guides that inform us in each circumstance how to act in the way that more detailed rules and judgments do.

We defend several types of rules that specify principles (and thereby provide specific guidance): substantive rules, authority rules, and procedural rules.

Substantive rules. Rules of truth-telling, confidentiality, privacy, and various rules about forgoing treatment, physician-assisted suicide, informed consent, and the rationing of health care provide more specific guides to action than do abstract principles. Consider a simple example of a rule that sharpens the requirements of the principle of respect for autonomy for certain contexts: "Follow a patient's advance directive whenever it is clear and relevant." To indicate how this rule specifies the principles of respect for autonomy, we may state it more fully as: "Respect the autonomy of patients by following all clear and relevant formulations in their advance directives." This formulation shows how the initial norm remains but becomes specified. ...

Authority rules. We also defend rules about decisional authority – that is, rules regarding who may and should perform actions. For example, *rules of surrogate authority* determine who should serve as surrogate agents in making decisions for incompetent persons, and *rules of professional authority* determine who, if anyone, should make decisions to override or to accept a patient's decisions if those decisions are medically damaging and poorly considered. Another example appears in *rules of distributional authority* that determine who should make decisions about allocating scarce medical resources.

Authority rules do not delineate substantive standards or criteria for making decisions. However, authority rules and substantive rules do interact. For instance, authority rules are justified, in part, by how well particular authorities can be expected to respect and express substantive rules and principles.

Procedural rules. We also defend rules that establish procedures to be followed. Procedures for determining eligibility for scarce medical resources and procedures for reporting grievances to higher authorities are typical examples. We often resort to procedural rules when we run out of substantive rules and when authority rules are incomplete or inconclusive. For example, if substantive or authority rules are inadequate to determine which patients should receive scarce medical resources, we resort to procedural rules such as first-come-first-served, queuing, and lottery.

Rights, Virtues, Emotions, and Other Moral Considerations

Our framework of principles and rules, as outlined above, does not mention the rights of persons, the character and virtues of the agents who perform actions, or moral emotions. These aspects of the moral life all merit attention in a comprehensive theory. ... Rights, virtues, and emotional responses are as important as principles and rules for a comprehensive vision of the moral life. For example, an ethics of virtue helps us see why good moral choices often depend more on character than principles, and it also allows us to assess a person's moral character in a richer way than does an ethics of principles and rules. ...

The Prima Facie Nature of Moral Norms

Principles, rules, and rights are not unbending standards that disallow compromise. Although "a person of principle" is sometimes regarded as strict and unyielding, we must specify principles for various circumstances and weigh them against other moral norms.

W. D. Ross's distinction between *prima facie* and *actual* obligations is basic for our analysis. A *prima facie* obligation must be fulfilled unless it conflicts on a particular occasion with an equal or stronger obligation. This type of obligation is always binding *unless* a competing moral obligation overrides or outweighs it in a particular circumstance. Some acts are at once prima facie wrong and prima facie right, because two or more norms conflict in the circumstances. Agents must then determine what they ought to do by finding an actual or overriding (in contrast to prima facie) obligation. That is, they must locate what Ross called "the greatest balance" of right over wrong. Agents can determine their *actual* obligations in such situations by examining the respective weights of the competing prima facie obligations (the relative weights of all competing prima facie norms). What agents ought to do is, in the end, determined by what they ought to do *all things considered*.

For example, imagine that a psychiatrist has confidential medical information about a patient who happens also to be an employee in the hospital where the psychiatrist practices. The employee is seeking advancement in a stress-filled position, but the psychiatrist has good reason to believe this advancement would be devastating for both the employee and the hospital. The psychiatrist has several duties in these circumstances, including confidentiality, nonmaleficence, and beneficence. Should the psychiatrist break confidence in light of the other duties? Could the psychiatrist handle this matter by making thin disclosures only to a hospital administrator and not to the personnel office? Are such disclosures consistent with a psychiatrist's general commitment to rules of medical confidentiality? Addressing these questions through a process of moral deliberation and justification is required to establish an agent's actual duty in the face of conflicting prima facie duties.

No moral theorist or professional code of ethics has successfully presented a system of moral rules free of conflicts and exceptions, but this fact is not cause for either skepticism or alarm. Ross's distinction between prima facie and actual obligations conforms closely to our experience as moral agents and provides indispensable categories for biomedical ethics. Almost daily we confront situations in which we must choose among plural and conflicting values in our personal lives, and we must balance several considerations. Some choices are moral, many nonmoral. For example, our budget may require that we choose between buying books and buying a train ticket to see our parents. Not having the books will be an inconvenience and a loss, while not visiting home will make our parents unhappy. The choice is not easy, perhaps, but usually we can think through the alternatives, deliberate, balance, and reach a conclusion. The moral life presents many similar circumstances of choice.

Thomas F. McMahon, *A Brief History of American Business Ethics*

Alongside medical ethics, perhaps the most prominent dimension of professional ethics is in the business world. Here concerns are frequently raised about ethical standards expected of individuals and corporations, the manner in which companies relate to wider society, particularly the disadvantaged, and in recent years the responsibility taken by organizations towards ecological concerns.

Thomas F. McMahon (1928–2004) was a Viatorian Catholic priest who taught for many years at Loyola University in Chicago. Whereas the previous passage suggests medical ethics is about time-independent objective ethical criteria, this passage demonstrates the way business ethics has emerged in relation to ever-changing circumstances and norms in wider society.

Thomas F. McMahon. "A Brief History of American Business Ethics." In *A Companion to Business Ethics*, ed. Robert Frederick. Oxford: Blackwell, 1999. From pages 342–50.

Origins and Underlying Ideologies 1700–1776

As a result of the USA's status as a British colony, American business ethics in its earliest stage reflected English law and business practices. An example was accepting monopolization of certain products, such as tobacco and textiles. During most of the 1700s, businessmen were primarily brokers and wholesalers since industrial production did not develop until after the Revolution. It was not until 1840 that the factory replaced the home as producer of goods. When machinery replaced handicraft production, businessmen became producers as well as wholesalers and suppliers.

During this period, the religious underpinnings of business were very important. Two basic ideologies developed. The first viewed wealth as a divine favor. Cotton Mather and Benjamin Franklin subscribed to this idea. The second viewpoint was expressed by John Woolman, a lawyer and a merchant, who incorporated William Penn's precept that merchants are stewards or trustees for the public good. During the eighteenth century and into the latter half of the nineteenth century, these two traditions created a tension that motivated businessmen toward good deeds. Gathering wealth and acting as stewards to the less fortunate became symbolic of the religious dimension of business, so much so that what has been called the "divine right of businessmen" appeared with the advent of the factory system. Businessmen perceived their role as business persons as directly related to God. However, in later years, a more restrictive view was that God gave control of property to Christian men who would protect the laborer. Still later, a more popular, broader perspective traced business stewardship indirectly to God, while subscribing to Social Darwinism and supporting the doctrines of Adam Smith and *laissez-faire* economists. Daniel Drew and John D. Rockefeller exemplified this latter view of the "Divine Right of Businessmen."

Underlying business ideologies evolved considerably over the forty years after the revolution. In his visit in 1831, Alexis de Tocqueville described in detail the American view of living, and especially of work. He perceived it as an "enlightened self-interest," a perspective that encourages daily self-denial for the sake of future prosperity. Furthermore, it is related to individualism. In his view, both tended to narrow a person's perspective. Another ideology that permeated business ethics, and is still felt today, is found in Adam Smith's *An Inquiry into the Wealth of Nations* (1776). Its overwhelming impact came with the development of the factory system and the advocates of big business and Social Darwinism – the idea that, in society, only the fittest should survive. Herbert Spencer, William Graham Sumner and other prophets of the new evolutionary social ideology, while concerned with the suffering of the poor, felt that progress could only come through long work, savings, and self-discipline. ...

Earlier American Business Ethics 1777–1890

Newer underlying ideologies of American business ethics can be found in the philosophical writings, especially in John Locke's position on private property and Jean Jacques Rousseau's proposals concerning the social contract. Practical applications of these views are exemplified in Andrew Carnegie's *Gospel of Wealth* and Henry Ford's *Gospel of Production*. John Locke, who made significant contributions in many areas of philosophy, had considerable influence first on the Founding Fathers and indirectly on the American constitution, and later on the development of the American business creed. He subscribed to the concept of natural human rights, and defended the right to private property. He argued that a person's right to self-preservation guarantees a right to those resources which are required to accomplish this goal, and that a person's labor is what contributes primarily to self-preservation. It is by "mixing" labor with land that a person acquires a right to land needed for sustaining himself and his family. For Locke, the primary function of society was to protect the natural rights of individuals, including the right to property. ...

In terms of business ethics, property and contract became important underlying philosophical ideologies. With reservations, Andrew Carnegie and Henry Ford applied Locke's and Rousseau's philosophical beliefs to the practical world of business. When the Industrial Revolution was in full swing, the belching of heavy smoke from the chimneys of factories was seen as a sign of successful manufacturing. Production – making things – was all important. Survival of the fittest became more important to business than the aforementioned stewardship tied to an earlier concept of business ethics. Carnegie believed that only the wealthy could endow society with what is necessary for cultural development. ... Carnegie indeed espoused survival of the fittest in a practical way that reflected the business ethic of the time. It is no wonder that workers began seriously to form power groups by supporting labor unions, which led to large-scale confrontations between management and labor. These clashes signaled the death knell of the stewardship ideal. The 1886 Haymarket riots in Chicago exemplify the conflict between employer and employees during this period of industrial growth. By this time, the extensive and the expansive power of the so-called Robber Barons was perceived by the public as divisive and devastating to society in general, and to the small business person and the working class in particular.

The Robber Barons of the late nineteenth century followed business ideologies that were very different from previous ones. Unlike earlier business persons, for them God was no longer in business in any real sense. Self-interest became self-aggrandizement. Stewardship gave way to gaining power for personal use. The certainty of social purpose was lost, and means and ends were confused. Not surprisingly, the Robber Barons, in addition to building up their own empires, also set the stage for public resentment that led to legislation (such as the Sherman Antitrust Act in 1890 and the establishment of the Interstate Commerce Commission in 1886), muckraking newspaper reports on different industries (such as meat-packing), and paved the road to the New Deal. It seemed that business ethics was all business and no ethics. Names such as Mellon, Drew, Vanderbilt, Gould and Astor are still well known, but not as exemplars of business ethics, either then or now.

Another name that is still well known is Ford. Henry Ford was the leading advocate of what might be called the Gospel of Production. In a sense, this approach to business was refreshing. His goal was to organize production to do as much good as possible for everybody. Ford's ideas about production applied to some degree the principles of "scientific management" devised by Frederick Taylor as a means to greater productivity. By favoring higher wages, shorter hours, and planned activities for workers on the job, Taylor's ideas undermined Spencer's "survival of the fittest," and led to a new phase in the history of American business ethics. Thus, in his own way, Henry Ford initiated a new era in American business ethics in addition to a new approach to production. ...

A Mature American Business Ethics 1891–1963

The failure of controls in the late nineteenth century were reflected in the economic collapse of 1929 and in the years leading up to the New Deal. It was said that in the early twentieth century there was "poverty in the midst of plenty." According to some historians, the ideology of the time incorporated the philosophy of pragmatism, the psychology of behaviorism and the economics of institutionalism. ...

One of the first comprehensive business ethics books – actually a textbook for college students – appeared in 1957. The author, Herbert Johnston, covered topics on a chapter-by-chapter basis. He included brief cases to illustrate in a practical manner the issues of a business situation. Each chapter generally commenced with a brief philosophical presentation (generally, the Natural Law theory) followed by acceptable ethical principles derived from the philosophical presentation. Ordinarily, there was a conclusion describing the correct ethical approach. The author dealt extensively with employee rights and obligations, like the "living wage." ...

Between 1957 and 1963, the years in which the books mentioned above were published, three important changes took place in the world of business that influenced and concerned business persons about their legal and ethical environment. First, the government proved that an alleged price fixing conspiracy among members of the electrical industry was true and punished the offenders with jail sentences and fines. Second, contrary to business's claims that only the electrical industry behaved illegally and unethically, an empirical study showed that most businesses, if not all, had unethical practitioners. Third, the 1964 Civil Rights Act and subsequent social legislation shifted the emphasis of business ethics from the individual business executive and manager to corporate activity. ...

The Rise of Social Issues in Business Ethics 1962–1970

The third change in business ethics came rather quickly after the price-fixing trouble and seemed to follow a shift in society's values in the post-Kennedy era. Beginning with the Supreme Court's *Brown vs the School Board of Topeka, Kansas* decision, the attitude towards racial discrimination began to change. The power of the federal government was felt in states where segregation was practiced in schools (including law and business schools), employment, police and fire departments, and even churches. ... The *Brown* case, which was written by Chief Justice Earl Warren, stated that it was "unconscionable" for there to be this separation in education. From then on, the shift to genuine equality began its slow, painful course. States were forced by federal law to integrate their schools and the spirit of equality among races began to spread to other institutions, including business. A notable aid in achieving this goal was the historic 1964 Civil Rights Act, which Congress passed during the Johnson administration. President Lyndon Johnson then added Executive Order 11246 whereby any corporate entity (including businesses, schools, health care facilities, and so forth) which wanted a government contract had to engage in affirmative actions to accelerate the movement of minorities, including women, into the workforce. ...

After the 1964 Civil Rights Act and Executive Order 11246, discrimination in the work place was illegal. Eventually, it was perceived as unethical. Some classes of employees were "protected" against discrimination by law, and the 1964 Civil Rights Act (as amended) prohibited discrimination against all employees in hiring, promotion, termination, pay, fringe benefits and other aspects of employment on the basis of race, color, religion, sex, or national origin. Although much, but not all, discrimination in business had been directed against African Americans and women, other laws, such as the *Americans with Disabilities Act of 1990*, were passed to protect groups that were not covered in the original legislation. ...

However, problems concerning discrimination were not the only focus of business ethics. Leading the world (and needing its cooperation) in assessing the needs of the environment, Americans were faced with the pollution of land, air and water. As the government passed legislation to limit the amount of pollution, businesses had to rethink their role in society. Up to this time, business did not fret about sending toxic materials into the ground, the air or the water. It was believed, if it was considered at all, that nature would eventually recover. As the Earth became more populous, the disposal of waste became first a concern, then a problem, and finally a critical strategy for preserving the needs of society in the present and the future. The general approach was for government to set the standards and business to comply, but this strategy met with considerable resistance. ...

The debate about environment problems took American business ethics to another turn in its history. This change in direction might be called "environmental business ethics." Ethicists began to see the environment as something more than land, air and water, and business ethicists began to see environmental protection as human protection. This new way of viewing the environment took an entirely different perspective on the relation between people and the environment, one that included more than could be physically measured in standard environmental impact statements. Environmental ethics thus attempted to shift the responsibility of business, its executives and its managers from simply controlling pollution, to issues of the overall quality of life. Consequently, in addition to fulfilling the mandates of civil rights legislation, business now had the responsibility to protect and, in some situations, to enhance the environment. This responsibility was given legal force in 1970, when the United States Environmental Act created the Environmental Protection Agency (EPA) as an independent agent to administer federal laws dealing with environmental issues. Businesses could no longer escape the consequences of environmental degradation they caused.

Social and ethical problems in discrimination, and health, safety, and the environment were only the beginning of what by now had become almost a revolution in the way business is practiced. Still other social and ethical issues, especially those with implications for trading with foreign countries, soon became a part of the everyday concerns of business executives and managers. ... Business also became concerned about political and social structures that permitted persons to be treated in an inhumane manner. These included apartheid, child labor, land division in less developed countries, and repressive political regimes.

Chapter Four

The Story of Christian Ethics

This chapter seeks to synthesize the previous three chapters. Chapter One explored what it means to regard the Bible as integral to Christian ethics. Chapter Two affirmed that ethics is not fundamentally about authors and arguments and decisions, but is rooted in the contexts and customs and common life of Christian communities over time. Chapter Three surveyed those themes that, while not generally regarded as part of the story of the church, are nonetheless significant for understanding ethics. This combination of scripture, history, and philosophy provides the essential grounding for understanding what has in recent times become the discipline of Christian ethics.

While the understanding of this book as a whole is that ethics is really about the practices of Christian communities, for newcomers to locate themselves in the field of Christian ethics it is necessary to offer an account of the way Christian ethics emerges as a distinct discipline in the most recent two centuries of the church. In the modern period the metaphysical and historical presuppositions of premodern Christianity were called into question (for example, by the development of Newtonian science and critical historical scholarship). Those who still wanted to give a rationale for Christian practice and truth-claims did so by trying to find a generally acceptable basis for them that could be shared by Christians and non-Christians alike: their aims were to secure relevance and consensus.

Thus "Christian ethics" emerged as a special discipline, commending itself in the marketplace of ideas, and scarcely rooted in ecclesial life and activity. It became commonplace, normal, and even required

that principles, judgments, and values be separated from prayer, sacrament, and works of mercy. This detachment from the soil that gave it life has in turn meant that the discipline of "Christian ethics" has played into the widespread view of its surrounding environment that "ethics" is about universal laws and rights on the one hand, and individual decision-making on the other, rather than being about the formation of character through a rhythm of corporate practice. This is why the move from the premodern era to the modern period is a move from a story whose chief characters have their center of gravity in the church to a story whose chief characters have their center of gravity in the academy – working in a field that can be distinguished if not isolated from the liturgical life, daily habits, and elementary practices of the church.

To read back into earlier centuries a discipline called Christian ethics is therefore in some ways an anachronism, and in other ways the only way to preserve the discipline from being hijacked by contemporary secular concerns. Either way, certain key figures stand out as significant voices in an emerging tradition, setting standards against which all subsequent work must be judged. This chapter offers readings from a number of these key figures.

Foundations

The great figures who shaped what we would now call Christian ethics prior to Augustine included Justin

Martyr, Tertullian, Basil of Caesarea, Gregory of Nyssa, and Ambrose of Milan. For such people, discipleship in the church was a whole context of worshipful practice. That it generated and informed particular forms of behavior did not mean that this needed analysis in a special field of its own, distinguished from the study of liturgy or doctrine. To get a flavor of some of the writing from the period prior to Augustine, the readings in Chapter Two may be helpful. However, the two figures that stand out in the pre-Reformation period are Augustine of Hippo and Thomas Aquinas. Extracts from their key works are offered below.

Augustine, *The City of God*

Augustine of Hippo (354–430) is a highly significant figure in Western Christianity. Prior to his conversion he pursued a Manichean philosophy that held to the eternal balance of good and evil. At 30 he was a professor of rhetoric in Milan, perhaps the most prestigious academic post in the Latin world. After his conversion to Christianity in 386 he gave away his possessions and became a monk. He returned to Africa in 391 and became Bishop of Hippo in 396. Many of his writings emerged out of the controversies of his time, for example his understandings of original sin and the validity of the sacraments (regardless of the failings of the priest) in response to the heresies of Pelagius and the Donatist sect, respectively.

The City of God (426) locates Christianity in relation to contemporary philosophies and religions. Its overarching theme is the coexistence of two cities, the earthly city and the heavenly city. The earthly city is flawed: "though it be mistress of nations, it itself is ruled by its lust of rule." The city of God, by contrast, is "surpassingly glorious, whether we view it as it still lives by faith in this fleeting course of time, as sojourns a stranger in the midst of the ungodly, or as it shall dwell in the fixed stability of its eternal seat."

The excerpt below has been very influential in contemporary theology. Augustine points out that there has never been a truly just government: not even the ideal picture drawn by Cicero of the commonwealth meets the essential requirements. Earlier (in Book 2) Augustine has argued that a people is not "every assemblage or mob, but an assemblage associated by a common acknowledgment of law and by a community of interests." According to this definition, there was never a people in Rome, and thus Rome was never a state or commonwealth, since it never had true justice. However, he notes that "true justice has no existence save in that republic whose founder and ruler is Christ."

Here in Book 19 he reasserts that there is no republic without true justice. He maintains there can be no true justice without true worship. Augustine assumes that those who don't serve God serve demons, and the serving of demons is the practice of injustice. Only a community where people serve and love God can exhibit justice, because only in such a commonwealth does each truly give to each their due.

St. Augustine. *The City of God*. Trans. Henry Bettenson. New York: Penguin Books, 1972, 1984. Book XIX, pages 879–83, 890–1. Available online in the Christian Classics Ethereal Library at www.ccel.org/ccel/schaff/npnf102.toc.html.

19. The dress and behaviour of the Christian people

... As for the three kinds of life, the life of leisure, the life of action, and the combination of the two, anyone, to be sure, might spend his life in any of these ways without detriment to his faith, and might thus attain to the everlasting rewards. What does matter is the answers to those questions: What does a man possess as a result of his love of truth? And what does he pay out in response to the obligations of Christian love? For no one ought to be so leisured as to take no thought in that leisure for the interest of his neighbour, nor so active as to feel no need for the contemplation of God. The attraction of a life of leisure ought not to be the prospect of lazy inactivity, but the chance for the investigation and discovery of truth, on the understanding that each person makes some progress in this, and does not grudgingly withhold his discoveries from another.

In the life of action, on the other hand, what is to be treasured is not a place of honour or power in this life, since "everything under the sun is vanity" but the task itself that is achieved by means of that place of honour and that power – if that achievement is right and helpful, that is, if it serves to promote the well-being of the common people, for, as we have already argued, this well-being is according to God's intention. …

20. The fellow-citizens of the saints are in this life made happy by hope

We see, then, that the Supreme Good of the City of God is everlasting and perfect peace, which is not the peace through which men pass in their mortality, in their journey from birth to death, but that peace in which they remain in their immortal state, experiencing no adversity at all. In view of this, can anyone deny that this is the supremely blessed life, or that the present life on earth, however full it may be of the greatest possible blessings of soul and body and of external circumstances, is, in comparison, most miserable? For all that, if anyone accepts the present life in such a spirit that he uses it with the end in view of that other life on which he has set his heart with all his ardour and for which he hopes with all his confidence, such a man may without absurdity be called happy even now, though rather by future hope than in present reality. Present reality without that hope is, to be sure, a false happiness, in fact, an utter misery. For the present does not bring into play the true goods of the mind; since no wisdom is true wisdom if it does not direct its attention, in all its prudent decisions, its resolute actions, its self-control and its just dealings with others, towards that ultimate state in which God will be all in all, in the assurance of eternity and the perfection of peace.

21. Scipio's definition of a commonwealth. Was it ever a reality at Rome?

This brings me to the place where I must fulfil, as briefly and clearly as I may, the promise I gave in the second book [Book II, Chapter 21]. I there promised that I would show that there never was a Roman commonwealth answering to the definitions advanced by Scipio in Cicero's On the Republic. For Scipio gives a brief definition of the state, or commonwealth, as the "weal of the people." Now if this is a true definition there never was a Roman commonwealth, because the Roman state was never the "weal of the people," according to Scipio's definition. For he defined a "people" as a multitude "united in association by a common sense of right and a community of interest." He explains in the discussion what he means by "a common sense of right," showing that a state cannot be maintained without justice, and where there is no true justice there can be no right. For any action according to right is inevitably a just action, while no unjust action can possibly be according to right. For unjust human institutions are not to be called or supposed to be institutions of right, since even they themselves say that right is what has flowed from the fount of justice; as for the notion of justice commonly put forward by some misguided thinkers, that it is "the interest of the strongest," they hold this to be a false conception.

Therefore, where there is no true justice there can be no "association of men united by a common sense of right," and therefore no people answering to the definition of Scipio, or Cicero. And if there is no people then there is no "weal of the people," but some kind of a mob, not deserving the name of a people. If, therefore, a commonwealth is the "weal of the people," and if a people does not exist where there is no "association by a common sense of right," and there is no right where there is no justice, the irresistible conclusion is that where there is no justice there is no commonwealth. Moreover, justice is that virtue which assigns to everyone his due. Then what kind of justice is it that takes a man away from the true God and subjects him to unclean demons? Is this to assign to every man his due? Or are we to say that a man is unjust when he takes an estate from a man who has bought it and hands it over to someone who has no right to it, while we give the name of just to a man who takes himself away from the Lord God who made him, and becomes the servant of malignant spirits? …

Now in serving God the soul rightly commands the body, and in the soul itself the reason which is subject to its Lord God rightly commands the lusts and the other perverted elements. That being so, when a man does not serve God, what amount of justice are we to suppose to exist in his being? For if a soul does not serve God it cannot with any kind of justice command the body, nor can a man's reason control the vicious elements in the soul. And if there is no justice in such a man, there can be no sort of doubt that there is no justice in a gathering which consists of such men. Here, then, there is not that "consent to the law" which makes a mob into a people, and it is "the weal of the people" that is said to make a "commonwealth." As for the "community of interest" in virtue of which, according to our definition, a gathering of men is called a "people," is there any need for me to talk about this? Although, to be sure, if you give the matter careful thought, there are no advantages for men who live ungodly lives, the lives of all those who do not serve God, but serve demons – demons all the more blasphemous in that they desire that sacrifice be offered to them as to gods, though in fact they are most unclean spirits. However, I consider that what I have said about "a common sense of right" is enough to make it apparent that by this definition people amongst whom there is no justice can never be said to have a commonwealth. …

24. An alternative definition of "people" and "commonwealth"

If, on the other hand, another definition than this is found for a "people," for example, if one should say, "A people is the association of a multitude of rational beings united by a common agreement on the objects of their love," then it follows that to observe the character of a particular people we must examine the objects of its love. And yet, whatever those objects, if it is the association of a multitude not of animals but of rational beings, and is united by a common agreement about the objects of its love, then there is no absurdity in applying to it the title of a "people." And, obviously, the better the objects of this agreement, the better the people; the worse the objects of this love, the worse the people. By this definition of ours, the Roman people is a people and its estate is indubitably a commonwealth. But as for the objects of that people's love – both in the earliest times and in subsequent periods – and the morality of that people as it proceeded to bloody strife of parties and then to the social and civil wars, and corrupted and disrupted that very unity which is, as it were, the health of a people – for all this we have the witness of history;

and I have had a great deal to say about it in my preceding books. And yet I shall not make that a reason for asserting that a people is not really a people or that a state is not a commonwealth, so long as there remains an association of some kind or other between a multitude of rational beings united by a common agreement on the objects of its love. However, what I have said about the Roman people and the Roman commonwealth I must be understood to have said and felt about those of the Athenians and of any other Greeks, or of that former Babylon of the Assyrians, when they exercised imperial rule, whether on a small or a large scale, in their commonwealths – and indeed about any other nation whatsoever. For God is not the ruler of the city of the impious, because it disobeys his commandment that sacrifice should be offered to himself alone. The purpose of this law was that in that city the soul should rule over the body and reason over the vicious elements, in righteousness and faith. And because God does not rule there the general characteristic of that city is that it is devoid of true justice.

25. True virtues impossible without true religion

The fact is that the soul may appear to rule the body and the reason to govern the vicious elements in the most praiseworthy fashion; and yet if the soul and reason do not serve God as God himself has commanded that he should be served, then they do not in any way exercise the right kind of rule over the body and the vicious propensities. For what kind of a mistress over the body and the vices can a mind be that is ignorant of the true God and is not subjected to his rule, but instead is prostituted to the corrupting influence of vicious demons? Thus the virtues which the mind imagines it possesses, by means of which it rules the body and the vicious elements, are themselves vices rather than virtues, if the mind does not bring them into relation with God in order to achieve anything whatsoever and to maintain that achievement. For although the virtues are reckoned by some people to be genuine and honourable when they are related only to themselves and are sought for no other end, even then they are puffed up and proud, and so are to be accounted vices rather than virtues. For just as it is not something derived from the physical body itself that gives life to that body, but something above it, so it is not something that comes from man, but something above man, that makes his life blessed; and this is true not only of man but of every heavenly dominion and power whatsoever.

Thomas Aquinas, *Of War*

Thomas Aquinas (1225–1274) was an Italian Dominican friar whose summaries and organization of medieval theology form the bedrock of Roman Catholic moral theology to the present day. He divides his great work, the *Summa Theologica*, into an elaborate series of questions. Each one follows a method of thesis and antithesis. First Aquinas asks the question; then he states the antithesis, listing significant objections; then he gives the thesis and good arguments for it; finally he refutes each of the objections with careful replies.

Aquinas stresses the difference between the use of force by a public authority for public benefit (*bellum* – war) and the use of force on private authority (*duellum* – literally, a duel). He has no time for the latter. Contemporary concern about just war has tended to prioritize the just cause, but Aquinas' emphasis is on legitimate authority. The three requirements for Aquinas are sovereign authority, just cause, and right intention (which positively aims for peace, punishes evildoers and uplifts the good, and negatively disdains aggrandizement or cruelty).

In addition to his concentration on legitimate authority, Aquinas sees war as an aspect of the sovereign's duty to ensure the common good. Responsibility for the common good follows from the possession of sovereign authority. Thus war is defended as an aspect of pursuing the common good, rather than fundamentally a matter of self-defense.

Thomas Aquinas. *Summa Theologica*. 5 vols. Notre Dame: Christian Classics, 1948. Also available online at www.ccel.org/ccel/aquinas/summa.html. From Secunda Secundae [The Second Part of the Second Part], Question 40, pages 1353–7.

We must now consider war, under which head there are four points of inquiry:

1 Whether some kind of war is lawful?
2 Whether it is lawful for clerics to fight?
3 Whether it is lawful for belligerents to lay ambushes?
4 Whether it is lawful to fight on holy days?
5 Whether it is always sinful to wage war?

Article 1. Whether it is always sinful to wage war?

Objection 1: It would seem that it is always sinful to wage war. Because punishment is not inflicted except for sin. Now those who wage war are threatened by Our Lord with punishment, according to Matt. 26:52: "All that take the sword shall perish with the sword." Therefore all wars are unlawful.

Objection 2: Further, whatever is contrary to a Divine precept is a sin. But war is contrary to a Divine precept, for it is written (Matt. 5:39): "But I say to you

not to resist evil"; and (Rom. 12:19): "Not revenging yourselves, my dearly beloved, but give place unto wrath." Therefore war is always sinful.

Objection 3: Further, nothing, except sin, is contrary to an act of virtue. But war is contrary to peace. Therefore war is always a sin.

Objection 4: Further, the exercise of a lawful thing is itself lawful, as is evident in scientific exercises. But warlike exercises which take place in tournaments are forbidden by the Church, since those who are slain in these trials are deprived of ecclesiastical burial. Therefore it seems that war is a sin in itself.

On the contrary, Augustine says in a sermon on the son of the centurion: "If the Christian Religion forbade war altogether, those who sought salutary advice in the Gospel would rather have been counselled to cast aside their arms, and to give up soldiering altogether. On the contrary, they were told: 'Do violence to no man ... and be content with your pay' [Lk. 3:14]. If he commanded them to be content with their pay, he did not forbid soldiering."

I answer that, In order for a war to be just, three things are necessary. First, the authority of the sovereign by whose command the war is to be waged. For it is not the business of a private individual to declare war, because he can seek for redress of his rights from the tribunal of his superior. Moreover it is not the business of a private individual to summon together the people, which has to be done in wartime. And as the care of the common weal is committed to those who are in authority, it is their business to watch over the common weal of the city, kingdom or province subject to them. And just as it is lawful for them to have recourse to the sword in defending that common weal against internal disturbances, when they punish evil-doers, according to the words of the Apostle (Rom. 13:4): "He beareth not the sword in vain: for he is God's minister, an avenger to execute wrath upon him that doth evil"; so too, it is their business to have recourse to the sword of war in defending the common weal against external enemies. Hence it is said to those who are in authority (Ps. 81:4): "Rescue the poor: and deliver the needy out of the hand of the sinner"; and for this reason Augustine says (Contra Faust. xxii, 75): "The natural order conducive to peace among mortals demands that the power to declare and counsel war should be in the hands of those who hold the supreme authority."

Secondly, a just cause is required, namely that those who are attacked, should be attacked because they deserve it on account of some fault. Wherefore Augustine says (QQ. in Hept., qu. x, super Jos.): "A just war is wont to be described as one that avenges wrongs, when a nation or state has to be punished, for refusing to make amends for the wrongs inflicted by its subjects, or to restore what it has seized unjustly."

Thirdly, it is necessary that the belligerents should have a rightful intention, so that they intend the advancement of good, or the avoidance of evil. Hence Augustine says (De. Verb. Dom.): "True religion looks upon as peaceful those wars that are waged not for motives of aggrandizement, or cruelty, but with the object of securing peace, of punishing evil-doers, and of uplifting the good." For it may happen that the war is declared by the legitimate authority, and for a just cause, and yet be rendered unlawful through a wicked intention. Hence Augustine says (Contra Faust. xxii, 74): "The passion for inflicting harm, the cruel thirst for vengeance, an unpacific and relentless spirit, the fever of revolt, the lust of power, and such like things, all these are rightly condemned in war."

Reply to Objection 1: As Augustine says (Contra Faust. xxii, 70): "To take the sword is to arm oneself in order to take the life of anyone, without the command or permission of superior or lawful authority." On the other hand, to have recourse to the sword (as a private person) by the authority of the sovereign or judge, or (as a public person) through zeal for justice, and by the authority, so to speak, of God, is not to "take the sword," but to use it as commissioned by another, wherefore it does not deserve punishment. And yet even those who make sinful use of the sword are not always slain with the sword, yet they always perish with their own sword, because, unless they repent, they are punished eternally for their sinful use of the sword.

Reply to Objection 2: Such like precepts, as Augustine observes (De Serm. Dom. in Monte i.19), should always be borne in readiness of mind, so that we be ready to obey them, and, if necessary, to refrain from resistance or self-defense. Nevertheless it is necessary sometimes for a man to act otherwise for the common good, or for the good of those with whom he is fighting. Hence Augustine says (Ep. ad Marcellin. cxxxviii): "Those whom we have to punish with a kindly severity, it is necessary to handle in many ways against their will. For when we are stripping a man of the lawlessness of sin, it is good for him to be vanquished, since nothing is more hopeless than the happiness of sinners, whence arises a guilty impunity, and an evil will, like an internal enemy."

Reply to Objection 3: Those who wage war justly aim at peace, and so they are not opposed to peace, except to the evil peace, which Our Lord "came not to send upon earth" (Matt. 10:34). Hence Augustine says (Ep. ad Bonif. clxxxix): "We do not seek peace in order to be at war, but we go to war that we may have peace. Be peaceful, therefore, in warring, so that you may vanquish those whom you war against, and bring them to the prosperity of peace."

Reply to Objection 4: Manly exercises in warlike feats of arms are not all forbidden, but those which are inordinate and perilous, and end in slaying or plundering. In olden times warlike exercises presented no such danger, and hence they were called "exercises of arms" or "bloodless wars," as Jerome states in an epistle.

Article 2. Whether it is lawful for clerics and bishops to fight?

… It was said to Peter as representing bishops and clerics (Matt. 16:52): "Put up again thy sword into the scabbard [Vulg.: 'its place'] ['Scabbard' is the reading in Jn. 18:11]." Therefore it is not lawful for them to fight.

Several things are requisite for the good of a human society: and a number of things are done better and quicker by a number of persons than by one, as the Philosopher [Aristotle] observes (*Polit.* i.1), while certain occupations are so inconsistent with one another, that they cannot be fittingly exercised at the same time; wherefore those who are deputed to important duties are forbidden to occupy themselves with things of small importance. Thus according to human laws, soldiers who are deputed to warlike pursuits are forbidden to engage in commerce.

Now warlike pursuits are altogether incompatible with the duties of a bishop and a cleric, for two reasons. The first reason is a general one, because, to wit, warlike pursuits are full of unrest, so that they hinder the mind very much from the contemplation of Divine things, the praise of God, and prayers for the people, which belong to the duties of a cleric. Wherefore just as commercial enterprises are forbidden to clerics, because they unsettle the mind too much, so too are warlike pursuits, according to 2 Tim. 2:4: "No man being a soldier to God, entangleth himself with secular business." The second reason is a special one, because, to wit, all the clerical Orders are directed to the ministry of the altar, on which the Passion of Christ is represented sacramentally, according to 1 Cor. 11:26: "As often as you shall eat this bread, and drink the chalice, you shall show the death of the Lord, until He come." Wherefore it is unbecoming for them to slay or shed blood, and it is more fitting that they should be ready to shed their own blood for Christ, so as to imitate in deed what they portray in their ministry. For this reason it has been decreed that those who shed blood, even without sin, become irregular. Now no man who has a certain duty to perform, can lawfully do that which renders him unfit for that duty. Wherefore it is altogether unlawful for clerics to fight, because war is directed to the shedding of blood. ...

Article 3. Whether it is lawful to lay ambushes in war?

... Augustine says (*QQ. in Heptateuch.*, qu. x, *Super Jos.*): "Provided the war be just, it is no concern of justice whether it be carried on openly or by ambushes": and he proves this by the authority of the Lord, Who commanded Joshua to lay ambushes for the city of Hai (Joshua 8:2).

The object of laying ambushes is in order to deceive the enemy. Now a man may be deceived by another's word or deed in two ways. First, through being told something false, or through the breaking of a promise, and this is always unlawful. No one ought to deceive the enemy in this way, for there are certain "rights of war and covenants, which ought to be observed even among enemies," as Ambrose states (*De Offic.* i).

Secondly, a man may be deceived by what we say or do, because we do not declare our purpose or meaning to him. Now we are not always bound to do this, since even in the Sacred Doctrine many things have to be concealed, especially from unbelievers, lest they deride it, according to Matt. 7:6: "Give not that which is holy, to dogs." Wherefore much more ought the plan of campaign to be hidden from the enemy. For this reason among other things that a soldier has to learn is the art of concealing his purpose lest it come to the enemy's knowledge, as stated in the Book on Strategy by Frontinus. Such like concealment is what is meant by an ambush which may be lawfully employed in a just war. Nor can these ambushes be properly called deceptions, nor are they contrary to justice or to a well-ordered will. For a man would have an inordinate will if he were unwilling that others should hide anything from him.

Article 4. Whether it is lawful to fight on holy days?

... It is written (1 Mac. 2:41): The Jews rightly determined ... saying: "Whosoever shall come up against us to fight on the Sabbath-day, we will fight against him."

The observance of holy days is no hindrance to those things which are ordained to man's safety, even that of his body. Hence Our Lord argued with the Jews, saying (Jn. 7:23): "Are you angry at Me because I have healed the whole man on the Sabbath-day?" Hence physicians may lawfully attend to their patients on holy days. Now there is much more reason for safeguarding the common weal (whereby many are saved from being slain, and innumerable evils both temporal and spiritual prevented), than the bodily safety of an individual. Therefore, for the purpose of safeguarding the common weal of the faithful, it is lawful to carry on a war on holy days, provided there be need for doing so: because it would be to tempt God, if notwithstanding such a need, one were to choose to refrain from fighting. However, as soon as the need ceases, it is no longer lawful to fight on a holy day, for the reasons given.

Revisions

While the Catholic Reformation was significant in shaping dogmatic and moral theology to the present day, the Reformation's significance for Christian ethics lies chiefly in creating three (or more) rival strands in Protestant ethics – the Lutheran, Reformed, and radical traditions. (One may speak of Anglican ethics, but in the form it is known today, particularly in its social tradition, it dates largely from the nineteenth rather than the sixteenth century.) We have already seen something of Calvin's work; so here we look at Lutheran and radical traditions more closely.

Martin Luther, *Temporal Authority*

Martin Luther (1483–1546) believed salvation is the free, gracious gift of God, and could not be earned by merit or bought by works. This central conviction motivated his challenge to and departure from the Church of Rome and the beginning of the Magisterial Reformation.

His views on church and state are especially significant, given that the Lutheran Reformation depended so heavily on the support of rulers in central Europe for its survival and expansion. In this excerpt we see his very influential distinction between the kingdom of God and the kingdom of the world, sometimes referred to as God's right hand (grace) and left hand (law). Members of the former kingdom recognize Christ as king and "need no temporal law or sword." The latter is like the constraint of a savage beast; people cannot practice their wickedness with impunity.

Thus both governments are needed: "the one to produce righteousness, the other to bring about external peace and prevent evil deeds." Luther makes clear that "you are under obligation to serve and assist the sword by whatever means you can, with body, goods, honor, and soul. For it is something which you do not need, but which is very beneficial and essential for the whole world and for your neighbor." Thus, "you satisfy God's kingdom inwardly and the kingdom of the world outwardly."

Martin Luther. "Temporal Authority: To What Extent it Should Be Obeyed." *Martin Luther's Basic Theological Writings*. Ed. Timothy F. Lull. Minneapolis: Fortress Press, 1989. From pages 659–70. Available online at www.uoregon. edu/~sshoemak/323/texts/luther~1.htm or in pdf format at www.isn.ethz.ch/isn/Digital-Library/Primary-Resources/Detail/?ots591=69F57A17-24D2-527C-4F3B-B63B07201CA1&lng=en&ord520=grp2&id=27215. Copyright © 1989 Fortress Press. Used by permission of Augsburg Fortress.

First, we must provide a sound basis for the civil law and sword so no one will doubt that it is in the world by God's will and ordinance. The passages which do this are the following: Romans 13, "Let every soul [*seele*] be subject to the governing authority, for therein no authority except from God; the authority which everywhere [*allenthalben*] exists has been ordained by God. He then who resists the governing authority resists the ordinance of God, and he who resists God's ordinance will incur judgment." Again, in I Peter 2 [:13–14], "Be subject to every kind of human ordinance, whether it be to the king as supreme, or to governors, as those who have been sent by him to punish the wicked and to praise the righteous."

The law of this temporal sword has existed from the beginning of the world. For when Cain slew his brother Abel, he was in such great terror of being killed in turn that God even placed a special prohibition on it and suspended the sword for his sake, so that no one was to slay him [Gen. 4:14–15]. He would not have had this fear if he had not seen and heard from Adam that murderers are to be slain. Moreover, after the Flood, God re-established and confirmed this in unmistakable terms when he said in Genesis 9 [:6], "Whoever sheds the blood of man, by man shall his blood be shed." This cannot be understood as a plague or punishment of God upon murderers, for many murderers who are punished in other ways or pardoned altogether continue to live, and eventually die by means other than the sword. Rather, it is said of the law of the sword, that a murderer is guilty of death and in justice is to be slain by the sword. …

In addition, Christ also confirms it when he says to Peter in the garden, "He that takes the sword will perish by the sword" [Matt. 26:52], which is to be interpreted exactly like the Genesis 9 [:6] passage, "Whoever sheds the blood of man," etc. Christ is undoubtedly referring in these words to that very passage which he thereby wishes to cite and confirm. John the Baptist also teaches the same thing. When the soldiers asked him what they should do, he answered, "Do neither violence nor injustice to any one, and be content with your wages" [Luke 3:14]. If the sword were not a godly estate, he should have directed them to get out of it, since he was supposed to make the people perfect and instruct them in a proper Christian way. Hence, it is certain and clear enough that it is God's will that the temporal sword and law be used for the punishment of the wicked and the protection of the upright. …

Third. Here we must divide the children of Adam and all mankind into two classes, the first belonging to the kingdom of God, the second to the kingdom of the world. Those who belong to the kingdom of God are all true believers who are in Christ and under Christ, for Christ is King and Lord in the kingdom of God, as Psalm 2 [:6] and all of Scripture says. For this reason he came into the world, that he might begin God's kingdom and establish it in the world. Therefore, he says before Pilate, "My kingdom is not of the world, but every one who is of the truth hears my voice" [John 18:36–37]. In the gospel he continually refers to the kingdom of God, and says, "Amend your ways, the kingdom of God and his righteousness" [Matt. 6:33]. He also calls the gospel a gospel of the kingdom of God; because it teaches, governs, and upholds God's kingdom.

Now observe, these people need no temporal law or sword. If all the world were composed of real Christians, that is, true believers, there would be no need for benefits from prince, king, lord, sword, or law. They would serve no purpose, since Christians have in their heart the Holy Spirit, who both teaches and makes them to do injustice to no one, to love everyone, and to suffer injustice and even death willingly and cheerfully at the hands of anyone. Where there is nothing but the unadulterated doing of right and bearing of wrong, there is no need for any suit, litigation, court, judge, penalty, law, or sword. …

Fourth. All who are not Christians belong to the kingdom of the world and are under the law. There are few true believers, and still fewer who live a Christian life, who do not resist evil and indeed themselves do no evil. For this reason God has provided for them a different government beyond the Christian estate and kingdom of God. He has subjected them to the sword so that, even though they would like to, they are unable to practice their wickedness, and if they do practice it they cannot do so without their wickedness, and if they do practice it they cannot do so without fear or with success and impunity. In the same way a savage wild beast is bound with chains and ropes so that it cannot bite and tear as it would normally do, even though it would like to; whereas a tame and gentle animal needs no restraint, but is harmless despite the lack of chains and ropes.

If this were not so, men would devour one another, seeing that the whole world is evil and that among thousands there is scarcely a single true Christian. No one could support wife and child, feed himself, and serve God. The world would be reduced to chaos. For this reason God has ordained two governments: the spiritual, by which the Holy Spirit produces Christians and righteous people under Christ; and the temporal, which restrains the un-Christian and wicked so that – no thanks to them – they are obliged to keep still and to maintain an outward peace. Thus does St. Paul interpret the temporal sword in Romans 13 [:3], when he says it is not a terror to good conduct but to bad. And Peter says it is for the punishment of the wicked [I Peter 2:14]. …

For this reason one must carefully distinguish between these two governments. Both must be permitted to remain; the one to produce righteousness, the other to bring about external peace and prevent evil deeds. Neither one is sufficient in the world without the other. No one can become righteous in the sight of God by means of the temporal government, without Christ's spiritual government. Christ's government does not extend over all men; rather, Christians are always a minority in the midst of non-Christians. Now where temporal government or law alone prevails, there sheer hypocrisy is inevitable, even though the commandments be God's very own. For without the Holy Spirit in the heart no one becomes truly righteous, no matter how fine the works he does. On the other hand, where the spiritual government alone prevails over land and people, there wickedness is given free rein and the door is open for all manner of rascality, for the world as a whole cannot receive or comprehend it.

Now you see the intent of Christ's words ... from Matthew 5 [Matt 5:38–41], that Christians should not go to law or use the temporal sword among themselves. Actually, he says this only to his beloved Christians, those who alone accept it and act accordingly, who do not make "counsels" out of it as the sophists do, but in their heart are so disposed and conditioned [genaturt] by the Spirit that they do evil to no one and willingly endure evil at the hands of others. If now the whole world were Christian in this sense, then these words would apply to all, and all would act accordingly. Since the world is un-Christian, however, these words do not apply to all; and all do not act accordingly, but are under another government in which those who are not Christian are kept under external constraint and compelled to keep the peace and do what is good. ...

Fifth. But you say: if Christians then do not need the temporal sword or law, why does Paul say to all Christians in Romans 13 [:1], "Let all souls be subject to the governing authority," and St. Peter, "Be subject to every human ordinance" [I Pet. 2:13], etc., as quoted? Answer: I have just said that Christians, among themselves, need no law or sword, since it is neither necessary nor useful for them. Since a true Christian lives and labors on earth not for himself alone but for his neighbor, he does by the very nature of his spirit even what he himself has no need of, but it is needful and useful to his neighbor. Because the sword is most beneficial and necessary for the whole world in order to preserve peace, punish sin, and restrain the wicked, the Christian submits most willingly to the rule of the sword, pays his taxes, honors those in authority, serves, helps, and does all he can to assist the governing authority, that it may continue to function and be held in honor and fear. Although he has no need of these things for himself – to him they are not essential – nevertheless, he concerns himself about what is serviceable and of benefit to others, as Paul teaches in Ephesians 5 [:21–6:9].

Just as he performs all other works of love which he himself does not need – he does not visit the sick in order that he himself might be made well, or feed others because he himself needs food – so he serves the govern-

ing authority not because he needs it but for the sake of others, that they may be protected and that the wicked may not become worse. He loses nothing by this; such service in no way harms him, yet it is of great benefit to the world. If he did not serve he would be acting not as a Christian but even contrary to love; he would also be setting a bad example to others who in like manner would not submit to authority, even though they were not Christians. In this way the gospel would be brought into disrepute, as though it taught insurrection and produced self-willed people unwilling to benefit or serve others, when in fact it makes a Christian the servant of all. ...

Sixth. You ask whether a Christian too may bear the temporal sword and punish the wicked, since Christ's words, "Do not resist evil," are so clear and definite that the sophists have had to make of them a "counsel." Answer: You have now heard two propositions. One is that the sword can have no place among Christians; therefore, you cannot bear it among Christians or hold it over them, for they do not need it. The question, therefore, must be referred to the other group, the non-Christians, whether you may bear it there in a Christian manner. Here the other proposition applies, that you are under obligation to serve and assist the sword by whatever means you can, with body, goods, honor, and soul. For it is something which you do not need, but which is very beneficial and essential for the whole world and for your neighbor. Therefore, if you see that there is a lack of hangmen, constables, judges, lords, or princes, and you find that you are qualified, you should offer your services and seek the position, that the essential government authority may not be despised and become enfeebled or perish. ...

In this way two propositions are brought into harmony with one another: at one and the same time you satisfy God's kingdom inwardly and the kingdom of the world outwardly. You suffer evil and injustice, and yet at the same time you punish evil and injustice; you do not resist evil, and yet at the same time, you do resist it. In the one case, you consider yourself and what is yours; in the other, you consider your neighbor and what is his. In what concerns you and yours, you govern yourself by the gospel and suffer injustice toward yourself as a true Christian; in what concerns the person or property of others, you govern yourself according to love and tolerate no injustice toward your neighbor.

Menno Simons, *A Kind Admonition on Church Discipline*

Menno Simons (1496–1561) was a priest from Witmarsum in the Netherlands whose doubts about transubstantiation and infant baptism led him to read the scriptures for himself. Influenced by Desiderius Erasmus, Luther, and Martin Bucer, he nonetheless remained within the Roman Church. A decisive event in the Radical Reformation was the New Jerusalem set up by Jan Matthijs at Münster in Germany in 1534, and its ruthless suppression the following year. Inspired by the Münsterites and by Simons, 300 people tried (in vain) to storm the Olde Klooster, a monastery in the Netherlands. At this point Simons believed he had to choose between the church and the scriptures, and was baptized by the leader of the non-resistant Anabaptists in the Netherlands. He quickly became the leader of the peaceful Anabaptists in the Netherlands and northwestern Germany. Despite being relentlessly pursued, he died a natural death in 1561 in Schleswig-Holstein (Germany), 25 years after his withdrawal from the Catholic Church.

A Kind Admonition on Church Discipline was written in 1541. Simons is constantly looking to win back the wayward soul: "we do not want to expel any, but rather to receive; not to amputate, but rather to heal; not to discard, but rather to win back; not to grieve, but rather to comfort; not to condemn, but rather to save." The perils of Simons' own biography demonstrate the adversarial circumstances in which these words were written, and the significance of their generosity.

Menno Simons. *A Kind Admonition on Church Discipline.* Pages 407–18 in *The Complete Writings of Menno Simons.* Trans. Leonard Verdiun. Ed. John Christian Wenger. Scottdale: Herald Press, 1956. Excerpt from pages 409–15. Copyright © 1956, 1984 by Herald Press, Scottdale, PA 15683. Used by permission.

I do not doubt, most beloved brethren, that you know very well (if you are born with Christ of God the Father of the heavenly seed of the divine Word) that you must be conformed unto Christ in mind, spirit, heart, and will, both in doctrine and life, as Christ Jesus is conformed unto the nature and image of His blessed heavenly Father to which He was begotten so that He did nothing but that which He saw the Father do; that He taught nothing but the word of His Father. In the same manner those who are begotten of the living, saving Word of our beloved Lord Jesus Christ are by virtue of their new birth so joined to Christ, are become so like unto Him, so really implanted into Him, so converted into His heavenly nature, that they do not teach nor believe any doctrine but that which agrees with the doctrine of Christ; they practice no ceremonies but Christ's ceremonies which He has taught and commanded in His holy Gospel. ...

Behold, brethren, such regenerate and godly-minded persons live unblamably, according to the measure of the holy Gospel of Jesus Christ and His apostles. Therefore He kisses them as His beloved chosen ones, with the mouth of His peace, and calls them His church, His bride, flesh of His flesh, and bone of His bone, of which He begets with inexpressible pleasure by His powerful seed, His holy Word, the children of God, the children of promise, the children of righteousness, the children of truth, and the children of life eternal. But never of the Babylonian, Sodomite, harloting, adulterous, idolatrous, bloody, unbelieving, blind, and unclean wench with which they have for centuries fornicated in wood, stone, gold, silver, bread, wine, false doctrine, and of the very vain, accursed works of their own hands, contrary to Jesus Christ and His holy Word. ...

O brethren, how far some of us, alas, are still distant from the evangelical life which is of God! Notwithstanding that they stay out of the churches and are outwardly baptized with water, yet they are earthly and carnally minded in all things, thinking perhaps that Christianity consists in external baptism and staying away from the churches. Oh, dear, No! I tell you as truly as the Lord lives, before God no outward baptism counts, nor staying away from the churches, nor Lord's Supper, nor persecution, if there is no obedience to the commandments of God, and no faith which manifests itself in love, and no new creature. ...

These regenerated ones shun all false doctrine, all idolatry, all improper use of the sacramental signs in the church or out of the church. They seek the true teachers who are unblamable both in doctrine and life; the true religion as taught and expressed in Christ's Word, namely, the dying unto the flesh (Rom. 12; Gal. 5); the service of the afflicted (Matt. 15); and the visiting of the widows and orphans, as James says. They seek to keep themselves unblemished and unspotted from the world. These regenerated ones bear the cross of Christ with gladness of heart, are so established in Christ Jesus that they cannot be separated from the eternal truth and love of God by false doctrine nor by horrible torments; ever remembering their Lord's Word: Whosoever therefore shall confess me before men, him will I confess also before my Father which is in heaven. ...

Therefore take heed. If you see your brother sin, then do not pass him by as one that does not value his soul; but if his fall be curable, from that moment endeavor to raise him up by gentle admonition and brotherly instruction, before you eat, drink, sleep, or do anything else, as one who ardently desires his salvation, lest your poor erring brother harden and be ruined in his fall, and perish in his sin.

Do not act so unfaithfully as you have hitherto acted, not making the transgressions of your dying brother or sister known to those within the church or without. Exhort him, rather, and seek by prayer, by words, and by deeds, to convert him from the error of his way, to save his soul, and to cover the multitude of his transgressions. Jas. 5. Take heed, brethren, take heed that you allow no defamer among you, as Moses taught. Lev. 19. A double, lying, deceiving and backbiting tongue do not allow at any time, lest you fall into the wrath of God. Let every one take heed how, where, when, and what he speaks, lest his tongue transgress against God and his neighbor. But always remember the words of Ecclesiasticus: Honor and shame is in talk, and the tongue of man is his fall.

But do not have anything to do, as the holy Paul has taught and commanded, and do not eat, with people who being of age and driven by the Spirit were baptized into the body of Jesus Christ with us, that is, the church, but afterwards, whether through false doctrine or a vain and carnal life, reject and separate themselves from the body and fellowship of Christ, no matter whether it be father or mother, sister or brother, man or wife, son or daughter, no matter who he be, for God's Word applies to all alike and there is no respect of persons with God.

We say, avoid him if he rejects the admonition of his brethren, done in sighing, tears, and a spirit of compassion and of great love, and if he nevertheless continues in his Jewish doctrine of sword, kingdom, polygamy, and similar deceptions; in the doctrine of shameless confession to each other, of no shame [for shameful acts], of nakedness; as well as a doctrine that contradicts the cross of Christ, as, for example, that impurity is pure to the pure – all fellowship with evil work such as attending the preaching of worldly preachers, infant baptism, worldly Lord's Supper, and similar abominations, as also drunkenness, avarice, fornication, adultery, unseemly conversation, etc.

But if he affectionately receives the admonition of his faithful brethren, confesses his fall, is truly sorry, promises to do better, and brings forth fruits worthy of repentance, then no matter how he has transgressed, receive him as a returning, beloved brother or sister. But let him beware lest he mock his God, for restoration with the brethren does not avail without restoration before God. Let him be sure that his heeding the admonition, his sorrow, his promise of reformation, and his penitence, are sincere before God who searches the hearts and reins and knows all inward thoughts of men. If his heeding the admonition, his sorrow, promise, and penitence, are not sincere and from his heart, but half-hearted, put on, mechanical, and of hypocritical exhibition, just because he does not want to be thrown out of the community of the brethren, he is still excommunicated by Christ, and is a hypocrite in the sight of God. Nor will he be rated or judged by God as anything else. For God the righteous Judge does not judge according to the outward appearance, but according to the inward intention of the heart.

Tell me, beloved, inasmuch as this is the case, what does it avail to go by the mere name of a Christian brother if we have not the inward, evangelical faith, love, and irreproachable life of the true brother of Jesus Christ?

Or what does it profit to eat of the Holy Supper of our Lord Jesus Christ with the brethren if we have not the true symbolized fruits of this Supper, namely, the death of Christ, the love of the brethren, and the peaceful unity of faith in Christ Jesus? Similarly it profits nothing to move about in the outward communion of the brethren if we are not inwardly in the communion of our beloved Lord Jesus Christ.

Wherefore, brethren, understand correctly, no one is excommunicated or expelled by us from the communion of the brethren but those who have already separated and expelled themselves from Christ's communion either by false doctrine or by improper conduct. For we do not want to expel any, but rather to receive; not to amputate, but rather to heal; not to discard, but rather to win back; not to grieve, but rather to comfort; not to condemn, but rather to save. For this is the true nature of a Christian brother. Whoever turns from evil, whether it be false doctrine or vain life, and conforms to the Gospel of Jesus Christ, unto which he was baptized, such a one shall not and may not be expelled or excommunicated by the brethren forever.

But those whom we cannot raise up and repentingly revive by admonition, fear, warning, rebuke, or by any other Christian services and godly means, these we should put forth from us, not without great sadness and anguish of soul, sincerely lamenting the fall and condemnation of such a straying brother; lest we also be deceived and led astray by such false doctrine which eats as does a cancer (II Tim. 2); and lest we corrupt our flesh which is inclined to evil by the contagion. Thus we must obey the Word of God which teaches and commands us so to do; and this in order that the excommunicated brother or sister whom we cannot convert by gentle services may by such means be shamed unto repentance and made to acknowledge to what he has come and from what he is fallen. In this way the ban is a great work of love, notwithstanding it is looked upon by the foolish as an act of hatred. ...

By their apostasy, rebellious and carnal hatred, they are deprived of grace and the knowledge of God, and become increasingly more wicked, so that they see death in eternal life, and darkness in the heavenly light of divine truth. Therefore we declare before God and His holy angels that we are clear of their damnable false doctrine, of their sins, obduracy, and eternal death if we have done in vain toward them that which the Lord's Word has commanded us in regard to this matter. We desire not to have communion with them, no lot nor part unto eternity, so long as they do not sincerely renounce their false doctrine and reform their miserable, condemnable, earthly, carnal, and devilish life to the praise of the Lord. But if such things are found in them, in good faith, as before God who sees all things, then we say, Welcome, beloved brethren! Welcome, beloved sisters! And we rejoice beyond measure at the sincere conversion of such brethren and sisters as one rejoices at the restoration of an only son who is healed of a critical and deadly disease, or a lost sheep or penny that is found again, or at the appearance of a son who was given up as lost.

You see, brethren, I will let every apostate brother determine why, wherefore, with what kind of spirit, and with what intention this excommunication or ban was so diligently practiced, first by Christ Jesus and His apostles, and afterward by us, who are intent upon recovering again Christian doctrine and practice as may be learned from the quoted Scriptures.

Very well, dear brethren in the Lord, you who are baptized by one Spirit into one body, and have voluntarily entered into the communion of Christ Jesus, and you also who are of a good will, inasmuch as you must shun the apostate in accordance with the Word of God, take heed that while you shun them as diseased, foul, and unprofitable members unfit for the body of Christ, you yourselves may be found to be sound, fit, and profitable members in Christ Jesus. When you shun them as children of darkness and of death, see to it that you yourselves may be children of the light and of eternal life, so that the righteous sentence of God may not reach unto you, lest you who shun others on account of their evil-doing secretly commit worse things in the sight of God. Take heed lest you judge others of what you yourselves are guilty. Behold, brethren, in this way the ban or excommunication should be practiced in the house of the Lord, that is, in God's church. Nor has it any other weapon unto all eternity.

Legacies of Division

The modern era has been marked both by the proliferation of denominations and by an ecumenical convergence marked by a number of major figures in the field. John Wesley had perhaps too much evangelical passion to sit easily within the listless Church of England of his day. While his ethical writings are not extensive, he is the key figure in the emergence of Methodism as eventually a new denomination, with its own ethical emphases. The other figures quoted here represent what might be called the high water mark of twentieth-century social ethics, in the mid-century when the churches still claimed a public voice as the voice for all people of good will. Reinhold Niebuhr and William Temple represent perhaps the most influential voices of the twentieth century in social ethics in the United States and Great Britain, respectively.

John Wesley, *The Use of Money*

John Wesley (1703–1791) was a lifelong Anglican, but the theological and organizational renewal he initiated became the source of a new denomination, Methodism. His notion of perfection, embracing holiness of heart and life, stimulated both personal renewal and social reform.

One place where Wesley's practical and spiritual emphases came together was in his highly influential treatment of money. More than anyone else, John Wesley is responsible for the prominence of the theme of stewardship in the language of contemporary theology and discipleship. Wesley describes money as "that precious talent that contains the rest." Wealth in itself is neither good nor bad: the wealthy person may make of it something good or evil.

Christians should consider themselves no more and no less than simply the first among the poor they must care for. Wealth only becomes a problem when one possesses more than is working for the furtherance of God's will. Hence his memorable conclusion, "Gain all you can, save all you can, give all you can."

John Wesley. "The Use of Money." *The Works of John Wesley*. Vol. 6. *Sermons on Several Occasions*. Grand Rapids: Zondervan, 1958. From pages 124–35. Available online at www.new.gbgm-umc.org/umhistory/wesley/sermons/50/.

"I say unto you, Make to yourselves friends of the mammon of unrighteousness; that, when ye fail, they may receive you into everlasting habitations." Luke xvi. 9. ...

2. An excellent branch of Christian wisdom is here inculcated by our Lord on all his followers, namely, the right use of money; – a subject largely spoken of, after their manner, by men of the world; but not sufficiently considered by those whom God hath chosen out of the world. These, generally, do not consider, as the importance of the subject requires, the use of this excellent talent. Neither do they understand how to employ it to the greatest advantage; the introduction of which into the world is one admirable instance of the wise and gracious providence of God. It has, indeed, been the manner of poets, orators, and philosophers, in almost all ages and nations, to rail at this, as the grand corrupter of the world, the bane of virtue, the pest of human society. ... "The love of money," we know, "is the root of all evil"; but not the thing itself. The fault does not lie in the money, but in them that use it. It may be used ill: And what may not? But it may likewise be used well: It is full as applicable to the best, as to the worst uses. It is of unspeakable service to all civilized nations, in all the common affairs of life: It is a most compendious instrument of transacting all manner of

business, and (if we use it according to Christian wisdom) of doing all manner of good. ... In the hands of [God's] children, it is food for the hungry, drink for the thirsty, raiment for the naked: It gives to the traveller and the stranger where to lay his head. By it we may supply the place of an husband to the widow, and of a father to the fatherless. We may be a defence for the oppressed, a means of health to the sick, of ease to them that are in pain; it may be as eyes to the blind, as feet to the lame; yea, a lifter up from the gates of death!

3. It is, therefore, of the highest concern, that all who fear God know how to employ this valuable talent; that they be instructed how it may answer these glorious ends, and in the highest degree. And, perhaps, all the instructions which are necessary for this may be reduced to three plain rules, by the exact observance whereof we may approve ourselves faithful stewards of "the mammon of unrighteousness."

I. 1. The First of these is, (he that heareth, let him understand!) "Gain all you can." Here we may speak like the children of the world: We meet them on their own ground. And it is our bounden duty to do this: We ought to gain all we can gain, without buying gold too dear, without paying more for it than it is worth. But this it is certain we ought not to do; we ought not to gain money at the expense of life, nor (which is in effect the same thing) at the expense of our health. Therefore, no gain whatsoever should induce us to enter into, or to continue in, any employ, which is of such a kind, or is attended with so hard or so long labour, as to impair our constitution. Neither should we begin or continue in any business which necessarily deprives us of proper seasons for food and sleep, in such a proportion as our nature requires. ...

2. We are, Secondly, to gain all we can without hurting our mind, any more than our body. For neither may we hurt this: We must preserve, at all events, the spirit of an healthful mind. Therefore, we may not engage or continue in any sinful trade; any that is contrary to the law of God, or of our country. Such are all that necessarily imply our robbing or defrauding the king of his lawful customs. For it is, at least, as sinful to defraud the king of his right, as to rob our fellow-subjects: And the king has full as much right to his customs as we have to our houses and apparel. Other businesses there are which, however innocent in themselves, cannot be followed with innocence now; at least, not in England; such, for instance, as will not afford a competent maintenance without cheating or lying, or conformity to some custom which is not consistent with a good conscience: These, likewise, are sacredly to be avoided, whatever gain they may be attended with, provided we follow the custom of the trade; for, to gain money, we must not lose our souls. ...

3. We are, Thirdly, to gain all we can, without hurting our neighbour. But this we may not, cannot do, if we love our neighbour as ourselves. We cannot, if we love every one as ourselves, hurt any one *in his substance*. We cannot devour the increase of his lands, and perhaps the lands and houses themselves, by gaming, by over-grown bills, (whether on account of physic, or law, or any thing else,) or by requiring or taking such interest as even the laws of our country forbid. Hereby all pawn-broking is excluded: Seeing, whatever good we might do thereby, all unprejudiced men see with grief to be abundantly over-balanced by the evil. And if it were otherwise, yet we are not allowed to "do evil that good may come." We cannot, consistent with brotherly love, sell our goods below the market-price; we cannot study to ruin our neighbour's trade, in order to advance our own; much less can we entice away, or receive, any of his servants or workmen whom he has need of. None can gain by swallowing up his neighbour's substance, without gaining the damnation of hell!

4. Neither may we gain by hurting our neighbour *in his body*. Therefore we may not sell any thing which tends to impair health. ...

6. This is dear-bought gain. And so is whatever is procured by hurting our neighbour *in his soul*; by ministering, suppose, either directly or indirectly, to his unchastity, or intemperance; which certainly none can do, who has any fear of God, or any real desire of pleas-ing Him. It nearly concerns all those to consider this, who have anything to do with taverns, victualling-houses, opera-houses, play-houses, or any other places of public, fashionable diversion. If these profit the souls of men, you are clear; your employment is good, and your gain innocent; but if they are either sinful in themselves, or natural inlets to sin of various kinds, then, it is to be feared, you have a sad account to make. O beware, lest God say in that day, "These have perished in their iniquity, but their blood do I require at thy hands!"

7. These cautions and restrictions being observed, it is the bounden duty of all who are engaged in worldly business to observe that first and great rule of Christian wisdom, with respect to money, "Gain all you can." Gain all you can by honest industry. Use all possible diligence in your calling. Lose no time. If you understand yourself, and your relation to God and man, you know you have none to spare. If you understand your particular calling, as you ought, you will have no time that hangs upon your hands. Every business will afford some employment sufficient for every day and every hour. That wherein you are placed, if you follow it in earnest, will leave you no leisure for silly, unprofitable diversions. ...

II. 1. Having gained all you can, by honest wisdom, and unwearied diligence, the Second rule of Christian prudence is, "Save all you can." Do not throw the precious talent into the sea: Leave that folly to heathen philosophers. Do not throw it away in idle expenses, which is just the same as throwing it into the sea. Expend no part of it merely to gratify: the desire of the flesh, the desire of the eye, or the pride of life. ...

III. 1. But let not any man imagine that he has done anything, barely by going thus far, by "gaining and saving all he can," if he were to stop here. All this is nothing, if a man go not forward, if he does not point all this at a farther end. Nor, indeed, can a man properly be said to save anything, if he only lays it up. You may as well throw your money into the sea, as bury it in the earth. And you may as well bury it in the earth, as in your chest, or in the bank of England. Not to use, is effectually to throw it away. If, therefore, you would indeed "make yourselves friends of the mammon of unrighteousness," add the Third rule to the two preceding. Having, First, gained all you can, and, Secondly, saved all you can, Then "give all you can." ...

3. The directions which God has given us, touching the use of our worldly substance, may be comprised in the following particulars. If you desire to be a faithful and a wise steward, out of that portion of your Lord's

goods which he has for the present lodged in your hands, but with the right of resuming whenever it pleases him, First, provide things needful for yourself; food to eat, raiment to put on, whatever nature moderately requires for preserving the body in health and strength. Secondly, provide these for your wife, your children, your servants, or any others who pertain to your household. If, when this is done, there be an overplus left, then "do good to them that are of the household of faith." If there be an overplus still, "as you have opportunity, do good unto all men." In so doing, you give all you can; nay, in a sound sense, all you have: For all that is laid out in this manner is really given to God. You "render unto God the things that are God's," not only by what you give to the poor, but also by that which you expend in providing things needful for yourself and your household.

4. If, then, a doubt should at any time arise in your mind concerning what you are going to expend, either on yourself or any part of your family, you have an easy way to remove it. Calmly and seriously inquire, "(1) In expending this, am I acting according to my character? Am I acting herein, not as a proprietor, but as a steward of my Lord's goods? (2) Am I doing this in obedience to

his word? In what scripture does he require me so to do? (3) Can I offer up this action, this expense, as a sacrifice to God through Jesus Christ? (4) Have I reason to believe, that for this very work I shall have a reward at the resurrection of the just?" You will seldom need anything more to remove any doubt which arises on this head; but, by this four-fold consideration, you will receive clear light as to the way wherein you should go. ...

6. You see, then, what it is to "make yourselves friends of the mammon of unrighteousness," and by what means you may procure, "that when ye fail, they may receive you into the everlasting habitations." You see the nature and extent of truly Christian prudence, so far, as it relates to the use of that great talent, money. Gain all you can, without hurting either yourself or your neighbour, in soul or body, by applying hereto with unintermitted diligence, and with all the understanding which God has given you; – save all you can, by cutting off every expense which serves only to indulge foolish desire; to gratify either the desire of the flesh, the desire of the eye, or the pride of life; waste nothing, living or dying, on sin or folly, whether for yourself or your children; – and then, give all you can, or, in other words, give all you have to God.

Reinhold Niebuhr, *The Conflict Between Individual and Social Morality*

Reinhold Niebuhr (1892–1971) grew up as a Lutheran in a denomination that later united with Reformed traditions and eventually formed part of the United Church of Christ in 1957. He rejected the naïveté of pacifists and those who followed the progressive politics of the social gospel movement, because he believed they had an inadequate understanding of human nature. He viewed the interplay of self-interest in the political sphere as an unalterable aspect of human life, and made the doctrine of original sin the center of his theology. He thought it made little sense to talk about love at the level of institutions and political organizations until one had first addressed the need for justice – even if the highest aim of the Christian ethic remains selfless love.

In his *Moral Man and Immoral Society* (1932) Niebuhr makes a firm distinction between individual and social life. For the individual, he seeks a disinterested motive – what in Chapter Five we shall call "right intention." For society, he seeks justice, even justice achieved by dubious means – a pursuit we shall call "right outcome." (One could almost rename the book, "Deontological Man and Consequential Society.") Niebuhr believes the disinterested, even idealistic, individual, and the more pragmatic society have a beneficial effect on one another. (He often presents his ideas as a balance between two poles.) He maintains "the religious ideal in its purest form has nothing to do with the problem of social justice." This is because the religious ideal is limited to disinterestedness and thus does not embrace the true complexities of human relationships.

Reinhold Niebuhr. *Moral Man and Immoral Society: A Study in Ethics and Politics.* New York: Charles Scribner's Sons, 1932. From Chapter 10, "The Conflict Between Individual and Social Morality," pages 257–73. Reprinted with the permission of the Estate of Reinhold Niebuhr.

A realistic analysis of the problems of human society reveals a constant and seemingly irreconcilable conflict between the needs of society and the imperatives of a sensitive conscience. This conflict, which could be most briefly defined as the conflict between ethics and politics, is made inevitable by the double focus of the moral life. One focus is in the inner life of the individual, and the other in the necessities of man's social life. From the perspective of society the highest moral ideal is justice. From the perspective of the individual the highest ideal is unselfishness. Society must strive for justice even if it is forced to use means, such as self-assertion, resistance, coercion and perhaps resentment, which cannot gain the moral sanction of the most sensitive moral spirit. The individual must strive to realise his life by losing and finding himself in something greater than himself.

These two moral perspectives are not mutually exclusive and the contradiction between them is not absolute. But neither are they easily harmonised. ... [T]he highest moral insights and achievements of the individual conscience are both relevant and necessary to the life of society. The most perfect justice cannot be established if the moral imagination of the individual does not seek to comprehend the needs and interests of his fellows. Nor can any non-rational instrument of justice be used without great peril to society, if it is not brought under the control of moral goodwill. Any justice which is only justice soon degenerates into something less than justice. It must be saved by something which is more than justice. The realistic wisdom of the statesman is reduced to foolishness if it is not under the influence of the foolishness of the moral seer. The latter's idealism results in political futility and sometimes in moral confusion, if it is not brought into commerce and communication with the realities of man's collective life. This necessity and possibility of fusing moral and political insights does not, however, completely eliminate certain irreconcilable elements in the two types of morality, internal and external, individual and social. ...

From the internal perspective the most moral act is one which is actuated by disinterested motives. The external observer may find good in selfishness. He may value it as natural to the constitution of human nature and as necessary to society. But from the viewpoint of the author of an action, unselfishness must remain the criterion of the highest morality. For only the agent of an action knows to what degree self-seeking corrupts his socially approved actions. Society, on the other hand, makes justice rather than unselfishness its highest moral ideal. Its aim must be to seek equality of opportunity for all life. If this equality and justice cannot be achieved without the assertion of interest against interest, and without restraint upon the self-assertion of those who infringe upon the rights of their neighbors, then society is compelled to sanction self-assertion and restraint. It may even, as we have seen, be forced to sanction social conflict and violence.

Historically the internal perspective has usually been cultivated by religion. For religion proceeds from profound introspection and naturally makes good motives the criteria of good conduct. It may define good motives either in terms of love or of duty, but the emphasis is upon the inner springs of action. Rationalised forms of religion usually choose duty rather than love as the expression of highest virtue (as in Kantian and Stoic morality), because it seems more virtuous to them to bring all impulse under the dominion of reason than to give any impulses, even altruistic ones, moral preeminence. The social viewpoint stands in sharpest contrast to religious morality when it views the behavior of collective rather than individual man, and when it deals with the necessities of political life. Political morality, in other words, is in the most uncompromising antithesis to religious morality.

Rational morality usually holds an intermediary position between the two. Sometimes it tries to do justice to the inner moral necessities of the human spirit rather than to the needs of society. If it emphasises the former it may develop an ethic of duty rather than the religious ethic of disinterestedness. But usually rationalism in morals tends to some kind of utilitarianism. It views human conduct from the social perspective and finds its ultimate standards in some general good and total social harmony. From that viewpoint it gives moral sanction to egoistic as well as to altruistic impulses justifying them because they are natural to human nature and necessary to society. It asks only that egoism be reasonably expressed. Upon that subject Aristotle said the final as well as the first authoritative word. Reason, according to his theory, establishes control over all the impulses, egoistic and altruistic, and justifies them both if excesses are avoided and the golden mean is observed. ...

The utilitarian attempt to harmonise the inner and outer perspectives of morality is inevitable and, within limits, possible. It avoids the excesses, absurdities and perils into which both religious and political morality may fall. By placing a larger measure of moral approval upon egoistic impulses than does religious morality and by disapproving coercion, conflict and violence more unqualifiedly than politically oriented morality, it manages to resolve the conflict between them. But it is not as realistic as either. It easily assumes a premature identity between self-interest and social interest and establishes a spurious harmony between egoism and altruism. With Bishop Butler most utilitarian rationalists in morals believe "that though benevolence and self-love are different ... yet they are so perfectly coincident that the greatest satisfaction to ourselves depends upon having benevolence in due degree, and that self-love is one chief security of our right behavior to society." Rationalism in morals therefore insists on less inner restraint upon self-assertion than does religion, and believes less social restraint to be necessary than political realism demands. ...

The more the moral problem is shifted from the relations of individuals to the relations of groups and collectives, the more the preponderance of the egoistic impulses over the social ones is established. It is therefore revealed that no inner checks are powerful enough to bring them under complete control. Social control must consequently be attempted; and it cannot be established without social conflict. The moral perils attending such a political strategy have been previously considered. They are diametrically opposite to the perils of religious morality. The latter tend to perpetuate injustice by discouraging self-assertion against the inordinate claims of others. The former justify not only self-assertion but the use of non-rational power in reinforcing claims. They may therefore substitute new forms of injustice for old ones and enthrone a new tyranny on the throne of the old. A rational compromise between these two types of restraint easily leads to a premature complacency toward self-assertion. It is therefore better for society to suffer the uneasy harmony between the two types of restraint than to run the danger of inadequate checks upon egoistic impulses. Tolstoi and Lenin both present perils to the life of society; but they are probably no more dangerous than the compromises with human selfishness effected by modern disciples of Aristotle.

If we contemplate the conflict between religious and political morality it may be well to recall that the religious ideal in its purest form has nothing to do with the problem of social justice. It makes disinterestedness an absolute ideal without reference to social consequences. It justifies the ideal in terms of the integrity and beauty of the human spirit. While religion may involve itself in absurdities in the effort to achieve the ideal by purely internal discipline, and while it may run the peril of deleterious social consequences, it does do justice to inner needs of the human spirit. The veneration in which a Tolstoi, a St. Francis, a crucified Christ, and the saints of all the ages have been held, proves that, in the inner sanctuary of their souls, selfish men know that they ought not be selfish, and venerate what they feel they ought to be and cannot be. ...

Nothing is clearer than that a pure religious idealism must issue in a policy of non-resistance which makes no claims to be socially efficacious. It submits to any demands, however unjust, and yields to any claims, however inordinate, rather than assert self-interest against another. "You will meekly bear," declared Epictetus, "for you will say on every occasion 'It seemed so to him.'" This type of moral idealism leads either to asceticism, as in the case of Francis and other Catholic saints, or at least to the complete disavowal of any political responsibility, as in the case of Protestant sects practicing consistent non-resistance, as, for instance, the Anabaptists, Mennonites, Dunkers and Doukhobors. The Quakers assumed political responsibilities, but they were never consistent non-resisters. They disavowed violence but not resistance.

While social consequences are not considered in such a moral strategy, it would be shortsighted to deny that it may result in redemptive social consequences, at least within the area of individual and personal relationships. Forgiveness may not always prompt the wrongdoer to repentance; but yet it may. Loving the enemy may not soften the enemy's heart; but there are possibilities that it will. Refusal to assert your own interests against another may not shame him into unselfishness; but on occasion it has done so. Love and benevolence may not lead to complete mutuality; but it does have that tendency, particularly within the area of intimate relationships. Human life would, in fact, be intolerable if justice could be established in all relationships only by self-assertion and counter-assertion, or only by a shrewd calculation of claims and counter-claims. The fact is that love, disinterestedness and benevolence do have a strong social and utilitarian value, and the place they hold in the hierarchy of virtues is really established by that value, though religion may view them finally from an inner or transcendent perspective. ... The paradox of the moral life consists in this: that the highest mutuality is achieved where mutual advantages are not consciously sought as the fruit of love. For love is purest where it desires no returns for itself; and it is most potent where it is purest. Complete mutuality, with its advantages to each party to the relationship, is therefore most perfectly realised where it is not intended, but love is poured out without seeking returns. That is how the madness of religious morality, with its trans-social ideal, becomes the wisdom which achieves wholesome social consequences. For the same reason a purely prudential morality must be satisfied with something less than the best. ...

The distinction between individual and group morality is a sharper and more perplexing one. The moral obtuseness of human collectives makes a morality of pure disinterestedness impossible. There is not enough imagination in any social group to render it amenable to the influence of pure love. Nor is there a possibility of persuading any social group to make a venture in pure love, except, as in the case of the Russian peasants, the recently liberated Negroes and other similar groups, a morally dubious social inertia should be compounded with the ideal. The selfishness of human communities must be regarded as an inevitability. Where it is inordinate it can be checked only by competing assertions of interest; and these can be effective only if coercive methods are added to moral and rational persuasion. Moral factors may qualify, but they will not eliminate, the resulting social contest and conflict. Moral goodwill may seek to relate the peculiar interests of the group to the ideal of a total and final harmony of all life. It may thereby qualify the self-assertion of the privileged, and support the interests of the disinherited, but it will never be so impartial as to persuade any group to subject its interests completely to an inclusive social ideal. The spirit of love may preserve a certain degree of appreciation for the common weaknesses and common aspirations which bind men together above the areas of social conflict. But again it cannot prevent the conflict. It may avail itself of instruments of restraint and coercion, through which a measure of trust in the moral capacities of an opponent may be expressed and the expansion rather than contraction of those capacities is encouraged. But it cannot hide the moral distrust expressed by the very use of the instrument of coercion. To some degree the conflict between the purest individual morality and an adequate political policy must therefore remain.

William Temple, *Christian Social Principles*

William Temple (1881–1944) was the 98th Archbishop of Canterbury, and son of the 95th. He holds a similar place in English social ethics to that held by Reinhold Niebuhr in American social ethics. He is most associated with his efforts to bring theological thinking in line with the enormous social changes in industrialized Britain. He was a key figure in the early years of the international ecumenical movement. He spoke up for the labor and union movement during the turbulent 1920s and 1930s and advocated for economic reforms. He was the first president (1908–1924) of the Workers' Educational Association and a member of the Labour Party. He convened the Malvern Conference (1941), which is seen as a landmark event in the years leading up to the introduction of the welfare state by the postwar Labour government. His death deprived the postwar era of a key leader.

Christianity and Social Order is his best-known work. It seeks to translate Christian principles into social expectations. Its three key themes are freedom, social fellowship, and service: he finds society wanting in each regard. He supports the notion of natural law as that which harmonized the urge to conserve with the desire to innovate. He has great confidence that social cohesion is possible, and that Christianity can provide it. There is an underlying Platonic idealism that holds up the central ideal of personality – an ideal enshrined in the incarnation of Jesus. Christianity, in Platonic fashion, is more about universals than particulars. In places he is close to Niebuhr (for example, his awareness of original sin). His description of politics – "a contention between different groups of self-interest" – is precisely the kind of account that ecclesial ethics challenges (see Chapter Seven). In common with ecclesial ethics, however, Temple's ethic has a teleological character – this excerpt concludes with reference to human destiny and the way social life should be ordered with that destiny in view.

William Temple. *Christianity and Social Order.* **London: SCM Press, 1950, 1955. From Chapter 4, "Christian Social Principles," pages 47–58.**

(A) Primary

The method of the Church's impact upon society at large should be two-fold. The Church must announce Christian principles and point out where the existing social order at any time is in conflict with them. It must then pass on to Christian citizens, acting in their civic capacity, the task of reshaping the existing order in closer conformity to the principles. For at this point technical knowledge may be required and judgments of practical expediency are always required. If a bridge is to be built, the Church may remind the engineer that it is his obligation to provide a really safe bridge; but it is not entitled to tell him whether, in fact, his design meets this requirement; a particular theologian may also be a competent engineer, and, if he is, his judgment on this point is entitled to attention; but this is altogether because he is a competent engineer and his theological equipment has nothing whatever to do with it. In just the same way the Church may tell the politician what ends the social order should promote; but it must leave to the politician the devising of the precise means to those ends.

This is a point of first-rate importance, and is frequently misunderstood. If Christianity is true at all it is a truth of universal application; all things should be done in the Christian spirit and in accordance with Christian principles. "Then," say some, "produce your Christian solution for unemployment." But there neither is nor could be such a thing. Christian faith does not by itself enable its adherent to foresee how a vast multitude of people, each one partly selfish and partly generous, and an intricate economic mechanism, will in fact be affected by a particular economic or political innovation – "social credit," for example. "In that case," says the reformer – or, quite equally, the upholder of the *status quo* – "keep off the turf. By your own confession you are out of place here." But this time the Church must say, "No; I cannot tell you what is the remedy; but I can tell you that a society of which unemployment (in peace time) is a chronic feature is a diseased society, and

that if you are not doing all you can to find and administer the remedy, you are guilty before God." Sometimes the Church can go further than this and point to features in the social structure itself which are bound to be sources of social evil because they contradict the principles of the Gospel. …

The political problem is concerned with men as they are, not with men as they ought to be. Part of the task is so to order life as to lead them nearer to what they ought to be; but to assume that they are already this will involve certain failure and disaster. It is not contended that men are utterly bad, or that they are more bad than good. What is contended is that they are not perfectly good, and that even their goodness is infected with a quality – self-centredness – which partly vitiates it, and exposes them to temptations so far as they achieve either freedom or power. This does not mean that freedom or power should be denied to them; on the contrary, it is fundamental to the Christian position that men should have freedom even though they abuse it; but it is also to be recognized that they certainly will abuse it except so far as they are won by devotion to truth or to beauty to that selfless outlook, which is only perfectly established in men by love which arises in them in answer to the redemptive love of God.

In any period worth considering, and probably to the end of earthly history, statesmen will themselves be men, and will be dealing with men, who abuse freedom and power. Now the most fundamental requirement of any political and economic system is not that it shall express love, though that is desirable, nor that it shall express justice, though that is the first ethical demand to be made upon it, but that it shall supply some reasonable measure of security against murder, robbery and starvation. If it can be said with real probability that a proposed scheme would in fact, men being what they are, fail to provide that security, that scheme is doomed. Christians have some clues to the understanding of human nature which may enable them to make a more accurate estimate than others of these points. But they will not, if they are true to their own tradition, approach the question with rosy-tinted spectacles. Its assertion of Original Sin should make the Church intensely realistic, and conspicuously free from Utopianism. …

1. God and His Purpose

All Christian thinking, and Christian thinking about society no less than any other, must begin not with man but with God. The fundamental conviction is that God is the creator of the world which could not begin or continue except by His will. The world is not necessary to God in the sense in which God is necessary to the world; for if there were no God, there would be no world; but if there were no world, God would be just what He is – only (presumably) about to make the world. For He is impelled to make the world by His love; as Plato saw, He is far removed from envy and wishes to share out His blessedness. The world is not necessary to God as the object of His love, for He has that within Himself in the relations of the Persons of the Blessed Trinity; but it results from His love; creation is a kind of overflow of the divine love. In making the world He brought into existence vast numbers of things which always have to obey His law for them – from stars and planets to atoms and electrons; these have no choice but to obey. But He also made creatures – men and women – who could disobey His law for them, and do so; He did this in order that among His creatures there might be some who gave Him a free obedience and answered His love with theirs. This involved the risk, amounting to a moral certainty, that they would take the self-centred outlook upon life, and then, partly by imitation and partly in self-defence, become hardened in selfishness, till society was a welter of competing selfishness instead of being a fellowship of love. That is what happened. To win them out of this, He came on earth and lived out the divine love in a human life and death. He is increasingly drawing men to Himself by the love thus shown. ...

2. Man: his Dignity, Tragedy and Destiny

The fundamental facts about man are two: he is made "in the image of God"; and this image is, so to speak, stamped upon an animal nature. Between these two there is constant tension resulting in perpetual tragedy.

The dignity of man is that he is the child of God, capable of communion with God, the object of the Love of God – such love as is displayed on the Cross – and destined for eternal fellowship with God. His true value is not what he is worth in himself or to his earthly state, but what he is worth to God; and that worth is bestowed on him by the utterly gratuitous Love of God.

All his life should be conducted and ordered with this dignity in view. The State must not treat him as having value only so far as he serves its ends, as

Totalitarian States do; the State exists for its citizens, not the citizens for the State. But neither must a man treat himself, or conduct his life, as if he were himself the centre of his own value; he is not his own end; his value is his worth to God and his end is "to glorify God and enjoy Him for ever." ...

Each individual is born into a family and a nation. In his maturity he is very largely what these have made him. The family is so deeply grounded in nature and the nation in history that anyone who believes in God as Creator and as Providence is bound to regard both as part of the divine plan for human life. Their claims have to be adjusted to one another, and so have the claims of the several families within each nation and of the several nations in the family of mankind. But any ordering of society which impairs or destroys the stability of the family stands condemned on that account alone; and any ordering of international life which obliterates the freedom of the several nations to develop their own cultural traditions is also condemned. The aim within the nation must be to create a harmony of stable and economically secure family units; the aim in the world as a whole must be to create a harmony of spiritually independent nations which recognize one another as reciprocally supplementary parts of a richly harmonious fellowship.

Such a harmony would be the earthly counterpart and "first fruits" (as St. Paul might call it) of the perfected Kingdom of God. It would supply the school, training the citizens of that Kingdom – of which the full life cannot be known under earthly conditions, for it is a fellowship of the servants of God in all generations alike with Him and with one another.

It is the tragedy of man that he conceives such a state of affairs and knows it for the only satisfaction of his nature, yet so conducts his life as to frustrate all hope of attaining that satisfaction. It is not only that his spirit and reason have as yet established but little control over the animal part of his nature; it is his spirit which is depraved, his reason which is perverted. His self-centredness infects his idealism because it distorts all his perspectives. ...

Anyhow, we all know that Politics is largely a contention between different groups of self-interest – e.g. the Haves and the Have-nots. It may be the function of the Church to lead people to a purely disinterested virtue (though this is at least debatable); a statesman who supposes that a mass of citizens can be governed without appeal to their self-interest is living in dreamland and is a public menace. The art of Government in fact is the art of so ordering life that self-interest prompts what justice demands. Thus it is enacted that thieves should be sent to prison; but the object of the law is not to imprison thieves, but to make men reflect that even if they are not honest it is still prudent to behave honestly.

Yet these expedients are not purely prudential, and though the cynic finds plenty of material for his malicious wit, the real truth about man eludes his grasp. Man is self-centred; but he always carries with him abundant proof that this is not the real truth of his nature. He has to his credit both capacities and achievements that could never be derived from self-interest. The image of God – the image of holiness and love – is still there, though defaced; it is the source of his aspirations; it is even – through its defacement – the occasion of his perversity. It is capable of response to the Divine Image in its perfection if ever this can be presented to it. This is the glory of the Gospel. It enables man to see "the light of the knowledge of the glory of God in the face of Jesus Christ," and so "with unveiled face, reflecting as a mirror the glory of the Lord," man may be "transformed into the same image from glory to glory."

That is man's destiny. And his social life, so far as it is deliberately planned, should be ordered with that destiny in view. He must be treated as what he actually is, but always with a view to what in God's purpose he is destined to become. For the law and the social order, is our schoolmaster to bring us to Christ.

Part Two

The Questions Christian Ethics Asks

Chapter Five

Universal Ethics

There are broadly three universal approaches to ethics, each of which assumes they apply to everybody but which differ on their understanding of the moment or place that is the key to the discipline.

The first approach sees ethics as concerning right *actions*, linked inextricably to right intentions. It is obvious because the popular understanding of morality tends to assume it is about doing good things rather than doing bad things. The means are everything, and a good end cannot justify the use of dubious means to bring it about.

By contrast, the second approach sees ethics as concerning right *outcomes*. In this case what is good is whatever produces the right result – the ends do, or at least may, justify the means.

The third approach gathers together a number of concerns not adequately addressed by the previous two approaches. It concentrates on right *relationships*. Here the priority is a good and healthy society, rather than right actions by or right outcomes for particular individuals. The third approach does not necessarily invalidate or even differ from either of the first two, but it places its emphasis elsewhere.

We shall look at each approach in turn.

Right Actions

Ethics that focuses on right action is most commonly known as deontological ethics, after the Greek noun *deon* meaning duty or obligation. Deontological ethics has many dimensions, including the scriptural tradition of the divine command, the ancient tradition of natural law, and the hugely influential categorical imperative of Immanuel Kant. These theories may be categorized respectively by what they take to be the source of the law – God, nature, or the conscience.

The readings in this section are designed to offer these traditions in some of their most characteristic voices. Karl Barth articulates the divine command; Thomas Aquinas and Thomas Hobbes give differing accounts of natural law; and Immanuel Kant expounds his categorical imperative.

Karl Barth, *The Command of God*

It may seem surprising to begin a chapter on universal ethics with a theologian so closely associated with ecclesial ethics. But the tradition of the divine command is one that assumes that God's decree is universal for all humankind, whether they accept the notion of God or the response of obedience or not. Hence Barth says, "we must first refuse to follow all those attempts at theological ethics which start from the assumption that it is to be built on, or to proceed from, a general human ethics, a 'philosophical' ethics." Here we see the tension between divine command ethics, which has universal claims, and philosophical ethics, which would usually exclude what it would see as the partial claims of theological ethics.

Barth defines goodness as obedience: "man does good in so far as he hears the Word of God and acts as a hearer of this Word." Resisting negative connotations of the term "command," Barth insists that what makes the command of God unique from all other commands is that "it is permission – the granting of a very definite freedom." The notion of command is never separated from the character of the God who commands – the one who commands is "the Lord who is gracious to us – gracious in the sense that He gave Himself for us in order that we might live before Him and with Him in peace and joy."

Barth acknowledges the appeal, but still more the weakness, of basing what we ought to do on what seems good or agreeable to *us*. A transcendent command cannot come from within – it must be something alien. The question of what we ought to do is always stated in the plural – and here it becomes clear that, though the command of God is universal, the ability to respond to that command is limited to "those who are elected in Jesus Christ to be covenant-partners with God." Finally, a command is an event rather than a rule: "We must divest ourselves of the fixed idea that only a universally valid rule can be a command."

Karl Barth. *Church Dogmatics*. Vol. 2, Part 2. Edinburgh: T & T Clark, 1949. From Section 36, "Ethics as a Task of the Doctrine of God"; Section 37, "The Command as the Claim of God"; and Section 38, "The Command as the Decision of God." Pages 543–8, 552, 585, 649–56, 672–3. By kind permission of Continuum International Publishing Group.

§ 36 Ethics as a Task of the Doctrine of God

2. The Way of Theological Ethics

It is the Christian doctrine of God, or, more exactly, the knowledge of the electing grace of God in Jesus Christ, which decides the nature and aim of theological ethics, of ethics as an element of Church dogmatics. It has its basis, therefore, in the doctrine of God Himself. For the God who claims man makes Himself originally responsible for man. The fact that He gives man His command, that He subjects man to His command, means that He makes Himself responsible not only for its authority but also for its fulfilment. Therefore we do not speak completely about God Himself if we do not go on at once to speak also about His command. But it is the Christian doctrine of God, or, more exactly, the knowledge of the

electing grace of God in Jesus Christ, which also decides the special way of theological ethics, the special form of its enquiry and reply, the attainment of its fundamental principles. ... Now the matter of theological ethics is the responsibility which God has assumed for us in the fact that He has made us accountable through His command. Its matter is the Word and work of God in Jesus Christ, in which the right action of man has already been performed and therefore waits only to be confirmed by our action.

In view of this matter, we must first refuse to follow all those attempts at theological ethics which start from the assumption that it is to be built on, or to proceed from, a general human ethics, a "philosophical" ethics. In the relationship between the command of God and the ethical problem, as we have defined it in its main features, there is not a universal moral element autonomously confronting the Christian. It is, therefore, quite out of the question methodically to subordinate the latter to the former, to build it on, or to derive it from, it. ...

The goodness of human action consists in the goodness with which God acts toward man. But God deals with man through His Word. His Word is the sum and plenitude of all good, because God Himself is good. Therefore man does good in so far as he hears the Word of God and acts as a hearer of this Word. In this action as a hearer he is obedient. Why is obedience good? Because it derives from hearing, because it is the action of a hearer, namely, of the hearer of the Word of God. It is good because the divine address is good, because God Himself is good. ...

The first thing that theological ethics has to show, and to develop as a basic and all-comprehensive truth, is the fact and extent that this command of God is an event. ... The proposition: "There is a command of God," is quite inadequate as a description of what concerns us. For we should naturally have to weigh against it the denial: No, "there is" no command of God. What "there is" is not as such the command of God. But the core of the matter is that God gives His command, that he gives Himself to be our Commander. God's command, God Himself, gives Himself to be known. And as He does so, He is heard. Man is made responsible. He is brought into that confrontation and fellowship with Jesus Christ. And his action acquires that determination. The command of God is the decision about the goodness of human action. As the divine action it precedes human action. It is only on the basis of this reality, which is not in any sense static but active, not in any sense general but supremely particular, that theological ethics has to make answer to the ethical question. ...

§ 37 The Command as the Claim of God

As God is gracious to us in Jesus Christ, His command is the claim which, when it is made, has power over us, demanding that in all we do we admit that what God does is right, and requiring that we give our free obedience to this demand.

3. The Form of the Divine Claim

... The form by which the command of God is distinguished from all other commands, the special form which is its secret even in the guise of another command, consists in the fact that it is permission – the granting of a very definite freedom. We know who it is that orders here, and what it is that makes this ordering peremptory. It is the God in whom we may believe as the Lord who is gracious to us – gracious in the sense that He gave Himself for us in order that we might live before Him and with Him in peace and joy. And we know what it is that is ordered. We have to live as those who accept as right what God does for us. We have not to do that which contradicts but that which corresponds to His grace as it is directed to us. We have to believe in Jesus Christ, and in and with the fact that

we live in this faith to do the right. The command of this Commander is a permission, and in this it is fundamentally and finally differentiated from all other commands. ...

§ 38 The Command as the Decision of God

1. The Sovereignty of the Divine Decision

What makes the divine command the transcendent decision of God over all other decisions? What distinguishes our (willing, free and joyful) obedience to it from disobedience? What makes the responsibility which we fulfil by our conduct something that is well-pleasing to God? When we put this question – which is the question of ethical meditation – we have to remember that what is well-pleasing to God, what makes our obedience obedience, and the command of God a sovereign decision, consists in the fact that our will is confronted by, and subjected to, an *ought* – and not conversely. Thus the ethical question: What *ought* we to do?, is not sincerely put if secretly or openly it means: What do we will to do? What do we will of ourselves, in virtue of the equally objective and indisputable claims of our own will, in responsibility – but not this time genuine responsibility – to the aims which our own promptings lead us to propose? Aims of this kind – in their various combinations – are usually what appears pleasing and useful and valuable to ourselves. What seems desirable and necessary to us, and even what we think to be true and good and beautiful, can in its own way seem to be obligatory and present itself in the form of an imperative. ...

Therefore when we ask: What *ought* we to do?, we must keep this question distinct from that of what seems to us to be desirable or necessary or even good and true and beautiful, from the whole question of even the supreme value of this or that action. However serious and deep our formulation of the latter, it can alter not at all the fact that we are asking about what we will – about what seems us to be most useful and therefore most real, most real and therefore most useful, and on this basis supremely desirable. But to the extent that our decisions are subject to the sovereign decision of the divine command, we have not to be answerable to ourselves, and therefore to our own ideas of what is supremely real and useful and desirable. With all our ideas and the resultant aims, we are answerable to the divine command, so that the question is whether, as those who entertain these ideas and set themselves these aims, we are good or bad according to God's command. What we consider desirable, useful and valuable may be very important to us as the truth of what we ought to do. But we can understand and claim it as our true obligation only in a conditional sense, i.e., as conditioned by ourselves. ... An imperative to which I owe absolute obedience must necessarily come in the most radical sense from within, in order that it may claim me most radically within. A command which transcends our actions cannot in the last analysis be merely a command which I have given myself on the basis of what I myself have seen and experienced and felt and judged of the good and the true and the beautiful. It must come to me as something alien, as the command of another, demanding as such that I should make its content the law of my life. If there is an *ought*, it must not be the product of my own will, but touch from outside the whole area of what I can will of myself. It must lay upon me the obligation of unconditioned truth – truth which is not conditioned by myself. Its authority and power to do so must be intrinsic and objective, and not something which I lend to it. Its validity must consist in the fact that the very question of its validity is quite outside the sphere of my own thinking and feeling; that I can no longer entertain the idea of making sure of its authority and power by seeking its basis in what I myself have understood or seen or felt or experienced; that I can no longer consider how it may best be proved and demonstrated. On the contrary, it establishes its own validity by asking concerning my own: whether and how far I can satisfy it and be justified and stand before it. The essence of the idea of obligation is not that I demand something from myself but that, with all that I can demand of myself, I am myself demanded. ...

What ought *we* to do? ... It is, of course, a question of what we are and will and do and do not do in the light of the fact that it is subject to the sovereign decision of God whether this is good or bad. It is a question of the divine judgment on human affairs concealed in the divine command. But the human element referred to is man, and that means ourselves. It is we who are the subject which derives from God's decision, which is now its object, and continually becomes its object. It is we who are and will and do and do not do. The command of God, His infinite promise and terrible threat – all have reference to us. It is we who are the covenant-partners of God. And therefore the question of our readiness for confrontation by the divine command is necessarily: What ought we to do? Two delimitations are necessary at this point. The first is that the question cannot be put impersonally: What ought *one* to do? We do not ask concerning the action of others, but concerning our own action and its corre-

spondence with the obligations of the command. We ask concerning ourselves. As the question of grace and election must find its ultimate and decisive answer in the fact that we ourselves, in faith in the election of Jesus Christ, dare to live in correspondence to the divine predestination of man, so the ethical question can be answered only as we make our own the necessary reflection of man on his confrontation by the divine command. As long as we do not do this, but think we can solve the ethical problem by concerning ourselves with human conduct in general, all ethics is ghostly, insubstantial. ...

This *we* of the ethical question is not an unqualified *we* but the highly qualified *we* of those who – whether they know and believe it or not, whether we can appeal to them on this ground, or whether this is not yet or no longer the case – are elected in Jesus Christ to be covenant-partners with God and therefore placed under the divine command. An unqualified *we* – the universal *we* of the human race, or the special *we* of a particular group or collective – would be no safeguard against an escape into irresponsibility along the two lines indicated. ... The *we* of those who are in Jesus Christ makes us unconditionally the subject of the ethical question. ...

2. The Definiteness of the Divine Decision

For, as the Lord of this history [in the biblical witness], God seems hardly to be interested at all in general and universally valid rules, but properly only in certain particular actions and achievements and attitudes, and this in the extremely simple and direct way of desiring from man (as a father from his child, or a master from his servant) that this or that must or must not happen. Nothing can be made of these commands if we try to generalise and transform them into universally valid principles (unless, of course, we artificially distort them). Their content is purely concrete and related to this or that particular man in this or that particular situation. It consists in what God wills that he should do or not do in a specific situation. Commands of this sort must be left as they stand. They belong directly to a specific history, and they must be left in all their historical particularity and uniqueness. What God wills and for what purpose He requires the active participation of man, for what purpose He claims his being and willing, what he does and does not do – this is the course of this history, which consists, therefore, in purely individual, concrete and specific events. Thus God's commanding can only be this individual, concrete and specific commanding. We must divest ourselves of the fixed idea that only a universally valid rule can be a command. We must realise that in reality a rule of this kind is not a command. We must be open to the realisation that the biblical witness to God's ruling is this: to attest God as the Father, or Lord, who in the process of the revelation and embodment of His grace, *hic et nunc* [here and now], orders or forbids His child, or servant, something quite specific, and in such a way that there can be no question of an appraisal or judgment by man of what is required (which would be legitimate and necessary if the command consisted in a universally binding rule), but the question put to man can be only that of his hearing and obeying.

Thomas Aquinas, *The Natural Law*

The Roman tradition of natural law left a significant unanswered question. Does natural law name humankind's difference from the animals or its similarity to them? Isidore of Seville (560–636) took a mediating path, seeing natural law as human reflection on natural circumstances. The tension between natural law as fundamentally about reason or fundamentally about nature runs through the work of Thomas Aquinas (1225–1274).

Aquinas distinguished between natural knowledge, which could be attained by reason, and supernatural knowledge, which required revelation from God. He sees human beings as shaped by reason, and he is aware that right action may not be the same for all or equally known by all (although the principle of natural law is simple: "good is to be done and pursued, and evil is to be avoided"). But he also refers to natural law as common to all animals and to the need for humans to accept their givenness as animals.

Thomas' hugely influential description of natural law assumes three orders of precepts. There is the precept shared with all beings, that of self-preservation. "Whatever is a means of preserving human life, and of warding off its obstacles, belongs to the natural law." Next there are the precepts shared with all animals, "such as sexual intercourse, education of offspring and so forth." Third, there is a uniquely human precept, an inclination to good – "to know the truth about God, and to live in society … for instance, to shun ignorance, to avoid offending those among whom one has to live" and so on. None of these precepts gives clear guidance except as they are articulated through positive law.

Thomas Aquinas. *Summa Theologica.* **5 vols. Notre Dame: Christian Classics, 1948. Also available online at www.ccel.org/ccel/aquinas/summa.html. From Prima Secundae [The First Part of the Second Part], Question 94, "Of the Natural Law," pages 1009–12.**

Question 94

Article 2. Whether the natural law contains several precepts, or only one?

… The precepts of the natural law in man stand in relation to practical matters, as the first principles to matters of demonstration. But there are several first indemonstrable principles. Therefore there are also several precepts of the natural law. … [T]he precepts of the natural law are to the practical reason, what the first principles of demonstrations are to the speculative reason; because both are self-evident principles. Now a thing is said to be self-evident in two ways: first, in itself; secondly, in relation to us. Any proposition is said to be self-evident in itself, if its predicate is contained in the notion of the subject: although, to one who knows not the definition of the subject, it happens that such a proposition is not self-evident. For instance, this proposition, "Man is a rational being," is, in its very nature, self-evident, since who says "man," says "a rational being": and yet to one who knows not what a man is, this proposition is not self-evident. Hence it is that, as Boethius says (*De*

Hebdom.), certain axioms or propositions are universally self-evident to all; and such are those propositions whose terms are known to all, as, "Every whole is greater than its part," and, "Things equal to one and the same are equal to one another."...

Now a certain order is to be found in those things that are apprehended universally. For that which, before aught else, falls under apprehension, is "being," the notion of which is included in all things whatsoever a man apprehends. Wherefore the first indemonstrable principle is that "the same thing cannot be affirmed and denied at the same time," which is based on the notion of "being" and "not-being": and on this principle all others are based ... Now as "being" is the first thing that falls under the apprehension simply, so "good" is the first thing that falls under the apprehension of the practical reason, which is directed to action: since every agent acts for an end under the aspect of good. Consequently the first principle of practical reason is one founded on the notion of good, viz. that "good is that which all things seek after." Hence this is the first precept of law, that "good is to be done and pursued, and evil is to be avoided." All other precepts of the natural law are based upon this: so that whatever the practical reason naturally apprehends as man's good (or evil) belongs to the precepts of the natural law as something to be done or avoided.

Since, however, good has the nature of an end, and evil, the nature of a contrary, hence it is that all those things to which man has a natural inclination, are naturally apprehended by reason as being good, and consequently as objects of pursuit, and their contraries as evil, and objects of avoidance. Wherefore according to the order of natural inclinations, is the order of the precepts of the natural law. Because in man there is first of all an inclination to good in accordance with the nature which he has in common with all substances: inasmuch as every substance seeks the preservation of its own being, according to its nature: and by reason of this inclination, whatever is a means of preserving human life, and of warding off its obstacles, belongs to the natural law. Secondly, there is in man an inclination to things that pertain to him more specially, according to that nature which he has in common with other animals: and in virtue of this inclination, those things are said to belong to the natural law, "which nature has taught to all animals," such as sexual intercourse, education of offspring and so forth. Thirdly, there is in man an inclination to good, according to the nature of his reason, which nature is proper to him: thus man has a natural inclination to know the truth about God, and to live in society: and in this respect, whatever pertains to this inclination belongs to the natural law; for instance, to shun ignorance, to avoid offending those among whom one has to live, and other such things regarding the above inclination. ...

Article 4. Whether the natural law is the same in all men?

... [T]o the natural law belongs those things to which a man is inclined naturally: and among these it is proper to man to be inclined to act according to reason. Now the process of reason is from the common to the proper ... The speculative reason, however, is differently situated in this matter, from the practical reason. For, since the speculative reason is busied chiefly with the necessary things, which cannot be otherwise than they are, its proper conclusions, like the universal principles, contain the truth without fail. The practical reason, on the other hand, is busied with contingent matters, about which human actions are concerned: and consequently, although there is necessity in the general principles, the more we descend to matters of detail, the more frequently we encounter defects. Accordingly then in speculative matters truth is the same in all men, both as to principles and as to conclusions: although the truth is not known to all as regards the conclusions, but only as regards the principles which are called common notions. But in matters of action, truth or practical rectitude is not the same for all, as to matters of detail, but only as to the general principles: and where there is the same rectitude in matters of detail, it is not equally known to all.

It is therefore evident that, as regards the general principles whether of speculative or of practical reason, truth or rectitude is the same for all, and is equally known by all. As to the proper conclusions of the speculative reason, the truth is the same for all, but is not equally known to all: thus it is true for all that the three angles of a triangle are together equal to two right angles, although it is not known to all. But as to the proper conclusions of the practical reason, neither is the truth or rectitude the same for all, nor, where it is the same, is it equally known by all. Thus it is right and true for all to act according to reason: and from this principle it follows as a proper conclusion, that goods entrusted to another should be restored to their owner. Now this is true for the majority of cases: but it may happen in a particular case that it would be injurious, and therefore unreasonable, to restore goods held in trust; for instance, if they are claimed for the purpose of fighting against one's country. And this principle will be found to fail the more, according as we descend further into detail, e.g. if one were to say that goods held in trust should be restored with such and such a guarantee, or in such and such a way; because the greater the number of conditions added, the greater the number of ways in which the principle may fail, so that it be not right to restore or not to restore.

Consequently we must say that the natural law, as to general principles, is the same for all, both as to rectitude and as to knowledge. But as to certain matters of detail, which are conclusions, as it were, of those general principles, it is the same for all in the majority of cases, both as to rectitude and as to knowledge; and yet in some few cases it may fail, both as to rectitude, by reason of certain obstacles (just as natures subject to generation and corruption fail in some few cases on account of some obstacle), and as to knowledge, since in some the reason is perverted by passion, or evil habit, or an evil disposition of nature; thus formerly, theft, although it is expressly contrary to the natural law, was not considered wrong among the Germans, as Julius Caesar relates.

Article 5. Whether the natural law can be changed?

... A change in the natural law may be understood in two ways. First, by way of addition. In this sense nothing hinders the natural law from being changed: since many things for the benefit of human life have been added over and above the natural law, both by the Divine law and by human laws.

Secondly, a change in the natural law may be understood by way of subtraction, so that what previously was according to the natural law, ceases to be so. In this sense, the natural law is altogether unchangeable in its first principles: but in its secondary principles, which are certain detailed proximate conclusions drawn from the first principles, the natural law is not changed so

that what it prescribes be not right in most cases. But it may be changed in some particular cases of rare occurrence, through some special causes hindering the observance of such precepts ...

Article 6. Whether the law of nature can be abolished from the heart of man?

... Augustine says: "Thy law is written in the hearts of men, which iniquity itself effaces not." But the law which is written in men's hearts is the natural law. Therefore the natural law cannot be blotted out. ... There belong to the natural law, first, certain most general precepts, that are known to all; and secondly, certain secondary and more detailed precepts, which are, as it were, conclusions following closely from first principles. As to those general principles, the natural law, in the abstract, can nowise be blotted out from men's hearts. But it is blotted out in the case of a particular action, in so far as reason is hindered from applying the general principle to a particular point of practice, on account of concupiscence or some other passion. But as to the other, i.e. the secondary precepts, the natural law can be blotted out from the human heart, either by evil persuasions, just as in speculative matters errors occur in respect of necessary conclusions; or by vicious customs and corrupt habits, as among some men, theft, and even unnatural vices, as the Apostle states (Romans 1), were not esteemed sinful.

Sin blots out the law of nature in particular cases, not universally, except perchance in regard to the secondary precepts of the natural law, in the way stated above.

Although grace is more efficacious than nature, yet nature is more essential to man, and therefore more enduring.

Thomas Hobbes, *Natural Law and Natural Right*

Whereas for the medieval thinkers natural law existed as part of a pattern of eternal, divine, and human laws, from the Enlightenment onwards speculation grew that no longer took eternal and divine law for granted. The work of Thomas Hobbes (1588–1679) emerged out of the chaos of the English Civil War. In his book *Leviathan* he vividly describes the dangerous existence of humankind in its natural condition. Hobbes thus derives self-protection from natural death as the highest necessity. A great deal of his argument is given over to demonstrating the necessity of a powerful central authority to avert the evil of civil war.

Hobbes expounds several laws of nature. Everyone ought to endeavor peace, as far as they have hope of obtaining it; for peace, and defense of themselves, to lay down their right to all things; and be content with so much liberty against others as they would allow others against themselves. They should keep their covenants, for the definition of injustice is the non-performance of a covenant. If someone receives grace from another, they should endeavor that the one who gives it has no cause to regret it. Everyone should strive to accommodate themselves to the rest, and pardon those who repent, not seek revenge, declare no hatred or contempt of another, and acknowledge others as their equal by nature. The significance of Hobbes' version of natural law is witnessed by the abiding resonance of his phraseology in contemporary discussions.

Here we see Hobbes articulate "natural right," which is "the liberty each man hath, to use his own power, as he will himself, for the preservation of his own nature." He distinguishes right from law. It is also interesting that he incorporates the Golden Rule, "whatsoever you require that others should do to you, that do ye to them" (Matthew 7:12), with no sense that it may in any significant way differ from his argument.

Thomas Hobbes. *Leviathan.* Oxford: Oxford University Press, 1998. On Man, Chapter 14, "Of the First and Second Natural Laws, and of Contracts." Pages 86–9. Available online at www.ebooks.adelaide.edu.au/h/hobbes/thomas/h68l/. By permission of Oxford University Press.

Of the First and Second Natural Laws, and of Contracts

1. THE RIGHT OF NATURE, which writers commonly call *jus naturale*, is the liberty each man hath, to use his own power, as he will himself, for the preservation of his own nature; that is to say, of his own life; and consequently, of doing any thing, which in his own judgment, and reason, he shall conceive to be the aptest means thereunto.

2. By LIBERTY, is understood, according to the proper signification of the word, the absence of external impediments: which impediments, may oft take away part of a man's power to do what he would; but cannot hinder him from using the power left him, according as his judgment, and reason shall dictate to him.

3. A LAW OF NATURE, (*lex naturalis*,) is a precept, or general rule, found out by reason, by which a man is forbidden to do, that, which is destructive of his life, or taketh away the means of preserving the same; and to omit, that, by which he thinketh it may be best preserved. For though they that speak of this subject, use to confound *jus*, and *lex*, *right* and *law*; yet they ought to be distinguished; because RIGHT, consisteth in liberty to do, or to forbear: whereas LAW, determineth, and bindeth to one of them: so that law, and right, differ as much, as obligation, and liberty; which in one and the same matter are inconsistent.

4. And because the condition of man, (as hath been declared in the precedent chapter) is a condition of war of every one against every one; in which case every one is governed by his own reason; and there is nothing he can make use of, that may not be a help unto him, in preserving his life against his enemies; it followeth, that in such a condition, every man has a right to every thing; even to one another's body. And therefore, as long as this natural right of every man to every thing endureth, there can be no security to any man, (how strong or wise soever he be,) of living out the time, which nature ordinarily alloweth men to live. And consequently it is a precept, or general rule of reason, *that every man, ought to endeavour peace, as far as he has hope of obtaining it; and when he cannot obtain it, that he may seek, and use, all helps, and advantages of war.* The first branch of which rule, containeth the first, and fundamental law of nature; which is, *to seek peace, and follow it.* The second, the sum of the right of nature; which is, *by all means we can, to defend ourselves.*

5. From this fundamental law of nature, by which men are commanded to endeavour peace, is derived this second law; *that a man be willing, when others are so too, as far-forth, as for peace, and defence of himself he shall think it necessary, to lay down this right to all things; and be contented with so much liberty against other men,*

as he would allow other men against himself. For as long as every man holdeth this right, of doing any thing he liketh; so long are all men in the condition of war. But if other men will not lay down their right, as well as he; then there is no reason for any one, to divest himself of his: for that were to expose himself to prey, (which no man is bound to) rather than to dispose himself to peace. This is that law of the Gospel; *whatsoever you require that others should do to you, that do ye to them.* And that law of all men, *quod tibi fieri non vis, alteri ne feceris* [do not do to others what you would not wish to be done to you].

6. To *lay down* a man's right to any thing, is to *divest* himself of the *liberty*, of hindering another of the benefit of his own right to the same. For he that renounceth, or passeth away his right, giveth not to any other man a right which he had not before; because there is nothing to which every man had not right by nature: but only standeth out of his way, that he may enjoy his own original right, without hindrance from him; not without hindrance from another. So that the effect which redoundeth to one man, by another man's defect of right, is but so much diminution of impediments to the use of his own right original.

7. Right is laid aside, either by simply renouncing it; or by transferring it to another. By *simply* RENOUNCING; when he cares not to whom the benefit thereof redoundeth. By TRANSFERRING; when he intendeth the benefit thereof to some certain person, or persons. And when a man hath in either manner abandoned, or granted away his right; then he is said to be OBLIGED, or BOUND, not to hinder those, to whom such right is granted, or abandoned, from the benefit of it: and that he *ought*, and it is his DUTY, not to make void that voluntary act of his own: and that such hindrance is INJUSTICE, and INJURY, as being *sine jure*; the right being before renounced, or transferred. So that *injury*, or *injustice*, in the controversies of the world, is somewhat like to that, which in the disputations of scholars is called absurdity. For as it is there called an *absurdity*, to contradict what one maintained in the beginning: so in the world, it is

called injustice, and injury, voluntarily to undo that, which from the beginning he had voluntarily done. The way by which a man either simply renounceth, or transferreth his right, is a declaration, or signification, by some voluntary and sufficient sign, or signs, that he doth so renounce, or transfer; or hath so renounced, or transferred the same, to him that accepteth it. And these signs are either words only, or actions only; or (as it happeneth most often) both words, and actions. And the same are the BONDS, by which men are bound, and obliged: bonds, that have their strength, not from their own nature, (for nothing is more easily broken than a man's word,) but from fear of some evil consequence upon the rupture.

8. Whensoever a man transferreth his right, or renounceth it; it is either in consideration of some right reciprocally transferred to himself; or for some other good he hopeth for thereby. For it is a voluntary act: and of the voluntary acts of every man, the object is some *good to himself.* And therefore there be some rights, which no man can be understood by any words, or other signs, to have abandoned, or transferred. As first a man cannot lay down the right of resisting them, that assault him by force, to take away his life; because he cannot be understood to aim thereby, at any good to himself. The same may be said of wounds, and chains, and imprisonment; both because there is no benefit consequent to such patience; as there is to the patience of suffering another to be wounded, or imprisoned: as also because a man cannot tell, when he seeth men proceed against him by violence, whether they intend his death or not. And lastly the motive, and end for which this renouncing, and transferring of right is introduced, is nothing else but the security of a man's person, in his life, and in the means of so preserving life, as not to be weary of it. And therefore if a man by words, or other signs, seem to despoil himself of the end, for which those signs were intended; he is not to be understood as if he meant it, or that it was his will; but that he was ignorant of how such words and actions were to be interpreted.

Immanuel Kant, *The Categorical Imperative*

Immanuel Kant (1724–1804) was searching for a grounding for truth and meaning and morality that would lead towards peace rather than endless conflict. He found it not in the starry heavens above, but in the moral law within – inside the conscience of the individual. Kant sought for the will to be subject only to its own nature – its mind and rational thought. This was true freedom, or autonomy. He saw freedom and rationality as essentially the same thing.

Kant's project is therefore to articulate a rule of morality that is binding yet ensures both the individual and morality itself remain autonomous, independent of history, tradition, or religious conviction. A rule that depends on the subject's prior interests and commitments is a hypothetical imperative – hypothetical because it starts with an assumption of what the subject wants to bring about. Hypothetical imperatives begin with the word "if"; thus, "If you wish to inherit the earth, you must be meek." What Kant is seeking is a *categorical* imperative – a rule that is binding *whatever* the subject desires or whatever outcome the subject has in mind – a rule that takes nothing for granted and makes no assumptions.

He gives three formulations of his categorical imperative:

1   Act only according to that maxim whereby you can at the same time will that it should become a universal law.
2   Act in such a way that you treat humanity, whether in your own person or in the person of any other, always at the same time as an end and never simply as a means.
3   All rational beings must so act as if they were through their maxims always legislating members in the universal kingdom of ends.

Kant is the preeminent exponent of deontological argument in ethics. His principle of universalizability and his emphasis on autonomy have been immensely influential in the post-Enlightenment era and remain so today.

Immanuel Kant. *Grounding for the Metaphysics of Morals.* 3rd edn. Trans. James W. Ellington. Indianapolis: Hackett, 1993. From Second Section: "Transition from Popular Moral Philosophy to a Metaphysics of Morals," Pages 23–30. Available online at www.sparknotes.com/philosophy/kants-grounding. Reprinted by permission of Hackett Publishing Company, Inc. All rights reserved.

All imperatives are expressed by an *ought* and thereby indicate the relation of an objective law of reason to a will that is not necessarily determined by this law because of its subjective constitution (the relation of necessitation). Imperatives say that something would be good to do or to refrain from doing, but they say it to a will that does not always therefore do something simply because it has been represented to the will as something good to do. That is practically good which determines the will by means of representations of reason and hence not by subjective causes, but objectively, i.e., on grounds valid for every rational being as such. It is distinguished from the pleasant as that which influences the will only by means of sensation from merely subjective causes, which hold only for this or

that person's senses but do not hold as a principle of reason valid for everyone.

A perfectly good will would thus be quite as much subject to objective laws (of the good), but could not be conceived as thereby necessitated to act in conformity with law, inasmuch as it can of itself, according to its subjective constitution, be determined only by the representation of the good. Therefore no imperatives hold for the divine will, and in general for a holy will; the *ought* is here out of place, because the *would* is already of itself necessarily in agreement with the law. Consequently, imperatives are only formulas for expressing the relation of objective laws of willing in general to the subjective imperfection of the will of this or that rational being, e.g., the human will.

Now all imperatives command either hypothetically or categorically. The former represent the practical necessity of a possible action as a means for attaining something else that one wants (or may possibly want). The categorical imperative would be one which represented an action as objectively necessary in itself, without reference to another end.

Every practical law represents a possible action as good and hence as necessary for a subject who is practically determinable by reason; therefore all imperatives are formulas for determining an action which is necessary according to the principle of a will that is good in some way. Now if the action would be good merely as a means to something else, so is the imperative hypothetical. But if the action is represented as good in itself, and hence as necessary in a will which of itself conforms to reason as the principle of the will, then the imperative is categorical.

An imperative thus says what action possible by me would be good, and it presents the practical rule in relation to a will which does not forthwith perform an action simply because it is good, partly because the subject does not always know that the action is good and partly because (even if he does know it is good) his maxims might yet be opposed to the objective principles of practical reason.

A hypothetical imperative thus says only that an action is good for some purpose, either possible or actual. In the first case it is a problematic practical principle; in the second case an assertoric one. A categorical imperative, which declares an action to be of itself objectively necessary without reference to any purpose, i.e., without any other end, holds as an apodeictic practical principle. …

There is, however, one end that can be presupposed as actual for all rational beings (so far as they are dependent beings to whom imperatives apply); and thus there is one purpose which they not merely can have but which can certainly be assumed to be such that they all do have by a natural necessity, and this is happiness. A hypothetical imperative which represents the practical necessity of an action as means for the promotion of happiness is assertoric. It may be expounded not simply as necessary to an uncertain, merely possible purpose, but as necessary to a purpose which can be presupposed a priori and with certainty as being present in everyone because it belongs to his essence. Now skill in the choice of means to one's own greatest well-being can be called prudence in the narrowest sense. And thus the imperative that refers to the choice of means to one's own happiness, i.e., the precept of prudence, still remains hypothetical; the action is commanded not absolutely but only as a means to a further purpose.

Finally, there is one imperative which immediately commands a certain conduct without having as its condition any other purpose to be attained by it. This imperative is categorical. It is not concerned with the matter of the action and its intended result, but rather with the form of the action and the principle from which it follows; what is essentially good in the action

consists in the mental disposition, let the consequences be what they may. This imperative may be called that of morality.

Willing according to these three kinds of principles is also clearly distinguished by dissimilarity in the necessitation of the will. To make this dissimilarity clear I think that they are most suitably named in their order when they are said to be either *rules of skill, counsels of prudence,* or *commands (laws) of morality.* For law alone involves the concept of a necessity that is unconditioned and indeed objective and hence universally valid, and commands are laws which must be obeyed, i.e., must be followed even in opposition to inclination. Counsel does indeed involve necessity, but involves such necessity as is valid only under a subjectively contingent condition, viz., whether this or that man counts this or that as belonging to his happiness. On the other hand, the categorical imperative is limited by no condition, and can quite properly be called a command since it is absolutely, though practically, necessary. The first kind of imperatives might also be called technical (belonging to art), the second kind pragmatic (belonging to welfare), the third kind moral (belonging to free conduct as such, i.e., to morals). …

The question as to how the imperative of morality is possible is undoubtedly the only one requiring a solution. For it is not at all hypothetical; and hence the objective necessity which it presents cannot be based on any presupposition, as was the case with the hypothetical imperatives. Only there must never here be forgotten that no example can show, i.e., empirically, whether there is any such imperative at all. Rather, care must be taken lest all imperatives which are seemingly categorical may nevertheless be covertly hypothetical. For instance, when it is said that you should not make a false promise, the assumption is that the necessity of this avoidance is no mere advice for escaping some other evil, so that it might be said that you should not make a false promise lest you ruin your credit when the falsity comes to light. But when it is asserted that an action of this kind must be regarded as bad in itself, then the imperative of prohibition is therefore categorical. Nevertheless, it cannot with certainty be shown by means of an example that the will is here determined solely by the law without any other incentive, even though such may seem to be the case. For it is always possible that secretly there is fear of disgrace and perhaps also obscure dread of other dangers; such fear and dread may have influenced the will. Who can prove by experience that a cause is not present? Experience only shows that a cause is not perceived. But in such a case the so-called moral imperative, which as such appears to be categorical and unconditioned, would actually be only a pragmatic precept which makes us pay attention to our own advantage and merely teaches us to take such advantage into consideration.

We shall, therefore, have to investigate the possibility of a categorical imperative entirely a priori, inasmuch as we do not here have the advantage of having its reality given in experience and consequently of thus being obligated merely to explain its possibility rather than to establish it. In the meantime so much can be seen for now: the categorical imperative alone purports to be a practical law, while all the others may be called principles of the will but not laws. The reason for this is that whatever is necessary merely in order to attain some arbitrary purpose can be regarded as in itself contingent, and the precept can always be ignored once the purpose is abandoned. Contrariwise, an unconditioned command does not leave the will free to choose the opposite at its own liking. Consequently, only such a command carries with it that necessity which is demanded from a law.

Secondly, in the case of this categorical imperative, or law of morality, the reason for the difficulty (of discerning its possibility) is quite serious. The categorical imperative is an a priori synthetic practical proposition; and since discerning the possibility of propositions of this sort involves so much difficulty in theoretic knowledge, there may readily be gathered that there will be no less difficulty in practical knowledge.

In solving this problem, we want first to inquire whether perhaps the mere concept of a categorical imperative may not also supply us with the formula containing the proposition that can alone be a categorical imperative. For even when we know the purport of such an absolute command, the question as to how it is possible will still require a special and difficult effort, which we postpone to the last section.

If I think of a hypothetical imperative in general, I do not know beforehand what it will contain until its condition is given. But if I think of a categorical imperative, I know immediately what it contains. For since, besides the law, the imperative contains only the necessity that the maxim should accord with this law, while the law contains no condition to restrict it, there remains nothing but the universality of a law as such with which the maxim of the action should conform. This conformity alone is properly what is represented as necessary by the imperative.

Hence there is only one categorical imperative and it is this: Act only according to that maxim whereby you can at the same time will that it should become a universal law.

Now if all imperatives of duty can be derived from this one imperative as their principle, then there can at least be shown what is understood by the concept of duty and what it means, even though there is left undecided whether what is called duty may not be an empty concept.

The universality of law according to which effects are produced constitutes what is properly called nature in the most general sense (as to form), i.e., the existence of things as far as determined by universal laws. Accordingly, the universal imperative of duty may be expressed thus: Act as if the maxim of your action were to become through your will a universal law of nature.

Right Outcomes

Ethics that focuses on right outcomes is most commonly known as consequential ethics. It represents a shift away from assuming that some things are simply set in stone, and towards a view of humanity as the shaper of its own destiny. (In this volume we make a distinction that is not always made: between consequentialism, which looks to the outcome of actions; and teleology, which looks to the ultimate goal of actions and which belongs with the ecclesial approaches explored in Chapter Seven.) Consequentialism refers to a family of theories that hold in common their rejection of deontological ethics, whether divine command, natural law, or Kantian in character. The theories differ on their answer to three questions: What counts as a good outcome? Good for whom? And who decides? The history of consequentialism, however, is by no means as long as that of deontological ethics. It begins in earnest with the utilitarianism of the late eighteenth century. Most other consequentialist views define themselves in relation to utilitarianism.

Here we look at three texts – the classical exposition of utilitarianism by John Stuart Mill; the moderate and nuanced Roman Catholic adaptation of consequentialism by Richard McCormick, known as proportionalism; and the more extreme Protestant view known as situation ethics, which leaves deontological norms behind altogether.

John Stuart Mill, *Utilitarianism*

Jeremy Bentham (1748–1832) was a legal and social reformer who resolved human experience into two poles, pain and pleasure, and sought to maximize pleasure among the maximum number of people. He aspired to a complete code of law based on "the greatest happiness of the greatest number."

Bentham's student John Stuart Mill (1806–1873) coined the term "utilitarianism" as the title of his 1863 book. Mill refines Bentham's account of pleasure by distinguishing between the lower, bodily, sensual pleasures and the higher, intellectual, mental pleasures. The former can evoke contentment, but only the latter can genuinely lead to happiness. Mill famously summarized this distinction with the words, "It is better to be a human being dissatisfied than a pig satisfied; better to be Socrates dissatisfied than a fool satisfied."

Mill begins this chapter by referring to Epicureanism, a Greek philosophy that is unfairly regarded as synonymous with hedonism, or simply fulfilling desire. Mill wishes to expand the notion of "pleasure" well beyond the sensual and transitory. He gives precedence to those pleasures that most people have preferred, placing great store by "the judgment of those who are qualified by knowledge" of the respective pleasures concerned. He thus concedes that utilitarianism can "only attain its end by the general cultivation of nobleness of character," a point that ecclesial ethicists might otherwise be quick to highlight. The potential of this philosophy for the nonhuman creation seems small, but is hinted at in the final words of this passage.

John Stuart Mill. *Utilitarianism*. Ed. Roger Crisp. Oxford: Oxford University Press, 1998. From Chapter 2, "What Utilitarianism Is," pages 55–9. Available online at www.utilitarianism.com/mill1.htm.

The creed which accepts as the foundation of morals, Utility, or the Greatest Happiness Principle, holds that actions are right in proportion as they tend to promote happiness, wrong as they tend to produce the reverse of happiness. By happiness is intended pleasure, and the absence of pain; by unhappiness, pain, and the privation of pleasure. To give a clear view of the moral standard set up by the theory, much more requires to be said; in particular, what things it includes in the ideas of pain and pleasure; and to what extent this is left an open question. But these supplementary explanations do not affect the theory of life on which this theory of morality is grounded – namely, that pleasure, and freedom from pain, are the only things desirable as ends; and that all desirable things (which are as numerous in the utilitarian as in any other scheme) are desirable either for the pleasure inherent in themselves, or as means to the promotion of pleasure and the prevention of pain.

Now, such a theory of life excites in many minds, and among them in some of the most estimable in feeling and purpose, inveterate dislike. To suppose that life has (as they express it) no higher end than pleasure – no better and nobler object of desire and pursuit – they designate as utterly mean and grovelling; as a doctrine worthy only of swine, to whom the followers of Epicurus were, at a very early period, contemptuously likened; and modern holders of the doctrine are occasionally made the subject of equally polite comparisons by its German, French and English assailants.

When thus attacked, the Epicureans have always answered, that it is not they, but their accusers, who represent human nature in a degrading light; since the accusation supposes human beings to be capable of no pleasures except those of which swine are capable. If this supposition were true, the charge could not be gainsaid, but would then be no longer an imputation; for if the sources of pleasure were precisely the same to human beings and to swine, the rule of life which is good enough for the one would be good enough for the other. The comparison of the Epicurean life to that of beasts is felt as degrading, precisely because a beast's pleasures do not satisfy a human being's conceptions of happiness. Human beings have faculties more elevated than the animal appetites, and when once made conscious of them, do not regard anything as happiness which does not include their gratification. I do not, indeed, consider the Epicureans to have been by any means faultless in drawing out their scheme of consequences from the utilitarian principle. To do this in any sufficient manner, many Stoic, as well as Christian elements require to be included. But there is no known Epicurean theory of life which does not assign to the pleasures of the intellect, of the feelings and imagination, and of the moral sentiments, a much higher value as pleasures than to those of mere sensation. It must be admitted, however, that utilitarian writers in general have placed the superiority of mental over bodily pleasures chiefly in the greater permanency, safety, uncostliness, &c., of the former – that is, in their circumstantial advantages rather than in their intrinsic nature. And on all these points utilitarians have fully proved their case; but they might have taken the other, and, as it may be called, higher ground, with entire consistency. It is quite compatible with the principle of utility to recognize the fact, that some kinds of pleasure are more desirable and more valuable than others. It would be absurd that while, in estimating all other things, quality is considered as well as quantity, the estimation of pleasures should be supposed to depend on quantity alone.

If I am asked, what I mean by difference of quality in pleasures, or what makes one pleasure more valuable than another, merely as a pleasure, except its being greater in amount, there is but one possible answer. Of two pleasures, if there be one to which all or almost all who have experience of both give a decided preference, irrespective of any feeling of moral obligation to prefer it, that is the more desirable pleasure. If one of the two is, by those who are competently acquainted with both, placed so far above the other that they prefer it, even though knowing it to be attended with a greater amount of discontent, and would not resign it for any quantity of the other pleasure which their nature is capable of, we are justified in ascribing to the preferred enjoyment a superiority in quality, so far outweighing quantity as to render it, in comparison, of small account. …

It may be objected, that many who are capable of the higher pleasures, occasionally, under the influence of temptation, postpone them to the lower. But this is quite compatible with a full appreciation of the intrinsic superiority of the higher. Men often, from infirmity of character, make their election for the nearer good, though they know it to be the less valuable; and this no less when the choice is between two bodily pleasures, than when it is between bodily and mental. They pursue sensual indulgences to the injury of health, though perfectly aware that health is the greater good. It may be further objected, that many who begin with youthful enthusiasm for everything noble, as they advance in years sink into indolence and selfishness. But I do not believe that those who undergo this very common change, voluntarily choose the lower description of pleasures in preference to the higher. I believe that before they devote themselves exclusively to the one, they have already become incapable of the other. Capacity for the nobler feelings is in most natures a very tender plant, easily killed, not only by hostile influences, but by mere want of sustenance; and in the majority of young persons it speedily dies away if the occupations to which their position in life has devoted them, and the society into which it has thrown them, are not favourable to keeping that higher capacity in exercise. Men lose their high aspirations as they lose their intellectual tastes, because they have not time or opportunity for indulging them; and they addict themselves to inferior pleasures, not because they deliberately prefer them, but because they are either the only ones to which they have access, or the only ones which they are any longer capable of enjoying. It may be questioned whether any one who has remained equally susceptible to both classes of pleasures, ever knowingly and calmly preferred the lower; though many, in all ages, have broken down in an ineffectual attempt to combine both.

From this verdict of the only competent judges, I apprehend there can be no appeal. On a question which is the best worth having of two pleasures, or which of two modes of existence is the most grateful to the feelings, apart from its moral attributes and from its consequences, the judgment of those who are qualified by knowledge of both, or, if they differ, that of the majority among them, must be admitted as final. And needs be the less hesitation to accept this judgment respecting the quality of pleasures, since there is no other tribunal to be referred to even on the question of quantity. What means are there of determining which is the acutest of two pains, or the intensest of two pleasurable sensations, except the general suffrage of those who are familiar with both? Neither pains nor pleasures are homogeneous, and pain is always heterogeneous with pleasure. What is there to decide whether a particular pleasure is worth purchasing at the cost of a particular pain, except the feelings and judgment of the experienced? When, therefore, those feelings and judgments declare the pleasures derived from the higher faculties to be preferable in kind, apart from the question of intensity, to those of which the animal nature, disjoined from the higher faculties, is susceptible, they are entitled on this subject to the same regard.

I have dwelt on this point, as being a necessary part of a perfectly just conception of Utility or Happiness, considered as the directive rule of human conduct. But it is by no means an indispensable condition to the acceptance of the utilitarian standard; for that standard is not the agent's own greatest happiness, but the greatest amount of happiness altogether; and if it may possibly be doubted whether a noble character is always the happier for its nobleness, there can be no doubt that it makes other people happier, and that the world in general is immensely a gainer by it.

Utilitarianism, therefore, could only attain its end by the general cultivation of nobleness of character, even if each individual were only benefited by the nobleness of others, and his own, so far as happiness is concerned, were a sheer deduction from the benefit. But the bare enunciation of such an absurdity as this last, renders refutation superfluous.

According to the Greatest Happiness Principle, as above explained, the ultimate end, with reference to and for the sake of which all other things are desirable (whether we are considering our own good or that of other people), is an existence exempt as far as possible from pain, and as rich as possible in enjoyments, both in point of quantity and quality; the test of quality, and the rule for measuring it against quantity, being the preference felt by those who, in their opportunities of experience, to which must be added their habits of self-consciousness and self-observation, are best furnished with the means of comparison. This, being, according to the utilitarian opinion, the end of human action, is necessarily also the standard of morality; which may accordingly be defined, the rules and precepts for human conduct, by the observance of which an existence such as has been described might be, to the greatest extent possible, secured to all mankind; and not to them only, but, so far as the nature of things admits, to the whole sentient creation.

Richard A. McCormick, *Ambiguity in Moral Choice*

Richard A. McCormick (1922–2000) was a Jesuit formed in the pre-Vatican II tradition of casuistry. Casuistry is a discipline that involves perceptive analysis of a situation, recognition of what is important and what is not, judicious perception of the wider ramifications of the issue, accurate comparison of the case with similar cases, and careful crafting of a solution. He often remarked that tradition is not the dead faith of the living, but the living faith of the dead, and this commitment marked his transition from a conservative to a more revisionist stance on several issues.

McCormick was among those who developed a theory of proportionalism to respond to the papal tendency (in encyclicals such as *Humanae Vitae*) to stress absolute norms in moral theology. This theory argued that one can directly do nonmoral evil as a means (never as an end), provided that there is a proportionate reason. (Nonmoral evil refers to evil that may cause pain or suffering, but is not bad in itself. The term derives from the distinction between evil arising from human free will – usually known as sin – and "natural" evil such as an earthquake. The point is that it is sometimes necessary to cause pain for the sake of a greater good.) Echoing the medieval principle of double effect, this reasoning has been very influential in questions such as war, euthanasia, and abortion.

In this summary lecture, McCormick proposes that a hierarchy of goods (*ordo bonorum*) be employed to determine proportionate responsibilities in challenging circumstances. It is a classic example of what ecclesial ethicists often call "decisionist" ethics. The reasoning is elaborate and is beyond the sophistication of most people likely to find themselves in the situations McCormick describes, but the rigor of the attempt to find faithful and sustainable solutions is absorbing.

Richard A. McCormick. *Ambiguity in Moral Choice.* The 1973 Pere Marquette Theology Lecture. Milwaukee: Marquette University Press, 1973. From pages 1–2, 69, 98–106. Copyright © 1973 by Marquette University Press. Used by permission of the publisher. All rights reserved. www.marquette.edu/mupress/.

The distinction between what is directly voluntary and indirectly voluntary has been a staple of Catholic moral thought for centuries. It has been used to face many practical conflict-situations where an evil can be avoided or a more or less necessary good achieved only when another evil is reluctantly caused. In such situations the evil caused as one goes about doing good has been viewed as justified or tolerable under a fourfold condition. (1) The action is good or indifferent in itself; it is not morally evil. (2) The intention of the agent is upright, that is, the evil effect is sincerely not intended. (3) The evil effect must be equally immediate causally with the good effect, for otherwise it would be a means to the good effect and would be intended. (4) There must be a proportionately grave reason for allowing the evil to occur. If these conditions are fulfilled, the resultant evil was referred to as an "unintended byproduct" of the action, only indirectly voluntary and justified by the presence of a proportionately grave reason.

The practical importance of this distinction can be gathered from the areas where it has been applied in decision-making: killing (self-defense, warfare, abortion, euthanasia, suicide), risk to life (dangerous missions, rescue operations, experimentation), sterilization, contraception, sexual reactions, cooperation in another's evil action, scandal. Its appeal is attested to by the long line of prominent theologians who have used it in facing problems of the first magnitude such as the conduct of war. The most articulate contemporary exponent of the just war theory (Paul Ramsey) appeals to it frequently in his writings much as did John C. Ford, S.J. in his excellent work on obliteration bombing. Many other theologians fall back on the distinction, sometimes unwittingly, sometimes when it suits a rather obvious purpose. So settled, indeed, had the usage become in theological circles that the direct-indirect distinction has achieved a decisive prominence in some of the most influential and authoritative documents of the Church's magisterium.

[McCormick summarizes what he calls "some of the recent attempts to deal with conflict situations in a sinful and imperfect world." With each of these attempts, McCormick shares a "dissatisfaction with the narrowly behavioral or physical understanding of

human activity that underlies the standard interpretation of direct and indirect," and attempts his own critical synthesis in the following points.]

1   There is a difference between an intending and permitting will, and therefore in the human action involving the one or the other.

2   In a conflict situation, the relation of the evil to the value sought is partially determinative of the posture of the will (whether intending or permitting).

3   The basic structure, however, in conflict situations is avoidable – unavoidable evil, the principle of the lesser evil.

4   Both the intending and the permitting will (where evil is involved) are to be judged teleologically (that is, by presence or absence of proportionate reason).

5   Proportionate reason means three things: (a) a value at stake at least equal to that sacrificed; (b) no other way of salvaging it here and now; (c) its protection here and now will not undermine it in the long run.

6   The notion of proportionate reason is analogous.

An explanation of each of these will provide the context for my own modified understanding of the moral relevance of the direct-indirect distinction.

[McCormick explains his sixth principle.] … The criterion of proportionality is that ordo bonorum viewed in Christian perspective, for it is the ordo bonorum which is determinative of the good one should attempt to do and the criterion of the objectively loving character of one's activity. In the light of this ordo bonorum are three distinct possible and general senses of "proportionate reason."

First, there is the situation where the only alternative to causing or permitting evil is greater evil. This is the instance where both mother and fetus will certainly die without an abortion but where at least the mother can be saved with abortion. It is also the case of the drowning swimmer where the hopeful rescuer cannot be of help because he cannot swim. The mother cannot save the child; under no condition can she do him any good. Similarly the bystander cannot save the drowning man. He can do him no good. It would be immoral to try. One who cannot save another but still tries is no longer governed by the ordo bonorum. For love (as involving, besides benevolentia, also beneficentia) is always controlled by the possible. There is no genuine beneficentia if no good can accrue to the individual through my sacrifice. An act of love (as beneficentia) is not measured by the mere desire or intention (benevolentia).

Therefore, in instances like this, abortion and not attempting to save the drowning swimmer are proportionately grounded decisions precisely because the harm cannot be avoided, whereas harm to the mother and prospective rescuer can and should be avoided. Into this first category of proportionality would fall also the standard cases where falsehood is uttered as the necessary means to protect a patient's confidence and reputation, etc.

Secondly, proportionate reason in a different sense is realized in situations where the alternatives are not so obvious. This is the instance where I lay down my life for another (or others). In this instance a good equal to what I sacrifice accrues to another and is the only way of securing that good for him. This is proportionate not because his life is preferable to mine – they are equally valuable as basic human goods – but because in case of conflict, it is a human and Christian good to seek to secure this good for my neighbor even at the cost of my life. Indeed, other things being equal, such sacrifice is the ultimate act of human love. It is an assertion-in-action that "greater love than this no man has than that he lay down his life for his friends." To deny that such sacrifice could be proportionately grounded would be to deny that self-giving love after the model of Christ is a human good and represents the direction in which we should all be growing.

By saying that self-sacrifice to save the neighbor can truly be proportionate, traditional theology has implied that the goods being weighed, the alternatives are not simply physical human life, my life v. that of another. Rather it has implied: (a) a world in which conflict occurs; (b) a world in which we are not mature in charity; (c) that the most maturing choices in such a world of conflict and sin are, other things being equal, those which prefer the good of others to self after the example of Christ. Preference of another to self is only thinkable as a good in a world both **objectively** and **subjectively** infected by sin and weakness: "objectively" in terms of conflict situations where death and deprivation are tragic possibilities that cannot be prevented except by corresponding or greater loss; "subjectively" in terms of the fact that being immature in grace and love, we tend to view such situations in terms of our own personal good exclusively and primarily – whereas our growth and perfection as human beings are defined in terms of our being, like the Triune God himself, ad alterum, a being for others.

Thirdly, some actions or omissions were said to be proportionately grounded because the preference of a good for or in another at the cost of that good in or for myself should not, in view of human weakness and immaturity, be demanded. To say anything else would be to impose perfect love on imperfect creatures under pain of separation from divine friendship. This would be disproportionate because it would crush human beings and turn them from God. ...

Could we approach it as follows? It is important, first of all, to admit that the allegation that Christ knew nothing of "excusing causes," "extraordinary measures," "excessive inconvenience," etc. where fraternal love was involved is assuredly correct. However, Christ was proclaiming an ideal after which we should strive and which we will realize perfectly only after this life and the purgations preparatory to eternal life. "Love one another as I have loved you" is a magnificent ideal. Our growth and maturity depend on our continued pursuit of it. But nobody has ever achieved it. This disparity between ideal and achievement suggests an explanation of the maxim under discussion which will show that it is not incompatible with, but even demanded by, the gospel message. That is, it suggests the imperfection of our charity in this life.

What I have in mind is something like this. To propose a deep knowledge of the physical science as desirable, as an ideal, is one thing. To demand of a ten-year-old that he master the subtleties of atomic physics under pain of deprivation of further instruction probably means that I will put an end to the individual's whole educational process. To propose bodily health as an ideal is proper and necessary. To demand that a tubercular patient recover his health all at once under pain of relapse into serious illness means that he is condemned to ill health. Similarly, to propose the Savior's love as an ideal is helpful and necessary. But to demand of men's charity the perfection of virtue exemplified and preached by Jesus under pain of deprivation of charity itself (mortal sin) would be to condemn men to life in mortal sin. This can hardly be thought to be the message of One who knew men so thoroughly that he came to redeem them. Hence, when one asserts limits to charity, he is not emasculating the gospel message; he is rather asserting it, but insisting that it was proclaimed to imperfect men who must grow to its fullness. One dare not forget this. For if charity can be minimalized out of existence, it can also be maximalized out of existence. When proclamation and immediate demand are confused, the proclamation can easily be lost in the impossibility of the demand.

The adage we are dealing with, therefore, simply recognizes human limits and the consequent imperfection of our charity. It is saying that we do not lose divine life for failing to have and express its fullness now. The ideal remains. It is therefore to be sought, pursued, struggled after. But it is precisely because its achievement demands constant pursuit that it would be inconsistent with the charity of the gospel message to assert that its demands exceed the limitations of the human pursuer. This is the third sense of "proportionate reason."

This study would very tentatively conclude, therefore, that the traditional distinction between direct and indirect is neither as exclusively decisive as we previously thought, nor as widely dispensable as some recent studies suggest. As descriptive of the posture of the will toward a particular evil (whether intending or permitting), it only aids us in understanding what we are doing. Whether the action so described represents integral intentionality more generally and overall depends on whether it is, or is not, **all things considered**, the lesser evil in the circumstances. This is

an assessment that cannot be collapsed into a mere determination of direct and indirect voluntariety. Hence the traditional distinction, while morally relevant, cannot be the basis for deontologically exceptionless norms – which is not to say that there are no virtually exceptionless norms. Quite the contrary in my judgment.

This conclusion will no doubt appear rationally somewhat untidy. But it is, I believe, a reflection of the gap that exists between our moral sensitivities and judgments, and our ability to systematize them rationally. Moral awareness and judgments are fuller and deeper than "rational arguments" and rational categories. They have the result of evidence in the broadest sense – which includes a good deal more than mere rational analysis. While moral judgments must continually be submitted to rational scrutiny in an effort to correct and nuance them, in the last analysis, rooting as they do in the intransigence and complexity of reality, they remain deeper and more obscure than the systems and arguments we devise to make them explicit.

Joseph Fletcher, *Situation Ethics*

In his book *Situation Ethics* (1963), the Episcopal priest Joseph Fletcher (1905–1991) presented his model of ethics as a mean between what he called legalist (natural law and divine command) and antinomian (entirely spontaneous and unprincipled) ethics. He saw all laws as merely useful to the extent they could bring about love; and he regarded his ethic as embodying the love commandment of Jesus – although he later renounced Christianity. The central purpose is *agape* – loving one's neighbor as oneself.

"Only the command to love is categorically good," says Fletcher. He arrays a variety of contemporary and historical sources to add weight to his claim. Anxious to show he is no antinomian who has no place for law, he maintains, "Our obligation is relative to the situation, but obligation in the situation is absolute." Situation ethics is thus a balance of absolute and relative. Taking the example of sports and games, Fletcher suggests that ethical rules are like general guidelines for good play: "The best players are those who know when to ignore them." Circumstances do not just alter cases – they "alter rules and principles." This Fletcher summarizes as "an effort to relate love to a world of relativities through a casuistry obedient to love."

Fletcher notoriously never gives a detailed account of "love" that might justify such a wholesale commitment to it. But in maintaining that "when the impersonal universal conflicts with the personal particular, the latter prevails" he epitomized the spirit of his age.

Joseph Fletcher. *Situation Ethics: The New Morality.* Louisville: Westminster Press, 1966, 1997. From pages 17–18, 26–31. Extracts from *Situation Ethics* are copyright © Joseph Fletcher, 1963. Used by permission of Hymns Ancient & Modern Ltd.

Three Approaches

There are at bottom only three alternative routes or approaches to follow in making moral decisions. They are: (1) the legalistic; (2) the antinomian, the opposite extreme – i.e., a lawless or unprincipled approach; and (3) the situational. All three have played their part in the history of Western morals, legalism being by far the most common and persistent. Just as legalism triumphed among the Jews after the exile, so, in spite of Jesus' and Paul's revolt against it, it has managed to dominate Christianity constantly from very early days. As we shall be seeing, in many real-life situations legalism demonstrates what Henry Miller, in a shrewd phrase, calls "the immorality of morality."

There is an old joke which serves our purposes. A rich man asked a lovely young woman if she would sleep the night with him. She said, "No." He then asked if she would do it for $100,000? She said, "Yes!" He then asked, "$10,000?" She replied, "Well, yes, I would." His next question was, "How about $500?" Her indignant "What do you think I am?" was met by the answer, "We have already established *that*. Now we are haggling over the price." Does any girl who has "relations" (what a funny way to use the word) outside marriage automatically become a prostitute? Is it always, regardless of what she accomplishes for herself or others – is it *always* wrong? Is extramarital sex inherently evil, or can it be a good thing in some situations? Does everybody have his price, and if so, does that mean we are immoral and ethically weak? Let's see if we can find some help in answering these questions.

[Fletcher summarizes the legalistic and antinomian positions, then moves on to the situational.]

3. Situationism

A third approach, in between legalism and antinomian unprincipledness, is situation ethics. (To jump from one polarity to the other would be only to go from the frying pan to the fire.) The situationist enters into every decision-making situation fully armed with the ethical maxims of his community and its heritage, and he treats them with respect as illuminators of his problems. Just the same he is prepared in any situation to compromise them or set them aside *in the situation* if love seems better served by doing so.

Situation ethics goes part of the way with natural law, by accepting reason as the instrument of moral judgment, while rejecting the notion that the good is "given" in the nature of things, objectively. It goes part of the way with Scriptural law by accepting revelation as the source of the norm while rejecting all "revealed" norms or laws but the one command – to love God in the neighbor. The situationist follows a moral law or violates it according to love's need. For example, "Almsgiving is a good thing *if* ..." The situationist never says, "Almsgiving is a good thing. Period!" His decisions are hypothetical, not categorical. Only the commandment to love is categorically good. "Owe no one anything, except to love one another" (Rom 13:8). If help to an indigent only pauperizes and degrades him, the situationist refuses a handout and finds some other way. He makes no law out of Jesus' "Give to every one who begs from you." It is only one step from that kind of Biblicist literalism to the kind that causes women in certain sects to refuse blood transfusions even if death results – even if they are carrying a quickened fetus that will be lost too. The legalist says that even if he tells a man escaped from an asylum where his intended victim is, if he finds and murders him, at least only one sin has been committed (murder), not two (lying as well)!

As [Emil] Brunner puts it, "The basis of the Divine Command is always the same, but its content varies with varying circumstances." Therefore, the "error of casuistry does not lie in the fact that it indicates the infinite variety of forms which the Command of love may assume; its error consists in deducing particular laws from a universal law ... as though all could be arranged beforehand. ... Love, however, is free from all this predefinition." We might say, from the situationist's perspective, that it is possible to derive general "principles" from whatever is the one and only universal law (*agapē* for Christians, something else for others), but not laws or rules. We cannot milk universals from a universal!

William Temple put it this way: "Universal obligation attaches not to particular judgments of conscience but to conscientiousness. What acts are right may depend on circumstances ... but there is an absolute obligation to will whatever may on each occasion be right." Our obligation is relative to the situation, but obligation in the situation is absolute. We are only "obliged" to tell the truth, for example, if the situation calls for it; if a murderer asks us his victim's whereabouts, our duty might be to lie. There is in situation

ethics an absolute element and an element of calculation, as Alexander Miller once pointed out. But it would
be better to say it has an absolute *norm* and a calculating
method. There is weight in the old saying that what is
needed is "faith, hope, and clarity." We have to find out
what is "fitting" to be truly ethical, to use H. R. Niebuhr's
word for it in his *The Responsible Self*. Situation ethics
aims at a contextual appropriateness – not the "good"
or the "right" but the *fitting*.

A cartoon in a fundamentalist magazine once
showed Moses scowling, holding his stone tablet with
its graven laws, all ten, and an eager stonecutter saying
to him, "Aaron said perhaps you'd let us reduce them
to 'Act responsibly in love.'" This was meant as a dig at
the situationists and the new morality, but the legalist
humor in it merely states exactly what situation ethics
calls for! With Dietrich Bonhoeffer we say, "Principles
are only tools in God's hands, soon to be thrown away
as unserviceable."

One competent situationist [E. LaB. Cherbonnier],
speaking to students, explained the position this way.
Rules are "like 'Punt on fourth down,' or 'Take a
pitch when the count is three balls.' These rules are
part of the wise player's know-how and distinguish
him from the novice. But they are not unbreakable.
The best players are those who know when to ignore
them. In the game of bridge, for example, there is a
useful rule which says 'Second hand low.' But have you
ever played with anyone who followed the rule slav-
ishly? You say to him (in exasperation), 'Partner, why
didn't you play your ace? We could have set the hand.'
And he replies, unperturbed, 'Second hand low!' What
is wrong? The same thing that was wrong when Kant
gave information to the murderer. He forgot the
purpose of the game. ... He no longer thought of
winning the hand but of being able to justify himself by
invoking the rule."

This practical temper of the activist or *verb*-minded
decision maker, versus contemplative *noun*-minded-
ness is a major Biblical rather than Hellenistic trait. In
Abraham Heschel's view, "The insistence upon generalization at the price of a total disregard of the particular
and concrete is something which would be alien to prophetic thinking. Prophetic words are never detached
from the concrete, historic situation. Theirs is not a
timeless, abstract message; it always refers to an actual
situation. The general is given in the particular and the
verification of the abstract is in the concrete." A "leap
of faith" is an action decision rather than a leap of
thought, for a man's faith is a hypothesis that he takes
seriously enough to act on and live by.

There are various names for this approach: situationism, contextualism, occasionalism, circumstantial-
ism, even actualism. These labels indicate, of course,
that the core of the ethic they describe is a healthy and
primary awareness that "circumstances alter cases" –
i.e., that in actual problems of conscience the situational
variables are to be weighed as heavily as the normative
or "general" constants.

The situational factors are so primary that we may
even say "circumstances alter rules and principles." It is
said that when Gertrude Stein lay dying she declared,
"It is better to ask questions than to give answers,
even good answers." This is the temper of situation
ethics. It is empirical, fact-minded, data conscious,
inquiring. It is antimoralistic as well as antilegalistic,
for it is sensitive to variety and complexity. It is
neither simplistic nor perfectionist. It is "casuistry"
(case-based) in a constructive and nonpejorative
sense of the word. We should perhaps call it "neocasuistry." Like classical casuistry, it is case-focused
and concrete, concerned to bring Christian imperatives
into practical operation. But unlike classical casuistry,
this neocasuistry repudiates any attempt to
anticipate or prescribe real-life decisions in their existential particularity. It works with two guidelines
from Paul: "The written code kills, but the Spirit gives
life" (II Cor. 3:6), and "For the whole law is fulfilled in
one word, 'You shall love your neighbor as yourself'"
(Gal. 5:14).

In the words of Millar Burrows' finding in Biblical
theology: "He who makes the law his standard is obligated to perform all its precepts, for to break one commandment is to break the law. He who lives by faith and
love is not judged on that basis, but by a standard infinitely high and at the same time more attainable." This
is why Msgr. Pietro Palazzini (Secretary of the Sacred
Congregation of the Council) freely acknowledges that
situation ethics "must not be understood as an escape
from the heavy burden of moral integrity. For, though
its advocates truly deny the absolute value of universal
norms, so are they motivated by the belief that in this
manner they are better safeguarding the eminent sovereignty of God."

As we shall see, *Christian* situation ethics has only
one norm or principle or law (call it what you will) that
is binding and unexceptionable, always good and right
regardless of the circumstances. That is "love" – the
agapē of the summary commandment to love God and
neighbor. Everything else without exception, all laws
and rules and principles and ideals and norms, are only
contingent, only valid *if they happen* to serve love in any

situation. Christian situation ethics is not a system or program of living according to a code, but an effort to relate love to a world of relativities through a casuistry obedient to love. It is the strategy of love. This strategy denies that there are, as Sophocles thought, any unwritten immutable laws of heaven, agreeing with [Rudolf] Bultmann that all such notions are idolatrous and a demonic pretension.

In non-Christian situation ethics some other highest good or *summum bonum* will, of course, take love's place as the one and only standard – such as self-realization in the ethics of Aristotle. But the *Christian* is neighbor-centered first and last. Love is for people, not for principles; i.e., it is personal – and therefore when the impersonal universal conflicts with the personal particular, the latter prevails in situation ethics.

Right Relationships

Both deontological and consequential theories of ethics have a habit of focusing on the individual as the center of ethics. In the period following the Enlightenment, however, two significant developments contributed to the emergence of what we might describe as a third strand in universal ethics, one with significant aspects in common with each of the first two. In the modern era, by which we mean the era bequeathed by the Enlightenment, it was no longer possible for Europeans to imagine the world as a seamless Christian whole, in the way that had been more common in the medieval era. Not only was there a split between Catholics and Protestants, there were increasingly vocal elements that rejected a theological frame of reference as a ground for ethics, at least in the public sphere, and sometimes in the personal sphere too. Meanwhile, huge economic,

social, and political changes were taking place across Europe, to which churches, theologians, and philosophers were seeking to adapt. Three themes emerged from the late nineteenth century onwards that have come to hold important places in contemporary conversations: responsibility, rights, and justice.

The four excerpts that follow represent some of the breadth of this very lively tradition. *Rerum Novarum*, the first papal social encyclical, initiated a profound theme in subsequent social ethics. The reading from Bartolomé de las Casas shows the circumstances from which this style of reasoning arose. The UN Declaration represents what many of these assertions turn into when framed in a nontheological context. And the excerpt from John Rawls identifies the most influential account of justice in the contemporary West.

Pope Leo XIII, *Rerum Novarum (On Capital and Labor)*

During the papacy of Leo XIII (1810–1903, pope from 1878), there began a series of encyclicals from the Vatican that acknowledged the changing social and economic circumstances of the modern era, and sought to address these new conditions with an approach based around natural law. From 1963 the popes recognized a need to speak not just to Roman Catholics but to the world community.

The popes often refer to the sanctity of life and the dignity of the human person. The basic unit of society is the family, and through communities, nations, and the global society, every person has a place in a kind of family. There is a varying degree of coolness toward socialism, whose methods of analysis are sometimes commended but whose materialism and atheism are intolerable, and capitalism, whose commitment to private property is endorsed but whose tendency to exacerbate class struggles is noted.

The popes make significant use of rights language. Everyone has a right to the necessities for a full and flourishing life, such as medical care, education, employment, and a living wage. Everyone has the right to property (as this passage underlines), but the right to use the world's resources comes with a duty to attend to those who lack access to basic goods. Hence, employers must not "look upon their work people as their bondsmen, but … respect in every man his dignity as a person ennobled by Christian character."

The tone of this passage is universal, but, as with all the encyclicals, there are moments when more ecclesial language breaks through (see, for example, paragraphs 21 and 24, below). The description of the manner in which godly power is exercised is very telling: "with a fatherly solicitude which not only guides the whole, but reaches also individuals."

Pope Leo XIII. *Rerum Novarum* (On Capital and Labor). 1891. www.vatican.va/holy_father/leo_xiii/encyclicals/documents/hf_l-xiii_enc_15051891_rerum-novarum_en.html. Reprinted by permission of the Libreria Editrice Vaticana.

Rights and Duties of Capital and Labor

3. In any case we clearly see, and on this there is general agreement, that some opportune remedy must be found quickly for the misery and wretchedness pressing so unjustly on the majority of the working class: for the ancient workingmen's guilds were abolished in the last century, and no other protective organization took their place. Public institutions and the laws set aside the ancient religion. Hence, by degrees it has come to pass that working men have been surrendered, isolated and helpless, to the hardheartedness of employers and the greed of unchecked competition. The mischief has been increased by rapacious usury, which, although more than once condemned by the Church, is nevertheless, under a different guise, but with like injustice, still practiced by covetous and grasping men. To this must be added that the hiring of labor and the conduct of trade are concentrated in the hands of comparatively few; so that a small number of very rich men have been able to lay upon the teeming masses of the laboring poor a yoke little better than that of slavery itself. …

8. The fact that God has given the earth for the use and enjoyment of the whole human race can in no way be a bar to the owning of private property. For God has granted the earth to mankind in general, not in the sense that all without distinction can deal with it as they like, but rather that no part of it was assigned to any one in particular, and that the limits of private possession have been left to be fixed by man's own industry, and by the laws of individual races. Moreover, the earth, even though apportioned among private owners, ceases not thereby to minister to the needs of all, inasmuch as there is not one who does not sustain life from what the land produces. Those who do not possess the soil con-

tribute their labor; hence, it may truly be said that all human subsistence is derived either from labor on one's own land, or from some toil, some calling, which is paid for either in the produce of the land itself, or in that which is exchanged for what the land brings forth. …

16. … Doubtless, this most serious question demands the attention and the efforts of others besides ourselves – to wit, of the rulers of States, of employers of labor, of the wealthy, aye, of the working classes themselves, for whom We are pleading. But We affirm without hesitation that all the striving of men will be vain if they leave out the Church. It is the Church that insists, on the authority of the Gospel, upon those teachings whereby the conflict can be brought to an end, or rendered, at least, far less bitter; the Church uses her efforts not only to enlighten the mind, but to direct by her precepts the life and conduct of each and all; the Church improves and betters the condition of the working man by means of numerous organizations; does her best to enlist the services of all classes in discussing and endeavoring to further in the most practical way, the interests of the working classes; and considers that for this purpose recourse should be had, in due measure and degree, to the intervention of the law and of State authority. …

21. But the Church, with Jesus Christ as her Master and Guide, aims higher still. She lays down precepts yet more perfect, and tries to bind class to class in friendliness and good feeling. The things of earth cannot be understood or valued aright without taking into consideration the life to come, the life that will know no death. … God has not created us for the perishable and transitory things of earth, but for things heavenly and everlasting; He has given us this world as a place of exile, and not as our abiding place. As for riches and the other things which men call good and desirable, whether we have them in abundance, or are lacking in them – so far as eternal happiness is concerned – it makes no difference; the only important thing is to use them aright. Jesus Christ, when He redeemed us with plentiful

redemption, took not away the pains and sorrows which in such large proportion are woven together in the web of our mortal life. He transformed them into motives of virtue and occasions of merit; and no man can hope for eternal reward unless he follow in the blood-stained footprints of his Saviour. "If we suffer with Him, we shall also reign with Him." ...

24. From contemplation of this divine Model, it is more easy to understand that the true worth and nobility of man lie in his moral qualities, that is, in virtue; that virtue is, moreover, the common inheritance of men, equally within the reach of high and low, rich and poor; and that virtue, and virtue alone, wherever found, will be followed by the rewards of everlasting happiness. Nay, God Himself seems to incline rather to those who suffer misfortune; for Jesus Christ calls the poor "blessed"; He lovingly invites those in labor and grief to come to Him for solace; and He displays the tenderest charity toward the lowly and the oppressed. These reflections cannot fail to keep down the pride of the well-to-do, and to give heart to the unfortunate; to move the former to be generous and the latter to be moderate in their desires. Thus, the separation which pride would set up tends to disappear, nor will it be difficult to make rich and poor join hands in friendly concord. ...

27. ... Of these facts there cannot be any shadow of doubt: for instance, that civil society was renovated in every part by Christian institutions; that in the strength of that renewal the human race was lifted up to better things – nay, that it was brought back from death to life, and to so excellent a life that nothing more perfect had been known before, or will come to be known in the ages that have yet to be. Of this beneficent transformation Jesus Christ was at once the first cause and the final end; as from Him all came, so to Him was all to be brought back. For, when the human race, by the light of the Gospel message, came to know the grand mystery of the Incarnation of the Word and the redemption of man, at once the life of Jesus Christ, God and Man, pervaded every race and nation, and interpenetrated them with His faith, His precepts, and His laws. And if human society is to be healed now, in no other way can it be healed save by a return to Christian life and Christian institutions. When a society is perishing, the wholesome advice to give to those who would restore it is to call it to the principles from which it sprang; for the purpose and perfection of an association is to aim at and to attain that for which it is formed, and its efforts should be put in motion and inspired by the end and object which originally gave it being. Hence, to fall away from its primal constitution implies disease; to go back to it, recovery. And this may be asserted with utmost truth both of the whole body of the commonwealth and of that class of its citizens – by far the great majority – who get their living by their labor.

28. Neither must it be supposed that the solicitude of the Church is so preoccupied with the spiritual concerns of her children as to neglect their temporal and earthly interests. Her desire is that the poor, for example, should rise above poverty and wretchedness, and better their condition in life; and for this she makes a strong endeavor. By the fact that she calls men to virtue and forms them to its practice she promotes this in no slight degree. Christian morality, when adequately and completely practiced, leads of itself to temporal prosperity, for it merits the blessing of that God who is the source of all blessings; it powerfully restrains the greed of possession and the thirst for pleasure – twin plagues, which too often make a man who is void of self-restraint miserable in the midst of abundance; it makes men supply for the lack of means through economy, teaching them to be content with frugal living, and further, keeping them out of the reach of those vices which devour not small incomes merely, but large fortunes, and dissipate many a goodly inheritance. ...

31. It cannot, however, be doubted that to attain the purpose we are treating of [to provide aid for the needy], not only the Church, but all human agencies, must concur. All who are concerned in the matter should be of one mind and according to their ability act together. It is with this, as with providence that governs the world; the results of causes do not usually take place save where all the causes cooperate. It is sufficient, therefore, to inquire what part the State should play in the work of remedy and relief.

32. By the State we here understand, not the particular form of government prevailing in this or that nation, but the State as rightly apprehended; that is to say, any government conformable in its institutions to right reason and natural law, and to those dictates of the divine wisdom which we have expounded in the encyclical *On the Christian Constitution of the State*. The foremost duty, therefore, of the rulers of the State should be to make sure that the laws and institutions, the general character and administration of the commonwealth, shall be such as of themselves to realize public well-being and private prosperity. This is the proper scope of wise statesmanship and is the work of the rulers. Now a State chiefly prospers and thrives through moral rule, well-regulated family life, respect for religion and justice, the moderation and fair impos-

ing of public taxes, the progress of the arts and of trade, the abundant yield of the land – through everything, in fact, which makes the citizens better and happier. Hereby, then, it lies in the power of a ruler to benefit every class in the State, and amongst the rest to promote to the utmost the interests of the poor; and this in virtue of his office, and without being open to suspicion of undue interference – since it is the province of the commonwealth to serve the common good. And the more that is done for the benefit of the working classes by the general laws of the country, the less need will there be to seek for special means to relieve them. ...

35. We have said that the State must not absorb the individual or the family; both should be allowed free and untrammelled action so far as is consistent with the common good and the interest of others. Rulers should, nevertheless, anxiously safeguard the community and all its members; the community, because the conservation thereof is so emphatically the business of the supreme power, that the safety of the commonwealth is not only the first law, but it is a government's whole reason of existence; and the members, because both philosophy and the Gospel concur in laying down that the object of the government of the State should be, not the advantage of the ruler, but the benefit of those over whom he is placed. As the power to rule comes from God, and is, as it were, a participation in His, the highest of all sovereignties, it should be exercised as the power of God is exercised – with a fatherly solicitude which not only guides the whole, but reaches also individuals.

36. Whenever the general interest or any particular class suffers, or is threatened with harm, which can in no other way be met or prevented, the public authority must step in to deal with it. Now, it is to the interest of the community, as well as of the individual, that peace and good order should be maintained; that all things should be carried on in accordance with God's laws and those of nature; that the discipline of family life should be observed and that religion should be obeyed; that a high standard of morality should prevail, both in public and private life; that justice should be held sacred and that no one should injure another with impunity; that the members of the commonwealth should grow up to man's estate strong and robust, and capable, if need be, of guarding and defending their country.

Bartolomé de las Casas, *History of the Indies*

Bartolomé de las Casas (1484–1566), Dominican friar and Bishop of Chiapas in southeast Mexico, was horrified by the conquistadores' atrocious treatment of the indigenous peoples of what became known as Latin America. He advocated for the self-determination of peoples, believing that power resides in the populace, and that rulers should serve the people and gain their consent when implementing significant actions.

In this prologue to his history of Latin America, he blends several significant kinds of arguments. He has a strongly teleological inclination: when he refers to "the goal for which divine Providence meant the discovery of those peoples and those lands" (i.e., the conversion and salvation of the Indian peoples) he is tracing ethics from the *telos* of salvation back to the evaluation of present-day actions. This is a style of argument associated with Aristotle and most closely associated, in today's debates, with ecclesial ethics. But he quickly goes on to assert "the dignity of any rational being ... singularly endowed over and above the universality of inferior creatures [i.e., animals]." This is language that puts him squarely among the forebears of the modern human rights tradition. It is interesting that he locates that dignity, not as self-evident in itself, but as under "divine care." Then he switches back to a more Aristotelian notion of natural law, with the words "nature works always, or almost always, for the perfection of all forms of inferior life" – and he uses this argument to plead for the native American peoples to be given time to emerge from ignorance to maturity, just as the Spanish themselves did many centuries before.

Bartolomé de las Casas. *History of the Indies.* Trans. and ed. Andrée Collard. New York: Harper and Row, 1971. From the Prologue, pages 4–8. Portions available online at www.columbia.edu/acis/ets/CCREAD/lascasas.htm. Copyright © 1971 by Andrée Collard, renewed © 1999 by Joyce J. Contrucci. Reprinted by permission of Joyce J. Contrucci.

Prologue

I can ... truly affirm that I was moved to write this book by the great and desperate need all Spain has of truth and enlightenment on all matters relating to this Indian world. What damage, calamities, disruptions, decimations of kingdoms, what millions of souls lost, how many unforgivable sins committed, what blindness and torpor of mind, what harms and evils past and present have been caused to the kingdoms of Castile by the shortcomings and mistakes of Spain! I am certain that they cannot ever be enumerated, weighed, measured and lamented enough from now until the final and fearful Day of Judgment.

I see that some have written of Indian things, not those they witnessed, but rather those they heard about, and not too well – although they themselves will never admit it. They write to the detriment of Truth, preoccupied as they are with a sterile, unfruitful arid superficiality, without penetrating that which would nourish and edify man's reason, to which everything must be subordinated. They waste their time telling about things that only fill the ears with air and satisfy our craving for novelty, the shorter the better, since that is least capable of wounding the reader's mind. And because they did not work the field of controversy with the plow of Christian discretion and prudence, they planted the arid, wild, sterile seed of their human and temporal feelings from which have sprung up and grown a deadly discord, scandalous and erroneous knowledge, and perverse conscience in a multitude of people, to such a degree that the Catholic Faith and the ancient Christian customs of the universal Church have suffered irreparable harm. The reason for this lies in the ignorance of the goal for which divine Providence meant the discovery of those peoples and those lands, which is none other, since we are mortal, than the conversion and salvation of those souls, to which end all temporal concerns must necessarily be subordinated. It lies in the ignorance, too, of the dignity of any rational being, never so unsheltered and destitute of divine care that he is not singularly endowed over and above the universality of inferior creatures. Hence it was not possible that over such extensive regions so many and innumerable kinds of men should be allowed to be born naturally and all-inclusively monstrous, that is to say, without reason and the ability to govern their domestic affairs. Since nature works always, or almost always, for the perfection of all forms of inferior life, so much the more then, since we deal with men, as will be evident throughout my *History*, are they gifted with better judgment and greater ability to rule themselves. In this the Indians surpass all other infidels; they even surpass, as we shall see, other self-presuming nations which hold them in contempt.

Such historians have also ignored another necessary and Catholic principle, that is to say, there is not and there has never been in the history of mankind a nation from which, especially after the Incarnation and Passion of the Saviour, there cannot be selected and composed that innumerable multitude of St. John's vision – Chapter 7 of the Apocalypse – that body of the Elect which St. Paul called the mystical Body of Christ and Church. Consequently, divine Providence must have naturally disposed these people for indoctrination and divine grace, reserving the time of their calling and conversion, as it did and we believe will always do toward all other nations outside the holy Church, as long as it endures. ... Since we believe that God predestined a few select ones from all parts of the world, appointing a time for their calling and glorification, and since we do not know who these might be, we must esteem and judge all men, trying to help them inasmuch as we desire their salvation. As for ourselves, we must see that our works be instrumental to their predestination as if we were all sure of being Elect ourselves. ...

Such historians make another mistake. If they had read the ancient historians, holy and profane, they would know that there never was a people, before or after the Flood, who, no matter how politically well organized and urbane it may be now, was not in its beginnings full of wild and irrational defects and abounding in grave and nefarious idolatry. Many nations, today smoothly organized and Christianized, lived like animals, without houses and without cities, before their conversion to the Faith. Therefore, since uncultivated soil produces only thistle and thorns but possesses the innate goodness to yield useful fruit if it is cultivated, so all manner of men, however barbaric or bestial, possess the use of reason and are capable of being taught. Consequently, no man and no nation in the world, however barbarian or inhuman, is incapable of bearing the reasonable fruit of excellence, if taught in the manner required for the natural condition of man, especially with the doctrine of the Faith. ... We could cite many examples of this, but let that of Spain suffice.

All historians know the barbaric simplicity and ferocity of the Spanish people, especially those of Andalusia and other provinces of Spain, at the time the Greeks first colonized Monviedro and when the pirate captain Alceus and the Phoenicians came to Cádiz. These were very astute people; the natives were like animals in comparison. Now see the foolishness and simplicity of the Andalusians! Who could fool them! And, by the grace of God, what nation surpasses Spain in matters of faith? It should be that much easier then to induce and persuade those who govern themselves by reason in their social life and human contacts – as for the most part do all the nations of these our Indies – to cultivate the true and perfect virtues of the Christian religion, the only religion that can cleanse uncultivated nations of their faults.

The lack of knowledge of ancient customs caused many ignorant people to marvel and hold as new and monstrous … the Indians' natural and moral defects, as if all of us were naturally and morally perfect and very holy in spiritual and Christian matters! Secondly, if they were not so ignorant, they would realize that all people experience difficulties in being converted and in converting: pain, labor, sweat, anguish, contradictions, incredible persecutions, schisms and controversies. Even among the Christians themselves, the Apostles and Disciples of Christ suffered by preaching and promulgating the Gospels in order to bring the Christian religion at all times and in all places, and so did all true preachers because God willed it so. Spain is a good example since in all of its territory St. James could win only seven or nine proselytes to Christ's militia.

As will be obvious to anyone who cares to look into it, ignorance of the above caused learned and non-learned men to make incomparably harmful mistakes about the inhabitants of this world. Some have inverted the spiritual end of this whole affair by making it the means; and the means – that is to say, temporal and profane things, which even pagan philosophers say must always be subordinate to virtue – have come to constitute the end of this Christian exercise. … From this grave transposition it necessarily follows that these nations are looked upon with contempt and their inhabitants held as beasts incapable of doctrine and virtue, used by the Spaniards with no more consideration than men use bread and wine and similar things, which merely by being used are consumed. The Indians contributed to this contempt and annihilation by being

toto genere gentle and humble, extremely poor, defenseless, very simple and, above all, people long-suffering and patient. For this reason our Spaniards had and still have today ample room to do whatever they wish with them, treating each and every one in a like manner, regardless of sex, age, status, or dignity, as my *History* will show. From this also springs the fact that they have no scruples or fear in despoiling and deposing their natural kings and nobles. God, nature and the common law of men made them rulers, confirmed and authorized by divine law. By ignoring this as well as the rules and dispositions of natural, divine and human law, one fails to take into account the three different kinds of infidels. One, those who usurp unjustly our lands and kingdoms. Two, those who molest, fatigue and oppose us, not only by disturbing or intending to disturb the temporal state of our Republic, but also the spiritual, by seeking, as their main objective, to overthrow our holy Faith, the Christian religion and the whole Catholic Church. Three, those who have never usurped anything from us and never owed us anything, who never disturbed or offended us, who never knew of the existence of our Christian religion or of ourselves, who lived in their own natural lands in kingdoms extremely different from ours. Whenever and wherever in the universe one discovers this last group, no matter how many grave sins they may possess – idolatry and others – we can only treat them with the love, peace and Christian charity which we owe them, attract them, as we would be attracted ourselves, to the holy Faith through sweet and humble evangelical preaching in the form established by Christ, Our Lord and Master. All the Indians of our transatlantic Indies belong to this third category of infidels. To this end and to no other was the Holy See able legally to establish, by the authority of Christ, the kings of Castile and Leon as sovereign and universal princes of all this vast Indian world. Their natural kings and nobles were to be maintained in their own kingdoms, land and subjects untouched, and each one required to recognize the kings of Castile and Leon as superior and universal princes, because it was considered necessary for the sowing and conservation of the Christian Faith throughout the Indies. And about this universal sovereignty, many have erred most grievously and perniciously, by believing blindly that it was not compatible with that of the natural lords of the Indians, as I have shown in a special treatise I wrote through divine grace.

General Assembly of the United Nations, Universal Declaration of Human Rights

The high water mark of human rights aspirations was the Universal Declaration of Human Rights adopted by the United Nations General Assembly in 1948. These rights were later, in 1966, divided into civil and political rights, and economic, social, and cultural rights. Specific rights named include the rights to life, liberty, security, equality before the law, to avoid enslavement or torture, to freedom of conscience and religion, to education, to work (in healthy conditions), to leisure, and to freedom of movement. Subsequent international legislation has sought to defend women, children, and those vulnerable to racism, genocide, or torture. The work of Amnesty International and other campaigning organizations has made human rights a central and popular global social cause.

The French Catholic theologian Jacques Maritain and the American stateswoman Eleanor Roosevelt were among those closely involved with the drafting. The preamble recognizes seven circumstances that the declaration regards as unarguable. These acknowledge the recent history of "barbarous acts": the Nazi atrocities, and the contradiction they constituted to any notion of historical moral progress, are fresh in the mind. They articulate the "highest aspiration" for humanity as "freedom of speech and belief and freedom from fear and want." But they also acknowledge that the notion of fundamental rights is a matter of "faith". There is nowhere in this document the same level of confidence as, for example, in the United States Constitution (1787), whose authors "hold these truths to be self-evident." Here, "universal respect for and observance of human rights and fundamental freedoms" are things members states do not simply identify, but "have pledged themselves to achieve."

Whereas recognition of the inherent dignity and of the equal and inalienable rights of all members of the human family is the foundation of freedom, justice and peace in the world,

Whereas disregard and contempt for human rights have resulted in barbarous acts which have outraged the conscience of mankind, and the advent of a world in which human beings shall enjoy freedom of speech and belief and freedom from fear and want has been proclaimed as the highest aspiration of the common people,

Whereas it is essential, if man is not to be compelled to have recourse, as a last resort, to rebellion against tyranny and oppression, that human rights should be protected by the rule of law,

Whereas it is essential to promote the development of friendly relations between nations,

Whereas the peoples of the United Nations have in the Charter reaffirmed their faith in fundamental human rights, in the dignity and worth of the human person and in the equal rights of men and women and have determined to promote social progress and better standards of life in larger freedom,

Whereas Member States have pledged themselves to achieve, in co-operation with the United Nations, the promotion of universal respect for and observance of human rights and fundamental freedoms,

Whereas a common understanding of these rights and freedoms is of the greatest importance for the full realization of this pledge,

Now, Therefore the General Assembly proclaims this Universal Declaration of Human Rights as a common standard of achievement for all peoples and all nations, to the end that every individual and every organ of society, keeping this Declaration constantly in mind, shall strive by teaching and education to promote respect for these rights and freedoms and by progressive measures, national and international, to secure their universal and effective recognition and observance, both among the peoples of Member States themselves and among the peoples of territories under their jurisdiction.

Article 1. All human beings are born free and equal in dignity and rights. They are endowed with reason and conscience and should act towards one another in a spirit of brotherhood.

Article 2. Everyone is entitled to all the rights and freedoms set forth in this Declaration, without distinction of any kind, such as race, colour, sex, language, religion, political or other opinion, national or social origin, property, birth or other status. Furthermore, no distinction shall be made on the basis of the political, jurisdictional or international status of the country or territory to which a person belongs, whether it be independent, trust, non-self-governing or under any other limitation of sovereignty.

Article 3. Everyone has the right to life, liberty and security of person.

Article 4. No one shall be held in slavery or servitude; slavery and the slave trade shall be prohibited in all their forms.

Article 5. No one shall be subjected to torture or to cruel, inhuman or degrading treatment or punishment.

Article 6. Everyone has the right to recognition everywhere as a person before the law.

Article 7. All are equal before the law and are entitled without any discrimination to equal protection of the law. All are entitled to equal protection against any discrimination in violation of this Declaration and against any incitement to such discrimination.

Article 8. Everyone has the right to an effective remedy by the competent national tribunals for acts violating the fundamental rights granted him by the constitution or by law.

Article 9. No one shall be subjected to arbitrary arrest, detention or exile.

Article 10. Everyone is entitled in full equality to a fair and public hearing by an independent and impartial tribunal, in the determination of his rights and obligations and of any criminal charge against him.

Article 11.

(1) Everyone charged with a penal offence has the right to be presumed innocent until proved guilty according to law in a public trial at which he has had all the guarantees necessary for his defence.

(2) No one shall be held guilty of any penal offence on account of any act or omission which did not constitute a penal offence, under national or international law, at the time when it was committed. Nor shall a heavier penalty be imposed than the one that was applicable at the time the penal offence was committed.

Article 12. No one shall be subjected to arbitrary interference with his privacy, family, home or correspondence, nor to attacks upon his honour and reputation. Everyone has the right to the protection of the law against such interference or attacks.

Article 13.

(1) Everyone has the right to freedom of movement and residence within the borders of each state.

(2) Everyone has the right to leave any country, including his own, and to return to his country.

Article 14.

(1) Everyone has the right to seek and to enjoy in other countries asylum from persecution.

(2) This right may not be invoked in the case of prosecutions genuinely arising from non-political crimes or from acts contrary to the purposes and principles of the United Nations.

Article 15.

(1) Everyone has the right to a nationality.

(2) No one shall be arbitrarily deprived of his nationality nor denied the right to change his nationality.

Article 16.

(1) Men and women of full age, without any limitation due to race, nationality or religion, have the right to marry and to found a family. They are entitled to equal rights as to marriage, during marriage and at its dissolution.

(2) Marriage shall be entered into only with the free and full consent of the intending spouses.

(3) The family is the natural and fundamental group unit of society and is entitled to protection by society and the State.

Article 17.

(1) Everyone has the right to own property alone as well as in association with others.

(2) No one shall be arbitrarily deprived of his property.

Article 18. Everyone has the right to freedom of thought, conscience and religion; this right includes freedom to change his religion or belief, and freedom, either alone or in community with others and in public or private, to manifest his religion or belief in teaching, practice, worship and observance.

Article 19. Everyone has the right to freedom of opinion and expression; this right includes freedom to hold opinions without interference and to seek, receive and impart information and ideas through any media and regardless of frontiers.

Article 20.

(1) Everyone has the right to freedom of peaceful assembly and association.

(2) No one may be compelled to belong to an association.

Article 21.

(1) Everyone has the right to take part in the government of his country, directly or through freely chosen representatives.

(2) Everyone has the right of equal access to public service in his country.

(3) The will of the people shall be the basis of the authority of government; this will shall be expressed in periodic and genuine elections which shall be by universal and equal suffrage and shall be held by secret vote or by equivalent free voting procedures.

Article 22. Everyone, as a member of society, has the right to social security and is entitled to realization, through national effort and international co-operation and in accordance with the organization and resources of each State, of the economic, social and cultural rights indispensable for his dignity and the free development of his personality.

Article 23.

(1) Everyone has the right to work, to free choice of employment, to just and favourable conditions of work and to protection against unemployment.

(2) Everyone, without any discrimination, has the right to equal pay for equal work.

(3) Everyone who works has the right to just and favourable remuneration ensuring for himself and his family an existence worthy of human dignity, and supplemented, if necessary, by other means of social protection.

(4) Everyone has the right to form and to join trade unions for the protection of his interests.

Article 24. Everyone has the right to rest and leisure, including reasonable limitation of working hours and periodic holidays with pay.

Article 25.

(1) Everyone has the right to a standard of living adequate for the health and well-being of himself and of his family, including food, clothing, housing and medical care and necessary social services, and the right to security in the event of unemployment, sickness, disability, widowhood, old age or other lack of livelihood in circumstances beyond his control.

(2) Motherhood and childhood are entitled to special care and assistance. All children, whether born in or out of wedlock, shall enjoy the same social protection.

Article 26.

(1) Everyone has the right to education. Education shall be free, at least in the elementary and fundamental stages. Elementary education shall be compulsory. Technical and professional education shall be made generally available and higher education shall be equally accessible to all on the basis of merit.

(2) Education shall be directed to the full development of the human personality and to the strengthening of respect for human rights and fundamental freedoms. It shall promote understanding, tolerance and friendship among all nations, racial or religious groups, and shall further the activities of the United Nations for the maintenance of peace.

(3) Parents have a prior right to choose the kind of education that shall be given to their children.

Article 27.

(1) Everyone has the right freely to participate in the cultural life of the community, to enjoy the arts and to share in scientific advancement and its benefits.

(2) Everyone has the right to the protection of the moral and material interests resulting from any scientific, literary or artistic production of which he is the author.

Article 28. Everyone is entitled to a social and international order in which the rights and freedoms set forth in this Declaration can be fully realized.

Article 29.

(1) Everyone has duties to the community in which alone the free and full development of his personality is possible.

(2) In the exercise of his rights and freedoms, everyone shall be subject only to such limitations as are determined by law solely for the purpose of securing due recognition and respect for the rights and freedoms of others and of meeting the just requirements of morality, public order and the general welfare in a democratic society.

(3) These rights and freedoms may in no case be exercised contrary to the purposes and principles of the United Nations.

Article 30. Nothing in this Declaration may be interpreted as implying for any State, group or person any right to engage in any activity or to perform any act aimed at the destruction of any of the rights and freedoms set forth herein.

John Rawls, *A Theory of Justice*

A Theory of Justice was published in 1971 by the Harvard philosopher John Rawls (1921–2002). Rawls outlines what he calls the "original position," which in some ways resembles the "state of nature" often recalled by Enlightenment thinkers. In the original position, human beings were self-interested, equally able to propose models of society, rational, equally in possession of the relevant facts, and, crucially, under a "veil of ignorance" about their future station in life, wealth, character, and abilities. This veil of ignorance ensures mutual benevolence, because no one would wish to make an enemy of a person they might later badly need as a friend. It excludes utilitarianism, because no one would take the risk that theirs would be the happiness that would be sacrificed for that of the greatest number.

Hence, Rawls derives two principles of justice:

1 Liberty – each person should have equal access to the most extensive total system of equal basic liberties compatible with a similar system of liberty for all.
2 Difference – social and economic inequalities are to be arranged so that they are both (a) to the greatest benefit of the least advantaged, and (b) attached to offices and positions open to all under conditions of fair equality of opportunity.

It is significant that Rawls rejects utilitarianism with the words "the principle of utility is incompatible with the conception of social cooperation among equals for mutual advantage." Meanwhile, "there is no injustice in the greater benefits earned by a few provided that the situation of persons not so fortunate is thereby improved."

This passage summarizes what has been perhaps the most influential account of justice in the post-World War II era. The final paragraph hints, for example, at the way rational choice theory would become a dominant mode of discourse in political science.

John Rawls. *A Theory of Justice*. Revised edn. Cambridge, MA: Belknap Press, 1999. From Chapter 1, "Justice as Fairness," pages 11–16. Reprinted by permission of the publisher. Copyright © 1971, 1999 by the President and Fellows of Harvard College.

My aim is to present a conception of justice which generalizes and carries to a higher level of abstraction the familiar theory of the social contract as found, say, in Locke, Rousseau, and Kant. In order to do this we are not to think of the original contract as one to enter a particular society or to set up a particular form of government. Rather, the guiding idea is that the principles of justice for the basic structure of society are the object of the original agreement. They are the principles that free and rational persons concerned to further their own interests would accept in an initial position of equality as defining the fundamental terms of their association. These principles are to regulate all further agreements; they specify the kinds of social cooperation that can be entered into and the forms of government that can be established. This way of regarding the principles of justice I shall call justice as fairness.

Thus we are to imagine that those who engage in social cooperation choose together, in one joint act, the principles which are to assign basic rights and duties and to determine the division of social benefits. Men are to decide in advance how they are to regulate their claims against one another and what is to be the foundation charter of their society. Just as each person must decide by rational reflection what constitutes his good, that is, the system of ends which it is rational for him to pursue, so a group of persons must decide once and for all what is to count among them as just and unjust. The choice which rational men would make in this hypothetical situation of equal liberty, assuming for the present that this choice problem has a solution, determines the principles of justice.

In justice as fairness the original position of equality corresponds to the state of nature in the traditional theory of the social contract. This original position is not, of course, thought of as an actual historical state of affairs, much less as a primitive condition of culture. It is understood as a purely hypothetical situation characterized so as to lead to a certain conception of justice. Among the essential features of this situation is that no one knows his place in society, his class position or social status, nor does any one know his fortune in the distribution of natural assets and abilities, his intelligence, strength, and the like. I shall even assume that the parties do not know their conceptions of the good or their special psychological propensities. The principles of justice are chosen behind a veil of ignorance. This ensures that no one is advantaged or disadvantaged in the choice of principles by the outcome of natural chance or the contingency of social circumstances. Since all are similarly situated and no one is able to design principles to favor his particular condition, the principles of justice are the result of a fair agreement or bargain. For given the circumstances of the original position, the symmetry of everyone's relations to each other, this initial situation is fair between individuals as moral persons, that is, as rational beings with their own ends and capable, I shall assume, of a sense of justice. The original position is, one might say, the appropriate initial status quo, and thus the fundamental agreements reached in it are fair. This explains the propriety of the name "justice as fairness": it conveys the idea that the principles of justice are agreed to in an initial situation that is fair. The name does not mean that the concepts of justice and fairness are the same, any more than the phrase "poetry as metaphor" means that the concepts of poetry and metaphor are the same.

Justice as fairness begins, as I have said, with one of the most general of all choices which persons might make together, namely, with the choice of the first principles of a conception of justice which is to regulate all subsequent criticism and reform of institutions. Then, having chosen a conception of justice, we can suppose that they are to choose a constitution and a legislature to enact laws, and so on, all in accordance with the principles of justice initially agreed upon. Our social situation is just if it is such that by this sequence of hypothetical agreements we would have contracted into the general system of rules which defines it. Moreover, assuming that the original position does determine a set

of principles (that is, that a particular conception of justice would be chosen), it will then be true that whenever social institutions satisfy these principles those engaged in them can say to one another that they are cooperating on terms to which they would agree if they were free and equal persons whose relations with respect to one another were fair. They could all view their arrangements as meeting the stipulations which they would acknowledge in an initial situation that embodies widely accepted and reasonable constraints on the choice of principles. The general recognition of this fact would provide the basis for a public acceptance of the corresponding principles of justice. No society can, of course, be a scheme of cooperation which men enter voluntarily in a literal sense; each person finds himself placed at birth in some particular position in some particular society, and the nature of this position materially affects his life prospects. Yet a society satisfying the principles of justice as fairness comes as close as a society can to being a voluntary scheme, for it meets the principles which free and equal persons would assent to under circumstances that are fair. In this sense its members are autonomous and the obligations they recognize self-imposed.

One feature of justice as fairness is to think of the parties in the initial situation as rational and mutually disinterested. This does not mean that the parties are egoists, that is, individuals with only certain kinds of interests, say in wealth, prestige, and domination. But they are conceived as not taking an interest in one another's interests. They are to presume that even their spiritual aims may be opposed, in the way that the aims of those of different religions may be opposed. Moreover, the concept of rationality must be interpreted as far as possible in the narrow sense, standard in economic theory, of taking the most effective means to given ends. I shall modify this concept to some extent, as explained later, but one must try to avoid introducing into it any controversial ethical elements. The initial situation must be characterized by stipulations that are widely accepted.

In working out the conception of justice as fairness one main task clearly is to determine which principles of justice would be chosen in the original position. To do this we must describe this situation in some detail and formulate with care the problem of choice which it presents. These matters I shall take up in the immediately succeeding chapters. It may be observed, however, that once the principles of justice are thought of as arising from an original agreement in a situation of equality, it is an open question whether the principle of utility would be acknowledged. Offhand it hardly seems likely that persons who view themselves as equals, entitled to press their claims upon one another, would agree to a principle which may require lesser life prospects for some simply for the sake of a greater sum of advantages enjoyed by others. Since each desires to protect his interests, his capacity to advance his conception of the good, no one has a reason to acquiesce in an enduring loss for himself in order to bring about a greater net balance of satisfaction. In the absence of strong and lasting benevolent impulses, a rational man would not accept a basic structure merely because it maximized the algebraic sum of advantages irrespective of its permanent effects on his own basic rights and interests. Thus it seems that the principle of utility is incompatible with the conception of social cooperation among equals for mutual advantage. It appears to be inconsistent with the idea of reciprocity implicit in the notion of a well-ordered society. Or, at any rate, so I shall argue.

I shall maintain instead that the persons in the initial situation would choose two rather different principles: the first requires equality in the assignment of basic rights and duties, while the second holds that social and economic inequalities, for example inequalities of wealth and authority, are just only if they result in compensating benefits for everyone, and in particular for the least advantaged members of society. These principles rule out justifying institutions on the grounds that the hardships of some are offset by a greater good in the aggregate. It may be expedient but it is not just that some should have less in order that others may prosper. But there is no injustice in the greater benefits earned by a few provided that the situation of persons not so fortunate is thereby improved. The intuitive idea is that since everyone's well-being depends upon a scheme of cooperation without which no one could have a satisfactory life, the division of advantages should be such as to draw forth the willing cooperation of everyone taking part in it, including those less well situated. The two principles mentioned seem to be a fair basis on which those better endowed, or more fortunate in their social position, neither of which we can be said to deserve, could expect the willing cooperation of others when some workable scheme is a necessary condition of the welfare of all. Once we decide to look for a conception of justice that prevents the use of the accidents of natural endowment and the contingencies of social circumstance as counters in a quest for political and economic advantage, we are led to these principles.

They express the result of leaving aside those aspects of the social world that seem arbitrary from a moral point of view.

The problem of the choice of principles, however, is extremely difficult. I do not expect the answer I shall suggest to be convincing to everyone. It is, therefore, worth noting from the outset that justice as fairness, like other contract views, consists of two parts: (1) an interpretation of the initial situation and of the problem of choice posed there, and (2) a set of principles which, it is argued, would be agreed to. One may accept the first part of the theory (or some variant thereof), but not the other, and conversely. The concept of the initial contractual situation may seem reasonable although the particular principles proposed are rejected. To be sure, I want to maintain that the most appropriate conception of this situation does lead to principles of justice contrary to utilitarianism and perfectionism, and therefore that the contract doctrine provides an alternative to these views. Still, one may dispute this contention even though one grants that the contractarian method is a useful way of studying ethical theories and of setting forth their underlying assumptions.

Justice as fairness is an example of what I have called a contract theory. ... The merit of the contract terminology is that it conveys the idea that principles of justice may be conceived as principles that would be chosen by rational persons, and that in this way conceptions of justice may be explained and justified. The theory of justice is a part, perhaps the most significant part, of the theory of rational choice. Furthermore, principles of justice deal with conflicting claims upon the advantages won by social cooperation; they apply to the relations among several persons or groups. The word "contract" suggests this plurality as well as the condition that the appropriate division of advantages must be in accordance with principles acceptable to all parties. The condition of publicity for principles of justice is also connoted by the contract phraseology. Thus, if these principles are the outcome of an agreement, citizens have a knowledge of the principles that others follow. It is characteristic of contract theories to stress the public nature of political principles. Finally there is the long tradition of the contract doctrine. Expressing the tie with this line of thought helps to define ideas and accords with natural piety. There are then several advantages in the use of the term "contract." With due precautions taken, it should not be misleading.

Chapter Six

Subversive Ethics

Perhaps the most quoted scriptural verse in subversive ethics is Galatians 3:28: "There is no longer Jew or Greek, there is no longer slave or free, there is no longer male and female; for all of you are one in Christ Jesus." This explicit identification of race ("Jew or Greek"), class ("slave or free"), and gender ("male and female") roots issues of difference at the heart of the gospel.

Four strands present themselves as prominent in discussions over subversive ethics:

- *Class.* This refers most specifically to the exclusion and oppression of the poor, but also to class struggle and questions of power and economics in general.
- *Race.* This most specifically refers to the way certain races have been subdued, suppressed, and exploited by certain other races, but also to the way questions of nation and ethnicity have influenced ethics.
- *Gender.* This refers to a concern for the subservient status of women within Christianity and across the human race, but also to minority forms of sexual orientation and identity and the bearing these perspectives have on ethics.
- *Disability and age.* The question in this case is whether justice is best understood as giving each person the same, or giving all persons their due – and thus whether rights language is sufficient to meet the particular and diverse needs of those whose "difference" is age or disability.

Class

Latin American liberation theology has been the most dynamic dimension of Christian ethical reflection on class in recent times.

The liberation theologians of Latin America emerged out of a combination of historical and theological circumstances. The culture of the early 1960s in South and Central America was one where the countryside was full of landless farmers harvesting cotton or coffee beans under a merciless sun for a pitiful wage, while malnourished children combed city dumping grounds for scraps of food or clothing. The economy was in the hands of transnational corporations who dominated the mining and manufacturing industries, and oligarchies who monopolized rural landholdings. Protest, in the form of developing self-help communities or organizing labor, was brutally suppressed.

The revolution in Cuba in 1959, the Second Vatican Council, and the growth of base ecclesial communities fostered an appetite for a new kind of theology. This made theological reflection a second, rather than the first, step. Many of those who later became liberation theologians had been educated in an intellectual environment that assumed contemplation was superior and prior to a kind of particular personal (and political) commitment that transforms the participant in the process of addressing injustice, known as "praxis."

Praxis comes to be used as something of a code term in liberation theology. While in theory it means any form of ethical conduct that takes social disadvantage and particularly poverty seriously, its use tends to assume activities such as the following: community organizing, particularly in the form of basic ecclesial communities and neighborhood associations; the introduction of educational programs designed to help people name their reality, denounce exploitation, and announce more humane structures; political gestures, particularly against oppression; bishops' letters expressing protests against governments or policies; sometimes the facing of harassment, torture, and even death from hostile forces both inside and outside the country; and in some cases violent resistance movements.

While class is a very broad concept and liberation theology is a diverse field, the work of Gustavo Gutiérrez is presented here as a foundational text.

Gustavo Gutiérrez, *The Church in the Process of Liberation*

The most famous liberation theologian is perhaps the Peruvian Dominican Gustavo Gutiérrez (b.1928). In his original groundbreaking work *A Theology of Liberation* (1971) he sees liberation as concerning not just the elimination of the causes of poverty and injustice, but also the opportunity for the poor to develop themselves freely and in dignity – as well as, crucially, concerning liberation from selfishness and sin, and restoration of right relationships.

In this passage Gutiérrez investigates three notions of poverty. One is poverty as degradation, expressed in terms like indigent and weak. This kind of poverty is an offense against God. Next, there is spiritual poverty. This was the state of the faithful remnant who anticipated restoration at the hands of God – a theme picked up in the New Testament in the Beatitudes. Finally, there is "poverty as a commitment of solidarity and protest." This recognizes that if material poverty is an evil, voluntary poverty cannot be a good; and that the point of spiritual poverty is total availability to God, which, for Gutiérrez, is "to struggle against human selfishness and everything that divides persons and enables there to be rich and poor." This is the pattern of Christ.

The conclusion is uncompromising: "Only by rejecting poverty and by making itself poor in order to protest against it can the Church preach something that is uniquely its own: 'spiritual poverty.'"

Gustavo Gutiérrez. *A Theology of Liberation: History, Politics, and Salvation*. Revised edn. London: SCM Press, 1988. Translation copyright 1988 by Orbis Books. From Chapter 13, "Poverty: Solidarity and Protest," pages 165–73. Reprinted by permission of the publisher SCM Press. Reprinted by permission of Orbis Books.

Poverty: A Scandalous Condition

In the Bible poverty is a scandalous condition inimical to human dignity and therefore contrary to the will of God.

This rejection of poverty is seen very clearly in the vocabulary used. ... The poor person is ... *ébyôn*, the one who desires, the beggar, the one who is lacking something and who awaits it from another. He is also *dal*, the weak one, the frail one; the expression *the poor of the land* (the rural proletariat) is found very frequently. The poor person is also *ani*, the bent over one, the one laboring under a weight, the one not in posses- sion of his whole strength and vigor, the humiliated one. And finally he is *anaw*, from the same root as the previous term but having a more religious connotation – "humble before God." In the New Testament the Greek term *ptokós* is used to speak of the poor person. *Ptokós* means one who does not have what is necessary to subsist, the wretched one driven into begging.

Indigent, weak, bent over, wretched are terms which well express a degrading human situation. These terms already insinuate a protest. They are not limited to description; they take a stand. This stand is made explicit in the vigorous rejection of poverty. The climate in which poverty is described is one of indignation. And it is with the same indignation that the cause of poverty is indicated: the injustice of oppressors. ...

But it is not simply a matter of denouncing poverty. The Bible speaks of positive and concrete measures to prevent poverty from becoming established among the People of God. In Leviticus and Deuteronomy there is very detailed legislation designed to prevent the accu- mulation of wealth and the consequent exploitation. ...

Behind these texts we can see three principal reasons for this vigorous repudiation of poverty. In the first place, poverty contradicts the very meaning of *the Mosaic religion*. Moses led his people out of the slavery, exploitation, and alienation of Egypt so that they might inhabit a land where they could live with human dignity. ...

The second reason for the repudiation of the state of slavery and exploitation of the Jewish people in Egypt is that it goes against *the mandate of Genesis* (1:26; 2:15). Humankind is created in the image and likeness of God and is destined to dominate the earth. Humankind fulfills itself only by transforming nature and thus entering into relationships with other persons. Only in this way do persons come to a full consciousness of themselves as subjects of creative freedom which is realized through work. The exploitation and injustice implicit in poverty make work into something servile and dehumanizing. Alienated work, instead of liberating persons, enslaves them even more. And so it is that when just treatment is asked for the poor, the slaves, and the aliens, it is recalled that Israel also was alien and enslaved in Egypt (Exod. 22:21–23; 23:9; Deut. 10:19; Lev. 19:34).

And finally, humankind not only has been made in the image and likeness of God; it is also *the sacrament of God*. ... The other reasons for the Biblical rejection of poverty have their roots here: to oppress the poor is to offend God; to know God is to work justice among human beings. We meet God in our encounter with other persons; what is done for others is done for the Lord.

In a word, the existence of poverty represents a sundering both of solidarity among persons and also of communion with God. Poverty is an expression of a sin, that is, of a negation of love. It is therefore incompatible with the coming of the Kingdom of God, a Kingdom of love and justice.

Poverty is an evil, a scandalous condition, which in our times has taken on enormous proportions. To eliminate it is to bring closer the moment of seeing God face to face, in union with other persons.

Poverty: Spiritual Childhood

There is a second line of thinking concerning poverty in the Bible. The poor person is the "client" of Yahweh; poverty is "the ability to welcome God, an openness to God, a willingness to be used by God, a humility before God."

The vocabulary which is used here is the same as that used to speak of poverty as an evil. But the terms used to designate the poor person receive an ever more demanding and precise religious meaning. This is the case especially with the term *anaw*, which in the plural (*anawim*) is the privileged designation of the spiritually poor.

The repeated infidelity to the Covenant of the people of Israel led the prophets to elaborate the theme of the "tiny remnant" (Isa. 4:3; 6:13). Made up of those who remained faithful to Yahweh, the remnant would be the Israel of the future. From its midst there would emerge the Messiah and consequently the first fruits of the New Covenant (Jer. 31:31–34; Ezek. 36:26–28). From the time of Zephaniah (seventh century BC), those who awaited the liberating work of the Messiah were "poor": "But I will leave in you a people afflicted and poor, the survivors in Israel shall find refuge in the name of the Lord" (Zeph. 3:12–13). In this way the term acquired a spiritual meaning. From then on poverty was presented as an ideal: "Seek the Lord, all in the land who live humbly by his laws, seek righteousness, seek a humble heart" (Zeph. 2:3). Understood in this way poverty is opposed to pride, to an attitude of self-sufficiency; on the other hand, it is synonymous with faith, with abandonment and trust in the Lord. ...

Spiritual poverty finds its highest expression in the Beatitudes of the New Testament. ... The poverty which is called "blessed" in Matt. 5:1 ("Blessed are the poor in spirit") is spiritual poverty as understood since the time of Zephaniah: to be totally at the disposition of the Lord. This is the precondition for being able to receive the Word of God. It has, therefore, the same meaning as the Gospel theme of spiritual childhood. God's communication with us is a gift of love; to receive this gift it is necessary to be poor, a spiritual child. This poverty has no direct relationship to wealth; in the first instance it is not a question of indifference to the goods of this world. It goes deeper than that; it means to have no other sustenance than the will of God. This is the attitude of Christ. ...

Solidarity and Protest

Material poverty is a scandalous condition. Spiritual poverty is an attitude of openness to God and spiritual childhood. Having clarified these two meanings of the term *poverty* we have cleared the path and can now move forward towards a better understanding of the Christian witness of poverty. We turn now to a third meaning of the term: poverty as a commitment of solidarity and protest.

We have laid aside the first two meanings. The first is subtly deceptive; the second partial and insufficient. In the first place, if *material poverty* is something to be rejected, as the Bible vigorously insists, then a witness of poverty cannot make of it a Christian ideal. This would be to aspire to a condition which is recognized as degrading to persons. It would be, moreover, to move against the current of history. It would be to oppose any idea of the domination of nature by humans and the consequent and progressive creation of better conditions of life. And finally, but not least seriously, it would be to justify, even if involuntarily, the injustice and exploitation which is the cause of poverty.

On the other hand, our analysis of the Biblical texts concerning *spiritual poverty* has helped us to see that it is not directly or in the first instance an interior detachment from the goods of this world, a spiritual attitude which becomes authentic by incarnating itself in material poverty. Spiritual poverty is something more complete and profound. It is above all total availability to the Lord. Its relationship to the use or ownership of economic goods is inescapable, but secondary and partial. Spiritual childhood – an ability to receive, not a passive acceptance – defines the total posture of human existence before God, persons, and things.

How are we therefore to understand the evangelical meaning of the witness of a real, material, concrete poverty? *Lumen gentium* [one of the principal documents of Vatican II] invites us to look for the deepest meaning of Christian poverty *in Christ*: "Just as Christ carried out the work of redemption in poverty and under oppression, so the Church is called to follow the same path in communicating to others the fruits of salvation. Christ Jesus, though He was by nature God … emptied himself, taking the nature of a slave (Phil. 2:6), and being rich, he became poor (2 Cor. 8:9) for our sakes. Thus, although the Church needs human resources to carry out her mission, she is not set up to seek earthly glory, but to proclaim humility and self-sacrifice, even by her own example." …

The taking on of the servile and sinful human condition, as foretold in Second Isaiah, is presented by Paul as an act of voluntary impoverishment: "For you know how generous our Lord Jesus Christ has been: He was rich, yet for your sake he became poor, so that through his poverty you might become rich" (2 Cor. 8:9). This is the humiliation of Christ, his *kenosis* (Phil. 2:6–11). But he does not take on the human sinful condition and its consequences to idealize it. It is rather because of love for and solidarity with others who suffer in it. It is to redeem them from their sin and to enrich them with his poverty. It is to struggle against human selfishness and everything that divides persons and enables there to be rich and poor, possessors and dispossessed, oppressors and oppressed.

Poverty is an act of love and liberation. It has a redemptive value. If the ultimate cause of human exploitation and alienation is selfishness, the deepest reason for voluntary poverty is love of neighbor. Christian poverty has meaning only as a commitment of solidarity with the poor, with those who suffer misery and injustice. The commitment is to witness to the evil which has resulted from sin and is a breach of communion. It is not a question of idealizing poverty, but rather of taking it on as it is – an evil – to protest against it and to struggle to abolish it. As Ricoeur says, you cannot really be with the poor unless you are struggling against poverty. Because of this solidarity – which must manifest itself in specific action, a style of life, a break with one's social class – one can also help the poor and exploited to become aware of their exploitation and seek liberation from it. Christian poverty, an expression of love, is solidarity *with the poor* and is a protest *against poverty*. This is the concrete, contemporary meaning of the witness of poverty. It is a poverty lived not for its own sake, but rather as an authentic imitation of Christ; it is a poverty which means taking on the sinful human condition to liberate humankind from sin and all its consequences. …

We must pay special attention to the words we use. The term *poor* might seem not only vague and churchy, but also somewhat sentimental and aseptic. The "poor" person today is the oppressed one, the one marginated from society, the member of the proletariat struggling for the most basic rights; the exploited and plundered social class, the country struggling for its liberation. In today's world the solidarity and protest of which we are speaking have an evident and inevitable "political" character insofar as they imply liberation. To be with the oppressed is to be against the oppressor. In our times and on our continent to be in solidarity with the "poor," understood in this way, means to run personal risks – even to put one's life in danger. …

Only by rejecting poverty and by making itself poor in order to protest against it can the Church preach something that is uniquely its own: "spiritual poverty," that is, the openness of humankind and history to the future promised by God. Only in this way will the Church be able to fulfill authentically – and with any possibility of being listened to – its prophetic function of denouncing every human injustice. And only in this way will it be able to preach the word which liberates, the word of genuine fellowship.

Race

Black theology stands in relation to the theology and ethics of race rather as Latin American liberation theology stands in relation to the theology and ethics of class: that is to say, it by no means exhausts the agenda and the literature, but its concerns significantly shape, and are often taken to represent, the whole field.

The civil rights movement was undoubtedly a crucible for African American theology. Martin Luther King, Jr. (1929–1968) articulated the call to and possibility of nonviolent liberation in a way that captured the imagination of a generation. King saw all humankind as siblings. He saw the incoming tide of justice as inexorable, if not rapid. He had a profound faith in the principles underlying the American Revolution and Constitution; thus there could be no separatism and only an appeal to the oppressors' good

will could bring about sustainable change. Studying the career and ethos of Gandhi led King to reread the Sermon on the Mount as a political program. Meanwhile, in the late 1960s and early 1970s, the Black Power movement, espoused by people such as the Student Nonviolent Coordinating Committee leader Stokely Carmichael (1941–1998), emerged out of the experience of the depth and intractability of white racism and the obstacles to black people entering the circles of power. In contrast to King's movement, the Black Power advocates encouraged the establishment of black political and cultural institutions to advance black interests, values, and autonomy.

An excerpt from the work of James Cone is presented here as representative of a diverse and complex field.

James Cone, *Black Theology of Liberation*

The most prominent African American proponent of black theology is James Cone (b. 1938), a Methodist from Arkansas and since 1970 professor at Union Theological Seminary in New York City. In *Black Theology and Black Power* (1969) Cone argues that both these evocative terms aspire to help black people find freedom through a new dignity and self-determination. The black churches have largely neglected this key dimension of black power, becoming passive and quiescent in the face of racism.

For Cone, blackness is a physiological characteristic – black skin – but also an ontological status – attained by those participating in the struggle of black people for liberation from oppression. By contrast whiteness denotes sickness and oppression. In this sense, because God is still concerned for the injustice against his people (a concern consistent since the time of the Exodus), God is black. Cone's view of Jesus is that Jesus is fully divine, fully human, and fully committed to liberating the oppressed. Jesus is black – because God becomes present in a form that restores the image of God among the oppressed of the earth. Jesus' resurrection demonstrates the divine commitment to and human possibility of throwing off oppression.

Like the Latin American liberation theologians, he has a realized eschatology that sees salvation as a present and attainable social reality, to be reached out for by people infused with God's Spirit. Cone does not rule out violence: he takes a line similar to proportionalism, suggesting that slavery, hunger, and exploitation are all forms of violence and may need to be thrown aside by violence if there is no better way.

James H. Cone. *A Black Theology of Liberation*. Twentieth Anniversary Edition. Maryknoll: Orbis Books, 1986, 1990. From Part I: A Black Theology of Liberation; Chapter 1: "The Content of Theology," pages 1–8. Reprinted by permission of Orbis Books.

Liberation as the Content of Theology

Christian theology is a theology of liberation. It is a rational study of the being of God in the world in light of the existential situation of an oppressed community, relating the forces of liberation to the essence of the gospel, which is Jesus Christ. This means that its sole reason for existence is to put into ordered speech the meaning of God's activity in the world, so that the community of the oppressed will recognize that its inner thrust for liberation is not only consistent with the gospel but is the gospel of Jesus Christ. There can be no Christian theology that is not identified unreservedly with those who are humiliated and abused. In fact, theology ceases to be a theology of the gospel when it fails to arise out of the community of the oppressed. For it is impossible to speak of the God of Israelite history, who is the God revealed in Jesus Christ, without recognizing that God is the God of and for those who labor and are over laden. ...

The definition of theology as the discipline that seeks to analyze the nature of the Christian faith in the light of the oppressed arises chiefly from biblical tradition itself.

1   Though it may not be entirely clear why God elected Israel to be God's people, one point is evident. The election is inseparable from the event of the exodus ... (Ex 19:4–5a). Certainly this means, among other things, that God's call of this people is related to its oppressed condition and to God's own liberating activity already seen in the exodus. *You have seen what I did!* By delivering this people from Egyptian bondage and inaugurating the covenant on the basis of that historical event, God is revealed as the God of the oppressed, involved in their history, liberating them from human bondage.

2   Later stages of Israelite history also show that God is particularly concerned about the oppressed within the community of Israel. The rise of Old Testament prophecy is due primarily to the lack of justice within that community. The prophets of Israel are prophets of social justice, reminding the people that Yahweh is the author of justice. It is important to note in this connection that the righteousness of God is not an abstract quality in the being of God, as with Greek philosophy. It is rather God's active involvement in history, making right what human beings have made wrong. The consistent theme in Israelite prophecy is Yahweh's concern for the lack of social, economic, and political justice for those who are poor and unwanted in society. Yahweh, according to Hebrew prophecy, will not tolerate injustice against the poor; God will vindicate the poor. Again, God is revealed as the God of liberation for the oppressed.

3   In the New Testament, the theme of liberation is reaffirmed by Jesus himself. The conflict with Satan and the powers of this world, the condemnation of the rich, the insistence that the kingdom of God is for the poor, and the locating of his ministry among the poor – these and other features of the career of Jesus show that his work was directed to the oppressed for the purpose of their liberation. To suggest that he was speaking of a "spiritual" liberation fails to take seriously Jesus' thoroughly Hebrew view of human nature. Entering into the kingdom of God means that Jesus himself becomes the ultimate loyalty of humankind, for *he is the kingdom*. This view of existence in the world has far-reaching implications for economic, political, and social institutions. They can no longer have ultimate claim on human life; human beings are liberated and thus free to rebel against all powers that threaten human life. That is what Jesus had in mind when he said: "The Spirit of the Lord is upon me, because he has anointed me to preach good news to the poor. He has sent me to proclaim release to the captives and recovering of sight to the blind, to set at liberty those who are oppressed, to proclaim the acceptable year of the Lord" (Luke 4:18–19).

In view of the biblical emphasis on liberation, it seems not only appropriate but necessary to define the Christian community as the community of the oppressed which joins Jesus Christ in his fight for the liberation of humankind. The task of theology, then, is to explicate the meaning of God's liberating activity so that those who labor under enslaving powers will see that the forces of liberation are the very activity of God. Christian theology is never just a rational study of the being of God. Rather it is a study of God's liberating activity in the world, God's activity in behalf of the oppressed. ...

Liberation and Black Theology

Unfortunately, American white theology has not been involved in the struggle for black liberation. It has been basically a theology of the white oppressor, giving religious sanction to the genocide of Amerindians and the enslavement of Africans. From the very beginning to the present day, American white theological thought has been "patriotic," either by defining the theological task independently of black suffering (the liberal northern approach) or by defining Christianity as compatible with white racism (the conservative southern approach). In both cases theology becomes a servant of the state, and that can only mean death to blacks. It is little wonder that an increasing number of black religionists are finding it difficult to be black *and* be identified with traditional theological thought forms.

The appearance of black theology on the American scene then is due primarily to the failure of white religionists to relate the gospel of Jesus to the pain of being black in a white racist society. It arises from the need of blacks to liberate themselves from white oppressors. Black theology is a theology of liberation because it is a theology which arises from an identification with the oppressed blacks of America, seeking to interpret the gospel of Jesus in the light of the black condition. It believes that the liberation of the black community is God's liberation.

The task of black theology, then, is to analyze the nature of the gospel of Jesus Christ in the light of oppressed blacks so they will see the gospel as inseparable from their humiliated condition, and as bestowing on them the necessary power to break the chains of oppression. This means that it is a theology of and for the black community, seeking to interpret the religious dimensions of the forces of liberation in that community.

There are two reasons why black theology is Christian theology. First, there can be no theology of the gospel which does not arise from an oppressed community. This is so because God is revealed in Jesus as a God whose righteousness is inseparable from the weak and helpless in human society. The goal of black theology is to interpret God's activity as related to the oppressed black community.

Secondly, black theology is Christian theology because it centers on Jesus Christ. There can be no Christian theology which does not have Jesus Christ as its point of departure. Though black theology affirms the black condition as the primary datum of reality to be reckoned with, this does not mean that it denies the absolute revelation of God in Jesus Christ. Rather it affirms it. Unlike white theology, which tends to make the Jesus-event an abstract, unembodied idea, black theology believes that the black community itself is precisely where Jesus Christ is at work. The Jesus-event in twentieth-century America is a black-event – that is, an event of liberation taking place in the black community in which blacks recognize that it is incumbent upon them to throw off the chains of white oppression by whatever means they regard as suitable. This is what God's revelation means to black and white America, and why black theology is an indispensable theology for our time.

It is to be expected that some will ask, "Why black theology? Is it not true that God is color-blind? Is it not true that there are others who suffer as much as, if not in some cases more than, blacks?" These questions reveal a basic misunderstanding of black theology and also a superficial view of the world at large. There are at least three points to be made here.

First, in a revolutionary situation there can never be nonpartisan theology. Theology is always identified with a particular community. It is either identified with those who inflict oppression or with those who are its victims. A theology of the latter is authentic Christian theology, and a theology of the former is a theology of the Antichrist! Insofar as black theology is a theology arising from an identification with the oppressed black community and seeks to interpret the gospel of Jesus Christ in the light of the liberation of that community, it is Christian theology. American white theology is a theology of the Antichrist insofar as it arises from an identification with the white community, thereby placing God's approval on white oppression of black existence.

Secondly, in a racist society, God is never color-blind. To say God is color-blind is analogous to saying that God is blind to justice and injustice, to right and wrong, to good and evil. Certainly this is not the picture of God revealed in the Old and New Testaments. Yahweh takes sides. On the one hand, Yahweh sides with Israel against the Canaanites in the occupancy of Palestine. On the other hand, Yahweh sides with the poor within the community of Israel against the rich and other political oppressors. In the New Testament, Jesus is not for *all*, but for the oppressed, the poor and unwanted of society, and against oppressors. The God of the biblical tradition is not uninvolved or neutral regarding human affairs; God is decidedly involved. God is active in human history, taking sides with the oppressed of the land. If God is not involved in human history, then all theology is useless, and Christianity itself is a mockery, a hollow, meaningless diversion.

The meaning of this message for our contemporary situation is clear: the God of the oppressed takes sides with the black community. God is not color-blind in the black – white struggle, but has made an unqualified identification with blacks. This means that the movement for black liberation is the very work of God, effecting God's will among men.

Thirdly, there are, to be sure, many who suffer, and not all of them are black. Many white liberals derive a certain joy from reminding black militants that two-thirds of the poor in America are white. Of course I could point out that this means that there are five times as many poor blacks as there are poor whites, when the ratio of each group to the total population is taken into account.

But it is not my intention to debate white liberals on this issue, for it is not the purpose of black theology to minimize the suffering of others, including whites. Black theology merely tries to discern the activity of the Holy One in achieving the purpose of the liberation of humankind from the forces of oppression. ...

The extermination of Amerindians, the persecution of Jews, the oppression of Mexican-Americans, and every other conceivable inhumanity done in the name of God and country – these brutalities can be analyzed in terms of the white American inability to recognize humanity in persons of color. If the oppressed of this land want to challenge the oppressive character of white society, they must begin by affirming their identity in terms of the reality that is antiwhite. Blackness, then, stands for all victims of oppression who realize that the survival of their humanity is bound up with liberation from whiteness.

This understanding of blackness can be seen as the most adequate symbol of the dimensions of divine activity in America. And insofar as this country is seeking to make whiteness the dominating power throughout the world, whiteness is the symbol of the Antichrist. Whiteness characterizes the activity of deranged individuals intrigued by their own image of themselves, and thus unable to see that they are what is wrong with the world. Black theology seeks to analyze the satanic nature of whiteness and by doing so to prepare all nonwhites for revolutionary action.

Gender

Susan Parsons describes a feminist as "one who takes most seriously the practical concerns of women's lives, the analysis and the critique of those conditions of life, and the ways in which women's lives may become more fulfilling." Feminist Christian ethics has rapidly become a very large dimension of the discourse in Christian ethics as a whole. With the ethics of class and race already examined, it shares a far-reaching critique of universal ethics. That critique dwells on the misuse of the Bible, the false association of divine qualities and universal rationality with maleness, and the devaluation of women's projected and genuine capabilities, callings, and spheres of influence. Further critiques have emerged as the initial generation of feminist theologians has been examined for its own race and class location.

We may perceive three broad constructive approaches within contemporary feminist Christian ethics:

1 *Incorporating women into a universal paradigm.* Standing in the liberal political tradition that emerges from the Enlightenment, this approach has confidence in the individual woman, through her behavior and decision-making, to bring about a gender-equal society without social revolution. Like many movements rooted in the Enlightenment, it attributes social ills to superstition, false religion, outdated science, and obscure tradition, and it retains a profound social optimism that such ills can be removed, and once rid of them, society will flourish as never before. The key terms are rights, equality, and the dignity of the human person.

2 *Restoring a universal paradigm.* This rests on the assertion that there are indeed profound differences between men and women, and that the problem lies not in the differences, but in the ways "male" tendencies and characteristics have been exalted and "female" ones demeaned or neglected. Whereas the revised paradigm or "liberal" approach relates to the universal Kantian and rights traditions, the restored or "romantic" version appeals more explicitly to a particular notion of natural law. It sees nature as intrinsically linked to the body, and thus biology and psychology play an important role in understanding its contours. It sees reproduction not as accidental to human nature and differentiation, but

as foundational. Such arguments can be extremely controversial because they seem to undermine the ethos and gains established by the liberal branch of feminism.

3 *Rejecting the universal project in ethics.* For a great many feminists, including significant thinkers in Christian ethics, feminism has to abandon the idea of a universal paradigm for ethics: it has to recognize the inherently conflictual nature of human life, particularly the institutional power relationships shaped by gender, and cease to hold to the fantasy that if the right theory emerged with the right application, a peaceable existence would break out.

Among this third group, a number of diverse themes have emerged, including womanism (which describes the experience of women of color – particularly African American women), lesbian ethics (which suggests that the goods held up for women by patriarchal culture – sacrifice and self-denial – should be replaced by values such as self-creation, freedom, and liberation), and ecofeminism (the study of the symbolic, psychological, and ethical patterns of destructive relations of humans with nature and the quest to replace this with a life-affirming culture).

The readings below attempt to survey this broad, diverse, and dynamic field.

Rosemary Radford Ruether, *Sexism and God-Talk*

Rosemary Radford Ruether (b. 1936) is a Roman Catholic feminist theologian who writes in a mixture of the first and third strands outlined above. Some of her work sounds like an incorporation of women into what remains a universal paradigm, now shorn of its patriarchal assumptions. Some of her work, by contrast, tends in a more explicitly ecofeminist direction which comes close to rejecting the universal project in ethics.

This passage explores Ruether's anthropology. Egalitarianism (a term at the heart of the first strand of feminism) is the key. She distances herself from the second strand by insisting that gender identity is limited to reproductive roles only, and by making little space for speculation on whether physiological differences might have any psychological or social implications. Sexuality is an acquired characteristic: there are no legitimate distinctions between standards for those of differing orientations.

The passage includes reflections on the person and role of Christ in feminist theology. Ruether notes positively, "the Jesus of the synoptic Gospels can be recognized as a figure remarkably compatible with feminism." Yet while Jesus of Nazareth is "a positive model of redemptive humanity, ... we need other clues and models as well, models drawn from women's experience, from many times and cultures." She concludes that "the maleness of Jesus has no ultimate significance."

Rosemary Radford Ruether. *Sexism and God-Talk: Towards a Feminist Theology.* London: SCM Press, 1983, 1992. From Chapter 4, "Anthropology" (pages 92–7) and Chapter 5, "Christology" (pages 113–16). Reprinted by permission of the publisher SCM Press. Copyright 1983 by Beacon Press. Reproduced with permission of Beacon Press in the format Textbook via Copyright Clearance Center.

Toward a Feminist Anthropology Beyond Liberalism and Romanticism

Contemporary feminism inherits the traditions of both liberal and romantic feminism. It becomes divided and confused over the opposite values and directions espoused by each viewpoint. Both liberalism and romanticism are inadequate and yet both testify to important truths that I wish to affirm. A more adequate feminist anthropology would be one that finds a creative synthesis between the two. Liberal feminism too readily identifies normative human nature with those capacities for reason and rule identified with men and with the public sphere. It claims that women, while appearing to have lesser capacities for these attributes, actually possess them equally; they have simply been denied the educational cultivation of them and the opportunity to exercise them. Opening up equal education and equal political rights to women will correct this and allow women's suppressed capacities for reason and rule to appear in their actual equivalence to men's.

There is important truth to this. Women, through the opening of equal education and political rights, have indeed demonstrated their ability to exercise the "same" capacities as men. But liberalism does not entirely recognize the more complex forms of women's psychological and economic marginalization that result in only token integration of women into "equal" roles in the public sphere. Liberalism assumes the traditional male sphere as normative and believes it is wrong to deny people access to it on the basis of gender. But once women are allowed to enter the public sphere, liberalism offers no critique of the modes of functioning within it.

Romanticism, in contrast, recognizes the moral ambiguity of the roles traditionally associated with masculinity. It idealizes the home, the private sphere of interpersonal relations, and places of "unspoiled nature" outside of urbanization and industrialization as havens of a more integrated humanity. It idealizes women precisely in their segregation from this ambiguous world. It tends to overlook the ambiguity and violence present in the sphere of private relationships, both the violation of women to keep them there and the way in which unexpressed angers and frustrations from the work world can be unleashed in the home. Altruism and service, while compensating women for acquiescence to relations of domination, also become a means of passive aggression masquerading as "helping others."

Romanticism is not entirely wrong in believing there are clues to a better humanity in the virtues relegated to women and the home in bourgeois society. But these virtues exist in deformed and deforming ways within the institutionalization of "woman's sphere." Moreover, the capacities traditionally associated with men and with public life also contain some important human virtues that women should not be forbidden to cultivate.

Thus neither masculinity traditionally defined nor femininity traditionally defined discloses an innately good human nature, and neither is simply an expression of evil. Both represent different types of alienation of humanity from its original potential. Socially, both home and work represent realms of corruption. If women will not be automatically redeemed by being incorporated into male political power and business in its present form, men will not automatically be redeemed by learning to nurture infants and keep house.

Androgyny has been used in recent feminist thought to express the human nature that all persons share. *Androgyny* refers to the possession by both males and females of both halves of the psychic capacities that have been traditionally separated as masculinity and femininity. The word *androgyny* is misleading, however, because it suggests that males and females possess both "masculine" and "feminine" sides to their psychic capacity. The term thus continues to perpetuate the ideas that certain psychic attributes are to be labeled masculine and others are to be labeled feminine and that humans, by integrating these "masculine" and "feminine" sides of themselves, become "androgynous."

There is no valid biological basis for labeling certain psychic capacities, such as reason, "masculine" and others, such as intuition, "feminine." To put it bluntly, there is no biological connection between male gonads and the capacity to reason. Likewise, there is no biological connection between female sexual organs and the capacity to be intuitive, caring, or nurturing. Thus the labeling of these capacities as masculine and feminine simply perpetuates gender role stereotypes and imports gender complementarity into each person's identity in a confusing way. Moreover, the idea of androgyny still preserves the idea of complementarity in complex form, since it suggests that males should integrate their androgynous identity around a "masculine" core of psychic capacities and females should integrate their androgyny around a "feminine" core. We need to affirm not the confusing concept of androgyny but rather that all humans possess a full and equivalent human nature and personhood, *as male and female*. …

Thus the recovery of holistic psychic capacities and egalitarian access to social roles point us toward that lost full human potential that we may call "redeemed humanity." Redeemed humanity, reconnected with the *imago dei*, means not only recovering aspects of our full psychic potential that have been repressed by cultural gender stereotypes, it also means transforming the way these capacities have been made to function socially. We need to recover our capacity for relationality, for hearing, receiving, and being with and for others, but in a way that is no longer a tool of manipulation or of self-abnegation. ...

In traditional Christian theology, Christ is the model for this redeemed humanity that we have lost through sin and recover through redemption. But Christ as symbol is problematic for feminist theology. The Christological symbols have been used to enforce male dominance, and even if we go back behind masculinist Christology to the praxis of the historical Jesus of the synoptic Gospels, it is questionable whether there is a single model of redeemed humanity fully revealed in the past. This does not mean that feminist theology may not be able to affirm the person of Jesus of Nazareth as a positive model of redemptive humanity. But this model must be seen as partial and fragmentary, disclosing from the perspective of one person, circumscribed in time, culture, and gender, something of the fullness we seek. We need other clues and models as well, models drawn from women's experience, from many times and cultures.

The fullness of redeemed humanity, as image of God, is something only partially disclosed under the conditions of history. We seek it as a future self and world, still not fully achieved, still not fully revealed. But we also discover it as our true self and world, the foundation and ground of our being. When we experience glimpses of it, we recognize not an alien self but our own authentic self. We experience such glimpses through encounters with other persons whose own authenticity discloses the meaning of such personhood. By holding the memory of such persons in our hearts and minds, we are able to recognize authenticity in ourselves and others.

The life and death of Jesus of Nazareth is one such memory, one such paradigm. It is no less paradigmatic when we recognize that it is partial and needs to be joined by other models, other memories, particularly those that disclose the journey to redemptive personhood from women's experience. Thus the question of anthropology leads us, theologically, to the problem of Christology. Has Christology, in fact, been a model of redemptive personhood for women, or has it become a tool for enforcing female subjugation in patriarchal society? What are the possibilities, and limits, of discovering an alternative, usable Christology, a paradigm of redemptive personhood, for women in the praxis of the historical Jesus? ...

A Feminist Christology?

... A Christology that identified the maleness of the historical Jesus with normative humanity and with the maleness of the divine *Logos* must move in an increas-

ingly misogynist direction that not only excludes woman as representative of Christ in ministry but makes her a second-class citizen in both creation and redemption. Androgynous Christologies try to affirm the female side in the vision of a Christ that is "neither male nor female." But the identification of this androgynous Christ with the male Jesus continues to give an androcentric bias to the vision of redemptive humanity. Woman can represent only the "feminine" side of a male-centered symbol the fullness of which is disclosed only in a male person.

Spirit Christologies begin by affirming that the risen Christ continues to be disclosed through spirit-possessed persons who may be male or female. But the splitting of the past revelation of Christ as the historical Jesus from the ongoing Spirit leads eventually to a revolt against a Christ encapsulated in the past. Institutionalized revelation becomes inadequate to the disclosure of new possibilities, specifically female possibilities. Where does this leave the quest for a feminist Christology? Must we not say that the very limitations of Christ as a male person must lead women to the conclusion that he cannot represent redemptive personhood for them? That they must emancipate themselves from Jesus as redeemer and seek a new redemptive disclosure of God and of human possibility in female form?

A starting point for this inquiry must be a reencounter with the Jesus of the synoptic Gospels, not the accumulated doctrine about him but his message and praxis. Once the mythology about Jesus as Messiah or divine *Logos*, with its traditional masculine imagery, is stripped off, the Jesus of the synoptic Gospels can be recognized as a figure remarkably compatible with feminism. This is not to say, in an anachronistic sense, that "Jesus was a feminist," but rather that the criticism of religious and social hierarchy characteristic of the early portrait of Jesus is remarkably parallel to feminist criticism.

Fundamentally, Jesus renews the prophetic vision whereby the Word of God does not validate the existing social and religious hierarchy but speaks on behalf of the marginalized and despised groups of society. Jesus proclaims an iconoclastic reversal of the system of religious status: The last shall be first and the first last. The leaders of the religious establishment are blind guides and hypocrites. The outcasts of society – prostitutes, publicans, Samaritans – are able to hear the message of the prophet. This reversal of social order doesn't just turn hierarchy upside down, it aims at a new reality in which hierarchy and dominance are overcome as principles of social relations. ...

Women play an important role in this Gospel vision of the vindication of the lowly in God's new order. ...

The role played by women of marginalized groups is an intrinsic part of the iconoclastic, messianic vision. It means that the women are the oppressed of the oppressed. They are the bottom of the present social hierarchy and hence are seen, in a special way, as the last who will be first in the Kingdom of God.

This role is quite different from doctrines of romantic complementarity. The Gospels do not operate with a dualism of masculine and feminine. The widow, the prostitute, and the Samaritan woman are not representatives of the "feminine," but rather they represent those who have no honor in the present system of religious righteousness. As women they are the doubly despised within these groups. They carry the double burden of low class and low gender status. The protest of the Gospels is directed at the concrete sociological realities in which maleness and femaleness are elements, along with class, ethnicity, religious office, and law, that define the network of social status. ...

Theologically speaking, then, we might say that the maleness of Jesus has no ultimate significance. It has social symbolic significance in the framework of societies of patriarchal privilege. In this sense Jesus as the Christ, the representative of liberated humanity and the liberating Word of God, manifests the *kenosis of patriarchy*, the announcement of the new humanity through a lifestyle that discards hierarchical caste privilege and speaks on behalf of the lowly. In a similar way, the femaleness of the social and religiously outcast who respond to him has social symbolic significance as a witness against the same idolatrous system of patriarchal privilege. This system is unmasked and shown to have no connection with favor with God. Jesus, the homeless Jewish prophet, and the marginalized women and men who respond to him represent the overthrow of the present world system and the sign of a dawning new age in which God's will is done on earth.

But this relation of redeeming Christ and redeemed women should not be made into ultimate theological gender symbols. Christ is not necessarily male, nor is the redeemed community only women, but a new humanity, female and male. We need to think in terms of a dynamic, rather than a static, relationship between redeemer and redeemed. The redeemer is one who has been redeemed, just as Jesus himself accepted the baptism of John. Those who have been liberated can, in turn, become paradigmatic, liberating persons for others.

Delores S. Williams, *Womanist Theology*

Delores S. Williams (b. 1937) is an African American theologian and longtime faculty member at Union Theological Seminary in New York. She defines womanist theology this way:

> Womanist theology is a prophetic voice concerned about the well-being of the entire African-American community, male and female, adults and children. Womanist theology attempts to help black women see, affirm, and have confidence in the importance of their experience and faith for determining the character of the Christian religion in the African-American community. Womanist theology challenges all oppressive forces impeding black women's struggle for survival and for the development of a positive, productive quality of life conducive to women's and the family's freedom and well-being. Womanist theology opposes all oppression based on race, sex, class, sexual preference, physical ability, and caste.

She identifies the black woman's experience with that of Sarah's slave Hagar, mother of Abraham's son Ishmael. Whereas white women may identify with Sarah, and the status motherhood bestows on them in the world, black women are more likely to identify with Hagar, whose motherhood is coerced and who is exploited by both a woman and a man. White feminists have continually neglected or ignored the role of white women in exploiting black women. Hagar survives in the wilderness with only God to help her, and remains homeless. This wilderness experience characterizes what it means to be an African American. Williams concludes: "It is God's continuing work in the African-American community's ever-present struggle for economic justice, for physical and emotional survival and for positive quality of life that forms 'the stuff' of black Christians' doctrines of resistance."

While much womanist writing exposes the class and race location of much feminist writing, this passage presents the constructive aspirations of womanism.

Delores S. Williams. "Womanist Theology: Black Women's Voices." *Christianity and Crisis* 47, 3 (March 2, 1987): 66–70.

DAUGHTER: Mama, why are we brown, pink, and yellow, and our cousins are white, beige, and black?
MOTHER: Well, you know the colored race is just like a flower garden, with every color flower represented.
DAUGHTER: Mama, I'm walking to Canada and I'm taking you and a bunch of slaves with me.
MOTHER: It wouldn't be the first time.

In these two conversational exchanges, Pulitzer Prize-winning novelist Alice Walker begins to show us what she means by the concept "womanist." The concept is presented in Walker's *In Search of Our Mother's Gardens*, and many women in church and society have appropriated it as a way of affirming themselves as *black* while simultaneously owning their connection with feminism and with the Afro-American community, male and female. The concept of womanist allows women to claim their roots in black history, religion, and culture.

What then is a womanist? Her origins are in the black folk expression "You acting womanish," meaning, according to Walker, "wanting to know more and in greater depth than is good for one ... outrageous, audacious, courageous and willful behavior." A womanist is also "responsible, in charge, serious." She can walk to Canada and take others with her. She loves, she is committed, she is a universalist by temperament.

Her universality includes loving men and women, sexually or nonsexually. She loves music, dance, the spirit, food and roundness, struggle, and she loves herself. "Regardless."

Walker insists that a womanist is also "committed to survival and wholeness of entire people, male and female." She is no separatist, "except for health." A womanist is a black feminist or feminist of color. Or as Walker says, "Womanist is to feminist as purple to lavender." ...

Codes and Contents

In her definitions Walker provides significant clues for the development of womanist theology. Her concept contains what black feminist scholar Bell Hooks in *From Margin to Center* identifies as cultural codes. These are words, beliefs, and behavioral patterns of a people that must be deciphered before meaningful communication can happen cross-culturally. Walker's codes are female-centered and they point beyond themselves to conditions, events, meanings, and values that have crystalized in the Afro-American community *around women's activity* and formed traditions. ...

Walker's allusion to skin color points to an historic tradition of tension between black women over the matter of some black men's preference for light-skinned women. Her reference to black women's love of food and roundness points to customs of female care in the black community (including the church) associated with hospitality and nurture.

These cultural codes and their corresponding traditions are valuable resources for indicating and validating the kind of data upon which womanist theologians can reflect as they bring black women's social, religious, and cultural experience into the discourse of theology, ethics, biblical and religious studies. Female slave narratives, imaginative literature by black women, autobiographies, the work by black women in academic disciplines, and the testimonies of black church women will be authoritative sources for womanist theologians.

Walker situates her understanding of a womanist in the context of nonbourgeois black folk culture. The literature of this culture has traditionally reflected more egalitarian relations between men and women, much less rigidity in male-female roles, and more respect for female intelligence and ingenuity than is found in bourgeois culture.

The black folk are poor. Less individualistic than those who are better off, they have, for generations, practiced various forms of economic sharing. For example, immediately after Emancipation mutual aid societies pooled the resources of black folk to help pay for funerals and other daily expenses. *The Book of Negro Folklore* describes the practice of rent parties which flourished during the Depression. The black folk stressed togetherness and a closer connection with nature. They respect knowledge gained through lived experience monitored by elders who differ profoundly in social class and world view from the teachers and education encountered in American academic institutions. Walker's choice of context suggests that womanist theology can establish its lines of continuity in the black community with non-bourgeois traditions less sexist than the black power and black nationalist traditions.

In this folk context, some of the black female-centered cultural codes in Walker's definition (e.g., "Mama, I'm walking to Canada and I'm taking you and a bunch of slaves with me") point to folk heroines like Harriet Tubman, whose liberation activity earned her the name "Moses" of her people. This allusion to Tubman directs womanist memory to a liberation tradition in black history in which women took the lead, acting as catalysts for the community's revolutionary action and for social change. Retrieving this often hidden or diminished female tradition of catalytic action is an important task for womanist theologians and ethicists. Their research may well reveal that female models of authority have been absolutely essential for every struggle in the black community and for building and maintaining the community's institutions.

Freedom Fighters

The womanist theologian must search for the voices, actions, opinions, experience, and faith of women whose names sometimes slip into the male-centered rendering of black history, but whose actual stories remain remote. … By uncovering as much as possible about such female liberation, the womanist begins to understand the relation of black history to the contemporary folk expression: "If Rosa Parks had not sat down, Martin King would not have stood up."

While she celebrates and *emphasizes* black women's culture and way of being in the world, Walker simultaneously affirms black women's historic connection with men through love and through a shared struggle for survival and for productive quality of life (e.g., "wholeness"). This suggests that two of the principal concerns of womanist theology should be survival and community building and maintenance. The goal of this community building is, of course, to establish a positive quality of life – economic, spiritual, educational – for black women, men, and children. Walker's understanding of a womanist as "not a separatist" ("except for health"), however, reminds the Christian womanist theologian that her concern for community building and maintenance must *ultimately* extend to the entire Christian community and beyond that to the larger human community.

Yet womanist consciousness is also informed by women's determination to love themselves. "Regardless." This translates into an admonition to black women to avoid the self-destruction of bearing a disproportionately large burden in the work of community building and maintenance. Walker suggests that women can avoid this trap by connecting with women's communities concerned about women's rights and well-being. Her identification of a womanist as also a feminist joins black women with their feminist heritage extending back into the nineteenth century in the work of black feminists like Sojourner Truth, Frances W. Harper, and Mary Church Terrell.

In making the feminist-womanist connection, however, Walker proceeds with great caution. While affirming an organic relationship between womanists and feminists, she also declares a deep shade of difference between them ("Womanist is to feminist as purple to lavender.") This gives womanist scholars the freedom to explore the particularities of black women's history and culture without being guided by what white feminists have already identified as women's issues. …

Womanist Theology and Method

Womanist theology is already beginning to define the categories and methods needed to develop along lines consistent with the sources of that theology. Christian womanist theological methodology needs to be informed by at least four elements: (1) a multidialogical intent, (2) a liturgical intent, (3) a didactic intent, and (4) a commitment both to reason *and* to the validity of female imagery and metaphorical language in the construction of theological statements.

A multidialogical intent will allow Christian womanist theologians to advocate and participate in dialogue and action with *many* diverse social, political, and religious communities concerned about human survival and productive quality of life for the oppressed. The genocide of cultures and peoples (which has often been instigated and accomplished by Western white Christian groups or governments) and the nuclear threat of omnicide mandates womanist participation in such dialogue/action. But in this dialogue/action the womanist also should keep her speech and action focused upon the slow genocide of poor black women, children, and men by exploitative systems denying them productive jobs, education, health care, and living space. Multidialogical activity may, like a jazz symphony, communicate some of its most important messages in what the harmony-driven conventional ear hears as discord, as disruption of the harmony in both the black American and white American social, political, and religious status quo.

If womanist theological method is informed by a liturgical intent, then womanist theology will be relevant to (and will reflect) the thought, worship, and action of the black church. But a liturgical intent will also allow womanist theology to challenge the thought/worship/action of the black church with the discordant and prophetic messages emerging from womanist participation in multidialogics. This means that womanist theology will consciously impact *critically* upon the foundations of liturgy, challenging the church to use justice principles to select the sources that will shape the content of liturgy. The question must be asked: "How does this source portray blackness/darkness, women and economic justice for nonruling-class people?" A negative portrayal will demand omission of the source or its radical reformation by the black church. The Bible, a major source in black church liturgy, must also be subjected to the scrutiny of justice principles.

A didactic intent in womanist theological method assigns a teaching function to theology. Womanist theology should teach Christians new insights about moral life based on ethics supporting justice for women, survival, and a productive quality of life for poor women, children, and men. This means that the womanist theologian must give authoritative status to black folk wisdom (e.g., Brer Rabbit literature) and to black women's moral wisdom (expressed in their literature) when she responds to the question, "How ought the Christian to live in the world?" Certainly tensions may exist between the moral teachings derived from these sources and the moral teachings about obedience, love, and humility that have usually buttressed presuppositions about living the Christian life. Nevertheless, womanist theology, in its didactic intent, must teach the church the different ways God reveals prophetic word and action for Christian living. ...

Who Do You Say God Is?

... Walker's mention of the black womanist's love of the spirit is a true reflection of the great respect Afro-American women have always shown for the presence and work of the spirit. In the black church, women (and men) often judge the effectiveness of the worship service not on the scholarly content of the sermon nor on the ritual nor on orderly process. Rather, worship has been effective if "the spirit was high," i.e., if the spirit was actively and obviously present in a balanced blend of prayer, of cadenced word (the sermon), and of syncopated music ministering to the pain of the people.

The importance of this emphasis upon the spirit is that it allows Christian womanist theologians, in their use of the Bible, to identify and reflect upon those biblical stories in which poor oppressed women had a special encounter with divine emissaries of God, like the spirit. In the Hebrew Testament, Hagar's story is most illustrative and relevant to Afro-American women's experience of bondage, of African heritage, of encounter with God/emissary in the midst of fierce survival struggles. Kate Cannon among a number of black female preachers and ethicists urges black Christian women to regard themselves as Hagar's sisters.

In relation to the Christian or New Testament, the Christian womanist theologian can refocus the salvation story so that it emphasizes the beginning of revelation with the spirit mounting Mary, a woman of the poor: ("... the Holy Spirit shall come upon thee, and the power of the Highest shall overshadow thee ..." Luke 1:35). Such an interpretation of revelation has roots in 19th-century black abolitionist and feminist Sojourner Truth. Posing an important question and response, she refuted a white preacher's claim that women could not have rights equal to men's because Christ was not a woman. Truth asked, "Whar did your Christ come from? ... From God and a woman! Man had nothin' to do wid Him!" This suggests that womanist theology could eventually speak of God in a well-developed theology of the spirit. The sources for this theology are many. Harriet Tubman often "went into the spirit" before her liberation missions and claimed her strength for liberation activity came from this way of meeting God. Womanist theology has grounds for shaping a theology of the spirit informed by black women's political action.

Ada María Isasi-Díaz, *Mujerista Theology*

Ada María Isasi-Díaz (b. 1943) was born and raised in Cuba, and came to the USA as a political refugee in 1960. She has been teaching at Drew University in New Jersey since 1991. Mujerista theology, originally known as Hispanic Women's Liberation Theology, began to be articulated in 1987.

In this passage Isasi-Díaz shows how mujerista theology strives to make Latinas the subject of theology in their own right and thus alter the sense of what counts as normative in mainline theology. Latinas need to understand and change oppressive structures, articulate their eschatological and desired future, and recognize their personal responsibility for internalizing their own oppression. Latinas are a culturally and racially mixed people, made up of black, white, and native people in Latin America and the Caribbean.

The passage includes an uncompromising denunciation of "any and all objectivity," which is no more than "the subjectivity of those who have the authority and/or power to impose their point of view." Instead, theology "has to start with self-disclosure," which is intended to "situate the subject." The action of God is perceived fundamentally in the present, rather than primarily in the past.

Ada María Isasi-Díaz. *Mujerista Theology: A Theology for the Twenty-First Century.* Maryknoll: Orbis, 1996. From Chapter 4, "Mujerista Theology," pages 61–6, 76–81. Reprinted by permission of Orbis Books.

Mujerista is the word we have chosen to name devotion to Latinas' liberation.

A *mujerista* is someone who makes a preferential option for Latina women, for our struggle for liberation. Because the term *mujerista* was developed by a group of us who are theologians and pastoral agents, the initial understandings of the term came from a religious perspective. At present the term is beginning to be used in other fields such as literature and history. It is also beginning to be used by community organizers working with grassroots Hispanic women. Its meaning, therefore, is being amplified without losing as its core the struggle for the liberation of Latina women.

Mujeristas struggle to liberate ourselves not as individuals but as members of a Hispanic community. We work to build bridges among Latinas/os while denouncing sectarianism and divisive tactics. ...

Turning to theology specifically, *mujerista* theology, which includes both ethics and systematic theology, is a liberative praxis: reflective action that has as its goal liberation. As a liberative praxis *mujerista* theology is a process of enablement for Latina women which insists on the development of a strong sense of moral agency

and clarifies the importance and value of who we are, what we think, and what we do. Second, as a liberative praxis, *mujerista* theology seeks to impact mainline theologies, those theologies which support what is normative in church and, to a large degree, in society – what is normative having been set by non-Hispanics and to the exclusion of Latinas and Latinos, particularly Latinas.

Mujerista theology engages in this two-pronged liberative praxis, first by working to enable Latinas to understand the many oppressive structures that almost completely determine our daily lives. It enables Hispanic women to understand that the goal of our struggle should be not to participate in and to benefit from these structures but to change them radically. In theological and religious language this means that *mujerista* theology helps Latinas discover and affirm the presence of God in the midst of our communities and the revelation of God in our daily lives. Hispanic women must come to understand the reality of structural sin and find ways of combating it because it effectively hides God's ongoing revelation from us and from society at large.

Second, *mujerista* theology insists on and aids Latinas in defining our preferred future: What will a radically different society look like? What will be its values and norms? In theological and religious language this means that *mujerista* theology enables Hispanic women to understand the centrality of eschatology in the life of every Christian. Latinas' preferred future breaks into our present oppression in many different ways. Hispanic women must recognize those eschatological glimpses, rejoice in them, and struggle to make those glimpses become our whole horizon.

Third, *mujerista* theology enables Latinas to understand how much we have already bought into the prevailing systems in society – including the religious systems – and have thus internalized our own oppression. *Mujerista* theology helps Hispanic women to see that radical structural change cannot happen unless radical change takes place in each and every one of us. In theological and religious language this means that *mujerista* theology assists Latinas in the process of conversion, helping us see the reality of sin in our lives. Further, it enables us to understand that to resign ourselves to what others tell us is our lot and to accept suffering and self-effacement is not a virtue. ...

Locus Theologicus. The *locus theologicus*, the place from which we do *mujerista* theology, is our *mestizaje* and *mulatez*, our condition as racially and culturally mixed people; our condition of people from other cultures living within the USA; our condition of people living between different worlds, a reality applicable to the Mexican Americans living in the Southwest, but also to the Cubans living in Miami and the Puerto Ricans living in the Northeast of the USA.

Mestizaje refers to the mixture of white people and native people living in what is now Latin America and the Caribbean. *Mulatez* refers to the mixture of black people and white people. We proudly use both words to refer both to the mixture of cultures as well as the mixture of races that we Latinas and Latinos in the USA embody. ...

Mestizaje and *mulatez* are what "socially situates" us Hispanics in the USA. This means that *mestizaje* and *mulatez* as the *theological locus* of Hispanics delineates the finite alternatives we have for thinking, conceiving, expressing our theology. For example, because *mestizaje* and *mulatez* socially situate our theology, our theology cannot but understand all racism and ethnic prejudice as sin and the embracing of diversity as virtue. This means that the coming of the kin-dom of God has to do with a coming together of peoples, with no one being excluded and at the expense of no one. Furthermore, *mestizaje* and *mulatez* mean that the unfolding of the kin-dom of God happens when instead of working to become part of structures of exclusion we struggle to do away with such structures. Because of the way mainline society thinks about *mestizas* and *mulatas*, we cannot but think about the divine in nonelitist, nonhierarchical ways. ...

"Epistemological vigilance"

... Now, what understandings are encompassed within this term "epistemological vigilance?" First, we *mujerista* theologians make a very serious and ongoing effort to be aware of our subjectivity. ... We work hard at being aware of our ideological biases and, though it is not easy, we work hard at revealing such biases. This means that we have to be aware of how our own social situation colors our analysis of the religion of our communities and colors the way we say what we say in our theological writings.

Second, epistemological vigilance here refers to the constant need to evaluate how our theological enterprise contributes to the liberation of our people. And here I am referring not only to the results of our theology, our writings, but also to the way in which we conduct our research. The question "Who benefits from this?" should never be far away from our minds. We need to apply a hermeneutics of suspicion to our constructive proposals, to our narratives, to our whole theological enterprise.

Third, epistemological vigilance refers to the need to avoid avoidance. *Mujerista* theologians need to be able to grapple with differences, with contradictions. We need to engage each other, to press each other for greater clarity, to question each other. In order to do this we need to work very hard at maintaining our sense of community, at not giving in to destructive competition or, what is worse, ignoring each other.

Now, all of this is a challenge to traditional theology because one of the key elements of traditional theology is its so-called objectivity, its so-called immutability, its sense of being "official" and, precisely because it is official, of being the only perspective that is correct.

Mujerista theology denounces any and all so-called objectivity. What passes as objectivity in reality merely names the subjectivity of those who have the authority and/or power to impose their point of view. So instead of objectivity what we should be claiming is responsibility for our subjectivity. All theology has to start with self-disclosure. Self-disclosure as part of theology should give all those who in one way or another come into contact with our theological work our "actional route." As a theologian I am obliged to reveal my concrete story within the framework of the social forces I have lived in. I am called to reveal the pivotal forces and issues that have formed me and that serve as my main points of reference. The idea in this kind of self-disclosure is to situate the subject, in this case myself, so that my discourse is understandable to others not only out of their own experience but insofar as they have the ability to go beyond the limits of their experience and see how my experience, because it is part of the processes of living, relates to and intersects with their experience, no matter how different both experiences are. …

Because subjectivity embraces the question "Who benefits from this?" *mujerista* theology challenges the so-called objectivity of traditional theology that refuses to recognize that it often tends to benefit the status quo at the expense of those who are marginal in church and society. The status quo is not a natural arrangement but rather a social construct originating with and maintained mainly by white, Euro-American males. Traditional theology offers intellectual backing for religious understandings and practices at the core of our churches, and it is easy to see who are those in charge of our churches.

Finally, *mujerista* theology's insistence on recognizing and disclosing subjectivity challenges the official status of traditional theology that results in avoidance of engagement. Traditional theology has clothed itself with the immutability that it claims is God's. Or does perhaps not that traditional theology make God immutable because it makes God in its own image and likeness?

Theology as a Communal Task

Our second challenge to traditional theology has to do with the centrality which community has in our Latino culture and in our theology. This means that we will continue to use the lived-experience of our grassroots communities as the source of our theology. So the themes of our theology are those that are suggested to us by the religious understandings and practices of our communities and not by the doctrines and dogmas of our churches. The goal of *mujerista* theology is not to come up with a *Summa*, or with three volumes entitled *Systematic Theology #1, #2, and #3*. The themes *mujerista* theology deals with are those that are required by Latinas' struggle for liberation. Thus, in our first book we dealt with what grounds the struggle for many of us, our understanding of God. The second book dealt with issues of self-identity – of ethnicity – and of moral agency. And now we are working on issues of embodiment, for what is most commonly used against us, to oppress us, is our bodies. …

In a way traditional theology, even the best of traditional theology, by insisting on following the patterns established long ago in my opinion, closes itself to the ongoing revelation of the divine in our midst. Those who do traditional theology call their way of proceeding "faithfulness to the past." I call it "blindness to the present" and "ignoring the God-in-our-midst today."

The Importance of Differences

A third challenge *mujerista* theology presents to traditional theology has to do with *mestizaje* and *mulatez*, with how we understand and deal with diversity, with differences. For us differences are not something to be done away with but rather something to be embraced. … Usually in mainline discourse, in traditional theological discourse, difference is defined as absolute otherness, mutual exclusion, categorical opposition. This is an essentialist meaning of difference in which one group serves as the norm against which all others are to be measured. Those of us who do not measure up are considered to be deviant, and our ideas are heretical. Difference of opinion, difference of perspective, arising most of the time from different life-experiences, any and all differences are defined as exclusion and opposition.

This way of defining difference expresses a fear of specificity and a fear of making permeable the boundaries between oneself and the others, between one's ideas and those of others. Specificity tends to be understood as unique – lending it a certain air of "the unknown" of which one is afraid or which is romanticized as exotic.

In *mujerista* theology we posit embracing differences as a moral option. We work at seeing those who are different from us as mirrors of ourselves and what we think. Ideas that are different from ours are mirrors – not the only ones – we have for our ideas (ideas similar to ours, of course, also are mirrors of our ideas) for they do make us see our ideas in a new light, maybe even make it possible for us to better understand our own ideas, to clarify them for ourselves and for others, a result that might not be achieved if we were to ignore ideas different from ours.

To embrace differences we have to stop being lazy and have to know what others really think. But that requires self-conscious interaction, and we are afraid of interacting with those with whom we disagree. Also, to be able to interact with others we have to affirm difference as something positive, we have to affirm plurality, to make permeable the boundaries of our categories. All of this requires embracing ambiguity, something those of us who live at the margins know much about. But traditional theology is not willing to do that because instead of risking ambiguity it rests secure in its impermeable and immutable center.

Age and Disability

The literature of subversive ethics clusters around questions of class, race, and gender. But the logic of subversive ethics stretches to other social groups whose "difference" has historically been seen negatively or is frequently seen today as related to social disadvantage. The paucity of literature in these areas perhaps speaks for itself about the degree of social exclusion involved.

Much secular discourse about disability concerns whether disability lies primarily in the body or mind of the impaired person (the medical model) or primarily in the discriminatory perceptions and the exclusive social structures brought about by the nondisabled person (the social model). Jean Vanier's words below are presented in the light of this discourse. Meanwhile, age is emerging as a growing area of concern and discussion, represented here by a speech given by Rowan Williams.

Jean Vanier, *In the Presence of the Poor*

Jean Vanier (b. 1928) is the founder of L'Arche, an international organization that creates communities in which people with developmental disabilities and those who assist them share life together. He explores in works such as *Community and Growth* (1989) the ways disability both inhibits and enables the expression and reception of the vulnerable areas in the lives of both the developmentally disabled and those who assist them. His L'Arche communities are one of the greatest living examples of the engagement of Christians with an issue that requires a life-transforming personal response.

One of the key issues in ethics surrounding disability is whether the disabled person is treated as a subject, or primarily as an object of the attention (or neglect) of carers, who themselves are regarded as subjects. Much work in disability discourse is concerned to promote ways in which those with a disability may be or become subjects in their own right. Of course, the term disability covers an enormous range of issues in developmental and physical dimensions. Vanier is speaking about those with profound developmental disabilities, and so his writing is less concerned with enabling such people to be subjects, and more concerned with enabling others to see them as at the center of God's purposes. That is what this passage is about.

Jesus Is the Poor

Jesus reveals an even greater unity between the personal contemplation of the Eternal and the personal relationship and bonding with people who are broken and rejected. This is perhaps the great secret of the Gospels and of the heart of Christ. Jesus calls his disciples not only to serve the poor but to discover in them his real presence, a meeting with the Father. Jesus tells us that he is hidden in the face of the poor, that he is in fact the poor. And so with the power of the Spirit, the smallest gesture of love towards the least significant person is a gesture of love towards him. Jesus is the starving, the thirsty, the prisoner, the stranger, the naked, the homeless, the sick, the dying, the oppressed, the humiliated. To live with the poor is to live with Jesus; to live with Jesus is to live with the poor (cf. Matt 25). "Whosoever welcomes one of these little ones in my name, welcomes me; and whosoever welcomes me, welcomes the Father" (Luke 9:48).

People who gather together to live the presence of Jesus among people in distress are therefore called not just to do things for them, or to see them as objects of charity, but rather to receive them as a source of life and of communion. These people come together not just to liberate those in need, but also to be liberated by them; not just to heal their wounds, but to be healed by them; not just to evangelise them but to be evangelised by them. ...

Those who come close to people in need do so first of all in generous desire to help them and bring them relief; they often feel like saviours and put themselves on a pedestal. But once in contact with them, once touching them, establishing a loving and trusting relationship with them, the mystery unveils itself. At the heart of the insecurity of people in distress there is a presence of Jesus. And so they discover the sacrament of the poor and enter the mystery of compassion. People who are poor seem to break down the barriers of powerfulness, of wealth, of ability and of pride; they pierce the armour the human heart builds to protect itself; they reveal Jesus Christ. They reveal to those who have come to "help" them their own poverty and vulnerability. These people also show their "helpers" their capacity for love, the forces of love in their hearts. A poor person has a mysterious power: in his weakness he is able to open hardened hearts and reveal the sources of living water within them. It is the tiny hand of the fearless child which can slip through the bars of the prison of egoism. He is the one who can open the lock and set free. And God hides himself in the child.

The poor teach us how to live the Gospel. That is why they are the treasures of the Church.

In l'Arche, assistants discover that they are called to announce good news to people in need and to reveal to them the immense love God has for them. Sometimes these assistants truly lead people with a handicap over the threshold and into faith. But once over the threshold, people with a handicap truly lead the assistants deeper into faith; they become our teachers. ...

Inner Pain

The cry for love and communion and for recognition that rises from the hearts of people in need reveals the fountain of love in us and our capacity to give life. At the same time, it can reveal our hardness of heart and our fears. Their cry is so demanding, and we are frequently seduced by wealth, power and the values of our societies. We want to climb the ladder of human promotion; we want to be recognised for our efficiency, power and virtue. The cry of the poor is threatening to the rich person within us. We are sometimes prepared to give money and a little time, but we are frightened to give our hearts, to enter into a personal relationship of love and communion with them. For if we do so, we shall have to die to all our selfishness and to all the hardness of our heart. ...

People come to l'Arche to serve the needy. They only stay if they have discovered that they themselves are needy, and that the good news is announced by Jesus to the poor, not to those who serve the poor.

Mission, then, does not imply an attitude of superiority or domination, an attitude of: "We know, you don't, so you must listen to us if you want to be well off. Otherwise you will be miserable." Mission springs necessarily from poverty and an inner wound, but also from trust in the love of God. Mission is not elitism. It is life given and flowing from the tomb of our beings which has become transformed into a source of life. It flows from the knowledge that we have been liberated through forgiveness; it flows from weakness and vulnerability. It is announcing the good news that we can live in humility, littleness and poverty, because God is dwelling in our hearts, giving us new life and freedom. We have received freely: we can give freely.

As long as there are fears and prejudices in the human heart, there will be war and bitter injustice. It is only when hearts are healed, and become loving and open, that the great political problems will be solved. ... The response to war is to live like brothers and sisters. The response to injustice is to share. The response to despair is a limitless trust and hope. The response to prejudice and hatred is forgiveness. To work for community is to work for humanity. To work for peace in community, through acceptance of others as they are, and through constant forgiveness, is to work for peace in the world and for true political solutions; it is to work for the Kingdom of God. It is to work to enable everyone to live and taste the secret joys of the human person united to the eternal. ...

Through the years, I am discovering that there is no contradiction between my life with those in need and my life of prayer and union with God. Of course Jesus reveals himself to me in the Eucharist and I need to spend time with him in silent prayer. But he reveals himself too in this life with my brothers and sisters. My fidelity to Jesus is also realised in my fidelity to my brothers and sisters of l'Arche and especially the poorest. If I give retreats, it is because of this covenant, which is the basis of my life. The rest is only service. ...

The Eyes of the Poor

Sometimes the greatest resource of all can be a small gesture of kindness from someone who is poor. It is often a gentle look from someone who is vulnerable which relaxes us, touches our heart and reminds us of what is essential. One day I went with some sisters of Mother Teresa to a slum in Bangalore where they were looking after people with leprosy. The sores stank and, humanly speaking, it was revolting. But the people there had light in their eyes. All I could do was hold the instruments the sisters were using, but I was glad to be there. The expressions and smiles of the people seemed to reach right into me and renew me. When I left, I felt an inexplicable joy, and it was they who had given it to me. I remember too an evening in a prison in Calgary, in Canada, where I spent three hours with the members of "Club 21" – the men who are serving more than 21 years for murder. They touched me and recharged my spirit. They changed something in me. …

The poor are always prophetic. As true prophets always point out, they reveal God's design. That is why we should take time to listen to them. And that means staying near them, because they speak quietly and infrequently; they are afraid to speak out, they lack confidence in themselves because they have been broken and oppressed. But if we listen to them, they will bring us back to the things that are essential. …

When I feel tired, I often go to La Forestière. This is a house in my community which welcomes very handicapped people; none of the ten who live there can talk, several can't walk, and in many ways they have only their hearts and the relationships they express through their face and bodies. The assistants who feed, bathe and care for them have to do this, not at their own rhythm, but at that of the people with a handicap. Things have to go at a pace which can welcome their least expression; because they have no verbal skills, they have no way of enforcing their views by raising their voice. So the assistants have to be the more attentive to the many non-verbal communications, and this adds greatly to their abilities to welcome the whole person. They become increasingly people of welcome and compassion. The slower rhythm and even the presence of the people with severe disabilities makes them slow down, switch off their efficiency motor, rest and recognise the presence of God. The poorest people have an extraordinary power to heal the wounds in hearts. If we welcome them, they nourish us.

Communities, if they close themselves off from the poor, close themselves off from God. That does not mean that every contemplative monastery should open its doors to the poor. No. But every contemplative monastery, every Christian, must be concerned by the poor and broken of the world. Every one must be close to the poor who are close by and who are calling us to love – these might be the sick and the old in a monastery; they might be those who hunger and ask for food and shelter for a few days. It might be those who are close by and who are in pain, calling out for a word of comfort. Every follower of Jesus is called to compassion and to walk with the poor and the broken and to pray for them.

It is not possible to eat the broken Body of Christ in the Eucharist and to drink his blood shed for us through torture, and not open our hearts to the broken and the crucified people in our world today.

Rowan Williams, *The Gifts Reserved for Age*

Rowan Williams (b. 1950) taught at Cambridge and Oxford universities before becoming Bishop of Monmouth and subsequently being named Archbishop of Canterbury in 2002. This address is typical of his work as archbishop, in that it seeks to affirm the evidence of the "kingdom" in a world often regarded as very secular, and meanwhile affirms underlying Christian claims and presuppositions in the purpose of reframing familiar questions and highlighting new and challenging ones.

Like disability, literature on age exhibits a tension between two tendencies: one is to advocate for autonomy and respect for those of advanced age, noting the wisdom and experience that can be neglected and overlooked, let alone the abuses to which some older people can be subject. The other is to take the infirm (for example, sufferers from profound memory loss) as the key subject in question, and examine good ways to care alongside finding ways to perceive God in distress and fragility.

In this speech, given to mark the centenary of an advocacy organization known as Friends of the Elderly, Williams earns the right to be heard in the second of these modes by beginning in the first. He uses the language of "dignity," so important to the autonomy approach, and then moves to a more reflective exploration of dementia, characteristic of the second approach, before returning to public policy questions.

Rowan Williams. "The Gifts Reserved for Age: A lecture to mark the Centenary of Friends of the Elderly, Church House, Westminster, September 6, 2005." www.archbishopofcanterbury.org/956?q=gifts+reserved+for+age. © Rowan Williams.

Of course, ageing brings much that is bound to be threatening; of course it entails the likelihood of sickness and disability and that most frightening of all prospects, the loss of mental coherence. But if this is combined with an unspoken assumption that the elderly are socially insignificant because they are not prime consumers or producers, the public image of ageing is bound to be extra bleak; and that is the message that can so easily be given these days. In contrast to a setting where age means freedom from having to justify your existence, age in our context is often implicitly presented as a stage of life when you exist "on sufferance." You're not actually pulling your weight; you're not an important enough bit of the market to be targeted in most advertising, except of a rather specialised and often rather patronising kind. In an obsessively sexualised world of advertising and other images, age is often made to look pathetic and marginal. And in the minds of most people there will be the picture of the geriatric ward or certain kinds of residential institution.

To borrow the powerful expression used of our prisons by Baroness Kennedy, this is "warehousing" – stacking people in containers because we can think of nothing else to do with them. From time to time, we face those deeply uncomfortable reports about abuse or even violence towards the vulnerable. Terrible as this is, we need to see it as an understandable consequence of a warehousing mentality. As the Friends of the Elderly make plain in their literature, even if not precisely in these terms, the question of how we perceive age is essentially a spiritual one. If you have a picture of human life as a story that needs pondering, retelling, organising, a story that is open to the judgement and mercy of God, it will be natural to hope for time to do

this work, the making of the soul. It will be natural to ask how the life of older people can be relieved of anxiety, and how the essentially creative work of reflection can be helped. It is not an exaggeration to say that, in such a perspective, growing old will make the greatest creative demands of your life. Furthermore, if we are all going to have the opportunity of undertaking reflection like this, it will be important that older people have the chance to share the task with the rest of us. The idea that age necessarily means isolation will be challenged. There is a sense that what matters for our own future thinking through of our life stories doesn't depend on the sort of things that go in and out of fashion. That is why, in most traditional societies, the term "elder" is a title of honour – as it is, of course, in the Christian Church, where the English word "priest" is an adaptation of the Greek for "elder." A person who has been released from the obligation to justify their existence is one who can give a perspective on life for those of us who are still in the middle of the struggle; their presence ought to be seen as a gift. …

We must not be sentimental. Age doesn't automatically confer wisdom, and the authority of "elders" of one sort or another can be oppressive, unrealistic and selfish. But when we completely lose sight of any idea that older people have a crucial role in pointing us to the way we might work to make better sense of our lives, we lose something vital. We lose the assumption that there is a perspective on our human experience that is bigger than the world of production and consumption. Work, sex, the struggle to secure our position or status, the world in which we constantly negotiate our demands and prove ourselves fit to take part in public life – what is there outside all this that might restore some sense of a value that is just given, a place that doesn't have to be earned? A healthy attitude to the elderly, I believe, is one of the things that can liberate us from the slavery of what we take for granted as the "real" world. Giving dignity to the elderly – and dignity is a crucial word for the mission of Friends of the Elderly – is inseparable from recognising the dignity of human beings as such. Contempt for older citizens, the unthinking pushing of them to the edges of our common life, is a sure sign of a shrivelled view of what it is to be human. ...

To digress just for a moment, I want to mention one specific kind of enterprise which crosses several frontiers in addressing the needs of older people. I have seen at close quarters some of the positive effects of oral history projects. Such a project can involve very young people, schoolchildren especially; it affirms the value of older people's memories; it allows them a chance to do some of that work we have already been thinking about, of ordering and reflecting on a life history. ...

But mention of memory at once raises the dark shadow that is for most of us one of the most deeply threatening aspects of ageing. As your annual review points out, a generally ageing population means an increase in the number of people likely to be afflicted with dementia. A large percentage of the population (and I should say that I am among them) has experience of the dilemmas of care that arise here. So far, a lot of what I have said might presuppose a more sunny prospect for older people than is in fact the case for a significant proportion of them.

Our understanding of dementia conditions is growing all the time, and we have seen a number of promising theories developed about contributory causes or about aspects of lifestyle that might defer or prevent the onset of these distressing states. But much is still mysterious, and we are not remotely likely to have resolved the problems in the next few decades. Here perhaps we are most challenged; it is not a matter of respecting age because of the freedom of older people to reflect and share their reflection. The question is whether we can respect and love those who may seem to have no clear picture of themselves or others at all. These are the people who most of all have no obvious stake in society, no justifying role. Yet how we treat them is as clear an index of our social vision as is the issue of how we treat children – almost more so, since these are not people who will grow and change in obviously positive ways. Are we truly committed to giving place and respect to those who can return nothing (as it seems)? ...

Yet in the harsh world of limited funding and personnel, how do we go on defending the expenditure of money and skill on such situations? As we've seen, there is always the temptation to "warehousing" in substandard geriatric care. But I have to say too in this context that the current drift towards a more accepting attitude to assisted suicide and euthanasia in some quarters gives

me a great deal of concern. What begins as a compassionate desire to enable those who long for death because of protracted pain, distress or humiliation to have their wish can, with the best will in the world, help to foster an attitude that assumes resources spent on the elderly are a luxury. Investment in palliative medicine, ensuring that access to the best palliative care is universally available, continuing research not only into the causes but into the behavioural varieties of dementia and so on – how secure would these be as priorities if there were any more general acceptance of the principle that it was legitimate to initiate a process designed to end someone's life? I am certainly not ascribing to the defenders of euthanasia or assisted dying any motive but the desire to spare people unnecessary suffering. But I think we have to ask the awkward question about how this might develop in a climate of anxiety about scarce resources.

I do not have a quick solution to the undeniable problem of resources. Nor, frankly, does anyone, independently of a deepened motivation to guarantee just treatment and high quality care for all, a motivation that honestly faces the demands on public and private finance that this will make. The fundamental question is whether we see this as expenditure that honours a human dignity we care about, or whether it is thought of as at best an unwelcome and rather irrational obligation. What I have tried to do in these brief observations is to argue that age deserves honour in any society which is serious about two things – about the fact that we all have the task of making sense of our lives by telling our stories without pressure, and about the fact that the value of our lives is not ultimately linked with the level of how much we produce or how much we consume.

If we do not accept that we ought to be serious about these things, we shall not only fail the elderly and treat them more and more as marginal to the real business of human communities: we shall run the risk of building in to our society a far wider disregard for the disadvantaged, those who are not in the forefront of producing and consuming. The Friends of the Elderly first came into existence because of the recognition that people living lives of poverty needed literal friends and advocates; the current profile of the charity reflects the awareness that older citizens are still constantly among the most high risk groups where economic and social privation are concerned. Taking the poor seriously means taking the elderly seriously, even those older people who do not suffer the most obviously acute forms of material deprivation.

Friends of the Elderly has for the last century had the task of speaking and acting for the sake of what we now fashionably call "social inclusion" – speaking for the poor, but more and more speaking for those whose lives are now lived outside the realm of "getting and spending." And this has meant speaking against certain things, against the over-functional narrowness that fails to see inherent dignity in everyone, against any idea that people don't deserve space and respect to become themselves more deeply and lastingly as they grow older. The task remains; it has not got easier and it is not likely to. But we should remember the millions of people who still have the instinctive feeling … that something is owed to our older citizens and that something crucial can be learned from them. Our job is to affirm that instinct without reservation or apology and to keep it linked to a whole sense of what we properly are as men and women – people who live in time, who learn who they are as they pursue both inner and outer dialogues, who need to be released from the tyrannies of producing and performing which so dominate our lives. The respect we learn and practice with our seniors is not something slavish or immature; it is a mark of our own maturity, indeed, our respect for our own humanity. Showing that and sharing that will give us work for a good many more centuries.

Chapter Seven

Ecclesial Ethics

Ecclesial ethics names a strand that has always been present in Christianity, but has attracted particular attention in the last generation under the leadership of some of the foremost names in contemporary theology. Whereas universal ethics concentrates on what is right for anyone and everyone, and subversive ethics points out the particular perspective of the marginalized and excluded, ecclesial ethics suggests that Christian ethics should first of all be concerned with the life made possible in Christ for Christians. It is not that Christians are better or more deserving of attention than others; it is that Christians are (or should be) those who look first to the transformation brought in Christ, rather than the contours of human society, for the sources of ethics.

It would be hard to ignore the polemical nature of much of the recent writing in this strand. Prominent writers have set out grand and far-reaching arguments suggesting (in most cases) that the current ethical establishment represents a loss of crucial commitments and assumptions from an earlier era, the recovery of which is indispensable for articulating and embodying a Christian ethic.

One key point of consensus for ecclesial ethics is that ethics in general and Christian ethics in particular has tended to concentrate on moments of decision and thus to neglect other significant issues. The description and evaluation of these other issues form the constructive dimension of ecclesial ethics.

While the protagonists among the advocates of ecclesial ethics are often associated together and have spent little time criticizing one another's work, there are in fact some significant differences between their respective emphases. In particular the role of Jesus in ethics is seen as normative by some but not by all, and this question among others has far-reaching implications for ethics.

Persuasive Narratives

Several of the most notable writers in the field of ecclesial ethics capture the imaginations of their readers with a story that goes broadly as follows. Western society is coming to the end of an era known by many names, the most common of which is modernity. Modernity describes a prevailing ethos and system of thought that gradually replaced an earlier consensus, stretching back to the medieval period or beyond. The key features of modernity for Christian ethics are that it tends to put humanity, particularly the individual person, at the center of enquiry – rather than God and the ways of God; that it tends to achieve consensus by avoiding public discussion of truth and purpose, thus privileging the bureaucratic facility of getting things done; and that it justifies its understanding and practice of authority by the more or less evident alternative of violence and chaos.

For some writers, the emergence of postmodernity, with its relentless suspicion of established systems, privileged narratives, and confident authorities, constitutes a significant challenge to modernity; for others, postmodernity is simply an outworking of one aspect of the logic of modernity. In this context, the narratives outlined by those associated with ecclesial ethics have a backward- and a forward-looking aspect. They look back to a time when communal and institutional life was shaped around particular practices derived from and dependent on particular perceptions of truth. And they look forward to the reassertion of confidence in those institutions – notably the church – that survive but which are currently shorn (or losing sight) of the practices that give their continued existence meaning.

The excerpts below are taken from perhaps the two most-discussed declension narratives in the area of ecclesial ethics, the foundational work of Alasdair MacIntyre and the provocative work of John Milbank.

Alasdair MacIntyre, *After Virtue*

Alasdair MacIntyre (b. 1929) is a Scottish-born philosopher who has been based in the United States since 1970. The decisive period of his writing is 1981–1999, with the publication of his four major works *After Virtue* (1981/1984), *Whose Justice? Which Rationality?* (1988), *Three Rival Versions of Moral Enquiry* (1990), and *Dependent Rational Animals* (1999). These books retain his earlier antagonism to liberal capitalism, but ground his constructive alternative in a restoration of the assumptions made about ethics by Aristotle and Thomas Aquinas.

The opening and closing passages of *After Virtue* are among the most celebrated rhetorical flourishes in modern philosophy. MacIntyre paints an imaginary picture of enlightened people trying to restore the discipline of science after it had fallen into such disrepute that almost all laboratories, textbooks, and research had been destroyed or lost. Such is the state of moral discourse today, argues MacIntyre. The assertions of rival positions have become no more than expressions of attitude and feeling. This impasse constitutes the failure of secular moral philosophy, a situation MacIntyre describes as "emotivism."

MacIntyre traces the roots of this condition to the failure of what he calls the Enlightenment project. Thinkers like David Hume, Jeremy Bentham, Denis Diderot, and Immanuel Kant set out to replace traditional and (in their view) superstitious forms of morality with a new universal morality that would elicit the assent of any rational person. The legacy of their various attempts is a set of rival models that each claims to be the only rational approach – as witnessed in endless disputes between Kantian deontologists and utilitarian consequentialists. Another legacy is the emergence of "a set of moral concepts which derive from their philosophical ancestry an appearance of rational determinateness and justification which they do not in fact possess." These include human rights and utility or welfare, which MacIntyre calls "useful fictions."

MacIntyre concludes that only a return to Aristotle avoids the critique that Nietzsche directed against both deontologists and consequentialists – and he famously brings his account to a climax (below) by advocating withdrawal to secluded communities.

Alasdair MacIntyre. *After Virtue: A Study in Moral Theory*. 2nd edn. London: Gerald Duckworth, 1990. From Chapter 18, "After Virtue: Nietzsche *or* Aristotle, Trotsky *and* St. Benedict," pages 256–9, 263. Published by Gerald Duckworth & Co. Ltd., copyright Alasdair MacIntyre 1981, 1985, 2007.

In Chapter 9 I posed a stark question: Nietzsche *or* Aristotle? The argument which led to the posing of that question had two central premises. The first was that the language – and therefore also to some large degree the practice – of morality today is in a state of grave disorder. That disorder arises from the prevailing cultural power of an idiom in which ill-assorted conceptual fragments from various parts of our past are deployed together in private and public debates which are notable chiefly for the unsettlable character of the controversies thus carried on and the apparent arbitrariness of each of the contending parties.

The second was that ever since belief in Aristotelian teleology was discredited moral philosophers have attempted to provide some alternative rational secular account of the nature and status of morality, but that all these attempts, various and variously impressive as they have been, have in fact failed, a failure perceived most clearly by Nietzsche. Consequently Nietzsche's negative proposal to raze to the ground the structures of inherited moral belief and argument had, whether we have regard to everyday moral belief and argument or look instead to the constructions of moral philosophers, and in spite of its desperate and grandiose quality, a certain plausibility – unless of course the initial rejection of the moral tradition to which Aristotle's teaching about the virtues is central turned out to have been misconceived and mistaken. Unless that tradition could be rationally vindicated, Nietzsche's stance would have a terrible plausibility.

Not that, even so, it would be easy in the contemporary world to be an intelligent Nietzschean. The stock characters acknowledged in the dramas of modern social life embody all too well the concepts and the modes of the moral beliefs and arguments which an Aristotelian and a Nietzschean would have to agree in rejecting. The bureaucratic manager, the consuming aesthete, the therapist, the protester and their numerous kindred occupy almost all the available culturally recognizable roles; the notions of the expertise of the few and of the moral agency of everyone are the presuppositions of the dramas which those characters enact. To cry out that the emperor had no clothes on was at least to pick on one man only to the amusement of everyone else; to declare that almost everyone is dressed in rags is much less likely to be popular. But the Nietzschean would at least have the consolation of being unpopularly *in the right* – unless, that is, the rejection of the Aristotelian tradition turned out to have been mistaken.

The Aristotelian tradition has occupied two distinct places in my argument: first, because I have suggested that a great part of modern morality is intelligible only as a set of fragmented survivals from that tradition, and indeed that the inability of modern moral philosophers to carry through their projects of analysis and justification is closely connected with the fact that the concepts with which they work are a combination of fragmented

survivals and implausible modern inventions; but in addition to this the rejection of the Aristotelian tradition was a rejection of a quite distinctive kind of morality in which rules, so predominant in modern conceptions of morality, find their place in a larger scheme in which the virtues have the central place; hence the cogency of the Nietzschean rejection and refutation of modern moralities of rules, whether of a utilitarian or of a Kantian kind, did not necessarily extend to the earlier Aristotelian tradition.

It is one of my most important contentions that against that tradition the Nietzschean polemic is completely unsuccessful. The grounds for saying this can be set out in two different ways. The first I already suggested in Chapter 9; Nietzsche succeeds if all those whom he takes on as antagonists fail. Others may have to succeed by virtue of the rational power of their positive arguments; but if Nietzsche wins, he wins by default.

He does not win. I have sketched in Chapters 14 and 15 the rational case that can be made for a tradition in which the Aristotelian moral and political texts are canonical. For Nietzsche or the Nietzscheans to succeed that case would have to be rebutted. Why it cannot be so rebutted is best brought out by considering a second way in which the rejection of Nietzsche's claims can be argued. Nietzschean man, the *Übermensch*, the man who transcends, finds his good nowhere in the social world to date, but only in that in himself which dictates his own new law and his own new table of the virtues. Why does he never find any objective good with authority over him in the social world to date? The answer is not difficult: Nietzsche's portrait makes it clear that he who transcends is wanting in respect of both relationships and activities. Consider part of just one note (962) from *The Will To Power*. "A great man – a man whom nature has constructed and invented in the grand style – what is he? ... If he cannot lead, he goes alone; then it can happen that he may snarl at some things he meets on the way ... he wants no 'sympathetic' heart, but servants, tools; in his intercourse with men he is always intent on *making* something out of them. He knows he is incommunicable: he finds it tasteless to be familiar; and when one thinks he is, he usually is not. When not speaking to himself, he wears a mask. He rather lies than tells the truth: it requires more spirit and *will*. There is a solitude within him that is inaccessible to praise or blame, his own justice that is beyond appeal."

This characterization of "the great man" is deeply rooted in Nietzsche's contention that the morality of European society since the archaic age in Greece has been nothing but a series of disguises for the will to power and that the claim to objectivity for such moral-ity cannot be rationally sustained. It is because this is so that the great man cannot enter into relationships mediated by appeal to shared standards or virtues or goods; he is his own only authority and his relationships to others have to be exercises of that authority. But we can now see clearly that, if the account of the virtues which I have defended can be sustained, it is the isola-tion and self-absorption of "the great man" which thrust upon him the burden of being his own self-suf-ficient moral authority. For if the conception of a good has to be expounded in terms of such notions as those of a practice, of the narrative unity of a human life and of a moral tradition, then goods, and with them the only grounds for the authority of laws and virtues, can only be discovered by entering into those relationships which constitute communities whose central bond is a shared vision of and understanding of goods. To cut oneself off from shared activity in which one has initially to learn obediently as an apprentice learns, to isolate oneself from the communities which find their point and purpose in such activities, will be to debar oneself from finding any good outside of oneself. It will be to condemn oneself to that moral solipsism which consti-tutes Nietzschean greatness. Hence we have to conclude not only that Nietzsche does not win the argument by default against the Aristotelian tradition, but also, and perhaps more importantly, that it is from the perspec-tive of that tradition that we can best understand the mistakes at the heart of the Nietzschean position.

The attractiveness of Nietzsche's position lay in its apparent honesty. When I was setting out the case in favor of an amended and restated emotivism, it appeared to be a consequence of accepting the truth of emotivism that an honest man would no longer want to go on using most, at least, of the language of past morality because of its misleading character. And Nietzsche was the only major philosopher who had not flinched from this conclusion. Since moreover the language of modern morality is burdened with pseudo-concepts such as those of utility and of natural rights, it appeared that Nietzsche's resoluteness alone would rescue us from entanglement by such concepts; but it is now clear that the price to be paid for this liberation is entanglement in another set of mistakes. The concept of the Nietzschean "great man" is also a pseudo-concept, although not always perhaps – unhappily – what I earlier called a fiction. It represents individualism's final attempt to escape from its own consequences. And the Nietzschean stance turns out not to be a mode of escape from or an alternative to the conceptual scheme of liberal individualist modernity, but rather one more representative moment in its internal unfolding. And we may therefore expect liberal individualist societies to breed "great men" from time to time. Alas!

So it was right to see Nietzsche as in some sense the ultimate antagonist of the Aristotelian tradition. But it now turns out to be the case that in the end the Nietzschean stance is only one more facet of that very moral culture of which Nietzsche took himself to be an implacable critic. It is therefore after all the case that the crucial moral opposition is between liberal individual-ism in some version or other and the Aristotelian tradi-tion in some version or other.

The differences between the two run very deep. They extend beyond ethics and morality to the understand-ing of human action, so that rival conceptions of the social sciences, of their limits and their possibilities, are intimately bound up with the antagonistic confronta-tion of these two alternative ways of viewing the human world. This is why my argument has had to extend to such topics as those of the concept of fact, the limits to predictability in human affairs and the nature of ideol-ogy. And it will now, I hope, be clear that in the chapters dealing with those topics I was not merely summing up arguments *against* the social embodiments of liberal individualism, but also laying the basis for arguments in favor of an alternative way of envisaging both the social sciences and society, one with which the Aristotelian tradition can easily be at home.

My own conclusion is very clear. It is that on the one hand we still, in spite of the efforts of three centuries of moral philosophy and one of sociology, lack any coher-ent rationally defensible statement of a liberal individu-alist point of view; and that, on the other hand, the Aristotelian tradition can be restated in a way that restores intelligibility and rationality to our moral and social attitudes and commitments. ...

It is always dangerous to draw too precise parallels between one historical period and another; and among the most misleading of such parallels are those which have been drawn between our own age in Europe and North America and the epoch in which the Roman empire declined into the Dark Ages. Nonetheless certain parallels there are. A crucial turning point in that earlier history occurred when men and women of good will turned aside from the task of shoring up the Roman *imperium* and ceased to identify the continuation of civility and moral community with the maintenance of that *imperium*. What they set themselves to achieve instead – often not recognizing fully what they were doing – was the construction of new forms of community within which the moral life could be sustained so that both morality and civility might survive the coming ages of barbarism and darkness. If my account of our moral condition is correct, we ought also to conclude that for some time now we too have reached that turning point. What matters at this stage is the construction of local forms of community within which civility and the intellectual and moral life can be sustained through the new dark ages which are already

upon us. And if the tradition of the virtues was able to survive the horrors of the last dark ages, we are not entirely without grounds for hope. This time however the barbarians are not waiting beyond the frontiers; they have already been governing us for quite some time. And it is our lack of consciousness of this that constitutes part of our predicament. We are waiting not for a Godot, but for another – doubtless very different – St. Benedict.

John Milbank, *Theology as a Social Science*

The story told by the English Anglican theologian John Milbank (b. 1952) goes as follows.

Once there was no secular. Every aspect of life was defined by its relationship with the transcendent sphere of existence – the creator God. There was thus no such thing as a material world of "nature": instead, all was "creation," what Milbank calls a "charged immanence" shaped with a transcendent orientation. Thus there was no objective, autonomous reason, no state, no public or private realm – and no form of existence that was not inherently ordered towards creaturely praise of the creator. Christianity is "the coding of transcendental difference as peace." The story of grace-infused creation runs from Plato to Gregory of Nyssa to Augustine to Thomas Aquinas.

But the harmony of participation in this seamless universe was broken, and the name for this fracture is "modernity." This transformation began with the medieval theologian John Duns Scotus (1266–1308), who detached the immanent world from the transcendent heaven, thus bringing under discussion a sphere of being unhinged from participation in the divine. This new realm was one of neutral, objective, autonomous universal reason, described by Milbank as the "univocity of being." Instead of a harmonious communion of enriching friendships, reality was constructed from the starting point of an isolated individual subject – the thinker of René Descartes, who became also the autonomous subject of Immanuel Kant, the owner of inalienable rights of John Locke, and the competitive aggregate of self-interested preservation instincts of Thomas Hobbes and Adam Smith. In place of participatory communion there was now self-interest; in place of worship there was now fundamental antagonism.

Postmodernity is upon us, and it is founded on Friedrich Nietzsche's profound questioning of interests and ability to trace genealogies of power. However, postmodernity's nihilism – its thoroughgoing skepticism that finds no resting place for suspicion and doubt – is no more than an extension of modernity's assumptions about the "univocity of being" – that is, the restriction of philosophy to considering the secular, detached from the divine. A true postmodernity would correct this philosophical error and return to contemplating and acting in a universe suffused with the transcendent and thus presuming the configuration of difference as benign.

In this passage Milbank acknowledges that "a gigantic claim to be able to read, criticize, say what is going on in other human societies, is absolutely integral to the nature of the Christian Church, which itself claims to exhibit the exemplary form of human community." What some regard as arrogance, Milbank regards as a renunciation of a false humility. This claim rests not on political conquest but on the centrality of forgiveness, as the final paragraphs of this passage show.

John Milbank. *Theology and Social Theory: Beyond Secular Reason*. 2nd edn. Oxford: Blackwell, 2006. From Part IV, "Theology and Difference"; Chapter 12, "The Other City: Theology as a Social Science," pages 387–8, 409–11.

Metanarrative Realism

... [W]e do not relate to the story of Christ by schematically applying its categories to the empirical content of whatever we encounter. Instead, we interpret this narrative in a response which inserts us in a narrative relation to the "original" story. First and foremost, the Church stands in a narrative relationship to Jesus and the Gospels, within a story that subsumes both. This must be the case, because no *historical* story is ever "over and done with." Furthermore, the New Testament itself does not preach any denial of historicity, nor any disappearance of our own personalities into the monistic truth of Christ. Quite to the contrary, Jesus's mission is seen as inseparable from his preaching of the Kingdom, and inauguration of a new sort of community, the Church. Salvation is available for us after Christ, because we can be incorporated into the community which he founded, and the response of this community to Christ is made possible by the response to the divine Son of the divine Spirit, from whom it receives the love that flows between Son and Father. The association of the Church with the response of the Spirit which arises "after" the Son, and yet is fully divine, shows that the new community belongs from the beginning within the new narrative manifestation of God. Hence the metanarrative is *not* just the story of Jesus, it is the continuing story of the Church, already realized in a finally exemplary way by Christ, yet still to be realized universally, in harmony with Christ, and yet *differently*, by all generations of Christians.

The metanarrative, therefore, is the genesis of the Church, outside which context one could only have an ahistorical, gnostic Christ. But once one has said this, one then has to face up to the real implication of a narrative that is at one and the same time a recounting of a "real history," and yet has also an interpretative, regulative function with respect to all other history. The real

implication is this: one simply cannot exhibit in what its "meta" character consists, without *already* carrying out this interpretation, this regulation, to the widest possible extent. One has to pass from [George] Lindbeck's "Kantian" narrative epistemology of scheme and content to a "Hegelian" metanarrative which is "a philosophy of history," though based on faith, not reason. For the Christological-ecclesial narrative *arises*, in the first place, not simply as an "identification" of the divine, but also as a "reading" and a critique-through-practice of all historical human community up to that point. Initially, it defines itself as both in continuity and discontinuity with the community of Israel; later on it defines itself as in still greater discontinuity with the "political" societies of the antique world. This account of history and critique of human society is in no sense an appendage to Christianity – on the contrary, it belongs to its very "essence." For first of all, its break with Judaism arises from Christianity's denial that the Jewish law is the final key to true human community and salvation. And secondly, Christianity's universalist claim that incorporation into the Church is indispensable for salvation assumes that other religions and social groupings, however virtuous-seeming, were, in their own terms alone, finally on the path of damnation.

In this fashion a gigantic claim to be able to read, criticize, say what is going on in other human societies, is absolutely integral to the nature of the Christian Church, which itself claims to exhibit the exemplary form of human community. For theology to surrender this claim, to allow that other discourses – "the social sciences" for example – carry out yet more fundamental readings, would therefore amount to a denial of theological truth. The *logic* of Christianity involves the claim that the "interruption" of history by Christ and his bride, the Church, is the most fundamental of events, interpreting all other events. And it is *most especially* a social event, able to interpret other social formations, because it compares them with its own new social practice.

A genuine "metanarrative realism" does full justice to the internal tension within narrative. In particular, the temporality of the syntagmatic dimension is not betrayed, because the metanarrative ceases, as we have just seen, to be *only* a privileged set of events, but rather becomes the whole story of human history which is still being enacted and interpreted in the light of those events. This ensures that the "redescription" of Christianity advocated by Lindbeck and the Yale school will now have a fully social and political dimension. ...

The Critique of Virtue

Exactly why does Augustine deny the existence of true justice and virtue in pagan society? The main reason he gives is that the pagans failed to offer the worship, *latria*, in justice owed to the true God. This, however, does not mean that Augustine's real criticism lies solely at the level of religious practice. On the contrary, Augustine believes that the form taken by true worship of the true God is (as Rowan Williams stresses) first of all the subordination of the passing to the abiding (God and immortal souls). This subordination exposes all desire to make worldly *dominium* an ultimate end to be idolatry and the prime source of injustice. It is therefore the *lack* of "otherworldliness" that promotes social inequity. In the second place it is the offering of mutual forgiveness in the community; at one point he associates absence of the practice of forgiveness ("true sacrifice") with the absence of monotheism. In addition, thought of God the Father seems for Augustine to have been quite inseparable from the thought of heaven, our Mother, or the eternal community of all unfallen and redeemed creatures enjoying the vision of the infinite Trinity. Thus, when he says that the pagans failed to "refer" all earthly *usus* to the peace of the one true God, he adjoins to this a failure of referral to the peace of the heavenly community. Without "mutual forgiveness" and social peace, says Augustine, "no-one will be able to see God." The pagans were for Augustine unjust, because they did not give priority to peace and forgiveness.

Augustine acknowledges that the pagans tried to ensure that the soul ordered the body. But the true principle of this ordering, he argues, was lacking, because they ignored a third level beyond the soul, which places the soul itself in order. This is the dimension of God/heaven/peace. But the way in which the pagans thought the soul ordered the body is not comparable to the way in which Augustine thought the third level ordered the soul. The soul violently constrains the body and represses the passions, but in the third dimension the soul realizes its true desire, and enters into reciprocal relationships of affirmation with other souls. In right relation to this level, not just the soul, but rather now the whole person, the soul-body continuum, just

is as it should be, affirmed in its correct external positioning, which still involves hierarchical subordination, yet no longer coercive suppression. After all, according to Augustine's *musical* ontology, both soul and body are different intensities of the same "numerical" stuff — both emerging, not from matter, but from nothing. Augustine's doctrine is that nothing that properly is, by nature, resists other natures, and therefore one must pass beyond suppression of passion towards the rectification of desire, and a peaceful order that is a pure consensus.

Justice that is content with less than absolute social consensus and harmony is therefore less than justice, not because justice is only founded in conventional agreement, but because one has faith in an infinite justice, in the idea that there is a temporally "proper" (even if changing) position for everything, without any chaotic remainder. But the pagans, Augustine implies, were resigned to inherently unruly social elements, which had to be disciplined somehow or other. Similarly, they were resigned to the existence of unruly and inherently dangerous psychic elements which had to be eternally held at bay. Public virtue, in consequence, was for them at base military virtue, the securing of inner dominance of one class over another, and outer security against enemies, both in the interests of the "whole" over the parts. If the city encourages virtue in individuals this is, nonetheless, fundamentally private virtue, for it is the glorious out-stripping of rivals in the defence of the city, related to an achievement of inward control of the passions and vices.

Augustine here rightly detects a fundamental individualism at work in the heroic ideals of antiquity, an individualism both of public *imperium* and private *dominium*. This is necessarily present, because whole and part are turn and turn about subordinated to each other, and the part/whole ratio is given predominance over the relational sequence which endlessly threatens to break out of any totality. And between the whole and the part, as between soul and body, there persists a kind of fundamental discontinuity, as between two different *media*, which means that subordination of the one by the other can only be forceful, and not a matter of continuity in a series, or isomorphic echo. By contrast, the Christian social ontology, linked to the neo-Platonic idea of an emanative procession of all reality from a single divine source, abolishes this duality which supports the idea of an ineradicable ontological violence.

Antique ethics, therefore, were not really, for Augustine, "ethical," because not finally about the realization of community as itself the final goal. They failed to arrive at a relational perspective and therefore, when deconstructed, can be seen as celebrating the greater strength shown by the *polis* or the *soul* in its control of its members or its body. From the viewpoint of antiquity, it must appear that, in heaven, where there is only harmony and tranquillity, there is no scope for virtue at all, whereas for Augustine, after St Paul, it is only here that virtue, and the full range of human powers, will be properly displayed. All the antique virtues are for him ambiguously virtuous, because each is necessitated by an absence of charity and peace. In all of them there lurks an element of "excessive" compulsion, or an arbitrary ordering of what can only be properly ordered if it responds with a true desire. By contrast, in heaven, in a sense, only charity remains, because this concerns a gratuitously received exchange, and not the necessary inhibition of something threatening. This is not to say that other virtues altogether disappear; it is just that they are no longer in any sense "in addition" to charity. Charity indeed is *not* for Augustine a matter of mere generous intention: on the contrary, it involves that exact appropriateness of reciprocal action necessary to produce a "beautiful" order, and, in this sense, charity is the very consummation of both justice and prudence.

How does it help though (one might protest) to imagine a state of total peace, when we are locked in a world of deep-seated conflict which it would be folly to deny or evade? It helps, because it allows us to unthink the necessity of violence, and exposes the manner in which the assumption of an inhibition of an always prior violence helps to preserve violence in motion. But it helps more, because it indicates that there is a way to act in a violent world which assumes the ontological priority of non-violence, and this way is called "forgiveness of sins."

Augustine asserts that, for us, the approach to divine perfection cannot be by any achieved excellence of virtue, but only through forgiveness. This does not, I think, imply a Protestant resignation to sinfulness. Instead, the assertion belongs with the social character of his thought: given the persistence of the sin of others (as well as our own sinfulness, which we cannot all at once overcome, but remains alien to our better desires) there is only one way to respond to them which would not itself be sinful and domineering, and that is to anticipate heaven, and act as if their sin was not there (or rather acting with a "higher realism" which releases what is positive and so alone real in their actions from negative distortion) by offering reconciliation. Augustine's real and astounding point is this: virtue cannot properly operate (in any degree) except when collectively possessed, when all are virtuous and to the extent that all concur in the sequence of their differences; hence the actual, "possessed," realized virtues which we lay claim to, *least of all* resemble true, heavenly virtues. On the contrary, the only thing really like heavenly virtue is our constant attempt to compensate for, substitute for, even short-cut this total absence of virtue, by not taking offence, assuming the guilt of others, doing what they should have done, beyond the bounds of any given "responsibility." Paradoxically, it is only in this exchange and sharing that any truly actual virtue is really present. Thus Augustine contrasts Cain's name, "possession," with Seth's name, "resurrection." Only the bodies which we have in common arise.

A New Aristotelianism

The philosophy of Alasdair MacIntyre and the theology of Stanley Hauerwas have spearheaded a broad consensus within ecclesial ethics around a number of key themes. One is their decisive break with universal ethics. Universal ethics tends to focus on the moment of decision as the central question in ethics. Ecclesial ethicists point out a number of flaws in this approach. They argue it offers an inadequate description of an ethical situation if the circumstances, commitments, and characters of those most closely involved are not taken into account. Ecclesial ethics seeks to broaden the perspective so that all the information excluded by universal ethics becomes relevant again. Universal ethics excludes such information because it seems particular, and thus must be excluded if ethics is to concentrate on phenomena that have been or could be replicated in many other contexts. Ecclesial ethics points out that it is precisely this particular information, which universal ethics shuns, that makes ethics comprehensible.

A second theme is the account of virtue. This is a theme recovered from Aristotle, Augustine, and Aquinas. It is accompanied by the notions of practice (a cooperative activity that defines excellence or human ends), *telos* (the final purpose of life), and tradition (which requires virtue to be sustained).

A third theme is habit formation. Forming character is like learning a language. Character is formed by the regular and disciplined performance of practices that after long exercise emerge as habits. The aim is to shape the imagination of persons by so training them in community through habit formation within a tradition that they learn to take the right things for granted and thus at the moment of decision act apparently effortlessly without anxiety or dismay.

A fourth theme is that of narrative. As MacIntyre points out, "I can only answer the question 'What am I to do?' if I can answer the prior question 'Of what story or stories do I find myself a part?'" Meanwhile, manners, culture, and social roles are embedded in narratives: "There is no way to give us an understanding of any society, including our own, except through the stock of stories which constitute its initial dramatic resources."

The readings below offer one foundational and one contemporary account of what is generally known as "virtue ethics," together with a key text outlining the place of narrative.

Thomas Aquinas, *Of the Virtues*

Aristotle's account of virtue in his *Nicomachean Ethics* is widely, though not universally, accepted in ecclesial ethics circles. Aristotle sees three dimensions of the human soul – passions, faculties, and states of character. "Passions" refer to desires and feelings; these arise involuntarily in response to circumstances, and are not the cause of praise or blame, and are thus not virtues. "Faculties" refer to natural capacities or abilities, which again attract praise or blame only when suitably applied. "States of character," by contrast, are dispositions to act in particular ways in particular circumstances – and it is here that virtue resides. But not all states of character are virtues. Here the key term is the "mean." Virtues, in the most influential (but not the only) description offered by Aristotle, are those states of character that lie at the mean between excess and deficiency.

Augustine recognized, in addition to the four cardinal virtues, three theological virtues: faith, hope, and love. Instead of love being a function of the virtues, the virtues become functions of our love for God. Virtue is thus "rightly ordered love." Thomas Aquinas, who followed Augustine closely in relation to these matters, yet incorporated most of Aristotle's understanding of virtue, described love as the form of the virtues.

In this passage, Aquinas, with his characteristic elegant simplicity, lays out the nature of virtue ("a good quality of the mind, by which we live righteously, of which no one can make bad use, which God works in us, without us"), the four cardinal virtues (which lead us to happiness in accord with our nature) and their relation to one another, the three theological virtues (which lead us to happiness beyond our nature), and the unity of the virtues. In a summary statement he concludes, "The perfect moral virtue is a habit that inclines us to do a good deed well."

Thomas Aquinas. *Summa Theologica*. 5 vols. Notre Dame: Christian Classics, 1948. Also available online at www.ccel.org/ccel/aquinas/summa.html. From Prima Secundae [First Part of the Second Part], Treatise on Habits. Question 55, "Of the Virtues, As to Their Essence"; Question 61, "Of the Cardinal Virtues"; Question 62, "Of the Theological Virtues"; Question 65, "Of the Connection of Virtues." Pages 819, 821–2, 846–8, 851, 861–4.

Question 55, "Of the Virtues"

Article 1. Whether human virtue is a habit?

… Virtue denotes a certain perfection of a power. Now a thing's perfection is considered chiefly in regard to its end. But the end of power is act. Wherefore power is said to be perfect, according as it is determinate to its act.

Now there are some powers which of themselves are determinate to their acts; for instance, the active natural powers. And therefore these natural powers are in themselves called virtues. But the rational powers, which are proper to man, are not determinate to one particular action, but are inclined indifferently to many: and they are determinate to acts by means of habits … Therefore human virtues are habits.

Reply to Objection 1. Sometimes we give the name of a virtue to that to which the virtue is directed, namely, either to its object, or to its act: for instance, we give the name Faith, to that which we believe, or to the act of believing, as also to the habit by which we believe. When therefore we say that "virtue is the limit of power," virtue is taken for the object of virtue. For the furthest point to which a power can reach, is said to be its virtue; for instance, if a man can carry a hundredweight and not more, his virtue is put at a hundredweight, and not at sixty. …

Article 4. Whether virtue is suitably defined?

Objection 1. It would seem that the definition, usually given, of virtue, is not suitable, to wit: "Virtue is a good quality of the mind, by which we live righteously, of which no one can make bad use, which God works in us, without us." …

I answer that, This definition comprises perfectly the whole essential notion of virtue. For the perfect essential notion of anything is gathered from all its causes. Now the above definition comprises all the causes of virtue. For the formal cause of virtue, as of everything, is gathered from its genus and difference, when it is defined as "a good quality": for "quality" is the genus of virtue, and the difference, "good." But the definition would be more suitable if for "quality" we substitute "habit," which is the proximate genus.

Now virtue has no matter "out of which" it is formed, as neither has any other accident; but it has matter "about which" it is concerned, and matter "in which" it exits, namely, the subject. The matter about which virtue is concerned is its object, and this could not be included in the above definition, because the object fixes the virtue to a certain species, and here we are giving the definition of virtue in general. And so for material cause we have the subject, which is mentioned when we say that virtue is a good quality "of the mind."

The end of virtue, since it is an operative habit, is operation. But it must be observed that some operative habits are always referred to evil, as vicious habits: others are sometimes referred to good, sometimes to evil; for instance, opinion is referred both to the true

and to the untrue: whereas virtue is a habit which is always referred to good: and so the distinction of virtue from those habits which are always referred to evil, is expressed in the words "by which we live righteously": and its distinction from those habits which are sometimes directed unto good, sometimes unto evil, in the words, "of which no one makes bad use."

Lastly, God is the efficient cause of infused virtue, to which this definition applies; and this is expressed in the words "which God works in us without us." If we omit this phrase, the remainder of the definition will apply to all virtues in general, whether acquired or infused. …

Question 61, "Of the Cardinal Virtues"

Article 2. Whether there are four cardinal virtues?

… Things may be numbered either in respect of their formal principles, or according to the subjects in which they are: and either way we find that there are four cardinal virtues.

For the formal principle of the virtue of which we speak now is good as defined by reason; which good is considered in two ways. First, as existing in the very act of reason: and thus we have one principal virtue, called "Prudence." Secondly, according as the reason puts its order into something else; either into operations, and then we have "Justice"; or into passions, and then we need two virtues. For the need of putting the order of reason into the passions is due to their thwarting reason: and this occurs in two ways. First, by the passions inciting to something against reason, and then the passions need a curb, which we call "Temperance." Secondly, by the passions withdrawing us from following the dictate of reason, e.g. through fear of danger or toil: and then man needs to be strengthened for that which reason dictates, lest he turn back; and to this end there is "Fortitude."

In like manner, we find the same number if we consider the subjects of virtue. For there are four subjects of the virtue we speak of now: viz. the power which is rational in its essence, and this is perfected by "Prudence"; and that which is rational by participation, and is threefold, the will, subject of "Justice," the concupiscible faculty, subject of "Temperance," and the irascible faculty, subject of "Fortitude." …

Article 3. Whether any other virtues should be called principal rather than these?

… [T]hese four are reckoned as cardinal virtues, in respect of the four formal principles of virtue as we understand it now. These principles are found chiefly in certain acts and passions. Thus the good which exists in the act of reason, is found chiefly in reason's command, but not in its counsel or its judgment ... Again, good as defined by reason and put into our operations as something right and due, is found chiefly in commutations and distributions in respect of another person, and on a basis of equality. The good of curbing the passions is found chiefly in those passions which are most difficult to curb, viz. in the pleasures of touch. The good of being firm in holding to the good defined by reason, against the impulse of passion, is found chiefly in perils of death, which are most difficult to withstand.

Accordingly the above four virtues may be considered in two ways. First, in respect of their common formal principles. In this way they are called principal, being general, as it were, in comparison with all the virtues: so that, for instance, any virtue that causes good in reason's act of consideration, may be called prudence; every virtue that causes the good of right and due in operation, be called justice; every virtue that curbs and represses the passions, be called temperance; and every virtue that strengthens the mind against any passions whatever, be called fortitude. Many, both holy doctors, as also philosophers, speak about these virtues in this sense: and in this way the other virtues are contained under them. ...

Question 62, "Of the Theological Virtues"

Article 1. Whether there are any theological virtues?

... The precepts of the Law are about acts of virtue. Now the Divine Law contains precepts about the acts of faith, hope, and charity: for it is written (*Ecclus.* 2:8, *seqq.*): "Ye that fear the Lord believe Him," and again, "hope in Him," and again, "love Him." Therefore faith, hope, and charity are virtues directing us to God. Therefore they are theological virtues.

Man is perfected by virtue, for those actions whereby he is directed to happiness ... Now man's happiness is twofold ... One is proportionate to human nature, a happiness, to wit, which man can obtain by means of his natural principles. The other is a happiness surpassing man's nature, and which man can obtain by the power of God alone, by a kind of participation of the Godhead, about which it is written (2 Pet. 1:4) that by Christ we are made "partakers of the Divine nature." And because such happiness surpasses the capacity of human nature, man's natural principles which enable him to act well according to his capacity, do not suffice to direct man to this same happiness. Hence it is necessary for man to receive from God some additional principles, whereby he may be directed to supernatural

happiness, even as he is directed to his connatural end, by means of his natural principles, albeit not without Divine assistance. Such like principles are called "theological virtues": first, because their object is God, inasmuch as they direct us aright to God: secondly, because they are infused in us by God alone: thirdly, because these virtues are not made known to us, save by Divine revelation, contained in Holy Writ. ...

Question 65, "Of the Connection of Virtues"

Article 1. Whether the moral virtues are connected with one another?

... Moral virtue may be considered either as perfect or as imperfect. An imperfect moral virtue, temperance for instance, or fortitude, is nothing but an inclination in us to do some kind of good deed, whether such inclination be in us by nature or by habituation. If we take the moral virtues in this way, they are not connected: since we find men who, by natural temperament or by being accustomed, are prompt in doing deeds of liberality, but are not prompt in doing deeds of chastity.

But the perfect moral virtue is a habit that inclines us to do a good deed well; and if we take moral virtues in this way, we must say that they are connected, as nearly all are agreed in saying. For this two reasons are given, corresponding to the different ways of assigning the distinction of the cardinal virtues. For ... some distinguish them according to certain general properties of the virtues: for instance, by saying that discretion belongs to prudence, rectitude to justice, moderation to temperance, and strength of mind to fortitude, in whatever matter we consider these properties to be. In this way the reason for the connection is evident: for strength of mind is not commended as virtuous, if it be without moderation or rectitude or discretion: and so forth. This, too, is the reason assigned for the connection by Gregory, who says (*Moral.* xxii, 1) that "a virtue cannot be perfect" as a virtue, "if isolated from the others: for there can be no true prudence without temperance, justice and fortitude": and he continues to speak in like manner of the other virtues. Augustine also gives the same reason (*De Trin.* vi, 4).

Others, however, differentiate these virtues in respect of their matters, and it is in this way that Aristotle assigns the reason for their connection (*Ethic.* vi, 13). Because ... no moral virtue can be without prudence; since it is proper to moral virtue to make a right choice, for it is an elective habit. Now right choice requires not only the inclination to a due end, which inclination is the direct outcome of moral virtue, but also correct choice of things conducive to the end, which choice is made by prudence, that counsels, judges, and commands in those things that are directed to the end. In like manner one cannot have prudence unless one has the moral virtues: since prudence is "right reason about things to be done," and the starting point of reason is the end of the thing to be done, to which end man is rightly disposed by moral virtue. Hence, just as we cannot have speculative science unless we have the understanding of the principles, so neither can we have prudence without the moral virtues: and from this it follows clearly that the moral virtues are connected with one another. ...

Article 3. Whether charity can be without moral virtue?

... All the moral virtues are infused together with charity. The reason for this is that God operates no less perfectly in works of grace than in works of nature. Now, in the works of nature, we find that whenever a thing contains a principle of certain works, it has also whatever is necessary for their execution: thus animals are provided with organs whereby to perform the actions that their souls empower them to do. Now it is evident that charity, inasmuch as it directs man to his last end, is the principle of all the good works that are referable to his last end. Wherefore all the moral virtues must needs be infused together with charity, since it is through them that man performs each different kind of good work.

It is therefore clear that the infused moral virtues are connected, not only through prudence, but also on account of charity: and, again, that whoever loses charity through mortal sin, forfeits all the infused moral virtues.

Samuel Wells, *Forming Habits*

Samuel Wells (b. 1965) was shaped by Scottish and English traditions in theology and now works at Duke University in North Carolina. His work has sought to articulate the constructive dimension of ecclesial ethics.

In his *Improvisation* he draws an analogy between the practice, skills, and habits of theatrical improvisation and the insights emerging in the field of ecclesial ethics about the nature, formation, and practice of Christian discipleship. Forming habits is one of six similar practices he identifies between theatrical improvisation and ecclesial ethics.

In this passage he summarizes the way habit, character, and formation displace decision as the heart of Christian ethics. He tells the story of a surgeon whose mistake in an operating theatre was due not to bad luck but to lack of application in medical school. He then tells a further story of an army chaplain who in a crisis found an unexpected purpose for an otherwise obscure dimension of his studies. The first story illustrates training for expected situations; the second story illustrates the nature of character formation in preparing disciples for the unexpected.

Samuel Wells. *Improvisation: The Drama of Christian Ethics*. Grand Rapids: Brazos, 2004. From Chapter 5, "Forming Habits," pages 73–9.

"The battle of Waterloo was won on the playing fields of Eton." The Duke of Wellington's famous reflection on the climax of the Napoleonic wars was not a statement of personal modesty. It was a recognition that success in battle depends on the character of one's soldiers. It was a statement that Britain had institutions that formed people with the kind of virtues that could survive and even thrive in the demanding circumstances of war.

... The moral life is more about Eton than it is about Waterloo. Eton and Waterloo represent two distinct aspects of the moral life. Eton represents the long period of preparation. Waterloo represents the tiny episode of implementation – the moment of decision, or "situation."

Contemporary ethics seems to offer a series of baffling dilemmas. The moral life seems to be an impossible negotiation of hopeless quandaries. Why is this? The reason is that it has become conventional to study Waterloo without studying Eton – in practice, to study Waterloo as if there were no Eton. Ethics has become the study of the battlefield without much recognition of the training ground. This has happened because ethics has come to be understood as the study of what is right always, everywhere, and for everybody. In other words, ethics considers what all people have in common, not the areas where they differ. It concentrates on the general, not the particular. In the case of the Duke of Wellington's observation, Waterloo is perceived to be what people have in common – a battle is a battle. Eton is considered to be an area where they differ – the French education system was different from the British.

To put the matter in more conventional terms, ethics has become the study of right and wrong actions – because actions are considered to be common to all people always and everywhere. The focus of ethics has come to rest on the choice that an individual in a situation faces between one action and another. The great debates in ethics are perceived to be between those who believe some actions are inherently right and others inherently wrong, and between those who judge actions by the relative desirability of their likely consequences. Ethics is seldom perceived to be about the people doing the actions, because these people's characters are inevitably varied.

But this is where the Duke of Wellington's remark is so significant. He says that one cannot understand Waterloo without understanding Eton. In fact, what went on at Eton was more important than what went on at Waterloo. At Eton, people were trained to shoulder the kind of responsibility they were later to encounter at Waterloo. The real decisions that took place at Waterloo, decisions that shaped the future of European history, had been taken many years earlier. The Duke of Wellington is saying that ethics is about people, not about actions. The heart of ethics lies in the formation of character. Once out in the "battlefield" it is too late. The following story illustrates his point.

One day in the 1950s, in an Edinburgh hospital, a child died tragically on an operating table. Later that week, two friends were talking over the sad events. One of the friends expressed sympathy for the surgeon involved, since he had encountered an unexpected complication. The other, a colleague of the surgeon, strongly disagreed, in these words:

I think the man is to blame. If anybody had handed me ether instead of chloroform I would have known from the weight it was the wrong thing. You see, I know the man well. We were students together at Aberdeen, and he could have become one of the finest surgeons in Europe if only he had given his mind to it. But he didn't. He was more interested in golf. So he just used to do enough work to pass his examinations and no more. And that is how he has lived his life – just enough to get through, but no more; so he has never picked up those seemingly peripheral bits of knowledge that can one day be crucial. The other day in that theatre a bit of "peripheral" knowledge was crucial and he didn't have it. But it wasn't the other day that he failed – it was thirty-nine years ago, when he only gave himself half-heartedly to medicine.

The Duke of Wellington's observation about a Belgian field applies equally well to the Edinburgh operating table. Just as the battle of Waterloo was won on the playing fields of Eton, so the battle for the sick child's life was lost on the golf course. An athlete trains for months for a marathon race, and no amount of enthusiasm on the day can make up for deficiencies in preparation. A student studies for years for an exam: again, no amount of thought on the day can make up for deficiencies in preparation. A doctor studies and trains and practises for years to excel in surgery: no amount of good will on the day can make up for deficiencies in preparation.

Ethics is not primarily about the operating theater: it is about the lecture theater, the training field, the practice hall, the library, the tutorial, the mentoring session. There are two times – one, the time of moral effort, the other, the time of moral habit. The time for moral effort is the time of formation and training. This is "Eton." Training requires commitment, discipline, faithfulness, study, apprenticeship, practice, cooperation, observation, reflection – in short, moral effort. The point of this effort is to form skills and habits – habits that mean people take the right things for granted and skills that give them ability to do the things they take for granted. The time for moral habit is the "moment of decision." This is "Waterloo," or "the operating room." Waterloo and the operating room separate those whose instincts have been appropriately formed from those whose character is inadequately prepared. In every moral "situation," the real decisions are ones that have been taken some time before. To live well requires both effort and habit. There is a place for both. But no amount of effort at the moment of decision will make up for effort neglected in the time of formation.

The moral life should not be experienced as an agony of impossible choice. Instead, it should be a matter of habit and instinct. Learning to live well is about gaining the right habits and instincts, rather than making the right choices. If one has the right assumptions and instincts and habits, many of the things others might experience as crises of choice will pass without one being aware of them. Meanwhile, if one has not developed such habits, decisions that do arise are likely to be insoluble. In the story of the surgeon, the moment of moral effort came in the student's commitment to his studies in the face of the lure of the golf course. If the commitment had been sufficient at the time of formation, habit and instinct in the operating room would have meant that a moment of crisis would have passed without anyone being aware of it. As it was, the patient died. By putting all the emphasis on the operating room, contemporary ethics makes the moral life seem like an agony of impossible choice. For those living in a disconnected present tense, guessing about an unknown future, considering of value only those things that they share with all people everywhere and always, this may well be so. But contemporary ethics neglects the only time from which liberation from this paralysis can come – the past. For it is only moral effort and formation in the past that can offer freedom from impossible moral effort in the present. ...

Forming the right kinds of instincts is really about developing the imagination. It is through the imagination that one aspires or desires, perseveres or reveres, envies or sympathizes. One may distinguish two kinds of imagination, rather as one may distinguish between habit and effort. There is the imagination that one uses in one's ordinary perception of the world. This "ordinary" imagination enables one to take for granted those things that one needs to be able to rely on. But there is also the imagination that is inventive and revolutionary, perceiving objects as symbols of things beyond themselves. ...

This ability ... is the creative force of training in how to live well – otherwise known as moral formation. The pain and care of schooling in a tradition is about learning to see the ambiguity of the world truthfully, yet maintaining hope. The practice of the moral life, meanwhile, is not so much about being creative or clever as it is about taking the right things for granted. Thus what I am here calling the "creative" imagination corresponds to what I earlier called moral effort. This is what moral training is about. Meanwhile what I am here

calling the "ordinary" imagination corresponds to what I earlier called habit. When one comes to a moment of crisis, one depends on the habits one has already formed.

Imagination, in this twofold sense, is a key element in the moral life. It is important to stress this because imagination tends to be perceived as the opposite of morality. Imagination tends to be associated with spontaneity and originality, while morality is assumed to be about worthy but dull things like fulfilling expectations and maintaining trust. It is much better to recognise that both imagination and morality are concerned with describing the world in which people perceive themselves to live and act, helping communities form practices consistent with life in such a world.

I have argued that there are two stages in the moral life. There is the stage of the moral situation, the stage that requires the ordinary imagination to respond from habit and instinct. And there is the prior stage of moral formation, the stage that requires the creative imagination to form character through moral effort. I have suggested that this stage of moral formation is vital and has been neglected in conventional ethics, because it attends to aspects where people differ, rather than to aspects that they have in common. ...

The church's faith is that, in story, sacrament, and Spirit, God has given his people all that they need to live with him. The church's creative energies are largely concerned with preparing its members to be able to respond by habit to unforeseeable turns of events. It is not the church's role to speculate on what the future may hold. The church's task is to be prepared for whatever the future may bring. It prepares through discipleship to be open to grace.

Back in the 1930s at the huge Roman Catholic seminary at Ushaw near Durham there was a man studying for the priesthood named Gerald Culkin. One day he read a play by Anton Chekhov and was so thrilled with it that he went out and bought *Teach Yourself Russian*. Last thing each night when his studies were finished he left the other students playing billiards and went to his room on his own to learn the language. By the time he was ordained he could read it fairly well. Soon afterwards the Second World War started and Gerald went to Beirut as an army chaplain. He met lots of Russians there, but couldn't make himself understood with his *Teach Yourself* way of speaking. Eventually he learned to speak real Russian with them.

Gerald was moved to Egypt and spent a lot of time comforting the wounded and dying. After a particularly heavy battle, with many injured, he came back to his tent exhausted, to be told that there was one more man to see. The man was in a desperate state, and Gerald could see that he didn't have long. Gerald spoke to him in English, but got no response. So he tried with his few words of French, and his fewer words of Italian, German, Spanish, even Arabic. Gerald was on the point of giving up when the dying man, on his stretcher, slowly and painfully made the sign of the cross in the Orthodox manner. Gerald suddenly realized that the man was Russian. In the last hour of the man's life he was able to hear a few words of confession, give absolution, and help the man through the Lord's Prayer. He held the man's hand until he died.

One can picture Gerald coming out of the tent and recalling all those nights at the seminary in Ushaw, all those times he was tempted to give up learning Russian and instead have a game of billiards or a chat with the others. And in retrospect it is clear that all that effort had been a time of preparation; perhaps his whole life had been a time of preparation: and it had all been worth it just for this last hour with the dying man. Moral effort, for Gerald, lay in choosing Russian over billiards: when the crisis came, he acted from habit.

Gerald Culkin's story illustrates all the themes of this chapter. The time for creative imagination, moral effort and discipleship was at Ushaw. The time for ordinary imagination, habit, and grace was in Egypt. The great majority of life is spent in preparation: this is where the emphasis in Christian ethics needs to be. And the experience of grace in the moment of crisis, of decision – the "situation" – came not through being clever or inspired in the moment, but through falling back on something he had once worked hard at and now took for granted.

Stanley Hauerwas, *The Narrative Character of Christian Ethics*

In relation to ecclesial ethics, there are broadly four uses of the term narrative, and they help to distinguish different emphases within this emerging tradition.

The first identifies the ways the self (or agent) is situated in a context, or rather a number of contexts, from which it cannot simply be abstracted for the purpose of coming to a moment of decision. The second credits narrative with the ability to make a coherent whole out of separate events and realities in one's life: an individual who can do this has established an identity; a community that can do this has established a tradition. These two claims about narrative would belong in a subdivision of universal ethics.

The third use of the term refers to the way MacIntyre and Milbank especially, but a number of imitators after them, have traced a "declension narrative" from a time when ethics made some kind of sense to a period (today) when it no longer does.

The fourth sense of narrative, which eventually becomes dominant in Hauerwas' thinking, is explicitly about Christian ethics in particular. It marks the difference between *teleology*, which is about an ultimate (but humanly attainable) goal, and *eschatology*, which is about a final destiny that can only be received as a gift from God. In this early passage the tensions in the different understandings of the term narrative are evident. In his later work, more influenced by Yoder, Hauerwas develops the full philosophical implications of ecclesial ethics by recognizing how the notion of nature needs to be redescribed once the cross and resurrection are placed at the center of history.

Stanley Hauerwas. *The Peaceable Kingdom: A Primer in Christian Ethics.* Notre Dame: University of Notre Dame Press, 1983. From Chapter 2, "A Qualified Ethic: The Narrative Character of Christian Ethics," pages 24–33. Extracts from *The Peaceable Kingdom: A Primer in Christian Ethics* are copyright © Stanley Hauerwas, 1983. Used by permission of Hymns Ancient & Modern Ltd.

The Narrative Character of Christian Convictions

The nature of Christian ethics is determined by the fact that Christian convictions take the form of a story, or perhaps better, a set of stories that constitutes a tradition, which in turn creates and forms a community. Christian ethics does not begin by emphasizing rules or principles, but by calling our attention to a narrative that tells of God's dealing with creation. To be sure, it is a complex story with many different subplots and digressions, but it is crucial for us at this point in the book to see that it is not accidentally a narrative. ...

My contention is that the narrative mode is neither incidental nor accidental to Christian belief. There is no more fundamental way to talk of God than in a story. The fact that we come to know God through the recounting of the story of Israel and the life of Jesus is decisive for our truthful understanding of the kind of God we worship as well as the world in which we exist. Put directly, the narrative character of our knowledge of God, the self, and the world is a reality-making claim that the world and our existence in it are God's creations; our lives, and indeed, the existence of the universe are but contingent realities. ...

Just as narrative is a crucial category for the knowledge of the self, so it is for our knowledge of God. "God," we must remember, is a common name, to which we can ascribe attributions only as we learn of God through a history. This, of course, follows from the basic theological claim that knowledge of God and knowledge of the self are interdependent. But once the formal nature of this claim is fleshed out in terms of narrative, we see its implications for the Christian life. Not only is knowledge of self tied to knowledge of God, but we know ourselves truthfully only when we know ourselves in relation to God. We know who we are only when we can place our selves – locate our stories – within God's story.

This is the basis for the extraordinary Christian claim that we participate morally in God's life. For our God is a God who wills to include us within his life. This is what we mean when we say, in shorthand as it were, that God is a God of grace. Such shorthand can be dangerous if it is mistaken for the suggestion that our relationship with God has an immediacy that makes the journey of the self with God irrelevant. Grace is not an eternal moment above history rendering history irrelevant; rather it is God's choice to be a Lord whose kingdom is furthered by our concrete obedience through which we acquire a history befitting our nature as God's creatures. ...

... [T]he emphasis on narrative as theologically central for an explication of Christian existence reminds us of at least three crucial claims. First, narrative formally displays our existence and that of the world as creatures – as *contingent* beings. Narrative is required precisely because the world and events in the world do not exist by necessity. Any attempt to depict our world and ourselves non-narratively is doomed to failure insofar as it denies our contingent nature. Correlatively, narrative is epistemically fundamental for our knowledge of God and ourselves, since we come to know ourselves only in God's life.

Second, narrative is the characteristic form of our awareness of ourselves as *historical* beings who must give an account of the purposive relation between temporally discrete realities. Indeed, the ability to provide such an account, to sustain its growth in a living tradition, is the central criterion for identifying a group of people as a community. Community joins us with others to further the growth of a tradition whose manifold storylines are meant to help individuals identify and navigate the path to the good. The self is subordinate to the community rather than vice versa, for we discover the self through a community's narrated tradition. ...

Third, God has revealed himself narratively in the history of Israel and in the life of Jesus. While much of Scripture does not take narrative literary form, it is perhaps not incidental that the Gospels do. In any case, Scripture as a whole tells the story of the covenant with Israel, the life, death, and resurrection of Jesus, and the ongoing history of the church as the recapitulation of that life. This empirical observation is not merely an interesting one; this notion of the essential nature of *narrative as the form of God's salvation* is why we rightly attribute to Scripture the truth necessary for our salvation.

Of course, we cannot be brought to understanding without training, for we resist at least the part of the narrative which describes us as sinful creatures. We can only know God by having our lives transformed through initiation into the kingdom. Such a transformation requires that we see the world as it is, not as we want it to be – that is, as sinful and ourselves as sinners. Thus the story requires transformation as it challenges the presumption of our righteousness and teaches us why we so badly need to be reborn through the baptism offered by this new community.

Narrative as a Reality-making Claim

As I have tried to show, emphasis on narrative is not an attempt to beg the question of the truthfulness of Christian convictions by turning them into a provocative account of human existence. On the contrary, attention to the narrative character of God's activity and our life reveals the nature of reality. Since our existence is historically determined, we should not be surprised to discover that our moralities are historical; they require a qualifier. We are unable to stand outside our histories in midair, as it were; we are destined to discover ourselves only within God's history, for God is our beginning and our end.

Christian ethics, therefore, is not first of all concerned with "Thou shalt" or "Thou shalt not." Its first task is to help us rightly envision the world. Christian ethics is specifically formed by a very definite story with determinative content. If we somehow discover the world is not as that story suggests, then we have good grounds for not believing in, or more accurately, not worshipping the God revealed in the life, cross, and resurrection of Jesus. In other words, the enterprise of Christian ethics primarily helps us to see. We can only act within the world we can envision, and we can envision the world rightly only as we are trained to see. We do not come to see merely by looking, but must develop disciplined skills through initiation into that community that attempts to live faithful to the story of God. Furthermore, we cannot see the world rightly unless we are changed, for as sinners we do not desire to see truthfully. Therefore Christian ethics must assert that by learning to be faithful disciples, we are more able to see the world as it is, namely God's creation.

But Christians must learn that the world, in spite of God's good creation, is also in fundamental rebellion. Such rebellion includes humanity, but is not limited to it. The revolt reaches to every aspect of our existence, since through humanity's sin all of creation has been thrown out of joint. Any suggestion that the world is sinful cannot be limited to "moralistic" claims about our petty crimes. The Christian story trains us to see that in most of our life we act as if this is not God's world and therein lies our fundamental sin. Moreover, when we so act, we find that our actions have far-reaching consequences, since in effect we distort our own and the world's nature. Therefore sin implies not just a claim about human behavior but a claim about the way things are.

That our existence is sinful adds new perspective to the claim that we must be transformed if we are to see the world truthfully. The new vision afforded us in such a transformation includes the appropriation of a truthful language. If we can see, so we can speak. That does not mean that we do not observe things we sometimes do not know how to describe, but that our *learning* to see them and our ability to interpret and share our vision with others depends on having a language appropriate to what we have seen.

Christian convictions constitute a narrative, a language, that requires a transformation of the self if we are to see, as well as be, truthful. The gospel commands us to submit to a vigorous and continuing discipleship if we are to recognize our status as subjects and properly understand the requirements for participation in the kingdom. Furthermore, to be a Christian is not principally to obey certain commandments or rules, but to learn to grow into the story of Jesus as the form of God's kingdom. We express that by saying we must learn to be disciples; only as such can we understand why at the center of creation is a cross and resurrection.

On Learning to Be a Sinner

Our lesson is most disconcerting when the narrative asks us to understand ourselves not only as friends of the crucified, but as the crucifiers. We must be trained to see ourselves as sinners, for it is not self-evident. Indeed, our sin is so fundamental that we must be taught to recognize it; we cannot perceive its radical nature so long as we remain formed by it. Sin is not some universal tendency of humankind to be inhumane or immoral, though sin may involve inhumanity and immorality. We are not sinful because we participate in some general human condition, but because we deceive ourselves about the nature of reality and so would crucify the very one who calls us to God's kingdom.

We only learn what our sin is as we discover our true identity through locating the self in God's life as revealed to us through the life, death, and resurrection of Jesus Christ. Only when we recognize ourselves as sinners of this kind can we receive the redemption that comes with assurance that because we have beheld God's glory in the cross of Jesus, our perception of ourselves as sinners will not destroy us.

The story Christians tell of God exposes the unwelcome fact that I am a sinner. For without such a narrative the fact and nature of my sin cannot help but remain hidden in self-deception. Only a narrative that helps me place myself as a creature of a gracious God can provide the skills to help me locate my sin as fundamentally infidelity and rebellion. As a creature I have been created for loyalty – loyalty to the truth, to the love that moves the sun and the stars and yet is found on a cross – but I find myself serving any powers but the true one in the hopes of being my own lord. The ironic result is that by seeking to possess I become possessed.

Christian tradition has at various times and places characterized this fundamental sin in quite different ways. Our basic sin has been said to be pride, self-love, infidelity, lust, sloth, all of which have some claim to the doubtful honor of being the father of all sins. I doubt, however, whether there is any one term sufficient to suggest the complex nature of our sin. That is exactly why we see we need the set of stories we find in Scripture and displayed by the church to recognize our sin. As narrative-determined creatures we must learn to locate our lives in God's life if we are to have the means to face, as well as do something about, our infidelity and rebellion against our true creator.

Just to the extent I refuse to be faithful to God's way, to live as part of God's life, my life assumes the character of rebellion. Our sin is not merely an error in overestimating our capacities. Rather it is the active and willful attempt to overreach our powers. It is the attempt to live *sui generis*, to live as if we are or can be the authors of our own stories. Our sin is, thus, a challenge to God's authorship and a denial that we are characters in the drama of the kingdom. ...

Of course, Christians are not just asked to see themselves as sinners. We are to do something about our sin. We are called to be disciples and even to count ourselves among the righteous. Our call is not a general admonition to be good, but a concrete and definite call to take up the way of life made possible by God's redemptive action for us in the cross. To be redeemed ... is nothing less than to learn to place ourselves in God's history, to be part of God's people. To locate ourselves within that history and people does not mean we must have some special experience of personal salvation. Redemption, rather, is a change in which we accept the invitation to become part of God's kingdom, a kingdom through which we acquire a character befitting one who has heard God's call. Now an intense personal experience may be important for many, but such experiences cannot in themselves be substitutes for learning to find the significance of our lives only in God's ongoing journey with creation.

The Christological Turn

For John Howard Yoder and the later work of Stanley Hauerwas, non-violence becomes the key to Christian ethics. All the perceptions of neo-Aristotelian ethics described above – virtue, character, habits, practices, formation, narrative – need to be reassessed from the point of view of the two central decisions – God's decision to be fully revealed in the fully human and fully divine Christ, and God's decision in Christ to face the world's rejection and enmity by going voluntarily to the cross rather than responding with conformity or violence. For Yoder and Hauerwas, non-violence is not a clever tactic that harnesses public relations and mass movements and thus resolves conflict more effectively; it may do this, but sometimes it will actually make the world a more violent place. Yet it is faithful simply because it is following the way of Christ, and is thus in line with the grain of the universe.

Non-violence – and its explicitly Christological derivation – emerges as the fault line that runs between two overlapping but fundamentally distinct traditions in ecclesial ethics. On the one hand there is the tradition represented most explicitly by Alasdair MacIntyre, which prizes the classical tradition of the virtues and sees narrative and the church in largely generic categories as part of the vocabulary and practice of generating people of character that can engage in the public sphere while seeking goods that have a genuinely teleological, or ultimate, dimension. On the other hand lies John Howard Yoder, for whom there are no general categories, only the specific revelation of the cross and resurrection of Jesus as the axis of history and the political manifestation of Jesus' journey to the cross as the definitive response of Christians to conflict and violence.

The text below demonstrates the diversity of ecclesial ethics when placed alongside the concerns of figures like MacIntyre and Milbank. For Yoder, non-violence is the key to Christian ethics because it is the key to understanding who Jesus is and what his death and resurrection mean.

John Howard Yoder, *The Possibility of a Messianic Ethic*

John Howard Yoder's most influential book is *The Politics of Jesus*. This is a sustained study, based on the Gospel of Luke, in how Jesus charted a path between establishment quietism (represented by the Sadducee party in Israel at the time), or withdrawal (represented by the Essene sect, whose records have been found near the Dead Sea), and the temptation to violent revolution (represented by the Zealot party of the time). It is perhaps the most significant single volume that makes the case for how Christian pacifism is not only an active (rather than passive) practice but is fundamentally grounded in the character of God and the achievement of Christ.

Yoder begins his book with a methodical walk through the conventional objections to seeing Jesus as the norm for Christian ethics. In doing so he identifies the assumptions of most of his theological forebears, and attempts to dismantle them in turn. He then goes on to survey such other norms as are held up as alternative aspirations for Christians – and finds that "social responsibility" features prominently. To this understanding of ethics he finally poses two questions. What does it say about revelation if the ethic of Jesus is so readily abandoned? And what does it say about Jesus' incarnation if his example is so easily ignored?

John Howard Yoder. *The Politics of Jesus*. 2nd edn. Grand Rapids: Eerdmans, 1994. From Chapter 1, "The Possibility of a Messianic Ethic," pages 4–11.

Mainstream Ethics: Jesus Is Not the Norm

The first and most substantial affirmation of this classic defense against an ethic of imitation is the observation that Jesus is simply not relevant in any immediate sense to the questions of social ethics. The great variety of ways of grounding this negative statement can perhaps not unfairly be summarized in three theses, the first being the sixfold claim of Jesus' irrelevance.

1 The ethic of Jesus is an ethic for an "Interim" which Jesus thought would be very brief. It is possible for the apocalyptic Sermonizer on the Mount to be unconcerned for the survival of the structures of a solid society because he thinks the world is passing away soon. His ethical teachings therefore appropriately pay no attention to society's need for survival and for the patient construction of permanent institutions. The rejection of violence, of self-defense, and of accumulating wealth for the sake of security, and the footlooseness of the prophet of the kingdom are not permanent and generalizable attitudes toward social values. They make sense only if it be assumed that those values are coming to an imminent end. Thus at any point where social ethics must

deal with problems of duration, Jesus quite clearly can be of no help. ...

2 Jesus was, as his Franciscan and Tolstoyan imitators have said, a simple rural figure. He talked about the sparrows and the lilies to fishermen and peasants, lepers and outcasts. His radical personalization of all ethical problems is only possible in a village sociology where knowing everyone and having time to treat everyone as a person is culturally an available possibility. The rustic "face-to-face model of social relations" is the only one he cared about. There is thus in the ethic of Jesus no intention to speak substantially to the problems of complex organization, of institutions and offices, cliques and power and crowds.

3 Jesus and his early followers lived in a world over which they had no control. It was therefore quite fitting that they could not conceive of the exercise of social responsibility in any form other than that of simply *being* a faithful witnessing minority. Now, however, that Christianity has made great progress in history represented symbolically by the conversion of Constantine and practically by the "Judeo-Christian" assumptions underlying our entire Western culture, the Christian is obligated to answer questions which Jesus did not face. The individual Christian, or all Christians together, must accept responsibilities that were inconceivable in Jesus' situation.

4   The nature of Jesus' message was ahistorical by definition. He dealt with spiritual and not social matters, with the existential and not the concrete. What he proclaimed was not a social change but a new self-understanding, not obedience but atonement. Whatever he said and did of a social and ethical character must be understood not for its own sake but as the symbolic or mythical clothing of his spiritual message. If the Gospel texts were not sufficiently clear on this point, at least we are brought to a definitive clarity by the later apostolic writings. Especially Paul moves us away from the last trace of the danger of a social misunderstanding of Jesus and toward the inwardness of faith.

5   Or to say it just a little differently, Jesus was a radical monotheist. He pointed people away from the local and finite values to which they had been giving their attention and proclaimed the sovereignty of the only One worthy of being worshiped. The impact of this radical discontinuity between God and humanity, between the world of God and human values, is to relativize all human values. The will of God cannot be identified with any one ethical answer, or any given human value, since these are all finite. But the practical import of that relativizing, for the substance of ethics, is that these values have become autonomous. All that now stands above them is the infinite.

6   Or the reason may be more "dogmatic" in tone. Jesus came, after all, to give his life for the sins of humankind. The work of atonement or the gift of justification, whereby God enables sinners to be restored to his fellowship, is a forensic act, a gracious gift. For Roman Catholics this act of justification may be found to be in correlation with the sacraments, and for Protestants with one's self-understanding, in response to the proclaimed Word; but never should it be correlated with ethics. Just as guilt is not a matter of having committed particular sinful acts, so justification is not a matter of proper behavior. How the death of Jesus works our justification is a divine miracle and mystery; how he died, or the kind of life which led to the kind of death he died, is therefore ethically immaterial.

It results from this consideration of the type of thinking and teaching Jesus was doing, that it cannot have been his intention – or at least we cannot take it to have been his achievement – to provide any precise guidance in the field of ethics. His apocalypticism and his radical monotheism may teach us to be modest; his personalism may teach us to cherish the values of face-to-face relationships, but as to the stuff of our decision-making, we shall have to have other sources of help.

What Other Norm Is There?

The second substantial affirmation of the mainstream ethical consensus follows from the first. Since, as we have seen, Jesus himself (either his teachings or his behavior) is not finally normative for ethics, there must be some kind of bridge or transition into another realm or into another mode of thought when we begin to think about ethics. This is not simply a bridge from the first century to the present, but from theology to ethics or from the existential to the institutional. A certain very moderate amount of freight can be carried across this bridge: perhaps a concept of absolute love or humility or faith or freedom. But the substance of ethics must be reconstructed on our side of the bridge.

Third, therefore, the reconstruction of a social ethic on this side of the transition will derive its guidance from common sense and the nature of things. We will measure what is "fitting" and what is "adequate"; what is "relevant" and what is "effective." We shall be "realistic" and "responsible." All these slogans point to an epistemology for which the classic label is the *theology of the natural*: the nature of things is held to be adequately perceived in their bare givenness; the right is that which respects or tends toward the realization of the essentially given. Whether this ethic of natural law be encountered in the reformation form, where it is called an ethic of "vocation" or of the "station," or in the currently popular form of the "ethic of the situation," or in the older catholic forms where "nature" is known in other ways, the structure of the argument is the same: it is by studying the realities around us, not by hearing a proclamation from God, that we discern the right.

Once these assumptions about the sources of a relevant social ethic and about the spirituality of Jesus' own message have been made, we may then observe a kind of negative feedback into the interpretation of the New Testament itself. We now know, the argument runs, that Jesus could not have been practicing or teaching a relevant social ethic. Then the Jewish and Roman authorities, who thought he was doing just that and condemned him for it, must have misunderstood very seriously what he was about. This is an evidence of the hardness of their hearts. Matthew as well, who organized and interpreted the teachings of Jesus so as to make of them a simple kind of ethical catechism, misunderstood Jesus: from his misunderstanding arises that regrettable phenomenon which Protestant historians call "Early Catholicism."

Fortunately before long, the explanation continues, things were put into place by the apostle Paul. He corrected the tendency to neo-Judaism or to early catholicism by an emphasis upon the priority of grace and the secondary significance of works, so that ethical matters could never be taken too seriously. ...

The second Pauline correction was that the apparent social radicality of Jesus himself (not only the Judaizing misinterpretation of Jesus) was clarified and put in its place. Positive respect for the institutions of society, even the subordination of woman and slavery, acceptance of the divinely sanctioned legitimacy of the Roman government, and the borrowing of Stoic conceptions of ethics conformed to nature were some of the elements of Paul's adjustment, so that the church was ready to construct an ethic to which the person and character – and especially the career – of Jesus made no unique or determining contribution.

Looking back over this hastily sketched pattern of prevalent structures of ethical thought, systematic and historical theology will need to ask some careful questions. There is the question of the authority of these hermeneutic assumptions. If the meaning of Jesus is this different from what he was understood by his Palestinian disciples and adversaries to mean, and if those ordinary meanings need to be filtered through a hermeneutic transposition and replaced by an ethic of social survival and responsibility, what then has come of the concept of revelation? Is there such a thing as a *Christian* ethic at all? If there be no specifically Christian ethic but only natural human ethics as held to by Christians among others, does this thoroughgoing abandon of particular substance apply to ethical truth only? Why not to all other truth as well?

A second kind of question we will need to ask is: What becomes of the meaning of incarnation if Jesus is not normatively human? If he is human but not normative, is this not the ancient ebionitic heresy? If he be somehow authoritative but not in his humanness, is this not a new gnosticism?

There could be problems of inner consistency as well. Why should it be important for Christians to exercise social responsibility within the power structures, if what they do there is to be guided by the same standards which non-Christians apply?

But this would not be biblical study if we were to pursue those questions now from the systematic and historical end. What I propose here is rather that, once we are sensitized by those questions, we might begin at the front again by seeking to read one portion of the New Testament without making the usual prior negative assumptions about its relevance. Or let me say it more sharply: I propose to read the Gospel narrative with the constantly present question, "Is there here a social ethic?" I shall, in other words, be testing the hypothesis that runs counter to the prevalent assumptions: the hypothesis that the ministry and the claims of Jesus are best understood as presenting to hearers and readers not the avoidance of political options, but one particular social-political-ethical option.

Part Three

The Questions Asked of Christian Ethics

The first part of this book set the *context* for the discipline of Christian ethics. The second part discussed the *method* and *audience* of Christian ethics, recognizing that there is no single approach, nor even one single group of approaches, but several overlapping and contrasting approaches to the discipline. This third part looks at the *subject matter* of Christian ethics, namely those issues and questions that present themselves to Christians and others as pressing and controversial. These are topics on which people of good conscience disagree, and yet because they are, or have a close bearing on, what Augustine called "common objects of love," they are matters on which careful deliberation is necessary if not vital for personal and communal well-being.

Each chapter considers three related issues, and for each issue there are three perspectives: one universal, one subversive, and one ecclesial. Needless to say, many of the texts overlap between these categories, just as many of the arguments overlap between issues. Nonetheless the intention is that in each case the three readings give perspectives that not only illuminate the issue, but highlight the qualities of the other readings and shed light on the categories of universal, subversive, and ecclesial themselves.

Part Three

The Questions Asked of Christian Ethics

Chapter Eight

Good Order

Jesus suggested to those who asked him about the lawfulness of paying taxes to Caesar, "Give to Caesar what is Caesar's, and give to God what is God's." The ambiguity of what belongs to Caesar and what belongs to God, the question of whether the answer is true to Israel's heritage or transformed by Jesus' cross and resurrection, and the uncertainty over whether the answer varies depending on the context, are among the biggest in Christian ethics. The issues are so large that they can hardly be rendered in deontological or consequentialist terms (although some groups, such as Mennonites in their withdrawal from participation in the state, have sought to do so) and are largely ones of right relationships. The church has sometimes been an oppressed minority, sometimes been an oppressive majority, sometimes been hand-in-glove with the state, sometimes been at odds with the state: all these have affected the questions of governance, authority, justice, punishment, war, and revolution that make up this chapter.

The State

The modern nation-state – with a developed idea of its own sovereignty within its territories, and a right to freedom from interference by other similarly sovereign states – owes much to political developments in the seventeenth century. The forms of political authority that make their appearance in the Old and New Testaments are not always easy to transfer onto our own circumstances. The same is true of the feudal orders of medieval Christendom. Augustine does not refer to the state as we now know it. His concern is with the sum of the values, or loves, of a people's individual members. A republic is "an assemblage of reasonable beings bound together by a common agreement concerning the objects of their love." It is not an entity in itself; it is the solidarity of the human beings of which it is composed, and its character is determined by the character of its citizens. Like all who followed him, Augustine was balancing the positive view of government in Romans 13 with the much more negative view expressed in the Book of Revelation.

The medieval period, with its high view of natural law, had in general a positive view of the state, in accordance with the hierarchical ordering of created nature for the promotion of social good. Calvin had if anything an even higher view of the state, because he saw a profound harmony in the workings of divine sovereignty, and therefore a harmony between the form of "earthly" government established to administer the lives of humans in society, and the requirements of life in the church, preparing them for heaven.

In the early modern period, as Christendom broke up into violently competing religious groups, a central political concern became how to manage these differences in a way that still allowed for collective human flourishing. It seemed necessary to try to prise people free from their "lethal allegiances" to religious viewpoints that could not be reconciled because they were of too great an import for the people who held them. So the idea of a "state of nature" was deployed, in which (it was argued) human beings exist as individuals, prior to any allegiances. The human individual is free. That freedom means equality with every other individual. The state of nature is a condition untrammeled by any claim of tradition, church, class, or location.

In the modern era central concerns have been the all-powerful state and the threat of totalitarianism; the emergence of complex national (and, increasingly, international) problems that require large-scale action; the idea of *rights* as the property of individuals to limit the power of the sovereign state over them; and attempts to use the state to help human flourishing through the provision of crucial services and systems of support to those in need.

The readings in this section begin with the papal social encyclical tradition, seeking out all people of good will. The subversive and ecclesial readings arise out of crisis moments in twentieth-century history: the South African apartheid era and the Nazi takeover in 1930s Germany.

Universal

Pope Pius XI, *Quadragesimo Anno (On Reconstruction of the Social Order);* Pope John XXIII, *Pacem in Terris (On Establishing Universal Peace in Truth, Justice, Charity, and Liberty)*

Quadragesimo Anno (On Reconstruction of the Social Order) was issued by Pope Pius XI on May 15, 1931, to celebrate the 40th anniversary of the encyclical *Rerum Novarum* (On Capital and Labor). The background for the encyclical is the turbulent times of the Great Depression – the obvious shortcomings of unregulated capitalism and the totalitarian menace of Soviet communism. The Pope continually steers a middle course, for example seeing private property as essential to human flourishing but as subordinate to the common good. A fair wage may be determined in relation to the needs of a worker's family, the economic capacity of the enterprise, and the general state of the economy. *Quadragesimo Anno* is famous for developing the notion of subsidiarity. Subsidiarity steers between capitalism and socialism by holding that a central authority should have a subsidiary function, performing only those tasks which cannot be performed effectively at a more immediate or local level. This has become a foundational element of European Union law.

Pacem in Terris (On Establishing Universal Peace in Truth, Justice, Charity, and Liberty) was issued on April 11, 1963, by Pope John XXIII shortly before his death. It is addressed not to Catholics only but to all people of good will. Its context is the Cold War and specifically the Cuban missile crisis. In addition, there was the end of the colonial era in Africa, the growing legislation protecting the rights of workers, and the increasing emergence of women in public life. The Pope explicitly endorses the notion of human rights – "to life, to bodily integrity, and to the means which are suitable for the proper development of life" – and sees these as the path that leads to peace.

Pope Pius XI. *Quadragesimo Anno* (On Reconstruction of the Social Order). 1931. www.vatican.va/holy_father/pius_xi/encyclicals/documents/hf_p-xi_enc_19310515_quadragesimo-anno_en.html.

Pope John XXIII. *Pacem in Terris* (On Establishing Universal Peace in Truth, Justice, Charity, and Liberty). 1963. www.vatican.va/holy_father/john_xxiii/encyclicals/documents/hf_j-xxiii_enc_11041963_pacem_en.html. **Reprinted by permission of the Libreria Editrice Vaticana.**

Quadragesimo Anno

78. When we speak of the reform of institutions, the State comes chiefly to mind, not as if universal well-being were to be expected from its activity, but because things have come to such a pass through the evil of what we have termed "individualism" that, following upon the overthrow and near extinction of that rich social life which was once highly developed through associations of various kinds, there remain virtually only individuals

and the State. This is to the great harm of the State itself; for, with a structure of social governance lost, and with the taking over of all the burdens which the wrecked associations once bore, the State has been overwhelmed and crushed by almost infinite tasks and duties.

79. As history abundantly proves, it is true that on account of changed conditions many things which were done by small associations in former times cannot be done now save by large associations. Still, that most weighty principle, which cannot be set aside or changed, remains fixed and unshaken in social philosophy: Just as it is gravely wrong to take from individuals what they can accomplish by their own initiative and industry and give it to the community, so also it is an injustice and at the same time a grave evil and disturbance of right order to assign to a greater and higher association what lesser and subordinate organizations can do. For every social activity ought of its very nature to furnish help to the members of the body social, and never destroy and absorb them.

80. The supreme authority of the State ought, therefore, to let subordinate groups handle matters and concerns of lesser importance, which would otherwise dissipate its efforts greatly. Thereby the State will more freely, powerfully, and effectively do all those things that belong to it alone because it alone can do them: directing, watching, urging, restraining, as occasion requires and necessity demands. Therefore, those in power should be sure that the more perfectly a graduated order is kept among the various associations, in observance of the principle of "subsidiary function," the stronger social authority and effectiveness will be and the happier and more prosperous the condition of the State.

81. First and foremost, the State and every good citizen ought to look to and strive toward this end: that the conflict between the hostile classes be abolished and harmonious cooperation of the Industries and Professions be encouraged and promoted.

Pacem in Terris

II. Relations Between Individuals and the Public Authorities

46. Human society can be neither well-ordered nor prosperous without the presence of those who, invested with legal authority, preserve its institutions and do all that is necessary to sponsor actively the interests of all its members. And they derive their authority from God, for, as St. Paul teaches, "there is no power but from God."

In his commentary on this passage, St. John Chrysostom writes: "What are you saying? Is every ruler appointed by God? No, that is not what I mean, he says, for I am not now talking about individual rulers, but about authority as such. My contention is that the existence of a ruling authority – the fact that some should command and others obey, and that all things not come about as the result of blind chance – this is a provision of divine wisdom."

God has created men social by nature, and a society cannot "hold together unless someone is in command to give effective direction and unity of purpose. Hence every civilized community must have a ruling authority, and this authority, no less than society itself, has its source in nature, and consequently has God for its author." ...

An Appeal to Conscience

48. Hence, a regime which governs solely or mainly by means of threats and intimidation or promises of reward, provides men with no effective incentive to work for the common good. And even if it did, it would certainly be offensive to the dignity of free and rational human beings. Authority is before all else a moral force. For this reason the appeal of rulers should be to the individual conscience, to the duty which every man has of voluntarily contributing to the common good. But since all men are equal in natural dignity, no man has the capacity to force internal compliance on another. Only God can do that, for He alone scrutinizes and judges the secret counsels of the heart.

49. Hence, representatives of the State have no power to bind men in conscience, unless their own authority is tied to God's authority, and is a participation in it.

50. The application of this principle likewise safeguards the dignity of citizens. Their obedience to civil authorities is never an obedience paid to them as men. It is in reality an act of homage paid to God, the provident Creator of the universe, who has decreed that men's dealings with one another be regulated in accordance with that order which He Himself has established. And we men do not demean ourselves in showing due reverence to God. On the contrary, we are lifted up and ennobled in spirit, for to serve God is to reign. ...

Attainment of the Common Good is the Purpose of the Public Authority

53. Men, both as individuals and as intermediate groups, are required to make their own specific contributions to the general welfare. The main consequence

of this is that they must harmonize their own interests with the needs of others, and offer their goods and services as their rulers shall direct – assuming, of course, that justice is maintained and the authorities are acting within the limits of their competence. Those who have authority in the State must exercise that authority in a way which is not only morally irreproachable, but also best calculated to ensure or promote the State's welfare.

54. The attainment of the common good is the sole reason for the existence of civil authorities. In working for the common good, therefore, the authorities must obviously respect its nature, and at the same time adjust their legislation to meet the requirements of the given situation. ...

Responsibilities of the Public Authority, and Rights and Duties of Individuals

60. It is generally accepted today that the common good is best safeguarded when personal rights and duties are guaranteed. The chief concern of civil authorities must therefore be to ensure that these rights are recognized, respected, co-ordinated, defended and promoted, and that each individual is enabled to perform his duties more easily. For "to safeguard the inviolable rights of the human person, and to facilitate the performance of his duties, is the principal duty of every public authority." ...

Duty of Promoting the Rights of Individuals

63. ... [H]eads of States must make a positive contribution to the creation of an overall climate in which the individual can both safeguard his own rights and fulfill his duties, and can do so readily. For if there is one thing we have learned in the school of experience, it is surely this: that, in the modern world especially, political, economic and cultural inequities among citizens become more and more widespread when public authorities fail to take appropriate action in these spheres. And the consequence is that human rights and duties are thus rendered totally ineffective.

64. The public administration must therefore give considerable care and thought to the question of social as well as economic progress, and to the development of essential services in keeping with the expansion of the productive system. Such services include road-building, transportation, communications, drinking-water, housing, medical care, ample facilities for the practice of religion, and aids to recreation. The government must also see to the provision of insurance facilities, to obviate any likelihood of a citizen's being unable

to maintain a decent standard of living in the event of some misfortune, or greatly increased family responsibilities.

The government is also required to show no less energy and efficiency in the matter of providing opportunities for suitable employment, graded to the capacity of the workers. It must make sure that working men are paid a just and equitable wage, and are allowed a sense of responsibility in the industrial concerns for which they work. It must facilitate the formation of intermediate groups, so that the social life of the people may become more fruitful and less constrained. And finally, it must ensure that everyone has the means and opportunity of sharing as far as possible in cultural benefits. ...

Connection Between the Common Good and Political Authority

136. Now, if one considers carefully the inner significance of the common good on the one hand, and the nature and function of public authority on the other, one cannot fail to see that there is an intrinsic connection between them. Public authority, as the means of promoting the common good in civil society, is a postulate of the moral order. But the moral order likewise requires that this authority be effective in attaining its end. Hence the civil institutions in which such authority resides, becomes operative and promotes its ends, are endowed with a certain kind of structure and efficacy: a structure and efficacy which make such institutions capable of realizing the common good by ways and means adequate to the changing historical conditions.

137. Today the universal common good presents us with problems which are world-wide in their dimensions; problems, therefore, which cannot be solved except by a public authority with power, organization and means co-extensive with these problems, and with a world-wide sphere of activity. Consequently the moral order itself demands the establishment of some such general form of public authority.

Public Authority Instituted by Common Consent and Not Imposed by Force

138. But this general authority equipped with worldwide power and adequate means for achieving the universal common good cannot be imposed by force. It must be set up with the consent of all nations. If its work is to be effective, it must operate with fairness, absolute impartiality, and with dedication to the common good of all peoples. The forcible imposition by the more

powerful nations of a universal authority of this kind would inevitably arouse fears of its being used as an instrument to serve the interests of the few or to take the side of a single nation, and thus the influence and effectiveness of its activity would be undermined. For even though nations may differ widely in material progress and military strength, they are very sensitive as regards their juridical equality and the excellence of their own way of life. They are right, therefore, in their reluctance to submit to an authority imposed by force, established without their co-operation, or not accepted of their own accord.

The Universal Common Good and Personal Rights

139. The common good of individual States is something that cannot be determined without reference to the human person, and the same is true of the common good of all States taken together. Hence the public authority of the world community must likewise have as its special aim the recognition, respect, safeguarding and promotion of the rights of the human person. This can be done by direct action, if need be, or by the creation throughout the world of the sort of conditions in which rulers of individual States can more easily carry out their specific functions.

The Principle of Subsidiarity

140. The same principle of subsidiarity which governs the relations between public authorities and individuals, families and intermediate societies in a single State, must also apply to the relations between the public authority of the world community and the public authorities of each political community. The special function of this universal authority must be to evaluate and find a solution to economic, social, political and cultural problems which affect the universal common good. These are problems which, because of their extreme gravity, vastness and urgency, must be considered too difficult for the rulers of individual States to solve with any degree of success.

Subversive

The Kairos Document

The Kairos Document: Challenge to the Church: A Theological Comment on the Political Crisis in South Africa, with 150 signatures but no stated author, emerged from the township of Soweto two months after the apartheid government's declaration of a state of emergency in July 1985. The document is addressed to a church divided over how to relate to an oppressive government. It has five brief chapters: (1) The Moment of Truth; (2) Critique of "State Theology"; (3) Critique of "Church Theology"; (4) Towards a Prophetic Theology; (5) Challenge to Action; and a short conclusion. *Kairos* is the Greek for special moment or time.

It condemns "the theological justification of the status quo with its racism, capitalism and totalitarianism" and the corresponding misuse of theological concepts and scriptural texts, which it calls "state theology." It criticizes the other-worldly "church theology" of the English-speaking Methodists, Anglicans, and Lutherans, who speak of reconciliation without recognizing the need for justice, who over-emphasize individual conversion to the neglect of structural injustice, and who see the violence of the oppressed but not of their oppressors. Instead, it proposes "prophetic theology," which maintains a tyrant has lost the right to govern, and claims: "It is therefore not primarily a matter of trying to reconcile individual people but a matter of trying to change unjust structures so that people will not be pitted against one another as oppressor and oppressed." Finally, the document advocates for church involvement in the anti-apartheid struggle and a campaign of civil disobedience.

The Kairos Document. Challenge to the Church: A Theological Comment on the Political Crisis in South Africa. **From Chapter Two, Critique of State Theology. Available online at www.bethel.edu/~letnie/ AfricanChristianity/SAKairos.html.**

Chapter Two, Critique of State Theology

2.4 The God of the State

The State in its oppression of the people makes use again and again of the name of God. Military chaplains use it to encourage the South African Defence Force, police chaplains use it to strengthen policemen and cabinet ministers use it in their propaganda speeches. But perhaps the most revealing of all is the blasphemous use of God's holy name in the preamble to the new apartheid constitution. In humble submission to Almighty God, who controls the destinies of nations and the history of peoples; who gathered our forebears together from many lands and gave them this their own; who has guided them from generation to generation; who has wondrously delivered them from the dangers that beset them.

This god is an idol. It is as mischievous, sinister and evil as any of the idols that the prophets of Israel had to contend with. Here we have a god who is historically on the side of the white settlers, who dispossesses black people of their land and who gives the major part of the land to his "chosen people."

It is the god of superior weapons who conquered those who were armed with nothing but spears. It is the god of the casspirs and hippos, the god of teargas, rubber bullets, sjamboks, prison cells and death sentences. Here is a god who exalts the proud and humbles the poor – the very opposite of the God of the Bible who "scatters the proud of heart, pulls down the mighty from their thrones and exalts the humble" (Lk 1:51–52). From a theological point of view the opposite of the God of the Bible is the devil, Satan. The god of the South African State is not merely an idol or false god, it is the devil disguised as Almighty God – the antichrist.

The oppressive South African regime will always be particularly abhorrent to Christians precisely because it makes use of Christianity to justify its evil ways. As Christians we simply cannot tolerate this blasphemous use of God's name and God's Word. "State Theology" is not only heretical, it is blasphemous. Christians who are trying to remain faithful to the God of the Bible are even more horrified when they see that there are Churches, like the White Dutch Reformed Churches and other groups of Christians, who actually subscribe to this heretical theology. "State Theology" needs its own prophets and it manages to find them from the ranks of those who profess to be ministers of God's Word in some of our Churches. …

Chapter Four, Towards a Prophetic Theology

Our present KAIROS calls for a response from Christians that is biblical, spiritual, pastoral and, above all, prophetic. It is not enough in these circumstances to repeat generalized Christian principles. We need a bold and incisive response that is prophetic because it speaks to the particular circumstances of this crisis, a response that does not give the impression of sitting on the fence but is clearly and unambiguously taking a stand.

Social Analysis

The first task of a prophetic theology for our times would be an attempt at social analysis or what Jesus would call "reading the signs of the times" (Mt 16:3) or "interpreting this KAIROS" (Lk 12:56). It is not possible to do this in any detail in the document but we must start with at least the broad outlines of an analysis of the conflict in which we find ourselves.

It would be quite wrong to see the present conflict as simply a racial war. The racial component is there but we are not dealing with two equal races or nations each with their own selfish group interests. The situation we are dealing with here is one of oppression. The conflict is between an oppressor and the oppressed. The conflict between two irreconcilable *causes or interests* in which the one is just and the other is unjust.

On the one hand we have the interests of those who benefit from the status quo and who are determined to maintain it at any cost, even at the cost of millions of lives. It is in their interests to introduce a number of reforms in order to ensure that the system is not radically changed and that they can continue to benefit from the system because it favors them and enables them to accumulate a great deal of wealth and to maintain an exceptionally high standard of living. And they want to make sure that it stays that way even if some adjustments are needed.

On the other hand we have those who do not benefit in any way from the system the way it is now. They are treated as mere labor units, paid starvation wages, separated from their families by migratory labor, moved about like cattle and dumped in homelands to starve – and all for the benefit of a privileged minority. They have no say in the system and are supposed to be grateful for the concessions that are offered to them like crumbs. It is not in their interests to allow this system to continue even in some "reformed" or "revised" form. They are determined to change the system radically so that it no longer benefits only the privileged few. And they are willing to do this even at the cost of their own lives. What they want is justice for all.

This is our situation of civil war or revolution. The one side is committed to maintaining the system at all costs and the other side is committed to changing it at all costs. There are two conflicting projects here and no compromise is possible. Either we have full and equal justice for all or we don't. ...

Tyranny in the Christian Tradition

... There are indeed some differences of opinion in the Christian tradition about the means that might be used to replace a tyrant but there has not been any doubt about our Christian duty to refuse to co-operate with tyranny and to do whatever we can to remove it. ...

The traditional Latin definition of a tyrant is *hostis boni communis* – an enemy of the common good. The purpose of all government is the promotion of what is called the common good of the people governed. To promote the common good is to govern in the interests of, and for the benefit of, all the people. Many governments fail to do this at times. There might be this or that injustice done to some of the people. And such lapses would indeed have to be criticized. But occasional acts of injustice would not make a government into an enemy of the people, a tyrant.

To be an enemy of the people a government would have to be hostile to the common good in principle. Such a government would be acting against the interests of the people as a whole and permanently. This would be clearest in cases where the very policy of a government is hostile towards the common good and where the government has a mandate to rule in the interests of some of the people rather than in the interests of all the people. Such a government would be in principle irreformable. Any reform that it might try to introduce would not be calculated to serve the common good but to serve the interests of the minority from whom it received its mandate. ...

Apartheid is a system whereby a minority regime elected by one small section of the population is given an explicit mandate to govern in the interests of, and for the benefit of, the white community. Such a mandate or policy is by definition hostile to the common good of all the people. In fact because it tries to rule in the exclusive interests of whites and not in the interests of all, it ends up ruling in a way that is not even in the interests of those same whites. It becomes an enemy of all the people. A totalitarian regime. A reign of terror. ...

A regime that is in principle the enemy of the people cannot suddenly begin to rule in the interests of all the people. It can only be replaced by another government – one that has been elected by the majority of the people with an explicit mandate to govern in the interests of all the people.

A regime that has made itself the enemy of the people has thereby also made itself the enemy of God. People are made in the image and likeness of God and whatever we do to the least of them we do to God (Mt 25:49, 45).

To say that the State or the regime is the enemy of God is not to say that all those who support the system are aware of this. On the whole they simply do not know what they are doing. Many people have been blinded by the regime's propaganda. They are frequently quite ignorant of the consequences of their stance. However, such blindness does not make the State any less tyrannical or any less of an enemy of the people and an enemy of God.

On the other hand the fact that the State is tyrannical and an enemy of God is no excuse for hatred. As Christians we are called upon to love our enemies (Mt 5:44). It is not said that we should not or will not have enemies or that we should not identify tyrannical regimes as indeed our enemies. But once we have identified our enemies, we must endeavor to love them. That is not always easy. But then we must also remember that the most loving thing we can do for both the oppressed and for our enemies who are oppressors is to eliminate the oppression, remove the tyrants from power and establish a just government for the common good *of all the people.*

Chapter Five, Challenge to Action

5.5 Civil Disobedience

Once it is established that the present regime has no moral legitimacy and is in fact a tyrannical regime certain things follow for the Church and its activities. In the first place the Church cannot collaborate with tyranny. It cannot or should not do any thing that appears to give legitimacy to a morally illegitimate regime. Secondly, that Church should not only pray for a change of government, it should also mobilize its members in every parish to begin to think and work and plan for a change of government in South Africa. We must begin to look ahead and begin working now with firm hope and faith for a better future. And finally the moral illegitimacy of the apartheid regime means that the Church will have to be involved at times in civil disobedience. A Church that takes its responsibilities seriously in these circumstances will sometimes have to confront and to disobey the State in order to obey God.

5.6 Moral Guidance

The people look to the Church, especially in the midst of our present crisis, for moral guidance. In order to provide this the Church must first make its stand absolutely clear and never tire of explaining and dialoguing about it. It must then help people to understand their rights and their duties. There must be no misunderstanding about the moral duty of all who are oppressed to resist oppression and to struggle for liberation and justice. The Church will also find that at times it does need to curb excesses and to appeal to the consciences of those who act thoughtlessly and wildly.

But the Church of Jesus Christ is not called to be a bastion of caution and moderation. The Church should challenge, inspire and motivate people. It has a message of the cross that inspires us to make sacrifices for justice and liberation. It has a message of hope that challenges us to wake up and to act with hope and confidence. The Church must preach this message not only in words and sermons and statements but also through its actions, programmes, campaigns and divine services.

Ecclesial

The Barmen Declaration

The Theological Declaration of Barmen was issued from the first national synod of the Confessing Church in Barmen, a suburb of Wuppertal in North Rhine-Westphalia, Germany, in 1934. It is set out in imitation of the classical declarations of faith, affirming scriptural teaching and condemning those who attempted to accommodate the Christian faith to the Nazi ideology. It sets out to remind the world that the world is not the church. That is the tenor of the words, "We repudiate the false teaching that there are areas of life in which we belong not to Jesus Christ, but to some other lord, areas in which we do not need justification and sanctification through him."

But this prophetic message is also designed to remind the church that it is not the world. Dietrich Bonhoeffer (1906–1945) was a sometimes lonely voice striving to ensure the Confessing Church remained a church, and did not simply become synonymous with the opposition to Hitler. Hideous, ruthless, and reckless as Hitler's regime already was, Bonhoeffer could see that what was required was not simply the removal of Hitler, but a wholesale renewal of the church in Germany. That was what the Confessing Church was really about. For the Evangelical Church's support of Hitler had not come out of the blue, but was of a piece with a theology that had been flawed for some time.

The Barmen Declaration. From *The Church's Confession Under Hitler* by Arthur C. Cochrane. Philadelphia: Westminster Press, 1962, pages 237–42. Accessed at www.creeds.net/reformed/barmen.htm.

I. An Appeal to the Evangelical Congregations and Christians in Germany

The Confessional Synod of the German Evangelical Church met in Barmen, May 29–31, 1934. Here representatives from all the German Confessional Churches met with one accord in a confession of the one Lord of the one, holy, apostolic Church. In fidelity to their Confession of Faith, members of Lutheran, Reformed, and United Churches sought a common message for the need and temptation of the Church in our day. With gratitude to God they are convinced that they have been given a common word to utter. It was not their intention to found a new Church or to form a union. For nothing was farther from their minds than the abolition of the confessional status of our Churches. Their intention was, rather, to withstand in faith and unanimity the destruction of the Confession of Faith, and thus of the Evangelical Church in Germany. In opposition to attempts to establish the unity of the German Evangelical Church by means of false doctrine, by the use of force and insincere practices, the Confessional Synod insists that the unity of the Evangelical Churches in Germany can come only from the Word of God in faith through the Holy Spirit. Thus alone is the Church renewed.

Therefore the Confessional Synod calls upon the congregations to range themselves behind it in prayer, and steadfastly to gather around those pastors and teachers who are loyal to the Confessions.

Be not deceived by loose talk, as if we meant to oppose the unity of the German nation! Do not listen to the seducers who pervert our intentions, as if we wanted to break up the unity of the German Evangelical Church or to forsake the Confessions of the Fathers!

Try the spirits whether they are of God! Prove also the words of the Confessional Synod of the German Evangelical Church to see whether they agree with Holy Scripture and with the Confessions of the Fathers. If you find that we are speaking contrary to Scripture, then do not listen to us! But if you find that we are taking our stand upon Scripture, then let no fear or temptation keep you from treading with us the path of faith and obedience to the Word of God, in order that God's people be of one mind upon earth and that we in faith experience what he himself has said: "I will never leave you, nor forsake you." Therefore, "Fear not, little flock, for it is your Father's good pleasure to give you the kingdom."

II. Theological Declaration Concerning the Present Situation of the German Evangelical Church

According to the opening words of its constitution of July 11, 1933, the German Evangelical Church is a federation of Confessional Churches that grew out of the Reformation and that enjoy equal rights. The theological basis for the unification of these Churches is laid down in Article 1 and Article 2(1) of the constitution of the German Evangelical Church that was recognized by the Reich Government on July 14, 1933:

Article 1. The inviolable foundation of the German Evangelical Church is the gospel of Jesus Christ as it is attested for us in Holy Scripture and brought to light again in the Confessions of the Reformation. The full

powers that the Church needs for its mission are hereby determined and limited.

Article 2 (1). The German Evangelical Church is divided into member Churches (*Landeskirchen*).

We, the representatives of Lutheran, Reformed, and United Churches, of free synods, Church assemblies, and parish organizations united in the Confessional Synod of the German Evangelical Church, declare that we stand together on the ground of the German Evangelical Church as a federation of German Confessional Churches. We are bound together by the confession of the one Lord of the one, holy, catholic, and apostolic Church.

We publicly declare before all evangelical Churches in Germany that what they hold in common in this Confession is grievously imperiled, and with it the unity of the German Evangelical Church. It is threatened by the teaching methods and actions of the ruling Church party of the "German Christians" and of the Church administration carried on by them. These have become more and more apparent during the first year of the existence of the German Evangelical Church. This threat consists in the fact that the theological basis, in which the German Evangelical Church is united, has been continually and systematically thwarted and rendered ineffective by alien principles, on the part of the leaders and spokesmen of the "German Christians" as well as on the part of the Church administration. When these principles are held to be valid, then, according to all the Confessions in force among us, the Church ceases to be the Church and the German Evangelical Church, as a federation of Confessional Churches, becomes intrinsically impossible.

As members of Lutheran, Reformed, and United Churches we may and must speak with one voice in this matter today. Precisely because we want to be and to remain faithful to our various Confessions, we may not keep silent, since we believe that we have been given a common message to utter in a time of common need and temptation. We commend to God what this may mean for the interrelations of the Confessional Churches.

In view of the errors of the "German Christians" of the present Reich Church government which are devastating the Church and also therefore breaking up the unity of the German Evangelical Church, we confess the following evangelical truths:

1. "I am the way, and the truth, and the life; no one comes to the Father, but by me." (John 14:6) "Truly, truly, I say to you, he who does not enter the sheepfold by the door, but climbs in by another way, that man is

a thief and a robber. ... I am the door; if anyone enters by me, he will be saved." (John 10:1, 9)

Jesus Christ, as he is attested for us in Holy Scripture, is the one Word of God which we have to hear and which we have to trust and obey in life and in death.

We reject the false doctrine, as though the church could and would have to acknowledge as a source of its proclamation, apart from and besides this one Word of God, still other events and powers, figures and truths, as God's revelation.

2. "Christ Jesus, whom God has made our wisdom, our righteousness and sanctification and redemption." (1 Cor. 1:30)

As Jesus Christ is God's assurance of the forgiveness of all our sins, so, in the same way and with the same seriousness he is also God's mighty claim upon our whole life. Through him befalls us a joyful deliverance from the godless fetters of this world for a free, grateful service to his creatures.

We reject the false doctrine, as though there were areas of our life in which we would not belong to Jesus Christ, but to other lords – areas in which we would not need justification and sanctification through him.

3. "Rather, speaking the truth in love, we are to grow up in every way into him who is the head, into Christ, from whom the whole body [is] joined and knit together." (Eph. 4:15, 16)

The Christian Church is the congregation of the brethren in which Jesus Christ acts presently as the Lord in Word and sacrament through the Holy Spirit. As the Church of pardoned sinners, it has to testify in the midst of a sinful world, with its faith as with its obedience, with its message as with its order, that it is solely his property, and that it lives and wants to live solely from his comfort and from his direction in the expectation of his appearance.

We reject the false doctrine, as though the Church were permitted to abandon the form of its message and order to its own pleasure or to changes in prevailing ideological and political convictions.

4. "You know that the rulers of the Gentiles lord it over them, and their great men exercise authority over them. It shall not be so among you; but whoever would be great among you must be your servant." (Matt. 20:25, 26)

The various offices in the Church do not establish a dominion of some over the others; on the contrary, they are for the exercise of the ministry entrusted to and enjoined upon the whole congregation.

We reject the false doctrine, as though the Church, apart from this ministry, could and were permitted to give itself, or allow to be given to it, special leaders vested with ruling powers.

5. "Fear God. Honor the emperor." (1 Peter 2:17)

Scripture tells us that, in the as yet unredeemed world in which the Church also exists, the State has by divine appointment the task of providing for justice and peace. [It fulfills this task] by means of the threat and exercise of force, according to the measure of human judgment and human ability. The Church acknowledges the benefit of this divine appointment in gratitude and reverence before him. It calls to mind the Kingdom of God, God's commandment and righteousness, and thereby the responsibility both of rulers and of the ruled. It trusts and obeys the power of the Word by which God upholds all things.

We reject the false doctrine, as though the State, over and beyond its special commission, should and could become the single and totalitarian order of human life, thus fulfilling the Church's vocation as well.

We reject the false doctrine, as though the Church, over and beyond its special commission, should and could appropriate the characteristics, the tasks, and the dignity of the State, thus itself becoming an organ of the State.

6. "Lo, I am with you always, to the close of the age." (Matt. 28:20) "The word of God is not fettered." (2 Tim. 2:9)

The Church's commission, upon which its freedom is founded, consists in delivering the message of the free grace of God to all people in Christ's stead, and therefore in the ministry of his own Word and work through sermon and sacrament.

We reject the false doctrine, as though the Church in human arrogance could place the Word and work of the Lord in the service of any arbitrarily chosen desires, purposes, and plans.

The Confessional Synod of the German Evangelical Church declares that it sees in the acknowledgment of these truths and in the rejection of these errors the indispensable theological basis of the German Evangelical Church as a federation of Confessional Churches. It invites all who are able to accept its declaration to be mindful of these theological principles in their decisions in Church politics. It entreats all whom it concerns to return to the unity of faith, love, and hope.

Justice and Punishment

The term justice is used in several overlapping ways in Christian ethics. The distinctively ecclesial way to speak of justice is as a virtue, indeed one of the four cardinal virtues, and thus to point out that there can be no just society without just people to make it so. More universal ways to think about justice may take a human turn, and see it as a complementary or alternative form of love – in some cases, the form love takes when it is translated into social relationships; or they may take a theological turn, and be rooted in the notion of justice as an attribute of God. In such accounts there is often some concern over whether forgiveness and justice are identical, opposite, complementary, or in some other relationship with one another. Meanwhile, both universal and subversive accounts refer to a further notion of justice, that of the sustainable distribution of rights and responsibilities, entitlements and duties among citizens. In this last sense it is now commonplace to point out that there is likely to be no lasting peace without justice, and to call for peace in the absence of justice may be inappropriate (or may betray a particular social location). Thus, civil disobedience is an appeal to a deeper conviction about justice.

As to punishment, the tension in Christian tradition is similar to that between love and justice. Thus, pun- ishment may be seen as a form of love, always a tough means to a generous end, and in that sense for the benefit of the offender as much as anyone else (hence the beginnings of incarceration in the solitary confinement of recalcitrant monks); or it may be seen as an assertion of natural justice, necessary to make a public restoration and restatement of the proper order of things in the face and wake of transgression. Commitment to capital punishment, and to the existence of hell (even if empty), are statements of the second kind. Views of punishment vary as to whether the primary beneficiary is taken to be the victim, the offender, the civil law or moral order (sometimes represented in the monarch), or the kingdom of God. Again, the place of forgiveness in relation to punishment, as to justice, is complex, especially for universal ethics, committed as it is to publicly applicable systems and procedures.

The readings below are more eclectic than in some other sections. Oliver O'Donovan takes issue with the Pope's treatment of capital punishment; Dan and Philip Berrigan explore the moments at which breaking the law is more loyal than keeping it; and Timothy Gorringe describes the theological issues at stake in the language of justice.

Universal

Oliver O'Donovan, The Death Penalty in *Evangelium Vitae*

Evangelium Vitae (On the Value and Inviolability of Human Life) was issued by Pope John Paul II on March 25, 1995. It articulates the value and inviolability of human life in particular relation to murder, abortion, euthanasia, and the death penalty. It notes the only potentially acceptable use of the death penalty arises when it would not otherwise be possible to defend society, a situation that is "rare if not practically non-existent" today.

In his response, Oliver O'Donovan begins by noting a puzzling silence regarding the resurrection in John Paul's treatment of capital punishment in *Evangelium Vitae*. The Pope presents the cross as the conquest of death, but not as a death itself, which leads O'Donovan to propose that *Evangelium Vitae* lacks a view of the cross as capital punishment. O'Donovan is concerned with the ideology of capital punishment in political ethics around the world, as well as the necessity for an ecumenical discussion that takes seriously the moral heritage of the church as traditionally permitting the death penalty within certain limits. He offers two readings of the Pope's position, first from the formal discussion of the topic in paragraph 56, and then from passing references elsewhere in the document.

The heart of O'Donovan's argument lies in the sentence "Our great-grandfathers and grandmothers thought the death penalty absolutely required, since only life could witness to the sanctity of life," and in his consequent claim that "punishment is an 'expressive' act, an acted declaration of the truth about the offense in relation to the moral order of society." Hence O'Donovan places the argument in squarely deontological terms rather than consequential ones. Punishment is a "symbolic construct," not a simple calculation. Capital punishment declares the truth about what has taken place – a truth it would be hard to declare any other way. O'Donovan concludes: "Absolute inviolability belongs only to *innocent* human life, so a society that has a necessity for capital punishment is not wrong to practice it." As he insists, "Death is the gold standard from which the currency of punishment draws its credit."

Oliver O'Donovan. "The Death Penalty in *Evangelium Vitae*." Pages 213–36 in *Ecumenical Ventures in Ethics: Protestants Engage Pope John Paul II's Moral Encyclicals.* Ed. Reinhard Hütter and Theodor Dieter. Grand Rapids: Eerdmans, 1998. Excerpt from pages 220–7, 233–5.

Paragraph 56 occurs near the beginning of the third chapter of the encyclical, which contains the bulk of its special ethics. From the command "You shall not kill" we are led to the only formal qualification which, in his view, this command is susceptible of: "legitimate defense," which includes not only personal self-defense but actions taken in responsibility for "the common good of the family or of the State." This brings us to the section on the death penalty which unfolds as follows:

(56a)   He observes "a growing tendency," in and beyond the church, to favor limitation or abolition.

(56b)   A methodological statement: The context must be "a system (*regul*) of penal justice ever more in line with human dignity."

(56c)   There follows a concise statement of the classical purposes of punishment: first, retribution, or "redress"; in a secondary place, the defense of public order and the rehabilitation of the offender.

(56d)   The "nature and extent of the punishment" (*modum et genus*) – what kind of punishment and how much – has to be ordered "carefully" to the achievement of these purposes.

(56e)   Capital punishment – "the extreme of executing the offender" – ought not to be invoked except in "cases of absolute necessity." This phrase is then explained to mean "when it would not be possible otherwise to defend society."

(56f)   There follows disconcertingly upbeat generalization, clearly intended to emphasize the marginal nature of the concession just made to capital punishment: "Today … as a result of steady improvements in the organisation of the penal system, such cases are very rare, if not practically non-existent."

(56g)   The section then concludes with a quotation from [the New Catholic Catechism] reinforcing the point that the principle of proportion requires "bloodless means" to protect public safety wherever they are sufficient.

… Three points are particularly in need of clarification. In the first place, what general state of affairs does the "upbeat generalization" (56f) suppose? In the second, what kind of situation does his talk of "absolute necessity" envisage? In the third, a more theoretical question: why, since the aims of punishment are stated, in a highly classical form, as primarily retributive and only secondarily defensive and remedial ("In this way authority also fulfils the purpose …" 56c), should the principle of proportionate defense (56e, 56g) exercise an overall constraint on the "nature and extent" of the punishment we inflict?

In the first place, we must suppose that in 56f John Paul is thinking only of modern, well-governed law-states. … One possibility is that he regards advanced economic development as the normal and normative condition of human civilization, an interpretation of which we might properly be cautious in the case of this pope, not only in view of the modernity-criticism adopted by the present encyclical, but in view of his warnings about the idea of development in *Sollicitudo Rei Socialis*. It may be enough for the moment to say that this idealist characterization of the current situation is simply raised as a thought experiment on which no weight in the argument is reposed.

The second question can be answered on the basis of indications in 56f. Cases of "absolute necessity" may be very rare (at least in well-governed law-states) *by virtue of the better organization of the penal system*. This separates the pope from any version of the thesis that certain types of crime, simply by virtue of their extreme gravity, constitute the necessity that justifies the extreme penalty. This is most striking since the Catechism gives every impression of supporting this thesis; when it authorizes "penalties commensurate with the gravity of the crime, not excluding, in cases of extreme gravity, the death-penalty." We must suppose that the pope understood the phrase "not excluding" to imply "but not requiring either.""Absolute necessity" is not a matter of the gravity of the crime alone – be it police-murder, child-murder, torture, indiscriminate terrorism, or whatever – but implies an element of *crisis*. Only so could the pope say that it arises very rarely in well-governed law-states; for, unhappily, no type of heinous crime is "rare if not practically non-existent" in well-governed law-states, which, indeed, have even tended to see the emergence of new types of specially heinous crime, pedophile child-murder for example. On the other hand, it does not seem that a *political* crisis fulfils the conditions either. If it is rare in well-governed law-states that a state is threatened with disaster from subversion or civil war, that is credit not to the organization of its penal system but to the stabilizing effects of its democratic polity. ...

The only scenario that seems to fit the description is a *breakdown of law and order*, in which government loses its control of crime and fails to protect society against its depredations. An organized penal system (i.e. a "system of justice," broadly understood to include detection, arrest, and conviction as well as punishment) has had much to do with obviating this type of emergency in developed societies; yet it is also plausible to think that in less elaborately organized societies the death penalty has played a significant role in containing forces of lawlessness and upholding public order. So on this reading John Paul sees the burden of maintaining order shifted, in well-governed states, from capital punishment to a sophisticated apparatus of detection and imprisonment. Given that the principle of proportionate defense demands a "bloodless" means where possible (56g), he thinks that this shift should be welcomed and consolidated; yet the liminal possibility of breakdown means that the death penalty is not disallowed categorically.

The third, more theoretical, question was why, if there are three purposes of punishment and retribution is the primary one, an overall constraint upon means of punishment should be that of proportionate defense. A consensus from the late eighteenth and nineteenth centuries would have said that *retributive appropriateness* was the final criterion for means of punishment. Our great-grandfathers and grandmothers thought the death penalty absolutely required, since only life could witness to the sanctity of life. ...

If we know what we are about when we speak of a "retributive" function of punishment, we mean that punishment is an "expressive" act, an acted declaration of the truth about the offense in relation to the moral order of society. A punishment must pronounce judgment on the offense, describing it, disowning it, and refounding the moral basis for the common life which the offense has challenged. In this sense punishment "gives back" the offense, not as an act of mere retaliation, returning evil for evil, but in the sense of a true statement, representing rightly that which has been done. If we then call retribution the "primary" end, we mean simply that such a pronouncement is what punishing *is*; just as telling the truth is the primary end of making a statement, because that is what "stating" is. Private vengeance or retaliation would be extrinsic, arbitrary ends; the distinction between retaliation and the proper sense of "retribution" is essential to any serious discussion of punishment. ...

Punishment is a kind of enacted language, and like all linguistic utterances, any one act of punishment can have a different meaning in different social contexts. There is no absolute vocabulary. Rather, as history has shown, there is a variety of possible systems of penal practice all of which satisfy the formal demand that offenses should be discriminatingly judged and pronounced on. The rule called by the Romans *lex talionis*, the infliction of equal and opposite harm, *appears* to promise an exact and universal tariff, but this is a chimera. Distinguished philosophers, Kant at their head, have sometimes confused it with the retributive form of punishment itself and so inferred that certain crimes (such as murder) must, as a moral principle, be answered with equal and opposite harm (the death penalty). Aristotle much more judiciously rejected the view that retaliation constituted just punishment, and so should we. The chief usefulness of *lex talionis* is in assessing damages, not punishments. The equivalence of punishment to crime has to be a symbolic construct. Punishment is a language that evolves as the symbolic meaning of certain acts within the context of social expectation changes. ...

So far, then, we have extracted from paragraph 56 of *Evangelium Vitae* [EV] an account of John Paul's views on capital punishment that broadly supports Western trends towards abolition yet sufficiently acknowledges their contingency to keep faith with the tradition. On this reading paragraph 56 of EV seems to me to provide a hopeful foundation for a possible ecumenical consensus. It has not broken faith with the permissive end of the tradition, as represented by Innocent III's insistence that a magistrate might employ the death penalty without mortal sin if he did so responsibly; the only doctrine ruled out is that of Kant, Hegel, and their theological followers, that murder *requires* the death penalty as a matter of moral fitness. Yet its center of gravity lies closer to the patristic consensus summed up in Ambrose's "You will be excused if you use it, admired if you refrain." Absolute inviolability belongs only to *innocent* human life, so a society that has a necessity for capital punishment is not wrong to practice it. Yet there is a presumption that this situation will tend to disappear. A society that succeeds in responsible abolition is, to that extent, morally more advanced; while one that fails to abolish it once it has become disproportionate to its needs is at fault. ...

[O'Donovan explores the other passing references to the death penalty in *Evangelium Vitae* in order to propose an alternate reading of the Pope's position; he concludes that this second account finds him "less respectful of tradition and more convinced of the universal moral unfitness of the penalty of death." O'Donovan finds this a less preferable and more inconsistent position.]

So wide and unbridgeable a gulf is made between death and all other kinds of penalty, that it quite escapes notice that the other punishments are coercive too. But all forms of coercion exercise their hold upon us through our mortality. Punishments are effected against the person, property, or liberty of the offender; an attack on any of these is an attack on the limited and irrecoverable powers which any individual human being can dispose of in order to live his or her life. Two years in prison are "two good years of my life," two out of a finite number less than a hundred. A heavy fine is a drain on resources that I need to feed, clothe, and house myself if I am to live my full term of days. And so on. A flexible penal system has a wide range of intermediate penalties that stop short of taking an offender's life. But that *ultima ratio* is indeed the *ratio* of all the penultimate measures. If we were not mortal, none of them would have any meaning. Death is the gold standard from which the currency of punishment draws its credit. Failure to see the intrinsic relation between death and punishment means failure to see what we *always* do when we punish; failure, therefore, to see that the state, in exacting the death penalty, is doing just what it always does, one way or another, in response to crime. ...

I return in closing to the theological issue raised at the start: the failure of the encyclical to achieve a clear focus on the resurrection and its tendency to put the cross in its place, central to the salvation history of life but unrelated to the phenomenology of death. Now I can suggest a reason for this. John Paul's failure, on the side of civil justice, to identify the link between judgment and mortality is reflected in a failure, on the side of death, to link mortality and judgment. Politically we have justice without death, anthropologically death without judgment. ...

The symbolic links of judgment and execution stand at the heart of what we understand about Christ's reconciling death. We may be rid of ordinary uses of the death penalty in most Western states; I am glad to live in one where we are. We may one day be rid of it elsewhere, in Third World countries, Muslim societies, and so on. If we can achieve that responsibly, it will be a fine achievement – though we must be on our guard against irresponsible, crusading attitudes which fail to take the context (legal, economic, social, and moral) seriously. But we cannot be rid of the symbolic role that the death penalty plays in relating death to judgment. There will always be a death penalty in the mind – if, that is, we are all to learn to "die with Christ," understanding our own deaths as a kind of capital punishment.

Subversive

Daniel and Philip Berrigan, *Civil Disobedience*

Daniel Berrigan (b. 1921) and Philip Berrigan (1923–2002) were shaped by the activist theology that emerged from the concentration camps and resistance movements of World War II Europe, by the French examples of worker-socialist-priests, and by ideas of civil disobedience.

The Catonsville Nine were nine Roman Catholics who burned draft files in protest of the Vietnam War. On May 17, 1968, they went to the draft board in Catonsville, Maryland, took 378 draft files, brought them to the parking lot in wire baskets, dumped them out, poured homemade napalm over them, and set them on fire. Two participants had previously poured blood on draft records as members of the "Baltimore Four," and were out on bail when they burned the records at Catonsville. The Catonsville Nine statement was written by Philip Berrigan, a former Josephite priest, and signed by eight others. After their conviction, Fr. Daniel Berrigan, Philip's brother, a Jesuit priest, wrote, "Our apologies, good friends, for the fracture of good order, the burning of paper instead of children."

From 1970 to 1995 Dan Berrigan spent a total of nearly seven years in prison, having continued his "witness-bearing" against militarism, nuclear arms, racism, and injustice. He called his post-Catonsville pacifist efforts "Plowshares," after the phrase "they shall beat their swords into plowshares" (Micah 4:3). Their protests mostly focused on disabling nuclear weapons.

While overlapping with universal and ecclesial approaches, these texts are subversive in the sense that they explicitly identify with and advocate for the victims of America's belligerent policies. Like the authors of the Kairos Document, they point out that peace and justice look and sound different depending on who is promoting them. Dan Berrigan here identifies the heart of his work as "the use and misuse of symbols, their seizure by secular power; then the struggle to keep the symbols in focus." As his closing words make clear, the question is always one of the mission of the church and its relationship to the state.

Daniel Berrigan: Poetry, Drama, Prose. Ed. Michael True. Maryknoll: Orbis Books, 1988. From Philip Berrigan et al., "Statement of the Catonsville Nine" (pp. 155–7) and Daniel Berrigan, "Swords into Plowshares" (pp. 179–82). As reprinted in *Daniel Berrigan: Poetry, Drama, Prose.* Ed. Michael True. Maryknoll, NY: Orbis Books, 1988.

Statement of the Catonsville Nine

Today, May 17, 1968, we enter Local Board #33, Catonsville, Maryland, to seize the Selective Service records and to burn them outside with homemade napalm. (The recipe for napalm we took from the Special Forces Handbook, published by the Army's School of Special Warfare at Ft. Bragg, North Carolina.)

As American citizens, we have worked with the poor in the ghetto and abroad. In the course of our Christian ministry, we have watched our country produce more victims than an army of us could console or restore. Two of us face immediate sentencing for similar acts against Selective Service. All of us identify with the victims of American oppression all over the world. We submit voluntarily to their involuntary fate.

We use napalm on these draft records because napalm has burned people to death in Vietnam, Guatemala, and Peru; and because it may be used in America's ghettos. We destroy these draft records not only because they exploit our young men, but because these records represent misplaced power, concentrated in the ruling class of America. Their power threatens the peace of the world; it isolates itself from public dissent and manipulates parliamentary process. And it reduces young men to a cost-efficiency item through the draft. In effect – if not in intent – the rulers of the United States want their global wars fought as cheaply as possible.

Above all, our protest attempts to illustrate why our country is torn at home and harassed abroad by enemies of its own creation. For a long time the United States has been an empire, and today it is history's richest nation. Representing 6 per cent of the world's people, our country controls half the world's productive capacity and two-thirds of its finance. It holds Northern and Southern America in an economic vise. In fifteen years time, economists think that its industry in Europe will be the third greatest industrial power in the world, after the United States and the Soviet Union. Our foreign profits run substantially higher than domestic profits. So industry flees abroad under Government patronage and protection from the CIA, counter-insurgency, and conflict management teams.

The military participates with economic and political sectors to form a triumvirate of power which sets and enforces policy. With an annual budget of more than 80 billion dollars, our military now controls over half of all Federal property (53 per cent, or 183 billion dollars) while U.S. nuclear and conventional weaponry exceeds that of the whole remaining world.

Peace negotiations with the North Vietnamese have begun in Paris. With other Americans, we hope a settlement will be reached, thus sparing the Vietnamese a useless prolongation of their suffering. However, this alone will not solve our nation's problems. The Vietnam War could end tomorrow and leave undisturbed the quality of our society, and its world role. Thailand, Laos, and the Dominican Republic have already been Vietnams. Guatemala, the Canal Zone, Bolivia, and Peru could be Vietnams overnight. Meanwhile, the colonies at home rise in rage and destructiveness. Our black people have concluded that after 350 years, their human acceptance is long overdue.

Injustice is the great catalyst of revolution. A nation that found life in revolution has now become the world's foremost counter-revolutionary force, not because the American people would have it that way, but because an expanding economy and continuing profits require an insistence on the *status quo*. Competitive capitalism as a system, and capitalists in general, must learn the hard lessons of justice, or a country may be swept away and humanity with it.

We believe that some property has no right to exist. Hitler's gas ovens, Stalin's concentration camps, atomic-bacteriological-chemical weaponry, files of conscription, and slum properties have no right to exist. When people starve for bread and lack decent housing, it is usually because the rich debase themselves with abuse of property, causing extravagance on their part and oppression and misery in others.

We are Catholic Christians who take the Christian gospel seriously. We hail the recent Papal encyclical, *The Development of Peoples*. Quotes like the following give us hope:

"No one is justified in keeping for his exclusive use what he does not need, when others lack necessities.

A revolutionary uprising – save where there is open, manifest, and long-standing tyranny which does great damage to fundamental personal rights and dangerous harm to the common good of the country – produces new injustices, throws more elements out of balance, and brings on new disasters.

It is a question of building a world where every man, no matter what his race, religion, or nationality, can live a fully human life, freed from slavery imposed on him by other men or natural forces, a world where the poor man Lazarus can sit down at the same table with the rich man.

The hour for action has now sounded. At stake are the survival of so many children and so many families overcome by misery, with no access to conditions fit for human beings; at stake are the peace of the world and the future of civilization."

Despite such stirring words, we confront the Catholic church, other Christian bodies, and the synagogues of America with their silence and cowardice in the face of our country's crimes. We are convinced that the religious bureaucracy in this country is racist, guilty of complicity in war, and hostile to the poor. In utter fidelity to our faith, we indict religious leaders and their followers for their failure to serve our country and humankind.

Finally, we are appalled by the ruse of the American ruling class invoking pleas for "law and order" to mask and perpetuate injustice. Let our President and the pillars of society speak of "law and justice" and back up their words with deeds. Then there will be "order." We have pleaded, spoken, marched, and nursed the victims of their injustice. Now this injustice must be faced, and this we intend to do, with whatever strength of mind, body, and grace that God will give us. May He have mercy on our nation.

Rev. Daniel Berrigan, Rev. Philip Berrigan,
Bro. David Darst, John Hogan, Thomas Lewis,
Majorie Bradford Melville, Thomas Melville,
George Mische, Mary Moylan

Swords into Plowshares

*On September 9, 1980, the Plowshares Eight, including
Daniel Berrigan, entered a General Electric nuclear missile
plant in King of Prussia, Pennsylvania, and damaged two
nose cones of the Mark 12A reentry missile.*

September 9, 1980. We rose at dawn after (to speak
for myself) a mostly sleepless night. ... We had passed
several days in prayer together, an old custom indeed,
as old as our first arrests in the late sixties. We were
mostly vets of those years, survivors too, survivors of
the culture and its pseudos and counters, survivors of
courts and jails, of the American flare of conscience and
its long hibernation, survivors in our religious communities, in our families (they have survived us!). By an
act of God and nothing of our own, survivors of America
– its mimes, grimaces, enticements, abhorrences, shifts
and feints, masks, counter-masks. Survivors (barely) of
the demons who, challenged, shouted their name
– Legion!

We knew for a fact (the fact was there for anyone who
bothered to investigate) that General Electric in King of
Prussia manufactures the reentry cones of Mark 12A
missiles. We learned that Mark 12A is a warhead that will
carry an H-bomb of 335 kilotons to its target. That three
of these weapons are being attached to each of three
hundred Minuteman III missiles. That because of Mark
12A accuracy and explosive power, it will be used to
implement U.S. counterforce or first-strike policy.

We knew these hideous cones ("shrouds" is the GE
word) were concocted in a certain building of the
General Electric complex. The building is huge: we had
no idea exactly where the cones could be found.

Of one thing we were sure. If we were to reach the
highly classified area of shipping and delivery and were
to do there what we purposed, Someone must intervene, give us a lead.

After our deed, a clamor arose among the FBI and
state and county and GE (and God knows what other)
police who swarmed into the building. "Did they have
inside information? Was there a leak?" Our answer: of
course we had Inside Information, of course there had
been a Leak. Our Informant is otherwise known in the
New Testament as Advocate, Friend, Spirit. We had
been at prayer for days.

And the deed was done. We eight looked at one
another, exhausted, bedazzled with the ease of it all. We

had been led in about two minutes, and with no interference to speak of, to the heart of the labyrinth.

They rounded us up, trundled us out in closed vans.
We spent the day uncommonly cheerful in that place of
penitence, in various cells of police headquarters. We
underwent what I came to think of as a "forced fast,"
the opposite of forced feeding and undoubtedly less
perilous to life and limb. Around the corridors of the
spiffy new building (we were in GE country, the local
economy is 40 percent GE, GE brings good things to
life) the atmosphere was one of hit and miss, cross-
purpose, barely concealed panic. How the hell did they
get into the building so easily? How about the jobs of
those of us who were purportedly guarding the nuclear
brews and potions?

Lines to Justice Department, Pentagon, FBI were red
hot. Why can't you get your act together up there? And
what are we to do with these religious doomsayers? Let
them go, let them off light, let them off never? Please
advise!

About noon another ploy got underway. They
loaded us in vans again; back to the scene of the crime.
... They carried four of five of us out of the van into
that big warehouse room with the bloody floor, the
bloody torn blueprints stamped "Top Secret." And then
the missile cones, broken, bloodied, useless. No more
genocide in our name! And the wall of faces, police,
employees, silent as the grave, furious, bewildered, a
captive nation. ...

Blood and hammers. The symbolic aspect of our GE
action appealed to some and appalled others. But
almost no one who has heard of the action lacks an
opinion about it, usually a passionately stated one. ...

Some who hear grow furious; some of the furious
are Catholics; Catholics also guard us, judge us, prosecute us. This is an old story that need not long
detain us.

What is of peculiar and serious interest here is the
use and misuse of symbols, their seizure by secular
power; then the struggle to keep the symbols in focus,
to enable them to be seen, heard, tasted, smelled, lived
and died for, in all their integrity, first intent.

Their misuse. How they are leveled off, made consistent with the credo of the state. Thus, to speak of King
of Prussia and our symbol there: blood. Its outpouring
in the death of Christ announced a gift and, by implication, set a strict boundary, a taboo. No shedding of
blood, by anyone, under any circumstances, since this,
my blood, is given for you. Blood as gift.

Hence the command: no killing, no war. Which is
to say, above all, no nuclear weapons. And thence the

imperative: resist those who research, deploy, or justify on whatever grounds such weaponry.

Thus the drama; the symbol outpoured implies a command. Do this; so live, so die. Clear lines are drawn for public as well as personal conduct. Church and state, the "twin powers," always in danger of becoming Siamese twins, are in fact kept from a mutually destructive symbiosis by imperative and taboo. More, they are revealed for what they in fact are – radically opposed spiritual powers, as in Revelation 13. Church can never be state; state is forbidden to ape or absorb church. And this mutual Opposition, this nonalignment, this friction and fraying, erupts from time to time in tragic and bloody struggle. The church resists being recast as Caesarian icon. The state, robust, in firm possession, demands that the church knuckle under, bend knee, bless war, pay taxes, shut up. Church, thy name is trouble.

Ecclesial

Timothy Gorringe, *Atonement, Retribution, and Forgiveness*

Timothy Jervis Gorringe (b. 1946) teaches at the University of Exeter. Here he explores the satisfaction theory of the atonement: in particular the way in which it was closely connected to the retributive theory of punishment. The satisfaction theory, most closely associated with Anselm of Canterbury (1033–1109), teaches that Christ went to the cross as a substitute for humankind, thereby satisfying the demands of God's honor by his infinite merit. Later modifications saw the issue more in terms of God's justice than God's honor.

Gorringe draws on the work of René Girard (b. 1923) for insight into the way in which Christian understandings of redemption and atonement have contributed to a rhetoric of violence and retribution. Girard has built a philosophical system based around the central role in human culture of sacrifice as the climax of mimetic, or imitative, violence between rivals. Gorringe explores the close connection of expiation and criminal law in the Old Testament. He then argues that the New Testament, "far from underscoring retributivism, actually deconstructs it." Christ's crucifixion is not expiation for our guilt but "the absorption of violence, the redefinition of power, and the establishment of the possibility of forgiveness." In his final chapter he presents an alternative understanding of Christ's death as it relates to reconciliation and the rehabilitation of offenders.

This excerpt represents a significant strand in ecclesial ethics because it demonstrates how ethics is deeply caught up in theological presuppositions.

Timothy Gorringe. *God's Just Vengeance: Crime, Violence and the Rhetoric of Salvation*. Cambridge Studies in Ideology and Religion 9. Cambridge: Cambridge University Press, 1996. From Chapter 10, "Forgiveness, Crime and Community," pages 262–71. © Cambridge University Press, reproduced with permission.

The challenge we face ... is to structure a genuine *community* – where values as well as material goods such as energy resources or means of transport are held in common – which does not at the same time repress and marginalise those who are different and which does not rule by a false normalisation. I wish to make the, at first slightly implausible, suggestion that there may be resources for this project within the Christian tradition.

In his discussion of the rise of nationalism, Benedict Anderson coins the phrase "imagined community." All communities are "imagined," he argues, in that the image of their communion lives in the mind of each member. The nations of the modern world are held together not primarily by ethnic ties, but by constructed stories. ... The Christian church was from the very beginning, I would like to argue, an "imagined community," not just in Anderson's sense but also in the sense of a utopian community, not rooted in kinship (Mark 3.31f.), whose purpose was to provide a messianic "home," or rooting, for human beings. In a society characterised by very stable, religiously under-girded family ties Jesus calls into being a community of *voluntary* commitment, willing to take on the hostility of this society. It was as a utopian, imagined, community that it both structured and sought further to envisage the possibilities of redemption, seeking to break down the fundamental barriers of the ancient world (Gal. 3.25). ... It could be argued, then, that the situation analysed by postmodern theory is precisely the situation envisaged by the church from the beginning, namely one in which rooted communities are often barriers to redemption, and in which redemption, the restoration of relationships, is brought about only by the creation of an "imagined" community athwart all existing communities. The community called "church" contributes to that struggle and negotiation for forms of social life properly called human by faithfulness to and proclamation of this tradition and, in every period and culture, by the creation of such communities. ...

Do we need to talk about the church at all? I believe that it continues to make sense to do so because the creation of a different kind of social space, in which people can find creative ways of coping with difference, disagreement and sheer downright evil, presupposes the immense work of education which we call the reappropriation of tradition. If there is anything in claims that the gospel is redemptive, this must be in virtue of the fact that the founts of the tradition themselves, "Scripture," constantly deconstruct positions of power and privilege, and therefore positions which legitimate oppressive normality. The church "semper reformanda" is the church constantly reconscientised. With Pieter Spierenberg Christians believe that human sensibilities can change for the better, and that the gospel plays a crucial part in this. ... [T]he church, on the ground of its founding texts, needs to attack the related ideologies of neoliberal economics and retributivism, to contribute to their deconstruction. At the heart of this attack lies a conception of human life grounded not on violence, and the logic of an eye for an eye, but on forgiveness.

The Logic of Forgiveness

In holding before us the claims of an imagined community the New Testament, far from providing legitimation for retributivist practice, in fact advanced the claims of an alternative, nonviolent, way of life. Forgiveness, I shall argue, lies at the heart of that – not as a benign doctrine, but as a remorselessly difficult *praxis*.

A repeated retributivist claim, as we have seen, is that to forgive without punishing is to condone evil, to reduce grace to sentimentality. Behind such claims seems to lurk the idea that to forgive is to let someone off, but this is absolutely not what happens in forgiveness. When Jesus forgives the woman taken in adultery (John 8.1–11), he neither insists on her punishment nor condones her sin. Forgiveness is a creative act, *sui generis*, which heals by restoring people to community, by recognising the mutuality of guilt ("Let him without sin cast the first stone").

The story of the healing of the paralysed man in Mark's gospel is a parable of the power of forgiveness (Mark 2.1–12). The sinner is paralysed by sin and guilt, a burden to all (he is carried by four friends). It is forgiveness which "looses" him, enables him to stand on his feet, rejoin society and begin a new life. Only retribution, it is claimed, recognises guilt and therefore responsibility, but this is false, for a recognition of guilt and responsibility is *implicit* in any real act of forgiveness. Forgiveness, in fact, changes both the past and the future. "If you forgive," writes Brian Frost, "often you can free a trapped yesterday and make possible a different tomorrow. In other words a paradigm shift occurs and a new ingredient has become available whose impact can be not only the changing of perceptions ... but roles and regulations too." ...

Iris Murdoch ... draws attention to the way in which forgiveness itself can be an exercise of power, but that such power is refused is what is redemptive in the crucifixion. As she puts it in another novel: "To love and to reconcile and to forgive, only this matters. All power is sin and all law is frailty. Love is the only justice. Forgiveness, reconciliation, not law." Despite the difficult questions about who could possibly be authorised to forgive, apart from the victims, we have to recognise that it is forgiveness alone which breaks the vicious circle by which disrespect breeds disrespect, and alienation causes alienation.

Forgiveness and Sacramental Praxis

I have argued that the church was from the beginning an "imagined community," and that at the heart of its gospel is a praxis of costly forgiveness. How does this relate to the current retributive penal climate, and to the strategies of reconciliation I have outlined? We have seen that the conclusion of two centuries of penal experimentation seems to indicate that, although crime will never be eliminated, the only way of tackling it effectively is through "mainstream processes of socialisation" and not through retribution. The imagined community called church is not this community of redemption *in toto*, but it is so *sacramentally*. The General Synod [of the Church of England] working group finely note that Christian experience shows that God's response to human misdeeds does not require suffering or pain as a condition for acceptance, or demand retaliation or condemn or exclude the offender. It does not primarily aim to express divine wrath. Instead "God accepts the offender without condoning the offence; requires the offender to face up to the reality of that offence; invites the offender into a community of reconciliation; encourages the offender to lead life with a new attitude; declares the offender to be free from the offence; invites the person to follow in service as a 'disciple.'" The community of reconciliation (not the church, but the church sacramentally) is the means through which atonement is effected, which is the reason, presumably, Christ bequeathed us not a set of doctrines or truths but a community founded on betrayal and the survival of betrayal.

Pierre Allard, Director of Chaplaincy Correctional Service in Canada, has a moving story to illustrate this. He has taken it as an axiom that prisoners cannot be ministered to by "chaplains," but only by a community of faith. In his experience it takes five to ten years to educate a faith community about prisoners. In one congregation, after a number of years addressed by prison chaplains and other prison workers an ex-offender was finally invited to speak:

"As he shared his story with much effort, the people's hearts were touched. This church of 800 people gave him a standing ovation. Two weeks after, he was still shedding tears over it. The ovation did more for him than many of our more sophisticated programmes, to help him believe that he had a place again in our community."

This story shows very clearly how the work of conscientisation, of the creation of new sensibilities, goes on. In reflecting on what it is God has done for us in Christ we need to shift the centre of our reflection from satisfaction to the biblical roots of redemption and reconciliation. Christ "redeems" us from the principalities and powers, from the social structures which warp human behaviour and produce violence and crime, partly by laying bare the way in which they scapegoat and exclude, but also, correlatively, by inaugurating a continuing practice of reconciliation.

The faith community, then, if it is true to its founding insights, is constituted as a sign or parable of how "offenders" should be treated, just as seventeenth- and eighteenth-century Protestants maintained, though to very different effect. For earlier Protestantism, the offender was the sign of the sinner in all of us, and his or her punishment a dreadful warning. According to satisfaction theory it was judgement which made reconciliation possible. By analogy, the offender had to make satisfaction before reconciliation could take place. The great Victorian prisons all proclaim the need to make satisfaction. Their high walls are at least as much about the exclusion of the scapegoat as they are about protecting "the public." Liberal theologians like [Friedrich] Schleiermacher and Hastings Rashdall complained that the imagery of satisfaction theory went back to "the crudest human conditions." In this they were not wrong. Their mistake was, first, to suppose that we might have outgrown such conditions and, second, to fail to see the immense power implicit in the rhetoric of satisfaction. For all its power, however, we have seen that the sub-text of the doctrine is a subtle rhetoric of violence, a violence which has underwritten both state sadism and individual masochism. Nothing is gained by simply inveighing against this rhetoric. Its engagement with the springs of human action has to be recognised. The point, however, as [Karl] Marx says, is not just to understand it but to change it. This can only be done through an alternative praxis.

A different construal of redemption, a recognition that it is about enabling those excluded to be included, enabling the acceptance of blame and penance by those who share the blame and must also do penance, calls for a different regime for offenders. In such a regime the faith community is, or ought to be, the sign of what human community, at large, is on the way to becoming – the community of forgiven sinners, the community always in need of reformation. The church, argues John Milbank, has to recognise the tragic necessity of alien punishment – the need, for example, for society to be defended against serial killers. However, it must also seek to be an asylum, a social space where a different, forgiving and restitutionary practice is pursued. The good of order, the need both to express and work through moral outrage, the need for guilt to be shriven, all have to find expression in the creation of such alternative space, as also does the acceptance of difference. In such a praxis, as [R.C.] Moberly argued, the work of atonement is continued by the church. Satisfaction theory has expressed some of the deepest human needs, but it has at the same time distorted them. The redeeming power of the cross needs to find deeper, and more effective, expression, in which the realities of human wickedness and guilt, on the side of both the offender *and* the judiciary, are creatively addressed. Over the past two centuries it has been shown beyond peradventure that the idea that punishment functions to deter offenders is an illusion: it has no statistical basis. The need to show that justice is done, to satisfy the moral *sensus communis*, is real, but this is not equivalent to saying that we are compelled to continue in present policies of imprisonment. The upshot of two centuries of penal experimentation is that nothing but "mainstream processes of socialisation" is of any use in rehabilitating offenders. The demand that the church should offer an alternative social space, therefore, and that it might be this which is the redemptive alternative to retribution, is neither nostalgia for a vanished past nor facile Pickwickian optimism. It is, rather, a sober account of the only realistic and creative way of dealing with human fecklessness and evil which we have discovered.

War and Violence

One may think of three broad approaches to war in the Christian tradition, each with a classical and contemporary face.

Classical pacifism is a theological conviction that because Jesus was the end of sacrifice, the sacrifice of war is contrary to faith in God's peace. It is a deontological position with strong ecclesial dimensions that operates largely outside a consequential frame of reference. Contemporary pacifism sometimes takes this form, but often also (or alternatively) has a much more consequential character, in that, inspired by such as Gandhi and King, it sees non-violence as an effective mechanism for achieving social results, especially when the oppressor has a moral conscience worth appealing to. When there is no such conscience (Nazi Germany; the ultranationalist government in 1940s Japan) consequentialist pacifism appears flawed.

The classical crusade refers to the eight Crusades that followed the seizure of Jerusalem by the Turks in 1072, concluding in 1270. While in the middle ages these endeavors were considered formative for chivalry, today they are invariably cited as nadirs of Christian brutality. A more contemporary account of the crusade might be cited wherever people believe a war is a tool they can use to achieve the cultural enhancement of the body of people with whom they are at war. The language of crusade can be regarded as referring today to any war that is not restricted to members of the armed forces but requires wholesale civilian attention. Once war is seen as a deontological good rather than an (apparently) unavoidable consequential necessity, the crusade becomes the likely descriptor.

Classical just war theory emerged as the way the pacifism of the early centuries of the church became adapted to the circumstances of the Christian empire and its successors. The key figures are Augustine, the twelfth-century Italian canon lawyer Gratian, the twelfth-century Parisian Peter Lombard, Thomas Aquinas, Martin Luther, and the seventeenth-century Dutch jurist Hugo Grotius. The conventional criteria require a legitimate authority, a right intention, and an overwhelming balance of injustice on one side. In such circumstances, such an authority, waging war as a last resort with a strong probability of success and a high expectation that the good to be achieved will outweigh the inevitable damage to be done, may consider the declaration of a war to be just. Contemporary just war theory, as evidenced by the reading from Paul Ramsey below, is often concerned with questions such as whether there can be any just war if nuclear weapons obliterate the principle of noncombatant immunity.

The excerpts in this section offer accounts of these three main themes. Not all universal accounts are just war arguments; not all liberation accounts invite guerrilla responses (by any means!); not all ecclesial accounts are pacifist. Nonetheless these texts are illustrative of the breadth of literature in these traditions.

Universal

Paul Ramsey, *Justice in War*

Paul Ramsey (1913–1988) was a Methodist who taught for many years at Princeton University. His ethic centers on what it means to love the neighbor; this love is defined by what it means for God to love humanity. The Old and New Testaments show God's love to mean fidelity to the flourishing of human beings, who are treasured for their own sake.

In relation to war, loving regard for innocent victims of violent force used in unjust attack yields a recovery of the notion of a "just" war. As Ramsey expresses it below, "What do you think Jesus would have made the Samaritan do if he had come upon the scene while the robbers were still at their fell work?" A just war is inherently limited because it would not be just to attack enemy noncombatants. As Ramsey says in this excerpt, "The same considerations which justify killing the bearer of hostile force by the same stroke prohibit non-combatants from ever being directly attacked with deliberate intent."

In this excerpt Ramsey looks not at just causes for going to war (*ius ad bellum*) but just conduct of a war once started (*ius in bello*). The context of this is the relatively recent invention of nuclear weapons and the considerable anxiety concerning the inception and conduct of the war in Vietnam (*The Just War* was published in 1968). Ramsey here shows how "the justice of sometimes resorting to armed conflict originated in the interior of the ethics of Christian love." He resists treating war as a special case, either especially wrong or an exceptional circumstance where things otherwise inexcusable are justified: "the *laws* of war are only an extension, where war is the only available means, of the rules governing any use of political power." On these grounds there can be no just nuclear war, because of the high noncombatant casualties.

Paul Ramsey. *The Just War: Force and Political Responsibility*. Lanham: Rowman and Littlefield, 1986, 2002. From Part Two: The Morality of War; Chapter 6, "Justice in War," pages 142–6. Reprinted by permission of Rowman & Littlefield Publishers, Inc.

I want to deal with the *origin* and the *meaning* of another criterion for the morality of war's conduct. It is [an] intrinsic [question], having to do with the justice or injustice of an *act* of war, considered apart from its consequences. In the course of tracing its origin, the systematic meaning of "just conduct" in war will be exhibited. This is the distinction between *legitimate* and *illegitimate* military actions. This distinction cuts across all distinctions among weapons systems and applies to them all, even though it is nuclear weapons that have decisively raised the question whether there are just and unjust acts of war by raising the question whether these

particular weapons can possibly be used in a just manner. To learn the meaning of "justice in war" (and its origin out of love-informed-reason) will be to learn what it means to say, in connection with military policy, that the end does not justify the means and that it can never be right to do wrong for the sake of some real or supposed good.

The western theory of the just war originated, not primarily from considerations of abstract or "natural" justice, but from the interior of the ethics of Christian love, or what John XXIII termed "social charity." It was a work of charity for the Good Samaritan to give help to the man who fell among thieves. But one step more, it may have been a work of charity for the inn-keeper to hold himself ready to receive beaten and wounded men, and for him to have conducted his business so that he was solvent enough to extend credit to the Good Samaritan. By another step it would have been a work of charity, and not of justice alone, to maintain and serve in a police patrol on the Jericho road to prevent such things from happening. By yet another step, it might well be a work of charity to resist, by force of arms, any external aggression against the social order that maintains the police patrol along the road to Jericho. This means that, where the enforcement of an ordered community is not effectively present, it may be a work of justice and a work of social charity to resort to other available and effective means of resisting injustice: what do you think Jesus would have made the Samaritan do if he had come upon the scene while the robbers were still at their fell work?

Now, I am aware that this is no proper way to interpret a parable of Jesus. Yet, these several ways of retelling the parable of the Good Samaritan quickly exhibit something that is generally true about the teachings of Jesus – namely, that by deed and word he showed the individual the meaning of being perfectly ready to have the will of God reign and God's mercy shed abroad by his life and actions. These versions quickly exhibit how a social ethic emerged from Christian conscience formed by this revelation, and what the early Christians carried with them when they went out into the world to borrow, and subsequently to elevate and refine, Stoic concepts of natural justice.

While Jesus taught that a disciple in his own case should turn the other cheek, he did not enjoin that his disciples should lift up the face of another oppressed man for *him* to be struck again on *his* other cheek. It is no part of the work of charity to allow this to continue to happen. Instead, it is the work of love and mercy to deliver as many as possible of God's children from tyranny, and to protect from oppression, if one can, as many of those for whom Christ died as it may be possible to save. When choice *must* be made between the perpetrator of injustice and the many victims of it, the latter may and should be preferred – even if effectively to do so would require the use of armed force against some evil power. This is what I mean by saying that the justice of sometimes resorting to armed conflict originated in the interior of the ethics of Christian love.

Thus Christian conscience shaped itself for effective action. It allowed even the enemy to be killed only because military personnel and targets stood objectively there at the point where intersect the needs and claims of many more of our fellow men. For their sakes the bearer of hostile force may and should be repressed. Thus, participation in war (and before that, the use of any form of force or resistance) was justified as, in this world to date, an unavoidable necessity if we are not to omit to serve the needs of men in the only concrete way possible, and maintain a just endurable order in they may live.

There was another side to this coin. The justification of participation in conflict at the same time severely limited war's conduct. What justified also limited! Since it was for the sake of the innocent and helpless of earth that the Christian first thought himself obliged to make war against an enemy whose objective deeds had to be stopped, since only for their sakes does a Christian justify himself in resisting by any means even an enemy-neighbor, he could never proceed to kill equally innocent people as a means of getting at the enemy's forces. Thus was twin-born the justification of war and the limitation which surrounded non-combatants with moral immunity from direct attack. Thus was twin-born the distinction between combatant and non-combatant in all Christian reflection about the morality of warfare. This is the distinction between *legitimate* and *illegitimate* military objectives. The same considerations which justify killing the bearer of hostile force by the same stroke prohibit non-combatants from ever being directly attacked with deliberate intent.

This understanding of the moral economy in the just use of political violence contains, then, two elements: (1) a specific justification for sometimes killing another human being; and (2) severe and specific restrictions upon anyone who is under the hard necessity of doing so. Both are exhibited in the use of force proper to the domestic police power. It is never just for a policeman to forget the distinction between the bearer of hostile force who must be stopped and the "innocent" bystanders (no matter how mixed-up they are). He may hit some innocent party accidentally; but it would never be right for him to "enlarge the target" and deliberately and directly kill any number in the crowd on Times Square *as a means* of preventing some criminal from injurious action. Nor do we allow the police the right to get a criminal's children into their power as hostages and threaten to kill them in order to "deter" him. Yet the source of the justification of such limited use of force is evidently to be found in "social charity." This is clear from the fact that a man, who in one situation could legitimately be killed if that were the only way to save other lives, would himself in another situation be saved at grave risk to the lives of the very same policemen – i.e. if that man alone is in need of rescue because he has gone off his rocker and is threatening to jump from the ledge of a building twenty stories up.

This is the moral economy which regulates the use of force *within* political communities, where it is both *morally* and *legally* binding. This same moral economy is *morally* if *not* legally binding upon the use of force between nations. It will become *both* legally and morally binding if ever there is world law and order abolishing the nation-state system. War may *in fact* be more than an extension of politics in another form, but the *laws* of war are only an extension, where war is the only available means, of the rules governing any use of political power. We are not apt ever to "abolish war" if we keep on denying that there is a morality *of* war, which is only a concise summary of right and charitable reason in the simultaneous *justification* and the *limitation* of the use of power necessary to the political life of mankind.

To summarize the theory of just or civilized conduct in war as this was developed within Christendom: love for neighbors threatened by violence, by aggression, or tyranny, provided the grounds for admitting the legitimacy of the use of military force. Love for neighbors at the same time required that such force should be limited. The Christian is commanded to do anything a realistic love commands (and so sometimes he must fight). But this also prohibits him from doing anything for which such love can find no justification (and so he can never approve of unlimited attack upon any human life not closely cooperating in or directly engaged in the force that ought to be repelled).

This means that nuclear war against the civil centers of an enemy population, the A-Bomb on Hiroshima, or obliteration bombing perpetrated by both sides in World War II were all alike immoral acts of war; and that Christians can support such actions only by dismissing the entire western tradition of civilized warfare that was originally born in the interior of that supreme compassion which always seeks if possible to wound none whom by His wounds Christ died to save. This theory of just and severely limited conflict has guided action and served as the regulative norm for military conduct for nineteen centuries. If a man cannot irresponsibly forsake those who need to be saved from an oppressor, neither can he directly and indiscriminately attack innocent people in order to restrain that same oppressor. If to protect his own children he should resist an aggressor, that gives him no leave directly to intend and directly to do the death of the aggressor's children as a means of dissuading him from his evil deeds. ...

I can only briefly indicate that this distinction between combatant and non-combatant never supposed that the latter were to be roped off like ladies at a medieval tournament. The fact of twilight, as Dr. Johnson said, does not mean you cannot tell day from night. So with noncombatant status, and the difference between discriminant and indiscriminant acts of war. Moreover, it was never supposed that non-combatants were immune from all damage but only from direct, intended attack. The range of indirect, unintended, collateral damage might be quite large. Moreover, closeness of civilian cooperation, in contrast to some degree of remoteness from the force used, was sufficient to bring the civilian under the category of "combatant." But these qualifications were never the same as "enlarging the target" to include the whole of civil society as a legitimate military objective, directly damaging whole peoples in order to get at their leaders and fighters. Translated into modern terminology, this means that just or limited warfare must be *forces*-counter-*forces* warfare, and that *people*-counter-*people* warfare is wholly unjust.

At stake in preserving this distinction is not only whether warfare can be kept barely civilized, but whether civilization can be kept from barbarism. Can civilization survive in the sense that we can continue in political and military affairs to *act civilized,* or must we accept total war on grounds that clearly indicate that we have already become *totalitarian* – by reducing everyone without discrimination and everyone to the whole extent of his being to a mere means of achieving political and military goals? Even if an enemy government says that is all its people are, a Christian or any truly just man cannot agree to this.

Subversive

Camilo Torres, *Love and Revolution*

Father Camilo Torres Restrepo (1929–1966) was a Roman Catholic priest from Colombia. He was also a member of the National Liberation Army guerrillas. He taught sociology at the National University of Colombia from 1960, but his involvement in student and political movements led to his persecution, whereupon he joined the guerrilla movement in hiding. He was killed on the occasion of his first combat action, when the National Liberation Army ambushed a Colombian military patrol. He is known for the statement, "If Jesus were alive today, He would be a guerrillero."

This excerpt is an early work in liberation theology. Torres' commitment to violent action is rooted in his support for the poor. The role of his sociological training is shown by his observation, "A group acting against its own interests would be a sociological absurdity." His general argument is consequential: hence, "If it is necessary in order for men to love each other, the Christian must be revolutionary." Similarly, while it is traditional for priests to withdraw from direct action, in these circumstances Torres believes this is a rule that may, indeed must, be broken. Here the reasoning resembles situation ethics. Perhaps the most telling sentence is, "For love to be genuine, it must seek to be effective." This takes us to the heart of consequential ethics.

It should be noted that most liberation theologians have been and remain committed to a traditional account of just war, and some are pacifist. Torres' views are therefore not representative of South American liberation theology as a whole, but represent a challenge to explore the depth and extent of liberation and the sacrifices it requires.

Camilo Torres. *Revolutionary Priest: The Complete Writings and Messages of Camilo Torres*. Ed. John Gerassi. New York: Random House, 1971. From Chapter 25, "Crossroads of the Church in Latin America" (pp. 329–32) and Chapter 29, "Message to Christians" (pp. 367–9).

Crossroads of the Church in Latin America

A real Christian can be identified by the love he demonstrates. When the people speak of Catholics, they refer to external observances. The church seems to be made up of a majority of persons who fulfill their external obligations and do not understand the Christian faith; they practice it only externally. Can either of these be said to be Christian? If they have bad faith, certainly not. Those who love, even if they are fetishists or believe they are atheists, are Christians. These people belong in spirit to the church, and if they are baptized they belong to the church in body as well.

The situation seems totally abnormal. Those who love do not have faith, and those who have faith – at least as faith is externally defined – do not love. "… he who loves his neighbor has fulfilled the Law," says Saint Paul (Romans 13:8). "Love and you may do what you please," says Saint Augustine. The surest proof of predestination is love for our fellow man.

Saint John tells us: "If anyone says, 'I love God,' and hates his brother, he is a liar. For how can he who does not love his brother, whom he sees, love God, whom he does not see?" (I John 4:20).

However, this love for fellow man must be effective. We will not be judged by our good intentions alone but principally by our actions serving Christ, Who is represented in each of our fellow men: "For I was hungry, and you did not give me to eat; I was thirsty and you gave me no drink" (Matthew 25:42).

In Latin America, in the conditions that exist here today, we see that it is not possible to feed, provide clothing for, or house the majority of our people. Those who are in power constitute that economic minority which dominates through its control over those who hold political power, cultural power, military power, and – unfortunately – even ecclesiastical power in countries in which the church has temporal goods. This minority will not make decisions against its own interests. Therefore, governmental decisions are not made in favor of the majorities. To give them food, drink, and clothing requires basic decisions that can only come from the government. We already have the technical solutions – or we will have them. But who decides whether to apply them? The minority, against its own interests? A group acting against its own interests would be a sociological absurdity.

Then the seizure of power by the majorities must be preached. The majority must take over the government to change the structures through economic, social, and political reforms that favor the majority. This is called revolution. If it is necessary in order for men to love each other, the Christian must be revolutionary. How difficult it is for those who believe themselves Catholics to understand this! But how easy it is to understand it if we reflect on what we have just said about the church!

Christians, Catholics, seem to be stoical spectators at the collapse of a world that seems not to be their concern. They do not commit themselves to the struggle. In reading the phrase "My kingdom is not of this world" (John 18:36), they take "world" to mean "present life," not "sinful life," which is its real meaning. They forget Christ's prayer to His Father: "I do not pray that thou take them out of the world, but that thou keep them from evil" (John 17:15).

Many times, men leave the world but are not kept from evil. If the members of the community love each other, the priest offers the Eucharist more genuinely. This is not an individual but rather a collective offering. An offering should be made to God only if those who offer it love one another.

Hence, if the laity is not committed to the fight for well-being of their brothers, the priesthood tends to become ritualistic, individualistic, and superficial. The priest has the obligation to take the place of the laity in its temporal commitment if the love of fellow man so demands. When this love seems no longer to be considered exclusive patrimony of the church, it is necessary to testify that the communal spirit of the church is love. Unfortunately, the public does not recognize the testimony of the laity as the testimony of the church. The priest, in this case, should give the testimony of the church until the public is educated to understand that the testimony of every baptized person is a testimony of the church.

To see a priest involved in political struggles, abandoning the external practices of his priesthood, is something repugnant to our traditional mentality. However, let us consider for a while that his priestly testimony and love for fellow man may impel him to this commitment to be true to his own conscience and, hence, to be true to God.

When Christians live fundamentally motivated by love and teach others to love, when faith is manifest in life and especially in divine life, in the life of Jesus and the church, then the external rites will be the true expressions of love within the Christian community; then we will be able to say that the church is strong, not in economic or political power but in love. If a priest's temporal commitment in political struggles contributes to this end, his sacrifice would appear to be justified.

Message to Christians

The convulsions caused by the political, religious, and social events of recent times may have sown a great deal of confusion among Colombian Christians. At this decisive moment in our history, we Christians must take a firm stand on the essential bases of our religion.

In Catholicism the main thing is love for one's fellow man: "… he who loves his fellow man has fulfilled the Law" (Romans 13:8). For this love to be genuine, it must seek to be effective. If beneficence, alms, the few tuition-free schools, the few housing projects – in general, what is known as "charity" – do not succeed in feeding the hungry majority, clothing the naked, or teaching the unschooled masses, we must seek effective means to achieve the wellbeing of these majorities. These means will not be sought by the privileged minorities who hold power, because such effective means generally force the minorities to sacrifice their privileges. For example, employment could be increased by investing the capital now leaving Colombia in dollars in the creation of new job opportunities here in the country. But, due to the virtually daily devaluation of the Colombian peso, those with money and power are never going to prohibit currency exportation, because it frees them from devaluation.

Thus, power must be taken from the privileged minorities and given to the poor majorities. If this is done rapidly, it constitutes the essential characteristic of a revolution. The revolution can be a peaceful one if the minorities refrain from violent resistance. Revolution is, therefore, the way to obtain a government that will feed the hungry, clothe the naked, and teach the unschooled. Revolution will produce a government that carries out works of charity, of love for one's fellows – not for only a few but for the majority of our fellow men. This is why the revolution is not only permissible but obligatory for those Christians who see it as the only effective and far-reaching way to make the love of all people a reality. It is true that "there exists no authority except from God" (Romans 13:1). But St. Thomas teaches that it is the people who concretely have the right to authority.

When the existing authority is against the people, it is not legitimate, and we call it a tyranny. We Christians can and must fight against tyranny. The present government is tyrannical because it receives the support of only twenty percent of the voters and because its decisions emanate from the privileged minorities.

The temporal defects of the church must not shock us. The church is human. The important thing is to believe that it is also divine and that if we Christians fulfill our obligation to love our fellow man, we are thereby strengthening the church.

I have given up the duties and privileges of the clergy, but I have not ceased to be a priest. I believe that I have given myself to the revolution out of love for my fellow man. I have ceased to say Mass to practice love for my fellow man in the temporal, economic, and social spheres. When my fellow man has nothing against me, when he has carried out the revolution, then I will return to offering Mass, God permitting. I think that in this way I follow Christ's injunction: "Therefore, if thou art offering thy gift at the altar, and there rememberest that thy brother has anything against thee, leave thy gift before the altar and go first to be reconciled to thy brother, and then come and offer thy gift" (Matthew 5:23–24). After the revolution we Colombians will be aware that we are establishing a system oriented toward the love of our neighbor. The struggle is long; let us begin now.

Ecclesial

Dorothy Day, *Our Country Passes from Undeclared War to Declared War; We Continue Our Christian Pacifist Stand*

Dorothy Day (1897–1980) was, with Peter Maurin, the founder of the Catholic Worker movement, an association of around 200 houses of hospitality that embody the works of mercy by ministering to and advocating for the poor and dispossessed. They also founded the monthly newspaper *Catholic Worker* in 1933, to articulate the justice and mercy of Jesus and to disseminate Catholic social teaching at a time when some were drawn to communism.

This article was published in the *Catholic Worker* in January 1942 and reflects on the United States' entry into World War II. It picks up many familiar themes of ecclesial ethics. Day speaks of the habits that will abide – "we will quote our Pope, our saints, our priests." She stresses the weapons of the weak – "We will try daily, hourly, to pray for an end to the war." She refers to almsgiving, penance, and fasting. She points out in characteristic Catholic Worker style that "Our works of mercy may take us into the midst of war."

Christian pacifism comes in several guises. The kind that advocates pacifism as a better strategy for achieving success in many ways belongs among universal arguments. Some ecclesial arguments such as those of John Howard Yoder and Stanley Hauerwas rest squarely on the conviction that cross and resurrection represent the true dynamic of history and are truly more powerful than war. While Day's closing remarks hint at this second view, the thrust of this article lies in a third view, namely that "Our manifesto is the Sermon on the Mount" – in other words, pacifism is primarily about following Jesus' teaching and example, rather than being rooted specifically in Jesus' death and resurrection.

Dear fellow workers in Christ:

Lord God, merciful God, our Father, shall we keep silent, or shall we speak? And if we speak, what shall we say?

I am sitting here in the church on Mott Street writing this in your presence. Out on the streets it is quiet, but you are there too, in the Chinese, in the Italians, these neighbors we love. We love them because they are our brothers, as Christ is our Brother and God our Father.

But we have forgotten so much. We have all forgotten. And how can we know unless you tell us. "For whoever calls upon the name of the Lord shall be saved." How then are they to call upon Him in whom they have not believed? But how are they to believe Him whom they have not heard? And how are they to hear, if no one preaches? And how are men to preach unless they be sent? As it is written, "How beautiful are the feet of those who preach the gospel of peace." (Romans X)

Seventy-five thousand Catholic Workers go out every month. What shall we print? We can print still what the Holy Father is saying, when he speaks of total war, of mitigating the horrors of war, when he speaks of cities of refuge, of feeding Europe …

We will print the words of Christ who is with us always, even to the end of the world. "Love your enemies, do good to those who hate you, and pray for those who persecute and calumniate you, so that you may be children of your Father in heaven, who makes His sun to rise on the good and the evil, and sends rain on the just and unjust."

We are at war, a declared war, with Japan, Germany and Italy. But still we can repeat Christ's words, each day, holding them close in our hearts, each month printing them in the paper. In times past, Europe has been a battlefield. But let us remember St. Francis, who spoke of peace and we will remind our readers of him, too, so they will not forget.

In The Catholic Worker we will quote our Pope, our saints, our priests. We will go on printing the articles which remind us today that we are all "called to be saints," that we are other Christs, reminding us of the priesthood of the laity.

We are still pacifists. Our manifesto is the Sermon on the Mount, which means that we will try to be peacemakers. Speaking for many of our conscientious objectors, we will not participate in armed warfare or in making munitions, or by buying government bonds to prosecute the war, or in urging others to these efforts.

But neither will we be carping in our criticism. We love our country and we love our President. We have been the only country in the world where men of all nations have taken refuge from oppression. We recognize that while in the order of intention we have tried to stand for peace, for love of our brother, in the order of execution we have failed as Americans in living up to our principles.

We will try daily, hourly, to pray for an end to the war, such an end, to quote Father Orchard, "as would manifest to all the world, that it was brought about by divine action, rather than by military might or diplomatic negotiation, which men and nations would then only attribute to their power or sagacity."

"Despite all calls to prayer," Father Orchard concludes, "there is at present all too little indication anywhere that the tragedy of humanity and the desperate need of the world have moved the faithful, still less stirred the thoughtless masses, to turn to prayer as the only hope for mankind this dreadful hour.

"We shall never pray until we feel more deeply, and we shall never feel deeply enough until we envisage what is actually happening in the world, and understand what is possible in the will of God; and that means until sufficient numbers realize that we have brought things to a pass which is beyond human power to help or save.

"Those who do feel and see, however inadequately, should not hesitate to begin to pray, or fail to persevere, however dark the prospects remain. Let them urge others to do likewise; and then, first small groups, and then the Church as a whole, and at last the world, may turn and cry for forgiveness, mercy and deliverance for all.

"Then we may be sure God will answer, and effectually; for the Lord's hand is not shortened that it cannot save, nor His ear heavy that it cannot hear." Let us add, that unless we combine this prayer with almsgiving, in giving to the least of God's children, and fasting in order that we may help feed the hungry, and penance in recognition of our share in the guilt, our prayer may become empty words.

Our works of mercy may take us into the midst of war. As editor of The Catholic Worker, I would urge our friends and associates to care for the sick and the wounded, to the growing of food for the hungry, to the continuance of all our works of mercy in our houses and on our farms. We understand, of course, that there is and that there will be great differences of opinion even among our own groups as to how much collaboration we can have with the government in times like these. There are differences more profound and there will be many continuing to work with us from necessity, or from choice, who do not agree with us as to our position on war, conscientious objection, etc. But we beg that there will be mutual charity and forbearance among us all.

This letter, sent to all our Houses of Hospitality and to all our farms, and being printed in the January issue of the paper, is to state our position in this most difficult time.

Because of our refusal to assist in the prosecution of war and our insistence that our collaboration be one for peace, we may find ourselves in difficulties. But we trust in the generosity and understanding of our government and our friends, to permit us to continue, to use our paper to "preach Christ crucified."

May the Blessed Mary, Mother of love, of faith, of knowledge and of hope, pray for us.

Chapter Nine

Good Life

While the previous chapter addressed questions that largely concerned the state, this chapter is more concerned with civil society – the realm of relations carried out by individuals and groups under the authority of a state but excluding familial or political relations. A somewhat different understanding would see civil society as the arena of true politics, as distinct from simply governmental processes. A very significant change in the modern era – the period since the Reformation, the emergence of the nation-state and the Enlightenment – is the increasing tendency to give an account of social relations without a teleological dimension – in other words, without an assumption that all was ordered by, for, and to God.

A theological reaction to modernity has come through the recovery by many theologians in the late twentieth century of a social doctrine of the Trinity which sees the history of salvation as the story of the inclusion of creation into the mutual indwelling of the Trinitarian persons. This prevents any totalitarianism based on monotheism and any paternalism based on the monarchy of the Father. Domination is replaced by communion, conquest by participation. Such perspectives highlight the interaction between an understanding of God and an understanding of human social relations.

The issues raised in this chapter, concerning economics, wealth, poverty, work, business, management, and the media, by no means exhaust the array of possible topics, but do provide a broad sample of the range of issues and point to some characteristic ethical engagements.

Economics, Wealth, and Poverty

For most of the world's human history its population was either agrarian or hunter-gatherer. Markets in the modern sense arose in the early medieval period but still presupposed an agrarian economy until the twentieth century. Urban and industrial wealth and urban poverty are thus recent phenomena. The rural and urban poverty of parts of the developing world is closely related to the difficulty of adapting to a money economy and the way in which the technological harnessing of natural resources has concentrated wealth in fewer hands.

Since the emergence of the modern urbanized industrial economy, of which Adam Smith was perhaps the most prominent prophet, three major forces have been at work. One is the abiding culture of kinship networks and agrarian or quasi-agrarian communities, accompanied by much debate over whether these networks were "natural" (and thus abiding, or at least overridden at human peril). Another is the power of the market, which has never been given untrammeled rein, since its tendencies would highlight human needs and desires and generate a level of casualties seldom thought morally acceptable. In between has been a greater or lesser introduction of the welfare state, which handles the fallout from the kinship network – brought about largely by industrial urbanization – by bureaucratic means. The readings in this section highlight the ways in which these questions look very different depending on one's social location.

Universal

Adam Smith, *The Invisible Hand*

Adam Smith (1723–1790) was a professor at Glasgow University and a key figure in the Scottish Enlightenment, and is regarded as the founder of modern economics. His *A Theory of Moral Sentiments* (1759) referred to the "invisible hand" by which society benefits when people behave in their own interests. The observation of others makes people more aware of the morality of their own actions, and they find it in their own interest to develop sympathy – that is, an understanding that earns the respect of the impartial observer.

In *An Inquiry into the Nature and Causes of the Wealth of Nations* (1776) Smith advocates for three principles: the division of labor, the pursuit of self-interest, and the freedom of trade. While his religious views were either deist or agnostic, Smith describes the invisible hand in quasi-religious terms: through the vehicle of competition, human selfishness and greed were transformed into social good by combining low prices with an incentive to buy.

This excerpt shows the power of Smith's hugely influential reasoning. Human beings prevail if they engage not just others' benevolence, but their self-interest. We never talk to others "of our own necessities but of their advantages." Smith's reasoning becomes foundational for modern economic thought the way Immanuel Kant's reasoning becomes foundational for ethical thought: one can disagree with it, but one cannot ignore it.

Adam Smith. *An Inquiry into the Nature and Causes of the Wealth of Nations.* Vol. 1. Ed. R. H. Campbell and A. S. Skinner. Oxford: Clarendon Press, 1976, 1979. From Book I, Chapter 2, "Of the Principle which gives occasion to the Division of Labour" (pp. 25–8); Book IV, Chapter 2, "Of Restraints upon the Importation from foreign Countries of such Goods as can be produced at Home" (pp. 454–7). Available online at www.econlib.org/library/Smith/smWN.html.

Of the Principle which gives occasion to the Division of Labour

This division of labour, from which so many advantages are derived, is not originally the effect of any human wisdom, which foresees and intends that general opulence to which it gives occasion. It is the necessary, though very slow and gradual consequence of a certain propensity in human nature which has in view no such extensive utility; the propensity to truck, barter, and exchange one thing for another.

Whether this propensity be one of those original principles in human nature, of which no further account can be given; or whether, as seems more probable, it be the necessary consequence of the faculties of reason and speech, it belongs not to our present subject to enquire. It is common to all men, and to be found in no other race of animals, which seem to know neither this nor any other species of contracts. ... In almost every other race of animals each individual, when it is grown up to maturity, is entirely independent, and in its natural state has occasion for the assistance of no other living creature. But man has almost constant occasion for the help of his brethren, and it is in vain for him to expect it from their benevolence only. He will be more likely to prevail if he can interest their self-love in his favour, and shew them that it is for their own advantage to do for him what he requires of them. Whoever offers to another a bargain of any kind, proposes to do this. Give me that which I want, and you shall have this which you want, is the meaning of every such offer; and it is in this manner that we obtain from one another the far greater part of those good offices which we stand in need of. It is not from the benevolence of the butcher, the brewer, or the baker, that we expect our dinner, but from their regard to their own interest. We address ourselves, not to their humanity but to their self-love, and never talk to them of our own necessities but of their advantages. Nobody but a beggar chuses to depend chiefly upon the benevolence of his fellow-citizens. Even a beggar does not depend upon it entirely. The charity of well-disposed people, indeed, supplies him with the whole fund of his subsistence. But though this principle ultimately provides him with all the necessaries of life which he has occasion for, it neither does nor can provide him with them as he has occasion for them. The greater part of his occasional wants are supplied in the same manner as those of other people, by treaty, by barter, and by purchase. With the money which one man gives him he purchases food. The old cloaths which another bestows upon him he exchanges for other old cloaths which suit him better, or for lodging, or for food, or for money, with which he can buy either food, cloaths, or lodging, as he has occasion.

As it is by treaty, by barter, and by purchase, that we obtain from one another the greater part of those mutual good offices which we stand in need of, so it is this same trucking disposition which originally gives occasion to the division of labour. In a tribe of hunters or shepherds a particular person makes bows and arrows, for example, with more readiness and dexterity than any other. He frequently exchanges them for cattle or for venison with his companions; and he finds at last that he can in this manner get more cattle and venison, than if he himself went to the field to catch them. From a regard to his own interest, therefore, the making of bows and arrows grows to be his chief business, and he becomes a sort of armourer. Another excels in making the frames and covers of their little huts or moveable houses. He is accustomed to be of use in this way to his neighbours, who reward him in the same manner with cattle and with venison, till at last he finds it his interest to dedicate himself entirely to this employment, and to become a sort of house-carpenter. In the same manner a third becomes a smith or a brazier, a fourth a tanner or dresser of hides or skins, the principal part of the clothing of savages. And thus the certainty of being able to exchange all that surplus part of the produce of his own labour, which is over and above his own consumption, for such parts of the produce of other men's labour as he may have occasion for, encourages every man to apply himself to a particular occupation, and to cultivate and bring to perfection whatever talent or genius he may possess for that particular species of business . ...

Of Restraints upon the Importation from foreign Countries of such Goods as can be produced at Home

Every individual is continually exerting himself to find out the most advantageous employment for whatever capital he can command. It is his own advantage, indeed, and not that of the society, which he has in view. But the study of his own advantage naturally, or rather necessarily leads him to prefer that employment which is most advantageous to the society.

First, every individual endeavours to employ his capital as near home as he can, and consequently as much as he can in the support of domestick industry; provided always that he can thereby obtain the ordinary, or not a great deal less than the ordinary profits of stock. ...

Secondly, every individual who employs his capital in the support of domestick industry, necessarily endeavours so to direct that industry, that its produce may be of the greatest possible value.

The produce of industry is what it adds to the subject or materials upon which it is employed. In proportion as the value of this produce is great or small, so will likewise be the profits of the employer. But it is only for the sake of profit that any man employs a capital in the support of industry; and he will always, therefore, endeavour to employ it in the support of that industry of which the produce is likely to be of the greatest value, or to exchange for the greatest quantity either of money or of other goods.

But the annual revenue of every society is always precisely equal to the exchangeable value of the whole annual produce of its industry, or rather is precisely the same thing with that exchangeable value. As every individual, therefore, endeavours as much as he can both to employ his capital in the support of domestick industry, and so to direct that industry that its produce may be of the greatest value; every individual necessarily labours to render the annual revenue of the society as great as he can. He generally, indeed, neither intends to promote the publick interest, nor knows how much he is promoting it. By preferring the support of domestick to that of foreign industry, he intends only his own security; and by directing that industry in such a manner as its produce may be of the greatest value, he intends only his own gain, and he is in this, as in many other cases, led by an invisible hand to promote an end which was no part of his intention. Nor is it always the worse for the society that it was no part of it. By pursuing his own interest he frequently promotes that of the society more effectually than when he really intends to promote it. I have never known much good done by those who affected to trade for the publick good. It is an affectation, indeed, not very common among merchants, and very few words need be employed in dissuading them from it.

What is the species of domestick industry which his capital can employ, and of which the produce is likely to be of the greatest value, every individual, it is evident, can, in his local situation, judge much better than any statesman or lawgiver can do for him. The statesman, who should attempt to direct private people in what manner they ought to employ their capitals, would not only load himself with a most unnecessary attention, but assume an authority which could safely be trusted, not only to no single person, but to no council or senate whatever, and which would nowhere be so dangerous as in the hands of a man who had folly and presumption enough to fancy himself fit to exercise it.

To give the monopoly of the home-market to the produce of domestick industry, in any particular art or manufacture, is in some measure to direct private people in what manner they ought to employ their capitals, and must, in almost all cases, be either a useless or a hurtful regulation. If the produce of domestick can be brought there as cheap as that of foreign industry, the regulation is evidently useless. If it cannot, it must generally be hurtful. It is the maxim of every prudent master of a family, never to attempt to make at home what it will cost him more to make than to buy. The taylor does not attempt to make his own shoes, but buys them of the shoemaker. The shoemaker does not attempt to make his own cloaths, but employs a taylor. The farmer attempts to make neither the one nor the other, but employs those different artificers. All of them find it for their interest to employ their whole industry in a way in which they have some advantage over their neighbours, and to purchase with a part of its produce, or what is the same thing, with the price of a part of it, whatever else they have occasion for.

What is prudence in the conduct of every private family can scarce be folly in that of a great kingdom. If a foreign country can supply us with a commodity cheaper than we ourselves can make it, better buy it of them with some part of the produce of our own industry, employed in a way in which we have some advantage. The general industry of the country, being always in proportion to the capital which employs it, will not thereby be diminished, no more than that of the above-mentioned artificers; but only left to find out the way in which it can be employed with the greatest advantage. It is certainly not employed to the greatest advantage, when it is thus directed towards an object which it can buy cheaper than it can make. The value of its annual produce is certainly more or less diminished, when it is thus turned away from producing commodities evidently of more value than the commodity which it is directed to produce. According to the supposition, that commodity could be purchased from foreign countries cheaper than it can be made at home. It could, therefore, have been purchased with a part only of the commodities, or, what is the same thing, with a part only of the price of the commodities, which the industry employed by an equal capital, would have produced at home, had it been left to follow its natural course. The industry of the country, therefore, is thus turned away from a more, to a less advantageous employment, and the exchangeable value of its annual produce, instead of being increased, according to the intention of the lawgiver, must necessarily be diminished by every such regulation.

Subversive

Medellín Conference

The Second General Conference of Latin American Bishops (CELAM) took place in Medellín, Colombia, in 1968. It came shortly after the conclusion of the Second Vatican Council (1962–1965), which was widely seen as making the Roman Catholic Church more open to the world. The conference included many calls from radicals to adopt non-violent protest and resistance and enter into partnership with nonchurch groups to bring about social change; some argued for violent means to be endorsed in circumstances of tyranny. It was time to transform a gospel of obedience and fatalism into one of liberation, and a politics of collaboration with entrenched interests into one of solidarity with the poor. The final document, quoted here, was highly divisive: for radical clergy, monks, and nuns it was a manifesto for change and a call to action; for conservatives, it sparked a backlash that led to the control of CELAM passing back into conservative hands in 1972. The document is the foundation stone of Latin American liberation theology.

Here the bishops distinguish between different kinds of poverty: the involuntary poverty of lacking basic goods, and the commitment to poverty of following Christ. A poor church witnesses to the value of the poor in God's eyes and to solidarity with those who suffer. Human advancement is the goal of these endeavors. Conversion is required to overcome the culture of centuries: "A sincere conversion has to change the individualistic mentality into another one of social awareness and concern for the common good."

Medellín document: "'The Church in the Present-Day Transformation of Latin America in the Light of the Council' (August 26–September 6, 1968)." In *Liberation Theology: A Documentary History*. Ed. Alfred T. Hennelly, SJ. Maryknoll: Orbis Books, 1990. From "Document on the Poverty of the Church," pages 114–18. Available online at www.providence.edu/las/documents.htm#Medell%C3%ADn%20Conference.

Document on the Poverty of the Church

Latin American Scene

1. The Latin American bishops cannot remain indifferent in the face of the tremendous social injustices existent in Latin America, which keep the majority of our peoples in dismal poverty, which in many cases becomes inhuman wretchedness.

2. A deafening cry pours from the throats of millions of men and women asking their pastors for a liberation that reaches them from nowhere else. "Now you are listening to us in silence, but we hear the shout which arises from your suffering," the pope told the campesinos in Colombia.

And complaints that the hierarchy, the clergy, the religious, are rich and allied with the rich also come to us. On this point we must make it clear that appearance is often confused with reality. Many causes have contributed to create this impression of a rich hierarchical church. The great buildings, the rectories and religious houses that are better than those of the neighbors, the often luxurious vehicles, the attire, inherited from other eras, have been some of those causes.

The system of taxes and tuition to support clergy and maintain educational endeavors has become discredited and has led to the formation of erroneous opinions about the amount of money received. To this has been added the exaggerated secrecy in which the finances of high schools, parishes, and dioceses have been shrouded, favoring a mysterious atmosphere which magnifies shadows to gigantic proportions and helps to create fictions. Besides, isolated cases of reprehensible opulence have been generalized.

All this has helped substantiate the argument that the Latin American church is rich.

3. The reality of the very great number of parishes and dioceses that are extremely poor, and the exceeding number of bishops, priests, and religious who live in complete deprivation and give themselves with great abnegation to the service of the poor, generally escapes the appreciation of many and does not succeed in dissipating the prevailing distorted image.

Within the context of the poverty and even of the wretchedness in which the great majority of the Latin American people live, we, bishops, priests, and religious, have the necessities of life and a certain security, while the poor lack that which is indispensable and struggle between anguish and uncertainty. And incidents are not lacking in which the poor feel that their bishops, or pastors and religious, do not really identify themselves with them, with their problems and afflictions, that they do not always support those who work with them or plead their cause.

Doctrinal Motivation

4. We must distinguish:

(a) Poverty, as a lack of the goods of this world necessary to live worthily as human beings, is in itself evil. The prophets denounce it as contrary to the will of the Lord and most of the time as the fruit of human injustice and sin.

(b) Spiritual poverty is the theme of the poor of Yahweh. Spiritual poverty is the attitude of opening up to God, the ready disposition of one who hopes for everything from the Lord. Although he values the goods of this world, he does not become attached to them and he recognizes the higher value of the riches of the kingdom.

(c) Poverty as a commitment, through which one assumes voluntarily and lovingly the conditions of the needy of this world in order to bear witness to the evil it represents and to spiritual liberty in the face of material goods, follows the example of Christ who took to Himself all the consequences of our sinful condition and who "being rich became poor" in order to redeem us.

5. In this context a poor church:

• denounces the unjust lack of this world's goods and the sin that begets it;
• preaches and lives in spiritual poverty, as an attitude of spiritual childhood and openness to the Lord;
• is itself bound to material poverty. The poverty of the church is, in effect, a constant factor in the history of salvation.

6. All members of the church are called to live in evangelical poverty, but not all in the same way, as there are diverse vocations to this poverty, that tolerate diverse styles of life and various modes of acting. Among religious themselves, although they all have a special mission to witness within the church, there will be differences according to personal charismas.

7. Against this background, it will be necessary to reemphasize strongly that the example and teaching of Jesus, the anguished condition of millions of the poor in Latin America, the urgent exhortations of the pope and of the council, place before the Latin American church a challenge and a mission that it cannot sidestep and to which it must respond with a speed and boldness adequate to the urgency of the times.

Christ, our savior, not only loved the poor, but rather "being rich he became poor," he lived in poverty. His mission centered on advising the poor of their liberation and he founded his church as the sign of that poverty among men and women.

The church itself has always tried to fulfill that vocation, notwithstanding "very great weaknesses and flaws in the past." The Latin American church, given the continent's conditions of poverty and underdevelopment, experiences the urgency of translating that spirit of poverty into actions, attitudes, and norms that make it a more lucid and authentic sign of its Lord. The poverty of so many brothers and sisters cries out for justice,

solidarity, open witness, commitment, strength, and exertion directed to the fulfillment of the redeeming mission to which it is committed by Christ.

The present situation, then, demands from bishops, priests, religious and laypersons the spirit of poverty which, "breaking the bonds of the egotistical possession of temporal goods, stimulates the Christian to order organically the power and the finances in favor of the common good."

The poverty of the church and of its members in Latin America ought to be a sign and a commitment – a sign of the inestimable value of the poor in the eyes of God, an obligation of solidarity with those who suffer.

Pastoral Orientations

8. Because of the foregoing, we wish the Latin American church to be the evangelizer of the poor and one with them, a witness to the value of the riches of the kingdom, and the humble servant of all our people. Its pastors and the other members of the people of God have to correlate their life and words, their attitudes and actions, to the demands of the gospel and the necessities of the people of Latin America.

Preeminence and Solidarity

9. The Lord's distinct commandment to "evangelize the poor" ought to bring us to a distribution of resources and apostolic personnel that effectively gives preference to the poorest and most needy sectors and to those segregated for any cause whatsoever, animating and accelerating the initiatives and studies that are already being made with that goal in mind.

We, the bishops, wish to come closer to the poor in sincerity and fellowship, making ourselves accessible to them.

10. We ought to sharpen the awareness of our duty of solidarity with the poor, to which charity leads us. This solidarity means that we make ours their problems and their struggles, that we know how to speak with them. This has to be concretized in criticism of injustice and oppression, in the struggle against the intolerable situation that a poor person often has to tolerate, in the willingness to dialogue with the groups responsible for that situation in order to make them understand their obligations.

11. We express our desire to be very close always to those who work in the self-denying apostolate with the poor in order that they will always feel our encouragement and know that we will not listen to parties interested in distorting their work.

Human advancement has to be the goal of our action on behalf of the poor and it must be carried out in such a manner that we respect their personal dignity and teach them to help themselves. With that end in mind we recognize the necessity of the rational structuring of our pastoral action and the integration of our efforts with those of other entities.

Testimony

12. We wish our houses and style of life to be modest, our clothing simple, our works and institutions functional, without show or ostentation.

We ask priests and faithful to treat us in conformity with our mission as fathers and pastors, for we desire to renounce honorable titles belonging to another era.

13. With the help of all the people of God we hope to overcome the system of fees, replacing it with other forms of financial cooperation not linked to the administration of the sacraments.

The administration of diocesan or parish properties has to be entrusted to competent laypersons and put to better use for the welfare of the whole community.

14. In our pastoral work we will trust above all in the strength of God's word; when we have to employ technical means we will seek those most adequate to the environment in which they will be used and will put them at the disposal of the community.

15. We exhort priests also to give testimony of poverty and detachment from material goods, as so many do, particularly in rural areas and poor neighborhoods. With great diligence we will procure for them a just though modest sustenance and the necessary social security. To this end we will seek to establish a common fund among all the parishes and the diocese itself; also among the dioceses of the same country.

We encourage those who feel themselves called to share the lot of the poor, living with them and even working with their hands, in accord with the decree *Presbyterorum Ordinis* [Decree on the Ministry and Life of Priests].

16. The religious communities by virtue of their special vocation ought to witness to the poverty of Christ. We encourage those who feel themselves called to form among their members small communities, truly incarnated in the poor environment; they will be a continual call to evangelical poverty for all the people of God.

We hope also that religious communities will be able more and more to effect the sharing of their goods with others, especially with the most needy, dividing among them not only superfluities, but also necessities, and disposed to put at the disposal of the human community the buildings and instruments of their work. The distinction between what belongs to the community and what pertains to the work will facilitate this distribution. It will likewise permit the searching for new forms to accomplish those works, in whose administration or ownership other members of the Christian community will participate.

17. These authentic examples of detachment and freedom of spirit will make the other members of the people of God give a similar witness to poverty. A sincere conversion has to change the individualistic mentality into another one of social awareness and concern for the common good. The education of children and youth at all levels, beginning in the home, ought to include this fundamental aspect of the Christian life.

This feeling of love of neighbor is evinced when one studies and works above all with the intention of performing a service for the community; when one organizes power and wealth for the benefit of the community.

Service

18. No earthly ambition impels the church, only its wish to be the humble servant of all.

We need to stress this spirit in Latin America.

We want our Latin American church to be free from temporal ties, from intrigues and from a doubtful reputation; to be "free in spirit as regards the chains of wealth," so that its mission of service will be stronger and clearer. We want it to be present in life and in secular works, reflecting the light of Christ, present in the construction of the world.

We want to recognize all the value and legitimate autonomy of temporal works; aiding them we do not wish to take away their substance or divert them from their distinctive ends.

We desire sincerely to respect all persons and listen to them in order to serve them in their problems and afflictions. Thus, the church, carrying on the works of Christ, "who made himself poor for us, being rich in order to enrich us with his poverty," will present before the world a clear and unmistakable sign of the poverty of its Lord.

Ecclesial

Martin Luther King, Jr., *I See The Promised Land*

This is an excerpt from the speech given by Martin Luther King, Jr. (1929–1968) on April 3, 1968, at Mason Temple, the World Headquarters of the Church of God in Christ, to the striking sanitation workers of Memphis, Tennessee, the day before his assassination. Because he was so closely associated with the civil rights movement, he might be thought to represent subversive ethics, but this speech is deeply ecclesial.

The rhetoric crosses over from the teleological to the eschatological: "When people get caught up with that which is right and they are willing to sacrifice for it, there is no stopping point short of victory." His unique skill is to unite those who see America's Constitution as its Bible, and those who see America's Bible as its Constitution. Thus, in the former approach, he says, "All we say to America is, 'Be true to what you said on paper.'" This is the language of universal ethics. When he talks of building a different economic base and withdrawing custom from businesses, this is the language of subversive ethics. But the heart of the sermon comes when he switches to the latter approach and speaks out of his own tradition of the parable of the Good Samaritan. He acknowledges the fear, and switches the question around from "If I help him, what will happen to me?" to "If I don't help him, what will happen to him?" This is a call for the renewal of the church.

Martin Luther King, Jr. "I See the Promised Land."
Source: www.mlkonline.net/promised.html.

I can remember, I can remember when Negroes were just going around as Ralph [Abernathy] has said, so often, scratching where they didn't itch, and laughing when they were not tickled. But that day is all over. We mean business now, and we are determined to gain our rightful place in God's world.

And that's all this whole thing is about. We aren't engaged in any negative protest and in any negative arguments with anybody. We are saying that we are determined to be men. We are determined to be people. We are saying that we are God's children. And that we don't have to live like we are forced to live. …

Secondly, let us keep the issues where they are. The issue is injustice. The issue is the refusal of Memphis to be fair and honest in its dealings with its public servants, who happen to be sanitation workers. Now, we've got to keep attention on that. That's always the problem with a little violence. You know what happened the other day, and the press dealt only with the window-breaking. I read the articles. They very seldom got around to mentioning the fact that one thousand, three hundred sanitation workers were on strike, and that Memphis is not being fair to them, and that Mayor

Loeb is in dire need of a doctor. They didn't get around to that.

Now we're going to march again, and we've got to march again, in order to put the issue where it is supposed to be. And force everybody to see that there are thirteen hundred of God's children here suffering, sometimes going hungry, going through dark and dreary nights wondering how this thing is going to come out. That's the issue. And we've got to say to the nation: we know it's coming out. For when people get caught up with that which is right and they are willing to sacrifice for it, there is no stopping point short of victory.

We aren't going to let any mace stop us. We are masters in our nonviolent movement in disarming police forces; they don't know what to do. I've seen them so often. I remember in Birmingham, Alabama, when we were in that majestic struggle there we would move out of the 16th Street Baptist Church day after day; by the hundreds we would move out. And Bull Connor would tell them to send the dogs forth and they did come; but we just went before the dogs singing, "Ain't gonna let nobody turn me round." Bull Connor next would say, "Turn the fire hoses on." And as I said to you the other night, Bull Connor didn't know history. He knew a kind of physics that somehow didn't relate to the transphysics that we knew about. And that was the fact that there was a certain kind of fire that no water could put out. And we went before the fire hoses; we had known water. If we were Baptist or some other denomination, we had been immersed. If we were Methodist, and some others, we had been sprinkled, but we knew water.

That couldn't stop us. And we just went on before the dogs and we would look at them; and we'd go on before the water hoses and we would look at it, and we'd just go on singing. "Over my head I see freedom in the air." And then we would be thrown in the paddy wagons, and sometimes we were stacked in there like sardines in a can. And they would throw us in, and old Bull would say, "Take them off," and they did; and we would just go in the paddy wagon singing, "We Shall Overcome." And every now and then we'd get in the jail, and we'd see the jailers looking through the windows being moved by our prayers, and being moved by our words and our songs. And there was a power there which Bull Connor couldn't adjust to; and so we ended up transforming Bull into a steer, and we won our struggle in Birmingham.

Now we've got to go on to Memphis just like that. I call upon you to be with us Monday. Now about injunctions: We have an injunction and we're going into court tomorrow morning to fight this illegal, unconstitutional injunction. All we say to America is, "Be true to what you said on paper." If I lived in China or even Russia, or any totalitarian country, maybe I could understand the denial of certain basic First Amendment privileges, because they hadn't committed themselves to that over there. But somewhere I read of the freedom of assembly. Somewhere I read of the freedom of speech. Somewhere I read of the freedom of the press. Somewhere I read that the greatness of America is the right to protest for right. And so just as I say, we aren't going to let any injunction turn us around. We are going on. …

Now the other thing we'll have to do is this: Always anchor our external direct action with the power of economic withdrawal. Now, we are poor people, individually, we are poor when you compare us with white society in America. We are poor. Never stop and forget that collectively, that means all of us together, collectively we are richer than all the nations in the world, with the exception of nine. Did you ever think about that? After you leave the United States, Soviet Russia, Great Britain, West Germany, France, and I could name the others, the Negro collectively is richer than most nations of the world. We have an annual income of more than thirty billion dollars a year, which is more than all of the exports of the United States, and more than the national budget of Canada. Did you know that? That's power right there, if we know how to pool it.

We don't have to argue with anybody. We don't have to curse and go around acting bad with our words. We don't need any bricks and bottles, we don't need any Molotov cocktails, we just need to go around to these stores, and to these massive industries in our country, and say, "God sent us by here, to say to you that you're not treating his children right. And we've come by here to ask you to make the first item on your agenda – fair treatment, where God's children are concerned. Now, if you are not prepared to do that, we do have an agenda that we must follow. And our agenda calls for withdrawing economic support from you." …

But not only that, we've got to strengthen black institutions. I call upon you to take your money out of the banks downtown and deposit your money in Tri-State Bank – we want a "bank-in" movement in Memphis. So go by the savings and loan association. I'm not asking you something that we don't do ourselves at SCLC. Judge Hooks and others will tell you that we have an account here in the savings and loan association from the Southern Christian Leadership Conference. We're just telling you to follow what we're doing. Put your money there. You have six or seven black insurance companies in Memphis. Take out your insurance there. We want to have an "insurance-in."

Now there are some practical things we can do. We begin the process of building a greater economic base. And at the same time, we are putting pressure where it really hurts. I ask you to follow through here.

Now, let me say as I move to my conclusion that we've got to give ourselves to this struggle until the end. Nothing would be more tragic than to stop at this point, in Memphis. We've got to see it through. And when we have our march, you need to be there. Be concerned about your brother. You may not be on strike. But either we go up together, or we go down together.

Let us develop a kind of dangerous unselfishness. One day a man came to Jesus; and he wanted to raise some questions about some vital matters in life. At points, he wanted to trick Jesus, and show him that he knew a little more than Jesus knew, and through this, throw him off base. Now that question could have easily ended up in a philosophical and theological debate. But Jesus immediately pulled that question from mid-air, and placed it on a dangerous curve between Jerusalem and Jericho. And he talked about a certain man, who fell among thieves. You remember that a Levite and a priest passed by on the other side. They didn't stop to help him. And finally a man of another race came by. He got down from his beast, decided not to be compassionate by proxy. But with him, administered first aid, and helped the man in need. Jesus ended up saying, this was the good man, because he had the capacity to project the "I" into the "thou," and to be concerned about his brother. Now you know, we use our imagination a great deal to try to determine why the priest and the Levite didn't stop. At times we say they were busy going to church meetings – an ecclesiastical gathering – and they had to get on down to Jerusalem so they wouldn't be late for their meeting. At other times we would speculate that there was a religious law that "One who was engaged in religious ceremonials was not to touch a human body twenty-four hours before the ceremony." And every now and then we begin to wonder whether maybe they were not going down to Jerusalem, or down to Jericho, rather to organize a "Jericho Road Improvement Association." That's a possibility. Maybe they felt that it was better to deal with the problem from the causal root, rather than to get bogged down with an individual effort.

But I'm going to tell you what my imagination tells me. It's possible that these men were afraid. You see, the Jericho road is a dangerous road. I remember when Mrs. King and I were first in Jerusalem. We rented a car and drove from Jerusalem down to Jericho. And as soon as we got on that road, I said to my wife, "I can see why Jesus used this as a setting for his parable." It's a winding, meandering road. It's really conducive for ambushing. ... And you know, it's possible that the priest and the Levite looked over that man on the ground and wondered if the robbers were still around. Or it's possible that they felt that the man on the ground was merely faking. And he was acting like he had been robbed and hurt, in order to seize them over there, lure them there for quick and easy seizure. And so the first question that the Levite asked was, "If I stop to help this man, what will happen to me?" But then the Good Samaritan came by. And he reversed the question: "If I do not stop to help this man, what will happen to him?"

That's the question before you tonight. Not, "If I stop to help the sanitation workers, what will happen to all of the hours that I usually spend in my office every day and every week as a pastor?" The question is not, "If I stop to help this man in need, what will happen to me?" "If I do not stop to help the sanitation workers, what will happen to them?" That's the question.

Let us rise up tonight with a greater readiness. Let us stand with a greater determination. And let us move on in these powerful days, these days of challenge to make America what it ought to be.

Work, Business, and Management

The attitude of Christians toward work and trade has historically covered the full range from deep suspicion to wholehearted endorsement and pursuit. Both views look back to the creation account. The positive view sees God as the archetypal worker and artisan (in contrast to Greek mythology, in which the gods did not work). The negative view goes back to the account of the Fall in Genesis 3, where work in general seems to be a form of punishment. Such a view is reflected in the Latin words *otium* (leisure) and *negotium* (business, literally non-leisure). There is also the traditional ban on usury found in Exodus 22:24. This was ardently maintained through the middle ages, such that usurers were excommunicated from 1179.

Alongside the condemnation of usury came the tradition of the just price, which held that it was unethical to gain financially without actually creating something, and in particular immoral to profiteer from market conditions of scarcity. The growth of medieval trade fairs, and particularly the Crusades, made transporting large quantities of money very difficult and encouraged the rise of banking. Banking was not in itself regarded as usury, and the papal banks became particularly influential. Jews had the same scriptural strictures as Christians – but they did not see those strictures as limiting their interactions with Gentiles. They were pushed to marginal professions such as collecting rents and taxes and lending money at interest: their role was needed as much as it was reviled.

Henry VIII's Act in Restraint of Usury (1545) marks a symbolic transformation in the attitude to trade and commerce brought about by the Reformation. The act allowed the charging of interest on any sum lent to a person or business. The focus of attention shifted from usury itself to the charging of excessive rates of interest. The Reformation brought a significant change from the generally positive medieval view of human endeavors to the perception that everyday occupations genuinely fell within the bounds of God's kingdom. Both Martin Luther and John Calvin saw trade and commerce, rather than simply works of mercy, as part of an economy of grace. Luther in particular extended the notion of vocation beyond the strictly "religious" roles of priest, monk, or nun to previously "secular" roles, thus bringing the world of commerce within the language of salvation.

The influential term "Protestant work ethic," coined by the German sociologist Max Weber (1864–1920), identifies the way Calvin's legacy made constant labor appear to be an indication of a person's membership of the elect. Weber argues that for Catholicism, salvation was assured by the blessing of the clergy and participa-

tion in the sacraments. But Protestants had no such assurance. They poured their religious zeal into their labor, but had few legitimate ways of spending their gains. Purchasing church adornments was excluded by the Protestant emphasis on relying on the Bible alone. Giving to the poor was frowned on because the poor should be encouraged to work harder. Personal luxury seemed to speak of greed. Weber cites this culture as fertile soil for the growth of mass production, for the industrial staple products suited this emphasis on stylistic understatement. Thus, Weber argues, surplus capital was invested and capitalism took hold.

The readings in this section address similar issues from significantly different perspectives. The first takes a pragmatic approach to the realities within which Christians operate. The second castigates those responsible for constructing an oppressive social order. The third sees management as a symbol of all that is wrong with a society that has lost its meaning and purpose.

Universal

Max L. Stackhouse, *Spirituality and the Corporation*

Max Stackhouse (b. 1935) has taught for many years at Princeton Theological Seminary. In this text he uses *oikos* to mean the agrarian "householder community" of the ancient Greeks, in which everyone's consumption was limited and everyone played a fixed role in production. It is also important to him that *oikos* is the root word for both economics and ecumenics. *Oikonomia* is defined as stewardship, referring either to the "whole inhabited world" (the structures of civilization), or to "the 'rule' or management of the household." Thus, stewardship (*oikonomia*) "is about the relationship of Word to world, of ecumenical theology to political economics." Stackhouse uses *oikoumene* to mean "the household of faith" of the early church, "a spiritual network of persons who were one in Christ who also formed a social-institution center independent of both the traditional *oikos* [i.e., household] and the regime."

This excerpt resolves the issues of ownership into three – socialism, corporative ownership, and the independent corporation – and settles on the last as the best. He then offers five theological motifs that may offer guidance to Christians in the face of what could otherwise seem a soulless enterprise.

Max L. Stackhouse. *Public Theology and Political Economy: Christian Stewardship in Modern Society.* Commission on Stewardship, National Council of Churches. Grand Rapids: Eerdmans, 1987. From Chapter 7, "Spirituality and the Corporation," pages 126–7, 130–5.

The Religious Roots of the Corporation

Throughout its early period, Christianity seems to have been most appealing precisely to those marginal groups that were not engaged in landholding, in agricultural production, or in the service of the rulers. It seems to have been quite attractive to urban workers – not only urban slaves but artisans, traders, tent-makers, and the like. In brief, Christianity has been linked from its inception to urbanized peoples involved in producing and trading. Those tied to the land and its duties of *oikos* were called pagans; those who gave primary loyalty to regime were called idolaters. Against these, the church developed its own corporate structures and disciplines that were to be the prototypes of later corporate structures of many kinds.

Much later, as the medieval cities developed, stimulated in part by the new methods of production introduced into northern Europe by the monastic missionaries, a series of legal provisions established the city itself as a corporation. Like the church, it was also independent of *oikos* and regime. In addition, hospitals, schools, and other charitable corporations were formed on the analogy of the church and its orders.

At the hands of Protestant lawyers, during the period when protodemocratic political institutions were also being formed, this long tradition was extended by the formation of the limited-liability corporation, developed specifically for commercial purposes. This made it possible for people to invest in companies without risking personal, familial, or political capital distinct from that which was invested. Imbued with the Protestant work ethic, a dedication to "covenantal relationships," an inclination to bring all aspects of life under disciplined rational control, a drive toward the democratization of piety, politics, and social relationships of all kinds, and a radicalization of the sense of vocation, the limited-liability corporation developed the concept of "trustee" and invented a new social form for stewardship. The patterns consequently developed contributed to and grew with the Industrial Revolution as it introduced modern technologies of production and new occupational possibilities on a massive scale. The ethos of the corporation, which still bears the marks of this history in its deepest fabric, continues to imbue all those working in the corporation with values rooted in this history: common economic action demands a work ethic, a set of values separate from familial and political control, a discipline guided by rational control, at least a sense of "profession," and a stewardship of wealth that is not one's own. Workers and managers in modern corporations continue to be drawn into an ethos wherein these moral and spiritual presuppositions are seen as "natural," although the overt theological foundations have largely been replaced by utilitarian and contractual understandings of human relationships, and mammon has become, for many, the reigning deity. ...

Reforming the Spirituality of the Corporation

... [I]f we are fundamentally committed to a public theology that hopes to make the Word enfleshed in this kind of world, what shall the *oikoumene* now offer to corporate life?

We will have to make some very fundamental and fateful decisions before we proceed very far. One involves answering a basic question: Which form of corporative organization do we want to champion? There are only three major choices institutionally. Shall we call for state-engineered corporative life, which is the socialist route? Shall we foster an *oikos*-based corporative model, which dominates the Third World? Or shall we endorse the model of the independent corporation, an endorsement implicit in the direction the West has taken in the past? The question could be put another way: Who do we want to have calculating and making the profits and thus controlling capitalization – governments, elite families, or stockholders? I do not think it will do for ecumenical leadership to continue to duck this issue by continuing to ignore the questions of production and concentrating only on distribution, however important it is to maintain ethical witness on that front.

I think that we had better choose the model of the independent corporation (although in some situations the state-socialist model may have to be employed temporarily to remove elite families from their present positions of economic exploitation). We should do so because, in the long run, it is the system most inclined to support and sustain the prospects for human rights, democratic participation in political life, and the reduction of feudal, patriarchal, and caste structure in family life. Of course, we must beware here, because making such a choice can easily be seen as simply a sanctification of Yankee corporate capitalism and a conscious or pre-conscious attempt to wrap the American way of life in the Christian flag and drape it around the world. These I do not intend, and hence any move in the direction I suggest must be coupled with simultaneous prophetic judgment against and pastoral reformation of many current corporate policies.

... It could be said that *oikos*-based feudalism has produced and still tends to produce its antithesis, capitalistic individualism; and that the synthesis, "robber barons," produces its antithesis of state capitalism. That has brought us the socialisms and fascisms of the twentieth century, against which the reactionary forces of individualistic and state capitalism are presently arrayed. We do not yet have a viable antithesis to this present state of affairs except the ideal of social democracy borne by the ecumenical church, which must, without extensive political, economic, or technological power, develop a new spirituality, based on a public theology, to transform the materialist and reductionist preoccupation of all present economic forms and ideologies. This is possible because already within the modern corporation are residual ecclesiological elements wherein spiritual matters are intrinsically related to social ones, and therefore are potentially related to new patterns of material and organizational embodiment. ...

What theological resources will we bring to bear on these facts of public life today, and what forms of spirituality ought we to attempt to cultivate for corporate life? To be sure, many argue that corporate life is inevitably spiritually vacuous, that corporations today are alienating and dehumanizing, and that a commercial enterprise surely cannot have any soul, any spirituality, for it is based, as it must be, on the making of a profit, the impersonality of the market, the mechanism of engineered needs, and finally the worship of mammon. And yet that judgment does not seem to be faithful either to the deeper history of the modern corporation (as it derived from ecclesiological, free-city, and charity-organization precedents) or to the human experience that people in our churches have in corporations. ...

Let me close this chapter by listing five motifs from the governing themes of a public theology that might become the counterpoints of preaching and teaching, pastoral care, and the development of a stewardly leadership able to carry their commitments and ministries into the world of the productive corporation:

1   Vocation. From the calling of Abraham and Moses to the calling of the prophets and disciples, through the various refinements in the history of the tradition, the notion that each person was put in the world by God to serve some particular purpose and is called to serve the whole of humanity in the economy of God is a profound and penetrating insight. A vocation is not simply a job or an occupation. It comes from God and may require sacrificial suffering, discipleship, and *kenosis*. The concept has its most important application in regard to personal life, but it has social dimensions as well. Further, every institution has *its* particular vocation. Schools are to seek the truth and understanding; hospitals are devoted to healing and the care of the sick; symphonies are meant for making music. Is it possible that corporations as cooperative endeavors, as well

as the people in them, have a vocation from God to do what they do? Surely this means that they must contribute to the material well-being of the human community with the particular skills and products they offer – plumbing supply, meat-packing, energy resources, or whatever – and that they must do so in a way that makes a profit. ...

2   Moral Law. In some circles today it seems quaint to speak of moral law, and many are so afraid of sounding self-righteous (as those who talk about it a great deal often do) that they avoid speaking of it. And yet the reluctance to speak clearly about fundamental principles of right and wrong allows people in corporate life to be satisfied on the one hand with mere legality, and on the other hand with whatever is strategic or efficient. This has allowed many to lose sight of the basic principles of human rights that must be met as a condition of any viable structure of economic life. Corporations, especially those in such places as South Africa and developing countries, must see to it that their activities enhance human rights. And if this is not the case, they must not be surprised if churches, workers' groups, opposition parties, and oppressed minorities form coalitions to convert them.

3   Liberation. In the West, millions of middle-class people have found their economic liberation – against the expectations of many – in the disciplined, cooperative sharing of vocations in corporations. Yet many on the underside of Western economies have not had this experience, and many more around the world are oppressed by corporations. If there is to be a remedy for this problem, it will mean that the long-range planning that every corporation now does and the intervening steps taken to carry out those plans must speak to this question: Does this project somehow contribute to the liberation of those not free in a way that draws them also into communities of economic responsibility?

4   Sin. There is something tragic in all of economic life. Every act of production involves the destruction of some resource that has been given to humanity in creation, and every pattern of distribution entails disproportionate gain for some at the expense of others, and every act of consumption involves waste. Further, every organized center of economic activity thus far developed involves the domination of some over others. Let us never think that we humans can find our salvation in economic activity and its rewards, or in the building of one specific kind of

economic order, including that centered in the corporation. Many corporations engender a kind of loyalty that borders on the totemic at best, on the idolatrous at worst. The tendencies to worship mammon are with us all, and can easily demand that the corporation become mammon's temple. Especially because the corporation can provide a kind of immortality, it can require human sacrifice on its altar. These perils are already suggested in the commandment that tells us that six days shall we labor, but that we must remember the Sabbath, to keep it holy. Our necessary efforts at production are disciplined and restrained by the constant and regular repair to the One who creates what we can never produce, distributes what no human system can apportion, and receives out of our willingness to consume less than we obviously could.

5 Covenant. In the face of our modern political economies, we must work out a covenantal structure for the corporation in ways framed by these other doctrines and in ways echoing the ecclesiological roots of the corporation. And we must attempt to structure economic influence by patterns that reflect what we have learned about political distributions of power. The future of corporate polity will surely demand the democratization of decision-making, the sharing of power, and the participation of labor in setting guidelines for corporate policy around the world. And this means the pluralization of economic authority and a political, social, and ethical openness to corporate formation in underdeveloped regions of the world, which state capitalisms of the left and the right do not presently encourage.

Subversive

Miguel A. de la Torre, *Corporate Accountability*

Miguel de la Torre (b. 1958) teaches at Iliff School of Theology in Denver, Colorado. This excerpt begins in explicitly subversive terms by recognizing that issues of capital and labor look very different depending on one's point of view. De la Torre privileges the point of view of workers, particularly exploited and oppressed workers. He describes the acceptance of theft in circumstances of necessity as situation ethics. It is subtly different from Joseph Fletcher's situation ethics because Fletcher takes a universal approach, imagining anyone could find themselves in a trying or desperate position of this kind, whereas de la Torre and those whom he quotes tend to treat the poor as a class with a different set of values and ethical codes from other classes.

Having made the case for a particular ethic for the excluded, de la Torre moves on to identify how a large employer can adversely affect not just its own workforce but the living standards of a whole country – a process he calls "the Wal-Martizing of America." Finally, he shows that exemplary personal virtues expressed by and admired in top executives are not enough to address the problem – a problem he describes as "institutionalized violence."

Miguel de la Torre. *Doing Christian Ethics from the Margins*. Maryknoll: Orbis Books, 2004. From Part IV: Case Studies on Business Relationships; Chapter 13, "Corporate Accountability," pages 211–21. Reprinted by permission of Orbis Books.

The exploitation of labor dehumanizes workers by reducing their existence to expendable commodities. Workers become non-persons who are prevented from living the abundant life promised to them by Christ. What the economic order values is how cheaply their labor can be extracted, regardless whether their wage affords the necessities of clothing, food, and shelter. Hence, what are perceived as moral vices (stealing and lying) may appear more as virtues than vices to the marginalized when dealing with those with power and privilege. For example, since the twelfth century, theologians have recognized the rights of the poor, specifically "theft arising from necessity." The bishop of Paris,

Guillaume d'Auxerre, insisted that the poor could take what they needed in order to survive. This right to steal to survive was proclaimed within the context of the famines and plagues common in that era.

Ethicist Cheryl Sanders continues this form of situation ethics in her analysis of slave testimonies. Slave masters would hire ministers to preach to the slaves about the virtues of speaking honestly and of not stealing from the owners of their bodies. A former slave, commenting on a sermon preached against stealing, said,

"I did not regard it as stealing then, I do not regard it as such now. I hold that a slave has a moral right to eat and drink and wear all that he needs, and that it would be a sin on his part to suffer and starve in a country where there is plenty to eat and wear within his reach. I consider that I had a just right to what I took, because it was the labor of my hands."

The ethics of the slaveholder, which defined the stealing of food by slaves as a vice, was a socially constructed ethics designed to protect their privilege within the social order. The real question to ask is did the slaves have a moral right to steal from their masters? Do the oppressed, whose labor is stolen from them, have an ethical right – or one could say, duty – to take what is produced through their labor to feed themselves and their family? Updating this question leads us to ask if employees today who are not paid a living wage also have a right to "steal" from their employers for the purpose of meeting their basic needs for food, clothes, and shelter? ...

Although one cannot compare the institution of slavery with the situation of marginalized employees, the same motivation of maximizing profit at the expense of others exists. When the economy experiences a downturn, some companies continue to grow and prosper on the backs of their employees. Not receiving a living wage contributes to individuals living a less than human existence. In effect, denying workers a living wage is stealing. Corporations steal from employees when they extract a full week of labor and refuse to compensate them with what is needed for basic necessities for the week.

Wal-Mart, the world's largest retailer with over 3,552 stores throughout the United States and employing more than 1.2 million workers (Wal-Mart likes to call them "associates"), provides a good example of these practices. With stores in nine countries, Wal-Mart produced $245 billion in revenue during 2002, an amount greater than the economies of all but thirty of the world's nations. Wal-Mart has also invaded Mexico,

making it that nation's largest private employer with over 100,000 workers in 633 outlets laboring for about $1.50 an hour. It is also the largest retailer in Canada. The practices employed at Wal-Mart exist, in varying degrees, in other corporations that employ predominantly the marginalized.

On December 20, 2002, a federal jury in Portland, Oregon, found Wal-Mart guilty of forcing its employees to work unpaid overtime. Employees in twenty-seven other states have similar class-action suits pending against the giant retailer. These employees were pressured to clock out after working forty hours, but to continue working, violating the Federal Labor Standards Acts that require employees receive time-and-a-half pay for all hours worked over forty within a week. According to testimony given during the Oregon trial, time cards were falsified by erasing hours worked in order to keep those hours below forty and thus avoid paying time-and-a-half. Failure to comply negatively affected promotions, raises, and employment security. This is not the first time Wal-Mart has faced such accusations. In 2000, Wal-Mart settled a class-action suit in Colorado for $50 million that asserted that its laborers were forced to work off the clock. ...

When employees at Wal-Mart attempted to unionize in order to have more leverage with management, union supporters were fired, intimidated, and threatened with the loss of bonuses. A union supporter at a Jacksonville, Texas, store was fired for supposedly stealing a banana. The only successful effort at organizing Wal-Mart employees occurred in the meat department in a Texas store. Within two weeks of unionizing, the department was disbanded by the company. A former Wal-Mart store manager who now works as a union organizer summed up the company's attitude: "They go after you any way they can to discredit you, to fire you. It's almost like a neurosurgeon going after a brain tumor: We got to get that thing out before it infects the rest of the store, the rest of the body." Such actions have led to over forty complaints filed with the National Labor Relations Board from 1999 through 2002. Eight cases were settled, ten cases were decided against Wal-Mart, and the rest are pending. According to Wal-Mart's senior vice president, Jay Allen, the reason Wal-Mart remains nonunion is because the company has done a great job in keeping its employees happy and paying them competitive wages. Yet nonunionized Wal-Mart employees average $8.50 an hour compared to $13 at unionized stores.

Wal-Mart's refusal to unionize negatively impacts those who work for Wal-Mart and threatens to undermine the wages being paid by other competitors like Sears, K-Mart, and Costco, who are now demanding contract concessions from unions so they can compete with Wal-Mart. They cite their inability to compete with Wal-Mart's wages and benefits, which are 20 percent below theirs.

In effect, Wal-Mart, the nation's largest corporate employer, is lowering the living standards for everyone by aggressively and artificially keeping wages depressed for the sake of profit. Because Wal-Mart is able to cut the cost of operations by paying employees less, Wal-Mart has been able to push over two dozen national supermarket chains into bankruptcy. Since 1990, Wal-Mart prices, on average, have been 14 percent lower than its competitors, partly due to substandard wages. The list of now defunct chains includes Grand Union, Bruno's of Alabama, Homeland Stores of Oklahoma, and, more recently, F.A.O. Schwarz. In February 2004, Wal-Mart opened its first of an expected forty supercenters in California. In California, unionized stockers and clerks average $17.90 an hour, with health benefits after two years, solidly placing them within the middle-class. Wal-Mart's employees, with an average starting pay of $8.50 an hour with little or no health insurance, find themselves living in poverty. The Wal-Martizing of America means that to compete, other supermarkets must race against Wal-Mart to the bottom of the labor pool or face their own demise. ...

Compare the plight of the marginalized working at Wal-Mart with the situation of their top executive officer, H. Lee Scott, whose total compensation for 2003 was $18.28 million. The connection between the privileged elite and the poor and marginalized workers is maintained through a corporate system that enriches the former at the expense of the latter. The privilege of top executives is protected through the creation of a professional-managerial class that then serves as a buffer zone between top management and those employees living in poverty due to low wages. ...

It would be erroneous to caricature the top executives of Wal-Mart as demonic or wicked people. In fact, many are considered virtuous, upright leading citizens and churchgoers. In his exposé of Wal-Mart culture, Bob Ortega reveals the disconnect between the Christian virtues expounded by top officials and their corporate practices. He concludes:

"David Glass [Wal-Mart's president] was considered by his friends to be a fine, upstanding, morally correct, and honest man. Don Soderquist [Wal-Mart's vice-chairman] was a devout Christian once named lay churchman of the year by a national Baptist organization. And yet these two ran a company that profited from the exploitation of children – and, in all likelihood, from the exploitation of Chinese prisoners, too. Time and again it was put before them, by *Dateline* [NBC revealed that some Wal-Mart products made in Bangladesh used illegal child labor], by Harry Wu [former Chinese political prisoner for nineteen years who alleged some Wal-Mart products were made with slave labor], by the *Wall Street Journal*, by others. And yet their response was to do the very least they could, to hold up, time and again their feeble code, as if its mere existence – forget monitoring, forget enforcement – was enough; as if by uttering once more "our suppliers know we have strict codes" would solve any problem. And nothing would change."

It is of little comfort to the marginalized that these top officials have certain personal virtues. Just as faith without works is dead (Jas. 2:20), so too are right virtues without right praxis meaningless. In teaching about the day of final judgment, Jesus tells a parable of two stewards in charge of the master's household – one conscientious, the other self-absorbed. The conscientious steward fulfilled his ethical obligations to both the master and his fellow servants. The self-absorbed steward instead beat those under his authority. Rather than providing his fellow servants with their fair share of profits from the work performed, the steward instead ate and drank what was stolen from the laborers. The steward's master came home unexpectedly and, seeing how both stewards had behaved, he rewarded the conscientious one while he condemned the oppressive one, casting off the latter to where there is "constant weeping and grinding of teeth" (Mt. 24:45–51). Through the parable Jesus prescribes the ethical responsibilities of those with power over workers. Increasingly, laws and government regulations tend to legitimize the power and privilege of multinational corporations – who have become the stewards of today's world. Because these new oppressive stewards "lord it" over the disenfranchised majority and contribute to their poverty, salvation becomes ever more elusive for them.

Rather than looking at the CEOs responsible for setting the wages of the employees, as well as their own compensation, our culture teaches us to blame the workers for their lot. Sometimes we justify this callousness through an ideology based on Charles Darwin's findings that argues for a natural selection that supposedly ensures the "survival of the fittest." Some economic philosophers have proposed that just as animals compete with each other to survive, so too do human beings. Social Darwinists maintain that free markets guarantee that only those who are aggressive enough will survive because they are the fittest in effect, the best human beings. Hence, those who fail deserve to fail because they are neither the fittest – nor the best. There is no reason then for the government to provide them with assistance (such as welfare, unemployment compensation, and so on) because preserving these economic "losers" would perpetuate inferior qualities in the next generation.

The Spirit of God runs counter to the exploitation of labor. When corporations create conditions that contribute to the poverty of workers – whether being disguised as a defense of democracy, open economic markets, or Christian virtues, these corporations in reality are complicit in establishing and maintaining institutionalized violence. Violence is never limited to the use of physical force, but incorporates power used to achieve wealth and privilege at the expense of others. Violence is anything that prevents an individual from

fulfilling the purpose of Christ's mission, that of giving life and giving it abundantly (Jn. 10:10).

Such violence (usually manifested as racism, classism, and sexism) becomes institutionalized when it is built into the very structure of the corporation. The violence experienced by the working poor through inadequate food, clothes, health care, and shelter brings profit to those within the corporation, specifically its officers, directors, and, to a lesser extent, the stockholders. Such exploitation of workers dehumanizes them, turning them into just another resource. Contrary to such common practices, biblical texts call for workers to be treated humanely and justly:

> You shall not oppress a poor and needy hired servant, neither among your compatriots nor an alien who is in your land or within your gates. You shall pay them for their work on the same day. The sun shall not set upon them, for they are poor and upon these wages their heart is lifted up. Let them not cry out against you to God, and it be sin against you. (Deut. 24:14–15)

Ecclesial

Alasdair MacIntyre, *"Fact," Explanation, and Expertise*

Alasdair MacIntyre (b. 1929) is a Scottish-born philosopher who has spent most of his career in the United States. After being closely associated with the Student Christian Movement, he became a Marxist, before converting to Catholicism in the early 1980s. He is a proponent of Thomistic Aristotelianism – that is, he advocates the tradition of the virtues as articulated by Aristotle and expressed through Thomas Aquinas, in contrast to what he sees as Enlightenment liberalism or the postmodern emphasis on suspicion and investigation into hidden motives. In theological circles his work has often been linked with that of Stanley Hauerwas, with whom he taught during spells at Notre Dame and Duke universities – although his work does not share Hauerwas' emphasis on Jesus, church, and, in particular, non-violence.

In his influential book *After Virtue* (1981, 1984) MacIntyre develops the notion of a practice, and laments that politics can no longer be described as a practice. A practice refers to "any coherent and complex form of socially established cooperative human activity through which goods internal to that form of activity are realized in the course of trying to achieve those standards of excellence which are appropriate to, and partially definitive of, that form of activity, with the result that human powers to achieve excellence, and human conceptions of the ends and goods involved, are systematically extended."

In this excerpt MacIntyre shows what happens when morality ceases to be about final causes. For Aristotle, there are four causes: the material (what a thing is made of), the formal (its shape), the efficient (the person who makes it what it becomes), and the final (its ultimate purpose). In the Enlightenment, says MacIntyre, action came to be understood either in terms of raw mechanistic process, or intention (which came to be the field of morality, wholly detached from science, which dealt with mechanisms). In other words, the quarrel was over rival accounts of efficient causes, and final causes (with their language of virtue, the qualities oriented towards ultimate purpose) disappeared altogether. It was not long before ethics desired to operate like a science, and thus seek law-like generalizations. But to do so meant excluding the language of intention altogether, because intention was too subjective to suit mechanistic science. This is the point where fact and value come apart completely, as MacIntyre vividly explains below.

MacIntyre then points out two ironies: (1) that those who try to manipulate others' behavior assume their behavior is not mechanistically predictable (but everyone else's is!); (2) that both the civil servants of the nineteenth century and their social reformist opponents swallowed the mechanistic model of human behavior. Citing Max Weber (1864–1920), the German sociologist, MacIntyre shows how the "expert" becomes the epitome of the bureaucrat who claims scientific knowledge of how systems work. Modern management and business schools rest on these same two claims (which MacIntyre shows to be ironies): value neutrality and manipulative power.

Alasdair MacIntyre. *After Virtue: A Study in Moral Theory.* 2nd edn. Notre Dame: University of Notre Dame Press, 1984, 2003. From Chapter 7, "'Fact,' Explanation and Expertise," pages 81–7.

For the middle ages mechanisms were efficient causes in a world to be comprehended ultimately in terms of final causes. ... The ends to which men as members of such a species move are conceived by them as goods, and their movement towards or away from various goods are to be explained with reference to the virtues and vices which they have learned or failed to learn and the forms of practical reasoning which they employ. Aristotle's *Ethics* and *Politics* (together of course with the *De Anima*) are as much treatises concerned with how human action is to be explained and understood as with what acts are to be done. ...

When in the seventeenth and eighteenth centuries the Aristotelian understanding of nature was repudiated, at the same time as Aristotle's influence had been expelled from both Protestant and Jansenist theology, the Aristotelian account of action was also rejected. "Man" ceases, except within theology – and not always there – to be what I called earlier a functional concept. The explanation of action is increasingly held to be a matter of laying bare the physiological and physical mechanisms which underlie action; and, when Kant recognizes that there is a deep incompatibility between

any account of action which recognizes the role of moral imperatives in governing action and any such mechanical type of explanation, he is compelled to the conclusion that actions obeying and embodying moral imperatives must be from the standpoint of science inexplicable and unintelligible. After Kant the question of the relationship between such notions as those of intention, purpose, reason for action and the like on the one hand and the concepts which specify the notion of mechanical explanation on the other becomes part of the permanent repertoire of philosophy. The former notions are however now treated as detached from notions of good or virtue; those concepts have been handed over to the separate subdiscipline of ethics. ...

But what is it to try to understand human action in mechanical terms, in terms that is of antecedent conditions understood as efficient causes? In the seventeenth and eighteenth century understanding of the matter – and in many subsequent versions – at the core of the notion of mechanical explanation is a conception of invariances specified by law-like generalizations. To cite a cause is to cite a necessary condition *or* a sufficient condition *or* a necessary and sufficient condition as the antecedent of whatever behavior is to be explained. So every mechanical causal sequence exemplifies some universal generalization and that generalization has a precisely specifiable scope. Newton's laws of motion which purport to be universal in scope provide the paradigm case of such a set of generalizations. Being universal they extend beyond what has actually been observed in the present or the past to what has escaped observation and to what has not yet been observed. ...

This ideal of mechanical explanation was transferred from physics to the understanding of human behavior by a number of English and French thinkers in the seventeenth and eighteenth centuries who differed a good deal among themselves over the details of their enterprise. And it was only somewhat later that the precise requirements that such an enterprise would have to meet could be spelled out. One such requirement, and a very important one, was identified only in our own time by W. V. Quine.

Quine argued that if there is to be a science of human behavior whose key expressions characterize that behavior in terms precise enough to provide us with genuine laws, those expressions must be formulated in a vocabulary which omits all reference to intentions, purposes, and reasons for action. Just as physics, to become a genuine mechanical science, had to purify its descriptive vocabulary, so must the human sciences. What is it about intentions, purposes and reasons that makes them thus unmentionable? It is the fact that all these expressions refer to or presuppose reference to the beliefs of the agents in question. The discourse which we use to speak about beliefs has two great disadvantages from the point of view of what Quine takes to be a science. First sentences of the form "*X* believes that *p*" (or for that matter, "*X* enjoys its being the case that *p*" or "*X* fears that *p*") have an internal complexity which is not truth-functional, which is to say that they cannot be mapped on to the predicate calculus; and in this they differ in a crucial respect from the sentences used to express the laws of physics. Secondly, the concept of a state or belief or enjoyment or fear involves too many contestable and doubtful cases to furnish the kind of evidence we need to confirm or disconfirm claims to have discovered a *law*.

Quine's conclusion is that therefore any genuine science of human behavior must eliminate such intentional expressions; but it is perhaps necessary to do to Quine what Marx did to Hegel, that is, to stand his argument on its head. For it follows from Quine's position that *if* it proved impossible to eliminate references to such items as beliefs and enjoyments and fears from our understanding of human behavior, that understanding could not take the form which Quine considers the form of human science, namely embodiment in law-like generalizations. An Aristotelian account of what is involved in understanding human behavior

involves an ineliminable reference to such items; and hence it is not surprising that any attempt to understand human behavior in terms of mechanical explanation must conflict with Aristotelianism.

The notion of "fact" with respect to human beings is thus transformed in the transition from the Aristotelian to the mechanist view. On the former view human action, because it is to be explained teleologically, not only can, but must be, characterized with reference to the hierarchy of goods which provide the ends of human action. On the latter view human action not only can, but must, be characterized without any reference to such goods. On the former view the facts about human action include the facts about what is valuable to human beings (and *not* just the facts about what they think to be valuable); on the latter view there are no facts about what is valuable. "Fact" becomes value-free, "is" becomes a stranger to "ought" and explanation, as well as evaluation, changes its character as a result of this divorce between "is" and "ought."

Another implication of this transition was noted somewhat earlier, by Marx in the third of his *Theses on Feuerbach*. It is clear that the Enlightenment's mechanistic account of human action included both a thesis about the predictability of human behavior and a thesis about the appropriate ways to manipulate human behavior. As an observer, if I know the relevant laws governing the behavior of others, I can whenever I observe that the antecedent conditions have been fulfilled predict the outcome. As an agent, if I know these laws, I can whenever I can contrive the fulfilment of the same antecedent conditions produce the outcome. What Marx understood was that such an agent is forced to regard his own actions quite differently from the behavior of those whom he is manipulating. For the behavior of the manipulated is being contrived in accordance with *his* intentions, reasons and purposes; intentions, reasons and purposes which he is treating, at least while he is engaged in such manipulation, as exempt from the laws which govern the behavior of the manipulated. To them he stands at least for the moment as the chemist does to the samples of potassium chloride and sodium nitrate with which he experiments; but in the chemical changes which the chemist or the technologist of human behavior brings about the chemist or the technologist must see exemplified not only the laws which govern such changes but the imprinting of his own will on nature or society. And that imprinting he will treat, as Marx saw, as the expression of his own rational autonomy and not the mere outcome of antecedent conditions. Of course the question remains open whether in the case of the agent who claims to be applying the science of human behavior we are genuinely observing the application of a real technology or rather instead the deceptive and self-deceptive histrionic mimicry of such a technology. Which it is depends upon whether we believe that the mechanistic programme for social science has or has not in fact been substantially achieved. And in the eighteenth century at least the notion of a mechanistic science of man remained programme and prophecy. But prophecies in this area may be translated *not* into real achievement, but into a social performance which disguises itself as such achievement. ...

The history of how intellectual prophecy became social performance is of course a complex one. It begins quite independently of the development of the concept of manipulative expertise with the story of how the modern state acquired its civil servants ... [A]s the functions of modern states become more and more the same, their civil services come to be more and more the same too; and while their various political masters come and go, civil servants maintain the administrative continuity of government and thus confer on the government much of its character.

The civil servant has as his nineteenth-century counterpart and opposite the social reformer: Saint Simonians, Comtians, utilitarians, English ameliorists such as Charles Booth, the early Fabian socialists. *Their* characteristic lament is: if only government could learn to be scientific! And the long-term response of government is to claim that it has indeed become scientific in just the sense that the reformers required. Government insists more and more that its civil servants themselves have the kind of education that will qualify them as experts. It more and more recruits those who claim to be experts into its civil service. And it characteristically recruits too the heirs of the nineteenth-century reformers. Government itself becomes a hierarchy of bureaucratic managers, and the major justification advanced for the intervention of government in society is the contention that government has resources of competence which most citizens do not possess.

Private corporations similarly justify *their* activities by referring to their possession of similar resources of competence. Expertise becomes a commodity for which rival state agencies and rival private corporations compete. Civil servants and managers alike justify

themselves and their claims to authority, power and money by invoking their own competence as scientific managers of social change. Thus there emerges an ideology which finds its classical form of expression in a pre-existing sociological theory, Weber's theory of bureaucracy. Weber's account of bureaucracy notoriously has many flaws. But in his insistence that the rationality of adjusting means to ends in the most economical and efficient way is the central task of the bureaucrat and that therefore the appropriate mode of justification of his activity by the bureaucrat lies in the appeal to his (or later her) ability to deploy a body of scientific and above all social scientific knowledge, organized in terms of and understood as comprising a set of universal law-like generalizations, Weber provided the key to much of the modern age.

... [M]odern theories of bureaucracy or of administration which differ widely from Weber's at many other points tend on this issue of managerial justification to agree with him and ... this consensus suggests strongly that what the books written by modern organization theorists describe is genuinely a part of modern managerial practice. So we can now see in bare skeletal outline a progress first from the Enlightenment's ideal for a social science to the aspirations of social reformers, next from the aspirations of social reformers to the ideals of practice and justification of civil servants and managers, then from the practices of management to the theoretical codification of these practices and of the norms governing them by sociologists and organization theorists and finally from the employment of the textbooks written by those theorists in schools of management and business schools to the theoretically informed managerial practice of the contemporary technocratic expert. ... [I]n every case the rise of managerial expertise would have to be the same central theme, and such expertise, as we have already seen, has two sides to it: there is the aspiration to value neutrality and the claim to manipulative power. Both of these, we can now perceive, derive from the history of the way in which the realm of fact and the realm of value were distinguished by the philosophers of the seventeenth and eighteenth centuries. Twentieth-century social life turns out in key part to be the concrete and dramatic re-enactment of eighteenth-century philosophy. And the legitimation of the characteristic institutional forms of twentieth-century social life depends upon a belief that some of the central claims of that earlier philosophy have been vindicated.

Media

The media are the various methods of encoding and delivering messages to a mass public. The term generally refers to both the form (television, Internet, newspapers, and so on) and the content of transmission. Ethical concern is both provoked and communicated by media; it is as pervasive as it is indispensable as it is troubling. Among areas of concern include advertising, which uses creativity to sell products which may benefit consumers but may also exploit them; publicity and the cult of celebrity, which tends to commodify human beings and encourage vicarious living; and cell (or mobile) phones, which foster a culture of perpetual communication with those not physically present.

Ethical responses vary between those that balance the positive and negative aspects of modern media, those that highlight (usually negative) features as symbolic of the culture as a whole, and those that reassert traditional or ancient practices – even manners – that become more difficult or unusual in a "fast-media" age. Underlying the theological debate is the notion of Christ as the embodied communication of God, and the scriptures as the written communication of the church across the centuries; two themes that show how integral are media questions to Christian self-understanding.

The readings below speak from the aspiration towards wisdom of the universal approach, the eye for the oppressed of the subversive approach, and the concern for practices and habit formation of the ecclesial approach.

Universal

Pope John Paul II, *Aetatis Novae (On Social Communications on the Twentieth Anniversary of Communio et Progressio)*

The encyclical *Aetatis Novae* (On Social Communications) was released by Pope John Paul II (1978–2005) on February 22, 1992, on the twentieth anniversary of *Communio et Progressio*, an encyclical emerging out of the Second Vatican Council. The earlier document saw the purpose of communications as the unity and advancement of people in society, and saw the press, the cinema, radio, and television as gifts of God. The later document describes new media as "new languages." It concludes: "It is not enough to use the media simply to spread the Christian message and the Church's authentic teaching. It is also necessary to integrate that message into the new culture created by modern communications … with new languages, new techniques, and a new psychology."

The popes have a very positive view of the potential of mass media: communication "mirrors the Church's own communion and is capable of contributing to it." It imitates Christ, who is the definitive embodiment of communication. However, mass media can diminish the God-given dignity and destiny of every person.

The encyclical has many deeply ecclesial commitments, and belongs as much in an ecclesial vein as in a universal one. Not only is communication rooted in Christ as the communication of God; it is given for transmitting the gospel in evangelization and the movement for justice; and for deepening the church's communion, mirroring that of the Trinity, by facilitating "the fundamental right of dialogue and information within the Church" – a right that the Pope carefully distinguishes from exerting the pressure of public opinion.

Like many encyclicals, a generally universal tone is interrupted from time to time by explicitly ecclesial reasoning, before a universal tone seems once again to be assumed. Thus the Pope says, in ecclesial voice,

Why does the Church insist that people have the right to receive correct information? Why does the Church emphasize its right to proclaim authentic Gospel truth? Why does the Church stress the responsibility of its pastors to communicate the truth and to form the faithful to do the same? It is because the whole understanding of what communication in the Church means is based upon the realization that the Word of God communicates himself.

This is perfect ecclesial reasoning, but it is surrounded by more general universal arguments and conclusions.

Pope John Paul II, Aetatis Novae (On Social Communications on the Twentieth Anniversary of *Communio et Progressio*). 1992. www.vatican.va/ roman_curia/pontifical_councils/pccs/documents/rc_ pc_pccs_doc_22021992_aetatis_en.html. **Reprinted by permission of the Libreria Editrice Vaticana.**

I. The Context of Social Communications

A. Cultural and social context

4. … The media can be used to proclaim the Gospel or to reduce it to silence in human hearts. As media become ever more intertwined with people's daily lives, they influence how people understand the meaning of life itself.

Indeed, the power of media extends to defining not only what people will think but even what they will think about. Reality, for many, is what the media recognize as real; what media do not acknowledge seems of little importance. Thus de facto silence can be imposed upon individuals and groups whom the media ignore; and even the voice of the Gospel can be muted, though not entirely stilled, in this way.

It is important therefore that Christians find ways to furnish the missing information to those deprived of it and also to give a voice to the voiceless.

The power of media either to reinforce or override the traditional reference points of religion, culture, and family underlines the continued relevance of the Council's words: "If the media are to be correctly employed, it is essential that all who use them know the principles of the moral order and apply them faithfully in this domain."

II. The Work of the Means of Social Communications

6. *Communio et Progressio* is rooted in a vision of communication as a way toward communion. For "more than the expression of ideas and the indication of emotion," it declares, communication is "the giving of self in love." In this respect, communication mirrors the

Church's own communion and is capable of contributing to it.

Indeed, the communication of truth can have a redemptive power, which comes from the person of Christ. He is God's Word made flesh and the image of the invisible God. In and through him God's own life is communicated to humanity by the Spirit's action. "Since the creation of the world, invisible realities, God's eternal power and divinity have become visible, recognized through the things he has made"; and now: "The Word has become flesh and made his dwelling among us, and we have seen his glory: the glory of an only Son coming from the Father, filled with enduring love."

Here, in the Word made flesh, God's self-communication is definitive. In Jesus' words and deeds the Word is liberating, redemptive, for all humankind. This loving self-revelation of God, combined with humanity's response of faith, constitutes a profound dialogue.

Human history and all human relationships exist within the framework established by this self-communication of God in Christ. History itself is ordered toward becoming a kind of word of God, and it is part of the human vocation to contribute to bringing this about by living out the ongoing, unlimited communication of God's reconciling love in creative new ways. We are to do this through words of hope and deeds of love, that is, through our very way of life. Thus communication must lie at the heart of the Church community.

A. Media at the service of persons and cultures

7. For all the good which they do and are capable of doing, mass media, "which can be such effective instruments of unity and understanding, can also sometimes be the vehicles of a deformed outlook on life, on the family, on religion and on morality – an outlook that does not respect the true dignity and destiny of the human person." It is imperative that media respect and contribute to that integral development of the person which embraces "the cultural, transcendent and religious dimensions of man and society."

One also finds the source of certain individual and social problems in the replacement of human interaction by increased media use and intense attachment to fictitious media characters. Media, after all, cannot take the place of immediate personal contact and interaction among family members and friends. But the solution to this difficulty also may lie largely in the media: through their use in ways – dialogue groups, discussions of films and broadcasts – which stimulate interpersonal communication rather than substituting for it.

B. Media at the service of dialogue with the world

8. The Second Vatican Council underlined the awareness of the People of God that they are "truly and intimately linked with mankind and its history." Those who proclaim God's Word are obliged to heed and seek to understand the "words" of diverse peoples and cultures, in order not only to learn from them but to help them recognize and accept the Word of God. The Church therefore must maintain an active, listening presence in relation to the world – a kind of presence which both nurtures community and supports people in seeking acceptable solutions to personal and social problems.

Moreover, as the Church always must communicate its message in a manner suited to each age and to the cultures of particular nations and peoples, so today it must communicate in and to the emerging media culture. This is a basic condition for responding to a crucial point made by the Second Vatican Council: the emergence of "social, technical, and cultural bonds" linking people ever more closely lends "special urgency" to the Church's task of bringing all to "full union with Christ." Considering how important a contribution the media of social communications can make to its efforts to foster this unity, the Church views them as means "devised under God's Providence" for the promotion of communication and communion among human beings during their earthly pilgrimage.

C. Media at the service of human community and progress

9. Communications in and by the Church is essentially communication of the Good News of Jesus Christ. It is the proclamation of the Gospel as a prophetic, liberating word to the men and women of our times; it is testimony, in the face of radical secularization, to divine truth and to the transcendent destiny of the human person; it is the witness given in solidarity with all believers against conflict and division, to justice and communion among peoples, nations, and cultures.

This understanding of communication on the part of the Church sheds a unique light on social communications and on the role which, in the providential plan of God, the media are intended to play in promoting the integral development of human persons and societies.

D. Media at the service of ecclesial communion

10. Along with all this, it is necessary constantly to recall the importance of the fundamental right of dialogue and information within the Church, as described in *Communio et Progressio*, and to continue to seek effective means, including a responsible use of media of social communications, for realizing and protecting this right. In this connection we also have in mind the affirmations of the Code of Canon Law, that, besides showing obedience to the pastors of the Church, the faithful "are at liberty to make known their needs, especially their spiritual needs, and their wishes" to these pastors, and that the faithful, in keeping with their knowledge, competence, and position, have "the right, indeed at times the duty, to express to the pastors their views on matters concerning the good of the Church."

Partly this is a matter of maintaining and enhancing the Church's credibility and effectiveness. But, more fundamentally, it is one of the ways of realizing in a concrete manner the Church's character as communion, rooted in and mirroring the intimate communion of the Trinity. Among the members of the community of persons who make up the Church, there is a radical equality in dignity and mission which arises from baptism and underlies hierarchical structure and diversity of office and function; and this equality necessarily will express itself in an honest and respectful sharing of information and opinions.

It will be well to bear in mind, however, in cases of dissent, that "it is not by seeking to exert the pressure of public opinion that one contributes to the clarification of doctrinal issues and renders service to the truth." In fact, "not all ideas which circulate among the People of God" are to be "simply and purely identified with the sense of the Faith."

Why does the Church insist that people have the right to receive correct information? Why does the Church emphasize its right to proclaim authentic Gospel truth? Why does the Church stress the responsibility of its pastors to communicate the truth and to form the faithful to do the same? It is because the whole understanding of what communication in the Church means is based upon the realization that the Word of God communicates himself.

E. Media at the service of a new evangelization

11. Along with traditional means such as witness of life, catechetics, personal contact, popular piety, the liturgy and similar celebrations, the use of media is now essential in evangelization and catechesis. Indeed, "the Church would feel guilty before the Lord if she did not utilize these powerful means that human skill is daily rendering more perfect." The media of social communications can and should be instruments in the Church's program of re-evangelization and new evangelization in the contemporary world. In view of the proven efficacy of the old principle "see, judge, act," the audiovisual aspect of media in evangelization should be given due attention.

But it will also be of great importance in the Church's approach to media and the culture they do so much to shape always to bear in mind that: "It is not enough to use the media simply to spread the Christian message and the Church's authentic teaching. It is also necessary to integrate that message into the 'new culture' created by modern communications ... with new languages, new techniques and a new psychology." Today's evangelization ought to well up from the Church's active, sympathetic presence within the world of communications.

III. Current Challenges

B. Solidarity and integral development

13. As matters stand, mass-media at times exacerbate individual and social problems which stand in the way of human solidarity and the integral development of the human person. These obstacles include secularism, consumerism, materialism, dehumanization, and lack of concern for the plight of the poor and neglected.

It is against this background that the Church, recognizing the media of social communications as "the privileged way" today for the creation and transmission of culture, acknowledges its own duty to offer forma-tion to communications professionals and to the public, so that they will approach media with "a critical sense which is animated by a passion for the truth"; it likewise acknowledges its duty to engage in "a work of defense of liberty, respect for the dignity of individuals, and the elevation of the authentic culture of peoples which occurs through a firm and courageous rejection of every form of monopoly and manipulation."

C. Policies and structures

14. Certain problems in this regard arise specifically from media policies and structures: for example, the unjust exclusion of some groups and classes from access to the means of communication, the systematic abridgement of the fundamental right to information which is practiced in some places, the widespread domination of media by economic, social, and political elites.

These things are contrary to the principal purposes, and indeed to the very nature, of the media, whose proper and essential social role consists in contributing to the realization of the human right to information, promoting justice in the pursuit of the common good, and assisting individuals, groups, and peoples in their search for truth. The media carry out these crucial tasks when they foster the exchange of ideas and information among all classes and sectors of society and offer to all responsible voices opportunities to be heard.

Conclusion

22. We affirm once again that the Church "sees these media as gifts of God which, in accordance with his providential design, unite men in brotherhood and so help them to cooperate with his plan for their salvation." As the Spirit helped the prophets of old to see the divine plan in the signs of their times, so today the Spirit helps the Church interpret the signs of our times and carry out its prophetic tasks, among which the study, evaluation, and right use of communications technology and the media of social communications are now fundamental.

Subversive

Mary E. Hess, *Growing Faithful Children in Media Cultures*

Mary Elizabeth Hess (b. 1963) teaches at Luther Seminary in St. Paul, Minnesota. This excerpt falls into the subversive category because (alone of the readings in this volume) it advocates for the child's point of view. Like many subversive texts, it deals extensively with the circumstances surrounding what might otherwise be taken to be a freestanding "issue." Hence, Hess points out, "Whereas three decades ago each family might have one television set (with a handful of channels), many families have more than one set – perhaps even more sets than they have actual family members." The same goes for computers. The result is "we no longer have shared databases to draw on as we make sense of the world around us, as we struggle to make sense of ourselves, let alone share our sense of our deep relationality."

Turning to children specifically, Hess highlights the paradox between the small role of children in generating media and their high visibility in media products. "Why can we find so many examples in popular culture that proclaim our desire to help and protect children, yet at the same time find so few examples of ways to provide real, material aid to improve the circumstances in their lives?"

To address this situation Hess draws on Ronald Heifetz's work and maintains that it requires an adaptive, rather than technical, response. What is required in relating to children is "deliberate cultural intervention" to promote more relational engagement and overcome isolation. By using several categories she ensures her critique of contemporary media culture is not a blanket one, but is nuanced around particular areas of concern.

Mary E. Hess. "Growing Faithful Children in Media Cultures." Chapter 5 in *The Ministry of Children's Education*. Professors of Christian Education at the ELCA Seminaries. Minneapolis: Fortress Press, 2004. From pages 134–42. Copyright © 2004 Fortress Press. Used by permission of Augsburg Fortress.

Media culture really is a *medium* in which meaning is made. Think of the definition of *medium* you learned in science classes: a substance in which something can be cultured or grown. Contrary to popular conception – a conception shared by many communities of faith – mass mediated popular culture is not simply a set of content that is enforced by sheer market presence on passive recipients. Rather, it is a meaning-making space where enormous amounts of material are provided for people to draw on. As noted earlier, effective learning engages *cognitive*, *affective*, and *psychomotor* elements. Mass mediated popular culture does this in a variety of ways, not the least of which is by fusing sound and image to representations of being.

Indeed, *media culture* is best understood as a dynamic medium in which meaning is produced, circulated, contested, and improvised with. That means that learning is taking place all of the time, all around us. That means that our relationships are often our most potent teachers. That means that when media culture encourages us to "reason by means of sympathetic identification" we are engaging one of its most powerful tools. If we truly do "know as we are known," what does it mean "to know" as media culture represents ourselves to ourselves and to each other?

First, and foremost, it means to know affectively, experientially. Media representations can be enormously powerful, pulling us into their worlds and helping us to suspend our disbelief. Unfortunately, it is also often the case that the sheer ubiquity of a particular representation captures our attention, limiting the database of possibilities we perceive as we engage in meaning-making, and focusing our attention on the "content" of that representation, rather than on its construction.

In addition, most media engagement in the United States in mainstream, middle-class families is increasingly happening in isolation. Whereas three decades ago each family might have one television set (with a handful of channels), many families have more than one set – perhaps even more sets than they have actual family members. Increasingly families are even buying more than one computer. So viewing screens (television or computer) is more often done in isolation. Movie theaters have evolved from showing one or perhaps two movies at a time, to big cineplexes where more than a dozen movies may be showing. Even families that go to the movie theater together may not see the same film. This reality cuts down on two important elements of media engagement – being in the same place at the same time when viewing media – so that people laugh together, cry together, yell at the absurdities, and so on – and being able to have shared conversations about media elements, being able to draw on the same database of meaning-making raw materials.

In this case a very tangible *psychomotor* element of the learning – that is, viewing done in relatively passive physical positions, and in relative isolation – contributes to some of the more challenging aspects of media practice. Mass mediated popular culture thrives on stories of relationality. Indeed, in some way, every genre of mass mediated pop culture, indeed almost every single piece of pop culture you can point to is at heart a reflection of relationality, whether *right* relationality, *broken* relationality, or at least *strained* relationality. Sitcoms tell stories about families and workplaces. News programs reflect our understanding of reality and its connection to our own experiences. Reality shows purport to represent how *real* people in *real* situations are responding to their relationships, or the lack thereof. Children's cartoons model relationships – some imaginary and some realistic. Indeed, communities of faith have always recognized how powerful a storyteller popular culture is, how much this storyteller reflects us to ourselves, and that is part of the reason we have been so reluctant for it to take center stage in our sharing of stories. ...

In our current contexts, we increasingly engage media in isolation, or at least in segmented groups – teens with teens, young children watching children's television, adults watching adult programming, and so on. The inter-generational, deeply relational patterns of practice with which we began engaging these media have broken down, and we find ourselves increasingly in a position in which the databases we draw on to make sense of our stories, literally to write our stories, are also segmented – intended for specific audiences. One painful consequence of this "target audience segmentation" is that we no longer have shared databases to draw on as we make sense of the world around us, as we struggle to make sense of ourselves, let alone share our sense of our deep relationality.

This is true of age-related programming. Think about the ways that various generations are identified, and all of the targeted marketing thrown at them. It is also true in terms of ideological and religious divides. People who share a particular view of the world can listen to particular radio shows and not encounter other views. People from a particular religious perspective – no matter how narrowly understood – can stay within a database of meanings that supports their background.

Indeed, many people engage mass media solely as a "window on the world" – without recognizing the shape of that window. That "frame," that specific construction of meaning may well be a good, solid, appropriate one, but it is nevertheless a construction of meaning. All of us need to be aware of the limited and narrow nature of any such construction. ...

Children ... are rarely present in the news, and almost never produce it. ... Indeed, the few attempts to provide opportunities for children to produce and report news have always been relegated to tiny local cable or public stations, or to very rare exceptions on national broadcasts (such as Peter Jennings's town meetings with kids following September 11, 2001). Indeed, children's active presence in news construction is so rare that perhaps instead of noting these as examples of an *implicit* curriculum, it would be more appropriate to note that children's role in news is instead part of the *null* curriculum of our current cultural contexts.

On the other hand, children are frequently at least present in entertainment genres, if not at the heart of the drama. Indeed, some of the most immediately resonant story lines on any number of prime time dramas are so moving precisely because children's lives are endangered (think about the children being hauled into the emergency room on a hospital drama, or the child dying on a mini-series). Children frequently stand as symbols of the most vulnerable of human beings, and of those most deserving of protection and support.

Yet in cold, crass terms, the sheer statistics on children in the United States are stunning. More and more children are sliding further into poverty, hunger, and homelessness. Our schools are increasingly stressed and unable to provide adequate instruction. Unemployment among teenagers is often higher than among any other group, and the few jobs that are available can feel demeaning. Why this enormous paradox? Why can we find so many examples in popular culture that proclaim our desire to help and protect children, yet at the same time find so few examples of ways to provide real, material aid to improve the circumstances in their lives?

I imagine there are numbers of possible answers to this question. I will not attempt to offer any here, although I think communities of faith ought to take the question very seriously. I suspect that our frameworks of understanding – particularly in terms of sinfulness and reconciliation – might have a lot to offer in response. Instead, I simply raise the question to point out that we are learning, in the midst of mass mediated popular culture, how to identify sympathetically with people experiencing any number of compelling problems, but rarely are we given any models to follow for responding in any way other than through vicarious emotional identification. …

Adaptive versus technical challenges

This is why the challenge that communities of faith face in mediated cultural contexts is so difficult, and why it is what Ronald Heifetz has termed an adaptive challenge, rather than simply a technical one. The distinction Heifetz is drawing gets at the center of the problems we face in this analysis. His classic example of the *adaptive versus technical* challenge comes from thinking about medical challenges. What a doctor needs to know to treat a broken bone, for instance, is quite different from what is involved in treating heart disease. Treating a broken bone is essentially a technical challenge, involving issues like realigning the broken bone in the proper position, applying the cast adequately, and so on. Whereas treating heart disease inevitably involves helping people to change elements of their lifestyles – to shift eating and exercise patterns, to handle stress differently, and so on.

If the challenge of supporting children in a mediated cultural context was simply a technical one, then communities of faith could choose the most effective media literacy curriculum to apply. We could try to provide the best vacation Bible school program, the best Bible translation, and so on. But it is not a technical challenge we're dealing with, but rather an adaptive one. We need to find ways to intervene in daily family practices that interrupt the narrowness and limited meaning-construction of relationality that is embedded in popular media, while at the same time affirming, expanding, and supporting those practices that encourage a deep relationality, that encourage and nurture rich religious life. While turning off the TV might be helpful once in a while, we can not hope to encourage the kind of adaptive practice necessary by ignoring mass mediated popular culture. We have to engage media, contest the elements that are narrow and limiting, and encourage those that help us to stretch our imagination and to feel deeply our global relationality. We need, in short, to envision children's ministry in this cultural context as a deliberate cultural intervention. …

A major part of the challenge we face with media culture is the narrowness of the range of representations of relationality available, and the limited nature of the actions in support of such relationality that are modeled. Churches need to become communities where a wide range of representations is shared, and where deeply relational patterns of practice are supported. We can only do that, however, if we know where our people are, if we have entered deeply into the meaning-making they are engaged in, if we have *confirmed* the reality where they are embedded.

The second element [of transformative education] that [Robert] Kegan speaks of is *contradiction*. This is an element in the learning process that arises in many ways. Teachers can introduce contradictions, but life also poses them unasked. I have already noted a number of ways that mass mediated popular culture on the one hand evokes our sympathetic identification with children, but then systematically excludes and impoverishes many of them, let alone encourages them in leadership. This is a major contradiction in our meaning frame.

People interested in supporting growing in faith in a mediated culture must help each other to sense and engage such contradictions. How to do so? The process of *confirmation* …, with its deep attention to listening, is a first step. What are the primary images and metaphors, for instance, that a family is using to describe their experiences? When children talk with excitement about something in their life, what is it they are talking about? When they make analogies, to what are they referring? This is part of the process of uncovering and *confirming* the reality that they are embedded in, but it is also part of discovering in what ways religious education might pose difficult contradictions to our meaning frames. If the images and stories children are using draw on biblical characters and biblical phrases, it may well be that engaging popular culture will seem a contradiction and thus be challenging. If the images and examples stem from popular Saturday morning cartoons or Disney movies, then a biblical imagination might at first seem strange or disorienting. To return to an earlier example, if the range of representation of relationship is primarily a mass mediated one, then the kind of "love of enemy" embodied in Christian gospel will not only seem far fetched, but deeply wrong. Living into an understanding of daily life that requires hospitality, that seeks to engage the stranger, that pours out love and power, rather than hoarding them – these are notions that deeply contradict the common representations of popular culture.

Ecclesial

Michael Budde, *Christian Formation in Global Culture Industries*

Michael L. Budde (b. 1958) is a Roman Catholic layman who teaches political science at DePaul University in Chicago. Like many in ecclesial ethics, Budde looks with favor on the practice of the early church before the Constantinian transformation of the fourth century. Like the contemporary Lutheran ecumenical theologian George Lindbeck, Budde sees the Christian formation practiced in the early church as like the process of learning a language and learning to inhabit a world. Budde sees this process as seriously hindered in a contemporary media-saturated world. This is a teleological argument because it judges media not in their own right but in relation to the extent to which they help or hinder the formation of Christians.

The destructive effects include the absorption of time and the reliance on superficial and secularly derived presentation of theological questions in the popular media. Budde refers to the sociologist Robert Bellah's term "Sheila-ism," coined in his influential book *Habits of the Heart*. Sheila Larson, a young nurse, says "I believe in God. … I can't remember the last time I went to church. My faith has carried me a long way. It's Sheilaism. Just my own little voice." This means "Just try to love yourself and be gentle with yourself [and] … Take care of each other."

Budde hints that these issues may be more significant for Catholics, because formation for Catholics has always paid especial attention to imagery, symbol, and sacrament – the areas where, as he says, "outside forces threaten to overwhelm, undermine, or drown out the communicative functions of religious symbols and images." In a stark conclusion, Budde does not see the problem to be solved by better content, but by a change of heart.

Michael Budde. *The (Magic) Kingdom of God: Christianity and Global Culture Industries.* Boulder: Westview Press, 1997. From "Christian Formation in Global Culture Industries," pages 69–72, 82–7, 90–6. Copyright © 1998 Michael Budde. Reprinted by permission of Westview Press, a member of the Perseus Books Group.

Whatever variations local churches practiced in the pre-Constantinian era, the formation of church members was generally a matter of great seriousness. It seemed to require:

- a substantial investment of time on the part of the initiate and the community;
- a process of *sequential learning,* with knowledge building upon knowledge and practice upon practice. People gradually developed the religious competencies and appetites necessary to appreciate and

benefit from later practices and lessons. There remained reserved knowledge and practice, things for which the initiated had to demonstrate themselves adequately prepared and formed;

- an apprenticeship with a church member, with the latter acting as an exemplar or role model for the neophyte. Processes of mimetic, or imitative learning, seemed of central importance;
- materials of instruction, most of which … were steeped in narratives of Jesus, stories of Israel and the church, and parables of the Kingdom;
- formal examination of candidates, with rejection a live possibility;
- obligations on the receiving community to live up to the standards expected of the catechumen and to walk with the newly baptized along the path of discipleship;
- a developed capacity for an interior spiritual life – in other words, the ability to pray as a Christian.

With such a process of formation as that of the early church, one could learn the faith (or a foreign language, to use [George] Lindbeck's metaphor) and come to inhabit its world. With such a formation process, I suspect, one could learn just about anything. But in our day, amidst the ceaseless flow of television, ubiquitous advertising and marketing messages, and interwoven data networks, processes of making Christians in a serious way are severely compromised. ...

Living in Television's World

... To argue as I do, that global culture industries influence significantly the maintenance and reproduction of the Christian community, is necessarily an argument built at least in part on speculative materials. If Christianity as a lived and incarnate movement transmits its heritage in the ways I think it does and if major culture industries work as I suggest they do ... , then it does not seem unreasonable to suggest conflicts in their fundamental cognitive, communal, and psychosocial processes. In this conflict, I argue that thus far the powers of religious formation have been overmatched by the formative capacities of television and other culture industries.

Although other analysts have sought to argue that religious formation remains healthy and well, much of that literature sees conventional behavioral or ideological evidence (church attendance, reported belief in God, etc.) as proof of the enduring effectiveness of religious socialization ... At the other end, media apologists and some scholars in the cultural studies movement have gone to great lengths to deny that culture industries (television, advertising) have *any* "power" or socially significant effects. ...

Implications for Christian Formation

Time Bandits

The first way through which global culture industries undermine practices of Christian formation is the easiest to present. Time spent with television, with recorded music, radio, movies, and the like is almost always time not spent being involved in the sorts of things that form people in practices and affections relevant to the radical demands of the gospel. Entering the world of commodified media, especially television, is so painless, so seductive in terms of form and content, that the hours not spent sleeping or working get absorbed – gradually but in large numbers – into the media whirl. If learning to live, think, and feel through the gospel requires serious learning and apprenticeship for most

people, the time-sponge called television leaves no time for such efforts. One would be hard-pressed to learn *any* demanding set of skills or competencies with the amount of time most Catholics in advanced industrial countries devote to their faith tradition. On the other hand, there are few competencies that *cannot* be acquired with 3 to 4 hours per day of time invested – and people in the West use that much time to develop "competence" in television-watching. I am not so stupid to assume that, were TV to disappear tomorrow, people would transfer all their newfound free time to becoming radical disciples of Jesus – indeed, that is the last thing I would expect ... I do know, however, that so long as people watch such large amounts of television (and work longer hours to pay for the products television has enticed them to buy ...), the gospel will remain a tepid nonessential.

We know how much time people invest with global culture industries. How much, under present circumstances, do they invest in expressing, deepening, or challenging their faith? Recall that behavioral measures of religious involvement (worship attendance, church activities, etc.) tend to be higher in the United States than in other advanced industrial countries (and self-reporting, typical of most U.S. studies, tends to exaggerate involvement). In the United States, according to the most ambitious study of Catholic parish life, only 3 percent of parish-registered Catholics spend 25 hours per month (roughly 6 hours per week) on parish activities outside Mass ... ; remember that for most American families (Catholic and non-Catholic), television viewing engages them 20 to 25 hours *per week*, or between three and four times as much. The percentages of these high-involvement Catholics would likely be even lower using a larger definition of Catholic membership than that used in this study. ... Such ratios may produce large numbers of experts on sitcoms and televised sports, but they won't produce saints, martyrs, teachers, or exemplars of the gospel's radical world.

Development of Christian sensibilities via printed media is, if possible, even less promising. In the course of a year, most American Catholics will read no books on contemporary or classical Catholicism, will subscribe to no Catholic periodicals (diocesan or independent, regional or national) – will do nothing, in short, to familiarize themselves with contemporary expression of the faith, diverse theological insights into contemporary problems, or even add to their information base regarding the faith tradition to which they are nominal adherents. The major source for news on Catholicism for American Catholics is the secular media. Under competitive pressures, most news organizations have eliminated specialized beat coverage in labor, religion, minority affairs, and the like, leaving it to nonspecialist reporters to fare as best they can. When the news media cover religion, it is to focus on controversy, scandal, the unusual, or freakish. Such coverage is of no help in nurturing an adult understanding of faith. Most adult Catholics in the United States have been more thoroughly "formed" in their affections and desires by television culture than by the gospel. ...

The Invasion of Social Space, the Collapse of Separation

... As I have argued elsewhere, the dominant ecclesiology of the Catholic Church in the United States and other advanced industrial countries is "loose" rather than "tight." A loose ecclesiology sees no fundamental incompatibilities between the gospel and the world and therefore sees no need for the Church to maintain any meaningful distance (sociologically or theologically) from the dominant culture. Churches with a loose ecclesiology do not demand or construct space apart, even on a modest scale, from postfordist [late industrial] culture for purposes of Christian formation; consequently they make possible people formed more by the gospel of wealth than the gospel of Jesus, people whose affective rhythms harmonize with the 15-second commercial and jump-cut better than the liturgical calendar.

With little or no social or theological space of their own, without the capacity to develop Christian affections and practices, the Catholic and mainline Protestant churches have left people to cobble together their own "spiritualities" from commercial culture, nationalist ideologies, and the fragments of Christian and other religious traditions. What emerges all too often is less than the sum of the parts, usually privileging the acquisitive, feel-good messages of the culture industries and bereft of critical capacities (except for the sort of self-criticism that can be assuaged by commercialist interventions). This sort of do-it-yourself spirituality (called "Sheila-ism" by Bellah and his colleagues), I argue, is utterly incapable of radical practices aimed at peace, the option for the poor, or any demanding exercises in transcending self-interest. There is no Amos or Jeremiah, no "Woe to you rich" in the canon of Sheila-ism. ...

Symbolic Predators

Learning to become a Christian has always involved more than learning doctrine. Especially (but not exclu-

sively) in the Catholic tradition, it has also involved learning how to respond to sacred symbols of the faith, how to use holy symbols as aids in prayer and meditation, and how to learn the stories, roles, and exemplars of faith through imagery, symbol, and sacrament. For Christian formation to work best, there must be some coherence to the sacred symbols employed by the Church in any given era (which does not preclude gradual change in the meaning of those symbols over time). While Christian formation does not require the non-Christian world to participate in the symbolic universe of Christians, the process is impeded when outside forces threaten to overwhelm, undermine, or drown out the communicative functions of religious symbols and images.

In recent decades, global culture industries like television and advertising have begun to exploit religious imagery in ever more overt, crass, and trivial ways. They have come to operate as "symbolic predators," cultural parasites seeking to profit from repositories of meaning and socialization they did not create and which they weaken by their encroachment. ...

Conclusion

... The amount of time invested by Christians in the enterprises of global culture industries (in advanced industrial countries and, increasingly, in other parts of the world), the seriousness with which these are pursued, and the surrender of Christians to the influences of these enterprises – all of these make authentic Christian formation increasingly difficult in ways not known to earlier generations. The "orchestrators of attention" benefit from techniques that may be more effectively distracting than the medieval festivals, the excesses of Corinth, or devotees of Canaanite cults.

To the extent that Catholics and other Christians have managed to resist the leveling and homogenizing effects of heavy television immersion ..., it is due largely to the persistence of socialization structures and habits developed in the times before media inundation. These socialization structures and processes, when deep and effective, offered the potential for critical reception of mediated flow, a chance (albeit limited) to be the "active audience" so celebrated by many cultural studies scholars. The capacity of audiences to construct "critical readings," or "subversive interpretations," of media texts, it seems to me, presupposes the presence and vitality of nonmedia ways of "forming" persons into an alternative story. And it is precisely these other ways of "forming" people that are withering in the cultural environment of postfordist capitalism.

"Making Christians" is a demanding process under the best of conditions – since the beginning, many interested persons have walked away when confronted with the radical demands of the gospel (Lk 18:18–23). In our day, after centuries of understating the demands of the Christian life, church leaders confront a situation in which the thin formation offered to the majority of Catholics is so easily overwhelmed by the global culture industries that have captured and monopolized the attention of nearly everyone in advanced industrial countries. Christians spend thousands of hours a year interacting with complex systems that, in ways not fully understood, impact our desires, temperament, predispositions, and sense of normality. Far from being distinctive in themselves, Christians see their once-distinctive stories and symbols deployed against them in efforts to make them buy, desire, and dream like everyone else. Liberal reform notions to the contrary, the main "problem" with global culture industries is not "bad" content and will not be addressed with "better" content. The church does not gain if the 20 to 30 hours of TV viewing each week changes from cops and sleaze to socially uplifting messages – it wouldn't gain from 20 to 30 hours of TV viewing of religious programming, for that matter. With so many hours of human existence in the thrall of commercial culture industries, with human attention surrounded by barkers and enticers and noisemakers, the quiet but single-minded call to the gospel cannot be heard.

Winning back members of the Body of Christ will not be done by imitating the techniques of the culture industries. Those who can be ransomed will be drawn to a radically reformed and revitalized vision of the church and its role in Jesus' mission – or they will not be ransomed at all.

Chapter Ten

Good Relationships

The questions addressed in this chapter cover three broad areas. What is the purpose and what is to be the nature of regular and sustained human interaction? What is the purpose and what is to be the form and quality of intimate and passionate human interaction? Are there specific kinds of relationships (for example, same-sex relationships) that may only ever be "regular and sustained," and may never be "intimate and passionate"?

Friendship

Friendship is a greater theme in ancient literature than in contemporary discourse. For Aristotle, *philia* (friendly love) is the virtue that holds the city-state together. Friendship depends on *koinonia* (community) – such as kinship, citizenship, a common project, or simple common humanity. There are three kinds of friendship – the noble, the pleasant, and the useful. For Cicero, friendship is "an accord in all things, human and divine, conjoined with mutual good will and affection." He sees friendship as arising from nature and not from need.

The Old Testament offers several examples of notable friendships, including Ruth and Naomi, David and Jonathan, and Esther and Mordecai, together with

warnings against false friends. The New Testament offers the fundamental command to love God and to love one's neighbor as oneself, but there remains a tension around whether these two loves are in any sense the same and whether the notion of neighbor challenges or supplants the notion of friend.

Augustine's work highlights several unresolved areas in friendship. Is love of self the opposite of loving God, or is it the same as loving God? Is another Christian a brother/sister or a friend?

For Thomas Aquinas, love is "to will good to someone," and this means there are two kinds of love – friendship-love (for the friend themselves) and desiring-love (for the goods we seek to acquire for the friend). But Aquinas insists these two loves are complementary. Our love for God is more the former than the latter, because God is greater than any of the benefits God brings us. In other words we love God more than ourselves. But love of self is next to love of God, and comes before love of neighbor.

The readings below reflect the wide range of themes explored in literature about friendship. C. S. Lewis seeks definitions and expressions that do not require ecclesial commitments; Mary Daly offers a provocative account that stresses a level of friendship only women can know; and Aelred places friendship in relation to friendship with God.

Universal

C. S. Lewis, *The Four Loves*

Clive Staples Lewis (1898–1963) was an Irish literature scholar at Oxford University who became a noted Anglican apologist after a conversion experience in the 1920s. *The Four Loves* explores the nature of pleasure, and then divides love into four Greek terms: affection, friendship, eros, and charity.

Affection (*storge*) is fondness through familiarity, especially between family members or people who have otherwise found themselves together by chance. *Eros* is passionate desire. Lewis warns that such love begins to be a demon the moment it begins to be a god. The greatest love is charity (*agape*), an unconditional love directed towards one's neighbor which is not dependent on any lovable qualities in that neighbor.

Friendship (*philia*) is a strong bond between those who share a common interest or activity. Friendship is narrower than mere companionship: it only exists if it is "about" something beyond itself. It is the least *natural* of loves, for it is not necessary like either affection (rearing a child), eros (creating a child), or charity (providing for a child). Because the relationship is selective, it is inevitably exclusive. Of the four loves, friendship has the least connection with impulse or emotion. It is the most admirable of loves because it looks not at the beloved but at something else – the substance or basis of the relationship. This frees the relationship from jealousy.

C. S. Lewis. *The Four Loves*. London: Geoffrey Bles, 1960. From Chapter 4, "Friendship," pages 69–85, 102–5. Copyright © 1960 by Helen Joy Lewis and renewed 1988 by Arthur Owen Barfield, reproduced by permission of Houghton Mifflin Harcourt Publishing Company.

To the Ancients, Friendship seemed the happiest and most fully human of all loves; the crown of life and the school of virtue. The modern world, in comparison, ignores it. We admit of course that besides a wife and family a man needs a few "friends." But the very tone of the admission, and the sort of acquaintanceships which those who make it would describe as "friendships," show clearly that what they are talking about has very little to do with that *Philia* which Aristotle classified among the virtues or that *Amicitia* on which Cicero wrote a book. It is something quite marginal; not a main course in life's banquet; a diversion; something that fills up the chinks of one's time. How has this come about?

The first and most obvious answer is that few value it because few experience it. And the possibility of going through life without the experience is rooted in that fact which separates Friendship so sharply from both the other loves. Friendship is – in a sense not at all derogatory to it – the least *natural* of loves; the least instinctive, organic, biological, gregarious and necessary. It has least commerce with our nerves; there is nothing throaty about it; nothing that quickens the pulse or turns you red and pale. It is essentially between individuals; the moment two men are friends they have in some degree drawn apart together from the herd. Without Eros none of us would have been begotten and without Affection none of us would have been reared; but we can live and breed without Friendship. …

Those who cannot conceive Friendship as a substantive love but only as a disguise or elaboration of Eros betray the fact that they have never had a Friend. The rest of us know that though we can have erotic love and friendship for the same person yet in some ways nothing is less like a Friendship than a love-affair. Lovers are always talking to one another about their love; Friends hardly ever about their Friendship. Lovers are normally face to face, absorbed in each other; Friends, side by side, absorbed in some common interest. Above all, Eros (while it lasts) is necessarily between two only. But two, far from being the necessary number for Friendship, is not even the best. …

… [T]rue Friendship is the least jealous of loves. Two friends delight to be joined by a third, and three by a fourth, if only the newcomer is qualified to become a real friend. They can then say, as the blessed souls say in Dante, "Here comes one who will augment our loves." For in this love "to divide is not to take away." Of course the scarcity of kindred souls – not to mention practical considerations about the size of rooms and the audibility of voices – set limits to the enlargement of the circle; but within those limits we possess each friend not less but more as the number of those with whom we share him increases. In this, Friendship exhibits a glorious "nearness by resemblance" to Heaven itself where the very multitude of the blessed (which no man can number) increases the fruition which each has of God. For every soul, seeing Him in her own way, doubtless communicates that unique vision to all the rest. That, says an old author, is why the Seraphim in Isaiah's vision are crying "Holy, Holy, Holy" *to one another* (*Isaiah* VI, 3). The more we thus share the Heavenly Bread between us, the more we shall all have. ...

Friendship arises out of mere Companionship when two or more of the companions discover that they have in common some insight or interest or even taste which the others do not share and which, till that moment, each believed to be his own unique treasure (or burden). The typical expression of opening Friendship would be something like, "What? You too? I thought I was the only one." We can imagine that among those early hunters and warriors single individuals – one in a century? one in a thousand years? – saw what others did not; saw that the deer was beautiful as well as edible, that hunting was fun as well as necessary, dreamed that his gods might be not only powerful but holy. But as long as each of these percipient persons dies without finding a kindred soul, nothing (I suspect) will come of it; art or sport or spiritual religion will not be born. It is when two such persons discover one another, when, whether with immense difficulties and semi-articulate fumblings or with what would seem to us amazing and elliptical speed, they share their vision – it is then that Friendship is born. And instantly they stand together in an immense solitude.

Lovers seek for privacy. Friends find this solitude about them, this barrier between them and the herd, whether they want it or not. They would be glad to reduce it. The first two would be glad to find a third. ...

The co-existence of Friendship and Eros may also help some moderns to realise that Friendship is in reality a love, and even as great a love as Eros. Suppose you are fortunate enough to have "fallen in love with" and married your Friend. And now suppose it possible that you were offered the choice of two futures: "*Either* you two will cease to be lovers but remain forever joint seekers of the same God, the same beauty, the same

truth, *or else*, losing all that, you will retain as long as you live the raptures and ardours, all the wonder and the wild desire of Eros. Choose which you please." Which should we choose? Which choice should we not regret after we had made it? ...

When I spoke of Friends as side by side or shoulder to shoulder I was pointing a necessary contrast between their posture and that of the lovers whom we picture face to face. Beyond that contrast I do not want the image pressed. The common quest or vision which unites Friends does not absorb them in such a way that they remain ignorant or oblivious of one another. On the contrary it is the very medium in which their mutual love and knowledge exist. One knows nobody so well as one's "fellow." Every step of the common journey tests his metal; and the tests are tests we fully understand because we are undergoing them ourselves. Hence, as he rings true time after time, our reliance, our respect and our admiration blossom into an Appreciative Love of a singularly robust and well-informed kind. If, at the outset, we had attended more to him and less to the thing our Friendship is "about," we should not have come to know or love him so well. You will not find the warrior, the poet, the philosopher or the Christian by staring in his eyes as if he were your mistress: better tight beside him, read with him, argue with him, pray with him.

In a perfect Friendship this Appreciative Love is, I think, often so great and so firmly based that each member of the circle feels, in his secret heart, humbled before all the rest. Sometimes he wonders what he is doing there among his betters. He is lucky beyond desert to be in such company. Especially when the whole group is together, each bringing out all that is best, wisest, or funniest in all the others. Those are the golden sessions; when four or five of us after a hard day's walking have come to our inn; when our slippers are on, our feet spread out towards the blaze and our drinks at our elbows; when the whole world, and something beyond the world, opens itself to our minds as we talk; and no one has any claim on or any responsibility for another, but all are freemen and equals as if we had first met an hour ago, while at the same time an Affection mellowed by the years enfolds us. Life – natural life – has no better gift to give. Who could have deserved it? ...

The mass of the people ... are hopelessly mistaken in their belief that every knot of friends came into existence for the sake of the pleasures of conceit and superiority. They are, I trust, mistaken in their belief that every Friendship actually indulges in these pleasures.

But they would seem to be right in diagnosing pride as the danger to which Friendships are naturally liable. Just because this is the most spiritual of loves the danger which besets it is spiritual too. Friendship is even, if you like, angelic. But man needs to be triply protected by humility if he is to eat the bread of angels without risk.

Perhaps we may now hazard a guess why Scripture uses Friendship so rarely as an image of the highest love. It is already, in actual fact, too spiritual to be a good symbol of Spiritual things. The highest does not stand without the lowest. God can safely represent Himself to us as Father and Husband because only a lunatic would think that He is physically our sire or that His marriage with the Church is other than mystical. But if Friendship were used for this purpose we might mistake the symbol for the thing symbolised. The danger inherent in it would be aggravated. We might be further encouraged to mistake that nearness (by resemblance) to the heavenly life which Friendship certainly displays for a nearness of approach. ...

[I]n Friendship ... we think we have chosen our peers. In reality, a few years' difference in the dates of our births, a few more miles between certain houses, the choice of one university instead of another, posting to different regiments, the accident of a topic being raised or not raised at a first meeting – any of these chances might have kept us apart. But, for a Christian, there are, strictly speaking, no chances. A secret Master of the Ceremonies has been at work. Christ, who said to the disciples "Ye have not chosen me, but I have chosen you," can truly say to every group of Christian friends "You have not chosen one another but I have chosen you for one another." The Friendship is not a reward for our discrimination and good taste in finding one another out. It is the instrument by which God reveals to each the beauties of all the others. They are no greater than the beauties of a thousand other men; by Friendship God opens our eyes to them. They are, like all beauties, derived from Him, and then, in a good Friendship, increased by Him through the Friendship itself, so that it is His instrument for creating as well as for revealing. At this feast it is He who has spread the board and it is He who has chosen the guests. It is He, we may dare to hope, who sometimes does, and always should, preside. Let us not reckon without our Host.

Subversive

Mary Daly, *The Fire of Female Friendship*

Mary Daly (b. 1928) is a radical post-Christian feminist who taught for many years at Boston College in Massachusetts. Her work falls squarely into the third of the three categories of feminist theology described in our treatment of subversive ethics. Daly's book *Beyond God the Father* (1973) explains and seeks to overcome male dominance in the interpretation and practice of Western Christianity. She develops a style of coining a new vocabulary made up of allusive and carefully crafted puns and parodies of conventional language. One such term is *Gyn/Ecology*, the title of her 1978 work, subtitled *The Metaethics of Radical Feminism*. Here she describes the "religion of patriarchy" – those patterns of life that perpetuate and uphold patriarchy.

In this passage she articulates a notion of friendship from what she sometimes calls the Background. (The foreground is the patriarchal realm, while the Background is the female world.) The language resonates as follows. Daly notes that the word Hag derives from an Old English word meaning harpy or witch. For Daly, *Hags* are strong, creative, self-directed women. Playing on the meanings of the word haggard, Daly describes Haggard women as "those who are intractable, willful, wanton, unchaste, and, especially, those who are reluctant to yield to wooing." *Crones* are described as the long-lasting Hags; "a woman becomes a Crone as a result of Surviving early stages of the Otherworld Journey and therefore having dis-covered depths of courage, strength, and wisdom in her self." Daly refers to the work of uncovering the lives of such women as Hag-ology (rather than hagiography), and to the writing of women's history as Crone-ology. The term *Fury* is essentially synonymous with Hag ("As Furies, women in the tradition of the Great Hags reject the curse of compromise," i.e., of allowing themselves to be wooed by men).

Mary Daly. *Gyn/Ecology: The Metaethics of Radical Feminism.* Boston: Beacon Press, 1978, 1990. From Chapter 9, "Sparking: The Fire of Female Friendship," pages 367–73, 382–4.

The Radical Friendship of Hags

It is Crone-logically important to re-call that the word *friend* is derived from an Old English term meaning to love, and that it is akin in its roots to an Old English word meaning free. The radical friendship of Hags means loving our own freedom, loving/encouraging the freedom of the other, the friend, and therefore *loving freely.* To those who might object that the word *friend* is an "old word," Crones who know what radical female friendship is can reply that it is indeed an Old Word and that we are re-calling it, re-claiming it as our heritage. The identity named by the Old Word *friend* is from our own Background. It names our Presence to each other on the Journey. It cannot be experienced by those who are under the spell of the Prepossessors. Nor can it be experienced by those who feel the need to prepossess others, for this need is evidence of inability to be radically alone, and thus of inability to be a friend. It is this lack that is hidden by the fraudulent claims of patriarchal males who name themselves The Proprietors of friendship itself, who propagate the Lie that "only men can be friends."

Crones journeying together find after a while that one of the most difficult parts of the journey is discovering the meaning of *together.* Those who have been journeying long enough to know Crone-ology can recall the euphoria experienced at the discovery of sisterhood. True, we had been "together" with women before we had learned to call our Selves feminists. But these prefeminist groupings had been essentially collections *of* women rather than *for* women. Then, with the rise of feminism, some women found each other, came to know each other in new ways. ...

There are many experiences which throw women back into a sense of loneliness and isolation. For example, many women who have experienced, as a result of coming to feminist consciousness, a burning desire to study, have found that precisely because of this deep awareness, patriarchal "education" is almost too disgusting to endure. Others, having struggled with a passion for justice to attain certain goals, for example, professional careers, have found that their very success turns to ashes when they realize the shoddiness of the professions. Crones are tempted, then, to lean upon friends/lovers out of frustration. However, when women bond out of weakness, there is a danger of victimizing each other. Searching for words to analyze this dilemma, Crones find that we have inherited a contaminated language. ...

Sisters and Friends

Women finding and creating deep bonds with each other seek to use the contaminated words of our patriarchal false heritage to express these. Women finding each other speak of sisters, friends, lovers. Yet the words often mysteriously bend back upon themselves, forming boomerangs rather than instruments for expression of bonding. Since the terms are all polluted with patriarchal associations, they function not only as means of expression, but also as mind pollutants.

Crones can begin to unsnarl the semantic problems that blind us into binding instead of bonding by examining some male definitions and distinctions. J. Glenn Gray offers the following enlightening distinction between male comradeship and friendship: "The essential difference between comradeship and friendship consists ... in a heightened awareness of the self in friendship and in the suppression of self-awareness in comradeship."

Since brotherhood/fraternity are roughly equivalent to male comradeship, males also perceive a sharp contrast between the bonding designated by these terms and their "bonding" in friendship.

Women breaking away from the feminine condition often tend at first to imitate male comradeship, initially misperceiving sisterhood as something like the female equivalent of brotherhood. However, Crones who have persisted in the Otherworld Journey have come to know deeply that sisterhood, like female friendship, has at its core the affirmation of freedom. Thus sisterhood differs radically from male comradeship/brotherhood, which functions to perpetuate the State of War.

Since sisterhood is deeply like female friendship, rather than being its opposite (as in the case of male semantic counterparts) it is radically Self-affirming. In this respect it is totally different from male comradeship/brotherhood, in which individuals seek to lose their identity. The difference between sisterhood and male comradeship, which is disguised by an apparent similarity of terms, would be almost impossible to exaggerate. An important clue to the essence of this difference is the fact that the epitome of male bonding in comradeship is experienced in war. Gray writes: "In mortal danger, numerous soldiers enter into a dazed condition in which all sharpness of consciousness is lost. When in this state they can be caught up into the fire of communal ecstasy and forget about death by losing their individuality, or they can function like cells in a military organism, doing what is expected of them because it has become automatic."

Such male merging in "the fire of communal ecstasy" or as "cells in a military organism" is necrophilic self-loss. In contrast to this, the Fire of Sisterhood results from the Sparking of Female Selves who are finding each other. It is the unleashing of biophilic energy. Furies spark new ideas, new words, new images, new feelings, new life, New Be-ing. This is the Fire of biophilic Self-finding. This Fire, unlike the male warrior's ecstasy, which causes him to stand outside himself, enables the Self-centering Spinster/Voyager to burn away the internalized false selves, so that she *is* deeper within her Self and outside the State of Possession, the fathers' foreground.

Since Sisterhood is the expression of biophilic energy burning through the encasements of the Necrophilic State of Staledom, it is more complex than mere male monogender merging. Since Bonding Furies are not primarily concerned with fighting, but with breaking boundaries, bounding free, our ecstasy is totally other than "war ecstasy." However, Crones also know that since the Female Self, who is Friend to her Self, is The Enemy of patriarchy, the bonding of our Selves is perceived by the warriors as the Ultimate Threat to be shot down with every big gun available. Given such conditions, besieged Furies *do* fight back, and thus there is a warrior element in Sisterhood. There is, then, an element in Haggard bonding which is "us versus a third," and which is Positively Furious. Yet Crones know that this warrior aspect of Amazon bonding becomes truly dreadless daring only when it is focused beyond fighting. Our inherited vocabulary is inadequate to express this complexity and its inherent priorities, since it has been dwarfed to accommodate the pale male experience of bonding. …

Far from being opposites, sisterhood and female friendship are not clearly distinct. A feminist thinks of her close friends as sisters, but she knows that she has many sisters – women extremely close in their temperaments, vision, commitment – whom she has never met. Sometimes she meets such women and some conversation unmasks the similarities between them. She may have an uncanny feeling that she has known these women for years, that the present conversation is merely one in a series of many with these women. The proximity that she feels is not merely geographic/spatial. It is psychic, spiritual, in the realm of inner life-time. She senses gynaesthetically that there is a convergence of personal histories, of wave-lengths. She knows that there is a network of communication present, and that on some level, at least potentially, it exists among women who have never met or heard of each other. Because of limitations of energy, time, space, these women are not actually her friends, but they are sisters, potential friends.

Only those who have the strength to be friends have the strength to bond in sisterhood. This sets sisterhood totally apart from male brotherhood or comradeship, which at best is a transitory and shallow substitute, dependent upon emergencies, upon violence, and upon the existence of The Enemy. Since the core, the Soul-Spark of sisterhood is friendship, it does not essentially depend upon an enemy for its existence and continued becoming. This friendship is the ultimate State of Enmity in relation to the War State, for it is the radical withdrawal of energy from warring patriarchy and transferral of this energy to women's Selves. Sisterhood exists precisely where women have found something better than the War State. …

Women loving women do not seek to lose our identity, but to express it, dis-cover it, create it. A Spinster/Lesbian can be and often is a deeply loving friend to another woman without being her "lover," but it is impossible to be female-identified lovers without being friends and sisters. The Presence of Enspiriting Female Selves to each other is a creative gynergetic flow that may assume different shapes and colors. The sparking of ideas and the flaming of physical passion emerge from the same source. The bonding of woman-loving women survives its transformations because its source is the Sister-Self. It survives because the very meaning of this bonding is Surviving, that is, Super-living. It is biophilic bonding. …

Separation: Room of One's Own

Whereas discussions of relations between men and women eulogize the so-called complementarity of opposites, an Amazonian analysis of female friendship/love dis-covers the fact that the basis of woman-identified relationships is neither biological differences nor socially constructed opposite roles. As Jan Raymond has observed, rather than accepting a standardized "difference" (femininity), Lesbians/Spinsters find in our authentic likeness to each other the opportunity to exhibit and develop genuine differences. Rather than relying upon stereotypic role relationships, Amazon friends/lovers/sisters cast our Selves into a creative variety of developing relationships with each other. Since there are no models, no roles, no institutionalized relationships to fall back upon, we move together and apart in ever-varying patterns of relating. ...

Paradoxically, then, it is the likeness of women that makes room for our otherness, our wildness, our strangeness. The creation of separate female-identified psychic, mythic, semantic, physical spaces is necessary for likeness and wild otherness to grow. Each individual Amazon must have such room of her own, and she must be free to communicate the light and warmth generated in the privacy of her own room to the hearts/hearths of other Hags, and to receive their luminous energy.

Isolation of female-identified women from each other – a basic tactic of patriarchy – does not quench the individual woman's Spark, but contains it in a dampening environment. Each such woman, locked into the damp dungeon assigned to her by the misogynistic State, must struggle to maintain her own sense of reality against the prevailing lies. When she makes contact with even one other Sparking Self, the combination is conflagration. Each woman sees her own knowledge of reality confirmed in her sister. The possessors' spell is broken. Their prisons are reduced to ashes as these Sparking Selves energize and re-energize each other, giving each other the incendiary incentive. ...

As this Sparking communication occurs, Hags do not haggle over "equality," for we know there is no equality among unique Selves. Noting that one definition of the term equal is "capable of meeting the requirements of a situation or a task," Jan Raymond observes that what each asks of the other is that she be equal to the task at hand. Crones expect and en-courage each other to become sister pyrotechnists, building the fire that is fueled by Fury, the fire that warms and lights the place where we can each have a loom of our own, where we can spin and weave the tapestries of Crone-centered creation.

Ecclesial

Aelred of Rievaulx, *Spiritual Friendship*

Aelred of Rievaulx (1110–1167) was a Cistercian abbot in Yorkshire, England, who, in common with many writers from the Benedictine monastic tradition, saw strict asceticism as a voluntary sharing in Christ's suffering in order to learn his way of love, and regarded the Song of Songs as the definitive allegory of mystical love. Aelred offers helpful distinctions between varieties of friendship. He delineates six kinds of inclination:

1 Spiritual – which can be holy or evil
2 Rational – which is admiration of virtue
3 Irrational – which is admiration of passing vanities
4 Dutiful – arising from service or gratitude
5 Natural – which is for relatives
6 Physical – arising from pleasant appearance – which can be good or neutral, but, if merely lust, is evil

We love our neighbor for one of three reasons: from nature – because they are like kin; from duty – because it is an obligation to love friends, even those we do not love as kin; or from the commandment – which ensures we love even enemies. The three loves – of self, of neighbor, and of God – are inseparable and complementary. "Each love is found in all, and all in each, nor can one be had without the other," although the love of God comes first. Unusually for his time, Aelred notes, "How beautiful it is that the second human being was taken from the side of the first, so that nature might teach us that human beings are equal and, as it were, collateral, and that there is in human affairs neither a superior nor an inferior, a characteristic of true friendship." Reflecting Cicero's contention that friendship is wisdom, Aelred transposed the language of 1 John 4:16 with the words, "God is friendship." If it were not for the Fall, which introduced avarice and envy, friendship would be evident as humankind's nature and destiny.

Aelred of Rievaulx. *Spiritual Friendship*. Trans. Mark F. Williams. Cranbury, NJ; London; Mississauga, Ontario: Associated University Presses, 1994. From Book I: What is Friendship? (pages 35–7); Book II: The Advantages of Friendship (pages 44–5); and Book III: The Requirements for Unbroken Friendship (pages 70–2, 77–81). Reprinted by permission of Associated University Presses.

What is Friendship?

37. Still, let us grant that, because of the similarity of emotions, even those friendships which are not true may be called friendships nonetheless, despite their being distinguished by certain marks from that friendship which is spiritual and therefore true. 38. So let us call one kind of friendship "carnal" and another "worldly" and yet another "spiritual." And carnal friendship is created by an agreement in vices, while hope of gain spurs on worldly friendship, and similarity of character, goals, and habits in life makes for a bond of friendship among good people. ...

42. Worldly friendship ... is created by desire for temporal goods and things. It is always full of deceit and deception; in it there is nothing certain, nothing constant, nothing secure. For this reason it is the sort of friendship that changes with fortune, and follows money. 43. Thus it is written: "He is a friend according to the time; and he will not remain fast on the day of tribulation." Take away the hope of gain, and immediately he will cease to be a friend. ...

45. For spiritual friendship, which is what we mean by true friendship, should be desired not with a view to any worldly good, nor for any reason extrinsic to itself, but from the worthiness of its own nature, and the feeling of the human heart, so that it offers no advantage or reward other than itself. 46. So the Lord says in the gospel of John, "I have chosen you, so that you may go and bear fruit," that is, so that you might love one another. For in this true friendship one makes progress by bettering oneself, and one bears fruit by experiencing the enjoyment of this increasing degree of perfection. And so spiritual friendship is born among good people through the similarity of their characters, goals, and habits in life. ...

The Advantages of Friendship

11. ... But what happiness, what security, what pleasure it is to have a friend "with whom you would dare to speak just as you would speak to yourself!" You would not fear to confide to a friend about your failings, nor would you blush to reveal to him your spiritual progress; and will you not entrust your plans for the future to the one to whom you have committed all the secrets of your heart? What then can be more pleasant than to unite one mind with another, and "to make one from two"? Among friends no boasting or suspicion need be feared, nor need one partner be saddened to receive correction from his friend, nor should the one note the other for having been praised and censure him for adulation. 12. "A friend," said the Wise Man, "is a medicine for life." And this is quite the case. For medicine is no more healthy or effective or excellent for our bodily wounds, than it is for us to have a friend who shows compassion to our every misfortune and shares our joy in every good thing. According to the Apostle, such friends bear one another's burdens, shoulder to shoulder with each other – except that each one bears his own injuries more lightly than those of his friend.

13. So friendship "makes favorable circumstances even more splendid, and adverse circumstances more bearable by sharing them." ...

14. Therefore, to the rich, friendship is like glory; to exiles, it is like a homeland; to the poor, it is like a family fortune; to the sick, it is like medicine; to the dead, it is like life; to the healthy, it is like grace; to the weak, it is like strength; to the strong, it is like a prize. ... [F]riendship is a path that leads very close to the perfection which consists of the enjoyment and knowledge of God, such that a man who is a friend of man is made into a friend of God, according to what the Savior said in the gospel: "Now I will not call you servants, but my friends." ...

The Requirements for Unbroken Friendship

62. In friendship there is nothing more outstanding than faithfulness, which seems to be both the nurse and the guardian of friendship. In all of life's turns, in adversity and prosperity, in joy and sadness, in delightful and bitter circumstances, it reveals itself to be comparable to friendship, holding in the same regard both the humble and the exalted, the poor and the rich, the strong and the weak, the well and the infirm. Thus the faithful man sees nothing in his friend that is alien to his own spirit; he honors virtue in its own proper place, but considers all other qualities external to his friend and does not test them much if he finds them present, nor seek them much if they are absent. 63. Still, this faithfulness is invisible when all is going well, but it comes to the fore in adversity. As someone has said, "In need, then, a friend is proved." The wealthy man has many friends, but a sudden decline into poverty shows whether they are true friends. "He who is a friend loves always," says Solomon, "and a brother is proved in straitened circumstances." ...

68. ... [O]ne must test a friend's intent. This is quite essential, for there are very many who recognize nothing good in human affairs unless it leads to some temporal gain. Thus these people love their friends just as they love their herds of cattle – "from them they hope to get" something useful. Indeed, they lack full spiritual friendship, which they ought to seek for its own sake – or rather, for God's sake and for its own sake; they do not contemplate the natural example of love in themselves, where its "strength and quality and magnitude" can be easily comprehended. 69. Our Lord and Savior himself prescribed for us the form of true friendship when he said, "Love your neighbor as yourself." Behold, here is the reflection of love: Do you love yourself? Yes, indeed, if you love God, and surely if you are the sort of person I described as worthy to be chosen for friendship. But do you think that you should give yourself some reward for this love of yourself? Not at all: Everyone holds himself dear. Therefore, unless you transfer this affection for yourself to another, and love your friend freely, because your friend is dear to you simply because of who he is, you will not be able to enjoy the pleasures of true friendship. 70. For then the person you love will become your alter ego once you have taken your esteem and poured it forth onto him. As the blessed Ambrose said, "Friendship does not exist to produce income, but rather is full of beauty and grace. Thus it is a virtue, not something to be acquired, because it is begotten not by money but by grace, not by bidding with prices but by competition in benevolence." Therefore the intent of the one you have chosen for friendship must be tested acutely, lest your friend desire to be joined with you simply out of hope for some kind of practical gain, thinking friendship more a matter of commerce than of grace.

This is why friendships among the poor are far more certain than those of the rich, since poverty removes the hope of gain from a friendship, so that it does not diminish but rather increases the joy of the friendship. 71. And so people oblige the rich so as to flatter them, but no one is disingenuous to a pauper. Whatever is granted to a pauper is genuine, because a friendship with a pauper lacks the inducements to envy. (By this I mean not that we should check a potential friend's social status, but that we should test his character.)

Thus one tests a friend's intent. If you see that your friend is more desirous of your goods than of yourself, and if he is always after some benefit which your diligence can provide – honor, wealth, glory, or freedom – if for all this you prefer the friendship of someone worthier than he, or (to be sure) if you are not able to provide him with what he seeks, you will easily see his intent in attaching himself to you. ...

90. ... It is a strong point of friendship that the superior becomes equal to the inferior. For often those who are lower in rank, class, dignity, or knowledge are received into friendship by those who outstrip them in some way. In these cases, it is proper for them to despise and to count as nothing, as mere vanity, whatever qualities come from sources other than nature. Instead, they should be mindful of the beauty of friendship, which is not decked out with silks and gems, nor enlarged by possessions or fattened with expensive

delicacies, not praised with high honors or inflated with dignities.

And so, returning to the principle of the origin of friendship, they should scrutinize the equality given by nature rather than the baubles which greed afford to mortals. 91. So also in friendship, which is the best gift of both nature and grace, the exalted come down and the lowly climb in status; the wealthy become poor and the poor abound in wealth; and so each partner shares his state with his friend, with the result that there is equality between them, as Scripture says: "He that gathered much did not have too much, and he that gathered little did not have too little." …

97. For those who do not maintain equality do not rightly cultivate friendship. Ambrose said, "Defer to a friend as you would to an equal; do not be ashamed to outstrip your friend in doing good. For friendship knows no pride." And so "a faithful friend is the medicine of life, and the grace of immortality." …

98. If we are expected to expend our money on behalf of our friends, how much more should we take account of our friends' advantages and needs! But everyone cannot do everything: one man has money in abundance, another has lands and possessions, a third has the gift of counsel, and yet another excels more in his positions of honor. In all these instances you should carefully consider what sort of person you should reveal yourself to be to your friend. Scripture deals well enough with money: "Spend your money on behalf of a friend," it says. But since a wise man has eyes in his head, we should do what the prophet says if we are ourselves members of the body and Christ is the head:

"My eyes are always on the Lord"; we should do this so that we can receive from him that formula for living about which it is written, "If anyone lacks wisdom, let him seek it from the Lord, who gives generously to all and does not reproach." 99. So you should give to a friend so as not to reproach him; do not look for gain in return; do not wrinkle your forehead, nor look the other way nor avert your eyes. Rather, with a serene and happy expression, and with pleasant speech, you should anticipate the request of a friend in need; help him with all goodwill, so that it seems you are granting his request without being asked. A man of honest spirit thinks nothing more embarrassing than to ask for a favor. Therefore, although there should be "one heart and one mind" between you and your friend, it is very harmful to your friendship if there is not also "one purse."

101. The wise man says that "men would lead the happiest life if they would get rid of these two words, 'my' and 'your.'" It is certain that a sanctified poverty offers much soundness to spiritual friendship, for although greed is destructive to friendship, once friendship is born it is certainly more easily preserved to the extent that the heart is found to be more pure of that contagion. However, there are other benefits in spiritual love, with which friends can render aid to each other. The first benefit is that friends are concerned for each other, pray for each other, one blushes for the other, another rejoices for the other, one mourns the fall of the other as he would his own, another regards the advantage of the other as his own.

The Family, Marriage, and Sex

The very considerable literature on the family, marriage, and sex can be grouped under three headings: when marriage and family go well, the boundaries of marriage and family, and when marriage and family go wrong.

The first area considers the disputed area of male and female complementarity, the ways marriage may be a means of grace, sexual intercourse as gift or threat, and the character of childhood. The second area considers whether sexual expression should be limited to marriage and whether and in what circumstances marriages may end. The third area considers the question of

whether children have rights and, if so, whether, how, and in what circumstances any bodies outside the family can or should intervene when family life has gone wrong.

In the modern era, these three areas – the goods, the boundaries, and the failures – are largely taken up by the three main strands of ethical discourse, respectively: universal ethics tends to concentrate on boundaries, subversive ethics is largely taken up with failures, and ecclesial ethics tends to look towards rearticulating goods. These themes are brought out amply in the passages below.

Universal

J. I. Packer, *Personal Standards*

James Packer (b. 1926) is a British-born Canadian Anglican with strong Calvinist commitments who has taught since 1979 at Regent College in Vancouver.

This article exhibits the general style of evangelical ethics in speaking with a universal voice. For example, in the first sentence "we" is used as a timeless descriptor of the human condition, in the third sentence as a contemporary Western collective pronoun. The list of those who "harp on sex endlessly" is long, but it is not clear whether artists, novelists, and others on the list are part of the "we" of the contemporary West or part of a "they" that lies outside the church.

The language of God's design, very accessibly expressed under the sequence of nature, disorder, and sanctification, locates sexuality within an ethic of creation and redemption. Packer's Calvinist logic appears in his notion of creation as fitting humanity to "to praise, serve, and glorify our Maker." The lament that Anglicans "were unanimous till very recently" hints at a declension narrative of the kind often found in ecclesial ethics. While compassion for gay and lesbian people is evident, such conditions are regarded as "skewed passions" and their sexual expression as "lapses." Perhaps the most significant paragraph is the first one under "The Family and the Call to Singleness," where Packer seamlessly harmonizes scriptural injunction, anthropological and sociological research, and human experience, in a way that most subversive approaches would find bewildering.

J. I. Packer. "Personal Standards." *Churchman* 111, 1 (1997): 19–26. [This article is a reprint of two chapters from Packer's Commentary on the Montreal Declaration of Anglican Essentials.] Available online at www.churchsociety.org/churchman/documents/ CMan_111_1_Packer.pdf. Reprinted by permission of *Churchman*.

The Standards of Sexual Conduct

Sexuality is a modern word that labels our biological gender, our experience of erotic attraction and mating urges, and our actions when these feelings are felt, as a single field of interest and study among the human sciences. The study itself is a very modern thing. The way we nowadays concentrate on sexuality, as if the deepest secret of life's meaning is hidden here, is historically unique. Artists, novelists, journalists, educationists, pop singers, media people, psychological pundits and counsellors, harp on sex endlessly; the pornography industry is able to rake in enormous sums of money by supplying demand; the advertising industry uses sex to sell cookies, clothes, cars, computers, cruises, cameras, and just about everything else; the sex-soddenness of modern minds can only be called stupendous. This is both demeaning and disturbing, doubly so when social pressure to act out our fantasies is strong, as today it is. The sexual revolution of the sixties that cracked up promiscuity as a recreational and therapeutic good; the establishing among young people in the seventies of a sexually experimental lifestyle; the AIDS plague of the eighties and nineties; and the drumbeat insistence of our pop culture that the greatest happiness on earth is found in good quality sexual intercourse, have together turned sexuality into a topic that is at once fascinating and fearful, titillating and traumatic, in a way that is not from any standpoint healthy either for individuals or for communal life. Bringing sex out into the open was expected to dispel sexual neuroses that had supposedly gripped our grandparents in the days when lifelong monogamous marriage was, if not invariable, at least usual. The effect of doing this, however, has actually been to make us far more neurotic and anxious on sexual subjects, and to render our marriages far less contented and stable, than was ever the case before. ...

Biblical Theology: God's Design

Biblical teaching on sexuality, on which Anglicans, with the rest of mainstream Christianity, were unanimous till very recently, can be summarized thus:

1. Our sexual *nature*, as such, is one strand in our identity as embodied persons (souls), or psycho-physical units, as we humans are sometimes called. God means us to live out his image, in which and for which he created us, through the material bodies he has given us. As is often said, God likes matter; he invented it; the whole physical universe displays his ingenuity with it, and the mind-boggling complexity, harmony, and adaptability of the human body is not the least part of this display. As our minds make possible for us modes of thinking, appreciating, planning, and relating that are not possible to animals, so our bodies make possible modes of experience, expression, enterprise and enjoyment that are not possible to angels. Human existence as God devised it is thus more varied and wide-ranging, and richer in its creative fusion of the intellectual and the emotional, than that of any other being in God's world. Now, the proper life's work of humankind, involving all our powers and energies, is to praise, serve, and glorify our Maker, and this requires that we relate both to him and to his creatures – first among these, our fellow-humans – in appropriate ways of admiration, valuation, and love. And this is where our sexuality comes in. Marriage and family are to be the building-blocks of society, and the use of our bodies in marital sexual intercourse (lovemaking) is meant to be a pilgrimage of mutual excitement and shared pleasure, divinely planned "not only for procreation" (though there is no procreation without it) "but also for the joyful expression of love, honour, and fidelity between wife and husband." That remains the formula for sexual action to the glory of God.

2. Our sexual *disorder* is however great and grievous, and has been so throughout the human race from the start. Humanity as we know it, in both ourselves and others, is fallen, inwardly disintegrated to a degree, and morally and spiritually misshapen. ... Sin is in essence playing God by self-centred self-service, with a mind-set that grabs rather than gives, especially where pleasure is concerned; so it was inevitable that in a sinful world God's delightful but delicate arrangement for the simultaneous joy-getting through simultaneous joy-giving of married couples would suffer. And so it does.

Because sin is self-indulgence, and the pleasure level of sexual action is high, exploitative sex, in which one partner uses the other in order to get a good feeling, abounds both within marriage and outside it, in the world of prostitution, where feelings become in effect a commodity for manufacture and sale. Again, because sin is lawless greed, the passion to possess sexually someone who is not your mate keeps recurring; lust joins hands with the equally sinful desire to dominate, and fornication, adultery, and child sexual abuse take place, if not in the flesh, then in the heart. Once more, because sin is egoism and sexual pleasure is a short-term ego-booster, rapists and seducers force sexual action on others by physical and psychological violence, anticipating a grand euphoric glow when it is done (which glow, be it said, does not always come: see 2 Samuel 13, especially verse 15). Victims of sexual violence are sometimes called sex slaves, but that phrase would apply even better to its lust-driven perpetrators. ... So many moderns are "sexually scarred" either as practitioners or as victims of sexual egoism and callousness, the "love" that is really self-absorbed lust, and it would be "sexual hypocrisy" (denial of the truth about ourselves) to pretend otherwise. Today's sexual mess is universal, and one way or another we are all in it together.

3. Our sexual *sanctification*, like every other part of God's renewing work in us, is real but not perfect in this world, and God's servants, like others, "struggle with ongoing sexual temptations" – temptations first to impurity of heart, which will then want to act itself out – all through their lives. There are, however, sources of strength for resistance, just as there is moral maturity to be gained through resistance. What Thomas Chalmers called "the explosive power of a new affection" will raise the hearts of the born-again above the mud flats of lust, and enable them to stop their ears against the lie told constantly by sexual desire, namely that its gratification is the most important thing in the world. A habit of watchfulness, and avoidance of persons, places and influences that tempt; fellowship, in which one shares one's struggles with fellow strugglers; prayer for the Holy Spirit's help, and keeping the eyes of one's faith fixed on Jesus as a model, mentor, and master (Heb 12:2); will make a big difference. Counselling may enable homosexuals to redirect their desires, though more often the skewed passions remain, and resisting them becomes a lifelong battle. As for married couples, they find that sustaining the quality of their mating as "the joyful expression of love, honour and fidelity" is by no means as easy as it sounds. For everyone, married or single, heterosexual or homosexual, living by God's sexual standards as they apply to oneself is a major task.

Congregations are corporately called to mutual nurture in Christ, and this requires of clergy and people together four things in the sphere of sex, as follows:

1   *Commitment* to God's sexual standards, which should be clearly taught in church; not, however, in isolation from the rest of Christian morality, nor in a legalistic way, as a workout in self-righteousness, but as part of the total truth of sanctification by the power of God. A communal cultivating of the virtues of modesty, self-control, restraint, and the capacity to feel shame, all of which our culture undermines, and all of which are integral to biblical holiness, will help very directly in establishing and maintaining this commitment.

2   *Care* for marriages, which are under constant attack in these days, and are not always seen as areas of vulnerability where pastoral support and help are required again and again. It never was the way of wisdom, and it is certainly not so today, to leave the marriages of Christians to look after themselves.

3   *Companionship* with single and homosexual individuals, for whom strong friendships with married and "straight" Christians prove constantly to be the most potent restraints from sexual lapses. Low self-esteem, which is common among the unmarried and those with same-sex inclinations, makes people specially vulnerable to emotionally-freighted temptations, and slow to reach out in friendship to those whom they see as different from themselves, and that means that the married and the "straight" must take the initiative in doing the reaching. This is a key element in healthy congregational life – healthy, that is, in the sense of practising authentic love.

4   *Compassion* for those who slip up sexually. While not compromising God's standards at convictional level, God's people must be quick to show neighbour-love to the pregnant unmarried, the unchaste gay or lesbian, and anyone else in sexual trouble. The pattern of neighbour-love in such cases is stated in Galatians 6:1–2: "Brothers, if someone is caught in a sin, you who are spiritual [Paul means, you who seek to live by the Holy Spirit's power] should restore him gently, but watch yourself, or you also may be tempted. Carry each other's burdens, and in this way you will fulfil the law of Christ."

The Family and the Call to Singleness

The idea of a family is of a stable human unit consisting of a father and a mother united in a permanent monogamous commitment, plus their children, with both generations linked to a wider kinship network (grandparents, aunts, uncles, nieces, nephews, cousins, in-laws, and so forth) – a network that is thought of as the family's "family circle." Differences from this in particular families and family patterns round the world are modifications of the basic idea. The Bible presents the family as the fundamental building-block of the human community since the world began, and lays upon us by precept and example the task of glorifying God through the quality of our family life. Anthropological and sociological research confirms that the nuclear family, "extended" when members of the kinship network live in the family home, is society's most primitive institution, and must ever be so if the needs of child-rearing are to be met. As experience constantly shows, there is no substitute for teaching and training in the family circle if we want our children to become mature and wise adults.

In the ideal family home, children find their shelter, space, and food, their base for exploring the world around them, and their primary experience of what an old slogan called "tender loving care" – care for their health, their growth, their standards of behaviour, their education, their reputation, their interests, their attitudes, values, and beliefs, their relationships, and their future as wage-earners, contributors to society, spouses and, ultimately, parents. In that ideal home children enjoy warm, intimate, and consistently dependable relations with their parents and others in the family circle, and are there given object lessons in self-discipline and prudence, reliability and responsibility, altruism and love, and the nature of manly maleness and womanly femaleness. There, too, they learn practical and social skills, and find patient help when in due course they reach for independent identity as adolescents, for stability in their early married years, and for know-how when their own children come along. ...

To all that has been said the Bible adds one more vital item: that it is in the home that the faith is to be passed on. By word and action parents are to rear their children "in the training and instruction of the Lord" (Eph 6:2). The family is to function as a spiritual unit, all of whose members pray separately and together. The [Canadian] *Book of Common Prayer* [of 1962] provides a section of "Forms of Prayer to be Used in Families," and Anglicans not long ago encouraged each other with the slogan, "The Family that Prays Together Stays Together." It is the special responsibility of fathers, as heads of their homes, to take initiatives to see that this happens.

Subversive

Rosemary Radford Ruether, *Reimagining Families*

As ever with subversive ethics, there is a twofold focus – both dismantling the assumptions of universal ethics and reconstructing an alternative pattern made possible by the toppling of "universal" assumptions that are in fact based on the supremacy of the white middle-class Western male subject. This is never more the case for feminism than on the subject of the family, marriage, and sex. So much of the polemical dimension of feminism has begun as a critique of conventional portrayals of these issues.

More complex is establishing a vision for the family, marriage, and sex beyond patriarchy. This is Rosemary Radford Ruether's project in her book *Christianity and the Making of the Modern Family*. Her positive proposal falls almost entirely into what we have called the first category of feminism, restoring the universal paradigm. Terms like "equality and partnership of men and women" and "equitable sharing of wealth" express optimism about establishing a new paradigm based on autonomy and good will. Rejected also is any notion of gender complementarity (the second strand of feminism): "men and women each possess the full range of all human capacities." Choice and diversity are significant goods, when qualified by commitments that are "mutual, sustaining, and life-affirming." Hence, gay unions and a variety of other relationships should be affirmed. Domestic-partnership contracts should belong to the state not to the church, which should instead be the "preparer and blesser of covenants and healer of those who need to move away from covenants that have broken down."

Ruether concludes with an ecclesial vision: "The church, God's messianic people, is a new family, an alternative, liberated community of chosen kin through which we can taste the messianic banquet." In this she seeks a reconciling position between subversive and ecclesial ethics.

Rosemary Radford Ruether. *Christianity and the Making of the Modern Family.* Boston: Beacon Press, 2000. From Chapter 9, "Reimagining Families: Home, Work, Gender, and Faith," pages 206–8, 212–14, 225–6, 228–30. Copyright 2000 by Beacon Press. Reproduced with permission of Beacon Press in the format Textbook via Copyright Clearance Center.

A black and white bumper sticker, given to me by a gay male friend, adorns the back bumper of my car. It reads "Hate is not a family value." The slogan is a critique of the failure of the Christian Right's "family values" campaign to embody an ethic of justice and reconciliation in American society in the late twentieth century. That failure is rooted in the underlying premises of the Christian Right's views of family and society, which turn on a view of the "order of Creation" that (divinely) mandates patriarchal hierarchy of men over women, Christians over non-Christians, rich over poor. ...

An Ecofeminist Family Ethic

The reimagining of families by progressive people of faith demands more than just protest against these consequences of Christian Right views. It calls for the articulation of alternative values that promote a more authentic ethic of human relationships. The alternative ethic for postmodern family social values that I will propose in this chapter may best be defined as an "ecofeminist" ethic, one based on the equality and partnership of men and women in family, work, and society, and on the reconfiguring of work-family relations and economic and political hierarchies to foster a more equitable sharing of wealth within sustainable communities. ...

Basic to an ecofeminist ethic is the full and equivalent humanity of women in partnership with men. A feminist ethic rejects both gender hierarchy and gender complementarity as distortions of the full humanness of women and men, and sources of the unjust relationship between them. Men are neither natural nor divinely mandated "heads" over women, to whom women are called to submit and subordinate themselves. Nor is the relationship appropriately one of complementary differences, of "masculine" rationality and agency and "feminine" intuition and altruism.

Whatever nuances of differences in style may exist through biology and socialization, men and women each possess the full range of all human capacities. We need to see a social development through the life cycle by which men and women, women and women, men and men across generations can be friends and partners in mutual agency and self-giving, in interdependent flourishing through and with one another, rather than at the expense of one another. Good families are families that nurture this kind of mutuality in self-giving and receiving.

What this means in terms of family relations is an ethic of sharing that is truly equivalent. One should not flourish at the expense of the other. Committed relationship also means an acceptance of self-limitation. One decides to commit oneself to particular relationships, to building particular communities, by forgoing infinite possibilities. Each partner gives up some options for the sake of the wellbeing and development of the other, but in a way that is equitable and shared, rather than rooted in a gender hierarchy in which women do most of the deferring and men have a right to most of the flourishing. This can never be a fixed and finalized format, but must be one that calls for constant reformulation in a process of growth and change. …

Better Policies to Support Families

We need to support a variety of family and household patterns. These include the single householder; the gay or lesbian couple, including partners raising children by adoption, former marriages, or artificial insemination; the single parent, male or female; the two-earner heterosexual couple; the three- or four-generation family; families blended through divorce and remarriage; and cohabiting partnerships of two, three, or more people that may or may not include a sexual pair. This diversity is already the reality of American life.

The exigencies of life in America at the dawn of the third millennium A.D. mean that people must support one another through a diversity of relationships. In all of these they should be encouraged by religious bodies to be as mutual, sustaining, and life-affirming as possible. These values of mutuality and commitment to flourishing life are not lessened but rather expanded when they are affirmed in many forms, and not in one form only that marginalizes and denigrates all the other forms by which people are sustaining their lives in community. We need to unmask the rhetoric that claims

that the affirmation of "holy unions" for gay couples somehow demeans marriage for heterosexuals. All of our unions are made holier by expanding the options for faithful relationship and taking seriously their careful preparation and joyful blessing.

Both the church and the state have a stake in stable, committed partnerships that provide the framework for child-raising, sustaining the wellbeing of related people over a period of time, and caring for others in crisis, illness, and old age. But I submit that the role of the state and that of the church in affirming such relationships differ. It is time to uncouple the legal role of the state in defining domestic-partner contracts from the role of the church as the preparer and blesser of covenants. …

The church should get out of the business of being a legal agent for the state in making marriage contracts through the performance of weddings. Domestic-partnership contracts belong to the state and should be available in a variety of forms, covering not only heterosexual couples but also homosexual couples; single parents who wish to appoint other persons legal guardians of their children in case of crisis; single persons who wish to designate friends as responsible for their medical needs in time of illness; and those who want to name others as receivers of their medical benefits or property. …

Hallowing Covenant Relations

Once the church is out of the business of being a surrogate for the state in making legal contracts, it can be freed to focus on its more important roles as preparer and blesser of covenants and healer of those who need to move away from covenants that have broken down, moving on to new lives and new kinds of relationships with former partners. It is the church's job to guide the spirituality and ethics of deepening relationship into sacramental bonding and redemptive promise.

The life-cycle ceremonies that have been available to Christians have focused on three moments: monogamous heterosexual marriage for life, baptism, and confirmation of children (as well as sickness and death). While surely important, these are no longer adequate to the complex realities of society, including the more diverse forms of family, such as homosexual couples; the ten- to fifteen-year gap between puberty and marriage for many people, occupied by experimental sexual relations; and the breakdown of marriages in divorce. We need to find pastoral and liturgical forms that can help people in these diverse situations and stages of life, which are currently ignored by the church or rejected as sinful and without redeeming value. …

Reimagining Families as Redemptive Communities

[T]he family model promoted by the Christian Right has its origins in the ideology of Victorian white/middle-class America, not in the Bible. The Bible, comprising Hebrew Scripture and the New Testament, reflects a variety of family patterns common in its era(s), all quite different from the model of the Victorian nuclear family. In fact, if there is a normative view of the family to be found in the New Testament, based as it is on the teachings of Jesus, it is the antifamily perspective of the Jesus movement and the early Pauline churches, a perspective later challenged by the deutero-Pauline strata that tried to reinstate the family of patriarchal slavocracy. ...

The antifamily tradition of the New Testament was rooted in a critique of the family systems of the day as an expression of the demonic powers and principalities of a fallen world. Family was seen as a locus of pride, power, and possessions by elites that marginalized most poor people (particularly in the urban world of empires) and denied them the benefits of family. Family systems constructed a hierarchy of men over women, masters over slaves, the old over the young, ruling nations over conquered ones. Real community was proscribed between these separated categories of people.

The Christian church, by contrast, defined itself as a new family that broke down such separations and brought together men and women, former masters and slaves, Jews and Greeks, the "clean" and the socially despised in table fellowship and a new kinship in Christ. This new family set itself against the existing family systems from which its members had come. It saw itself as awaiting a final transformation of the world in the Kingdom of God, when all Creation could feast together at the messianic banquet and all oppression would be overcome. ...

Today we face the breakdown of [the] Victorian pattern of the idealized family, with its segregation of male and female in separate spheres of work and home. The question now becomes, Is there some new way of reading marriage, family, sex, and procreation theologically that can support a more just and more sustainable harmony of women and men, home and work?

A new vision of family, of home and work, needs to be based on the mutuality of whole human beings, not on the truncation of such beings into separate parts, home for women and work for men. Women and men as whole human beings participate in the entirety of life, sharing in family nurture as well as in the larger paid economy, culture, and politics. We need to imagine new ways to knit these together in more organic wholes, allowing for better harmony and balance between areas of life in which men and women both participate as equals.

Theologically, this requires first of all a clear and explicit rejection of the doctrine that holds that the patriarchal family of male headship and female subordination is the "order of creation," mandated by God. The patriarchal family in its various forms, from the slavocracy of antiquity to the Victorian nuclear family, is a human construct, not a divine mandate. In antiquity it was founded on an oppressive power that benefited dominant men at the expense of women and the servant/slave classes, while the Victorian version of the patriarchal ideal was achievable only by a well-paid male elite that denied women full human development. Maintaining this family model today spells poverty for those women who lack a male "breadwinner," and economic struggle for many families with only a single, male earner.

These family systems, then, not only are not of God, but partake of demonic distortions that impede justice and wellbeing for many. They manifest the powers and principalities of an alienated "world." This judgment of family as alien to God and contrary to redemptive community underlay the antifamily tradition of the Jesus movement and the early church. Today, as in the early church, we need to realize that becoming a redemptive community means reimagining the family. The church, God's messianic people, is a new family, an alternative, liberated community of chosen kin through which we can taste the messianic banquet.

Reimagining families as redemptive communities does not mean setting creation against redemption, sex against holiness, or the reproduction of bodies against the cultivation of souls. These dualisms defeated the early Christian critique of family, as well as its sacramental promise in Catholic theology. Rather, we need to reimagine a dynamic interrelation of creation and new creation, of the reproducing and renewing of life. *Eros* needs to be integrated into *philia*, and *philia* into *agape*, in deepening relationships among lovers, friends, and partners seeking to shape life-enhancing communities.

Making love will then indeed become sacramental, a means of grace for redemptive life. The union of Christ and the church, messianic hope and redemptive community, is anticipated and prefigured in the union of lovers becoming friends, builders of nurturing families, and partners in the effort to bring about the reign of God's peace and justice on Earth.

Ecclesial

Vigen Guroian, *An Orthodox Ethic of Marriage and Family*

Vigen Guroian (b. 1948) is an American theologian based at Loyola College, Baltimore, and writes out of the Armenian Orthodox tradition. This passage offers an uncompromising view of marriage that makes clear that marriage is more than a building-block of society in general. For Guroian, marriage and family build up the church by being a training ground for "the belief, the trust and the caring love absolutely necessary for happiness." His strong emphasis on creation hints at a more universal voice than many ecclesial accounts.

Guroian sees a "'natural' sacramentality" in marriage, rooted in the second chapter of Genesis and its account of the relationship of man and woman within the created order. For Guroian, "Christian marriage is the beginning of a 'small church,' the smallest and most important social unit of Christ's Body in the world." It is striking that Guroian sees sexual love and the union arising from it (and not procreation) as "the primary good of marriage." Despite the intimacy of this connection, marriage is not a private matter, but a "conjugal community of being" that is always a witness to the life of the church. Guroian insists that the Orthodox view of marriage is not "utilitarian; it is eschatological." In other words, marriage is not a means to some further end, but a depiction of the eternal life of the kingdom.

Vigen Guroian. *Incarnate Love: Essays in Orthodox Ethics.* Notre Dame: University of Notre Dame Press, 1987. From Chapter 4, "An Ethic of Marriage and Family," pages 86–93, 113–14.

Christian theologians and churchpersons need to be much clearer than they have been about why the state of marriage and family, particularly among those who identify themselves as Christians, is of matter to the Church. This goal will not be served by immediately raising the cry that Christians need to have good marriages, raise children properly, and not divorce, because if they fail to do so the foundations of society will crumble. Christians who worry about the triumph of secularism or cultural relativism in American society would do well to direct their attention first to ecclesiology. There is nothing new in the observation that this world is fallen, however one puts it. The crucial issue for the Church always has been to maintain the well-being and good functioning of its own polity. This is an obligation owed to Christ who, for the world's sake, is married to the Church. Marriage, St. Paul tells us, is bound up with a profound mystery, that of "Christ and the church" (Eph. 5:32 RSV). If marriage has become a problem for the Church – if, from within the very life of the Church, marriage looks as if it is "out of joint" with the Church's norms – then it is incumbent upon Christians to deal with this problem as a vital ecclesiological matter. The Church, which is the gathering of Christ's faithful, is itself "made up of kinds of conduct that congeal into relationships and then sub-societies of the inclusive society." As Theodore Mackin goes on to observe: "Marriage is the most substantial of these sub-societies. If the Church does not understand marriage in its nature she does not understand her own. For the Church's nature is to be a society in which the belief, the trust and the caring love absolutely necessary for happiness are learned and carried on. But these are learned and carried on in families first and more than in any other relationship." When Christian marriages and families lose their sense of belonging and purpose within the community of faith, the Church is weakened; and lessened is its ability to witness to Christ and his Kingdom. This is a great loss to a world in need of redemption.

The Nature of Marriage

John L. Boojamra has observed that "even monasticism makes sense only in the context of family as a mutualistic paradigm and is justified only in the context of a fallen world, a world misshapen by sin and separation. In a world whose purpose was clear and undirectional … the family would be the norm as the Genesis account (Gen 2:18) makes clear." This basic theological affirmation about human sociality provides the source for an Orthodox ethic of marriage and family. The second chapter of Genesis illumines marriage (and the family) as a natural institution of human life rooted in the creative activity of God. Through marriage and family God enables human beings to participate in his creative activity and redemptive purpose. There belongs a "natural" sacramentality to marriage even in its fallen condition. This sacramentality, like the image of God in humankind, was not lost entirely with the primal act of disobedience and deviance from the normativity of being human. Marriage need not be reinvented by Christians. Its character and intentionality, however, must change from selfishness, carnality, and possessiveness to being married "in the Lord." Marriage must be reconnected with the divine purpose through its full integration into the sacramental life of the Church, centered, as that life is, in the renewing and nurturing actions of baptism and eucharistic assembly. …

[A]ccording to Orthodox teaching, marriage is founded in a sexual love which, when not deviant, aspires toward perfect union with the other. This union is the primary good of marriage. "Indeed from the beginning," wrote John Chrysostom in his homily on Ephesians 5:22–23, "God appears to have made a special provision for this union; and discoursing of the twain as one." This means that marriage is no mere agreement or contract between two individuals. As Basil exhorts in the *Hexaemeron*, "May the bond of nature, may the yoke imposed by the blessing make as one those who were divided." This union may be understood as an ethical imperative of marriage even as, paradoxically, it is also a divine gift, a blessed bond. Those who are married have an obligation to live a life together consistent with this norm of union. And this is not an obligation that the spouses owe only to themselves. It is an obligation owed to the Church which marries them. Marriage is not, as some contemporary views have it – e.g. the new "contractual marriages" – an utterly private, mutually agreed-upon relationship regulated by certain claims of one spouse upon the other and rights to certain goods or benefits which derive from living together. Such views deny the norms of unitive and communica-tive love as well as expansive community in marriage and replace them with a norm of separateness together for the sake of personal psychic satisfaction, self-fulfillment, and autonomous activity. An Orthodox ethic of marriage denies all claims of normative so-called natural egoism, self-interest, or autonomy. The first chapter of Genesis introduces the very first man and woman as one conjugal being, complementaries of one complete humanity. This is declared to be good. Only with the intrusion of the demonic is this conjugal community of being, this "Adam-Eve," divided into two who are alienated from one another and their relationship disrupted by sexual shame and antagonism. Nevertheless, conjugal union and communion become fundamental analogues and metaphors in the Old Testament prophets for the alliance between God and his people and the restoration of humanity's original relationship to God. In the New Testament marriage is a symbol for the personal, pleromic communion of God's Kingdom (Rev. 19). …

Orthodoxy understands sacramental marriage to be a gift bestowed upon the couple by God through the Church. The sacrament of marriage is a passage from natural and fallen marriage into the new order of Christ's Kingdom. Marriage which is of this order would be impossible indeed, were it dependent solely upon human will. But Christian marriage is itself a medicine which heals the ruptured relationship of men and women by uniting them through grace within the eschatological community of the Church. One great failure of the Western, particularly Roman Catholic, theology of marriage, is that it lost sight of this eschatological promise in marriage and the Christian vocation bestowed upon the couple by the Church. Roman Catholic moral theology went far toward reducing marriage to a legal contract, a guarantee of certain rights and privileges between the contracting individuals, which terminates in death. The language of the Coptic prayer insists upon the extralegal spiritual reality of marriage as communion with God and service to his Kingdom. God bestows upon the married couple the dispositions and virtues necessary for building up his Kingdom. And in all the Eastern rites children are counted as spiritual blessings which strengthen the little church of the family, increasing its service to God and extending it from one generation to the next until Christ's Second Coming. Lest there be any confusion about it, the force of this logic is not utilitarian; it is eschatological.

Again in contrast to earlier Roman Catholic moral theology, the Eastern theology could never define procreation as the primary purpose of marriage. Procreation obtains a fully human value only when it occurs within a relationship which is characterized by *unselfish and unitive love*. One of the oldest prayers of the Byzantine rite orders the goods of marriage with special clarity. "Unite them in one mind: wed them in one flesh, granting unto them of the fruit of the body and the procreation of fair children." And in typical Eastern fashion the Coptic prayer refers the blessing of children to the greater service to God to which all those married and "familied" "in the Lord" are called. "May they rejoice in gazing upon sons and daughters, and whoever they bring to birth may they be *useful in your one and only holy Catholic and Apostolic Church* [my emphasis], confirmed in Orthodox faith."

… [T]he special insight of the Armenian prayer is not only that children are gifts of God but that covenanted marriage "in the Lord" is the sort of relationship most fit for the nurture of children who will become heirs to God's promise of salvation which he made to the patriarchs and revealed fully in Jesus Christ. Children are a gift and blessing, a human reflection within the union of husband and wife of the power and plenitude of the divine nature. And children who become "a people unto God" are an even greater gift and reward of marriage well lived. Christian marriage is the beginning of a "small church," the smallest and most important social unit of Christ's Body in the world. Marriage envisioned as sacrament, lived out in marital fidelity, gives hope for steadfast love and enduring communion even beyond the brokenness of all human relationships, including marriage itself. Christian family is a promise, enfleshed in the form of children, of a future filled with joy.

Marriage as Christian Vocation

… The guiding question for the articulation of an Orthodox ethic of marriage and family is: "What can the Church do to restore a vision of Christian vocation to married and family living?" … The primary elements of the "living" catechesis needed to restore this vision are present already in the liturgy and worship of the Church. Certainly, the vision of marriage as a calling in service to God, Christ's Church, and the Kingdom redound in the rites of matrimony, baptism, and, of course, the Divine Liturgy. But the images, narratives, and symbols which compose this vision need to be taught by the Church in word and action more often than during the rites alone. Baptismal and wedding anniversaries should be celebrated and made the occasions for instruction and service. It is well that churches have begun the practice of premarital counseling. But why should this catechesis and discipline end with the wedding, as it often does? The sacrament of holy matrimony is an entrance into and beginning of the new life lived together in conjugal love. Christian catechesis and discipline ought to deepen and intensify with each year husband and wife live together. As their individual destinies become more intertwined, so should their marriage become identified increasingly with the mission and destiny of the Church. The last prayer of the Byzantine rite speaks directly to this imperative. It says: "May he who by his presence at the marriage feast in Cana of Galilee did declare marriage to be an honourable estate, Christ our true God; through prayers of his all-holy Mother; of the holy, glorious and all laudable Apostles, of the holy, God-crowned Kings and Saints-equal-to-the-Apostles Constantine and Helena; of the holy great martyr Procopius; and of all the Saints, have mercy upon you and save you, forasmuch as he is good, and loveth mankind."

Thus the final words said to the newly wedded couple and to all those gathered as witnesses to their wedding refer marriage to the apostles, to the martyrs, to St. Procopius, who exhorted spouses to go to martyrdom as to a wedding feast, and to Constantine and Helena, who in their missionary propagation of the faith were equal to the apostles. This prayer alone of the Byzantine rite is a powerful answer to the privatization and disestablishment of family in our society. It provides married people with a transcendent purpose, which society seems no longer capable of giving, for their coming together, remaining together, and raising children. It is a reminder to the Church, as well, that its ethics are not only founded in its evangelical witness but are dependent upon marriages and families equipped with the virtues and vision of the apostles, saints, and martyrs. In this light, the so-called crisis of the family becomes an opportunity for the Orthodox Church to reclaim marriage as an ecclesial entity and in so doing strengthen itself for the testimony it must bear to a despairing post-Christendom world of the hope in Christ's Kingdom.

Homosexuality

Few issues have generated more contemporary controversy than the question of homosexuality. The issue is an interesting study in the details of divine command deontological ethics – i.e., do the notorious seven scripture texts (appear to) rule out bodily homosexual expression because such expression is inherently wrong, or must such expression be treated as wrong, regardless of social, cultural, and historical developments, simply because the scripture texts require so? The controversy seems to be largely between those who see the seven texts as wholly or largely in keeping with the general spirit of the Bible, in which God has a (more or less) clear pattern for flourishing human life that reflects divine glory, and those who see these texts as (now, if not necessarily in their time) out of step with a broadly inclusive gospel in which Jesus had a particular heart for outcasts and in which difference, provided it does not generate specific harm, should be welcomed as enrichment rather than threat.

One can perceive four broad strands in the debate. There is the view that homosexuality does not exist – whether (from the ultra-conservative side) because it is a delusion or a willful perversion, or (from the ultra-liberal side) because there is no such thing as fixed sexuality. There is the moderate conservative consensus that homosexual orientation exists but homosexual behavior is wrong, on either natural law or scriptural grounds.

There is the moderate liberal view that homosexual orientation exists but homosexual behavior is a lesser good, a distraction from larger issues of unity, kingdom, and mission. And there is the more explicit liberal strand that homosexual orientation and behavior are goods equal to heterosexual orientation and behavior, to be embodied either in marriage like heterosexual marriage, in exclusive friendship, or in a new form – or new forms – of relationship. While the debate is frequently supplemented by consequential arguments, the core questions are all deontological.

The excerpts below reflect a regular theme of this volume, that views reflect to a large degree the location of those that hold them. Thus, John Boswell renarrates Paul's arguments from a different location to that in which they have generally been read; Eugene Rogers seeks to deepen an understanding of God through a more complete understanding of sexuality; and Stephen Pope strives to achieve consensus in characteristic universal fashion. It should be noted that while Pope and Rogers articulate open and affirming approaches to homosexual persons, there are many figures in both universal and ecclesial branches of Christian ethics that would take more conservative standpoints; and some who would be subversive on other issues find themselves less so on this one.

Universal

Stephen J. Pope, *Homosexuality and Natural Law*

Stephen J. Pope (b. 1955) teaches Christian social ethics at Boston College, Massachusetts. His article concerns "whether our growing but still very incomplete understanding of homosexuality influences our assessment of the ethical status of its expression in sexual activity." He rejects the assumption that once homosexuality is recognized as natural, ethical objections evaporate; but he also rejects the contrary view that scientific insights carry no weight. More specifically, he maintains (using Aristotelian language) that "the evolution, genetics, and physiology of homosexuality pertain to its efficient and material causes rather than to its final cause." In other words, ethics is concerned with how homosexuality may be incorporated into the purposes and destiny of God, and not so much with the nature and origins of homosexual affections.

He appeals to "revealed natural law," which rests on "the ordinary lived human experience of interpersonal love." As he puts it, "human flourishing is conceived much more strongly in affective and interpersonal terms than in strictly natural terms."

Because it is teleological, Pope's proposal has much in common with ecclesial approaches. Where many ecclesial accounts would differ from Pope is on whether, as he puts it, "interpersonal affection [is] the most important end of sexual relations." He concludes with concrete proposals for the positive benefit offered by natural law approaches for informing some of the more controversial aspects of this debate.

Stephen J. Pope. "Scientific and Natural Law Analyses of Homosexuality: A Methodological Study." *Journal of Religious Ethics* 25, 1 (Spring 1997): 89–126. Excerpt from pages 90–1, 100, 103, 110–11, 113, 118–21.

Natural law arguments have typically been used to prohibit rather than to justify or tolerate sexual activity among male homosexuals. In the *Laws*, Plato contrasted the "unnatural" homosexual activity of human beings with the "natural" heterosexual behavior of birds and other animals. Though Thomas Aquinas had a much more developed account of nature than did St. Paul, he agreed with the latter's general indictment of homosexual acts as "against nature" (Rom 1:26–27). Because the order of nature has been created by God, Thomas held, sins that violate this order offend God, its Author. Mitigating circumstances, good intentions, or beneficial consequences might diminish guilt but can never render sins *contra naturam* morally permissible. The "unnatural urges" of the sensitive appetite are to be entirely subjected to reason, and acts that express such urges are prohibited absolutely. In similar language, the pre-critical Immanuel Kant condemned homosexual activity as a "crime of the flesh contrary to our animal nature" (*crimina carnis contra naturam*). More recently, the Ramsey Colloquium has adamantly invoked the standard condemnation of homosexual activity as "unnatural." Natural law has sometimes even been enlisted to support the kind of inhumane and chilling moralism illustrated in Senator Jesse Helms's image of homosexuals who, by "deliberately engaging in unnatural acts," have nothing but their own "disgusting, revolting conduct" to blame for contracting AIDS, a view that echoes the sardonic contempt of Patrick Buchanan: "The poor homosexuals – they have declared war upon nature, and now nature is exacting an awful retribution."

An increasing number of contemporary scientists, on the other hand, have come to regard homosexuality as natural. Studies have shown homosexual conduct to be more common to animals than Plato or Thomas suspected. Rejecting the standard psychological judgment on human homosexuality, the American Psychological Association declared about twenty years ago, on the basis of a majority vote, that homosexuality is not pathological. While this vote itself represented an expression of political more than scientific judgment, since then an increasing number of scientists working in a variety of biological sub-disciplines, from microbiology to physiology, have come to accept the more positive claim that homosexuality is natural. Accepting this judgment, some ethicists, both theological and philosophical, make the further argument that the traditional prohibition against homosexual activity ought to be abandoned. When philosophers believed homosexual acts were unnatural, they argue, homosexuality could reasonably be said to be unethical. Now that a convergence of scientific evidence is beginning to indicate that homosexuality is natural, ethical objections from this quarter no longer hold.

This article examines the two claims just mentioned – that homosexuality is unnatural, and therefore immoral, and, conversely, that homosexuality is natural, and therefore not immoral. Both are found wanting. First of all, the connection between homosexuality as a sexual orientation and the morality of sexual activity between homosexuals is more complex than indicated in this simple option. The Roman Catholic Church, for example, teaches that homosexual acts are wrong, not that homosexuals as such are "bad." Whatever one's response to this ethical judgment, few theological ethicists will hold that homosexuality itself as a preordained state is sinful. The interesting question is whether our growing but still very incomplete understanding of homosexuality influences our assessment of the ethical status of its expression in sexual activity. This question, in other words, concerns whether descriptive analyses of homosexuality can or ought to influence our relevant normative judgments. ...

A Scientific Paradigm: Homosexuality As Natural

Proponents of one position, found in secular as well as in some religious ethics, argue that by overturning the traditional notion that homosexuality is unnatural, science destroys the basis for the traditional moral prohibition of homosexual acts. When philosophers believed homosexual acts were unnatural, they argue, homosexual acts could reasonably be said to be unethical. Now that science has replaced the speculation of philosophers with increasing empirical indications that homosexuality may be natural, rooted in genes and physiology, this kind of ethical objection no longer obtains. ...

"Revealed" Natural Law: Homosexuality As Unnatural

The second perspective is diametrically opposed to the first in the status it accords scientific information vis-à-vis natural law ethics. Though it may acknowledge that contemporary scientific studies of homosexuality might be able to produce a purely descriptive account of why some people might find it more difficult to conform to moral norms than others, this perspective flatly denies that contemporary scientific studies have any relevance to the formulation and justification of moral norms and virtues. According to this position, exemplified by the teachings of the current Roman Catholic magisterium, homosexuality as an orientation may be caused by genetic or other biological factors, acting in conjunction with psychological and social influences, and as such it is blameless as a predisposing condition. Homosexual conduct in sexual matters, on the other hand, is blameworthy to the extent to which it reflects a free decision to act in a manner that is against nature. ...

"Revisionist" Natural Law: Homosexuality Reconsidered

My argument is that these two extreme ways of relating science to the normatively natural ought to be avoided. The first ... assumes that because science depicts homosexuality as natural, moral reflection is complete. The second, displayed by proponents of revealed natural law, builds an impenetrable wall between scientific description of homosexuality and the moral status of particular acts. A middle way is found in the "revisionist" position, which relies on science to make a significant, if limited, contribution to natural law ethics. ...

The most distinctive feature of the revisionist approach to natural law, particularly when contrasted with its revealed natural law counterpart, is the relatively greater role it gives to the ordinary lived human experience of interpersonal love as the basis of moral insight. In this it develops the Thomistic notion that some moral truths are best grasped "by way of experience." Whereas the revealed natural law approach identifies the normatively human as what is given in the Scriptures and tradition and taught by the magisterium, the revisionist relies, *in addition* to these very important

sources, on what it takes to be reasonable interpretations and judgments of what actually constitutes genuine human flourishing in lived human experience. Human flourishing is conceived much more strongly in affective and interpersonal terms than in strictly natural terms. Interpersonal love is here the locus of human flourishing. I stress "in addition to" Scripture and tradition to avoid the impression that this position favors experience over revelation or ecclesially established norms; I think the revisionist regards experience not as a replacement for established sources of moral wisdom but rather as one basis for selectively modifying and revising an ongoing moral tradition. ...

Several important elements of a more careful revisionist natural law perspective can be noted if not thoroughly explicated. First, the revisionist rejects the tendency of Thomistic sexual ethics to equate the will of God with what was perceived to be the natural functioning of human reproductive and sexual biology (always, of course, in coordination with the higher ends also rooted in the intellect and will). The will of God, in this view, requires that sexual activity be marked by generosity of spirit, personal responsibility, permanent and monogamous commitment, deep interpersonal love and fidelity, and attentiveness to relevant contextual factors. The procreative purpose of sexual intercourse is a good in general but not necessarily a good in each and every concrete situation or even in each particular monogamous bond. Monogamy itself is regarded as a central value not because it constitutes the best context for procreation, the material support of women, or the stability and order of society but because it provides the best structural support for the affective relations of the partners.

At the same time, this position is teleological in that it grounds ethics on an account of the characteristic desires and ends of human nature, the most important of which are taken to be interpersonal and affective. By "desire" I mean a natural human tendency toward a good that is not yet possessed, for instance, toward friendship and affective communion, sexual fulfillment and social acceptance; by "end" I mean that which satisfies desire. For Thomas, all things incline toward the good, and they do so at the bidding of a deeply rooted intrinsic inclination toward what is suitable to them. Human beings naturally incline toward suitable goods, and among these inclinations is sexual appetite. All this, it seems to me, is assumed implicitly or explicitly by revisionists, but what is distinctive of their approach is the degree to which they affirm interpersonal affection as the most important end of sexual relations. ...

Conclusion: Science and Natural Law

It has to be admitted that, for all the important qualifications, specifications, and nuances upon which biblical scholars and historians would properly insist, the Scriptures, and even more strongly the Christian tradition, render an unmistakably negative judgment on every kind of homosexual activity. This judgment by no means ends the discussion, but it does imply that the burden of proof must be borne by those who would argue for the legitimacy of some kind of homosexual covenant. This presumption of doubt, however, does not gainsay the legitimate questions of an empirical nature pertaining to this matter, and these questions are precisely where science can provide some assistance to our understanding of human behavior.

Before I sketch the positive potential of science for natural law ethics, let me underscore its limits. Most importantly, the etiology of homosexuality is not determinative of its moral status. On this point, the revealed natural law position is correct. Using Aristotelian language of causality, we can say that studies on the evolution, genetics, and physiology of homosexuality pertain to its efficient and material causes rather than to its final cause. The crucial moral question identified here, however, pertains to final causality – that is, whether and how homosexual activity can take shape so as to promote rather than undermine the well-being of people with a homosexual orientation and the well-being of their communities. ...

Three positive contributions of science to natural law theory can be suggested. First, scientific sources can provide insights into the limits to and constraints placed upon human freedom. [Evolutionary psychologist Donald] Symons's work on male homosexual orientation is relevant at this point as a caveat for those who believe that monogamous commitment is simply a matter of good will and is easily accomplished. If Symons is correct in his depiction of evolved human nature, monogamous commitment strains powerfully against the grain of male sexuality, and simple conformity to the naturally human as it has evolved is morally out of the question. That monogamous commitment is not impossible, however, is indicated in the stable relationships (even if these are not always completely successful) of male heterosexuals. If modification of male sexual patterns has in fact been effected by conditions attending the formation of pair-bonds with females, perhaps the same is possible, if more difficult, in moral commitments of male same-sex partners.

Second, and in a much more speculative vein, social scientific studies on well-being might be extended to homosexuals. These kinds of studies, of course, are notoriously subject to philosophical as well as methodological objections, yet they are potentially relevant to aspects of the question of homosexual conduct and human flourishing. Empirical data regarding the psychological well-being and the moral development of monogamous homosexuals might assist moral reflection on this matter. It may be that in the future social scientists will be able to provide data regarding the effect of stable homosexual couples on the common good of their wider communities. This is a crucially important issue because critics charge that, even if good for the partners considered as two individuals, homosexual covenants should be prohibited because they undermine the value of heterosexual marriages and the centrality of the nuclear family to their local communities and the wider society.

Third and finally, scientists from various disciplines can shed light on human flourishing. Science can assist our understanding of the descriptively human, the base from which the normatively human is derived. It can certainly identify some conditions which undermine human flourishing; for example, medical science can detail the effect of toxic agents on physical health, and behavioral biology can trace the effect of extreme stress on the immune system. In this sense, science is an important source for natural law, even if it cannot provide the kind of indisputable and irrefutable foundation for ethics hoped for by [E. O.] Wilson.

If proponents of natural law of whatever stripe are genuinely interested in moral truth more than in defending entrenched positions, they will want to know whether, as an empirical matter of fact, active homosexuality, even in permanent and monogamous form, usually does undermine the human good. We can be assured that future scientific discoveries and theories will provide valuable and interesting bases for further moral reflection on this troubling and far from resolved moral and social question. Whatever the state of this question in scientific circles, however, natural law ethics must develop a more precise and comprehensive account of genuine human flourishing if it is to develop as a moral tradition which offers neither timeworn prohibitions nor vague platitudes but genuine moral wisdom.

Subversive

John Boswell, *Homosexuality in the Scriptures*

John Boswell (1947–1994) was a professor of history at Yale University and a Roman Catholic. His controversial book *Christianity, Social Tolerance, and Homosexuality* (1980) renarrated the reception of homosexuality in the West, arguing that the church had articulated no negative regard for the orientation or expression of homosexuality until the twelfth century.

In this passage he takes on what for many is the greatest obstacle, the apparent condemnation found in both Old and New Testaments. He points out that "the word 'homosexual' does not occur in the Bible"; he dismisses the assumption that the sin of Sodom was a sexual one; and he argues that the prohibitions of Leviticus are matters of ritual purity only. As for the New Testament, the most-cited passage in Romans 1 he regards as only an illustration of general infidelity, and more specifically as referring to "homosexual acts committed by apparently heterosexual persons"; and he suggests the term "against nature" has been overlaid with "associations inculcated by social taboos, patristic and Reformation theology, Freudian psychology, and personal misgivings." Boswell thus concludes that the source of Christian antipathy towards homosexuality is not to be found in the Bible, but must be sought elsewhere.

John Boswell. *Christianity, Social Tolerance, and Homosexuality: Gay People in Western Europe from the Beginning of the Christian Era to the Fourteenth Century.* Chicago: University of Chicago Press, 1980. From Chapter 4, "The Scriptures," pages 92–7, 100, 106–17. Reprinted by permission of the publisher The University of Chicago Press.

The Bible was not the only or even the principal source of early Christian ethics, and the biblical passages purportedly relating to homosexuality had little to do with early Christian misgivings on the subject. Very few influential theologians based objections to homosexual practices on the New Testament passages now claimed to derogate such behavior, and those who did invoked them only as support for arguments based primarily on other authorities. It is, moreover, quite clear that nothing in the Bible would have categorically precluded homosexual relations among early Christians. In spite of misleading English translations which may imply the contrary, the word "homosexual" does not occur in the Bible: no extant text or manuscript, Hebrew, Greek, Syriac, or Aramaic, contains such a word. In fact none of these languages ever contained a word corresponding to the English "homosexual," nor did any languages have such a term before the late nineteenth century.

Neither Hebrew nor Arabic has such a word today, nor does modern Greek, except as they coin words by analogy with the pseudo-Latin "homosexual." There are of course ways to get around the lack of a specific word in a language, and an action may be condemned without being named, but it is doubtful in this particular case whether a concept of homosexual behavior as a *class* existed at all.

The idea that homosexual behavior is condemned in the Old Testament stems from several passages. Probably the most well known, certainly the most influential, is the account of Sodom in Genesis 19. Sodom in fact gave its name to homosexual relations in the Latin language, and throughout the Middle Ages the closest word to "homosexual" in Latin or any vernacular was "sodomita." A purely homosexual interpretation of this story is, however, relatively recent. None of the many Old Testament passages which refer to Sodom's wickedness suggests any homosexual offenses, and the rise of homosexual associations can be traced to social trends and literature of a much later period. It is not likely that such associations played a large role in determining early Christian attitudes.

On the basis of the text alone, there would seem to be four inferences one could make about the destruction of Sodom: (1) the Sodomites were destroyed for the general wickedness which had prompted the Lord to send angels to the city to investigate in the first place; (2) the city was destroyed because the people of Sodom had tried to rape the angels; (3) the city was destroyed because the men of Sodom had tried to engage in homosexual intercourse with the angels ...; (4) the city was destroyed for inhospitable treatment of visitors sent from the Lord.

Although it is the most obvious of the four, the second possibility has been largely ignored by biblical scholars both ancient and modern, probably due to ambiguities surrounding homosexual rape. Since 1955 modern scholarship has increasingly favored interpretation (4), emphasizing that the sexual overtones to the story are minor, if present, and that the original moral impact of the passage had to do with hospitality. Briefly put, the thesis of this trend in scholarship is that Lot was violating the custom of Sodom (where he was himself not a citizen but only a "sojourner") by entertaining unknown guests within the city walls at night without obtaining the permission of the elders of the city. When the men of Sodom gathered around to demand that the strangers be brought out to them, "that they might *know* them," they meant no more than to "know" who they were, and the city was consequently destroyed not for sexual immorality but for the sin of inhospitality to strangers. ...

There are, moreover, numerous other references in the Old Testament to Sodom and its fate, and scholars have failed to accord this facet of the controversy the importance it deserves. Sodom is used as a symbol of evil in dozens of places, but not in a single instance is the sin of the Sodomites specified as homosexuality. Other sins, on the other hand, are explicitly mentioned. Ecclesiasticus says that God abhorred the Sodomites for their pride (16:8) ... In Ezekiel the sins of Sodom are not only listed categorically but contrasted with the sexual sins of Jerusalem as less serious: "As I live, saith the Lord God, Sodom thy sister hath not done ... as thou hast done. ... Behold, this was the iniquity of thy sister Sodom, pride, fulness of bread, and abundance of idleness was in her and her daughters, neither did she strengthen the hand of the poor and the needy" (16:48–49, KJV). ...

Stories of divine testing of human piety by dispatching beggars or wayfarers to demand the sacred right of hospitality ("theoxeny") are a commonplace of folklore in many cultures and occur elsewhere in the Old Testament as well (e.g., immediately before the Sodom story in Gen. 18; cf. Deut. 23:3–4 [KJV]). In nearly all such stories evil persons appear either as neighbors or other townsfolk who do not fulfill their obligation and

are punished, violently or by exclusion from some divine benefice, while the solitary upright family is rewarded with a gift or a prophecy of misfortunes to come. Genesis 19 obviously belongs in this context, no matter how many modern commentators may have ignored it, and a sexual element, if present at all, was probably intended only as the concrete expression of the Sodomites' lack of hospitality. ...

The only place in the Old Testament where homosexual acts per se are mentioned is Leviticus: "Thou shalt not lie with mankind, as with womankind: it is abomination (18:22). "If a man also lie with mankind, as he lieth with a woman, both of them have committed an abomination: they shall surely be put to death; their blood shall be upon them" (20:13, KJV). The Hebrew word "toevah," (תּוֹעֵבָה), here translated "abomination," does not usually signify something intrinsically evil, like rape or theft (discussed elsewhere in Leviticus), but something which is ritually unclean for Jews, like eating pork or engaging in intercourse during menstruation, both of which are prohibited in these same chapters. It is used throughout the Old Testament to designate those Jewish sins which involve ethnic contamination or idolatry and very frequently occurs as part of the stock phrase "toevah ha-goyim," "the uncleanness of the Gentiles" (e.g., 2 [4] Kings 16:3). ... Leviticus 18 is specifically designed to distinguish the Jews from the pagans among whom they had been living, or would live, as its opening remarks make clear ...

Saint Paul, whose commitment to Jewish law had taken up most of his life, never suggested that there was any historical or legal reason to oppose homosexual behavior: if he did in fact object to it, it was purely on the basis of functional, contemporary moral standards.

There are three passages in the writings of Paul which have been supposed to deal with homosexual relations. [Boswell argues that the two words in 1 Corinthians 6:9 and 1 Timothy 6:9 commonly translated "homosexual" are mistranslations of other concepts.]

The remaining passage, Romans 1:26–27, does not suffer from mistranslation, although little attention has been paid to the ramifications of its wording: "For this cause God gave them up unto vile affections: for even their women did change the natural use into that which is against nature: And likewise, also the men, leaving the natural use of the woman, burned in their lust one toward another; men with men working that which is unseemly, and receiving in themselves that recompense of their error which was meet" (KJV).

... [T]he point of the passage is not to stigmatize sexual behavior of any sort but to condemn the Gentiles for their general infidelity. There was a time, Paul implies, when monotheism was offered to or known by the Romans, but they rejected it (vv. 19–23). The reference to homosexuality is simply a mundane analogy to this theological sin; it is patently not the crux of this argument. Once the point has been made, the subject of homosexuality is quickly dropped and the major argument resumed (vv. 28ff.).

What is even more important, the persons Paul condemns are manifestly not homosexual: what he derogates are homosexual acts committed by apparently heterosexual persons. The whole point of Romans 1, in fact, is to stigmatize persons who have rejected their calling, gotten off the true path they were once on. It would completely undermine the thrust of the argument if the persons in question were not "naturally" inclined to the opposite sex in the same way they were "naturally" inclined to monotheism. What caused the Romans to sin was not that they *lacked* what Paul considered proper inclinations but that they *had* them: they held the truth, but "in unrighteousness" (v. 18), because "they did not see fit to retain Him in their knowledge" (v. 28). …

There is, however, no clear condemnation of homosexual acts in the verses in question. The expression "against nature" is the standard English equivalent of Paul's Greek phrase "παρὰ φύσιν" which was first used in this context by Plato. Its original sense has been almost wholly obscured by 2,000 years of repetition in stock phrases and by the accretion of associations inculcated by social taboos, patristic and Reformation theology, Freudian psychology, and personal misgivings.

The concept of "natural law" was not fully developed until more than a millennium after Paul's death, and it is anachronistic to read it into his words. For Paul, "nature" was not a question of universal law or truth but, rather, a matter of the *character* of some person or group of persons, a character which was largely ethnic and entirely human: Jews are Jews "by nature," just as Gentiles are Gentiles "by nature." "Nature" is not a moral force for Paul: men may be evil or good "by nature," depending on their own disposition. A possessive is always understood with "nature" in Pauline writings: it is not "nature" in the abstract but *someone's* "nature," the Jews' "nature" or the Gentiles' "nature" or even the pagan gods' "nature" ("When ye knew not God, ye did service unto them which by nature [i.e., by *their* nature] are no gods," Gal. 4:8, KJV). …

Paul believed that the Gentiles knew of the truth of God but rejected it and likewise rejected their true "nature" as regarded their sexual appetites, going beyond what was "natural" for them and what was approved for the Jews. It cannot be inferred from this that Paul considered mere homoerotic attraction or practice morally reprehensible, since the passage strongly implies that he was not discussing persons who were by inclination gay and since he carefully observed, in regard to both the women and the men, that they changed and abandoned the "natural use" to engage in homosexual activities. …

While Saint Paul did not specifically comment on gay feelings or lifestyles, he would have disapproved of any form of sexuality which had as its end purely sexual pleasure, and he might have disapproved of relationships directed chiefly at the expression of erotic passion. He did not, however, suggest any connection between sexuality and procreation – a link created by a later age – and he clearly regarded licit sexuality as that contained within a permanent and monogamous relationship. He not only permitted but urged Christians to satisfy the sexual needs of their spouses ("Do not refuse each other except by mutual consent, and then only for an agreed time, to leave yourselves free for prayer," 1 Cor. 7:5, JB). In recommending celibacy, and sexual abstinence even for the married, he did not adduce the evils of sexual pleasure or concupiscence as arguments against the liceity of sex but clearly indicated as the reason for Christian restraint in such matters the impending arrival of the Kingdom of God, before which *all* earthly concerns should seem secondary: "But this I say, brethren, the time is short: it remaineth, that both they that have wives be as though they had none; and they that weep, as though they wept not; … and they that buy, as though they possessed not" (1 Cor. 7:29–30, KJV). …

The New Testament takes no demonstrable position on homosexuality. To suggest that Paul's references to excesses of sexual indulgence involving homosexual behavior are indicative of a general position in opposition to same-sex eroticism is as unfounded as arguing that his condemnation of drunkenness implies opposition to the drinking of wine. At the very most, the effect of Christian Scripture on attitudes toward homosexuality could be described as moot. The most judicious historical perspective might be that it had no effect at all. The source of antigay feelings among Christians must be sought elsewhere.

Ecclesial

Eugene F. Rogers, *Sanctification, Homosexuality, and God's Triune Life*

Eugene Rogers (b. 1961) is a professor at the University of North Carolina (Greensboro). His has been the most sustained voice arguing for an ecclesial openness not just to homosexuality in general, but to gay marriage in particular. What makes his argument ecclesial is his profound concern to ground his proposals in the practices of the church. Thus, if gay and lesbian people are to be encouraged to form lifelong unions, these must be described as marriages, because marriages are what the church calls lifelong embodied unions. Likewise, marriage is not a concession to gay and lesbian people but an aspect of God's grace – a "means of redemption." In characteristic ecclesial style, Rogers is seeking not to make logical or compassionate exceptions to a rule but to renew an ancient church tradition.

Rogers has a very high regard for Rowan Williams' celebrated essay "The Body's Grace," which explores the risks and potential of sexuality, bodily identity, and desire. In Williams' own words, his essay seeks "A theology of the body's grace which can do justice to the experience of concrete sexual discovery, in all its pain and variety." In many ways Rogers' essay is an attempt to articulate the ecclesial assumptions and implications of Williams' essay. He longs for the church to recognize the love of gay and lesbian people not as its problem but as God's gift.

Eugene F. Rogers. "Sanctification, Homosexuality, and God's Triune Life." Pages 217–46 in *Theology and Sexuality: Classic and Contemporary Readings*. Ed. Eugene F. Rogers, Jr. Oxford: Blackwell, 2002. Excerpt from pages 217–18, 230, 232–8.

Along the wide spectrum of views about marriage for gay and lesbian couples, the extremes sometimes meet in claims that gay and lesbian marriages are irredeemable, on the far right because they are gay, on the far left because they are marriages. I claim the opposite: they can be a means of redemption.

Moreover, they can be a means of anticipating God's catching human beings up into that wedding feast that God celebrates in the life of the Trinity, an elevation that the tradition has had the wisdom to call consummation. The question for the right is: Given that gay and lesbian people are not going to go away, what shall the church *do* with them? The question for the left is: Given that gay and lesbian people are part of the church, how much shall it allow their bodies to *mean*? In the context of baptism, Eucharist, and (yes) monastic vows, the Spirit is now moving Christian communities to see marriage as the central symbol by which to test and renegotiate the fit of gay and lesbian bodies into the body of Christ.

Rowan Williams puts it this way:

The whole story of creation, incarnation, and our incorporation into the fellowship of Christ's body tells us that God desires us, *as if we were* God, as if we were that unconditional response to God's giving that God's self makes in the life of the Trinity. ... The life of the Christian community has as its rationale – if not invariably its practical reality – the task of teaching us this: so ordering our relations that human beings may see themselves as desired, as the occasion of joy.

The question for both sides is then this: By what sort of sacramental practices can the church best teach gay and lesbian Christians to see themselves as occasions of joy, that God desires them as if they were God? Marriage is peculiarly suited to teaching God's desire for human beings because it mirrors God's choosing of human beings for God's own. As Barth puts it, "In that the election of God is real, there is such a thing as love and marriage." God's election of Israel, like marriage, involves a discipline of faithfulness in which God permits human beings to become what God sees. God's election of the mostly gentile church, like marriage for gay and lesbian couples, is (in Paul's metaphor) God's overturning of nature to graft wild olives onto a domestic tree – to include them, that is, in a structure (the law of the Spirit) that allows their selves, their souls and bodies, to mean much more than they would by nature, to be caught up into the very life and love by which God loves God. …

The Body's Grace?

Williams's essay bears the title, "The Body's Grace." In it he claims that grace, like some sexual love, works a change in a human being by causing her to reperceive herself as loved by Another. …

The objection to a grace of the body, then, is this: it sounds as if it takes an all-too-general category, transformative, positive regard, as the primary analogate, of which God's grace is not the defining example, but a mere illustration, if the most impressive. To be theologically adequate, grace must be defined first of all as what God does, and the grace of the body related to that. But that is just what Williams does:

[T]he body's grace itself only makes human sense if we have a language of grace in the first place; and that depends on having a language of creation and redemption. To be formed in our humanity by the loving delight of another is an experience whose contours we can identify most clearly and hopefully if we have also learned or are learning about being the object of the causeless, loving delight of God, being the object of God's love for God through incorporation into the community of God's Spirit and the taking-on of the identity of God's Child.

The references to God's Spirit and Child are crucial. For if *God* defines what grace is, then grace is simply an impersonal name for the Holy Spirit. … Without saying so, Williams makes the word *grace* an analogy in the strict theological sense, where the grace of God supplies the primary analogate. The grace of the body only makes sense by reference to the grace of God identified in a community that tells certain stories of God's creation and redemption. Only thus can it emerge that the body is one of God's ways of catching human beings up in God's own life, and therefore a possible means, derivative and second or third hand, of grace. The body's grace, should it occur, is not a movement of the body up to God, but a movement of the Spirit down, so that human bodies will not be left out of salvation. …

[Rogers names ways in which salvation is itself bodily, particularly crucifixion and Eucharist.]

Thus gay and lesbian marriages can, like straight marriages, take bodies seriously in a handful of ways:

1 Since the true body, or the primary analogate of "body" in Christian discourse, is the body of Christ, any body is taken seriously that extends and deepens the Eucharistic entry into God's body. Marriage, gay or straight, receives its sacramental character not independently but from the welcoming of the one flesh, in soteriological ways a new body, into the eucharistic community.

The male-female version of the one flesh can be especially apt for representing the union of Christ with his bride the church, but not everyone need represent this union in the same way. The analogy is flexible enough already that both celibates and the married can represent it. Gay and lesbian couples also need not threaten the aptness of the relation between Christ and the church, but can be taken up into it. …

2 Any body is taken seriously in which the eucharistic community is built up. Weddings, gay or straight, build up the eucharistic community by contributing to the institutional stability of marriage and because weddings represent the trinitarian life. In a wedding, third parties guarantee, celebrate, witness, bless, testify to, and delight in the love of two. When Jesus says the kingdom of heaven is like a wedding feast, and theologians say that the role of the Spirit is to guarantee, celebrate, witness, bless, testify to, and delight in the love of the Father and the Son, they are speaking of the same reality. The Spirit incorporates the wedding guests into the public of love. It bears repeating that Augustine rejects the triad father, mother, child as an analogy for the Trinity, while the analogy of the Spirit to the guests at a wedding has implicit support in the parables of Jesus (Mt. 9:15, 22:2) – the second passage issuing a dire warning about those who do not celebrate the wedding, who refuse the Spirit's work.

3 Any body is taken seriously in which the Holy Spirit dwells so as to raise it from the dead. Anticipation of that resurrection is the bodily sanctification that marriage, as a form of ascetic practice, carries out. Note well, in the Christian view marriage is not for satisfaction, but for sanctification, of which satisfaction and enjoyment will be an inalienable part of its perfection. Marriage and monasticism have exactly the same end: the sanctification of the person by means of the body, by putting the body so in the power of others that one cannot escape their love and truth. Human beings imitate God when they take time and make space for each other, as God takes time and space for Israel and in Jesus; in so doing they honor the body that exists over time and in space. Sartre notoriously opined that "hell is other people"; so is holiness. Indeed, in Eastern

Orthodoxy the crowns placed over the heads of bride and groom are crowns of martyrdom. This leaves room for the fading of sexual urgency in marriage (gay or straight) and its being taken up into other forms of care for the partner and the community. So it is too that "in heaven they neither marry nor are given in marriage." ...

4   Any body is taken seriously in which a human being begins to fulfill the chief end for which she or he was made, which, according to the first answer of the Westminster catechism, is to "glorify God and enjoy him forever." Sanctification and the Eucharist and wedding feasts certainly glorify God. Properly understood, they enjoy God, too. And if human beings were so created to enjoy God, then the joy of sex, under sanctifying circumstances, cannot be unfitting. Sexual attraction is explicitly or implicitly concerned with real bodies. Gay and lesbian people care about bodies – otherwise many of them would take the easier route and settle for those of the opposite sex. There is *something* right about insert-tab-A-in-slot-B – or there is something in having tabs and slots. What is it? And why is it wrong that God should give it to some with tabs to admire the tabs of others? Or, to be less crude, the chests and shoulders? Even Augustine was able to speculate about the placement of nipples on a man's chest: "They articulate the space of the chest, and they prove that beauty is a value in itself, not tied inevitably to utility in the human body." Or better, the utility is for bodies made aware of grace, the utility of joy.

Williams puts it this way:

Same-sex love annoyingly poses the question of what the meaning of desire is – in itself, not considered as instrumental to some other process, such as the peopling of the world. We are brought up against the possibility not only of pain and humiliation without any clear payoff, but, just as worryingly, of nonfunctional joy – of joy, to put it less starkly, whose material "production" is an embodied person aware of grace.

Just because a body is pleasing to me I become vulnerable, and God has made us so to be vulnerable in one another's bodily presence. The embodiment of God's creation is borne in upon me and will not leave me alone. Neither monogamy nor celibacy cause these interventions of God through bodily forms of the neighbor to go away.

Perhaps this is the point to mention that the phenomenon of gay and lesbian desire, contrary to popular belief, can do a good job of articulating what celibacy is for in the Christian tradition. For celibacy also raises the question of nonfunctional joy. Both Jesus and Paul speak of sexual desire and fulfillment without mentioning children. If sex is for *God*, then the task of celibacy is to bear witness to that fact *directly* and *immediately*, whereas the task of people in sanctifying sexual relationships of whatever orientation is to bear witness to that fact *indirectly* and *mediately*. ...

5. Any body is taken seriously that is *ruled* by the *Spirit*. ... [R]eliance on the Spirit rather than on concrete forms of the created order, or the previously revealed order (such as that of circumcision), is not antinomian. On the contrary, the Spirit's work is also and precisely that of fidelity, or of keeping faith between the Father and the Son. Fidelity is a work proper to the Spirit, particularly "the Spirit of the One Who raised Christ Jesus from the dead," the *vinculum caritatis*, the one who "restores" the bond between Father and Son and works (much less successfully?) to restore unity also among human beings, even through the witnesses of the wedding to restore unity in a couple. ...

Gay and lesbian relationships not only must exhibit the spiritual fruits of faith, hope, and charity but must also exhibit them in sacramental form. Just as marriage gives form or rule to the sanctifying possibilities of heterosexual sex, so gay and lesbian people need sacramental forms, or inspired rules. ... Gay and lesbian relationships must wait upon a churchly form – call it sacramental if you think of marriage as a sacrament – to give their holiness ecclesial shape, just as heterosexual relationships had to wait centuries for the church to integrate them fully into its life with heterosexual marriage forms.

Chapter Eleven

Good Beginnings and Endings

The beginning and ending of life evoke awe and mystery – and profound emotion and argument. This is especially so in recent times, when research and technological breakthroughs have made possible the conception of new life, the potential amelioration of certain genetic diseases, and the prolongation of life in circumstances unimaginable in previous centuries. The tendency is for all issues in this area – notably genetic engineering, abortion, and euthanasia – to take the same shape: innovations are proposed on utilitarian grounds and opposed on deontological grounds. It sometimes seems like the head is in one place, the gut in another, and the heart is divided between the two. Perhaps more than in any other of the areas discussed in Part Three of this book, tension has gathered in this area around legislation. The need not only to guide behavior but to influence legislation has added an extra dimension to the questions raised in this chapter.

Contraception, Assisted Conception, and Genetic Engineering

These issues all converge on a single theme: the desire to have children, to have them at the right time, and to have children who have the greatest possible expectation and opportunity of flourishing and fulfillment in adult life. The ethical questions are similar in each case: while these are understandable desires, are they legitimate ones, and are there limits to the methods employed to attain them? One variable has been whether it is ever appropriate to discuss such matters outside the context of the relationships within which they arise. This question goes to the heart of the distinction between universal ethics – which tends to privilege the individual and the moment of decision – and ecclesial ethics, which tends to concentrate on the narratives and communities within which such dilemmas may be better understood. Subversive ethics tends to see these questions in more adversarial terms, highlighting the (often hidden) "losers" in the public debate.

The readings below include the papal encyclical *Humanae Vitae*, which is the most controversial text in this area; a broad outline of the issues from a moderate feminist perspective – recognizing that, since it concerns control of women's bodies, this is often seen as a key area in feminist ethics; and an early work of Oliver O'Donovan, a figure who in many ways bridges universal and ecclesial approaches.

Universal

Pope Paul VI, *Humanae Vitae (On the Regulation of Birth)*

After most Protestant denominations, following the lead of the Anglican Lambeth Conference of 1930, had relaxed their prohibitions on contraception, the Vatican responded with the encyclical *Casti connubii* (On Christian Marriage) in 1930, which reaffirmed the Catholic prohibition on birth control but allowed for natural methods of family planning. The marketing of oral contraceptives from 1960 provoked fresh debate, and a papal commission was initiated in 1963. It found no intrinsic evil in contraception.

So when Paul VI (1897–1978; pope from 1963 until his death) issued the encyclical *Humanae Vitae* it came as a surprise to many. It is arguably the most significant event in the recent history of the Roman Catholic Church, particularly in the relationship between its hierarchy and its lay people. Its position is simply stated: "An act of mutual love which impairs the capacity to transmit life which God the Creator, through specific laws, has built into it, frustrates His design which constitutes the norm of marriage, and contradicts the will of the Author of life" (13). Aware of the (consequential) implications of this uncompromising deontological line, particularly in the developing world, Paul VI nonetheless reiterated the words of his predecessor John XXIII: "No statement of the problem and no solution to it is acceptable which does violence to man's essential dignity; those who propose such solutions base them on an utterly materialistic conception of man himself and his life" (23).

[handwritten margin note: contraceptives inherently provide more options.]

While Paul VI's argument is squarely deontological and rooted in natural law, he does cite four consequential dimensions to supplement his reasoning. He says artificial contraception, and the culture of irresponsibility it encourages, leads to a general lowering of moral standards, to women being reduced to instruments of men's desires, to governments exercising coercive powers over women's bodies, and to an exaggerated assumption of personal autonomy.

[handwritten margin note: What is an exaggerated assumption of personal autonomy?]

Pope Paul VI. *Humanae Vitae* (On the Regulation of Birth). 1968. www.vatican.va/holy_father/paul_vi/ encyclicals/documents/hf_p-vi_enc_25071968_humanae-vitae_en.html. Reprinted by permission of the Libreria Editrice Vaticana.

The transmission of human life is a most serious role in which married people collaborate freely and responsibly with God the Creator. It has always been a source of great joy to them, even though it sometimes entails many difficulties and hardships.

The changes that have taken place are of considerable importance and varied in nature. In the first place there is the rapid increase in population which has made many fear that world population is going to grow faster than available resources, with the consequence that many families and developing countries would be faced with greater hardships. This can easily induce public authorities to be tempted to take even harsher measures to avert this danger. There is also the fact that now not only working and housing conditions but the greater demands made both in the economic and educational field pose a living situation in which it is frequently difficult these days to provide properly for a large family.

[handwritten margin note: now does contraception lead to this?]

Also noteworthy is a new understanding of the dignity of woman and her place in society, of the value of conjugal love in marriage and the relationship of conjugal acts to this love.

But the most remarkable development of all is to be seen in man's stupendous progress in the domination and rational organization of the forces of nature to the point that he is endeavoring to extend this control over every aspect of his own life – over his body, over his mind and emotions, over his social life, and even over the laws that regulate the transmission of life.

Responsible Parenthood

10. Married love, therefore, requires of husband and wife the full awareness of their obligations in the matter of responsible parenthood, which today, rightly enough, is much insisted upon, but which at the same time should be rightly understood. Thus, we do well to consider responsible parenthood in the light of its varied legitimate and interrelated aspects.

With regard to the biological processes, responsible parenthood means an awareness of, and respect for, their proper functions. In the procreative faculty the human mind discerns biological laws that apply to the human person.

With regard to man's innate drives and emotions, responsible parenthood means that man's reason and will must exert control over them.

With regard to physical, economic, psychological and social conditions, responsible parenthood is exercised by those who prudently and generously decide to have more children, and by those who, for serious reasons and with due respect to moral precepts, decide not to have additional children for either a certain or an indefinite period of time.

Responsible parenthood, as we use the term here, has one further essential aspect of paramount importance. It concerns the objective moral order which was established by God, and of which a right conscience is the true interpreter. In a word, the exercise of responsible parenthood requires that husband and wife, keeping a right order of priorities, recognize their own duties toward God, themselves, their families and human society.

From this it follows that they are not free to act as they choose in the service of transmitting life, as if it were wholly up to them to decide what is the right course to follow. On the contrary, they are bound to ensure that what they do corresponds to the will of God the Creator. The very nature of marriage and its use makes His will clear, while the constant teaching of the Church spells it out.

Observing the Natural Law

11. The sexual activity, in which husband and wife are intimately and chastely united with one another, through which human life is transmitted, is, as the recent Council recalled, "noble and worthy." It does not, moreover, cease to be legitimate even when, for reasons independent of their will, it is foreseen to be infertile. For its natural adaptation to the expression and strengthening of the union of husband and wife is not thereby suppressed. The fact is, as experience shows, that new life is not the result of each and every act of sexual intercourse. God has wisely ordered laws of nature and the incidence of fertility in such a way that successive births are already naturally spaced through the inherent operation of these laws. The Church, nevertheless, in urging men to the observance of the precepts of the natural law, which it interprets by its constant doctrine, teaches that each and every marital act must of necessity retain its intrinsic relationship to the procreation of human life.

Unlawful Birth Control Methods

14. Therefore We base Our words on the first principles of a human and Christian doctrine of marriage when We are obliged once more to declare that the direct interruption of the generative process already begun and, above all, all direct abortion, even for therapeutic reasons, are to be absolutely excluded as lawful means of regulating the number of children. Equally to be condemned, as the magisterium of the Church has affirmed on many occasions, is direct sterilization, whether of the man or of the woman, whether permanent or temporary.

Similarly excluded is any action which either before, at the moment of, or after sexual intercourse, is specifically intended to prevent procreation – whether as an end or as a means.

Neither is it valid to argue, as a justification for sexual intercourse which is deliberately contraceptive, that a lesser evil is to be preferred to a greater one, or that such intercourse would merge with procreative acts of past and future to form a single entity, and so be qualified by exactly the same moral goodness as these. Though it is true that sometimes it is lawful to tolerate a lesser moral evil in order to avoid a greater evil or in order to promote a greater good, it is never lawful, even for the gravest reasons, to do evil that good may come of it – in other words, to intend directly something which of its very nature contradicts the moral order, and which must therefore be judged unworthy of man, even though the intention is to protect or promote the welfare of an individual, of a family or of society in general. Consequently, it is a serious error to think that a whole married life of otherwise normal relations can justify sexual intercourse which is deliberately contraceptive and so intrinsically wrong.

Recourse to Infertile Periods

16. Now as We noted earlier, some people today raise the objection against this particular doctrine of the Church concerning the moral laws governing marriage, that human intelligence has both the right and respon-

sibility to control those forces of irrational nature which come within its ambit and to direct them toward ends beneficial to man. Others ask on the same point whether it is not reasonable in so many cases to use artificial birth control if by so doing the harmony and peace of a family are better served and more suitable conditions are provided for the education of children already born. To this question We must give a clear reply. The Church is the first to praise and commend the application of human intelligence to an activity in which a rational creature such as man is so closely associated with his Creator. But she affirms that this must be done within the limits of the order of reality established by God.

If therefore there are well-grounded reasons for spacing births, arising from the physical or psychological condition of husband or wife, or from external circumstances, the Church teaches that married people may then take advantage of the natural cycles immanent in the reproductive system and engage in marital intercourse only during those times that are infertile, thus controlling birth in a way which does not in the least offend the moral principles which We have just explained.

Neither the Church nor her doctrine is inconsistent when she considers it lawful for married people to take advantage of the infertile period but condemns as always unlawful the use of means which directly prevent conception, even when the reasons given for the later practice may appear to be upright and serious. In reality, these two cases are completely different. In the former the married couple rightly use a faculty provided them by nature. In the latter they obstruct the natural development of the generative process. It cannot be denied that in each case the married couple, for acceptable reasons, are both perfectly clear in their intention to avoid children and wish to make sure that none will result. But it is equally true that it is exclusively in the former case that husband and wife are ready to abstain from intercourse during the fertile period as often as for reasonable motives the birth of another child is not desirable. And when the infertile period recurs, they use their married intimacy to express their mutual love and safeguard their fidelity toward one another. In doing this they certainly give proof of a true and authentic love.

Consequences of Artificial Methods

17. Responsible men can become more deeply convinced of the truth of the doctrine laid down by the Church on this issue if they reflect on the consequences of methods and plans for artificial birth control. Let them first consider how easily this course of action could open wide the way for marital infidelity and a general lowering of moral standards. Not much experience is needed to be fully aware of human weakness and to understand that human beings – and especially the young, who are so exposed to temptation – need incentives to keep the moral law, and it is an evil thing to make it easy for them to break that law. Another effect that gives cause for alarm is that a man who grows accustomed to the use of contraceptive methods may forget the reverence due to a woman, and, disregarding her physical and emotional equilibrium, reduce her to being a mere instrument for the satisfaction of his own desires, no longer considering her as his partner whom he should surround with care and affection. ...

Limits to Man's Power

Consequently, unless we are willing that the responsibility of procreating life should be left to the arbitrary decision of men, we must accept that there are certain limits, beyond which it is wrong to go, to the power of man over his own body and its natural functions – limits, let it be said, which no one, whether as a private individual or as a public authority, can lawfully exceed. These limits are expressly imposed because of the reverence due to the whole human organism and its natural functions, in the light of the principles We stated earlier, and in accordance with a correct understanding of the "principle of totality" enunciated by Our predecessor Pope Pius XII.

Concern of the Church

18. It is to be anticipated that perhaps not everyone will easily accept this particular teaching. There is too much clamorous outcry against the voice of the Church, and this is intensified by modern means of communication. But it comes as no surprise to the Church that she, no less than her divine Founder, is destined to be a "sign of contradiction." She does not, because of this, evade the duty imposed on her of proclaiming humbly but firmly the entire moral law, both natural and evangelical. ...

In preserving intact the whole moral law of marriage, the Church is convinced that she is contributing to the creation of a truly human civilization. She urges man not to betray his personal responsibilities by putting all his faith in technical expedients. In this way she defends the dignity of husband and wife. This course of action shows that the Church, loyal to the example and teaching of the divine Savior, is sincere and unselfish in her regard for men whom she strives to help even now during this earthly pilgrimage "to share God's life as sons of the living God, the Father of all men."

now?

does contraception condone infidelity in women? what is the relationship here?

Subversive

Margaret A. Farley, *Feminist Theology and Bioethics*

Margaret Farley (b. 1935) is a member of the Roman Catholic religious order the Sisters of Mercy. She has taught at Yale Divinity School since 1971. This is a summary article looking at various issues, especially *in vitro* fertilization (IVF). Given the three-fold distinction within feminism made elsewhere in this volume, between reconstructionists, restorationists, and deconstructionists (those who respectively take a largely liberal, largely "romantic," and largely rejecting perspective on a universal paradigm in ethics), it is striking that Farley falls fairly neatly into the first designation. The key issue for Farley is women's autonomy.

Thus the arguments are largely consequential. Is a particular technological innovation likely to increase or decrease a woman's pain or independence – that is the question: not whether it is in accord with natural law or the character of God (as defined without reference to women's experience). Similar issues arise in relation to "reproductive technologies that divorce decisions for childbearing from childrearing." Farley's closing remarks appeal to another universal value – distributive justice. This is a subversive ethic that seeks earnestly to be incorporated into universal ethics.

Margaret A. Farley. "Feminist Theology and Bioethics." Pages 238–54 in *Feminist Theology: A Reader*. Ed. Ann Loades. Louisville: Westminster/John Knox Press, 1990. Excerpt from pages 249–53.

Feminist theology and bioethics

… The potentialities of reproductive technology have for some time caught the attention of feminists, though without unanimity of analysis. Some feminists have argued that the ultimate source of women's oppression is their physiological capability of bearing children. While physical motherhood can constitute individual and social power, it also renders women powerless – before nature, before men, before their children, before society (which judges and determines the conditions under which their children must grow). In the face of this powerlessness, and the suffering it entails, technology offers a solution. Indeed, in an extreme view, women's liberation can only be achieved with a revolution not only against forms of society, but against nature itself. Thus, Shulamith Firestone argued for the "freeing of women from the tyranny of their reproductive biology by every means available," including technology that could separate women once and for all from a gender-identified responsibility for reproduction.

This was a relatively early position, however, and strong disagreement came from other feminists on a variety of grounds. Many consider the analysis of the causes of oppression to be wrong. Others see in the development of reproductive technologies a new means of devaluing women, rendering them "expendable in the procreative process." Still others argue that some uses of technology, such as amniocentesis for the purpose of gender selection, will pit women against themselves.

Feminists agree, however, on at least two things in regard to these questions. First, the history of women's experience in relation to the power and process of reproduction is a history of great pain. While fertility, pregnancy and childbirth have been a source of women's happiness and fulfilment, and occasions for powerful expressions of great human love and enduring fidelity to duty, they have also been the locus of a cumulative burden of immense oppression and suffering. The twentieth-century incursion of technology into reproduction (the "medicalization" of pregnancy and childbirth) has often added to this suffering, extended this oppression.

Secondly, feminists agree that the development and use of reproductive technology cannot be evaluated apart from its concrete, sociocultural context. This context remains an "historically specific social order in which positions of power and privilege are dispropor- tionately occupied by men." As long as sexism contin- ues to characterize the lived world that women know, technology will have different consequences for women and for men. Far from freeing women from unneces- sary burdens in reproduction, further technological development may result in greater bondage.

Neither feminism in general nor feminist theology render wholly negative judgements on reproductive technology. One obvious reason is that such technology can take many forms. Evaluations of developments of contraceptives, childbirth procedures, methods of abortion, artificial insemination, *in vitro* fertilization, foetal diagnosis, cloning, and many other technologies can hardly be lumped together in a single comprehen- sive judgement. Generally, despite deep ambivalence towards reproductive technologies, feminists can affirm that "natural-scientific breakthroughs represent genuine gains in human self-understanding. The wide- spread social irresponsibility of medical practice, exac- erbated by male monopoly of the medical profession that is only now changing, must not be confused with the value of scientific discoveries." Science and technol- ogy have been instruments for reform at times, even in regard to sexism. ...

One place to begin a feminist analysis of *in vitro* fertilization (with embryo transfer or some other form of providing for gestation) is with women's experience to date of technology in the area of pregnancy and birth. As we have already noted, in many respects this is not a happy experience. Recent studies have helped to make visible the difficulties women have had. Recalling these difficulties can help us to formulate the questions that need to be asked of *in vitro* fertilization. The use of medical technology in relation to childbirth has con- tributed to the alienation of women from their bodies, their partners, and their children (by, for example, moving childbirth into settings appropriate primarily for the treatment of disease, isolating mothers both from "women's culture" and their spouses, regimenting the presence of mothers with their babies, etc.); and it has placed women in a network of professional relations which unjustifiably limit their autonomy (as "patient"). Does the development and use of *in vitro* fertilization hold this same potential for alienation, albeit in differ- ent ways? Does *in vitro* fertilization violate (or is it in accord with) feminist understandings of embodiment, norms for relationships, and concerns for the common good?

For many feminists the sundering of the power and process of reproduction from the bodies of women con-

stitutes a loss of major proportions. Hence, the notion of moving the whole process to the laboratory (using not only *in vitro* fertilization but artificial placentas, etc.) is not one that receives much enthusiasm. On the other hand, *in vitro* fertilization does not necessarily violate the essential embodying of reproduction. If its purpose is to enable women who would otherwise be infertile to conceive a child, it becomes a means precisely to mediate embodiment. Feminists generally oppose the sacralization of women's reproductive organs and functions that would prohibit all techno- logical intervention. In fact, desacralization in this regard is a necessary step in the breaking of feminine stereotypes and the falsification of anatomy as destiny. Moreover, feminist interpretations are very clear on the validity of separating sexuality from reproduction. Without contradiction, however, they also affirm reproduction as a significant potential dimension of sexuality. Yet feminists do not give an absolute value to a series of "natural" physical connections between sexual intercourse and the fertilization of an ovum by male sperm. It is a failure of imagination which sees this as the only way in which integrated sexuality can be related to reproduction. All in all, then, while human embodiment remains a central concern in a feminist analysis of *in vitro* fertilization, it does not thereby rule out the ethical use of this technology.

Feminists are generally clear on the need to under- stand and experience childbearing in an active way. Pregnancy and childbirth are not events in relation to which women should be wholly passive. Part of taking active control and responsibility regarding their repro- ductive power can include a willingness to use tech- nology in so far as it makes childbearing more responsible, less painful, and more safe. Sometimes discernment of just these consequences for technology is difficult, but the fact that it is called for indicates, again, that *in vitro* fertilization is not ruled out in principle.

Perhaps the most troubling aspect of *in vitro* fertil- ization, and other technologies that actually empower reproduction, is the question of primary agency and responsibility. Women's previous experience with reproductive technology suggests that women's own agency is likely to be submerged in the network of mul- tiple experts needed to achieve *in vitro* fertilization. Far from this accomplishing a liberation of women from childbearing responsibilities, it can entail "further alien- ation of our life processes." Moreover, efforts to restrict and share the agency of professionals often move only in the direction of what some feminists fear as collectivism or state control, the "total alienation of one's life to institutions external to one's own control and governed by a managerial elite." Without a drastic change in the composition of society and the professions, widespread use of *in vitro* fertilization could make it difficult for women to achieve or sustain control of human reproduction.

Does it matter whether women or men, parents or scientists, control reproduction? Feminists argue that those who will bear the responsibility for childrearing should have primary agency in decisions about childbearing – not just because it is their right if they are to bear the burden of such responsibility, but because this is required for the well-being of offspring. "Only those who are deeply realistic about what it takes to nourish human life *from birth onward* have the wisdom to evaluate procreative choice." Reproductive technologies that divorce decisions for childbearing from childrearing fail to take seriously the basic needs of children for not only material resources but personal relations and support, in contexts that allow the awakening of basic trust and the development of fundamental autonomy. It is not only women who, in principle, can make these choices, but it is "parents," not just "scientific facilitators" or society at large or any persons unprepared to take responsibility at an intimate and comprehensive level for our children. Such problems of agency are complex and sobering in the face of technological capabilities such as *in vitro* fertilization. They are not, in principle, intractable, perhaps not even in practice. They need not rule out the ethical use of *in vitro* fertilization. But they occasion grave moral caution.

Yet another consideration regards the developing capability for "selection" of offspring from among many candidates (differentiated by gender, bodily health, intellectual capacity, etc.). The problem of "discards" in *in vitro* fertilization is larger than the discernment of grave embryonic anomalies. For some feminists this capability can erode moral and religious obligation to accept all sorts of persons into the human community. In so doing, it undermines basic feminist principles of equality, inclusiveness, mutuality, and toleration of difference and of "imperfection." *In vitro* fertilization need not, of course, be used in this way. But once again, a voice of caution is raised.

Underlying all of these considerations is the need to measure *in vitro* fertilization according to norms of justice. If justice in its deepest sense can be understood as treating persons in truthful accordance with their concrete reality, then all the issues of embodiment, non-discrimination, agency, responsibility, inclusive care, are issues of justice. They are not focused only on individuals, but on the human community. They converge in the fundamental question, "How are we to reproduce ourselves as human persons?" They press us to new theories of justice which extend a requirement for "just parenting" in relation to all human children. They include, too, questions of the meaning and value of *in vitro* fertilization in a world threatened by overpopulation, in countries where not every existing child is yet cared for, in communities where grave needs of children require the resources of science and technology. Questions of macroallocation of scarce goods and services may finally be unresolvable, but they cannot be ignored. At the very least, in this instance, they preclude justifications of *in vitro* fertilization on the basis of any absolute right to procreate.

A feminist analysis of *in vitro* fertilization remains, then, provisional. It yields, however, the following position. Negatively, there are no grounds for an absolute prohibition of the development and use of technology such as *in vitro* fertilization. Positively, such technology may aid just and responsible human reproduction. The presence of certain circumstances, or certain conditions, sets limits to its ethical development and use – circumstances such as (1) high risk of injury to the well-being of either parent or child (2) a context unconducive to the growth and development of any child produced (unconducive because, for example, no one is prepared to offer the child a basic human personal relationship) (3) an intention to produce a child to be used as a means only, in relation to the producers' ends (as, for example, if the child is produced merely for the sake of the advance of scientific research, or for the duplication of one's own self without regard for the child's development into an autonomous self) (4) failure to meet criteria of distributive justice (when it is determined that other basic human needs place legitimate prior claims on the resources involved). Such conditions rule out spectres of human laboratory "farms." They also tell us something about the conditions for any ethical decisions regarding human reproduction, not just decisions made in the context of reproductive technology.

[Handwritten margin notes:]

what's the difference of screening + picking a man

"you can create perfect babies"

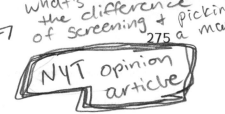

NYT opinion article

Ecclesial

Oliver O'Donovan, *Begotten or Made?*

Like much of O'Donovan's work, this passage lies close to the border between ecclesial and universal ethics. Its concluding remarks, however, place it firmly on the ecclesial side. O'Donovan appeals to the doctrine of creation. This doctrine is invoked in a general way very frequently in universal ethics, particularly when (as here) there are anxieties about "playing God" or about the natural order more broadly. But O'Donovan has a more nuanced theological appeal to creation.

His point is that the child born through *in vitro* fertilization (IVF) is "the creature of the doctors who assisted at her conception." In other words her creator is not God but the physicians and the society that makes such physicians possible. O'Donovan's argument pivots on the sanguine undertaking of risk, and the way those taking risks are not accountable to those who stand to suffer from the adverse consequences of those risks. Like other ecclesial ethicists, O'Donovan deftly portrays the outlines of a society shorn of the ability to think of God as creator, and thus exhibits a genuinely theological ethic, one that shows the ways human life and society are profoundly rooted in the character of God.

[Handwritten margin note:] Is it non-Christian to utilize IVF bc God did not create it directly?

Oliver O'Donovan. *Begotten or Made?* Oxford: Clarendon Press; New York: Oxford University Press, 1984. From Chapter 5, "In a Glass Darkly," pages 79–83, 85–6. By permission of Oxford University Press.

[O'Donovan begins his essay with a fairy-tale in which a fairy godmother magically grants pregnancy to a childless couple through IVF, but without the usual difficulties and uncertainties of the procedure. O'Donovan explores IVF through the doubts the couple may have had about the fairy godmother's solution to their lack of children.]

What, then, was achieved by discussing a fairy-tale? It enabled us to concentrate our attention on an ideal, hypothetical simple-case IVF pregnancy, and so evaluate the procedure in the abstract. That is an important step in the moral discussion, but not one at which we can stop. Many current discussions seem content to stop there; but if we are to evaluate IVF as it really is, and not as it might be in a world of magic wands, we must take account of certain contextual features which are inseparable from it in reality. I shall speak of two such features in particular, which I think to be of central importance.

In the first place there is the inextricable involvement of clinical *in vitro* fertilization with non-clinical research on early human embryos. I say "inextricable"

although I am aware that some practitioners in this field insist on keeping these two questions distinct (as, of course, in conceptual abstraction they are). And I do not undervalue the restraint which some practitioners exercise in their research activities precisely in order to commend their work on its merits as clinical practice. Nevertheless, the distinction between this clinical practice and the research which supports it cannot be maintained with much plausibility for very long. We may accept two simple statements of fact from Dr. R. G. Edwards: "Oocytes and embryos were grown during … early investigations without intention of replacing them in the uterus"; and: "This preliminary period is by no means completed, even in hospitals and clinics where many pregnancies have already been established by IVF. Improved methods are needed to assess the normality of growth of the embryos, and to sustain or monitor their development without impairing the development of those which are to be replaced in the mother." In other words: IVF did depend on non-clinical embryo-research in order to become established, and it still does depend on non-clinical embryo research in order to perfect its techniques. IVF is not the gift of a fairy-godmother; it is the gift of researchers. The suggestion that we can thank these researchers for their gift, make use of what they have achieved, and simultaneously declare all their research, past and future, to be illegitimate, is strikingly lacking both in consistency and realism. Our view of IVF, then, is necessarily determined by our view of non-clinical research on early embryos.

The second feature is the risk to the child who will be born; and in raising this issue it is necessary to specify rather carefully what kind of risk we are talking about and what its moral significance is. There may, in the first place, be risks of genetic or other defects which already arise in the course of natural procreation and which are replicated in artificial procreation. We may expect children born of IVF to show the same proportion of defects as children born in the course of nature; and such an event need not trouble us. There may, in the second place, be an *enhanced* risk of such defects, which is *indirectly* attributable to the IVF procedure. We may fear that more children may be born with inherited defects because the natural process of selection through foetal wastage is inhibited by the measures taken to ensure replacement. This will certainly trouble us, if it should turn out to be the case; but to what extent it will appear to be a decisive consideration will depend, no doubt, on the extent of the increment by which the natural risk is enhanced. It will be a matter of prudential judgement to decide whether this increment is compensated for by the great good of circumventing childlessness. I am speaking now about neither of these kinds of risk, but about risk *directly* attributable to the IVF procedure itself. Will there arise defects which are due, not to natural risk, not to the enhancement of natural risk indirectly, but directly to the procedure itself?

I do not claim to know, or even to suspect, the answer to that question. As I understand the situation, nobody knows the answer to it with certainty, even now. B. A. Liebermann and P. Dyer write of the "as yet undetermined incidence of chromosomal and other diagnosable defects peculiar to *in vitro* fertilization." Experience with embryos frozen for a long period before replacement is still very limited. But even if somebody does now know the answer, or suspects that he knows it, and even if that answer is as favourable to IVF as could be hoped, it is still the case that nobody knew the answer when the procedure was inaugurated. And it is *the willingness to take these risks*, rather than the favourableness or unfavourableness of the outcome, which in my view gives its most decisive characterization to the whole enterprise.

The risk is usually justified by an argument that runs something like this: since there are risks associated with natural conception (which in some cases can be very high), why should we be more reluctant to incur risks from artificial conception than we are to incur those? Thus H. W. Jones maintains: "This argument [i.e. the argument against risk-taking] could equally well be applied to a couple, the female of which is above the age of 35, where the expectation of an abnormality is measurable." And Gerald Elfstrom: "Natural conception entails its attendant risks for the unborn without offering any clearcut benefit to it." We must not confuse this reply with another, which sounds very similar and, as I have said, raises no problems. It does not mean that artificial conception merely reproduces risks already attendant on natural conception. It means that we must be prepared to take new risks, uniquely related to artificial conception, because we have hitherto been prepared to take old risks related to natural conception. The logic of the argument, it seems to me, is that we must lose all sense of difference between nature and artifice, between the constraints which are given to us as natural conditions for our lives, and the liabilities of projects which we have freely undertaken and might as freely not have undertaken. Thus Elfstrom revealingly concludes his argument: "Both kinds of event [i.e. defective births arising from natural and artificial causes] result from human actions, and therefore both kinds of risk to the unborn may be avoided by human restraint." That is the conclusion to which a technological society must certainly come. Even natural procreation is something which we may equally well undertake or not undertake, and it is subject to exactly the same cost-benefit calculus which we apply to all our projects. Thus having children "naturally" is just another instrumental means chosen to realize a project which could, if it proved more efficient, equally well be realized by technical means. The whole of life … comes to be interpreted in the light of technique.

We are faced with a choice, as Paul Ramsey rightly said in his reply to Elfstrom, in which "no one can long halt between two opinions: one favouring artificiality as more human, delivering us from the 'necessities' of nature, the other favouring the spontaneities of natural procreation." Like the people of Israel we must choose between Baal and Yahweh: but is it between the Baal of nature and the Yahweh of artifice (as an older generation of Old Testament critics liked to suggest) or between the Baal who may be manipulated by magic and the Yahweh who is sovereign Lord of man and creation? That, perhaps, is the fundamental form of our question. For the appearance of neutrality is only an appearance. Once we begin to justify the risks of artifice by analogy with the uncertainties of nature, we have put ourselves in a masterful position *vis-à-vis* the natural processes. The first step for any man to take in the understanding of divine providence, is to comprehend that God has evils at his disposal which he does not put at ours. Though he works good through war, death, disease, famine, and cruelty, it is not given to us to deploy these mysterious alchemies in the hope that we may bring forth good from them. There is the world of difference between accepting the risk of a disabled child (where that risk is imposed upon us by nature) and ourselves imposing that risk in pursuit of our own purposes. ...

Can we deny that risks taken in relation to a child's conception are risks for which the child can never properly hold anyone responsible? Can we deny, therefore, that the IVF practitioner, who takes these risks, not as a parent does, in renunciation to divine providence, but in calculation relating to his technical project, places himself in a quite unparalleled position *vis-à-vis* another human being? Is there another instance in our moral experience where someone may, in pursuit of a scheme of world-betterment, impose injuries upon another human being for which he cannot subsequently be held responsible? These paradoxes arise only because the beginning of a human being has come to be at the same time also a making; and that transformation has occurred, not, in my opinion, as a result of the separation of acts, but as a result of the taking of risks which place those who take them above the interrogation of those who suffer from them. I confess that I do not know how to think of an IVF child except (in some unclear but inescapable sense) as the *creature* of the doctors who assisted at her conception – which means,

also, of the society to which the doctor belongs and for whom he acts.

If anyone finds this conception grotesque and self-evidently wrong, I congratulate him on his good habits of thought – but with a warning. Good habits of thought teach us to find the notion of one human being as the creature of another odd and repulsive; but habit alone will not protect a culture against the "paradigm shift" in its perceptions which will occur when too much in what it observes and does is more obviously thought of in a new way. If our habits of thought continue to instruct us that the IVF child is radically equal to the doctors who produced her, then that is good – for the time being. But if we do not live and act in accordance with such conceptions, and if society welcomes more and more institutions and practices which implicitly deny them, then they will soon appear to be merely sentimental, the tatters and shreds which remind us of how we used once to clothe the world with intelligibility.

For myself, I do not *believe* that the doctor has become the child's creator. I do not believe it, though, as I have admitted, I do not know how to reconcile my unbelief with the obvious significance of *in vitro* fertilization. I can only confess, as a matter of Christian faith, that I believe in another and unique Creator who will not relinquish to others his place as the maker and preserver of mankind. To those who wish to make this confession with me let me put this closing question: should we not expect that a humanity which is so made will vindicate its maker, and his creatures, against every false claim to lordship?

Abortion

Abortion refers to the deliberate choice to terminate a pregnancy through an intervention which either forces the pre-viable fetus out of the womb or destroys the fetus within the womb. It is a hugely emotive issue because the terms used – death, murder, termination, fetus, blastocyst, embryo, person – are all contested, and the chosen vocabulary tends to presuppose the moral conclusion. While many look to scripture for specific guidance, it is hard to find such guidance precisely on the question of moral status of the unborn fetus.

The tendency in universal ethics has been to focus somewhat narrowly on the fetus and its competing

claims vis-à-vis its mother; while subversive ethics seeks to restore the mother's perspective; and ecclesial ethics generally seeks to portray this classic "decisionist" issue against a backdrop of wider concerns without which it is unintelligible and insoluble, such as the unexpectedness of all children and the role of hospitality in the capacity of all communities to receive life.

These three readings are each exemplary treatments from their respective strands, displaying the different qualities of universal, subversive, and ecclesial ethics as distinctly as any in this volume.

Universal

James M. Gustafson, *Abortion: An Ethical Case Study*

James M. Gustafson (b. 1925) has taught at Emory University in Atlanta, at Yale, and at the University of Chicago. He comes from the Reformed tradition, studied under H. Richard Niebuhr, and became with Paul Ramsey the leading Protestant ethicist of his generation. His major work, *Ethics from a Theocentric Perspective*, places a high value on scientific and other non-theological sources of knowledge and resists the assumption that humanity is the center of God's purposes. He sees ethics as about aligning human beings and all things in a manner appropriate to their relations to God.

This excerpt is in many ways a classic example of universal ethics. It soberly and sensitively presents the tragic situation, considers the various factors that need to be taken into consideration, offers reasons for and against each of the options, and declares a tentative conclusion. It is a "decisionist" model. It differs significantly from an ecclesial approach by not investigating the community of which the woman is a part (although it does consider her friendships), nor examining in detail the presuppositions behind what seem the only possible courses of action. It is not unaware of subversive considerations – it makes explicit reference to a bias toward the "widow, the orphan and the stranger."

Gustafson himself takes the view that human life begins at conception – but he develops several arguments that suggest this is not the only consideration. He locates his approach between what he regards as an extreme deontological view of "the manuals" (by which he means standard Catholic and Protestant textbooks inclined to pass judgment without regard to circumstantial detail) and the emotivist consequentialist view that simply trusts in the protagonist's feelings. The overall tenor of the argument is of specific principles tempered by profound awareness of complex and conflicting commitments.

James M. Gustafson. "A Protestant Ethical Approach." Pages 101–22 in *The Morality of Abortion: Legal and Historical Perspectives.* Ed. John T. Noonan, Jr. Cambridge, MA: Harvard University Press, 1970. Excerpt from pages 107–17.

II. A Discussion of a Human Choice

The pregnant woman is in her early twenties. She is a lapsed Catholic, with no significant religious affiliation at the present time, although she expresses some need for a "church." Her marriage was terminated by divorce; her husband was given custody of three children by that marriage. She had an affair with a man who "befriended" her, but there were no serious prospects for a marriage with him, and the affair has ended. Her family life was as disrupted and as tragic as that which is dramatically presented in Eugene O'Neill's *Long Day's Journey into Night*. Her alcoholic mother mistreated her children, coerced them into deceptive activity for her ends, and was given to periods of violence. Her father has been

addicted to drugs, but has managed to continue in business, avoid incarceration, and provide a decent income for his family. The pregnant woman fled from home after high school to reside in a distant state, and has no significant contact with her parents or siblings. She has two or three friends.

Her pregnancy occurred when she was raped by her former husband and three other men after she had agreed to meet him to talk about their children. The rapes can only be described as acts of sadistic vengeance. She is unwilling to prefer charges against the men, since she believes it would be a further detriment to her children. She has no steady job, partially because of periodic gastro-intestinal illnesses, and has no other income. There are no known physiological difficulties which would jeopardize her life or that of the child. She is unusually intelligent and very articulate, and is not hysterical about her situation. Termination of the pregnancy is a live option for her as a way to cope with one of the many difficulties she faces.

The Christian Moralist's Responsible Relationship

... The moralist responding to this woman can establish one of a number of ways of relating to her in his conversations. The two extremes are obvious. On the one hand, he could determine that no physiological difficulties seem to be present in the pregnancy, and thus seek to enforce her compliance with the standard rule against abortions. The manuals would decide what right conduct is; her predicament would be defined so that factors that are important for others who respond to her are not pertinent to the decision about abortion. Both the moralist and the woman could defer further moral responsibility to the textbooks. On the other hand, he could take a highly permissive approach to the conversation. In reliance on a theory of morality that would minimize the objective moral considerations, and affirm that what a person feels is best is morally right, he could affirm consistently what her own dominant disposition seemed to be, and let that determine the decision.

Somewhere between these is what I would delineate as a more responsible relationship than either of the two extremes. It would recognize that the moralist and the woman are in an interpersonal relationship; this is to say that as human beings they need to be open to each other, to have a high measure of confidence in each other, to have empathy for each other. ...

Salient Facts in One Christian Moralist's Interpretation

... In the personal situation under discussion, it is clear that if medical factors alone were to be considered grounds for an abortion, none would be morally permissible. The woman had three pregnancies that came to full term, and the children were healthy. To the best of her knowledge there are no medical problems at the present time. Periodic gastro-intestinal illnesses, which might be relieved with better medical care, would not be sufficient medical grounds. Although the present pregnancy is disturbing for many reasons, including both the occasion on which the pregnancy occurred and the future social prospects for the woman and the child, in the judgment of the moralist the woman is able to cope with her situation without serious threat to her mental health. The medical factors insofar as the moralist can grasp them, would not warrant a therapeutic abortion. ...

The moralist has to reckon with the financial plight of the woman. She is self-supporting, but her income is irregular. There are no savings. Application for welfare support might lead to the disclosure of matters she wishes to keep in confidence. If a legal abortion was possible, the physician would receive little or no remuneration from the patient. There are no funds in sight to finance an illegal abortion, and the medical risks involved in securing a quack rule that out as a viable prospect. The child, if not aborted, could be let out for adoption, and means might be found to give minimum support for the mother during pregnancy. If she should choose to keep the child, which is her moral right to do, there are no prospects for sufficient financial support, although with the recovery of her health the woman could join the work force and probably with her intelligence earn a modest income.

The spiritual and emotional factors involved are more difficult to assess. While the moralist is impressed with the relative calm with which the woman converses about her predicament, he is aware that this ability is probably the result of learning to cope with previous inhumane treatment and with events that led to no happy ending. Socially, she is sustained only by two or three friends, and these friendships could readily be disrupted by geographical mobility. She has no significant, explicit religious faith, and as a lapsed Catholic who views the Church and its priests as harsh taskmasters, she is unwilling to turn to it for spiritual and moral sustenance. She has a profound desire not merely to achieve a situation of equanimity, of absence of suffering and conflict, but also to achieve positive goals. ...

The more readily identifiable moral factors are three, though in the ethical perspective of this paper, this constitutes an oversimple limitation of the "moral" and of the nature of moral responsibility. One is the inviolability of life, the sanctity of life. My opinion is that since the genotype is formed at conception, all the genetic potentialities of personal existence are there. Thus it is to be preserved unless reasons can be given that make an exception morally justifiable. A second is rape – not only a crime, but a morally evil deed. The sexual relations from which the pregnancy came were not only engaged in against the woman's will, but were in her judgment acts of retaliation and vengeance. The third is the relation of morality to the civil law. ...

Salient Aspects of the Moralist's Perspective

... The perspective of the Christian moralist is informed and directed by his fundamental trust that the forces of life seek the human good, that God is good, is love. This is a matter of trust and confidence, and not merely a matter of believing certain propositions to be true. ...

God wills the creation, preservation, reconciliation, and redemption of human life. Thus, one can infer, it is better to give and preserve life than to take it away; it is better to prevent its coming into being than to destroy it when it has come into being. But the purposes of God for life pertain to more than physical existence: there are conditions for human life that need delineation: physical health, possibilities for future good and meaning that engender and sustain hope, relationships of trust and love, freedom to respond and initiate and achieve, and many others. The love of God, and in response to it, the loves of men, are particularly sensitive to "the widow, the orphan, and the stranger in your midst," to the oppressed and the weak.

These brief and cryptic statements are the grounds for moral biases: life is to be preserved, the weak and the helpless are to be cared for especially, the moral requisite of trust, hope, love, freedom, justice, and others are to be met so that human life can be meaningful. The bias gives a direction, a fundamental intention that does not in itself resolve the darknesses beyond the reach of its light, the ambiguities of particular cases. It begins to order what preferences one would have under ideal conditions and under real conditions. One would prefer not to induce an abortion in this instance. There is consistency between this preference and the Christian moralist's faith and convictions. But one would prefer for conception to arise within love rather than hate, and one would prefer that there would be indications that the unknowable future were more favorably disposed to the human well-being of the mother and the child.

The perspective of the Christian moralist is informed and directed by his understanding of the nature of human life, as well as his convictions about God. Abbreviated statements of some convictions are sufficient here. These would be first, that moral life is a life of action, in which intentions, judgments, the exercise of bodily power and other forms of power and influence give direction to our responses to past events, and direction to future events themselves. Persons are active, responsive, creative, reflective, self-aware, initiating. The second would be that we can discern something of the order of relationships and activity that sustains, preserves, and develops our humanity. The child conceived in love, within a marriage (an order of love), within an order of society that maintains justice, is more likely to have a higher quality of life than one who is conceived in other conditions. The decision to seek an abortion is human, the act of abortion would be human, the relationships before, during, and after the abortion are human. The consequences are not fully predictable

beyond the physical, and yet the human is more than perpetuation of the body. A moral order was violated in rape; are the human conditions present that would sustain and heal the humanity of the child and the mother in the future? The answer to that question is a finite, human answer, and how it will be answered by the mother and others deeply affects a most decisive act. ...

Pertinent Principles That Can Be Stipulated for Reflection

Neither the moralist nor the woman comes to a situation without some convictions and beliefs that begin to dissolve some of the complexity of the particularities into manageable terms. Perhaps the traditional Catholic arguments simply assume that one can begin with these convictions and principles, and need not immerse one's self in the tragic concreteness. The pertinent ones in this case have already been alluded to, but here they can be reduced to a simpler scheme.

1 Life is to be preserved rather than destroyed.
2 Those who cannot assert their own rights to life are especially to be protected.
3 There are exceptions to these rules.

Possible exceptions are:

a "medical indications" that make therapeutic abortion morally viable. Condition not present here.
b the pregnancy has occurred as a result of sexual crime. (I would grant this as a viable possible exception in every instance for reasons imbedded in the above discussion, if the woman herself were convinced that it was right. In other than detached academic discussions I would never dispatch an inquiry with a ready granting of the exception. If the woman sees the exception as valid, she has a right to more than a potentially legal justification for her decision; as a person she has the right to understand why it is an exception in her dreadful plight.)
c the social and emotional conditions do not appear to be beneficial for the well-being of the mother and the child. (In particular circumstances, this may appear to be a justification, but I would not resort to it until possibilities for financial, social, and spiritual help have been explored.) ...

The Decision of the Moralist

My own decision is: (a) if I were in the woman's human predicament I believe I could morally justify an abortion, and thus: (b) I would affirm its moral propriety in this instance. Clearly, logic alone is not the process by which a defense of this particular judgment can be given; clearly, the facts of the matter do not add up to a justification of abortion so that one can say "the situation determines everything." Nor is it a matter of some inspiration of the Spirit. It is a human decision, made in freedom, informed and governed by beliefs and values, as well as by attitudes and a fundamental perspective. It is a discernment of compassion for the woman, as well as of objective moral reflection. It may not be morally "right" in the eyes of others, and although we could indicate where the matters of dispute between us are in discourse, and perhaps even close the gap between opinions to some extent, argument about it would probably not be persuasive. The judgment is made with a sense of its limitations, which include the limitations of the one who decides (which might well result from his lack of courage, his pride, his slothfulness in thinking, and other perversities).

Subversive

Beverly Wildung Harrison with Shirley Cloyes, *Procreative Choice*

Beverly Wildung Harrison (b. 1932) taught for 34 years at Union Theological Seminary in New York and authored *Our Right to Choose: Toward a New Ethic of Abortion* (1983). Like the passage quoted above from Margaret Farley, this passage fits into the first strand of feminist ethics fairly succinctly. Harrison is quick to invoke the notion of rights – a clear appeal to a universal ethic that goes beyond simply honoring women's experience. She appeals to a dialectical understanding of creation that balances the givens of nature with the proven ability of humans in recent centuries to affect nature positively (and negatively).

Harrison's lament is that "Christian theology celebrates the power of human freedom to shape and determine the quality of human life except when the issue of procreative choice arises." She concludes therefore that the prohibition of abortion derives more from the "ancient power of misogyny rather than from any passion for the sacredness of human life." She calls for a "desacralization" of procreation and a deeper sacralization of social relationships instead. As a compelling example of the current paradox, she points out that "those who proclaim that a zygote at the moment of conception is a person worthy of citizenship continue to deny full social and political rights to women."

Perhaps the most sensitive paragraph addresses the question of whether abortion is murder. Harrison highlights the tendency toward biological reductionism; but she is more vociferous in pointing out that the same ethicists who argue vehemently against abortion are often much more sanguine about the taking of human life in other circumstances such as war and capital punishment. It remains unclear whether abortion is justifiable homicide or not homicide at all.

Beverly Wildung Harrison with Shirley Cloyes. "Theology and Morality of Procreative Choice." Pages 213–32 in *Feminist Theological Ethics: A Reader.* Ed. Lois K. Daly. Louisville: Westminster/John Knox Press, 1994. Excerpt from pages 213–16, 223–4, 227–8.

Much discussion of abortion betrays the heavy hand of misogyny, the hatred of women. We all have a responsibility to recognize this bias – sometimes subtle – when ancient negative attitudes toward women intrude into the abortion debate. It is morally incumbent on us to convert the Christian position to a teaching more respectful of women's concrete history and experience.

My professional peers who are my opponents on this question feel they own the Christian tradition in this matter and recognize no need to rethink their positions in the light of this claim. As a feminist, I cannot sit in silence when women's right to shape the use of our procreative power is denied. Women's competence as moral decision makers is once again challenged by the state even before the moral basis of women's right to procreative choice has been fully elaborated and recognized. Those who deny women control of procreative power claim that they do so in defense of moral sensibility, in the name of the sanctity of human life. We have a long way to go before the sanctity of human life will include genuine regard and concern for every female already born, and no social policy discussion that obscures this fact deserves to be called moral. We hope the day will come when it will not be called "Christian" either, for the Christian ethos is the generating source of the current moral crusade to prevent women from gaining control over the most life-shaping power we possess. ...

Abortion in Theological Context

... The elevation of procreation as the central image for divine blessing is intimately connected to the rise of patriarchy. In patriarchal societies it is the male's power that is enhanced by the gift of new life. Throughout history, women's power of procreation has stood in definite tension with this male social control. In fact, what we feminists call patriarchy – that is, patterned or institutionalized legitimations of male superiority – derives from the need of men, through male-dominated political institutions such as tribes, states, and religious systems, to control women's power to procreate the species. We must assume, then, that many of these efforts at social control of procreation, including some church teaching on contraception and abortion, were part of this institutional system. The perpetuation of patriarchal control itself depended on wresting the power of procreation from women and shaping women's lives accordingly.

In the past four centuries, the entire Christian story has had to undergo dramatic accommodation to new and emergent world conditions and to the scientific revolution. As the older theological metaphors for creation encountered the rising power of science, a new self-understanding including our human capacity to affect nature had to be incorporated into Christian theology or its central theological story would have become obscurantist. Human agency had to be introjected into a dialectical understanding of creation.

The range of human freedom to shape and enhance creation is now celebrated theologically, but only up to the point of changes in our understanding of what is natural for women. Here a barrier has been drawn that declares No Radical Freedom! The only difference between mainstream Protestant and Roman Catholic theologians on these matters is at the point of contraception, which Protestants more readily accept. However, Protestants like Karl Barth and Helmut Thielicke exhibit a subtle shift of mood when they turn to discussing issues regarding women. They follow the typical Protestant pattern: They have accepted contraception or family planning as part of the new freedom, granted by God, but both draw back from the idea that abortion could be morally acceptable. In *The Ethics of Sex*, Thielicke offers a romantic, ecstatic celebration of family planning on one page and then elaborates a total denunciation of abortion as unthinkable on the next. Most Christian theological opinion draws the line between contraception and abortion, whereas the *official* Catholic teaching still anathematizes contraception.

The problem, then, is that Christian theology celebrates the power of human freedom to shape and determine the quality of human life except when the issue of procreative choice arises. Abortion is anathema, while widespread sterilization abuse goes unnoticed. The power of man to shape creation radically is never rejected. When one stops to consider the awesome power over nature that males take for granted and celebrate, including the power to alter the conditions of human life in myriad ways, the suspicion dawns that the near hysteria that prevails about the immorality of women's right to choose abortion derives its force from the ancient power of misogyny rather than from any passion for the sacredness of human life. An index of the continuing misogyny in Christian tradition is male theologians' refusal to recognize the full range of human power to shape creation in those matters that pertain to women's power to affect the quality of our lives.

In contrast, a feminist theological approach recognizes that nothing is more urgent, in light of the changing circumstances of human beings on planet Earth, than to recognize that the entire natural-historical context of human procreative power has shifted. We desperately need a desacralization of our biological power to reproduce and at the same time a real concern for human dignity and the social conditions for personhood and the values of human relationship. And note that desacralization does not mean complete devaluation of the worth of procreation. It means we must shift away from the notion that the central metaphors for divine blessing are expressed at the biological level to the recognition that our social relations bear the image of what is most holy. …

Abortion and Moral Theory

… We need to remember that even in Roman Catholic natural law ethics, the definition of the status of fetal life has shifted over time and in all cases the status of prenatal life involves a moral judgment, not a scientific one. The question is properly posed this way: What status are we morally wise to predicate to prenatal human life, given that the fetus is not yet a fully existent human being? Those constrained under Catholic teaching have been required for the past ninety years to believe a human being exists from conception, when the ovum and sperm merge. This answer from one tradition has had far wider impact on our culture than most people recognize. Other Christians come from traditions that do not offer (and could not offer, given their conception of the structure of the church as moral community) a definitive answer to this question.

Even so, some contemporary Protestant medical ethicists, fascinated by recent genetic discoveries and experiments with deoxyribonucleic acid (DNA), have all but sacralized the moment in which the genetic code is implanted as the moment of humanization, which leaves them close to the traditional Roman Catholic position. Protestant male theologians have long let their enthrallment with science lead to a sacralization of specific scientific discoveries, usually to the detriment of theological and moral clarity. In any case, there are two responses that must be made to the claim that the fetus in early stages of development is a human life or, more dubiously, a human person.

First, the historical struggle for women's personhood is far from won, owing chiefly to the opposition of organized religious groups to full equality for women. Those who proclaim that a zygote at the moment of conception is a person worthy of citizenship continue to deny full social and political rights to women. Whatever one's judgment about the moral status of the fetus, it cannot be argued that that assessment deserves greater moral standing in analysis than does the position of the pregnant woman. This matter of evaluating the meaning of prenatal life is where morally sensitive people's judgments diverge. I cannot believe that any morally sensitive person would fail to value the woman's full, existent life less than they value early fetal life. Most women can become pregnant and carry fetal life to term

many, many times in their lifetimes. The distinctly human power is not our biologic capacity to bear children, but our power to actively love, nurture, care for one another and shape one another's existence in cultural and social interaction. To equate a biologic process with full normative humanity is crass biologic reductionism, and such reductionism is never practiced in religious ethics except where women's lives and well-being are involved.

Second, even though prenatal life, as it moves toward biologic individuation of human form, has value, the equation of abortion with murder is dubious. And the equation of abortion with homicide – the taking of human life – should be carefully weighed. We should also remember that we live in a world where men extend other men wide moral range in relation to justifiable homicide. For example, the just-war tradition has legitimated widespread forms of killing in war, and Christian ethicists have often extended great latitude to rulers and those in power in making choices about killing human beings. Would that such moralists extended equal benefit of a doubt to women facing life-crushing psychological and politicoeconomic pressures in the face of childbearing! Men, daily, make life-determining decisions concerning nuclear power or chemical use in the environment, for example, that affect the well-being of fetuses, and our society expresses no significant opposition, even when such decisions do widespread genetic damage. When we argue for the appropriateness of legal abortion, moral outrage rises. …

The Social Policy Dimensions of the Debate

We must always insist that the objective social conditions that make women and children already born highly vulnerable can only be worsened by a social policy of compulsory pregnancy. However one judges the moral quality of the individual act of abortion (and here, differences among us do exist that are morally justifiable), it is still necessary to distinguish between how one judges the act of abortion morally and what one believes a societywide policy on abortion should be. We must not let those who have moral scruples against the personal act ignore the fact that a just social policy must also include active concern for enhancement of women's well-being and, for that, policies that would in fact make abortions less necessary. To anathematize abortion when the social and material conditions for control of procreation do not exist is to blame the victim, not to address the deep dilemmas of female existence in this society.

Even so, there is no reason for those of us who celebrate procreative choice as a great moral good to pretend that resort to abortion is ever a desirable means of expressing this choice. I know of no one on the pro-choice side who has confused the desirability of the availability of abortion with the celebration of the act itself. We all have every reason to hope that safer, more reliable means of contraception may be found and that violence against women will be reduced. Furthermore, we should be emphatic that our social policy demands include opposition to sterilization abuse, insistence on higher standards of health care for women and children, better prenatal care, reduction of unnecessary surgery on women's reproductive systems, increased research to improve contraception, and so on. Nor should we draw back from criticizing a health care delivery system that exploits women. An abortion industry thrives on the profitability of abortion, but women are not to blame for this.

A feminist position demands social conditions that support women's full, self-respecting right to procreative choice, including the right not to be sterilized against our wills, the right to choose abortion as a birth control means of last resort, and the right to a prenatal and postnatal health care system that will also reduce the now widespread trauma of having to deliver babies in rigid, impersonal health care settings. Pro-lifers do best politically when we allow them to keep the discussion narrowly focused on the morality of the act of abortion and on the moral value of the fetus. We do best politically when we make the deep connections between the full context of this issue in women's lives, including this society's systemic or patterned injustice toward women.

Ecclesial

Stanley Hauerwas, *Abortion and the Church*

This passage displays several characteristic features of ecclesial ethics. Stanley Hauerwas constantly challenges the use of universal terms such as rights, choice, compassion, the "sanctity of life," or "wanted children," pointing out their weaknesses as theological designations. Instead, he calls for abortion, like other significant practices, to be set within the context of Christian worship. It is in worship, he believes, that Christians learn the "grammar" of their moral lives; worship provides the setting in which life under God makes sense. Outside the context of worship, moral lives are isolated, and what is held up as a defense of the "private" in fact becomes the abandonment of women, the neglect of children, and the permission for male promiscuity. Rather than begin by demanding the world should adhere to abstract ethical demands, ecclesial ethics should begin, Hauerwas contends, with deepening the practice of hospitality in accordance with the assumptions of baptism.

Thus Hauerwas offers a way of talking about medical ethics that is not in thrall to technological investigation. When Beverly Wildung Harrison says that "Protestant male theologians have long let their enthrallment with science lead to a sacralization of specific scientific discoveries" she is clearly not talking about Hauerwas.

Stanley Hauerwas. "Abortion, Theologically Understood." Pages 603–22 in *The Hauerwas Reader*. Ed. John Berkman and Michael Cartwright. Durham, NC: Duke University Press, 2001. Excerpt from pages 612–19.

The Church as True Family

We, as church, are ready to be challenged by the other. This has to do with the fact that in the church, every adult, whether single or married, is called to be a parent. All Christian adults have a parental responsibility because of baptism. Biology does not make parents in the church. Baptism does. Baptism makes all adult Christians parents and gives them the obligation to help introduce these children to the gospel. Listen to the baptismal vows; in them the whole church promises to be parent. The minister addresses the church with these words:

Will you nurture one another in the Christian faith and life and include [those being baptized] now before you in your care?

With God's help we will proclaim the good news and live according to the example of Christ. We will surround [those being baptized] with a community of love and forgiveness, that they may grow in their service to others. We will pray for [those being baptized], that they may be true disciples who walk in the way that leads to life.

By these vows the church reinvents the family. …

From the beginning we Christians have made singleness as valid a way of life as marriage. What it means to be the church is to be a group of people called out of the world, and back into the world, to embody the hope of the Kingdom of God. Children are not necessary for the growth of the Kingdom, because the church can call the stranger into her midst. That makes both singleness and marriage possible vocations. If everybody has to marry, then marriage is a terrible burden. But the church does not believe that everybody has to marry. Even so, those who do not marry are also parents within the church, because the church is now the true family. The church is a family into which children are brought and received. It is only within that context that it makes sense for the church to say, "We are always ready to receive children. We are *always* ready to receive children." The people of God know no enemy when it comes to children.

Why "When Life Begins" Is Not the Fundamental Question

… When many people start talking about abortion, what is the first thing they talk about? When life begins. And why do they get into the question of when life begins? Because they think that the abortion issue is determined primarily by the claims that life is sacred and that life is never to be taken. They assume that these claims let you know how it is that you ought to think about abortion.

Well, I want to know where Christians get the notion that life is sacred. That notion seems to have no reference at all to God. Any good secularist can think life is sacred. Of course, what the secularist means by the word *sacred* is interesting, but the idea that Christians are about the maintenance of some principle separate from our understanding of God is just crazy. As a matter of fact, Christians do not believe that life is sacred. I often remind my right-to-life friends that Christians took their children with them to martyrdom rather than have them raised pagan. Christians believe there is much worth dying for. We do not believe that human life is an absolute good in and of itself. Of course, our desire to protect human life is part of our seeing each human being as God's creature. But that does not mean that we believe that life is an overriding good.

To say that life is an overriding good is to underwrite the modern sentimentality that there is absolutely nothing in this world worth dying for. Christians know that Christianity is simply extended training in dying early. That is what we have always been about. Listen to the gospel! I know that today we use the church primarily as a means of safety, but life in the church should actually involve extended training in learning to die early.

When you frame the abortion issue in sacredness-of-life language, you get into intractable debates about when life begins. Notice that is an issue for legalists. By that I mean the fundamental question becomes, How do you avoid doing the wrong thing?

In contrast, the Christian approach is not one of deciding when life has begun, but hoping that it has. We hope that human life has begun! We are not the kind of people that ask: Does human life start at the blastocyst stage, or at implantation? Instead, we are the kind of people that hope life has started, because we are ready to believe that this new life will enrich our community. We believe this not because we have sentimental views about children. Honestly, I cannot imagine anything worse than people saying that they have children because their hope for the future is in their children. You would never have children if you had them for that reason. We are able to have children because our hope is in God, who makes it possible to do the absurd thing of having children. In a world of such terrible injustice, in a world of such terrible misery; in a world that may well be about the killing of our children, having children is an extraordinary act of faith and hope. But as Christians we can have hope in the God who urges us to welcome children. When that happens, it is an extraordinary testimony of faith.

Why "When Personhood Begins" Is Not the Fundamental Question

On the pro-choice side, you also get the abortion issue framed in a context that is outside of a communitarian structure. On the pro-choice side, you get the question about when the fetus becomes a "person," because only persons supposedly have citizenship rights. That is the issue of *Roe v. Wade*. It is odd for Christians to take this approach since we believe that we are first of all citizens of a far different kingdom than something called the United States of America. If we end up identifying persons with the ability to reason – which, I think, finally renders all of our lives deeply problematic – then we cannot tell why it is that we ought to care for the profoundly retarded. One of the most chilling aspects of the current abortion debate in the wider society is the general acceptance, even among antiabortion people, of the legitimacy of aborting severely defective children. Where do people get that idea? Where do people get the idea that severely defective children are somehow a less valuable gift from God? People get that idea by privileging rationality. We privilege our ability to reason. I find that morally indefensible.

We must remember that as Christians we do not believe in the inherent sacredness of life or in personhood. Instead, we believe that there is much worth dying for. Christians do not believe that life is a right or that we have inherent dignity. Instead, we believe that life is the gift of a gracious God. That is our primary Christian language regarding abortion: life is the gift of a gracious God. As part of the giftedness of life, we believe that we ought to live in a profound awe of the other's existence, knowing that in the other we find God. So abortion is a description maintained by Christians to remind us of the kind of community we must be to sustain the practice of hospitality to life. That is related to everything else that we do and believe. …

One of the reasons why the church's position about abortion has not been authentic is because the church has not lived and witnessed as a community in a way that challenges the fundamental secular presuppositions of both the pro-life side and the pro-choice side. We are going to have to become that kind of community if our witness is to have the kind of integrity that it must. …

Should Christians "Want" Children?

There is one other issue that I think is worth highlighting. It concerns how abortion in our society has dramatically affected the practice of having children. In discussions about abortion, one often hears that no "unwanted child" ought to be born. But I can think of no greater burden than having to be a wanted child.

When I taught the marriage course at the University of Notre Dame, the parents of my students wanted me to teach their kids what the parents did not want them to do. The kids, on the other hand, approached the course from the perspective of whether or not they should feel guilty for what they had already done. Not wanting to privilege either approach, I started the course with the question, "What reason would you give for you or someone else wanting to have a child?" And I would get answers like, "Well, children are fun." In that case, I would ask them to think about their brothers and sisters. Another answer was, "Children are a hedge against loneliness." Then I recommended getting a dog. Also I would note that if they really wanted to feel lonely, they should think about someone they had raised turning out to be a stranger. Another student reply was, "Kids are a manifestation of our love." "Well," I responded, "what happens when your love changes and you are still stuck with them?" I would get all kinds of answers like these from my students. But, in effect, these answers show that people today do not know why they are having children.

It happened three or four times that someone in the class, usually a young woman, would raise her hand and say, "I do not want to talk about this anymore." What this means is that they know that they are going to have children, and yet they do not have the slightest idea why. And they do not want it examined. You can talk in your classes about whether God exists all semester and no one cares, because it does not seem to make any difference. But having children makes a difference and the students are frightened that they do not know about these matters.

Then they would come up with that one big answer that sounds good. They would say, "We want to have children in order to make the world a better place." And by that, they think that they ought to have a perfect child. And then you get into the notion that you can have a child only if you have everything set – that is, if you are in a good "relationship," if you have your finances in good shape, the house, and so on. As a result, of course, we absolutely destroy our children, so to speak, because we do not know how to appreciate their differences.

Now, who knows what we could possibly want when we "want a child"? The idea of want in that context is about as silly as the idea that we can marry the right person. That just does not happen. Wanting a child is particularly troubling as it finally results in a deep distrust of mentally and physically handicapped children. The crucial question for us as Christians is what kind of people we need to be to be capable of welcoming children into this world, some of whom may be born disabled and even die.

Too often we assume compassion means preventing suffering and think that we ought to prevent suffering even if it means eliminating the sufferer. In the abortion debate, the church's fundamental challenge is to challenge this ethics of compassion. There is no more fundamental issue than that. People who defend abortion defend it in the name of compassion. "We do not want any unwanted children born into the world," they say. But Christians are people who believe that any compassion that is not formed by the truthful worship of the true God cannot help but be accursed. That is the fundamental challenge that Christians must make to this world. It is not going to be easy.

[handwritten margin note: hmm idk more so out of autonomy]

[handwritten note across page: laws targeting women who get abortions framed as murderers!]

Euthanasia and Suicide

The question of a good death is driven less by technological developments than by theological transformation. For much, perhaps most, of church history, the overriding concern was that one's life and one's death be such as to fit one for heaven. With the decline of belief in hell from the eighteenth century onwards and the consequent diminishing anxiety concerning the precarious nature of any afterlife, attention shifted gradually away from death in general and more towards dying in particular. The availability of anesthesia from the early nineteenth century onwards coincided with these theological developments. Euthanasia and suicide emerge more prominently than they had before because they emphasize two significant themes of the modern age: they highlight individual autonomy, the desire to be in control of the most bewildering force of all, one's own mortality; and they offer a response to human suffering, that most abiding of questions to modern minds.

The readings below set out with considerable subtlety the degree to which these issues connect with some of the deepest assumptions of Christians and non-Christians alike, and conclude in diverse places that disclose the characteristic methods of universal, subversive, and ecclesial approaches to ethics.

Universal

Richard A. McCormick, *Proportionalist Reasoning*

Richard McCormick (1922–2000) sets out with evident confidence in universal rationality. He refers to the "prethematic" grasp, that all people possess, that suicide and killing are generally wrong. Thus the question is of when exceptions may be made. Here he appeals to the notion of the lesser evil. This leads in to a discussion of McCormick's characteristic approach known as proportionalism. McCormick shows how proportionalism avoids absolutizing either life or death. He carefully explores the difference between omission and commission.

Given that the abandonment of absolutes locates McCormick in consequential territory, it is notable that he is at pains to distance himself from Joseph Fletcher's situationism – an approach regarded by many as more than a step too far from deontological reasoning. He concludes with the notion of a "virtually exceptionless" norm prohibiting euthanasia, on the grounds of "our past experience of human failure, inconstancy, and frailty, and our uncertainty with regard to long-term effects."

Richard A. McCormick. "The New Medicine and Morality." *Theology Digest* 21, 4 (Winter 1973): 308–21. (The Hillenbrand Lecture, delivered October 5, 1973, at Saint Louis University.) Excerpt from pages 315–20. Reprinted by permission of *Theology Digest*.

A Question of Exceptions

The first thing that must be said is that the issue is not precisely whether suicide and killing are generally wrong. This we grasp spontaneously and prethematically, a point well made by Germain Grisez and John Finnis. In this sense our basic moral commitments are not the result of discursive reflection. The issue is exception-making, and the form of moral reasoning that both supports and limits in an intelligible way the exceptions we tolerate. For it is precisely discursive moral reasoning that contains exceptions within our notion of the *humanum*. The issue is the marginal instance where "here-and-now values clash with always-and-every-where principles" as Walter Burghardt puts it. Since these always-and-everywhere principles root in our spontaneous inclinations toward basic human goods and remain, therefore, somewhat mysterious, exception-making where these same basic values are concerned will also remain somewhat mysterious. But a beginning must be made.

It can be made, I believe, with Burghardt's use of the word "clash." In trying to discover the most satisfying form of moral reasoning, one that will draw lines in a way truly promotive of the best interests of persons, we must attend to the conflict-model of human decision-making. Every human choice, being a finite choice, will fail to realize all possible values. It can realize only certain limited values, and in doing so must at times do so to the neglect of other values or at the expense of associated disvalues. In this light every choice represents the resolution of a conflict. We do not advert to this very often, since most of our day-to-day choices are either instinctive reactions, the product of habit, or shaped by and within larger vocational commitments. But even the choice to smoke a cigarette represents a conflict resolved. I need not do so, but I choose to do so. To the extent that I am rational that means I have decided, either here and now or by overall policy decision, that this is better for me, or at least, when compared to its alternative, acceptable and tolerable in light of all the values and considerations involved. When the stakes get bigger than a puff of smoke, we become clearly conscious, sometimes agonizingly so, of the conflicting alternatives. At any rate, this means that the concrete moral norms we develop to guide our conduct

and communicate our convictions and experience to others are all conclusions of and vehicles for a larger, more general assertion: in situations of conflict, where values are copresent and mutually exclusive, the reasonable thing is to avoid what is, *all things considered*, the greater evil or, positively stated, to do the greater good.

This means, of course, that we may cause or permit evils in our conduct only when the evil caused or permitted is, all things considered, the lesser evil in the circumstances. In other words, we may cause or permit premoral evils only when there is a truly proportionate reason. A careful analysis of traditional teachings on just warfare, capital punishment, surgical intervention, promise-keeping, etc., will show this structure operating beneath and in control of the ultimate normative statements. For instance, the traditional formulation "the direct killing of an innocent man is immoral" is as absolutely valid as the good to be realized through the killing stands in no proportionate relationship to the evil of destruction of life, a point Schüller has argued very persuasively.

In this light the traditional norms for caring for the dying must mean: (1) there is a proportionate reason for not using (omission) every means to save a life, or to prolong dying; (2) there is no proportionate reason for directly dispatching a terminal or dying patient. [Joseph] Fletcher has correctly identified this structure, but he has failed to show us why and in light of what criteria and values direct termination is truly proportionate.

Avoiding Absolutism

An examination of each one of these propositions may throw some light on the problem. First, the proportionate reason for not prolonging life at any cost and with every means. I take it as established and commonly accepted that there is a proportionate reason for not using (or withdrawing the use of – which is morally the same) every means in all circumstances to save a life or to prolong dying. Fletcher is right in saying that as a moral issue this is as dead as Queen Anne, even though notification of death has not reached all corners of the medical community.

However, if clarity is desired, we must pursue the implications of this proposition. I would approach it as follows. The prohibition against suicide and killing is based on the conviction that human life is a basic good and may not be taken except where higher values are at stake and cannot be preserved in any other way. This is the substance of moral reasoning on the matter within the Christian tradition. It led in the past to the legitimation of capital punishment. It is now leading us seriously to question that legitimation. I believe that once we say that at a certain point no artificial means need to be used to prolong life and prevent death – means we would ordinarily and in other circumstances be obliged to use – we are putting in some sense or other a different evaluation on that life than we would if it were non-dying life. ("Evaluation" here refers to the delineation of our duties to protect and support a good.) This suggests that the same basic value can call forth different obligations at various stages or phases of its existence. To say that there is a proportionate reason for not using all means to prolong life is to say simply that there is a point where we judge it to be to the good of the patient and all concerned to allow death to occur. What we judge to be to the good of the patient and all concerned is rooted in Christian attitudes on the meaning of life and death, attitudes that value life without absolutizing it, and that fear and avoid death without absolutizing it.

Does this difference in evaluation of dying life also lead to the conclusion that irreversibly dying life may be terminated directly, that there is a proportionate reason for direct termination? In other words, is it to the good of the patient and all concerned to respond to the irreversible dying process by direct termination? The two positions taken on this question I find dissatisfying. Those who argue the immorality of positive euthanasia by appeal only to the inherent value of all human life, even dying life, and therefore to the general disproportion at the heart of the prohibition of killing and suicide in general, forget that they have already abandoned this evaluation when they have provided for passive euthanasia. They have already said of the basic value of human life that it need not be supported while dying in the same way and with the same means as it need be while in a non-dying condition. In other words, they have evaluated dying life differently (in the above sense of evaluation) but then they return to and appeal to the evaluation of non-dying life where direct intervention is concerned. This is inconsistent.

On the other hand, to those who see no difference at all between omission and commission, the matter is settled, too. For them, if there is a truly proportionate reason to allow a person to die, then there is also thereby a proportionate reason to end the life by positive direct intervention. But is it true to say that at a certain point there is no difference between omission and commission? There is certainly a *descriptive* difference, rooted in the action and the accompanying intention. But is

there a genuine *moral* difference? Those who assert the identity of omission and commission at a certain stage are asserting the *moral* identity of the two. They are saying that there is no *moral* difference between the two and therefore that a reason that justifies one (omission) justifies the other (commission).

Does End Justify Means?

Is that the case? It is my opinion that it is not. Whether omission and commission are *morally* identical cannot be concluded simply from the inevitability of the dying process and the imminence of death – and the correspondence of these to the patient's desires. This is what many writers seem to suppose. They suppose that once death is inevitable and imminent, then it makes no difference how it occurs. However, descriptively different actions may have different short and/or long range implications and effects. And it is these effects, either feared, suspected, unknown, or clearly foreseen, that could spell, or at least reveal, the *moral* difference between omission and commission where the dying are concerned. In other words, mere omission may not entail, either logically or factually, the same consequences as direct commission would. And if this is so, a different calculus of proportion may be called for. For proportion must encompass the good of the patient and all concerned.

To rephrase the point, proportionate reason, if it is adequately developed, must include all the effects of a proposed course of action, its relationship to all the values. In this sense, it is not the end that justifies the means, as Fletcher contends, but the ends. Or to reword Fletcher, to know whether the benefit repays the cost, one has to count all the costs. When all the values are weighed, I would tentatively suggest that what is proportionate for allowing a terminal patient to die is not proportionate for directly causing death. And if this is true, it means that omission and commission are not *morally* identical, at least insofar as the moral significance is traceable to, or revealed by, effects. ...

A New Absolute Norm?

But is this an absolute, to be observed without exception? If it is – and I am strongly inclined to this view – how is it to be argued? If we regard norms of this type as "virtually exceptionless," we do so because of the prudential validity of what we refer to technically as a law established on the presumption of a common and universal danger (*lex lata in praesumptione periculi communis*). The notion of a presumption of universal danger is one most frequently associated with positive law. Its sense is that even if the action in question does not threaten the individual personally, there remains the further presumption that to allow individuals to make that decision for themselves will pose a threat for the common good. For instance, in time of drought, all outside fires are sometimes forbidden. This prohibition of outside fires is founded on the presumption that the threat to the common welfare cannot be sufficiently averted if private citizens are allowed to decide for themselves what precautions are adequate.

It seems to me that the exceptionless character of the norm prohibiting direct killing of any terminal patients would have to be argued in a way analogous to this. The risk in alternative policies is simply too great. There are enormous goods at stake, and both our past experience of human failure, inconstancy, and frailty, and our uncertainty with regard to long-term effects lead us to believe that we ought to hold some norms as virtually exceptionless, that this is the conclusion of prudence in the face of dangers too momentous to make risk tolerable.

Subversive

Jennifer A. Parks, *Gender and Euthanasia*

Jennifer A. Parks (b. 1968) teaches at Loyola University of Chicago. She identifies a significant tendency in feminist ethics: "Although feminists are concerned about the cultural context within which women make medical decisions, they have primarily focused on women's reproductive decisions; only recently have feminist bioethicists turned to issues beyond reproduction."

Parks questions whether autonomy should really be the only value in question in considering euthanasia. She argues that "unlike liberal accounts of the self, feminist approaches view the individual as a socially embedded, interdependent, relational subject whose choices are made within a complex web of social relationships." Her concern centers on the "widespread sexism that serves to undermine respect for women's choices." Parks' argument is a plea for attention to context: as she points out, "the less social weight a woman carries, the less likely she is to have her death requests taken seriously."

Jennifer A. Parks. "Why Gender Matters to the Euthanasia Debate: On Decisional Capacity and the Rejection of the Woman's Death Request." Hastings Center Report 30, 1 (2000): 30–6.

On Decisional Capacity and the Rejection of Women's Death Requests

The euthanasia debate has typically addressed the tension between patient autonomy and physician obligations. Where physician-assisted suicide and active euthanasia are concerned, ethicists balance a patient's request to die against both the physician's role as healer and her duty of nonmaleficence. The physician is seen to be in a moral dilemma in which her commitments to healing and saving lives conflict with her commitment to serving her patients' needs, respecting their autonomy, and maintaining their trust. The focal question for ethical debate has thus been: how much should patient autonomy govern the practices of physician-assisted suicide and active euthanasia?

Such questions are too narrowly formulated because they fail to address the background conditions that may affect a patient's death request. Besides individual agency, we must take into account the ways gender roles and social circumstances affect patients' requests to die; and the way those requests are received by our culture. Feminist approaches raise such contextual and cultural questions, yet there is little available feminist literature on physician-assisted suicide and euthanasia. Although feminists are concerned about the cultural context within which women make medical decisions, they have primarily focused on women's reproductive decisions;

only recently have feminist bioethicists turned to issues beyond reproduction.

Susan Wolf offers one of the few feminist treatments to date of euthanasia. She argues that women are more likely to request euthanasia and physician-assisted suicide in an attempt to avoid burdening their families – a perversion of the feminine ethic of care that takes women's caring for and about others to the extreme – and that physicians are simultaneously more likely to fulfill women's death requests, based on "the same historical valorization of women's self-sacrifice and the same background sexism." In a culture that valorizes their altruism and caring for others, women who suffer from severe pain or terminal illness may perceive themselves as failing in their appointed duties; unable to care for others, they may see themselves as actually burdening them. For Wolf, the authenticity and rationality of a woman's request to die seems suspect at the very least, given the extent to which cultural expectations about not burdening others have likely affected her. Indeed, Wolf chastens physicians "not to accede to the request for assisted suicide and euthanasia" for this very reason. …

I have isolated Wolf as an influential feminist voice because she brings depth to a debate that has, until recently, focused almost exclusively on the issue of patient autonomy. I suggest, however, that Wolf's reasoning may actually lead to very different conclusions. While some women in particular can exhibit a preoccupation with and overemphasis on relationships, terminally ill women's death requests can also, like men's, stem from basic personal concerns for pain, psychic suffering, and the determination that their lives have become meaningless or burdensome to them. In taking Wolf's feminist account seriously, I suggest that women's requests to die may be discounted, trivialized, and ignored for the same reasons that Wolf claims they are too likely to be heeded. By virtue of the expectation that women will be altruistic, self-abnegating caregivers, women's own voices, and their claims to autonomy in requesting death, are easily dismissed. I conclude that women's choices, their capacity to reason, and their ability to accurately represent their own interests are undermined in our culture and as a consequence that women's claims to pain and suffering are often disregarded. Yet in cases of intolerable pain and suffering, a woman's request to die should not be questioned on the grounds that she is incapable of determining her own good; women, like men, should be extended the right to decide when their life is burdensome, meaningless, and no longer worth living.

Some Background

Both in Canada and the United States there has been growing support for social policies that would legalize active euthanasia and physician-assisted suicide. This increasing support is not surprising given North Americans' commitment to an individualistic ethic: the primary focus, socially, politically, and medically, is on the individual, and the protection of his or her autonomy. Ethicists are also primarily concerned with the individual and his rights: their debates largely concern the conflict between patient and physician and how to navigate the tensions between these two parties and their conflicting goals. For example, Dan Brock argues that the patient has a right to choose active euthanasia or physician-assisted suicide because, "If self-determination is a fundamental value, then the great variability among people on this question makes it especially important that individuals control the manner, circumstances, and timing of their dying and death."

Conversely, arguments against euthanasia have also taken the individual's self-governance to be the main issue. Gay-Williams argues against euthanasia on the ground that, "Because death is final and irreversible, euthanasia contains within it the possibility that we will work against our own interest if we practice it or allow it to be practiced on us." Plainly, traditional liberal concerns for protecting individual autonomy remain the primary focus of debates over euthanasia. …

On the autonomy model, if the rights-bearer asserts her right to die, then the appropriate response is to secure her death. And while this model intends the positive goal of individuals pursuing their own good as they see fit, the liberal conception of the individual as a rational, independent, rights-bearing agent choosing her own time and mode of death is impoverished. By contrast, a feminist approach to the euthanasia debate regards women's experiences in a gendered culture as relevant to determinations regarding the legitimacy of their death requests.

The Importance of Context

The demand for euthanasia, and the interaction between the patient requesting death and the physician considering the request, is largely understood as a private matter. … But feminist ethicists argue that practices like active euthanasia and physician-assisted suicide are not merely cases of individualized decisionmaking: such individual decisions are made within a social context that informs and affects individuals' choices. Thus unlike liberal accounts of the self, feminist approaches view the individual as a socially embedded, interdependent, relational subject whose choices are made within a complex web of social relationships. Where the euthanasia debate is concerned, the situated subject is not an isolatable, independent, atomistic subject: her choice to die has implications for both self and society, and her choices can be either upheld or undermined by the prevailing social ethos.

That gender matters where physician-assisted suicide and active euthanasia are concerned is contentious. The individual expression of autonomy is held to be a right in which we all share an objective, equal interest. Thus the particular features of a patient's life are considered irrelevant once we have determined that her choices are unconstrained by coercion, irrationality, ignorance, or the limited options available to her. But here a feminist account of euthanasia departs from traditional liberal accounts; feminists assert that deep social inequalities affect individual agents in ways not recognized on traditional liberal approaches to autonomy. For example, liberal accounts of euthanasia fail to address the widespread sexism that serves to undermine respect for women's choices.

It is imperative that a feminist account of euthanasia consider the feminine ethic of care to which women have been held, an ethic that requires women's unselfish commitment to the nurturance and care of others, especially their husbands, children, and elderly parents. The imperative to care for others – to the point of giving up their sense of self completely – encourages people to dismiss women's self-concerns, and it makes society less willing to consider euthanasia for women. A liberal, rights-based account of euthanasia fails to account for such difficulties because it does not countenance contextual features of this sort. A feminist account, however, can show how sexism may lead to the medical and social rejection of a woman's request for death. ...

That "womanly" virtues require caring for and nurturing others to the detriment of women's self-concern relates to my worries about gender and euthanasia. For if women are expected to be deferential to others, self-effacing, and caring to the point of sacrificing their own happiness, then any self-interested and self-directed claims they make (in this case, the request to die) may be more easily discounted or dismissed as irrational. A woman's capacity for reason and self-determination is not validated in our culture (since women have been historically viewed as emotional, not rational, beings); the presence of severe pain or terminal illness may be

used as further support for the view that women are particularly incompetent when it comes to making even deeply personal life and death decisions. ...

So a physician's moral grounds for rejecting euthanasia or physician-assisted suicide will – at least partially – reflect a social refusal to acknowledge the legitimacy of such feelings of burdensomeness and meaninglessness in a culture that denies women's competency. Not only does our culture view women as self-abnegating caregivers who lack reason and autonomy: physicians discount or dismiss women's reasoning capacity and ability to govern themselves, making it easier for them to reject women's death requests. For determining that a patient's life has become "meaningless" or "burdensome" involves making a value judgment that, like most value judgments, reflects dominant cultural prejudices, among them (in our society) the assumption that women are primarily nurturers and caregivers who lack the competency to self-govern. That a man may experience his life as "meaningless" or "burdensome" is considered a rational self-evaluation so long as his life is marked by intolerable pain, personal suffering, or terminal illness. But women's similar experiences are much more likely to be rejected, discounted, or unheeded because their capacity for such determinations of personal suffering are questioned. Perhaps, as Kathryn Morgan claims, the denial of women's full moral agency stems from the view that, "simply by virtue of their embodiment as women, women just are closer to nature and, hence, not capable of the kind of thought that is necessary for human moral life." ...

Dismissing Suffering

While Wolf's feminist account provides a foundation for a rich ethical analysis of euthanasia, it is not clear that women are more likely than men to be euthanized or extended the means for physician-assisted suicide. Indeed, there is reason to think, and statistical evidence to support the thought, that women are far less likely to be taken seriously, listened to, and supported in their end of life choices than are their male counterparts. While I share Wolf's concern for the way in which the debate over euthanasia and physician-assisted suicide has been decontextualized and governed by an individualistic model, I believe that contextual considerations should lead us to question why women's death requests are taken less seriously and acted on less often than those of men.

Wolf acknowledges that some feminists "will see this problem differently. That may be especially true of women who feel in control of their lives, are less subject to subordination by age or race or wealth, and seek yet another option to add to their many." She makes an important point: contingencies such as poverty, poor education, age, and race are important to a feminist account of euthanasia. But rather than making a woman's death request more likely to be respected, these contingencies make it less so: the less social weight a woman carries, the less likely she is to have her death requests taken seriously. A woman who is white, well educated, articulate, wealthy, or politically powerful is far less likely to be denied decisionmaking capacity than is her uneducated, poor, powerless counterpart. The more a woman is like the autonomous, rational, independent agent that is the traditional focus of the euthanasia debate, the more likely her death request will be taken seriously.

Ecclesial

Gilbert Meilaender, *Suicide and Euthanasia*

Gilbert Meilaender (b. 1946) is Professor of Christian Ethics at Valparaiso University, Indiana and is a member of the President's Council on Bioethics. He is a member of the Evangelical Lutheran Church of America. His work has echoed many of the familiar themes of ecclesial ethics such as friendship and virtue, but its tone has sometimes had more of a universal character than his more strident ecclesial colleagues.

This passage from his short but influential book *Bioethics: A Primer for Christians* (1995, 2005) sets about its discussion in a typically ecclesial manner. It identifies the reasons advocates give for supporting euthanasia – the value of autonomy and the desire to alleviate suffering. Meilaender does not dismiss these arguments, but he does show how uneasily they rest within the terms in which they are conventionally set. He then proceeds to expose the tensions between these values and Christian commitments, before finally recognizing that if Christians are to maintain such commitments they need to be renewed in their understanding of God and their regular discipleship. Meilaender unequivocally asserts: "The principle that governs Christian compassion … is not 'minimize suffering.' It is 'maximize care.'"

Gilbert Meilaender. "Suicide and Euthanasia." *Bioethics: A Primer for Christians*. 2nd edn. Grand Rapids: Eerdmans, 1996, 2005. From Chapter 6, "Suicide and Euthanasia," pages 56–64.

Here is a recent story from the newspaper. A man named George Delury helped his wife of twenty-two years, Myrna Lebov, to commit suicide. Ms. Lebov was suffering from multiple sclerosis and near the end of her life was able only to wash her face and hands, feed herself if the food had already been cut, apply her makeup, and brush her teeth. In addition, her memory had begun to be affected. When she asked her husband if he would help her end her life, he reports that "I said, of course I'd help. I also said in effect that I was astonished she'd fought so hard and so long to keep going. I would have quit a lot sooner."

He learned that one of the medications his wife was taking could prove fatal if taken in a sufficiently large dose, so over several months she cut back on her dosage, saving enough of the medicine to kill herself. Then on Independence Day they shared their traditional celebrative meal of chicken and wine, and he diluted the pills to provide a drinkable mixture. She drank it and was dead the next morning.

"The primary project in her life was to be independent," Mr. Delury said, and so she exercised that independence one last time on July 4. He, for his part, hopes to write a book about death and, especially, about what he calls the "considerate hero" – an elderly person, for example, "who, facing serious illness, says, 'This money would be better spent elsewhere.'"

Here, in short, is the story of a woman whose suffering evokes our sympathy and also our fears, since we are uncertain what we would do in her circumstances. She is a woman whose "primary project" in life is to be independent, a project that surely calls for scrutiny, however great our sympathy for her. And her story, at least as told by her husband, invites us to consider whether we might be obligated to act "heroically" at some point in the future, ending our life in order to save resources that could be better spent on others. This is the sort of case that today makes news, and it turns our attention to two considerations – autonomy and suffering.

Christians have held that suicide is morally wrong because they have seen in it a contradiction of our nature as creatures, an unwillingness to receive life moment by moment from the hand of God without ever regarding it as simply "our" possession. We might think of ourselves as characters in a story of which God is the author. ... We are dependent beings, and to think otherwise – to make independence our project, however sincerely – is to live a lie, to fly in the face of reality.

Thus, suicide as a rational project expresses a desire to be only free and not also finite – a desire to be more like Creator than creature. Of course, suicide may often result from depression or other emotional illness. In such cases it is not a rational undertaking, and we do not regard a person in such a state as a responsible agent. But there is no reason to deny that suicide can sometimes be undertaken by those who are not emotionally ill and who are responsible for their actions. Such suicide has about it a Promethean quality, a rejection of our status as creatures. Precisely because this is true, it is important to state that, contrary to what Christians have often believed, such rational suicide does not necessarily damn one. The suicide dies, so to speak, in the moment of sinning, without opportunity to repent. But then, so may I be killed instantly in a car accident while plotting revenge against an enemy of mine. God judges persons, not individual deeds, and the moment in one's life when a sinful deed occurs does not determine one's fate. Even if I try to reject God and keep the light of his presence from my life, there is no guarantee that my creaturely action will be able to overcome his authorial ingenuity. ...

What should be clear, though, is that Christians do not approach this issue by first thinking in terms of a "right to life" or a "right to die with dignity." That is to say, we do not start with the language of independence. Within the story of my life I have the relative freedom of a creature, but it is not simply "my" life to do with as I please. I am free to end it, of course, but not free to do so without risking something as important to my nature as freedom: namely, the sense of myself as one who always exists in relation to God.

Caring (But Only Caring)

If my life is not simply my possession to dispose of as I see fit, as if the God-relation did not exist, the same is true of the lives of others. I have no authority to act as if I exercised lordship over another's life, and another has no authority to make me lord over his life and death. Hence, Christians should not request or cooperate in either assisted suicide or euthanasia.

In a chapter written a quarter century ago that remains to this day a classic discussion of the issues, Paul Ramsey sought to articulate an ethic of "(only) caring for the dying." Such an ethic, he suggested, would reject two opposite extremes: refusing to acknowledge death by continuing the struggle against it when that struggle is useless, or aiming to hasten the coming of death. Neither of these can count as *care* for one of our fellow human beings; each is a form of abandonment. We should always try to care for the dying person, but we should *only* care. To try to do more by seizing either of the extremes is always to give something other or less than care. ...

Why might we be tempted to ask for or to offer euthanasia? One of the reasons has already been suggested in the discussion of suicide: our commitment to autonomy or self-determination. I am tempted to believe that my life is my own to do with as I please – and tempted to believe that another's life is her own to do with as she pleases. A second reason, equally powerful and tempting, is our desire to bring relief to those who suffer greatly. The argument for euthanasia rests chiefly on these two points, taken either singly or together.

Usually in the public debates of our society these two reasons are presented as a package, as if they must be taken together. For the present, that is, advocates of euthanasia (or, as it is sometimes termed, assistance in dying) have tended to argue that it should be permitted only if the person euthanized both was suffering greatly and (while competent) had requested such assistance. ...

If self-determination is truly so significant that we have a right to help in ending our life, then how can we insist that such help can rightly be offered only to those who are suffering greatly? Others who are not suffering may still find life meaningless, the game not worth the candle. They, too, are autonomous, and, if autonomy is as important as the argument claims it is, then their autonomous requests for euthanasia should also be honored, even if they are not suffering greatly. Similarly, if the suffering of others makes so powerful a claim upon us that we should kill them to bring it to an end, it is hard to believe that we ought to restrict such merciful relief only to those who are self-determining, who are competent to request it. Surely, fully autonomous people are not the only human beings who can suffer greatly. Thus, from both directions, from each prong of the argument, there will be pressure to expand the class of candidates for euthanasia. Those who suffer greatly but cannot request relief and those who request help even though their suffering is not great will begin to seem more suitable candidates. …

For Christians, each person's life is a divine gift and trust, taken up into God's own eternal life in Jesus, to be guarded and respected in others and in ourself. However, because we are inclined to overemphasize our freedom and forget the limits of our finite condition, inclined to forget that life comes to us as a gift, death becomes the great reminder of those limits. In *The Death of Ivan Ilyich* Tolstoy powerfully captures Ilyich's surprise that he – and not just others – should come up against this limit, that his own existence should be included in the truth that all men are mortal. But try as we may to forget it, death is the starkest reminder of our limits. It is therefore a peculiar moment at which to attempt to seize ultimate control of our life and pretend that we are independent self-creators. That is simply one last way of living a lie.

Moreover, euthanasia is not simply an extension of personal autonomy; it is not simply "nonintervention" in another person's private choice. On the contrary, because it requires the participation of at least one other person, it becomes a communal act involving the larger society and giving its approval to an act of abandonment. If it becomes a permissible and acceptable practice, have our freedom and independence been enhanced? In one sense no doubt they have, since we are given a new option, the option to die when we wish. But it is also true that the pressure will build to exercise this option to be the "considerate hero" who does not stay alive too long using resources that might better be spent elsewhere. If and when euthanasia receives social approval what looks like more freedom is likely to turn out to be less. In short, there are good reasons not to acquiesce in the autonomy argument.

Christians are, I suspect, more likely to be drawn to the argument that describes euthanasia as compassionate relief of suffering. And, to be sure, we all know the fear of suffering and the frustration of being unable to relieve it fully in those whom we love. The principle that governs Christian compassion, however, is not "minimize suffering." It is "maximize care." Were our goal only to minimize suffering, no doubt we could sometimes achieve it by eliminating sufferers. But then we refuse to understand suffering as a significant part of human life that can have meaning or purpose. We should not, of course, pretend that suffering in itself is a good thing, nor should we put forward claims about the benefits others can reap from their suffering. Jesus in Gethsemane – who shrinks from the suffering to come but accepts it as part of his calling and obedience – should be our model here. The suffering that comes is an evil, but the God who in Jesus has not abandoned us in that suffering can bring good from it for us as for Jesus. We are called simply to live out our personal histories – the stories of which God is author – as faithfully as we can.

Our task is therefore not to abandon those who suffer but to "maximize care" for them as they live out their own life's story. We ought "always to care, never to kill." And it has, in fact, been precisely our deep commitment not to abandon those who suffer that has, in large measure, been a powerful motive force in the development of modern medicine. Our continued task is not to eliminate sufferers but to find better ways of dealing with their suffering. If we cannot always fully relieve the suffering, when we cannot relieve it, we must remember that even God does not really "solve" or take away the problem of suffering; rather, God himself lives that problem and bears it. His way is steadfast love *through* suffering, and it is the mystery of God's own being and power that this truly proves to be the way to maximize care for all who suffer.

Chapter Twelve

Good Earth

Ecological concerns have become central to Christian ethics in the last thirty years. While universal ethics has long had the dimension of attending to the good society, today it is impossible to conduct such a debate without reference to the nonhuman creation. The debate often divides on squarely deontological/consequential grounds: some see the crisis of climate change and species depletion as requiring active responses of a largely utilitarian nature; others see the human relationship with the living and inanimate environment as seriously awry regardless of sustainable consequences, and thus take a more explicitly deontological (or virtue/ecclesial) line. The questions in this chapter include the status of animals, the appropriateness or otherwise of genetically modified foods, and the sustainability of the earth's ecosystem.

Animals

One problematic area for theological ethics is the question of whether humanity is genuinely in the center of God's purposes, or whether the nonhuman (or even inanimate) creation has its own value independent of its instrumental usefulness to human flourishing. Perhaps the most controversial area in this regard is the status of animals. The areas in question include the hunting of wild animals, notably foxes; the intensification of breeding and slaughter systems; and the use of animals for biological, behavioral, medical, or cosmetic experimentation. While many Christians would be comfortable with the premature ending of the life of an

animal to achieve a direct human benefit, so long as the animal was well cared for in its lifetime, others would regard animals as moral subjects in much the same way they would regard humans, and thus would rule out all killing or maltreatment of animals.

The human-centered view of animals is that animals have no moral status. This was the dominant view until the last two centuries, despite the visibility of animals in biblical portrayals of the peaceable kingdom such as Genesis 1–2 and 8, Isaiah 11, and Romans 8. A contractual view of animals would suggest that rights accord with duties – and thus that because animals have no duties, they have no rights. These are deontological approaches. They are thus not neighbors to be loved alongside humans and God. A more humanitarian view would suggest that if a being is capable of feeling pain, one should avoid giving pain as much as possible, perhaps even as much as one would avoid giving pain to a human – given the general rule of avoiding innocent suffering. This is essentially a utilitarian theory that is not against suffering *tout court* but seeks to reduce it where possible. An animal rights theory would suggest on theological or philosophical natural law grounds that animals, being purposed by God, or at least by being complex creatures, have rights that are not bestowed but recognized. For some, the question centers on vegetarianism; for others, what is at stake is the entire social groundwork of contemporary culture.

In the readings below, Andrew Linzey offers a proposal for an account of animal rights, Carol Adams makes a case for vegetarianism, and Stephen Webb roots practices of eating in the Eucharist.

Universal

Andrew Linzey, *Reverence, Responsibility, and Rights*

Andrew Linzey (b. 1952) is an Anglican priest, a teacher of theology at the University of Oxford, and the director of the Oxford Centre for Animal Ethics. This excerpt sets out in unequivocally universal vein, speaking of the spiritual crisis of our civilization, assuming a very wide dimension to the "our." He cites Albert Schweitzer (1875–1965), the Alsatian theologian, musician, philosopher, and physician who won the Nobel Peace Prize for his philosophy and practice of reverence for life (or more accurately "awe of the mystery of life"). In true universal vein, Linzey highlights Schweitzer's principle as comprehensive, universal, and limitless. Linzey notes that this is a mystical, religious experience rather than an ethical code as such.

Linzey goes on to challenge Thomas Aquinas' teleological view of the human relationship to animals, which sees animal life as subordinate to the meaning and purpose of human life. Partly through the common experience of pain, Linzey brings animals within the language of justice: "Mental superiority does not justify moral abuse."

Linzey finally sets out the case for the rights of animals. He starts by affirming that creation exists for God – thus bypassing human utility. He then affirms that God is for *creation* – and not just for humanity. Thus human beings, imitating God, should be for creation too. The argument is deontological throughout.

It is [Albert] Schweitzer, of course, who is most well-known for his development of [the] concept [of the worth and rights of animals]. ... The answer to the "spiritual crisis" of our civilization, maintains Schweitzer, is the development of ethical thought which must seek to conceive life-affirmation as "a manifestation of an inward, spiritual relation to the world" and which does not "lapse into abstract thinking" but remains – as Schweitzer calls it – "elemental," that is, "understanding self-devotion to the world to be self-devotion of human life to every form of living being with which it can come into relation." From this, Schweitzer deduces a classic definition:

> Ethics consists, therefore, in my experiencing the compulsion to show to all will-to-live the same reverence as I do to my own. There we have given us that basic

principle of the moral which is a necessity of thought. It is good to maintain and encourage life; it is bad to destroy life or to obstruct it.

Three characteristics of this basic principle of reverence should be noted. First, the principle is comprehensive. Schweitzer does not posit reverence as one principle among many, even as the most satisfying or coherent principle, but as the *sole* principle of the moral. Love and compassion, for example, whilst important notions for Schweitzer, are entirely subsumed under the concept of reverence. Compassion which suggests only "interest in the suffering will-to-live" is regarded as "too narrow to rank as the total essence of the ethical." Whereas the ethics of reverence "include also feeling as one's own all the circumstances and all the aspirations of the will-to-live, its pleasures, too, and its longing to live itself out to the full, as well as its urge to self-perfecting."

Second, the principle is universal. Schweitzer sees reverence as applying to *all* life forms, human or animal, insect or vegetable. The ethical person "does not ask how far this or that life deserves one's sympathy as being valuable, nor, beyond that, whether and to what degree it is capable of feeling." "Life as such is sacred to him," maintains Schweitzer. ...

Third, the principle is limitless. Schweitzer is no exponent of casuistry. Apart from one possible exception, namely animal experimentation, he enters into no discussion about the relative rights and wrongs of this or that action when confronted with this or that dilemma. "Ethics," he insists with stark, perhaps unreasonable, simplicity, "are responsibility *without limit* to all that lives." ...

It is ... [an] experiential, mystical identification of individual life with life, and through life with Being itself, which lies at the heart of Schweitzer's philosophy. It is not so much a new law, code or maxim but essentially an unconditional religious experience of great power. The insight that lies at its heart is actually quite simple, namely an apprehension of the value of other life-forms as given by God. Life, in other words, is sacred or holy. ...

I want now to turn to the question of responsibility to animals. ... I propose to discuss two questions raised and answered by St Thomas in his *Summa Theologica*. The first concerns whether it is unlawful to kill any living thing. ... In summary, three elements distinguish Aquinas' view of the status of animal life: First, animals are irrational, possessing no mind or reason. Second, they exist to serve human ends by virtue of their nature and by divine providence. Third, they therefore have no moral status in themselves save in so far as some human interest is involved, for example, as human property. ...

Aquinas' doctrine has become the dominant Western religious position on animals since the thirteenth century. Those in any doubt about this should consult Keith Thomas' excellent survey entitled *Man and the Natural World*. Only in the eighteenth and nineteenth centuries do we find Aquinas seriously challenged. I want now to consider the best of these challenges made by a little-known eighteenth-century divine, Humphry Primatt. That so few should have even heard of Primatt may itself be suggestive of oblivion, but in a number of practical ways, his theology, if not his name, lives on.

Primatt's sole known work is his *Dissertation on the Duty of Mercy and the Sin of Cruelty to Brute Animals*, published in 1776. Without directly mentioning Aquinas, he takes on many of the key elements within the scholastic tradition. He appears to agree with Aquinas in rejecting the idea that creation has in some way "fallen" from the original designs of the Creator, but unlike Aquinas (who then goes on to postulate the innocency of parasitical existence and man's part in it), Primatt sees in nature "a transcript

of the divine goodness." Beginning from this starting-point that creation is fundamentally good, the outward result of a Creator who is "wise and just and good, and merciful," Primatt deduces the principle that "every creature of God is good in its kind; that is, it is such as it ought to be." It follows, according to Primatt, that whatever the "perfections or defects may be, they cannot be owing to any merit or demerit in the creature itself, being not prior, but consequential to its creation." ...

Whilst he accepts significant differences between humans and animals, he insists upon the common misery of pain:

> Pain is pain, whether it be inflicted on man or on beast; and the creature that suffers it, whether man or beast, being sensible of the misery of it whilst it lasts, suffers evil; and the sufferance of evil, unmeritedly, unprovokedly, where no offence has been given; and no good end can possibly be answered by it, but merely, to exhibit power or gratify malice, is Cruelty and Injustice in him that occasions it.

The appeal here to justice is significant. For Aquinas – whether he thought animals could feel pain or no – certainly did not include animals, even analogically, within the sphere of human justice. Indeed because, strictly speaking, animals could, for Aquinas, have no friendship with humans, and therefore be subject to charitable constraints, animals could not actually be wronged. The new note in Primatt is the insistence that what happens within the sphere of animal-human relations is not just a question of locating some human interest, hidden or otherwise, nor a question of taste or skill, but of plain justice. ...

And in a crucial step, Primatt – contrary to the Thomist tradition – places animals within this widening circle of sympathy and justice.

> Now, if amongst men, the differences of their powers of the mind, of their complexion, stature, and accidents of fortune, do not give any one man a right to abuse or insult any other man on account of these differences; for the same reason, a man can have no natural right to abuse and torment a beast, merely because a beast has not the *mental* powers of a man.

This further point that mental superiority does not justify moral abuse is developed by Primatt throughout his whole work. In short: unlike Aquinas, who found all-embracing support for the notion that humans had a right to kill animals precisely because of their rationality, Primatt insists that "superiority of rank or station may give ability to communicate happiness, and seems so intended; but it can give no right to inflict unnecessary or unmerited pain." ...

Again, contrary to Aquinas, the usefulness of animals is a sign of the very generosity of God which should inspire in humans a corresponding generosity towards them. For the purpose of animals is not to serve the human species but to glorify God. In other words, they have a justification for existence which humans themselves have yet to earn, and earn they may supremely through the exercise of mercy. Primatt does not pull his punches in this matter so central, as he sees it, to Christian faith:

> We may pretend to what religion we please, but cruelty is atheism. We may make our boast of Christianity; but cruelty is infidelity. We may trust to our orthodoxy, but cruelty is the worst of heresies. ...

I want now to turn to our third question, whether animals have rights. The language of rights is sometimes viewed within contemporary Christian circles as being a secular import into theological ethics. In fact it is the Christian theological tradition that has been one of the main inspirations for the language of rights, and for many centuries right up until the present day, Christians, both Catholic and Protestant, have placed notions of rights within their theological systems. The question is, however, should the language of rights extend to animals? ...

I want to propose ... that there is a Christian basis for what I shall term "the theos-rights" of animals that is consistent with those same notions of reverence and responsibility which the tradition has, at its better moments, espoused. At the heart of this proposal is the conviction that we need a theocentric view of creation. There are four aspects to this which require some brief elaboration.

The first is that creation exists *for* God. If the question be asked "What is creation for?" or "Why do animals exist?" there is only one satisfactory theological answer. Creation exists for its Creator. Years of anthropocentrism have almost completely obscured this simple but fundamental point. What follows from this is that animals should not be seen simply as means to human ends. The key to grasping this theology is the abandoning of the common but deeply erroneous view that animals exist in a wholly instrumental relationship to human beings. Even if humans are uniquely important in creation, it does not follow that everything in creation is made for us, to be pleasing for us, or that our pleasure is God's chief concern. ...

The second is that God is *for* creation. I mean by that that God, as defined by trinitarian belief, cannot be fundamentally indifferent, negative or hostile to the creation which is made. Creation, as [Karl] Barth suggests, is not only "actualization" but also "justification." Every creature is a blessed creature or it is no creature at all. The point is grasped by Oliver Wendell Holmes Sr who argued that "if a created being has no rights which his Creator is bound to respect, there is an end to all moral relations between them." There is a sense in which this dictum is false and another in which it is true. It is false if it supposes some rights that exist independently of divine graciousness, almost external constraints which must tie the hands of the Almighty to obey them. But the dictum is true if it conveys the sense that God the Creator is tied to what divine nature has created in creation. Since God's nature is love, and since God loves creation, it follows that what is genuinely given and purposed by that love must acquire some right in relation to the Creator. I do not see how God can be the kind of God as defined by trinitarian doctrine who is morally indifferent to the creation which is sustained, reconciled and which will in the end be redeemed. To posit that the Creator can be indifferent to creatures, especially those who are indwelt by the Spirit, is ultimately to posit a God indifferent to his or her own nature and being. ...

The fourth point or rather question is this: If creation exists for God, and if God is for creation, how can human beings be other than for creation? To the criticism that this theological perspective under-rates or minimizes the special, perhaps unique, gifts of human beings, we should reply that on the contrary, it may well be the special task of humans within creation to do what other creatures cannot do, at least in a consciously deliberate way, namely honour, respect and rejoice in the creation in which God rejoices. The notion of "theos-rights" then for animals means that God rejoices in the lives of those differentiated beings in creation enlivened by the Spirit. In short: If God is for them, we cannot be against them.

Subversive

Carol J. Adams, *Institutional Violence, Feminist Ethics, and Vegetarianism*

Carol J. Adams (b. 1951) is a vegetarian-feminist activist and author who lives in Dallas, Texas. Here she describes the eating of animals as institutional violence. One of the features of institutional violence is that its violence is invisible to most of its beneficiaries. In a provocative term, she calls the consumption of meat "corpse eating." She identifies the Genesis creation narrative as an "authorizing myth of dominance," shifting responsibility for killing and eating animals "from individual responsibility to divine intent." She highlights the way Genesis 1:29 contrasts with Genesis 1:26 – the former tends toward a vegetarian position. Citing Isaiah's eschatological vegetarian vision, she sees the eating of meat as a fallen practice lying between created purpose and eschatological restoration – and not a creation ordinance at all. She comes to see animals as having almost a liberation theology of their own. The choice is one of "institutionalized violence or feeding on grace."

Again, the argument is on entirely deontological grounds. While there is much to be said on the economics of meat eating, that is not the line that Adams takes: she is concerned with the inherent wrongness of the practice.

Carol J. Adams. *Neither Man Nor Beast: Feminism and the Defense of Animals.* New York: Continuum, 1994. From Chapter 9, "Feeding on Grace: Institutional Violence, Feminist Ethics, and Vegetarianism," pages 163–4, 171–8. Excerpt from *Neither Man Nor Beast: Feminism and the Defense of Animals* by Carol J. Adams, © 1995, 2001. Reprinted with the permission of the publisher, The Continuum International Publishing Group.

The eating of animals is a form of institutional violence. The corporate ritual that characterizes institutional violence deflects or redefines the fact that the eating of animals is exploitative. This is why conscientious and ethical individuals do not see corpse eating as a problem. … [T]he most frequent relationship the majority of Americans have with the other animals is with dead animals whom they eat. Because of institutional violence, corpse eating is conceived of neither as a relationship nor as the consuming of dead animals. We require an analysis of institutional violence to identify just why it is that feminist ethics ought to reconceptualize corpse eating. This chapter offers such an analysis and reconceptualization.

The Institutional Violence of Eating Animals

Through an understanding of institutional violence we will come to see the dynamics of exploitation vis-à-vis the other animals, and begin to recognize their suffering as ethically relevant in determining our own actions.

For something to be *institutional* violence it must be a significant, widespread, unethical practice in a society. As the second largest industry in this country, corpse production is both widespread and vitally important to the economy. Though corpse eating is now the normative expression of our relationship with other animals, a close examination of the functioning of institutional violence will reveal why I call it unethical.

Institutional violence is characterized by:

1 An infringement on or failure to acknowledge another's inviolability
2 Treatment and/or physical force that injures or abuses
3 Involving a series of denial mechanisms that deflect attention from the violence
4 The targeting of "appropriate" victims
5 Detrimental effects on society as a whole
6 The manipulation of the public (e.g., consumers) into passivity

Corpse eating fits this definition of institutional violence. In fact, the word *meat* itself illustrates several of these components. It renders animals appropriate victims by naming them as edible and deflects our attention from the violence inherent to killing them for food. …

Genesis and the Institutionalized Violence of Eating Animals

... In the context of the United States in which Christian interpretations have insinuated themselves into much cultural discourse, including ostensibly secular discussions, it is necessary for feminist ethics to acknowledge the way the early chapters of Genesis are appropriated to sanctify the institutional violence of eating animals. These chapters are invoked as an authorizing myth of dominance. Despite the secular nature of American culture, the early chapters of Genesis, mediated by a specifically Christian interpretation, offer a legitimization for the eating of animals that seems to let individuals off the hook. It functions as a myth of origins, explaining our nature as corpse eaters. ...

The same passage that establishes that humans are in the image of God, appears to bestow legitimacy on the exploitation of the other animals. Genesis 1:26 reads: "Then God said, 'Let us make humankind in our image, according to our likeness; and let them have dominion over the fish of the sea, and over the birds of the air, and over the cattle, and over all the wild animals of the earth, and over every creeping thing that creeps upon the earth.'" Genesis 1:26 is seen to be God's permission to dominate the other animals and make them instruments for humans' interests, thus de facto allowing corpse eating. By interpreting *dominion* to mean "God gave us permission to exploit animals for our tastes," several denial mechanisms are enacted. We are deflected from concern about animals by believing that we are absolved from the decision that has cast animals as flesh. The comforting nature of this belief derives from the fact that the onus of the decision to eat animals is shifted from individual responsibility to divine intent. (Someone, but not me, is responsible for these animals' deaths. If I am not responsible, I do not need to examine what I am doing and its consequences.) In this viewpoint, God as the author of and authority over our lives has created us as corpse eaters. In one act of authorization two ontological realities are simultaneously created: corpse eater and flesh. ...

When dominion is equated with exploitation, people are finding in the Genesis passages an origin myth that confirms their own preconceptions concerning their relationship with animals. This gravitation to a sacralized dominance reveals its own inconsistencies, however, for it requires separating Genesis 1:26 from the instructions to be vegetarian that follow three verses later: "See, I have given you every plant yielding seed that is upon the face of all the earth, and every tree with seed in its fruit; you shall have them for food." *The Interpreter's Bible* notes the difficulty of reconciling these two passages when it explicates Genesis 1:29: "Man is thus to be a vegetarian. This is something of a contradiction to verse 26, according to which he was to *have dominion over* all living creatures." For others "the human 'dominion' envisaged by Genesis 1 included no idea of using the animals for meat and no terrifying consequences for the animal world. Human exploitation of animal life is not regarded as an inevitable part of human existence, as something given and indeed encouraged by the ideal conditions of the original creation."

Genesis 1:26 does not supersede the meaning of creation that extends to include Genesis 1:29. When severed from the meaning of creation and the direction to be vegetarian, the passage becomes a historically justificatory defense of actions. This is a denial mechanism at the theological level.

These defenses continue when considering God's explicit permission to consume animals in Genesis 9:3, "Every moving thing that lives shall be food for you; and just as I gave you the green plants, I give you everything." On a certain view of Genesis, one must argue that corpse eating is a consequence of the fall. The end of vegetarianism is "a necessary evil," and the introduction of corpse eating has a "negative connotation." In his discussion of the Jewish dietary laws, Samuel H. Dresner argues that "the eating of meat [permitted in Genesis 9] is itself a sort of *compromise*," "*a divine concession to human weakness and human need.*" Adam, the perfect man, "is clearly meant to be a vegetarian." In pondering the fact that Isaiah's vision of the future perfect society postulates vegetarianism as well, Dresner observes:

"At the 'beginning' and at the 'end' man is, thus, in his ideal state, herbivorous. His life is not maintained at the expense of the life of the beast. In 'history' which takes place here and now, and in which man, with all his frailties and relativities, lives and works out his destiny, he may be carnivorous."

What is interposed between Genesis 1:29 and Isaiah is human history. In this sense, history is the concrete, social context in which we move. Moreover, history becomes our destiny.

Through a corporate sacred myth, the dominant Christian culture offers the idea that because an action of the past was condoned by God and thus the ethical norm of the time, it may continue unchanged and unchallenged into the present time. History becomes another authority manipulating and extending our pas-

sivity. It allows us to objectify the praxis of vegetarianism: it is an ideal, but not realizable. It is out of time,
not in time. When Genesis 9 is used to interpret back-
ward to Genesis 1 and forward to our own practice of
corpse eating, history is read into creation, and praxis
is superseded by an excused fallibility. History will then
immobilize the call to praxis – to stop the suffering, end
institutional violence, and side with the oppressed
animals. If vegetarianism is placed out of time, in the
Garden of Eden, then we need not concern ourselves
with it. ...

Resisting Institutionalized Violence

We are estranged from animals through institutionalized violence and have accepted inauthenticity in the
name of divine authority. We have also been estranged
from ways to think about our estrangement. Religious
concepts of alienation, brokenness, separation ought to
include our treatment of animals. Eating animals is an
existential expression of our estrangement and alienation from the created order.

Elisabeth Schüssler Fiorenza reminds us that "the
basic insight of all liberation theologies, including feminist theology, is the recognition that all theology, willingly or not, is by definition always engaged for or
against the oppressed." To side with history and posit
vegetarianism as unattainable is to side against the
oppressed animals; to side with the praxis of vegetarianism is to side with the oppressed and against institutional violence.

We are not bound by our histories. We are free to
claim an identity based on current understandings of
animal consciousness, ecological spoilage, and health
issues. No more crucifixions are necessary: animals,
who are still being crucified, must be freed from the
cross. The suffering of animals, our sacrificial lambs,
does not bring about our redemption but furthers suffering, suffering from the inauthenticity that institutional violence promotes. ...

Responding to the insights from the defense of
animals, individuals must ask questions about the institutional violence that permits them the personal satisfaction of eating flesh. "In effect, the [particular]
questions represent 'problems *raised by practices* that
have to be faced.'" Farming and slaughtering practices
such as caging, debeaking, liquid diets for calves,
twenty-four-hour starvation before death, transporting
and killing animals are all troublesome practices and
they raise particular questions that need to be addressed.

Ethical statements "always evolve 'as particular ways
of questioning in which people, individually or in

groups, *stake their lives* as they decide what they want
to do and what their solidarity is.' Thus, *if no one questions,* if no *practical engagement* takes place, no problem
exists." False naming and other denial mechanisms I
have mentioned cannot be overcome at a merely theoretical level. Practical engagement is required. Unless
we acquaint ourselves with the *practice* of farming and
slaughtering animals, we will not encounter the *problems* raised by these practices, such as the abuse of
animals, the environment, our health, and workers in
the corpse industry. If the problem is invisible, in a
sense mirroring the physical invisibility of intensively
farmed animals, then there will be ethical invisibility.

An ethical stance that would challenge the institutional violence of eating animals involves three connected parts: certain practices raise problems; practical
engagement and solidarity with the oppressed ensues
when these problematic practices are perceived; an
ethical position arises from this ongoing solidarity that
forges critical community consciousness. As we become
personally aware of the contradictions between feminist
ethics and the practice of eating animals, we find that
we must enter into a struggle regarding our own and
this culture's practice.

To overcome our failure to acknowledge another's
inviolability we need to find alternative ways of relating
to animals rather than eating them. Recall Beverly
Harrison's insight that "we know and value the world,
if we know and value it, through our ability to touch,
to hear, to see." This sensual knowing involves calling
upon second-person relationships with animals. The
epigraph to the book offers a model for this type of
knowing and its consequences: Alice Walker describes
an experience when she touches, hears, and encounters
an animal, when she has a second-person relationship
with an animal. With the horse Blue the depth of feeling
in his eyes recalls something she feels adults fail to
remember: "Human animals and nonhuman animals
can communicate quite well." Shortly after regaining
that knowledge, Walker experiences the injustice of a
steak: "I am eating misery" she thinks. Walker touches,
hears, sees, and describes interactions with very
specific animals with whom she has second-person
relationships, and she is changed by this, called to
authenticity.

We all have an option to dispense with the consumption of misery, we can feed instead on the grace of
vegetables. Virginia de Araújo describes such a perspective, that of a friend, who takes the barrenness of a
cupboard, filled only with "celery threads, chard stems,
avocado skins" and creates a feast, a grace

& says, On this grace I feed, I wilt
in spirit if I eat flesh, let the hogs,
the rabbits live, the cows browse,
the eggs hatch out chicks & peck seeds.

The choice is institutionalized violence or feeding on grace. Can one feed on grace and eat animals? Our goal

of living in right relationships and ending injustice is to have grace *in* our meals as well as *at* our meals. Feminist ethics must recognize that we are violating others in eating animals and in the process wilting the spirit. There are no appropriate victims. Let the hogs, rabbits, cows, chicks live. In place of misery, let there be grace.

Ecclesial

Stephen H. Webb, *The Lord's Supper as a Vegetarian Meal*

Stephen H. Webb (b. 1961) teaches at Wabash College in Crawfordsville, Indiana. In characteristic ecclesial style, Webb begins his discussion of eating with the paradigmatic meal – the Eucharist. He notes that this meal does not include meat. This is partly because it is a celebration of the end of sacrifice. But Webb also notes that meat-meals historically connect to hierarchy, rank, and wealth, partly for hygienic reasons. He also notes gender dimensions to meat eating, and adds several positive qualities of vegetarian eating. It is bread, not meat, that is the "staff of life." He concludes with the practice of praying before a meal, and notes how different such a practice is for vegetarians, because they have truly left behind any investment in sacrifice.

Stephen H. Webb. *Good Eating*. Grand Rapids: Brazos Press, 2001. From Chapter 6, "The Lord's Supper as a Vegetarian Meal," pages 144–8, 158–9. Reprinted by permission of Brazos, a division of the Baker Publishing Group.

Learning to Eat Like Christians

How Christians relate to the rest of the world is determined, in part, by how they eat, and how they eat is constituted by the paradigmatic meal of the Lord's Supper. In a book about the origins and evolution of table manners, food historian Margaret Visser has some very perceptive comments about the importance of the Lord's Supper for Christians. Just as children learn to behave and to act like adults at the dinner table, Christians learn what it means to be a Christian at communion. We learn what Christian behavior is by sharing a meal with each other, a meal that is a communion with God made possible by the death of Jesus Christ. All Christians are invited to the Lord's Table, and thus this is the most concrete expression of what it means to be a part of the body of Christ. Sharing the bread and the cup, no matter how it is done in the different Christian traditions, is the single act that demonstrates what Christian community is all about.

It is important, then, to reflect on what this meal actually is. Perhaps the most striking characteristic of the Eucharist is something that is often overlooked precisely because it is *not* a part of this meal. That is, the Eucharist does not include meat. Is this omission a mere accident of history, or does it say something fundamental about who Jesus was and what he taught? Visser calls communion a meal of peace, which makes sense because Jesus rejected the militaristic nationalism of many of his contemporaries and instead anticipated a more radical kingdom of God, where the whole world would be returned to an Edenic state of harmony and love. Meals of peace do not serve dead animal flesh for obvious reasons. Of course, the Eucharist operates on many different levels, and I am not suggesting that vegetarianism is its most fundamental message. The message of the Eucharist is that God is one with us through the life, death, and resurrection of Jesus Christ. Nevertheless, the medium of that message – the actual food eaten – is not irrelevant to the content of what the Eucharist conveys.

The question for us today is the same one that confronted the earliest Christians: How do we best remember, celebrate, and follow Jesus? Think about how inappropriate it would be to receive meat with the wine or grape juice and bread. As Visser explains, "In it [the Eucharist], animals are not killed because one message of the Eucharist is that, for believers, it reenacts the conclusive sacrifice; neither human beings nor animals need ever be immolated again, because the thing has been done." Moreover: "No animal and no new death is needed, no bridges required: God enters directly." It takes a food critic, perhaps, to understand how the Eucharist is a meal that comments on every other meal.

Meat could not be a part of the Eucharist not only because the death of Jesus puts an end to the need to sacrifice animals, but also because the whole ritual of eating meat is so different from the ritual of eating a vegetarian meal. When an animal is served for a meal, decisions must be made about how to carve and distribute it. The quality of meat varies from cut to cut. Moreover, meat could not be preserved very well, so it had to be passed out all at once, and thus when an animal was killed there would be a feast. The pieces of meat that were more desirable than others would be given to honored guests or people of merit and distinction. Thus, serving meat has always been one of the most visible signs of hierarchy, rank, and wealth.

Meat not only reflects and upholds class distinctions; it also creates gender differences. As religion scholar Nancy Jay has argued, sacrificial rituals serve to distinguish the roles of men and women by putting male priests in charge of the rituals that ancient people thought did the most to uphold social and even cosmic order. Throughout history men almost always have been in charge of the meat. This continues today, as any barbecue will demonstrate. Cooking meat on a fire, as with the ancient sacrifices, is a male-dominated activity. Killing animals was thought to be not dissimilar to going to war, and cutting meat involved the use of dangerous tools and knives. There are many ancient rituals that suggest that sacrificing animals is the only way to keep peace with the gods and promote social stability, and these rituals take for granted that the only people who can perform such serious duties are men.

A vegetarian meal has a totally different dynamic. As Visser explains, the preparation of vegetables in the ancient world, as today, was a more feminine activity. "Vegetables, on the other hand, were most often the result of the steady, unexalted, cooperative, and often mainly female work required for collecting them, or for tending them in the fields." Preparing vegetables has none of the drama of killing animals. In killing animals, men express their dominance over nature, their skill at using knives and controlling fire, and their willingness to shed blood for the good of their families. In preparing vegetables, women express their closeness to the earth and the equality of all those partaking of the meal, since there is no single portion of a vegetable dish that is better than any other portion.

Certainly the death of Jesus was very dramatic and bloody. But it is interesting that we remember that death in a vegetarian meal of fruit and bread, not in the further slaying of animals. The Bible often associates meat eating with gluttony, as is clear from the story of the sons of Eli, who were in a hurry to eat their meat before it was properly sacrificed on the altar (1 Samuel 2:12–17). It makes sense, then, that the Eucharist is a simple, frugal, and vegetarian meal. As Visser comments, "A joint of meat served for dinner restricts the number of guests invited; vegetarian meals permit far more elastic arrangements because they are easily shared and extended." Serving meat is a sign of wealth and power; thus, in remembering the humility and suffering of God in Jesus, meat would be out of place.

Unfortunately, today we eat meat with a regularity and passion that was unheard of in the premodern world. One consequence of our meat-heavy diet is that Christians no longer look at the communion as a real meal. Communion seems like a play meal, a ritual with nominal meaning, precisely because it does not include meat. In many churches today, Christians sip some juice from thimble-sized glasses, often made of disposable plastic, and they nibble a tiny, tasteless piece of bread, as if eating too much would be a sacrilegious act in the presence of God's holiness. In other churches, they carefully tear off a small piece of bread to dip in the chalice or hold out their cupped hands for a bread crumb or a pressed wafer. The Eucharist provides hardly enough food to constitute a snack, let alone a meal. Solemn music plays in the background, and everyone keeps their heads bowed. At family meals, people look at each other, but at this ceremonious meal people act like they are in a fancy restaurant, where they shun each other's eyes and try not to make a sound. It is almost as if Christians are ashamed of their need for food.

Certainly reverence is a part of this central Christian ritual, but the Lord's Supper should also be a festive occasion. We can only be embarrassed to eat before the Lord if we do not think that our bodies as well as our souls are saved by Jesus' death. The Lord's Supper tells us that all who come to the Lord's Table will not be turned away, that all who come to Jesus will be given sustenance and life. Communion is the heart of Christianity because in it we know and experience the fullness of God's abundant gifts to us. There is enough for all, the Eucharist proclaims. Meat is the food of the wealthy and the powerful. A meatless diet, by contrast, says that everyone can be cared for cheaply and without bloodshed. After all, a vegetarian diet can quite literally feed more people than a meat diet.

Bread, then, and not meat, is the staff of life. In many languages, the very word *bread* means simply food, and "breaking bread" means eating. We want bread with every meal. The word *companion*, from the Latin, literally means a person with whom we share bread. Jesus broke bread with the disciples on the road to Emmaus, and only then did they recognize him. When we eat the bread of communion we should be reminded that the essence of food is not a life that has been taken but a substance that gives life. Anthropologist Mary Douglas has recently suggested that the bread of the Eucharist could have reminded the early Christians of the cereal offerings that are detailed in Leviticus. She even argues that the existence of a cereal offering as a kind of alternative or parallel to the animal sacrifices in Judaism prepared the way for the early Christians to have a vegetable, not animal, sacrificial meal. Perhaps bread is treated as such a special food item throughout history precisely because it has always represented an alternative to animal sacrifices, something women would bake and share at home while the men were dividing up the meat.

… [T]o think about the Eucharist as a vegetarian meal does not involve any changes in what is served or how it is served. It would involve a change, however, in what we take away from this meal. It would ask Christians to think much more seriously about what they actually eat on Sunday mornings. John 4:34 says, "Jesus said to them, 'My food is to do the will of him who sent me and to complete his work.'" The will of God should be in our food, something that we are reminded of when we partake of the body and blood of Jesus Christ. Jesus is the perfect embodiment of God's will, so we should eat in a way that celebrates his life and what he represents. Perhaps today the bread and juice

together can be thought of as a vegetarian meal that witnesses to the sacrificial presence of Jesus Christ while also protesting against the way factory farms and slaughterhouses abuse animals.

God Bless This Meal

The most obvious Christian practice in the area of diet is the customary prayer before the meal. Because Christianity is a religion all about sacrifice, it can seem to make sense that Christians pray before meals that include meat. As Karl Barth has written, "The slaying of animals is really possible only as an appeal to God's reconciling grace, as its representation and proclamation." The logic goes like this: When Christians pray before a meal of meat, they are thanking God not only for the sacrifice of God's Son but also for the sacrifice of the life of the animal that they are about to eat. God had to give up something for us, just as animals give their lives for our benefit. Sacrifice might be a nasty business, whether it is the crucifixion on Golgotha or the animals packed into the slaughterhouses, but it is something that simply must be done, and we should be grateful to God for both the gentle obedience of God's Son and the tender morsels of meat on our plates.

Vegetarian Christians, however, see the death of animals differently. If an animal needs to be eaten to keep humans alive, then such a tragic choice must be made. But most of us live in a society where animals do not have to die for us. We have plenty of nonmeat alternatives for our protein. Thus, when Christian vegetarians say grace before a meal, they are thanking God that Jesus Christ came to end unnecessary suffering and to teach us how to live in peace with each other and with the world. The whole meal of the vegetarian is a supplication to the extent that it is an expression of confidence in God and an act of solidarity with the all-encompassing suffering of Jesus Christ. Christian vegetarians find the good in what they eat not by turning their diet into a new religion but by turning every meal into a plea for the good of all God's creatures.

Crops

People have long manipulated living organisms to make bread, cheese, and beer. In the last generation it has become possible to identify the genetic code of an organism and to modify that code by introducing particular genes from another organism. This includes *wide transfer* – where a gene from one organism, such

as a fish, is transferred into a very different organism, such as a tomato; *close transfer* – where genes are moved between similar organisms, such as a wild plants and commercial crops; and the alteration of activity levels of genes within the one organism, affecting, for example, the conditions in which a crop can flourish.

There is a deontological argument in favor – that of freedom of scientific (and entrepreneurial) endeavor – but most of the arguments in favor are on consequentialist grounds, particularly those reducing developing world hunger and enhancing Western consumer choice. The arguments against include the deontological concern about "playing God" but tend to be consequentialist too – universal accounts tend to stress the unforeseen and irreversible outcomes of significant innovation, while subversive accounts concentrate more on the imbalance and misuse of power over a basic human necessity, particularly in relation to transnational corporations dominating developing world food supply.

In the readings that follow, Derek Burke focuses on the question of technology, while Wendell Berry and Michael Northcott dwell from different perspectives on the relationship of the soil to the dinner table.

Universal

Derek Burke, *Genetic Engineering of Food*

Derek Burke (b. 1930) chaired the UK Advisory Committee on Novel Foods and Processes, 1988–1997, and was Vice-Chancellor of the University of East Anglia, 1987–1995. Here he argues the case for genetically modified (GM) foods on squarely consequentialist lines. The key factors are growing world population and the loss of land due to urbanization. He acknowledges that food shortages arise for largely economic and political reasons, but describes the move from this insight to a denial of GM technology as "perverse."

In response to the deontological question of whether scientists are "playing God," Burke lists scientific responses but describes them as "too glib." He reaffirms that the questions for him are consequential, by listing what he calls "technical" (but are in fact consequential) issues. Nonetheless, he does take on the deontological question of whether it is justified to interfere in the "natural" order. He disputes whether natural is always best, and has little time for making a firm line between the natural and the unnatural. He does not see that there is anything wrong in principle in interfering with the genetic constitution of living creatures. He refers to "the dehumanizing effect of the innate reductionism that is the basis of modern molecular biology," but sees the matter as largely about public perception. While he fears that responsibility to future generations has been neglected, the issue remains entirely a consequential one, all deontological questions having been ruled out.

Derek Burke. "Genetic Engineering of Food." In *Christians and Bioethics*. Ed. Fraser Watts. London: SPCK, 2000. From pages 21–34.

Biotechnology derives from three techniques discovered only in the last 20 years:

- The ability to cut and stitch DNA. Specific enzymes can be used to cut DNA into gene-sized pieces which are then inserted into bacteria. These transformed bacteria are used to amplify and separate the many different DNA pieces, which are then sequenced by a mixture of chemical and biochemical techniques.

Any of these pieces can be inserted into another DNA genome.

- The ability to move DNA and genes from one organism to another and, moreover, the ability to persuade new genes to work in the new organisms. This is possible because, rather broadly, the way genes work is universal, from bacteria to human beings. These two techniques are what is called "genetic modification."
- The ability to modify proteins by a process termed "protein engineering." This involves systematic alteration of the DNA sequence which will, in turn, alter the aminoacid sequence of a protein, thus altering its properties.

Some of the applications of this new technology are obvious; growth hormone can now be made in bacteria rather than extracted from cadavers, so providing a source that is free of contamination with the agent for the Creutzfeldt-Jakob Disease, and the supply of insulin for diabetics or of interferon for patients with Hepatitis B is no longer limited. We also need to grow more food, and soon farmers will be able to use less herbicide, and lose less of their corn crop to insects, because they will be growing plants resistant to the herbicides and pests. The world's population is increasing at about 1.5 per cent per year (about 87 million per year), and is estimated to grow from its present 5.9 billion to 8 billion by 2020. In addition, loss of land to urbanization means that the amount of cultivated land supporting food production has fallen from 0.44 ha per person in 1961 to 0.26 now, and is projected to fall to 0.15 ha per person by 2050. The need for irrigation is increasing, climate is changing and as people become more prosperous, they replace plant foods with animal foods – which are less efficient in trapping solar energy.

About one half of the grain produced in Europe, North America and Russia is already used as animal feed. Critics argue that the planet's food problems are due to economic and political problems, not because we cannot grow enough. There is truth in that, and we need to do better, but I very much doubt if we shall solve all our problems that way, and it seems perverse to me to walk away from a potential substantial increase in the world's food supply. ...

So what is biotechnology likely to do for food and crops? The most straightforward developments will be a whole series of new and improved enzymes for food processing and for the modification of existing foods, for example modification of fats by a process known as interesterification with the introduction of unsaturated fatty acids or fatty acids yielding fewer calories. A Mars bar which claims to yield fewer calories is already on sale in the US. The science is straightforward, and there seems to be little consumer concern.

There will also be many new crop products; of three general types:

- modifications of the genetic material of plants to extend their shelf life by slowing down the enzyme responsible for the breakdown of the plant cell walls, for example the new tomato, and a melon to come;
- modification of the genetic material of plants to produce novel parental lines for the production of new Fl hybrids, for example rape;
- modification of the genetic material of plants to introduce resistance to herbicides or pests, for example, soya, potatoes, cotton and corn. ...

... [S]ome think that scientists are playing God. The public asks "How do you know you are not going to release a new plague?" Scientists reply that they see living systems as a unity, knowing that cells, from bacteria to human beings, work in much the same way. So of course it is all right to move genes around – all we have to do is to explain it clearly, and people will be reassured. We are not abusing our position as the earth's most powerful species. We know what we are doing.

I think this is all too glib. There are, first of all, important technical issues to be talked about, particularly environmental issues. Will herbicide resistance spread to weeds, will antibiotic-resistant genes transfer from plants to humans through gut bacteria, will the use of the Bt gene in the potato, to provide protection against insect pests, also have a deleterious effect on the ladybird population, and so prevent their mopping up the aphids, as a recent report suggests? ...

But there are other issues. There is the natural/unnatural issue. Some think that it is unwise, even unethical, to disturb the natural world – and that genetic modification is unnatural because it crosses species barriers. Others believe that BSE resulted from the "unnatural," feeding of an animal foodstuff to a herbivore; in their view, BSE is a sort of divine judgement for upsetting the natural order of things. Now personally, I do not accept that all that is natural is best; fungal infection of crops with production of the ergot alkaloids is certainly not for the good of those who eat the crops. And why the yoghurt that I eat for my lunch is better for containing "natural" colouring defeats me! Is there an issue here, or are we too romantic about what is "natural"?

For the Christian, the fundamental question is whether any interference in "the natural" or created order is permitted or not. If so, what criteria are to be used in establishing the limits of such inteference? Biblical teaching sees human beings with the responsibility of stewardship for all creation, but this has not excluded us intervening in the natural world, ever since we ceased to be hunter-gatherers. The question, then, is whether the genetic constitution of living creatures, a constitution that has undoubtedly changed during the course of evolution, should have any specially protected status. That is, is it wrong *in principle*? I do not think so, though that is not to say that individual cases might not be unwise or even wicked, and should not proceed. ...

Let me try and sort out some of these different ethical issues and see how our Christian faith can help us. First, there is a clear warning to us scientists who are Christians, that in stressing the underlying simplicity and order of the complex world which modern biology reveals, and in stressing the power and effectiveness of modern technology, we must also stress its limits. We must be less assertive, less arrogant than is sometimes the case at present. We are too often driven by our love of new technology, and are unaware of the dehumanizing effect of the innate reductionism that is the basis of modern molecular biology. So we are regarded as arrogant, distant and uncaring. That is a warning to us all.

Second, we scientists working in the food area must be sensitive to the different way in which the general public regards new technology when it is applied to food. Let me digress for a moment. In both Greek and Latin, ethics and morals originally meant simply "custom" or "habit" – and we still have this meaning in English in the words "ethos" and "mores." Despite these origins, "ethics" and "morality" now usually entail "values" and "principles" which most people believe should not be reduced simply to "customs" and "habits." In our area of novel foods and processes both sets of meanings are involved. Food is surrounded by "customs" and "habits" which can properly change over time. Some of these customs derive from religious traditions (e.g. Jews and Muslims not eating pork) and others probably have secular origins (e.g. the English not eating dogs or horses). Breaking these customs can be very offensive to other people but it is not clear that they actually involve wrongdoing as such. They are, perhaps, much more to do with social and community identity, which of course is becoming weaker in our increasingly pluralistic world. However, other aspects of novel foods and processes are much more to do with values, especially the fundamental value of not harming the innocent. So allowing novel foods which risk harm to the innocent would be wrong. It is therefore a clear moral/ethical duty for those developing novel foods and processes to test their safety extremely carefully, and it may always be right to err on the side of caution when there might be risk. It is also necessary to be sensitive to the difference between the consumer's attitude to change in medicine and food; the practices are not simply transferable.

Third, there is the natural/unnatural issue that I raised earlier, and I think that there are a number of issues here.

First, although this is a distinction commonly made by non-scientists, it is a distinction that all scientists, including Christians, find difficult to understand. We who are Christians see no distinction between what we learn of the world through our faith and through our science; what we do in the laboratory is not "unnatural." It is all God's world.

Second, this distinction assumes a false, I believe, romantic view of "Nature," a view verging on pantheism. The world is not ideally left as it is; rivers do need taming, land use has to change if we are to feed our world, and all environments need managing. This view assumes that much modern agriculture is "unnatural," but I have an uneasy feeling that some of these concerns are only possible for us because we are so affluent and can afford to pay more, as we surely will, for (say) non-genetically modified soya – although the genetically modified form is a product which I believe carries no health risk. So if customers want to choose, then they will have to pay. That is not an option for many in the developing world, for they need the food.

Third, though it is impossible to distinguish between "natural" vanilla and that made by chemistry or fermentation, some want to buy "natural" vanilla because by doing so they are maintaining a Third World economy. But that is not a problem peculiar to biotechnology. Every time we replace an imported raw material by one derived from high technology (and there are many reasons for doing so) we are into this debate, which is much more complex than it sounds, and which too easily tempts well-intentioned but uninformed people into pronouncements about economics.

Fourth, there are environmental issues. It was Edmund Burke who said: "Society is indeed a contract [...] it becomes a partnership between not only those who are living, but between those who are living, those who are dead, and those who are yet to be born." This seems to me to be a deeply biblical idea. Have we got our present practices right? I am beginning to get concerned that we are being insufficiently careful as to our responsibility to future generations. We have to be very careful. ...

So, to sum up: I believe this new technology has the capacity to make food cheaper, safer and more nutritious. There are few quantifiable risks to the consumer, but their concerns, which are much more about moral acceptability, need to be handled thoughtfully and openly. We do not have the right to use a new technology unless the users or consumers, or at least most of them, are happy about it. That means open dialogue, and when in doubt, delay. With those provisos, we can thank God for another insight into this amazing world we live in, and our ability to use our knowledge for the good of all.

Subversive

Wendell Berry, *The Pleasures of Eating*

Wendell Berry (b. 1934) is a man of letters, an academic, cultural, and economic critic, and a farmer. He is a prolific author of novels, short stories, poems, and essays. He is a Baptist with wide religious sympathies, whose work is committed to and expressive of his place – rural Kentucky.

This excerpt comes under the subversive heading because it speaks from the soil in much the same way as other excerpts have spoken from the oppressed experience of race or gender. Berry begins by challenging the notion of food as an abstract idea and restoring the role of the eater within the annual cycle of planting and reaping. He demonstrates that the logic of industrialization would be to eradicate even chewing from the consumption process: "The condition of the passive consumer of food is not a democratic condition." He uses analogy very effectively: "Like industrial sex, industrial eating has become a degraded, poor, and paltry thing."

Berry narrates a sad tale of the doleful effects of separating the eater from the land whence the food arises. The result is a trap created by industrialism: "a walled city surrounded by valves that let merchandise in but no consciousness out." He offers seven suggestions for escaping this trap. His concern for the soil does not entail vegetarianism: he is concerned that people eat with "understanding and with gratitude." While there are many consequential elements to his argument, his main concern is right relationships: he concludes by saying, "Eating with the fullest pleasure – pleasure, that is, that does not depend on ignorance – is perhaps the profoundest enactment of our connection with the world."

I begin with the proposition that eating is an agricultural act. Eating ends the annual drama of the food economy that begins with planting and birth. Most eaters, however, are no longer aware that this is true. They think of food as an agricultural product, perhaps, but they do not think of themselves as participants in agriculture. They think of themselves as "consumers." If they think beyond that, they recognize that they are passive consumers. They buy what they want – or what they have been persuaded to want – within the limits of what they can get. They pay, mostly without protest, what they are charged. And they mostly ignore certain critical questions about the quality and the cost of what they are sold: How fresh is it? How pure or clean is it, how free of dangerous chemicals? How far was it transported, and what did transportation add to the cost? How much did manufacturing or packaging or advertising add to the cost? When the food product has been manufactured or "processed" or "precooked," how has that affected its quality or price or nutritional value?

Most urban shoppers would tell you that food is produced on farms. But most of them do not know what farms, or what kinds of farms, or where the farms are, or what knowledge or skills are involved in farming. They apparently have little doubt that farms will continue to produce, but they do not know how or over what obstacles. For them, then, food is pretty much an abstract idea – something they do not know or imagine – until it appears on the grocery shelf or on the table.

The specialization of production induces specialization of consumption. Patrons of the entertainment industry, for example, entertain themselves less and less and have become more and more passively dependent on commercial suppliers. This is certainly true also of patrons of the food industry, who have tended more and more to be *mere* consumers – passive, uncritical, and dependent. Indeed, this sort of consumption may be said to be one of the chief goals of industrial production. The food industrialists have by now persuaded millions of consumers to prefer food that is already prepared. They will grow, deliver, and cook your food for you and (just like your mother) beg you to eat it. That they do not yet offer to insert it, prechewed, into your mouth is only because they have found no profitable way to do so. We may rest assured that they would be glad to find such a way. The ideal industrial food consumer would be strapped to a table with a tube running from the food factory directly into his or her stomach. ...

There is, then, a politics of food that, like any politics, involves our freedom. We still (sometimes) remember that we cannot be free if our minds and voices are controlled by someone else. But we have neglected to understand that we cannot be free if our food and its sources are controlled by someone else. The condition of the passive consumer of food is not a democratic condition. One reason to eat responsibly is to live free.

But if there is a food politics, there are also a food esthetics and a food ethics, neither of which is dissociated from politics. Like industrial sex, industrial eating has become a degraded, poor, and paltry thing. Our kitchens and other eating places more and more resemble filling stations, as our homes more and more resemble motels. "Life is not very interesting," we seem to have decided. "Let its satisfactions be minimal, perfunctory, and fast." We hurry through our meals to go to work and hurry through our work in order to "recreate" ourselves in the evenings and on weekends and vacations. And then we hurry, with the greatest possible speed and noise and violence, through our recreation – for what? To eat the billionth hamburger at some fast-food joint hellbent on increasing the "quality" of our life? And all this is carried out in a remarkable obliviousness to the causes and effects, the possibilities and the purposes, of the life of the body in this world. ...

And this peculiar specialization of the act of eating is, again, of obvious benefit to the food industry, which has good reasons to obscure the connection between food and farming. It would not do for the consumer to know that the hamburger she is eating came from a steer who spent much of his life standing deep in his own excrement in a feedlot, helping to pollute the local streams, or that the calf that yielded the veal cutlet on her plate spent its life in a box in which it did not have room to turn around. And, though her sympathy for the slaw might be less tender, she should not be encouraged to meditate on the hygienic and biological implications of mile-square fields of cabbage, for vegetables grown in huge monocultures are dependent on toxic

chemicals – just as animals in close confinement are dependent on antibiotics and other drugs.

The consumer, that is to say, must be kept from discovering that, in the food industry – as in any other industry – the overriding concerns are not quality and health, but volume and price. For decades now the entire industrial food economy, from the large farms and feedlots to the chains of supermarkets and fast-food restaurants, has been obsessed with volume. It has relentlessly increased scale in order to increase volume in order (presumably) to reduce costs. But as scale increases, diversity declines; as diversity declines, so does health; as health declines, the dependence on drugs and chemicals necessarily increases. As capital replaces labor, it does so by substituting machines, drugs, and chemicals for human workers and for the natural health and fertility of the soil. The food is produced by any means or any shortcut that will increase profits. And the business of the cosmeticians of advertising is to persuade the consumer that food so produced is good, tasty, healthful, and a guarantee of marital fidelity and long life.

It is possible, then, to be liberated from the husbandry and wifery of the old household food economy. But one can be thus liberated only by entering a trap (unless one sees ignorance and helplessness as the signs of privilege, as many people apparently do). The trap is the ideal of industrialism: a walled city surrounded by valves that let merchandise in but no consciousness out. How does one escape this trap? Only voluntarily, the same way that one went in: by restoring one's consciousness of what is involved in eating; by reclaiming responsibility for one's own part in the food economy. One might begin with the illuminating principle of Sir Albert Howard's *The Soil and Health*, that we should understand "the whole problem of health in soil, plant, animal, and man as one great subject." Eaters, that is, must understand that eating takes place inescapably in the world, that it is inescapably an agricultural act, and that how we eat determines, to a considerable extent, how the world is used. This is a simple way of describing a relationship that is inexpressibly complex. To eat responsibly is to understand and enact, so far as one can, this complex relationship. What can one do? Here is a list, probably not definitive:

1   Participate in food production to the extent that you can. If you have a yard or even just a porch box or a pot in a sunny window, grow something to eat in it. Make a little compost of your kitchen scraps and use it for fertilizer. Only by growing some food for yourself can you become acquainted with the

beautiful energy cycle that revolves from soil to seed to flower to fruit to food to offal to decay, and around again. You will be fully responsible for any food that you grow for yourself, and you will know all about it. You will appreciate it fully, having known it all its life.

2   Prepare your own food. This means reviving in your own mind and life the arts of kitchen and household. This should enable you to eat more cheaply, and it will give you a measure of "quality control": you will have some reliable knowledge of what has been added to the food you eat.

3   Learn the origins of the food you buy, and buy the food that is produced closest to your home. The idea that every locality should be, as much as possible, the source of its own food makes several kinds of sense. The locally produced food supply is the most secure, the freshest, and the easiest for local consumers to know about and to influence.

4   Whenever possible, deal directly with a local farmer, gardener, or orchardist. All the reasons listed for the previous suggestion apply here. In addition, by such dealing you eliminate the whole pack of merchants, transporters, processors, packagers, and advertisers who thrive at the expense of both producers and consumers.

5   Learn, in self-defense, as much as you can of the economy and technology of industrial food production. What is added to food that is not food, and what do you pay for these additions?

6   Learn what is involved in the *best* farming and gardening.

7   Learn as much as you can, by direct observation and experience if possible, of the life histories of the food species.

The last suggestion seems particularly important to me. Many people are now as much estranged from the lives of domestic plants and animals (except for flowers and dogs and cats) as they are from the lives of the wild ones. This is regrettable, for these domestic creatures are in diverse ways attractive; there is much pleasure in knowing them. And farming, animal husbandry, horticulture, and gardening, at their best, are complex and comely arts; there is much pleasure in knowing them, too. ...

The pleasure of eating should be an *extensive* pleasure, not that of the mere gourmet. People who know the garden in which their vegetables have grown and know that the garden is healthy will remember the beauty of the growing plants, perhaps in the dewy first light of morning when gardens are at their best. Such a memory involves itself with the food and is one of the pleasures of eating. The knowledge of the good health of the garden relieves and frees and comforts the eater. The same goes for eating meat. The thought of the good pasture and of the calf contentedly grazing flavors the steak. Some, I know, will think it bloodthirsty or worse to eat a fellow creature you have known all its life. On the contrary, I think it means that you eat with understanding and with gratitude. A significant part of the pleasure of eating is in one's accurate consciousness of the lives and the world from which food comes. The pleasure of eating, then, may be the best available standard of our health. And this pleasure, I think, is pretty fully available to the urban consumer who will make the necessary effort.

I mentioned earlier the politics, esthetics, and ethics of food. But to speak of the pleasure of eating is to go beyond those categories. Eating with the fullest pleasure – pleasure, that is, that does not depend on ignorance – is perhaps the profoundest enactment of our connection with the world. In this pleasure we experience and celebrate our dependence and our gratitude, for we are living from mystery, from creatures we did not make and powers we cannot comprehend.

Ecclesial

Michael S. Northcott, *Faithful Feasting*

Michael S. Northcott (b. 1955) teaches ethics at the University of Edinburgh, Scotland. He is perhaps the leading voice among theological responses to the environmental crisis. In his *A Moral Climate* he offers an ethical, theological, and exegetical plea for action. For all the urgent consequential concern about planetary sustainability, for

Northcott it is fundamentally a deontological issue, not a consequential one. "The rituals encouraged by the recognition of global warming – turning off lights, turning down the heating, cycling or walking instead of driving, holidaying nearer to home, buying local food, shopping less and conversing more, addressing the issues of fuel poverty locally and nationally – are good because they are *intrinsically* right, not just because they have the consequence of reducing carbon emissions." It is quite simply wrong to enslave people and ecosystems to the high resource requirements of a corporately governed consumer economy.

Northcott offers ways to reconceptualize the relation of humanity to the planet. "It makes more sense to think of the human economy as a wholly owned subsidiary of the earth's systems rather than as a monetary system which is physically independent from the great economy of the earth and therefore endlessly expandable." His work is an excellent example of how subversive themes are made visible in an ecclesial framework.

This excerpt is explicitly ecclesial, in the way it makes the Eucharist the center of a theology of food. Northcott has been discussing the Eucharist in 1 Corinthians and the way in which the Eucharist meal is a microcosm for divine redemption of the whole creation. In this context, he comments on the rigorist third-century Roman theologian Novatian's essay *On Jewish Foods*, which treats the Jewish dietary laws as allegories of virtues (e.g., temperance) in the moral and spiritual life.

Michael S. Northcott. *A Moral Climate: The Ethics of Global Warming*. London: Darton, Longman, and Todd, 2007. From Chapter 8, "Faithful Feasting," pages 255–65. Published and copyright 2007, by Darton, Longman, and Todd Ltd., London, and used by permission of the publishers. Reprinted by permission of Orbis Books.

The Eucharist and Christian Eating

Novatian's account of the importance of moral virtue and spiritual worship in Christian eating indicates that for the early Christians *all* eating is potentially eating *with Christ*, and that there is a moral and ritual continuum between the Lord's Table and the household meal. This recognition is an important corrective to much Eucharistic practice and theology where the Eucharist has become a token meal, and as a memorial rite of the death of Christ conceived as a sacrifice. It indicates that not all ritual meals were associated in the Christian mind with sacrifice. Some Christian meal practices were open to sacrificial interpretation, but sacrifice is not the only way in which ritual eating is understood in the early Church. Equally strong are metaphors concerned with mission to the world beyond the Church, with the binding of the fellowship in the shared act of eating and drinking bread that has been broken and from a cup that is shared, and with blessing and gift giving. Furthermore, in certain crucial respects

Novatian's account indicates that there was no sharp distinction between the sacrality of a ritual meal and the profane eating of the household. All meals are indicative of the relationship of the guests with God and with one another; all meals constitute community and sociality and offer opportunities for conversation and table fellowship.

The elements and the rituals of Christian meals, then, are *all* theurgic (and hence the tradition of Christ as the unseen guest at every meal) and all are constitutive of Christian identity, and of the boundary between *ecclesia* and *seculum* in a pagan world. Analogously, food growing and the social economy of food are caught up in the divine economy of giving and receiving which Christ's many acts of blessing and breaking of bread set forth. …

Modern European culture has been profoundly shaped by the sacred-profane distinction which emanates into Christian theology from the medieval practice of the Mass. The medieval focus on priestly or cultic objects and sacred space paved the way for the emergence of the non-cultic as secular in succeeding centuries. In post-Christendom Europe and North America, profanity in relation to creation and food does not take the form of disrespecting the Host or refusing to honour the priest. In a sense both Host and priest are sidelined in modern secularism. It is now the creation itself which is profaned, while the sacred Host is set aside, replaced with the sacred dollar or euro. The contemporary form of idolatry is the devotion of the culture of food to money, from crop to table. This produces a new kind of profanity in which industrial food is debased while the soil is eroded, the land poisoned and the climate changed. By participating without critique in the fruits of modern agronomy, do Christians analogously "eat meat offered to idols" and imbibe a worldview which is contrary to the Gospel?

This point is sharpened by the recognition that most celebrations of the Eucharist in Europe and North America occur not in rural areas but in cities where the resonance of the agrarian references of the elements of bread and wine may be lost, either consciously or materially. Thus congregations that decide to use a real loaf of bread rather than communion wafers may use a loaf which has been made from petrochemically farmed wheat and then manufactured by the Chorleywood process. When a loaf which is the product of this novel structure of food growing, making and marketing is presented at the altar with words that declare that it is through the goodness of God that the people "have this bread to offer," and moreover that it is "fruit of the field, work of human hands," credibility is being stretched. Did the goodness of God intend that bread should be wrung from the land at the expense of the rape of the soil, the poisoning of ground water and the wasteful expenditure of fossil fuels, or that it should be manufactured in such a way as to turn it into the ambiguously convenient consumer product which is modern sliced bread? While it is the case that there is a foundational agrarian reference in the use of bread and wine as the elements of the Eucharist, it is questionable whether this agrarian reference is truly honoured and proclaimed in these circumstances.

The related claim I am making here is that food *is* politics, and that the Eucharist is therefore political food. Just as Eucharistic practice in Europe, both before and after the Reformation, represented a very different kind of politics than the revolutionary subordination of Christ and the apostles, so a Eucharistic practice which fails to challenge the profanation of the creation represented by modern agronomy is equally flawed. Profane eating, eating food offered to idols, has become the norm in the twenty-first century and like earlier cults, this idolatry involves sacrifices – of the soil, healthy rural communities, and now of the climate of the earth. ...

Wes Jackson and Wendell Berry ... suggest that in their neglect of the laws of ecology modern farmers, and the scientists, politicians and corporate managers who guide them, are not just myopic but morally deficient. By neglecting the wisdom of conserving soil quality for the next generation the modern farmer, and the politicians and consumers who collude with him, display "moral ignorance and weakness of character." Science-informed agriculture, far from liberating modern humans from natural necessities, has subjected them to a new form of slavery – the slavery of the machine and of untutored instinct. This mechanistic slavery takes a number of forms in the global food economy. And this enslavement is not of course confined to humans. Billions of animals are now caught up in a horrendous factory farming industry which is not only one of the largest single sources of greenhouse gas emissions but also a form of collective cruelty which is unique in human history. Never before did a civilisation rest upon such systemic cruelty to so many living creatures as does industrial civilisation. That this immoral treatment also has serious health implications for human beings in the form of novel viruses and toxins in our diet is still not seen as a cause for governments or food scientists to press the industry into more humane and sustainable approaches to animal husbandry. ...

Once again, we are faced with the systematic conflict between the neoliberal, corporately-driven economy of endless growth without moral limits, and the ecological and moral structures of the biosphere and of ecological and human community. The deregulated industrial food economy promoted by neoliberals advances a fundamental disconnect between the growing and eating of food. So remote have global food chains become that the *average* item of food in an American supermarket has travelled 1,500 miles. ...

Christian Worship and Spiritual Eating

If Christian worship is effectively to resist the devotion of modern civilisation to an increasingly heedless abuse of the precious resources of this good earth, and if it is to resist the particular threat posed to all life on earth by climate change, then there is an urgent need to recover the full agrarian and social significance of Eucharist in Christian worship. Breaking bread was the paradigmatic meal of first-century Palestinians and Romans. The early Christians worshipped sitting at tables where they blessed the cup and broke bread because it was a common meal, not just a "sacral" act. The social meanings attached to the meal traditions in which the Eucharist began have considerable resonances with the witness of the Church today in a situation where once again a global imperial economy is the source of oppression of both humanity and the land. The creatures which are the elements of bread and wine are transformed in the Eucharist into the new creation which is the body of Christ, the Church, and in this transformation lies the possibility of the end of the groaning of creation and the remaking of all things towards their peaceable destiny. The Eucharist does not only remake human politics and spaces but the politics and spaces of all creatures, human and nonhuman. ...

The claim that the Eucharist makes the Church, which in the twentieth century has been advanced by the Catholic theologian Henri de Lubac, needs also to be read in the light of the moral economy of food. Here both Catholic and Protestant may learn something from those Christian farmers who departed the shores of Europe in the face of bloody and extreme persecution and established the Anabaptist culture of North America, which still maintains a close relation to the land today. Just one of their major disagreements with Catholic and Protestant theologians was over the theology of the Lord's Supper. They claimed that the Lord's Supper was the constituting action of the body of Christ. For the Anabaptists it was not the priest or the altar, nor their mystical association with Christ, which made the elements holy but rather the gathering of the whole people of God and the holiness of lives. The crucial element in a proper invocation of the body of Christ *is* the body of Christ, where the body is conceived not as the material or mystical body of Jesus Christ but, as St Paul has it in 1 Corinthians 12, the community of the local church. As Yoder points out, Anabaptist ecclesiology broke with Reformation and Catholic theology over the question of the visibility of the Church and its capacity to act.

In Anabaptist perspective the Lord's Supper has no objective power, no mystical significance, apart from the participation of the people of God in the action of breaking bread. There is no invisible Church which resides behind the real, presently-existing Church as represented by the local congregation. Instead, the Church and the Lord's Supper are mutually constitutive because the local church in its gathering to break bread *is* the agent that breaks bread. The celebrant acts on behalf of the community, and the act of breaking bread creates and sustains the community. This approach places ethics and holy living at the centre of the Eucharist Church relationship, because it also

requires that those who gather to break bread are living in communities whose morality and order are modelled on the teachings of the Gospels. There is no objective sacramental mystery here. Only when the people of God act morally and live holy lives do they constitute a body of people who can break bread and so be the body of Christ. ...

The Anabaptist recognition of the foundational significance of Christian eating is surely not unconnected with the fact that they are unique among Protestant Christians in North America in resisting modern agricultural practices. Instead of pursuing the model of power over nature, and of agriculture as an extractive economy, they have sustained a model of holy agriculture in which communal dependence and the conservation of the soil go hand in hand. Instead of debt to banks and government to sustain the high inputs and machinery of chemical farming, they have been content with growing enough to sustain their communities, and this restraint, and freedom from debt, has made them not only the best conservers of the soil in North America, but, in recent decades, the most successful farmers, if success is measured in quality of life as well as quantity of production. As Wendell Berry says, only the Amish

> as a community, have carefully restricted their use of machine-developed energy, and so have become the only true masters of technology. They are mostly farmers, and they do most of their farm work by hand and by the use of horses and mules. They are pacifists, they operate their own local schools, and in other ways hold themselves aloof from the ambition of a machine-based society. And by doing so they have maintained the integrity of their families, their community, their religion, and their way of life. They have escaped the mainstream American life of distraction, haste, aimlessness, violence, and disintegration.

... If the connections I have sought to establish in this chapter between Eucharist, eating and ecology are to be recovered in the Christian practice of worship, Christians will be among those who will seek in future to know where their food has come from, how it was grown, by whom, and at what cost to the climate, farmers, species and soil. In this way Christians will begin to recover the revolutionary nature of the first Christian communities and their acting out of that spirit which "turned the world upside down" in their own moral economy of food.

Ecology

Augustine, in his *On Christian Doctrine*, draws an influential distinction between those things humans should "use" and those things humans should "enjoy." The latter were the abundant gifts of God, that never run out, and enjoying them was participating in the worship of God. The former were available to serve the latter. A tension that runs through the history of Christian ethics concerns whether the nonhuman creation is to be "used" or "enjoyed." That tension has become a matter of intense debate in recent times due to the deepening sense of ecological crisis.

There are broadly four dimensions to the contemporary ecological crisis. The most publicized issue is the overwhelming evidence of climate change, with a host of ancillary causes, such as the burning of fossil fuels, and effects, such as rising sea levels and the reduction in polar icecaps. There are at least three other issues besides global warming. There is the rapid depletion of species diversity, currently estimated at 10,000 annually. This has causes such as deforestation, extensive deep-sea fishing, and the widespread use of pesticides and herbicides. There is the rate of soil erosion and desertification, related to poor farming methods, overgrazing, and the use of inappropriate land for crop production. And finally there is the damaging appearance of chemical pollutants across the planet in air, land, oceans, and rivers.

Christian ethics responds to this crisis first by drawing on the theological theme of creation. Within the Genesis account there are two dimensions, sometimes seen in tension with one another. One suggests that humanity is called to dominate and subdue the nonhuman creation. It points to Genesis 1:28: "God blessed them, and God said to them, 'Be fruitful and multiply, and fill the earth and subdue it; and have dominion over the fish of the sea and over the birds of the air and over every living thing that moves upon the earth.'" The other dimension suggests that humanity is called to live in harmony with the nonhuman creation, with mutually beneficial results. It points to Genesis 2:15: "The Lord God took the man and put him in the Garden of Eden to till it and keep it."

A second key theological theme in relation to issues of ecology is that of resurrection. A foundational article by the historian Lynn White in 1967 entitled "The Historic Roots of Our Ecologic Crisis" put the blame for the alienation of the Christian imagination from the created world on early modern mechanistic views of the universe. But the blame has also been directed at views of salvation that seem to rescue humanity *from* the physical world, rather than *to* a renewed world. Hence the significance of the resurrection, by which God in Christ is restored to a world made new. The resurrection thus affirms the creation by showing how the earth is permanently a part of God's destiny for humanity and all his creation.

Jürgen Moltmann's text below straddles the boundary between universal, subversive, and ecclesial, bringing together themes from each approach. Sallie McFague draws out some of the theological ambiguities of a Christian commitment to see nature as the "new poor." Finally, Laura Yordy explores one particular virtue required to sustain ecological commitments.

Universal

Jürgen Moltmann, *An Ecological Doctrine of Creation*

Jürgen Moltmann (b. 1926) is Professor Emeritus of Systematic Theology at the University of Tübingen, Germany. His extensive theological works center on hope for the coming kingdom of God based on the cross and resurrection of Jesus Christ. His first major work, *A Theology of Hope* (1967), sees judgment as fundamentally vindication of the oppressed and suffering peoples of the present and past. He traces these themes through his later influential works on the crucifixion of God in Christ and on the Holy Spirit.

In *God in Creation* (1985) Moltmann sees God's creation as the double world of heaven and earth. Earth permeates heaven and heaven permeates earth. At the center of his doctrine of creation is the Sabbath as the crown of creation. In this excerpt he offers "Some Guiding Ideas for an Ecological Doctrine of Creation." While he speaks of "a deliberately and emphatically Christian doctrine of creation," his argument remains in largely universal terms. It is significant that he avoids drawing a firm distinction between creation and redemption: theologies that do so tend to find it difficult to articulate such an affirming role for creation itself, since they tend to see everything through the lens of the Fall. By contrast, Moltmann says "creation is aligned towards its redemption from the very beginning."

Perhaps his most fascinating insight is that it is the Sabbath that "distinguishes the view of the world as creation from the view of the world as nature." In other words the Sabbath gives purpose and shape to nature, identifying its relationship to God. Jesus' resurrection, along with the Sabbath, becomes the key place where creation and redemption, nature and grace, meet.

Whereas in many accounts creation is largely or wholly the work of the first person of the Trinity (hence inclusive-language nomenclature for God, which often replaces the term Father with the apparent synonym Creator), Moltmann is at pains to show how creation is the work of each member of the Trinity – not just Christ, but the Spirit too – and indeed he sees the Spirit as the key to a human response to the ecological crisis. His concluding words come close to the notion of pantheism – whereby God is present in all things; although Moltmann's developed understanding of the Holy Spirit seeks to ensure that, while God is indeed present in all things, those things do not constitute the whole of God.

Jürgen Moltmann. *God in Creation: An Ecological Doctrine of Creation.* Trans. Margaret Kohl. London: SCM Press, 1985. From Chapter 1, "God in Creation: Some Guiding Ideas for an Ecological Doctrine of Creation," pages 2–17. Reprinted by permission of the publisher SCM Press.

1. Knowledge of Nature as God's Creation is Participating Knowledge

To be alive means existing in relationship with other people and things. Life is communication in communion. And, conversely, isolation and lack of relationship means death for all living things, and dissolution even for elementary particles. So if we want to understand what is real *as* real, and what is living *as* living, we have to know it in its own primal and individual community, in its relationships, interconnections and surroundings.

But we shall then have to conceive of the inversion of this as well. We shall have to understand that everything real and everything living is simply a concentration and manifestation of its relationships, interconnections and surroundings. Integrating, and integral, thinking moves purposefully in this social direction towards the goal of an inclusiveness that is many-sided, and ultimately fully comprehensive. ...

Integrating and integral thinking serves to generate the community between human beings and nature which is necessary and promotes life. And here "nature" means both the natural world in which we share, and our own bodily nature. As a network and interplay of relationships is built up, a symbiotic life comes into being. ...

2. Creation for Glory

It is my intention to present a deliberately and emphatically Christian doctrine of creation. In this context I understand the word "Christian" in its original sense, as "messianic"; but messianic as the word has been moulded by Jesus' proclamation and his history. So a Christian doctrine of creation is a view of the world in the light of Jesus the Messiah; and it will be determined by the points of view of the messianic time which has begun with him and which he defines. It is directed towards the liberation of men and women, peace with nature, and the redemption of the community of human beings and nature from negative powers, and from the forces of death.

This messianic doctrine of creation therefore sees creation together with its future – the future for which it was made and in which it will be perfected. Ever since ancient times, "the future of creation" has been termed "the kingdom of glory." This symbol of cosmic hope is supposed to indicate that "creation in the beginning" is an open creation, and that its consummation will be to become the home and dwelling place of God's glory. Human beings already experience the indwellings of God in the Spirit here in history, even if as yet only partially and provisionally. That is why they hope that in the kingdom of glory God will dwell entirely and wholly and for ever in his creation, and will allow all the beings he has created to participate in the fullness of his eternal life. ...

3. The Sabbath of Creation

According to the biblical traditions, creation is aligned towards its redemption from the very beginning; for the creation of the world points forward to the sabbath, "the feast of creation." ... So when we present creation in the light of its future – "the glory of God," "existence as home" and the general "sympathy of all things" – then we are developing *a sabbath doctrine of creation.* What this means, factually and practically, is the aspect and prospect of creation which is perceived on the sabbath, and only then. The sabbath is the true hallmark of every biblical – every Jewish and also every Christian – doctrine of creation. The completion of creation through the peace of the sabbath distinguishes the view of the world as creation from the view of the world as nature; for nature is unremittingly fruitful and, though it has seasons and rhythms, knows no sabbath. It is the sabbath which blesses, sanctifies and reveals the world as God's creation. ...

Israel celebrates the sabbath in the time and context of her own history. But the sabbath which is repeated week by week does not merely interrupt the time for work and the time for living. It points beyond itself to the sabbatical year, in which the primordial conditions between human beings, and between human beings and nature, are supposed to be restored, according to the righteousness of the covenant of Israel's God. And this sabbatical year, in its turn, points in history beyond itself to the future of the messianic era. Every sabbath is a sacred anticipation of the world's redemption. ...

4. The Messianic Preparation of Creation to be the Kingdom

[Moltmann proposes a revision of the famous principle of medieval theology, *gratia non destruit, sed praesupponit et perfecit naturam*: grace does not destroy, but presupposes and perfects nature.]

I would therefore like to reformulate the second part of the theological tenet in the sense of a three-term dialectic, and say: *gratia non perfecit, sed praeparat naturam ad gloriam aeternam; gratia non est perfectio*

naturae, sed praeparatio messianica mundi ad regnum Dei [grace does not perfect, but prepares nature for eternal glory; grace is not the perfection of nature but messianic preparation of the world for the reign of God]. This principle proceeds from the assumption that the grace of God can be seen in the raising of Christ, and concludes that Christ's resurrection is the beginning of the new creation of the world. It follows from this that we have to talk about nature and grace, and the relationship between nature and grace, in a forward perspective, in the light of the coming glory, which will complete both nature and grace, and hence already determines the relationship between the two here and now. It also follows that God's covenant in history cannot already be called "the inner foundation" of creation. We can give this name only to the coming kingdom of God's glory, which his covenant in history promises and guarantees. And the third and last conclusion is that being a Christian is not yet in itself the completion, but represents only a messianic path towards a possible future consummation of the condition of being human. ...

In mediaeval Judaism, the Christian church in its evangelization of the nations was often viewed and valued as the divinely willed *praeparatio messianica* [messianic preparation] of the Gentile peoples. We shall take up this Jewish assessment of Christian existence and extend it beyond the world of the Gentiles to nature itself. For Christianity is intended to be the *praeparatio messianica naturae* [messianic preparation of nature] as well. ...

5. Creation in the Spirit

According to the Christian interpretation, creation is a trinitarian process: the Father creates through the Son in the Holy Spirit. The created world is therefore created "by God," formed "through God" and exists "in God." ...

According to the biblical traditions, all divine activity is pneumatic in its efficacy. It is always the Spirit who first brings the activity of the Father and the Son to its goal. It follows that the triune God also unremittingly breathes the Spirit into his creation. Everything that is, exists and lives in the unceasing inflow of the energies and potentialities of the cosmic Spirit. This means that we have to understand every created reality in terms of energy, grasping it as the realized potentiality of the divine Spirit. Through the energies and potentialities of the Spirit, the Creator is himself present in his creation. He does not merely confront it in his transcendence; entering into it, he is also immanent in it. ...

If the Holy Spirit is "poured out" on the whole creation, then he creates the community of all created things with God and with each other, making it that fellowship of creation in which all created things communicate with one another and with God, each in its own way. The existence, the life, and the warp and weft of interrelationships subsist in the Spirit: "*In him* we live and move and have our being" (Acts 17.28). But that means that the interrelations of the world cannot be traced back to any components, or universal foundations (or whatever name we may give to "elementary particles"). ... Everything exists, lives and moves *in others,* in one another, with one another, for one another, in the cosmic interrelations of the divine Spirit. So it is only the community of creation in the Spirit itself that can be called "fundamental." For only the Spirit of God exists *ex se* [from itself]; and it is therefore the Spirit who has to be seen as the sustaining foundation of everything else, which does not exist *ex se* but *ab alio et in aliis* [from another and in another]. The patterns and the symmetries, the movements and the rhythms, the fields and the material conglomerations of cosmic energy all come into being out of the community, and in the community, of the divine Spirit. ...

Creation in the Spirit is the theological concept which corresponds best to the ecological doctrine of creation which we are looking for and need today. With this concept we are cutting loose the theological doctrine of creation from the age of subjectivity and the mechanistic domination of the world, and are leading it in the direction in which we have to look for the future of an ecological world-community. The progressive destruction of nature by the industrial nations, and the progressive threat to humanity through the pile-up of nuclear armaments, have brought the age of subjectivity and the mechanistic domination of the world up against their definitive limits. Faced with these limits, we have only one realistic alternative to universal annihilation: the non-violent, peaceful, ecological worldwide community in solidarity. ...

6. God's Immanence in the World

An ecological doctrine of creation implies a new kind of thinking about God. The centre of this thinking is no longer the distinction between God and the world. The centre is the recognition of the presence of God *in* the world and the presence of the world *in* God.

... [A]n ecological doctrine of creation today must perceive and teach God's *immanence* in the world. This does not mean departing from the biblical traditions. On the contrary, it means a return to their original truth: through his cosmic Spirit, God the Creator of heaven and earth is present *in* each of his creatures and *in* the fellowship of creation which they share. "*Deus penetrat praesentia sua totum universum*" [God in his presence penetrates the whole universe]. God is not merely the Creator of the world. He is also the Spirit of the universe. Through the powers and potentialities of the Spirit, the Creator indwells the creatures he has made, animates them, holds them in life, and leads them into the future of his kingdom. In this sense the history of creation is the history of the efficacy of the divine Spirit. So even when we consider the original biblical traditions, it is one-sided to view creation only as the work of "God's hands" and, as his "work," something that has simply and solely to be distinguished from God himself. Creation is also the differentiated presence of God the Spirit, the presence of the One *in* the many. ...

7. The Principle of Mutual Interpenetration

The archetype of this dialectical movement is to be found in the Godhead itself. The doctrine of the Trinity is the formulation for the distinctions and the unity in God. Through the concept of perichoresis, the social doctrine of the Trinity formulates the mutual indwellings of the Father, the Son and the Holy Spirit, and the eternal community that is manifested through these indwellings. ...

In God there is no one-sided relationship of superiority and subordination, command and obedience, master and servant, as Karl Barth maintained in his theological doctrine of sovereignty, making this the starting point for his account of all analogously antithetical relationships: God and the world; heaven and earth; soul and body; and, not least, man and woman too. In the triune God is the mutuality and the reciprocity of love.

Our starting point here is that all relationships which are analogous to God reflect the primal, reciprocal indwelling and mutual interpenetration of the trinitarian perichoresis: God *in* the world and the world *in* God; heaven and earth *in* the kingdom of God, pervaded by his glory; soul and body united *in* the life-giving Spirit to a human whole; woman and man *in* the kingdom of unconditional and unconditioned love, freed to be true and complete human beings. There is no such thing as solitary life.

Subversive

Sallie McFague, *The Body of God*

Sallie McFague (b. 1933) is Professor Emeritus of Theology at Vanderbilt University. Her early work concerned literature, metaphor, and parable. Since the mid-1980s her emphasis has been upon ecology.

In this excerpt, she goes beyond the language of Jürgen Moltmann (see the passage quoted above) in ways that highlight some of the distinctions between universal and subversive ethics. To suggest that "the direction of creation is toward inclusive love for all, especially the oppressed, the outcast, the vulnerable" is not a surprise, although, as McFague acknowledges, it puts her in tension with evolutionary history. It is a more significant step to go on to suggest that the definition of the outcast be expanded "to include oppressed nonhuman animals and the earth itself." This results in her claim that "Nature is the 'new poor.'" This is not a utilitarian argument – McFague acknowledges it may be "useless in light of the ecological crisis we face" – but a call to rethink the notion of God.

One issue for all strands in ethics, but perhaps particularly focused in some aspects of subversive ethics, is to what extent the commitment to the oppressed is invited or inclined to adjust central doctrinal dimensions of Christianity. Here McFague makes the provocative statement that "the scandal of uniqueness is perhaps not the central claim of Christian faith." She is looking for ways to see the universe in a parallel relationship to God to that held by Jesus. Her language about Jesus makes frequent use of her characteristic term "parable," rather than the ancient vocabulary of two natures and incarnation.

This is one of the most pressing issues in subversive ethics – to what extent radical commitment to the oppressed permits or requires one to reexamine core tenets of doctrine, and to what extent the doctrine that emerges is able to meet the new challenges while remaining recognizably Christian.

Sallie McFague. *The Body of God: An Ecological Theology.* Minneapolis: Fortress Press, 1993. From Chapter 6, "The Body of God," pages 159–68.

Christology: The Body of God

"And the Word became flesh and lived among us" (John 1:14a). The scandal of uniqueness is absolutized by Christianity into one of its central doctrines, which claims that God is embodied in one place and one place only: in the man Jesus of Nazareth. ...

But the scandal of uniqueness is perhaps not the central claim of Christian faith. In the model of the universe as God's body, the important motifs are "became flesh" and "lived among us." It is the statement of faith that God is embodied and embodied paradigmatically as one of us, a human being, that is critical. It is not the exclusive claim that matters, for one would assume that the source, power, and goal of the universe, its life and breath, its enlivening energy, would be embodied in many forms through its vast reaches. Rather, it is both the concrete, physical availability of God's presence ("became flesh") and the likeness to ourselves, a human being ("lived among us") that matter. ...

From the paradigmatic story of Jesus we will propose that the direction of creation is toward inclusive love for all, especially the oppressed, the outcast, the vulnerable. This paradigm suggests a trajectory for creation, one that we cannot read off evolutionary history but, from our wager of faith in the destabilizing, nonhierarchical, inclusive life, teachings, and death of Jesus of Nazareth, we can read back into natural, historical, and cultural evolution as its goal. ...

While trinitarian reflection has had a number of purposes in Christian history, its greatest asset has probably been its value as a way to imagine divine transcendence and immanence in a unified manner. As suggested earlier, the Christian tradition has had great difficulty with this issue, often projecting a transcendent sky-God who becomes immanent only at the point of Jesus of Nazareth. This transcendent God is available to other human beings principally through the work of the spirit of Christ, that is, by means of the sacraments and the reading of Scripture. The rest of creation is more or less neglected in this view linking divine transcendence and immanence. We will suggest a different picture, one that agrees with the tradition that transcendence is available to us only immanently, only through the mundane, the physical, the bodily – but a body that is not limited to Jesus of Nazareth. It is a kind of trinitarian reflection that emphasizes both the mystery of God (the face or "first person") and the visible physicality of God (the body or "second person") both the radical transcendence and the radical immanence of God. The mystery and the mud, the invisible and the visible, are mediated by the spirit ("third person"), the dynamic life and breath that moves in all things. Once again, the Christic paradigm will give a particular shape to this reflection: immanence does not mean simply overcoming the spatial distance of transcendence but the radicality of love for the vulnerable and the oppressed, the embodied God identifying with all suffering bodies.

The Shape of the Body: The Christic Paradigm

... [W]e will be suggesting two interrelated moves in regard to christology: the first is to relativize the incarnation in relation to Jesus of Nazareth and the second is to maximize it in relation to the cosmos. In other words, the proposal is to consider Jesus as paradigmatic of what we find everywhere: everything that is is the sacrament of God (the universe as God's body), but here and there we find that presence erupting in special ways. Jesus is one such place for Christians, but there are other paradigmatic persons and events – and the natural world, in a way different from the self-conscious openness to God that persons display, is also a marvelous sacrament in its diversity and richness.

But if knowing and doing are embodied, are concrete and particular, as we have assumed throughout this essay, then we must begin with the story of Jesus, not with everything that is. We stand within particular historical, cultural communities and see the world through those perspectives. We gain our hints and clues, our metaphors of reality, through formative traditions that we also are called upon to re-form. Our first step, then, is to read the central story of Christian faith

from the perspective of the organic model. The Christic paradigm must precede the cosmic Christ; the hints and clues for an embodied theology should arise from the particular, concrete insights and continuities of the tradition's basic story. This in no way privileges Scripture as the first or last word, but only as the touchstone text that Christians return to as a resource (not *the* source) for helping them to construct for their own time the distinctiveness of their way of being in the world.

Christianity's Distinctive Embodiment: Inclusion of the Neglected Oppressed

... *The story of Jesus suggests that the shape of God's body includes all, especially the needy and outcast.* While there are many distinctive features of the Christian notion of embodiment, in an ecological age when the development of our sensibility concerning the vulnerability and destruction of nonhuman creatures and the natural environment is critical, we ought to focus on one: the inclusion of the neglected oppressed – the planet itself and its many different creatures, including outcast human ones. The distinctive characteristic of Christian embodiment is its focus on oppressed, vulnerable, suffering *bodies*, those who are in pain due to the indifference or greed of the more powerful. In an ecological age, this ought to include oppressed nonhuman animals and the earth itself.

We need to pause and consider this suggestion, for it is shocking by conventional human standards. Until recently, most people found the notion that the earth is vulnerable, that its many species as well as the ecosystems supporting life are victims, are oppressed, absurd. And many still do. Many will even deny that the destabilizing love that we see in Jesus' parables, which overturns the conventional dualisms of rich and poor, righteous and sinner, Jew and Gentile, should include the dualism of humans over nature. And yet a cosmological or ecological perspective demands this radicalization of divine love: God's love is unlimited and oriented especially toward the oppressed – whoever the oppressed turn out to be at a particular time. The definition of who falls into this group has changed over the centuries, most recently focusing not on the spiritually poor, but the physically poor, those oppressed through the deprivation of bodily needs or through discrimination because of skin color or gender. Thus, the liberation theologies based on oppression due to poverty, race, or gender (and their interconnections) have arisen to claim that the gospel of Jesus of Nazareth has a preferential option for the poor, the poor in body, those whose bodies and bodily needs are not included in the conventional hierarchy of value. These are bodies that are devalued, discarded, and destroyed; these are bodies that can claim no intrinsic value in themselves but are of worth only because they are useful to others. In the organic model, bodies are basic, we have suggested, and how they are treated – how they are fed and housed, valued in their differences, honored in their integrity – is the primary issue. One of the most fundamental aspects of the story of Jesus, the love that overturns conventional dualistic hierarchies to reach out to the outcast and the victim, ought, we suggest, be extended to another dualistic hierarchy, that of humanity over nature. Nature is the "new poor," and in an embodiment, organic perspective, this means bodily poverty.

It is important to be clear about this suggestion of nature as the new poor. It does not mean that the "old poor" – poor human beings – are being replaced, or that every microorganism is included in God's love in the same way as human beings are. It does, however, suggest that nature is the "also" poor, and that even microorganisms have their place in creation, a place that is not merely their usefulness (or threat) to human beings. ...

Nature as the new poor does not mean that we should sentimentalize nature or slip into such absurdities as speaking of "oppressed" mosquitoes or rocks. Rather, nature as the new poor means that *we have made nature poor*. It is a comment not about the workings of natural selection but of human sin. It is a hard, cold look at what one part of nature, we human beings, have done to the rest of it: we have broken the integrity of creation by the excesses of our population and lifestyle, by our utilitarian attitude toward other creatures as well as toward our own vulnerable sisters and brothers, by our refusal to acknowledge the value of each and every aspect of creation to itself and to God. Nature is not necessarily and as such poor; it is so only because of *one* species, our own, which threatens the vitality and viability of the rest of nature. To say that the inclusive love of Jesus' destabilizing parables ought to be extended to nature does not, then, imply a sentimental divine love for each and every cell or bacterium. Rather, it brings to mind the righteous judgment of the Creator whose body, composed of many valuable, diverse forms, is being diminished on our planet by one greedy, thoughtless, albeit self-conscious and hence responsible, part of that body – ourselves. It means that nature needs to be liberated and healed because *we* have enslaved it and made it sick. ...

A cosmological and theocentric perspective – valuing the natural bodies around us because they are intrinsically worthwhile in themselves and to God, rather than for our purposes – is conventionally alien to us, but so is the overturning of the other hierarchies in the message of Jesus. The central claim of the gospel is, then, not only that the Word became flesh, but the particular shape that flesh took – one that presented a shock to our natural way of considering things in terms of value to ourselves. And for us to admit that nature is the "new poor" is also a direct affront to our anthropocentric sensibility. Our first response, in fact, might well be that such a radical perspective, a theocentric-cosmological one, is useless in light of the ecological crisis we face, where increasing numbers of poor, needy people *must* use the natural environment to provide for their own basic needs. We do not need to add yet another category of the oppressed, especially that of nature. But the shape of the body of God from a Christian perspective suggests otherwise. That shape, we have suggested, is given its basic outlines from one of the central features of Jesus' ministry – his destabilizing parables that side with the outcast. Extended to the natural world, to our planet and its many nonhuman creatures, the parabolic ministry of Jesus names a new poor, which is by definition poor in body, for those creatures and dimensions of our planet are primarily body. An incarnational religion, a bodily tradition, such as Christianity, should not have to strain to include the natural world and its creatures, for they epitomize the physical. They are, as it were, the *representative* bodies. ...

Since Christians understand Jesus of Nazareth as at least paradigmatic of God, that his ministry is a place to gain hints and clues about divine concern, then the centrality of the healing stories stands full square against any minimizing of the body. Bodies *count*, claims the healing ministry of Jesus, in the eyes of God. ... If the parables are the deconstructive phase of Jesus' ministry, overturning the oppressive, dualistic hierarchies, then the healing stories are the middle or reconstructive phase, not promising the kingdom but only what in ecological terms is called "sustainability," the ability to function in terms of bodily needs. The healings are a modest statement in light of the radical character of the parables. And yet, in another sense, at least in a cosmological or ecological context, they deepen the radicality of the parables, for they imply that bodily health and well-being is a priority of the gospel – and given the inclusiveness of the parabolic message and its bias toward the needy, this must mean not just human bodies but other vulnerable ones as well.

Ecclesial

Laura Ruth Yordy, *The Church's Eco-Discipleship*

Laura Ruth Yordy (b. 1969) teaches at Bridgewater College near Harrisonburg, Virginia. She considers a virtue approach to ecological ethics and settles on the virtue of patience, which she identifies as part of the meaning of witness. Yordy sees patience not as a sign of human distinctiveness from creation, but as a sign of human oneness with creation. In this she differs from the views outlined by David Baily Harned in his book *Patience: How We Wait Upon the World* (1997). Yordy sets out here dimensions of patience: "enduring adversity; waiting (and looking) for moments of grace; and, finally, the attentive appreciation of something without desiring its mastery, possession, or improvement." Finally, she locates patience among the other ecological virtues and reasserts the difference between patience and passivity.

Laura Ruth Yordy. *Green Witness: Ecology, Ethics, and the Kingdom of God.* Eugene: Cascade Books, 2008. From Chapter 4, "The Church's Eco-Discipleship," pages 153–60. Used by permission of Wipf and Stock Publishers. www.wipfandstock.com.

Patience: The Ecological Virtue

In addition to faith, the central virtue for ecological discipleship is patience. The prima facie evidence for this claim is the obvious role that impatience has played in environmental destruction: the impatient ambition for absolute dominance over the "natural" world, the impatient disregard for biophysical limits, and the impatient greed for profit. Patience is by no means a cure-all for human destruction of God's creation; however, it is a necessary virtue for the development of a vigorous witness to God's care for the world. Ecological witness or Christian activism cannot come about in the absence of patience. Even the word "witness," in one of its meanings, signifies watching – and watching is an activity of patience.

Given the central role played by patience in eco-discipleship, then, it is important to understand the nature of patience, the ways in which it differs from passivity, and how it functions as a peculiarly Christian virtue with regard to ecological witness. David Baily Harned argues in favor of re-establishing patience in its central position among Christian virtues, where it can stand as an urgently needed corrective to the extreme *im*patience of the modern world. ...

Unfortunately, Harned anchors patience in human distinctiveness, rather than on the nature of creature-liness. He writes that waiting is an inevitable part of life, rather than a sign of human failure. "What is most important, however, is the recognition that waiting is at the center of things not because of the nature of the world, not because of the nature of society, but because of who we are – made to be dependent, incomplete in isolation from others." That is, humans are created in the image of a God who is Creator, Redeemer, and Sanctifier in eternal communion, so interdependence and love are essential to the very being of the divine. And such interdependence makes patience necessary because each person must, in some way, rely upon the presence or activity of another. In contrast with Harned's anthropocentrism, however, every part of creation reflects the creator in exactly this way: from the atom to the solar system, each created entity is interdependent with its neighbors. Sociality and dependence are not distinctive to human beings. In fact, regarding interdependence as a human distinction undercuts the very idea Harned is trying to articulate, for the interdependence he emphasizes is not limited to humans, but unites creatures of widely differing species. The effect of Harned's misstep is, ironically, to isolate humans from their non-human neighbors and biophysical environment.

This anthropocentric isolation is compounded when Harned writes, "faith in the creator demands unwearying and persevering effort in the confidence that the universe we have been given is a benign and appropriate context for the exercise of human liberty." Taken at face value, the statement is true, but it strongly implies that liberty is the most important aspect of being human, and that the universe was designed for the sake of that liberty – both claims that contradict the Christian doctrines of creation and sin.

In contrast, patience *is* woven into the web of the universe because this universe reflects – in dim and fractured ways – the divine patience of its creator. Part of the human need for patience (as well as other virtues) is the imperative for humans to re-align themselves with the patient character of God's creation. This is not to claim that nothing is distinctive about human patience, but that human patience is more about living into our humanity as creatures than into our suspected superiority as a species. All human virtues are more about human creatures' relationship with God than about human status vis-à-vis other creatures.

That said, Harned develops a coherent account of the different aspects of patience, which he delineates as disciplined endurance of adversity, undying expectancy of God's Kingdom, unselfish forbearance of the faults of oneself and others, and realistic perseverance in faithful living. My own view differs somewhat, following my different starting position. I see patience as having three fundamental aspects, all of which stem from the character of our existence as creatures and all of which have ecological consequences. Patience is enduring adversity; waiting (and looking) for moments of grace; and, finally, the attentive appreciation of something without desiring its mastery, possession, or improvement.

The first aspect is that of endurance: bearing the ills of life for the sake of faithfulness to God. It may be that God has sent the trial (although Christians should hesitate to move too quickly to this judgment) or that the adversity can only be combated by vicious or unfaithful actions. Thus Christians in the western United States may endure the threats of puma attacks, for instance, because the only certain way of eliminating the threat would be to eliminate the animals, an action clearly in conflict with the command to care for creation. Or Christians in the southeastern part of the country may decide to endure the nuisance of mosquito bites and the slight risk of mosquito-borne disease rather than buy a propane-fueled vacuum that promises to suck up every mosquito in one square acre. This aspect of patience contrasts most sharply with the dictum of late Western capitalism that any desire can and should be satisfied, any risk averted, and the means for the goal should be far greater than necessary.

It is not the case that Christians must never take action against "natural" threats or hardships, especially in defense of human life. But the importance of patience should proffer two cautions: First, if we are considering measures that harm the non-human creation, we must be as conservative as possible, and remain open to the alternative of enduring rather than easing the hardship.

Second, we should be aware that if life is extremely comfortable, our virtue might well be impaired. Sometimes, therefore, we should undertake an ecological reform as a discipline, rather than purely as a means to saving forests or oceans.

The second aspect of Christian patience is quintessentially eschatological. Resting on faith in God's loving providence and promise of the Kingdom of Heaven, patience remains hopefully alert to signs of the Spirit while awaiting the coming of Christ. It is crucial to the ability to continue eco-discipleship in the face of apparent failure. This aspect of patience is the core of Christian witness, for the patient community of faith perseveres in resisting evil and positing signs of God's grace in the midst of a fallen and violent world. Patience of this sort is exemplified in the life of Paul Farmer, an American physician who has spent years providing medical ministry to poor Haitians against impossible odds, and in the work of Floresta, a Christian organization that plants trees in regions where deforestation intensifies the poverty of communities and their land. This patience not only requires hope, but it also *generates* hope; for the persistence of peaceful struggle itself points to God's presence in the midst of violence and sorrow.

Finally, the third aspect of patience is appreciation, an attitude of receptive delight to the particularity of something. It might be expressed as gratitude and doxology (though not romanticism), connected with humility and responsiveness toward God's grace. It is neither the calculating gaze of the colonial gold-hunter, who sees a river only as a route to financial gain, nor the starry-eyed gaze of the Romantic, who yearns for a return to the Garden of Eden. In American history, this sort of patience is notable by its absence; it could have reveled in the grandeur of Niagara Falls and Yosemite, for instance, without needing to "improve" the falls with concrete and hydro-engineering, and to "perfect" Yosemite Valley by removing its Native American residents. It is, rather, an appreciation of the beauty, complexity, and diversity of the biophysical world that includes acknowledgement of nature's fallen character. Wendell Berry and Annie Dillard, both Christians who write in very different ways about land and creatures, display this aspect of patience in their work. *Pilgrim at Tinker Creek,* for instance, describes the skill of watching closely – not waiting for a particular event, but simply to take in the particularity and otherness of what she sees.

The second and third aspects of patience are closely allied with loving attention, described by Iris Murdoch as a "just and loving concentration upon some individual or situation." Attention is a patient way of seeing, acknowledging the otherness of what is seen and appreciating the divine reflection in God's creation. When we "seek and serve Christ in all persons," we pay *attention* to the particular other. We hold ourselves alert to her signals of joy, sorrow, or suffering; we receive her without consuming or enclosing her. Likewise, when we pay close attention to the world we gain an increased sense of the reality of its inhabitants, relationships, and needs. In Harned's words, "we wait upon the world."

All three aspects of patience together form the core of Christian witness, for the human virtue of patience reflects (but dimly) the patience of God. And in the arena of ecological discipleship, patience teaches Christians to inhabit the earth, to share its witness to the creator, rather than (try to) dominate it. It enables Christians to persevere in their concrete acts of witness to the redemption of all creation, despite the continued onslaught against animals, species, and ecosystems. We can see this sort of patience in Christina García's novel *The Agüero Sisters*. Ignacio, a Cuban naturalist living in the early twentieth century, is walking along the beach when he encounters a leatherback turtle; he reacts with awe and protectiveness, rather than his customary love-as-control:

> It was then I saw her. Her ridged back and the enormity of her flippers made identification easy, especially in the moonlight. She was over eight feet long, a half ton of slow magnificence. The leatherback turned her wrinkled, spotted neck and gazed at me, as if gauging my trustworthiness. I could see her eyes clearly, the inverse widow's peak of her beak. ... After what seemed interminable digging, the giantess brought her hind flippers together, craned her neck forward, and began to sway slightly to a private rhythm, finally laying her eggs in the sand. ... At dawn, a fat scavenging gull dropped onto the leatherback's buried nest. I cursed the bird and threw a fistful of sand at it. A moment later, more gulls appeared. ... What choice did I have? I sat on the leatherback's nest all that day and all the next night, guarding the eggs from predators, guarding the eggs for her.

Ignacio here displays the patience of endurance (sitting on a sweltering beach for eighteen hours), hopeful waiting, and appreciative attention. Moreover, he does not regard his action as a choice, but a "natural" response to what his patience enabled him to see.

Patience, as with all virtues, is characteristic of communities even more than of individuals. The church, by its very identity, is a patient community: "we await his coming in glory." The church narrates, practices, and teaches patience as a communal virtue; the community and its individual members acquire patience as they are formed by the stories (Scripture) and practices (sacraments as well as outreach and ecological practices) of that same community. Of course patience cannot stand alone; it is part of the constellation of virtues that make up a Christian life. Prudence, or wisdom, determines when patience is appropriate (its appropriateness in an "environmental crisis"), and when it is not. Courage makes patience possible in the face of danger or hostility. Justice ensures that patience is not merely endurance for its own sake, but perseverance toward right relationships with humans and nonhumans alike.

The importance of patience should not be enlisted in favor of any sort of passivism, or of waiting for God to rescue humans from their misdeeds; actions ought not be judged based on short-term effectiveness in the world. If, as Christians, we relinquish our grasp of environmental destruction as a crisis, and understand it as a call to strengthen the faithful virtue of faith communities, we are able to persevere and move forward in the frightening and laborious tasks of changing the way we live.

Source Credits

The editors and publisher gratefully acknowledge the permission granted to reproduce the copyright material in this book:

1 The Story of God

1 Tertullian. *Adversus Marcionem*. Ed. Ernest Evans. Oxford: Oxford University Press, 1972. From Book I Paragraph 10 (pp. 25–7); I.19 (pp. 49–51); IV.6–7 (pp. 257–85); IV.20 (pp. 365–71); IV.43 (p. 507). Available online at www.tertullian.org/articles/evans_marc/evans_marc_00index.htm. By permission of Oxford University Press.

2 Karl Barth. "Israel and the Church." *Church Dogmatics*. Volume 2, Part 2. Edinburgh: T & T Clark, 1949. From Section 34, "The Election of the Community," pages 195–205. By kind permission of Continuum International Publishing Group.

3 John Howard Yoder. *The Original Revolution: Essays on Christian Pacifism*. Scottdale: Herald Press, 1972. From "If Abraham is our Father," pages 91–111. Copyright © 1971, 1977, 2003 by Herald Press, Scottdale, PA 15683. Used by permission.

4 Oliver O'Donovan. *The Desire of the Nations: Rediscovering the Roots of Political Theology*. Cambridge: Cambridge University Press, 1996, 2002. From pages 30–49. © Cambridge University Press, reproduced with permission.

5 John Calvin. *Institutes of the Christian Religion*. 2 vols. Ed. John T. McNeill. Trans. Ford Lewis Battles. The Library of Christian Classics 20. Philadelphia: Westminster Press, 1960. From Vol. 1, Book II, Chapter 15, pages 494–502. Available online at www.reformed.org/master/index.html?mainframe=/books/institutes/.

6 Stanley Hauerwas. *The Peaceable Kingdom: A Primer in Christian Ethics*. Notre Dame: University of Notre Dame Press, 1983. From Chapter 5, "Jesus: The Presence of the Peaceable Kingdom," pages 72–90. Copyright © Stanley Hauerwas, 1983. Used by permission of Hymns Ancient & Modern Ltd.

7 John Calvin. *Institutes of the Christian Religion*. 2 vols. Ed. John T. McNeill. Trans. Ford Lewis Battles. The Library of Christian Classics 20. Philadelphia: Westminster Press, 1960. From Vol. 1, Book III, Chapter 7, pages 689–701. Available online at www.reformed.org/master/index.html?mainframe=/books/institutes/.

8 Dietrich Bonhoeffer. *The Cost of Discipleship*. London: SCM Press, 2001. From Chapter 1, "Costly Grace," pages 3–9. Available online at www.crossroad.to/Persecution/Bonhoffer.html. Reprinted by permission of the publisher SCM Press. Reprinted with the permission of Scribner, a Division of Simon & Schuster, Inc., from *The Cost of Discipleship* by Dietrich Bonhoeffer. Copyright © 1959 by SCM Press Ltd. All rights reserved.

2 The Story of the Church

9 The Epistle of Mathetes to Diognetus. Source: www.earlychristianwritings.com/text/diognetus-roberts.html.

10 Perpetua. "Martyrdom of Perpetua." From *In Her Words: Women's Writings in the History of Christian Thought*. Ed. Amy Oden. Nashville: Abingdon Press, 1994. From pages 26–37. Available online at www.newadvent.org/fathers/0324.htm.

11 St. Clement of Alexandria, "Who is the Rich Man That Shall Be Saved?" Source: www.early christianwritings.com/text/clement-richman. html. Originally published in "The Early Church Fathers and Other Works", Wm. B. Eerdmans Pub. Co. in English, Edinburgh, Scotland, beginning 1867. (ANF 2, Roberts and Donaldson).

12 Eusebius of Caesarea. "A Speech on the Dedication of the Holy Sepulchre Church." In *From Irenaeus to Grotius: A Sourcebook in Christian Political Thought 100–1625*. Ed. Oliver O'Donovan and Joan Lockwood O'Donovan. Translation adapted from E. C. Richardson, *Nicene and Post-Nicene Fathers*. Grand Rapids: Eerdmans, 1999. From pages 58–65.

13 *The Rule of St. Benedict*. Trans. Caroline White. New York: Penguin Books, 2008. From Chapter 4, "The Tools for Good Works" (pages 17–18) and Chapter 7, "Humility" (pages 22–6). Available online in multiple versions at www.osb.org/rb/.

14 John Howard Yoder. *The Priestly Kingdom*. 2nd edn. Notre Dame: University of Notre Dame Press, 1984, 2001. From Chapter 7, "The Constantinian Sources of Western Social Ethics," pages 135–47.

15 Ernst Troeltsch. *The Social Teaching of the Christian Churches*. Vol. 1. Trans. Olive Wyon. New York: Macmillan, 1931. From Chapter 1, "The Foundations in the Early Church"; Part 1: The Gospel. Page 61.

16 H. Richard Niebuhr. *Christ and Culture*. New York: HarperCollins, 1951, 2001. From Chapter 6, "Christ the Transformer of Culture," pages 190–6. Copyright © 1951 by Harper and Brothers. Renewed © 1979 by Florence M. Niebuhr. Introduction copyright © 1996 by Richard R. Niebuhr. Foreword copyright © 2003 by Martin E. Marty. Preface copyright © 2003 by James Gustafson. Reprinted by permission of HarperCollins Publishers.

3 The Story of Ethics

17 Plato. *The Republic*. Provided by the Internet Classics Archive. www.classics.mit.edu//Plato/republic.html. From Book IX and Book VII.

18 Aristotle. *Nicomachean Ethics*. Cambridge Texts in the History of Philosophy. Ed. Roger Crisp. Cambridge: Cambridge University Press, 2000. From Book II, pages 23–35. Available online at www.classics.mit.edu/Aristotle/nicomachean.html through the Internet Classics Archive. © Cambridge University Press, reproduced with permission.

19 Sumner B. Twiss. "Comparison in Religious Ethics." Chapter 16 in *The Blackwell Companion to Religious Ethics*, ed. William Schweiker. Oxford: Blackwell, 2005. Pages 148–54.

20 Mohandas K. Gandhi. *An Autobiography: The Story of My Experiments With Truth*. Trans. Mahadev Desai. Boston: Beacon Press, 1957. From pages xii–xiv, 135–8, 159–60, 503–5. Reprinted by permission of the Navajivan Trust.

21 His Holiness The Dalai Lama. *Ethics for the New Millennium*. New York: Riverhead Books, 1999. From Chapter Five, "The Supreme Emotion," pages 64–8, 70–4.

22 Tom L. Beauchamp and James F. Childress. *Principles of Biomedical Ethics*. 5th edn. Oxford: Oxford University Press, 2001. From pages 342–50. By permission of Oxford University Press, Inc.

23 Thomas F. McMahon. "A Brief History of American Business Ethics." In *A Companion to Business Ethics*, ed. Robert Frederick. Oxford: Blackwell, 1999. From pages 342–50.

4 The Story of Christian Ethics

24 St. Augustine. *The City of God*. Trans. Henry Bettenson. New York: Penguin Books, 1972, 1984. Book XIX, pages 879–83, 890–1. Available online in the Christian Classics Ethereal Library at www. ccel.org/ccel/schaff/npnf102.toc.html.

25 Thomas Aquinas. *Summa Theologica*. 5 vols. Notre Dame: Christian Classics, 1948. Also available online at www.ccel.org/ccel/aquinas/summa.html. From Secunda Secundae [The Second Part of the Second Part], Question 40, pages 1353–7.

26 Martin Luther. "Temporal Authority: To What Extent it Should Be Obeyed." *Martin Luther's Basic Theological Writings*. Ed. Timothy F. Lull.

Minneapolis: Fortress Press, 1989. From pages 659–70. Available online at www.uoregon.edu/~sshoemak/323/texts/luther~1.htm or in pdf form at www.isn.ethz.ch/isn/Digital-Library/Primary-Resources/Detail/?ots591=69F57A17-24D2-527C-4F3B-B63B07201CA1&lng=en&ord520=grp2&id=27215. Copyright © 1989 Fortress Press. Used by permission of Augsburg Fortress.

27 Menno Simons. *A Kind Admonition on Church Discipline*. Pages 407–18 in *The Complete Writings of Menno Simons*. Trans. Leonard Verduin. Ed. John Christian Wenger. Scottdale: Herald Press, 1956. Excerpt from pages 409–15. Copyright © 1956, 1984 by Herald Press, Scottdale, PA 15683. Used by permission.

28 John Wesley. "The Use of Money." *The Works of John Wesley*. Vol. 6. *Sermons on Several Occasions*. Grand Rapids: Zondervan, 1958. From pages 124–35. Available online at www.new.gbgm-umc.org/umhistory/wesley/sermons/50/.

29 Reinhold Niebuhr. *Moral Man and Immoral Society: A Study in Ethics and Politics*. New York: Charles Scribner's Sons, 1932. From Chapter 10, "The Conflict Between Individual and Social Morality," pages 257–73. Reprinted with the permission of the Estate of Reinhold Niebuhr.

30 William Temple. *Christianity and Social Order*. London: SCM Press, 1950, 1955. From Chapter 4, "Christian Social Principles," pages 47–58.

5 Universal Ethics

31 Karl Barth. *Church Dogmatics*. Vol. 2, Part 2. Edinburgh: T & T Clark, 1949. From Section 36, "Ethics as a Task of the Doctrine of God"; Section 37, "The Command as the Claim of God"; and Section 38, "The Command as the Decision of God." Pages 543–8, 552, 585, 649–56, 672–3. By kind permission of Continuum International Publishing Group.

32 Thomas Aquinas. *Summa Theologica*. 5 vols. Notre Dame: Christian Classics, 1948. Also available online at www.ccel.org/ccel/aquinas/summa.html. From Prima Secundae [The First Part of the Second Part], Question 94, "Of the Natural Law," pages 1009–12.

33 Thomas Hobbes. *Leviathan*. Oxford: Oxford University Press, 1998. On Man, Chapter 14, "Of the First and Second Natural Laws, and of

Contracts." Pages 86–9. Available online at www.ebooks.adelaide.edu.au/h/hobbes/thomas/h68l/. By permission of Oxford University Press.

34 Immanuel Kant. *Grounding for the Metaphysics of Morals*. 3rd edn. Trans. James W. Ellington. Indianapolis: Hackett, 1993. From Second Section: "Transition from Popular Moral Philosophy to a Metaphysics of Morals," Pages 23–30. Available online at www.sparknotes.com/philosophy/kants-grounding. Reprinted by permission of Hackett Publishing Company, Inc. All rights reserved.

35 John Stuart Mill. *Utilitarianism*. Ed. Roger Crisp. Oxford: Oxford University Press, 1998. From Chapter 2, "What Utilitarianism Is," pages 55–9. Available online at www.utilitarianism.com/mill1.htm.

36 Richard A. McCormick. *Ambiguity in Moral Choice*. The 1973 Pere Marquette Theology Lecture. Milwaukee: Marquette University Press, 1973. From pages 1–2, 69, 98–106. Copyright © 1973 by Marquette University Press. Used by permission of the publisher. All rights reserved. www.marquette.edu/mupress/.

37 Joseph Fletcher. *Situation Ethics: The New Morality*. Louisville: Westminster Press, 1966, 1997. From pages 17–18, 26–31. Extracts from *Situation Ethics* are copyright © Joseph Fletcher, 1963. Used by permission of Hymns Ancient & Modern Ltd.

38 Pope Leo XIII. *Rerum Novarum* (On Capital and Labor). 1891. www.vatican.va/holy_father/leo_xiii/encyclicals/documents/hf_l-xiii_enc_15051891_rerum-novarum_en.html. Reprinted by permission of the Libreria Editrice Vaticana.

39 Bartolomé de las Casas. *History of the Indies*. Trans. and ed. Andrée Collard. New York: Harper and Row, 1971. From the Prologue, pages 4–8. Portions available online at www.columbia.edu/acis/ets/CCREAD/lascasas.htm. Copyright © 1971 by Andrée Collard, renewed © 1999 by Joyce J. Contrucci. Reprinted by permission of Joyce J. Contrucci.

40 Universal Declaration of Human Rights. Available online at www.un.org/Overview/rights.html. © United Nations. Reproduced with permission.

41 John Rawls. *A Theory of Justice*. Revised edn. Cambridge, MA: Belknap Press, 1999. From Chapter 1, "Justice as Fairness," pages 11–16. Reprinted by permission of the publisher. Copyright © 1971, 1999 by the President and Fellows of Harvard College.

6 Subversive Ethics

42 Gustavo Gutiérrez. *A Theology of Liberation: History, Politics, and Salvation.* Revised edn. London: SCM Press, 1988. Translation copyright 1988 by Orbis Books. From Chapter 13, "Poverty: Solidarity and Protest," pages 165–73. Reprinted by permission of the publisher SCM Press. Reprinted by permission of Orbis Books.

43 James H. Cone. *A Black Theology of Liberation.* Twentieth Anniversary Edition. Maryknoll: Orbis Books, 1986, 1990. From Part I: A Black Theology of Liberation; Chapter 1: "The Content of Theology," pages 1–8. Reprinted by permission of Orbis Books.

44 Rosemary Radford Ruether. *Sexism and God-Talk: Towards a Feminist Theology.* London: SCM Press, 1983, 1992. From Chapter 4, "Anthropology" (pages 92–7) and Chapter 5, "Christology" (pages 113–16). Reprinted by permission of the publisher SCM Press. Copyright 1983 by Beacon Press. Reproduced with permission of Beacon Press in the format Textbook via Copyright Clearance Center.

45 Delores S. Williams. "Womanist Theology: Black Women's Voices." *Christianity and Crisis* 47, 3 (March 2, 1987): 66–70.

46 Ada María Isasi-Díaz. *Mujerista Theology: A Theology for the Twenty-First Century.* Maryknoll: Orbis, 1996. From Chapter 4, "Mujerista Theology," pages 61–6, 76–81. Reprinted by permission of Orbis Books.

47 Jean Vanier. *Community and Growth.* Revd. edn. London: Darton, Longman, and Todd, 1989. From Chapter 3, "Mission" (pp. 95–7, 98–101) and Chapter 5, "Nourishment: Give Us Our Daily Bread" (pp. 185–8). Published and copyright 1989, by Darton, Longman, and Todd, Ltd., London, and used by permission of the publishers. Copyright 1989 by Paulist Press. Reproduced with permission of Paulist Press in the format Textbook via Copyright Clearance Center.

48 Rowan Williams. "The Gifts Reserved for Age: A lecture to mark the Centenary of Friends of the Elderly, Church House, Westminster, September, 6, 2005." www.archbishopofcanterbury.org/956?q=gifts+reserved+for+age. © Rowan Williams.

7 Ecclesial Ethics

49 Alasdair MacIntyre. *After Virtue: A Study in Moral Theory.* 2nd edn. London: Gerald Duckworth, 1990. From Chapter 18, "After Virtue: Nietzsche or Aristotle, Trotsky *and* St. Benedict," pages 256–9, 263. Published by Gerald Duckworth & Co. Ltd., copyright Alasdair MacIntyre 1981, 1985, 2007.

50 John Milbank. *Theology and Social Theory: Beyond Secular Reason.* 2nd edn. Oxford: Blackwell, 2006. From Part IV, "Theology and Difference"; Chapter 12, "The Other City: Theology as a Social Science," pages 387–8, 409–11.

51 Thomas Aquinas. *Summa Theologica.* 5 vols. Notre Dame: Christian Classics, 1948. Also available online at www.ccel.org/ccel/aquinas/summa.html. From Prima Secundae [First Part of the Second Part], Treatise on Habits. Question 55, "Of the Virtues, As to Their Essence"; Question 61, "Of the Cardinal Virtues"; Question 62, "Of the Theological Virtues"; Question 65, "Of the Connection of Virtues." Pages 819, 821–2, 846–8, 851, 861–4.

52 Samuel Wells. *Improvisation: The Drama of Christian Ethics.* Grand Rapids: Brazos, 2004. From Chapter 5, "Forming Habits," pages 73–9. Reprinted with permission of Brazos, a division of the Baker Publishing Group.

53 Stanley Hauerwas. *The Peaceable Kingdom: A Primer in Christian Ethics.* Notre Dame: University of Notre Dame Press, 1983. From Chapter 2, "A Qualified Ethic: The Narrative Character of Christian Ethics," pages 24–33. Extracts from *The Peaceable Kingdom: A Primer in Christian Ethics* are copyright © Stanley Hauerwas, 1983. Used by permission of Hymns Ancient & Modern Ltd.

54 John Howard Yoder. *The Politics of Jesus.* 2nd edn. Grand Rapids: Eerdmans, 1994. From Chapter 1, "The Possibility of a Messianic Ethic," pages 4–11.

8 Good Order

55 Pope Pius XI. *Quadragesimo Anno* (On Reconstruction of the Social Order). 1931. www.vatican.va/holy_father/pius_xi/encyclicals/documents/hf_p-xi_enc_19310515_quadragesimo-anno_en.html. Pope John XXIII. *Pacem in Terris* (On Establishing Universal Peace in Truth, Justice, Charity, and Liberty). 1963. www.vatican.va/holy_father/john_xxiii/encyclicals/documents/hf_j-xxiii_enc_11041963_pacem_en.html. Reprinted by permission of the Libreria Editrice Vaticana.

56 *The Kairos Document. Challenge to the Church: A Theological Comment on the Political Crisis in South Africa.* From Chapter Two, Critique of State Theology. Available online at www.bethel. edu/~letnie/AfricanChristianity/SAKairos.html.

57 The Barmen Declaration. From *The Church's Confession Under Hitler* by Arthur C. Cochrane. Philadelphia: Westminster Press, 1962, pages 237–42. Accessed at www.creeds.net/reformed/barmen.htm.

58 Oliver O'Donovan. "The Death Penalty in *Evangelium Vitae.*" Pages 213–36 in *Ecumenical Ventures in Ethics: Protestants Engage Pope John Paul II's Moral Encyclicals.* Ed. Reinhard Hütter and Theodor Dieter. Grand Rapids: Eerdmans, 1998. Excerpt from pages 220–7, 233–5.

59 *Daniel Berrigan: Poetry, Drama, Prose.* Ed. Michael True. Maryknoll: Orbis Books, 1988. From Philip Berrigan et al., "Statement of the Catonsville Nine" (pp. 155–7) and Daniel Berrigan, "Swords into Plowshares" (pp. 179–82). As reprinted in *Daniel Berrigan: Poetry, Drama, Prose.* Ed. Michael True. Maryknoll, NY: Orbis Books, 1988.

60 Timothy Gorringe. *God's Just Vengeance: Crime, Violence and the Rhetoric of Salvation.* Cambridge Studies in Ideology and Religion 9. Cambridge: Cambridge University Press, 1996. From Chapter 10, "Forgiveness, Crime and Community," pages 262–71. © Cambridge University Press, reproduced with permission.

61 Paul Ramsey. *The Just War: Force and Political Responsibility.* Lanham: Rowman and Littlefield, 1986, 2002. From Part Two: The Morality of War; Chapter 6, "Justice in War," pages 142–6. Reprinted by permission of Rowman & Littlefield Publishers, Inc.

62 Camilo Torres. *Revolutionary Priest: The Complete Writings and Messages of Camilo Torres.* Ed. John Gerassi. New York: Random House, 1971. From Chapter 25, "Crossroads of the Church in Latin America" (pp. 329–32) and Chapter 29, "Message to Christians" (pp. 367–9).

63 Dorothy Day, "Our Country Passes from Undeclared War to Declared War; We Continue Our Christian Pacifist Stand" (1942). Pages 50–2 in *The Power of Nonviolence: Writings by Advocates of Peace.* Ed. Howard Zinn. Boston: Beacon Press, 2002. Also available on the Catholic Worker website at www.catholicworker.org/dorothyday/daytext.cfm?TextID=868. Copyright 2002 by Beacon Press. Reproduced with permission of

Beacon Press in the format Textbook via Copyright Clearance Center.

9 Good Life

64 Adam Smith. *An Inquiry into the Nature and Causes of the Wealth of Nations.* Vol. 1. Ed. R. H. Campbell and A. S. Skinner. Oxford: Clarendon Press, 1976, 1979. From Book I, Chapter 2, "Of the Principle which gives occasion to the Division of Labour" (pp. 25–8); Book IV, Chapter 2, "Of Restraints upon the Importation from foreign Countries of such Goods as can be produced at Home" (pp. 454–7). Available online at www.econlib.org/library/Smith/smWN.html.

65 Medellín document: "'The Church in the Present-Day Transformation of Latin America in the Light of the Council' (August 26–September 6, 1968)." In *Liberation Theology: A Documentary History.* Ed. Alfred T. Hennelly, SJ. Maryknoll: Orbis Books, 1990. From "Document on the Poverty of the Church," pages 114–18. Available online at www.providence.edu/las/documents.htm#Medell%C3%ADn%20Conference.

66 Martin Luther King, Jr. "I See the Promised Land." Source: www.mlkonline.net/promised.html.

67 Max L. Stackhouse. *Public Theology and Political Economy: Christian Stewardship in Modern Society.* Commission on Stewardship, National Council of Churches. Grand Rapids: Eerdmans, 1987. From Chapter 7, "Spirituality and the Corporation," pages 126–7, 130–5.

68 Miguel de la Torre. *Doing Christian Ethics from the Margins.* Maryknoll: Orbis Books, 2004. From Part IV: Case Studies on Business Relationships; Chapter 13, "Corporate Accountability," pages 211–21. Reprinted by permission of Orbis Books.

69 Alasdair MacIntyre. *After Virtue: A Study in Moral Theory.* 2nd edn. Notre Dame: University of Notre Dame Press, 1984, 2003. From Chapter 7, "'Fact,' Explanation and Expertise," pages 81–7.

70 *Aetatis Novae* (On Social Communications on the Twentieth Anniversary of *Communio et Progressio*). 1992. www.vatican.va/roman_curia/pontifical_councils/pccs/documents/rc_pc_pccs_doc_22021992_aetatis_en.html. Reprinted by permission of the Libreria Editrice Vaticana.

71 Mary E. Hess. "Growing Faithful Children in Media Cultures." Chapter 5 in *The Ministry of Children's Education.* Professors of Christian

Education at the ELCA Seminaries. Minneapolis: Fortress Press, 2004. From pages 134–42. Copyright © 2004 Fortress Press. Used by permission of Augsburg Fortress.

72   Michael Budde. *The (Magic) Kingdom of God: Christianity and Global Culture Industries.* Boulder: Westview Press, 1997. From "Christian Formation in Global Culture Industries," pages 69–72, 82–7, 90–6. Copyright © 1998 Michael Budde. Reprinted by permission of Westview Press, a member of the Perseus Books Group.

10 Good Relationships

73   C. S. Lewis. *The Four Loves.* London: Geoffrey Bles, 1960. From Chapter 4, "Friendship," pages 69–85, 102–5. Copyright © 1960 by Helen Joy Lewis and renewed 1988 by Arthur Owen Barfield, reproduced by permission of Houghton Mifflin Harcourt Publishing Company.

74   Mary Daly. *Gyn/Ecology: The Metaethics of Radical Feminism.* Boston: Beacon Press, 1978, 1990. From Chapter 9, "Sparking: The Fire of Female Friendship," pages 367–73, 382–4.

75   Aelred of Rievaulx. *Spiritual Friendship.* Trans. Mark F. Williams. Cranbury, NJ; London; Mississauga, Ontario: Associated University Presses, 1994. From Book I: What is Friendship? (pages 35–7); Book II: The Advantages of Friendship (pages 44–5); and Book III: The Requirements for Unbroken Friendship (pages 70–2, 77–81). Reprinted by permission of Associated University Presses.

76   J. I. Packer. "Personal Standards." *Churchman* 111, 1 (1997): 19–26. [This article is a reprint of two chapters from Packer's Commentary on the Montreal Declaration of Anglican Essentials.] Available online at www.churchsociety.org/churchman/documents/CMan_111_1_Packer.pdf. Reprinted by permission of *Churchman*.

77   Rosemary Radford Ruether. *Christianity and the Making of the Modern Family.* Boston: Beacon Press, 2000. From Chapter 9, "Reimagining Families: Home, Work, Gender, and Faith," pages 206–8, 212–14, 225–6, 228–30. Copyright 2000 by Beacon Press. Reproduced with permission of Beacon Press in the format Textbook via Copyright Clearance Center.

78   Vigen Guroian. *Incarnate Love: Essays in Orthodox Ethics.* Notre Dame: University of Notre Dame Press, 1987. From Chapter 4, "An Ethic of Marriage and Family," pages 86–93, 113–14.

79   Stephen J. Pope. "Scientific and Natural Law Analyses of Homosexuality: A Methodological Study." *Journal of Religious Ethics* 25, 1 (Spring 1997): 89–126. Excerpt from pages 90–1, 100, 103, 110–11, 113, 118–21.

80   John Boswell. *Christianity, Social Tolerance, and Homosexuality: Gay People in Western Europe from the Beginning of the Christian Era to the Fourteenth Century.* Chicago: University of Chicago Press, 1980. From Chapter 4, "The Scriptures," pages 92–7, 100, 106–17. Reprinted by permission of the publisher The University of Chicago Press.

81   Eugene F. Rogers. "Sanctification, Homosexuality, and God's Triune Life." Pages 217–46 in *Theology and Sexuality: Classic and Contemporary Readings.* Ed. Eugene F. Rogers, Jr. Oxford: Blackwell, 2002. Excerpt from pages 217–18, 230, 232–8.

11 Good Beginnings and Endings

82   Pope Paul VI. *Humanae Vitae* (On the Regulation of Birth). 1968. www.vatican.va/holy_father/paul_vi/encyclicals/documents/hf_p-vi_enc_25071968_humanae-vitae_en.html. Reprinted by permission of the Libreria Editrice Vaticana.

83   Margaret A. Farley. "Feminist Theology and Bioethics." Pages 238–54 in *Feminist Theology: A Reader.* Ed. Ann Loades. Louisville: Westminster/John Knox Press, 1990. Excerpt from pages 249–53.

84   Oliver O'Donovan. *Begotten or Made?* Oxford: Clarendon Press; New York: Oxford University Press, 1984. From Chapter 5, "In a Glass Darkly," Pages 79–83, 85–6. By permission of Oxford University Press.

85   James M. Gustafson. "A Protestant Ethical Approach." Pages 101–22 in *The Morality of Abortion: Legal and Historical Perspectives.* Ed. John T. Noonan, Jr. Cambridge, MA: Harvard University Press, 1970. Excerpt from pages 107–17.

86   Beverly Wildung Harrison with Shirley Cloyes. "Theology and Morality of Procreative Choice." Pages 213–32 in *Feminist Theological Ethics: A Reader.* Ed. Lois K. Daly. Louisville: Westminster/John Knox Press, 1994. Excerpt from pages 213–16, 223–4, 227–8.

87 Stanley Hauerwas. "Abortion, Theologically Understood." Pages 603–22 in *The Hauerwas Reader*. Ed. John Berkman and Michael Cartwright. Durham, NC: Duke University Press, 2001. Excerpt from pages 612–19.

88 Richard A. McCormick. "The New Medicine and Morality." *Theology Digest* 21, 4 (Winter 1973): 308–21. (The Hillenbrand Lecture, delivered October 5, 1973, at Saint Louis University.) Excerpt from pages 315–20. Reprinted by permission of *Theology Digest*.

89 Jennifer A. Parks. "Why Gender Matters to the Euthanasia Debate: On Decisional Capacity and the Rejection of the Woman's Death Request." Hastings Center Report 30, 1 (2000): 30–6.

90 Gilbert Meilaender. "Suicide and Euthanasia." *Bioethics: A Primer for Christians*. 2nd edn. Grand Rapids: Eerdmans, 1996, 2005. From Chapter 6, "Suicide and Euthanasia," pages 56–64.

12 Good Earth

91 Andrew Linzey. *Animal Theology*. Urbana: University of Illinois Press, 1995. From Chapter 1, "Reverence, Responsibility and Rights," pages 4–7, 12–17, 19, 24–5. Extracts from *Animal Theology* are copyright © Andrew Linzey, 1995. Used by permission of Hymns Ancient & Modern Ltd. From *Animal Theology*. Copyright 1994 by Andrew Linzey. Used with permission of the University of Illinois Press.

92 Carol J. Adams. *Neither Man Nor Beast: Feminism and the Defense of Animals*. New York: Continuum, 1994. From Chapter 9, "Feeding on Grace: Institutional Violence, Feminist Ethics, and Vegetarianism," pages 163–4, 171–8. Excerpt from *Neither Man Nor Beast: Feminism and the Defense of Animals* by Carol J. Adams, © 1995, 2001. Reprinted with the permission of the publisher, The Continuum International Publishing Group.

93 Stephen H. Webb. *Good Eating*. Grand Rapids: Brazos Press, 2001. From Chapter 6, "The Lord's Supper as a Vegetarian Meal," pages 144–8, 158–9. Reprinted by permission of Brazos, a division of the Baker Publishing Group.

94 Derek Burke. "Genetic Engineering of Food." In *Christians and Bioethics*. Ed. Fraser Watts. London: SPCK, 2000. From pages 21–34.

95 Wendell Berry. *What Are People For?* San Francisco: North Point Press, 1990. From "The Pleasures of Eating," pages 145–52. Copyright © 1990 by Wendell Berry from *What Are People For?: Essays*. Reprinted by permission of Counterpoint.

96 Michael S. Northcott. *A Moral Climate: The Ethics of Global Warming*. London: Darton, Longman, and Todd, 2007. From Chapter 8, "Faithful Feasting," pages 255–65. Published and copyright 2007, by Darton, Longman, and Todd Ltd., London, and used by permission of the publishers. Reprinted by permission of Orbis Books.

97 Jürgen Moltmann. *God in Creation: An Ecological Doctrine of Creation*. Trans. Margaret Kohl. London: SCM Press, 1985. From Chapter 1, "God in Creation: Some Guiding Ideas for an Ecological Doctrine of Creation," pages 2–17. Reprinted by permission of the publisher SCM Press.

98 Sallie McFague. *The Body of God: An Ecological Theology*. Minneapolis: Fortress Press, 1993. From Chapter 6, "The Body of God," pages 159–68.

99 Laura Ruth Yordy. *Green Witness: Ecology, Ethics, and the Kingdom of God*. Eugene: Cascade Books, 2008. From Chapter 4, "The Church's Eco-Discipleship," pages 153–60. Used by permission of Wipf and Stock Publishers. www.wipfandstock.com.

Every effort has been made to trace copyright holders and to obtain their permission for the use of copyright material. The publisher apologizes for any errors or omissions in the above list and would be grateful if notified of any corrections that should be incorporated in future reprints of editions of this book.

Names Index

Subject Index

Printed and bound by CPI Group (UK) Ltd, Croydon, CR0 4YY

26/01/2025

14632224-0003